M000274408

HARCOURT

Math

GEORGIA EDITION

Visit *The Learning Site!*
www.harcourtschool.com

Copyright © 2008 by Harcourt, Inc.

All rights reserved. No part of this publication may be reproduced or transmitted in any form or by any means, electronic or mechanical, including photocopy, recording, or any information storage and retrieval system, without permission in writing from the publisher.

Requests for permission to make copies of any part of the work should be addressed to School Permissions and Copyrights, Harcourt, Inc., 6277 Sea Harbor Drive, Orlando, Florida 32887-6777. Fax: 407-345-2418.

HARCOURT and the Harcourt Logo are trademarks of Harcourt, Inc., registered in the United States of America and/or other jurisdictions.

Source for Georgia Performance Standards for Mathematics: Georgia Department of Education

Printed in the United States of America

ISBN 13: 978-0-15-347154-4

ISBN 10: 0-15-347154-9

If you have received these materials as examination copies free of charge, Harcourt School Publishers retains title to the materials and they may not be resold. Resale of examination copies is strictly prohibited and is illegal.

ossession of this publication in print format does not entitle users to convert this blication, or any portion of it, into electronic format.

6 7 8 9 10 030 15 14 13 12 11 10 09 08 07

Senior Author

Evan M. Maletsky
Professor of Mathematics
Montclair State University
Upper Montclair, New Jersey

Mathematics Advisor

Margaret W. Faircloth
K–12 Mathematics Consultant
Georgia Presidential Award for Mathematics
Macon, Georgia

Authors

Angela Giglio Andrews
Math Teacher, Scott School
Naperville District #203
Naperville, Illinois

Jennie M. Bennett
Houston Independent School District
Houston, Texas

Grace M. Burton
Professor, Watson School of Education
University of North Carolina at Wilmington
Wilmington, North Carolina

Lynda A. Luckie
K–12 Mathematics Coordinator
Gwinnett County Public Schools
Lawrenceville, Georgia

Joyce C. McLeod
Visiting Professor
Rollins College
Winter Park, Florida

Vicki Newman
Classroom Teacher
McGaugh Elementary School
Los Alamitos Unified School District
Seal Beach, California

Tom Roby
Associate Professor of Mathematics
University of Connecticut
Storrs, Connecticut

Janet K. Scheer
Executive Director
Create A Vision
Foster City, California

Program Consultants and Specialist

Elsie Babcock
Director, Mathematics and Science Center
Mathematics Consultant
Wayne Regional Educational Service Agency
Wayne, Michigan

Dr. William O. Lacefield, III
Associate Professor of Mathematics Education
Tift College of Education
Mercer University
Atlanta, Georgia

William J. Driscoll
Professor of Mathematics
Department of Mathematical Sciences
Central Connecticut State University
New Britain, Connecticut

Rebecca Valbuena
Language Development Specialist
Stanton Elementary School
Glendora, California

Lois Harrison-Jones
Education and Management Consultant
Dallas, Texas

UNIT 1 Understand Numbers

CHAPTERS 1-2

NUMBER SENSE AND PLACE VALUE

Technology Link

Harcourt Mega Math
Chapter 1: pp. 2, 7
Chapter 2: p. 25
The Harcourt Learning Site:
www.harcourtschool.com
Multimedia Math Glossary:
rcourtschool.com/mathglossary

2 COMPARE, ORDER, AND ESTIMATE 20

UNIT WRAPUP

UNIT 2
CHAPTERS 3-6

Addition, Subtraction, Money, and Time

3 ADDITION .44

4 SUBTRACTION .68

Technology Link

Harcourt Mega Math
Chapter 3: p. 55; Chapter 5: pp. 89, 97
Chapter 6: p. 112
The Harcourt Learning Site: www.harcourtschool.com
Multimedia Math Glossary:
www.harcourtschool.com/mathglossary

UNIT 3
CHAPTERS 7-10

Multiplication Concepts and Facts

Technology Link

Harcourt Mega Math
Chapter 7: pp. 126, 130; Chapter 8: p. 150
Chapter 9: p. 168; Chapter 10: pp. 181, 184
The Harcourt Learning Site:
www.harcourtschool.com
Multimedia Math Glossary:
www.harcourtschool.com/mathglossary

9 MULTIPLICATION FACTS AND STRATEGIES . . 160

10 MULTIPLICATION FACTS AND PATTERNS 178

UNIT WRAPUP

UNIT 4 Division Concepts and Facts

CHAPTERS 11-13

11 UNDERSTAND DIVISION .200

DIVISION FACTS THROUGH 5 .220

Harcourt Mega Math
Chapter 11: p. 206; Chapter 12: p. 225
Chapter 13: pp. 238, 245
The Harcourt Learning Site:
www.harcourtschool.com
Multimedia Math Glossary:
www.harcourtschool.com/mathglossary

13 DIVISION FACTS THROUGH 10 236

UNIT WRAPUP

UNIT 5 Data and Measurement

CHAPTERS 14-15

14 COLLECT AND GRAPH DATA

Technology Link

Harcourt Mega Math
Chapter 14: p. 269
Chapter 15: pp. 284, 287
The Harcourt Learning Site:
www.harcourtschool.com
Multimedia Math Glossary:
www.harcourtschool.com/mathglossary

UNIT WRAPUP

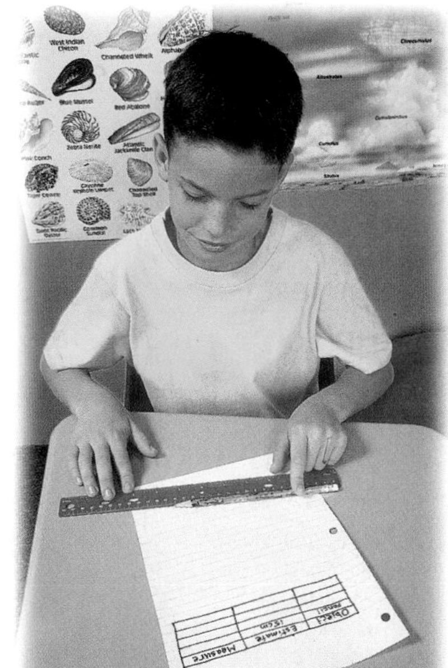

UNIT 6 Geometry and Patterns

CHAPTERS 16-19

18 PERIMETER AND AREA .348

19 ALGEBRA PATTERNS .368

UNIT WRAPUP

Technology Link

Harcourt Mega Math
Chapter 16: p. 318; Chapter 17: pp. 332, 336
Chapter 19: p. 376
The Harcourt Learning Site:
www.harcourtschool.com
Multimedia Math Glossary:
www.harcourtschool.com/mathglossary

UNIT 7 Fractions and Decimals

CHAPTERS 20-21

20 FRACTIONS .388

Technology Link

Harcourt Mega Math
Chapter 20: pp. 398, 402
Chapter 21: p. 416
The Harcourt Learning Site:
www.harcourtschool.com
Multimedia Math Glossary:
www.harcourtschool.com/mathglossary

$0.98
PER LB

UNIT 8 Multiply and Divide by 1-Digit Numbers

CHAPTERS 22-23

22 MULTIPLY BY 1-DIGIT NUMBERS .432

Technology Link

Harcourt Mega Math
Chapter 23: p. 457
The Harcourt Learning Site:
www.harcourtschool.com
Multimedia Math Glossary:
www.harcourtschool.com/mathglossary

23 DIVIDE BY 1-DIGIT NUMBERS 454

UNIT WRAPUP

GEORGIA CRCT HANDBOOK

GEORGIA CRCT HANDBOOK

OTHER RESOURCES

Using Math In Georgia

Building Success Now

You use patterns when you work with arts and crafts. ▼

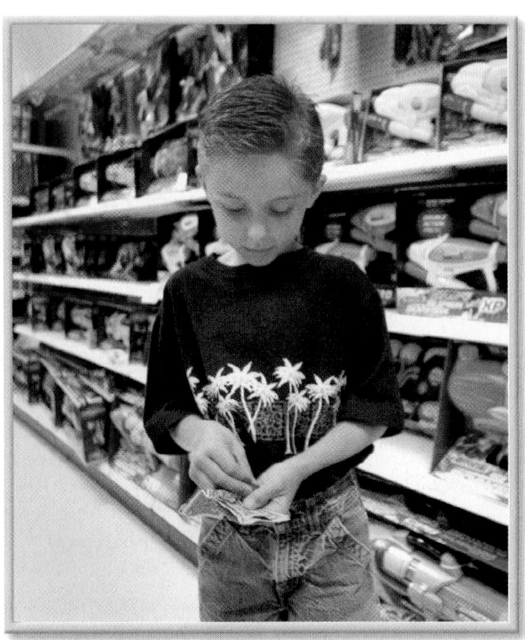

▲ You use addition to find the total cost of items you want to buy.

You use division when you share things with your friends. ▶

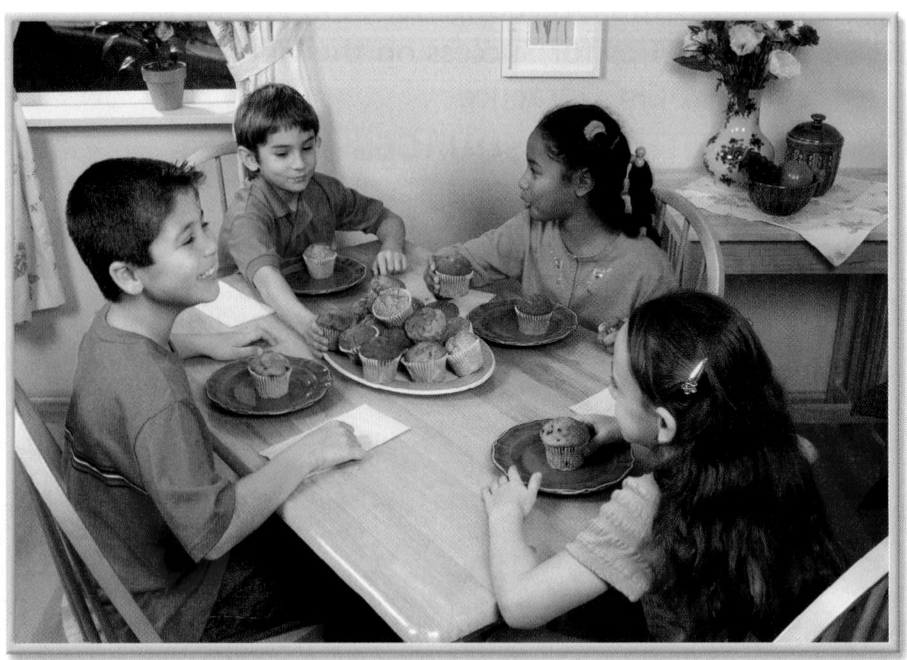

You will use the mathematics that you learn in **Harcourt Math** every day. The skills you learn will help you **build success** both now and in the future.

Building Success for the Future

Live Oak Public Library, Savannah, Georgia

◀ Architects use geometry to design different types of buildings.

Moultrie, Georgia

▲ Farmers use measurement to figure out how many crops they can plant.

Biomedical engineers use data and statistics to study illnesses and their treatments. ▼

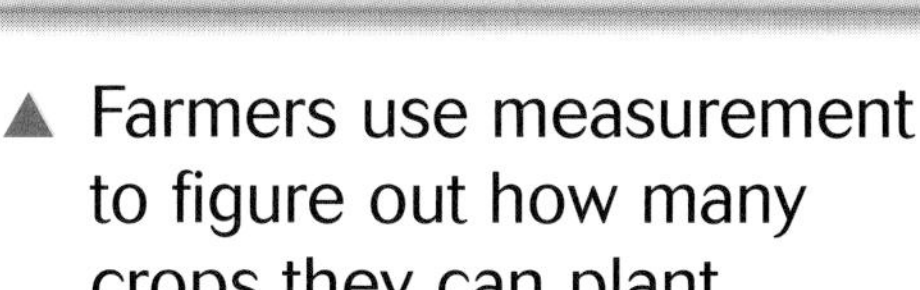

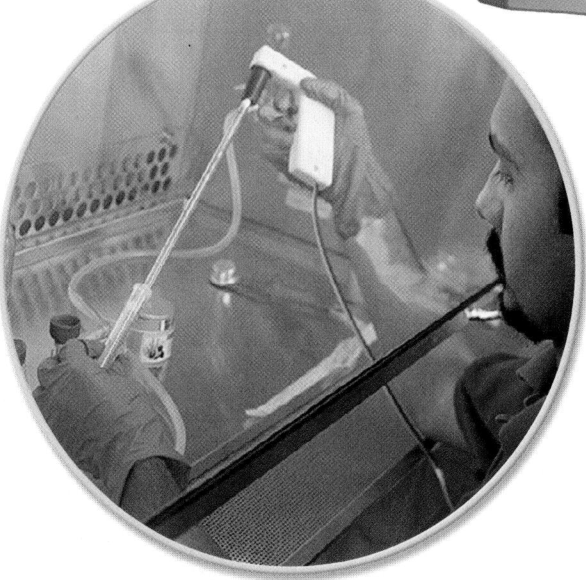

University of Georgia, Athens, Georgia

For CRCT preparation, see the CRCT Test Prep at the end of each chapter and the CRCT Practice at the end of this Pupil Edition.

Addition

Concepts/Skill to Maintain Addition & subtraction of multi-digit numbers

Model 3-digit addition with regrouping.

Add. 116
+146

STEP 1

Add the ones.
6 + 6 = 12
Regroup 12 ones to make 1 ten 2 ones.

Hundreds	Tens	Ones

	H	T	O
		1	
	1	1	6
+	1	4	6
			2

STEP 2

Add the tens.

Hundreds	Tens	Ones

	H	T	O
		1	
	1	1	6
+	1	4	6
		6	2

STEP 3

Add the hundreds.

Hundreds	Tens	Ones

	H	T	O
		1	
	1	1	6
+	1	4	6
	2	6	2

Practice

Find the sum.

1.

	H	T	O
		□	
	2	2	7
+	4	3	5

2.

	H	T	O
	□		
	3	8	4
+	1	2	3

3.

	H	T	O
	□	□	
	5	7	5
+	3	4	6

Subtraction

Concepts/Skill to Maintain Addition & subtraction of multi-digit numbers

Model 3-digit subtraction with regrouping.

Subtract. 281
−163

We are subtracting 163 from 281. We regrouped 8 tens 1 one as 7 tens 11 ones. What should we do next?

STEP 1

Show 281. Are there enough ones to subtract 3 ones?

Hundreds	Tens	Ones

	H	T	O
		□	□
	2	8	1
−	1	6	3

STEP 2

Regroup 1 ten as 10 ones to make 11 ones. Subtract the ones.

Hundreds	Tens	Ones

	H	T	O
		7	11
	2	~~8~~	~~1~~
−	1	6	3
			8

STEP 3

Subtract the tens. Subtract the hundreds.

Hundreds	Tens	Ones

	H	T	O
		7	11
	2	~~8~~	~~1~~
−	1	6	3
	1	1	8

Practice

Find the difference.

1.

	H	T	O
		□	□
	7	6	4
−	2	2	8

2.

	H	T	O
	□	□	
	8	2	7
−	4	6	1

3.

	H	T	O
	□	□	□
	9	3	6
−	1	4	7

CHAPTER 1

Number Sense and Place Value

FAST FACT • SCIENCE Horses have the largest eyes of any land mammal. Their large eyes help horses see almost directly behind themselves while facing forward. Horses need hay, oats, and fresh water to stay healthy.

Using Data

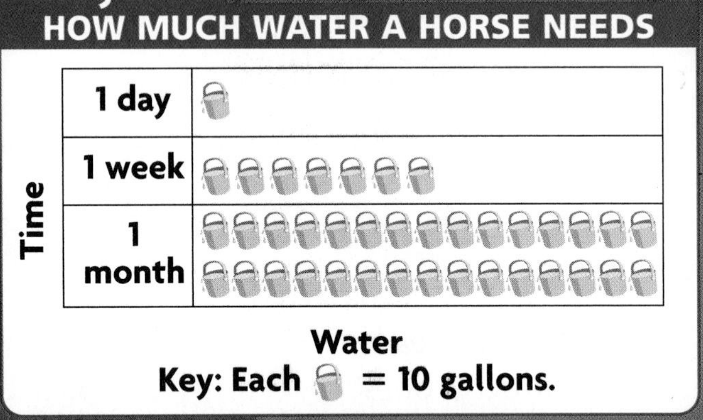

HOW MUCH WATER A HORSE NEEDS

Time	Water
1 day	
1 week	
1 month	

Water

Key: Each = 10 gallons.

INVESTIGATION Use the pictograph to find the number of gallons of water a horse needs in a week, a month, and a year. What other way can you use to show the same information?

Use this page to help you review and remember important skills needed for Chapter 1.

PLACE VALUE: 2-DIGIT NUMBERS

Write the value of the blue digit.

1. 40
2. 73
3. 65
4. 39
5. 28
6. 19
7. 32
8. 76
9. 27
10. 84

MODEL 3-DIGIT NUMBERS

Write the number that matches the model.

11. 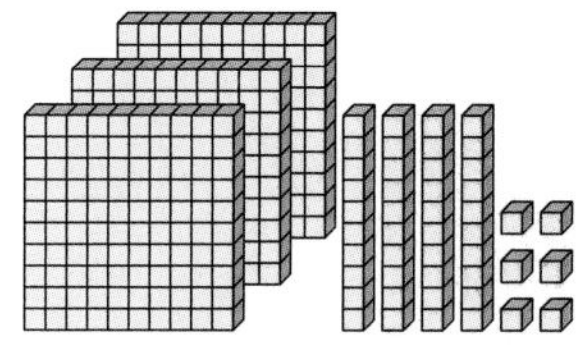

12. 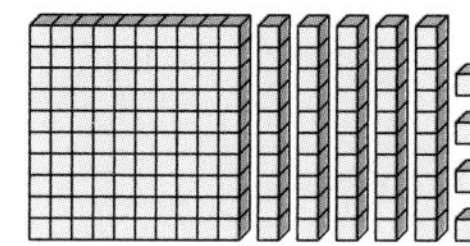

13. 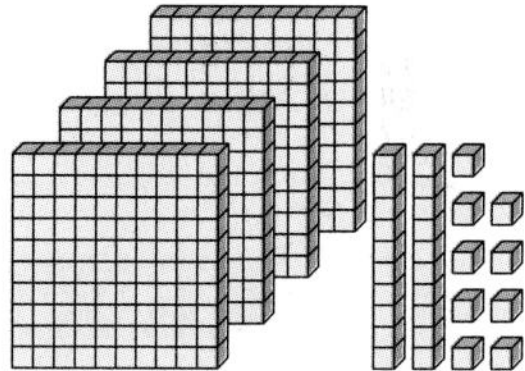

14. 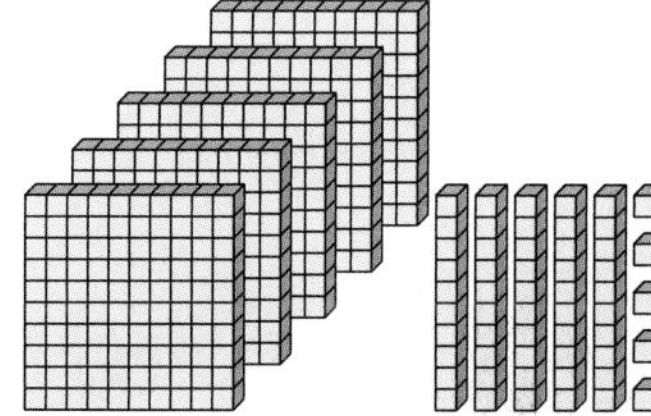

15. 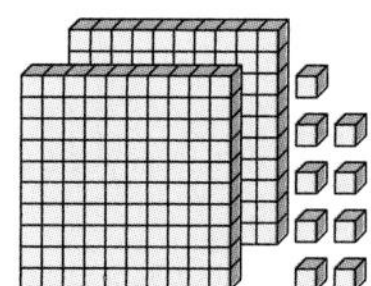

16. 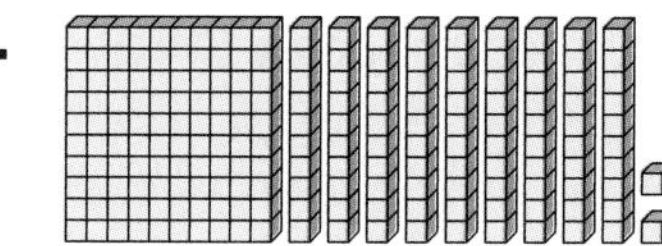

VOCABULARY POWER

REVIEW

number [num′bər] *noun*

A number tells you how many or how much. A number can be shown with words or symbols. Fifteen and 15 show the same number. Choose a number and write a word and a symbol to show it.

PREVIEW

whole number
standard form
expanded form
word form
pattern

www.harcourtschool.com/mathglossary

LESSON 1

HANDS ON

Patterns on a Hundred Chart

M3A1.a. Describe and extend numeric and geometric patterns. *also* M3A1.c., M3P2., M3P2.a., M3P2.b., M3P3.a., M3P3.b., M3P3.c., M3P3.d., M3P4., M3P5., M3P5.b., M3P5.c.

Quick Review

1. 3 + 3
2. 6 + 3
3. 9 + 3
4. 12 + 3
5. 15 + 3

MATERIALS
hundred chart, crayons

Explore

You can use a hundred chart to find number patterns.

STEP 1
Use a hundred chart.

STEP 2
Start at 3. Shade that box.

STEP 3
Skip-count by threes, and shade each box you land on.

1	2	3	4	5	6	7	8	9	10
11	12	13	14	15	16	17	18	19	20
21	22	23	24	25	26	27	28	29	30
31	32	33	34	35	36	37	38	39	40
41	42	43	44	45	46	47	48	49	50
51	52	53	54	55	56	57	58	59	60
61	62	63	64	65	66	67	68	69	70
71	72	73	74	75	76	77	78	79	80
81	82	83	84	85	86	87	88	89	90
91	92	93	94	95	96	97	98	99	100

- What is the next number in the pattern below?

  15, 18, 21, 24, ■

- Look at your shaded chart. What pattern do you see?

Technology Link
More Practice: Harcourt Mega Math The Number Games, *Tiny's Think Tank*, Level I

Try It

Use the hundred chart. Start at the beginning of the chart.

a. Skip-count by twos. Move 7 skips. What number do you land on?

b. Skip-count by fours. Move 6 skips. What number do you land on?

c. Skip-count by tens. What numbers do you land on? What pattern do you see?

REASONING Skip-count by fives. Will you land on the number 34? Explain.

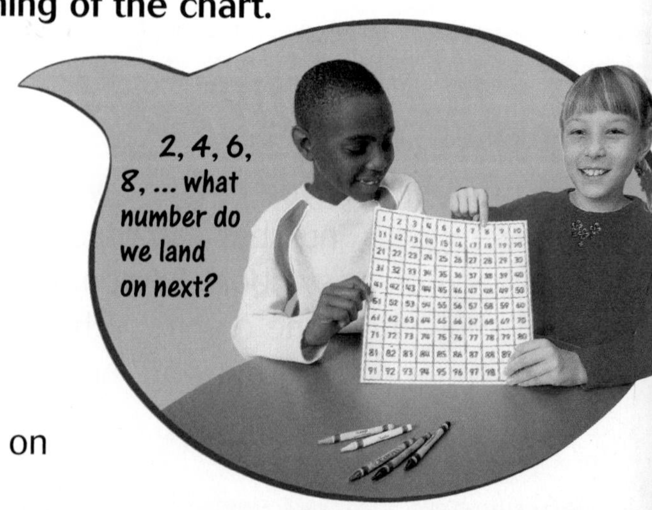

Connect

Use a hundred chart. Skip-count by fours, and shade each number you land on.

What number comes next?

16, 20, 24, 28, ■

72, 76, 80, 84, ■

Look at your shaded chart. What pattern do you see?

1	2	3	4	5	6	7	8	9	10
11	12	13	14	15	16	17	18	19	20
21	22	23	24	25	26	27	28	29	30
31	32	33	34	35	36	37	38	39	40
41	42	43	44	45	46	47	48	49	50
51	52	53	54	55	56	57	58	59	60
61	62	63	64	65	66	67	68	69	70
71	72	73	74	75	76	77	78	79	80
81	82	83	84	85	86	87	88	89	90
91	92	93	94	95	96	97	98	99	100

Practice and Problem Solving

Use the hundred chart to look for a pattern. Write the missing numbers.

1. 30, 40, 50, 60, ■
2. 12, 16, 20, 24, ■
3. 28, 30, 32, 34, ■
4. 55, 60, 65, 70, ■
5. 33, 36, 39, 42, ■
6. 60, 70, 80, 90, ■
7. 44, 46, 48, 50, ■
8. 63, 66, 69, 72, ■

Use the hundred chart.

9. Skip-count by fives. Move 4 skips. What number do you land on?
10. Skip-count by tens. Move 6 skips. What number do you land on?
11. The first five houses on Quinn's street are numbered 4, 8, 12, 16, and 20. What are the next three house numbers? Explain.
12. **REASONING** Marcos skip-counted. He started at 0. He landed on 15. Could he be skip-counting by twos? Why or why not?

Maintain Skills

13. Write the time.

CRCT Test Prep

14. M3N2.c. Jon has 12 red marbles and 17 blue marbles. How many marbles does he have in all?

A. 30 B. 29 C. 19 D. 5

LESSON 2

Place Value: 3-Digit Numbers

M3N1.a. Identify place values from tenths through ten thousands. *also* M3N1.b., M3P2.b., M3P2.d., M3P3.a., M3P3.b., M3P4.c.

Quick Review

Write the number.

1. 5 tens 1 one
2. 4 tens 3 ones
3. 7 tens 0 ones
4. 1 ten 9 ones
5. 2 hundreds 6 tens 8 ones

VOCABULARY

whole number
standard form
expanded form
word form

Learn

FARM FACTS Each of the numbers 1, 2, 3, 4, ... is called a **whole number**. The set of whole numbers goes on without end.

On Mr. Sam's farm there are 248 chickens. What does the number 248 mean?

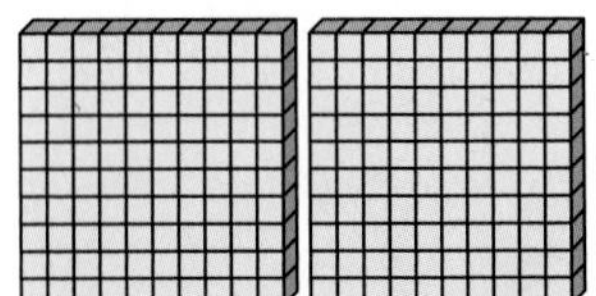

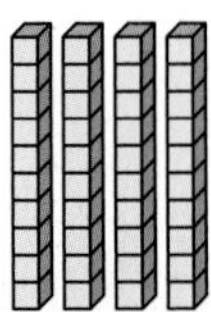

HUNDREDS	TENS	ONES
2	4	8

So, 248 means 2 hundreds + 4 tens + 8 ones or 200 + 40 + 8.

Remember

The symbols 0, 1, 2, 3, 4, 5, 6, 7, 8, and 9 are digits. Numbers are made up of digits.

MATH IDEA You can write a number in different ways: standard form, expanded form, and word form.

Standard form: 248

Expanded form: 200 + 40 + 8

Word form: two hundred forty-eight

- In the number 408, what is the meaning of the zero in the tens place?

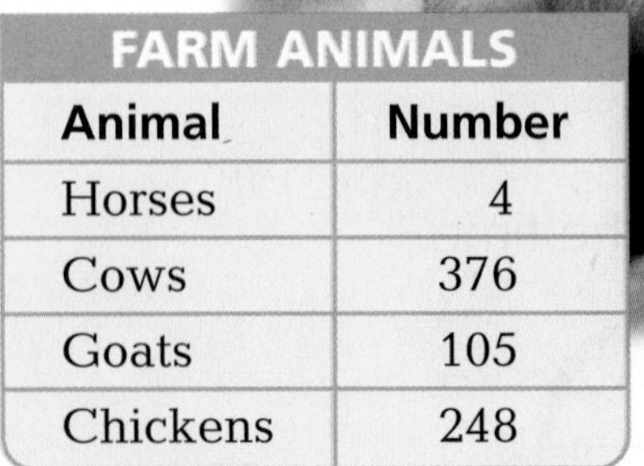

Check

USE DATA For 1–2, use the table.

FARM ANIMALS	
Animal	**Number**
Horses	4
Cows	376
Goats	105
Chickens	248

1. **Explain** why the value of the digit 3 is 300 in the number of cows on the farm.
2. Write the expanded form for the number of goats on the farm.

Write each number in standard form.

3. 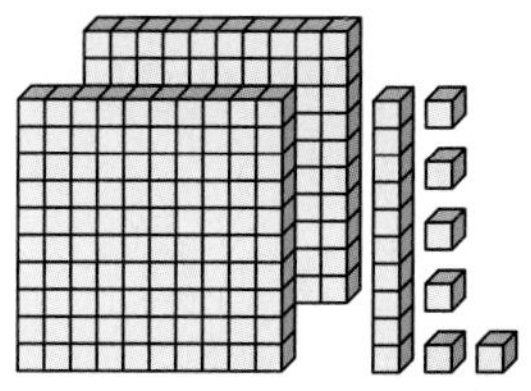

4. 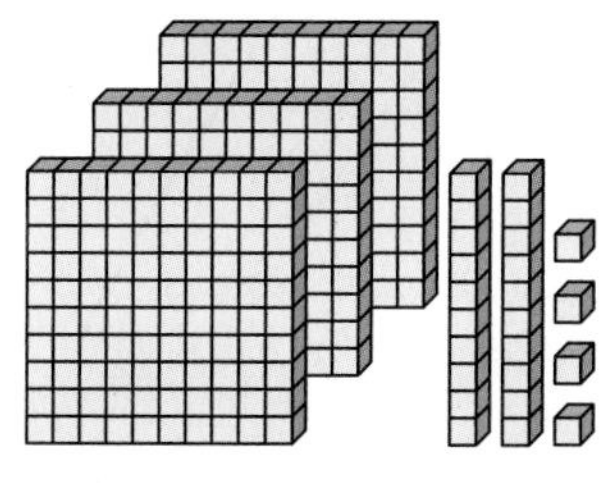

5. 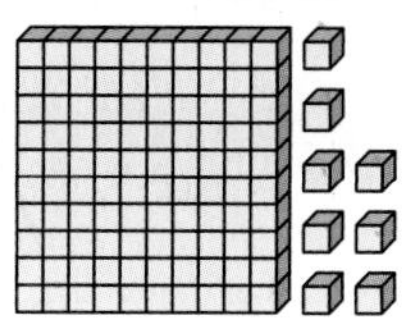

Practice and Problem Solving

Extra Practice, page 16, Set A

Write each number in standard form.

6. 100 + 50 + 3
7. 400 + 70 + 6
8. 600 + 30 + 9
9. 900 + 2
10. 4 hundreds 2 tens 1 one
11. 6 hundreds 8 tens 3 ones
12. 7 hundreds 2 tens 3 ones
13. 4 hundreds 5 ones
14. one hundred three
15. three hundred forty-five
16. six hundred eleven
17. nine hundred seventy-one

Write the value of the blue digit.

18. 846
19. 267
20. 493
21. 923
22. Mr. Sam put 297 bales of hay in one barn. There are still 86 bales of hay in the field. How many more bales of hay are in the barn than in the field?
23. **FAST FACT** • SCIENCE There are about 210 kinds of horses in the world. What is the value of the digit 2 in the number 210?
24. **Vocabulary Power** *Value* means "what something is worth." Use this meaning to describe the digit 5 in 527.
25. **REASONING** I am a digit in each of the numbers 312, 213, and 132. My value is different in all three numbers. What digit am I? What is my value in each number?

Maintain Skills

Find the sum or difference.

26. 24 + 35 = ■
27. 48 − 17 = ■
28. $\begin{array}{r} 64 \\ +21 \\ \hline \end{array}$
29. $\begin{array}{r} 78 \\ -54 \\ \hline \end{array}$

CRCT Test Prep

30. M3N1.a. What is the value of the blue digit in 513? (p. 4)

A. 1
B. 10
C. 100
D. 1,000

LESSON 3

Place Value: 4-Digit Numbers

M3N1.a. Identify place values from tenths through ten thousands. *also* M3N1.b., M3D1.b., M3P2., M3P2.a., M3P2.b., M3P2.c., M3P2.d., M3P5., M3P5.b., M3P5.c.

Quick Review

Write the value of the blue digit.

1. 246
2. 394
3. 714
4. 502
5. 802

Learn

HORSE SENSE The largest horse on record is a Belgian that stood 18 hands—or 6 feet—tall and weighed 3,174 pounds. You can use base-ten blocks to show the number of pounds.

HANDS ON

Activity

Materials: base-ten blocks

Make a model to show 3,174.

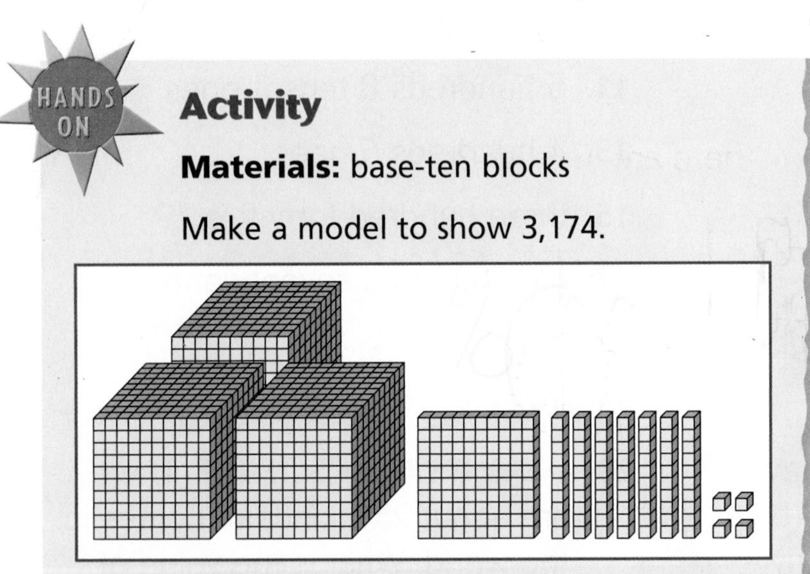

A place-value chart can help you understand the value of each digit in a number.

THOUSANDS	HUNDREDS	TENS	ONES
3,	1	7	4
↑ Value is 3,000.	↑ Value is 100.	↑ Value is 70.	↑ Value is 4.

Standard form: 3,174

A comma is used to separate the thousands and hundreds.

Expanded form: 3,000 + 100 + 70 + 4

Word form: three thousand, one hundred seventy-four

- What is the value of the digit 4 in 4,618?

Understanding Thousands

You can use place-value blocks to help you understand thousands.

There are 10 ones in 10.

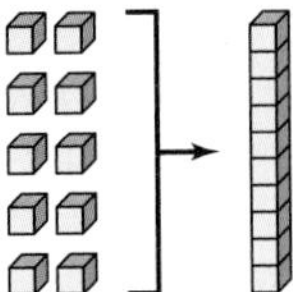

There are 10 tens in 100.

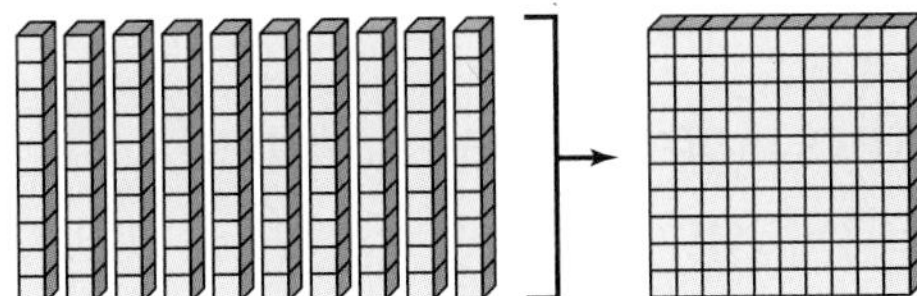

How many hundreds do you think there are in 1,000?

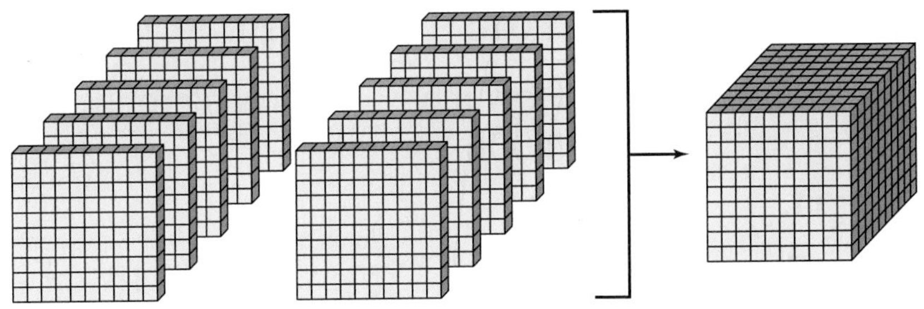

There are 10 hundreds in 1,000.

- How many hundreds do you think there are in 2,000?

Check

1. **Explain** the value of each digit in 5,403.

Write in standard form.

2.

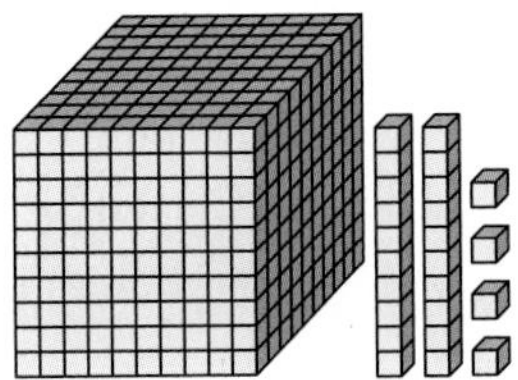

3.

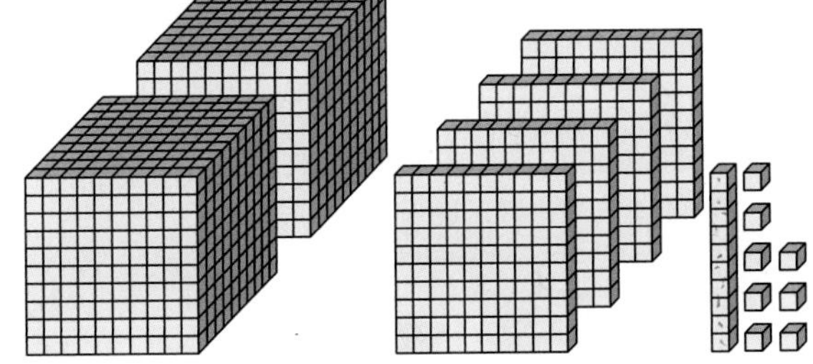

Write in expanded form.

4. 5,632 **5.** 7,401 **6.** 8,011 **7.** 462

8. How many tens are in 100? How many tens are in 200?

LESSON CONTINUES

Practice and Problem Solving

Extra Practice, page 16, Set B

Write in standard form.

9.

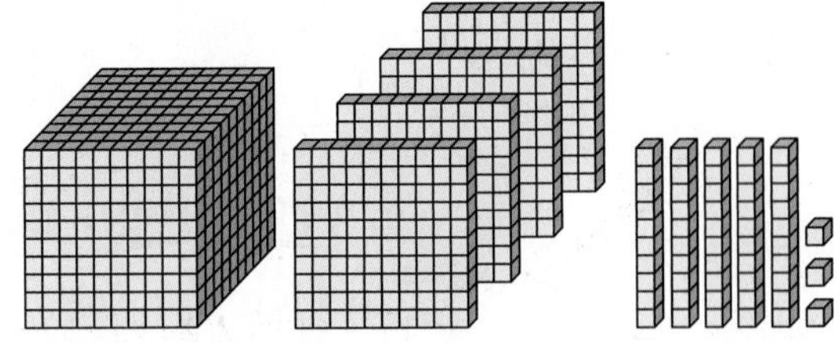

10.

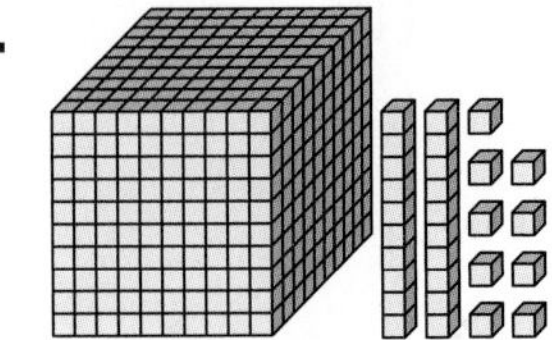

11. 5,000 + 400 + 50

12. 4,000 + 300 + 90 + 7

13. 700 + 20 + 3

14. 1,000 + 10 + 8

15. two thousand, four hundred eighty-three

16. six thousand, one hundred ninety-four

For 17–20, write in expanded form.

17. 1,234 **18.** 4,321 **19.** 3,016 **20.** 367

21. How many tens are in 400?

22. How many hundreds are in 3,000?

Write the value of the blue digit.

23. 1,548 **24.** 6,290 **25.** 971 **26.** 8,346

27. **USE DATA** The bar graph shows what Molly saw at the farm. How many animals did Molly see in all?

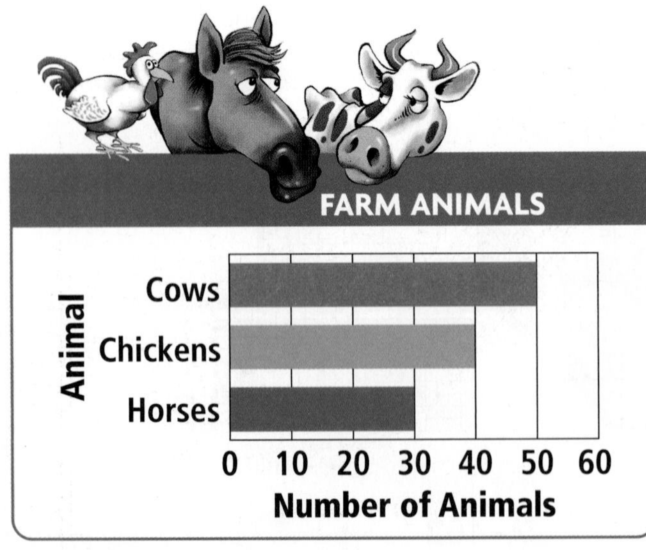

28. **REASONING** I am a 4-digit number. My thousands digit is 4 less than my tens digit. My hundreds digit equals the sum of my tens digit and my ones digit. My tens digit is 4 more than my ones digit. My ones digit is 1. What number am I?

29. What is the least possible number you can write with the digits 2, 9, 4, and 7? Use each digit only once.

30. **Write About It** Why do you have to use a zero when you write one thousand, six hundred four in standard form?

31. The number 124 is an even number. Write 5 more even numbers including one with 4 digits.

32. Show that each of the even numbers 6, 8, 10, and 12 can be written as the sum of a group of twos.

Maintain Skills

Compare the numbers. Write <, >, or = for each ●.

33. 94 ● 73 **34.** 28 ● 25

35. 36 ● 63 **36.** 87 ● 76

Find the sum.

37. 53 + 19 **38.** 46 + 29

39. 29 + 79 **40.** 59 + 37

Find the difference.

41. 77 − 19 **42.** 92 − 55

43. 31 − 17 **44.** 46 − 28

CRCT Test Prep

45. M3N1.a. What is the value of the blue digit in 804? (p. 4)

A. 8,000
B. 800
C. 80
D. 8

46. M3N1.a. Which digit is in the tens place in the number 9,374? (p. 6)

A. 3
B. 4
C. 7
D. 9

Problem Solving Thinker's Corner

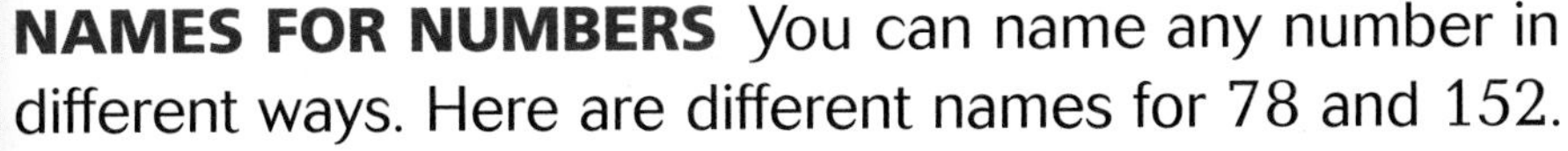

NAMES FOR NUMBERS You can name any number in different ways. Here are different names for 78 and 152.

78	152
70 + 8	100 + 50 + 2
25 + 25 + 25 + 3	50 + 50 + 52
80 − 2	155 − 3
100 − 22	200 − 48

Write two other names for each number.

1. 45 **2.** 215 **3.** 698 **4.** 1,523

LESSON 4

Problem Solving Strategy
Use Logical Reasoning

M3N1.b. Understand the relative sizes of digits in place value notation (10 times, 100 times, 1/10 of a single digit whole number) and ways to represent them. *also* M3D1.b., M3P1.a., M3P1.b., M3P1.c., M3P1.d., M3P2.a., M3P2.b., M3P2.d., M3P3.a., M3P3.b., M3P3.c., M3P3.d.

Quick Review

1. 400 + ■ + 9 = 499
2. ■ + 700 + 5 = 8,705
3. ■ + 60 + 3 = 763
4. 900 + 30 + ■ = 936
5. ■ + 400 + 7 = 1,407

PROBLEM Todd used base-ten blocks to model 243. He used 2 hundreds, 4 tens, 3 ones. What is another way he can show 243 with base-ten blocks?

UNDERSTAND

- What are you asked to find?
- Is there information you will not use? If so, what?

PLAN

- What strategy can you use to solve the problem?

  You can use *logical reasoning*.

SOLVE

- How can you use the strategy to solve the problem?

  Begin with 2 hundreds, 4 tens, 3 ones.

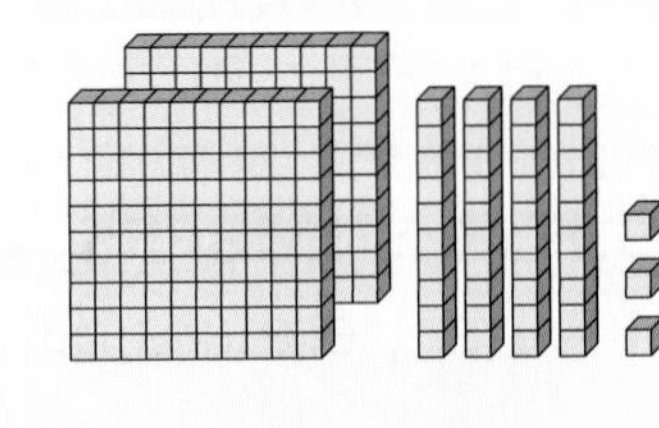

  Trade one of the hundreds for 10 tens. Add the 10 tens and the 4 tens. You now have 1 hundred, 14 tens, 3 ones.

  So, another way to show 243 is with 1 hundred, 14 tens, 3 ones.

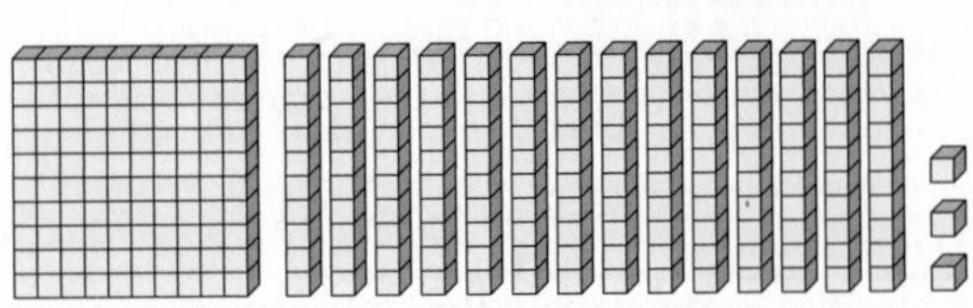

CHECK

- Look at the problem. Does your answer make sense? Explain.
- Explain how to model 243 with base-ten blocks a third way.

Problem Solving Practice

Use logical reasoning and solve.

1. **What if** Todd doesn't have any tens? How can he model 243 without using any tens?
2. Emily made a model for 156 using 1 hundred, 5 tens, 6 ones. What are two other ways she can show 156 using base-ten blocks?
3. Sage used 34 tens, 2 ones to model a number. What other way can she model the same number?

   A 3 hundreds, 4 tens
   B 3 tens, 2 ones
   C 3 hundreds, 2 ones
   D 3 hundreds, 4 tens, 2 ones

4. Louis used 1 thousand, 2 hundreds, 4 tens, 3 ones to model a number. What number did he model?

   F 143 **H** 1,423
   G 1,243 **J** 2,143

Strategies

Act It Out or Use Objects
Make a Picture or Diagram
Guess and Check
Use or Look for a Pattern
Use Logical Reasoning

Problem Solving

Mixed Strategy Practice

5. Write the greatest possible 4-digit number using the digits 3, 4, 5, and 6. Write the least possible 4-digit number.
6. **REASONING** A 3-digit number has the same number of ones, tens, and hundreds. If the sum of the digits is 9, what is the number?
7. **USE DATA** The bar graph shows farm animals. How many more sheep than horses are there? How many animals are there in all?
8. **Write a problem** about 8 hundreds, 4 tens, 6 ones. Tell how to solve the problem.

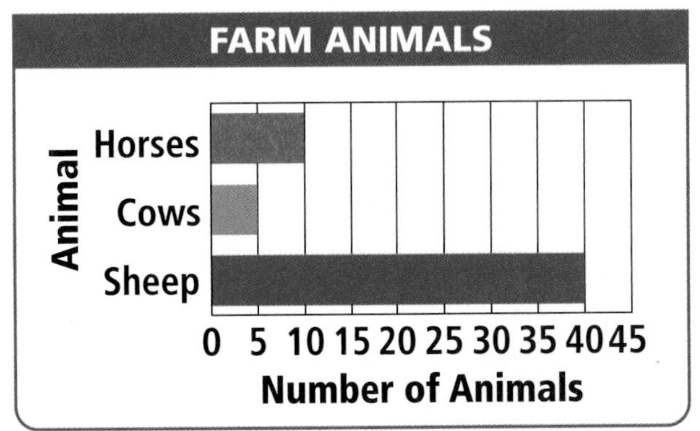

LESSON 5

Algebra: Number Patterns

M3A1.a. Describe and extend numeric and geometric patterns.
also M3P3.a., M3P3.b., M3P3.c., M3P3.d.

Learn

WHAT'S NEXT? A **pattern** is an ordered set of numbers or objects. The order helps you predict what will come next.

Examples

Predict the next number in each pattern.

A 8, 10, 12, 14, 16, ■

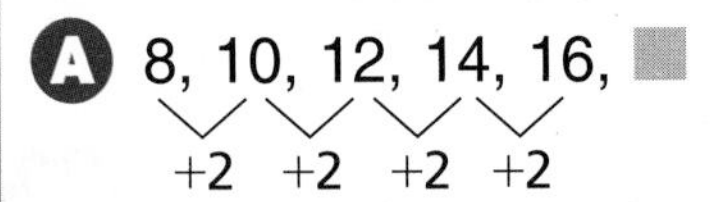

The next number will be 16 + 2, or 18.

B 25, 35, 45, 55, 65, ■

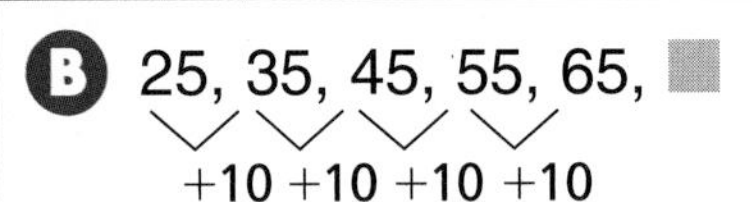

The next number will be 65 + 10, or 75.

C

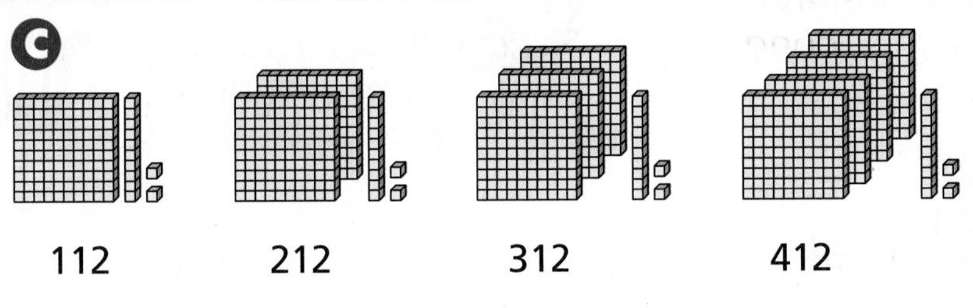

The numbers increase by 100, so the next number will be 412 + 100, or 512.

- **REASONING** What is the next number in the pattern 923, 823, 723, 623? Explain.

Quick Review

Find each missing number.

1. 17 + ■ = 21
2. 24 + ■ = 32
3. 55 + ■ = 65
4. 8 + ■ = 28
5. 393 – ■ = 293

VOCABULARY
pattern

Check

1. **Explain** what base-ten blocks are needed for the sixth number of the pattern in Example C.

Predict the next number in each pattern. Explain.

2. 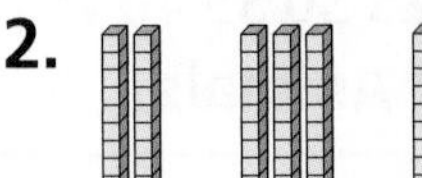 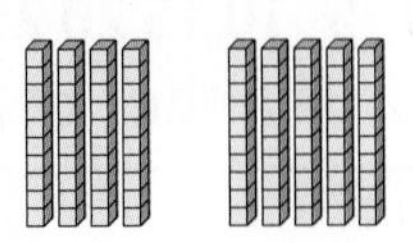

3.  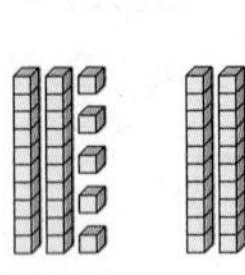 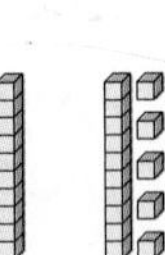

4. 30, 35, 40, 45, ■
5. 58, 68, 78, 88, ■
6. 13, 17, 21, 25, ■

Practice and Problem Solving

Extra Practice, page 16, Set C

Predict the next number in each pattern. Explain.

7.

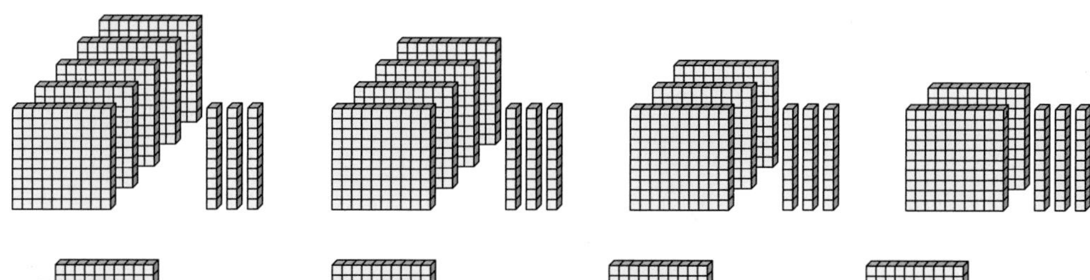

8.

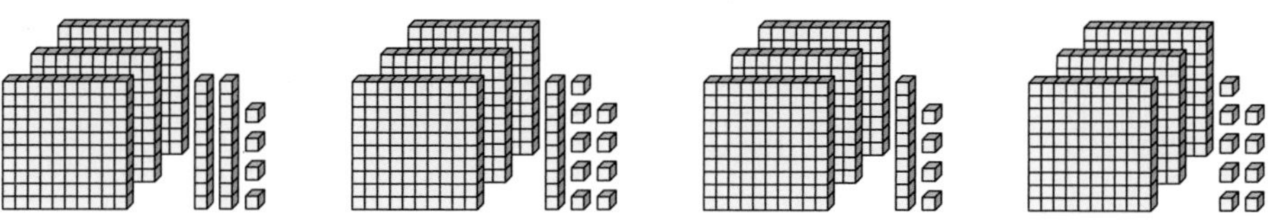

9. 50, 70, 90, 110, ■

10. 110, 105, 100, 95, ■

11. 580, 590, 600, 610, ■

12. 235, 335, 435, 535, ■

13. 657, 667, 677, 687, ■

14. 712, 715, 718, 721, ■

15. Adam skip-counts by thousands to write a number pattern. The first number is 1,495. The second number is 2,495. What are the third and fourth numbers?

16. **MULTISTEP** Drew rented 4 movies and 5 video games. Phillip rented 5 movies and 3 video games. Who rented more items? Explain.

17. **What's the Question?** Hans wrote the following number pattern.

432, 434, 436, 438

The answer is 446.

18. **Write a problem** about a number pattern. Exchange problems with a classmate and solve.

Maintain Skills

Find each sum or difference.

19. $18 + 42$

20. $17 + 56$

21. $60 + 12$

22. $49 - 27$

23. $72 - 54$

24. $98 - 19$

CRCT Test Prep

25. M3A1.a. Which number comes next in the pattern?

435, 430, 425, 420, □

A. 400
B. 405
C. 410
D. 415

LESSON 6

Place Value: 5-Digit Numbers

M3N1.a. Identify place values from tenths through ten thousands. *also* **M3N1.b., M3P2.a., M3P2.b., M3P2.d., M3P3.a., M3P3.b., M3P3.c., M3P3.d., M3P4.a.**

Quick Review

Write in expanded form.

1. 384 **2.** 51

3. 677 **4.** 9,240

5. 3,818

Learn

THE PEACH STATE Georgia has an area of 59,441 square miles. You can use a place-value chart to help you understand each digit in the number.

TEN THOUSANDS	THOUSANDS	HUNDREDS	TENS	ONES
5	9,	4	4	1

Remember

Put a comma between the thousands place and the hundreds place.

59,441

comma

You can write this number in three ways:

Standard form: 59,441

Expanded form: 50,000 + 9,000 + 400 + 40 + 1

Word form: fifty-nine thousand, four hundred forty-one

- How many ten thousands are in 59,441?

In 2004, there were 52,103 students in the public schools of Atlanta, the state capital. Look at this number in the place-value chart.

TEN THOUSANDS	THOUSANDS	HUNDREDS	TENS	ONES
5	2,	1	0	3

You can write this number in three ways:

Standard form: 52,103

Expanded form: 50,000 + 2,000 + 100 + 3

Word form: fifty-two thousand, one hundred three

- What is the value of the digit 5 in 52,103?

Check

1. **Explain** the value of each digit in 21,694.

Write in standard form.

2. 20,000 + 6,000 + 700 + 30 + 4
3. thirty-five thousand, nine hundred forty-seven

Write in expanded form.

4. 16,723
5. 52,019
6. 8,605

Practice and Problem Solving

Extra Practice, page 16, Set D

Write in standard form.

7. 20,000 + 6,000 + 700 + 30 + 4
8. 10,000 + 400 + 8
9. two thousand, three hundred fifteen
10. eighteen thousand, nine hundred

Write in expanded form.

11. 16,723
12. 119
13. 11,012
14. 49,207

Write the value of the blue digit.

15. 465
16. 62,817
17. 3,912
18. 19,273

Complete.

19. ■ + 2,000 + 600 + 50 + 1 = 12,651
20. 60,000 + ■ + 300 + 10 + 9 = 62,319

21. **REASONING** I am an even number between 51,680 and 51,700. The sum of my digits is 23. What number am I?

22. **What's the Error?** Karla wrote eleven thousand, forty-five as 1,145. Explain her error. Write the number correctly in standard form.

Maintain Skills

23. 98 − 52

24. 72 + 19

25. 28 + 63 = ■

26. 52 − 18 = ■

CRCT Test Prep

27. M3N1.a. What is the value of the blue digit in 5,789? (p. 6)

A. 7
B. 70
C. 700
D. 7,000

Extra Practice

Set A (pp. 4–5)

Write each number in standard form.

1. 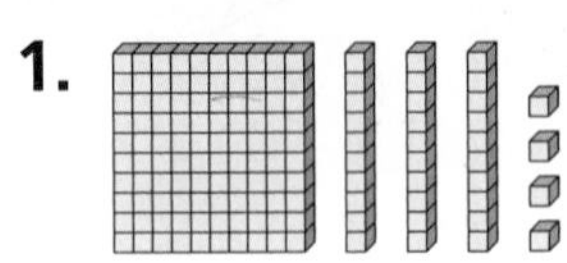

2.

3. 500 + 60 + 6

4. 700 + 4

5. four hundred seventy-six

6. nine hundred ninety-one

Write the value of the blue digit.

7. 346 **8.** 872 **9.** 13 **10.** 554

Set B (pp. 6–9)

Write in standard form.

1. 1,000 + 900 + 40 + 2

2. 5,000 + 700 + 80 + 3

3. two thousand, four hundred sixty-seven

4. eight thousand, eighteen

Write the value of the blue digit.

5. 5,487 **6.** 6,055 **7.** 6,170 **8.** 7,796

Set C (pp. 12–13)

Predict the next number in each pattern. Explain.

1. 310, 410, 510, 610, ■

2. 75, 70, 65, 60, ■

3. 503, 506, 509, 512, ■

4. 8,324, 7,324, 6,324, 5,324, ■

Set D (pp. 14–15)

Write in standard form.

1. 10,000 + 6,000 + 900 + 60 + 5

2. 50,000 + 3,000 + 6

3. fifty-one thousand, four hundred

4. twenty-two thousand, eighteen

Write the value of the blue digit.

5. 65,487 **6.** 76,055 **7.** 36,173 **8.** 47,796

Review/Test

CHECK VOCABULARY

Choose the best term from the box.

Vocabulary
whole number
expanded form
standard form
word form

1. The number 562 written in ? is 500 + 60 + 2. (p. 4)
2. Each of the numbers 1, 2, 3, 4, … is called a ? . (p. 4)

CHECK SKILLS

Write the missing number. (pp. 2–3)

3. 2, 4, 6, 8, ■
4. 12, 16, 20, 24, ■
5. 40, 50, 60, 70, ■
6. 18, 21, 24, 27, ■

Write in standard form. (pp. 4–9, 14–15)

7. 800 + 60 + 9
8. 3,000 + 700 + 10 + 1
9. 8,000 + 500 + 20 + 2
10. 30,000 + 4,000 + 700 + 5
11. 90,000 + 4,000 + 600 + 50 + 5
12. fifty-three thousand, eight hundred nineteen

Predict the next number in each pattern. (pp. 12–13)

13. 135, 235, 335, 435, ■
14. 250, 230, 210, 190, ■

Write the value of the blue digit. (pp. 4–9, 14–15)

15. 863
16. 9,845
17. 12,053
18. 72,859

CHECK PROBLEM SOLVING

Solve. (pp. 10–11)

19. Katie made a model using base-ten blocks. She used 3 hundreds, 12 tens, 8 ones. What number did she model?
20. Randy modeled 257 with base-ten blocks. He used 2 hundreds, 4 tens. How many ones did he use?

Chapter CRCT Test Prep

NUMBERS AND OPERATIONS

1. M3N1.a. What is the value of the digit 4 in 24,869?

   A. 4 tens
   B. 4 hundreds
   C. 4 thousands
   D. 4 ten thousands

2. M3N1.a. Which number shows 6 thousands, 2 hundreds, and 9 ones?

   A. 629
   B. 6,029
   C. 6,209
   D. 6,290

3. M3N1.a. In 2000, the population of Alpharetta, Georgia, was 34,854. Which digit is in the ten thousands place in the number 34,854?

   A. 3
   B. 4
   C. 5
   D. 8

NUMBERS AND OPERATIONS

4. M3N1.a. What is the value of the digit 7 in 375?

   A. 7
   B. 70
   C. 700
   D. 7,000

5. M3N1.b. Billy is playing a game with numbered tiles. He draws four tiles shown below from a pile.

   What is the greatest number that Billy can make from these four tiles?

   A. 9,863
   B. 3,689
   C. 8,639
   D. 9,368

6. M3N1.a. What is the value of the digit 6 in 5,046?

   A. 6,000
   B. 600
   C. 60
   D. 6

Chapter CRCT Test Prep

ALGEBRA

7. M3A1.a. Which number is next in the pattern?

   958, 858, 758, 658, □

   A. 657

   B. 648

   C. 558

   D. 458

8. M3A1.a. Marci is shading a pattern on a hundred chart as shown.

41	42	43	**44**	45	46	47	**48**	49	50
51	**52**	53	54	55	**56**	57	58	59	**60**
61	62	63	**64**	65	66	67	68	69	70

   What is the next number she should shade?

   A. 59

   B. 68

   C. 69

   D. 79

9. M3A1.a. Which number is next in the pattern?

   40, 48, 56, 64, □

   A. 68

   B. 72

   C. 74

   D. 81

ALGEBRA

10. M3A1.a. Joshua wrote the pattern 24, 27, 30, 33, 36. What is the next number in Joshua's pattern?

   A. 38

   B. 39

   C. 40

   D. 46

11. M3A1.a. Griffin's class is selling tickets to the fall festival. The table shows how many tickets they have sold in the first 3 days.

Tickets Sold

Day	Number of Tickets
1	6
2	12
3	18
4	□

   If the pattern continues how many tickets will the class sell on the fourth day?

   A. 30 tickets

   B. 28 tickets

   C. 24 tickets

   D. 20 tickets

CHAPTER 2

Compare, Order, and Estimate

FAST FACT • SOCIAL STUDIES The state of Georgia has many beautiful lakes. These lakes are used for boating, fishing, and other outdoor recreation activities.

INVESTIGATION The distance around a lake is called its shoreline. The graph shows the number of miles of shoreline for each Georgia lake.

Which lake has the most shoreline? Explain how to compare the length of the longest shoreline to the lengths of the other shorelines.

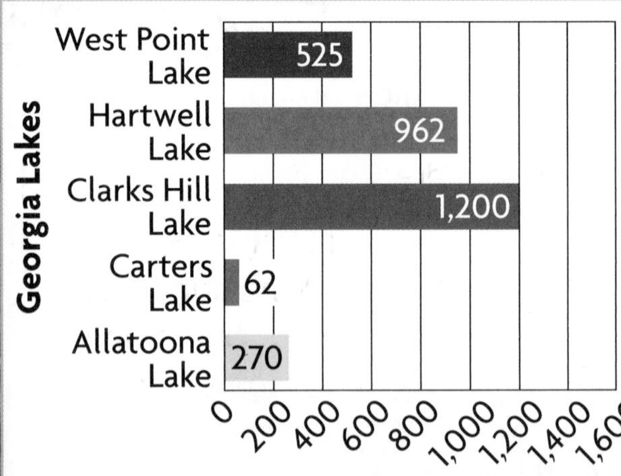

Use this page to help you review and remember important skills needed for Chapter 2.

COMPARE 2- AND 3-DIGIT NUMBERS

Write <, >, or = for each ●.

1. 34 ● 25
2. 45 ● 56
3. 239 ● 293
4. 67 ● 76
5. 342 ● 342
6. 706 ● 760

ORDER NUMBERS

Write the numbers in order from least to greatest.

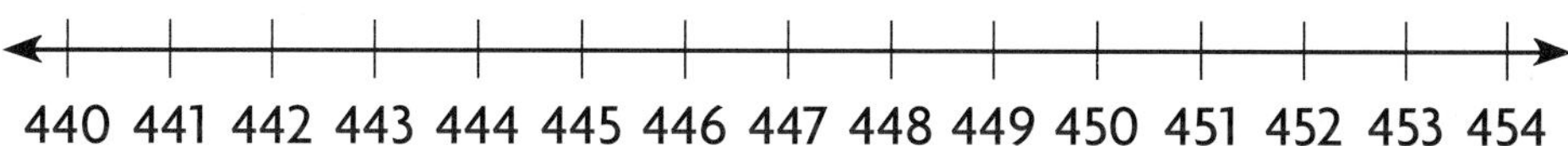

7. 451 442 448
8. 450 444 440
9. 452 441 449
10. 446 453 443

VOCABULARY POWER

REVIEW

hundred [hun′drəd] *noun*

The German word for hundred is *hundert*. Its value and meaning have changed over time. Its value is now 100. How many hundreds are in 672?

PREVIEW

benchmark numbers
is less than (<)
is greater than (>)
bar graph
is equal to (=)

www.harcourtschool.com/mathglossary

LESSON 1

Benchmark Numbers

Concepts/Skill to Maintain Addition & subtraction of multi-digit numbers
also M3P3.a., M3P3.b., M3P3.c., M3P3.d.

Quick Review

Which is greater?

1. 29 or 92
2. 101 or 1,001
3. 523 or 498
4. 7 or 70
5. 64 or 65

VOCABULARY

benchmark numbers

Learn

HOW MANY? Numbers that help you estimate the number of objects without counting them are called **benchmark numbers**. Any useful number can be a benchmark.

About how many jellybeans are in Jar B? You can use 25 as a benchmark to estimate.

There are 25 jellybeans in Jar A.

There are about ■ jellybeans in Jar B.

B

There are about twice as many jellybeans in Jar B.

So, there are about 50 jellybeans in Jar B.

Think about the number of students in your class, your grade, and your school. Which has about 25 students? Which has about 100 students? Which has about 500 students?

BENCHMARK	NUMBER TO BE ESTIMATED
25	students in your class
100	students in your grade
500	students in your school

- Suppose all the third and fourth-grade classes went on a field trip. About how many students went? What benchmark can you use?

Check

1. **Explain** how a benchmark could help you estimate the number of girls in your grade.

Estimate the number of jellybeans in each jar. Use Jars A and B as benchmarks.

Jar A has 10 jellybeans.

Jar B has about 50 jellybeans.

2. 

10 or 50?

3. 

25 or 50?

4.  

100 or 200?

Practice and Problem Solving

Extra Practice, page 36, Set A

5. Estimate the number of jellybeans in the jar at the right. Use Jars A and B above as benchmarks.

For 6–7, choose a benchmark of 10, 100, or 500 to estimate.

6. the number of players on a soccer team

7. the number of pretzels in a large bag

8. **MULTISTEP** Juan had 30 blocks. He gave 18 to Rick but got 14 from Ron. How many blocks does Juan have now?

9. **Write a problem** in which a benchmark is used to estimate. Solve.

Maintain Skills

10. Write the amount.

CRCT Test Prep

11. M3N1.a. What is the value of the blue digit in 15,688? (p. 14)

A. 6
B. 60
C. 600
D. 700

LESSON 2

Algebra: Compare Numbers

Concepts/Skill to Maintain Comparison of numbers
also **M3P5., M3P5.b., M3P5.c.**

Quick Review

Write how many tens each number has.

1. 15 **2.** 20 **3.** 54
4. 37 **5.** 82

VOCABULARY

is greater than (>)
is less than (<)
is equal to (=)

Learn

HOW NEAR? HOW FAR? Beth lives 262 miles from Homer and 245 miles from Lakewood. Which city does she live closer to?

Use a sign of equality (=) to show that two numbers are equal. Use a sign of inequality (< or >) to show that one number is less than or greater than the other.

is greater than (>) **is less than (<)**

One Way Use base-ten blocks.

Show 262 and 245. Compare from left to right.

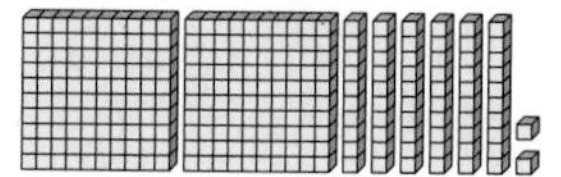

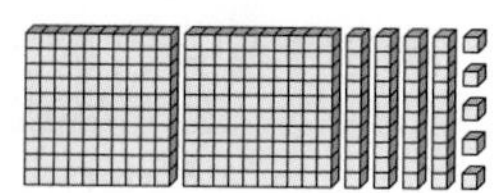

The hundreds are the same, so compare the tens.
6 tens > 4 tens.

262 > 245
262 is greater than 245.

245 < 262
245 is less than 262.

So, Beth lives closer to Lakewood.

Another Way Use a number line.

A Compare.

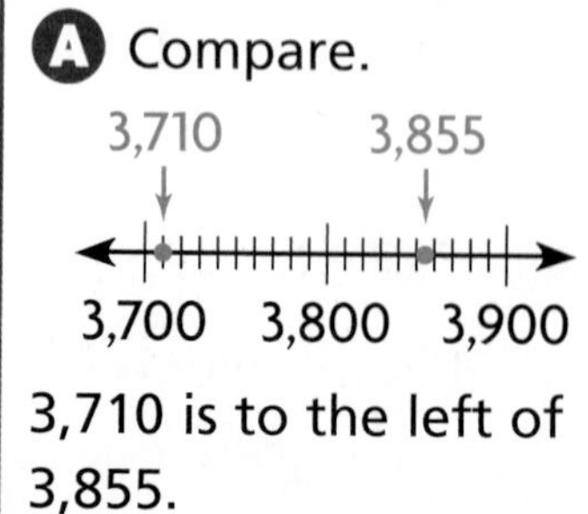

3,710 is to the left of 3,855.

3,710 < 3,855

B Compare.

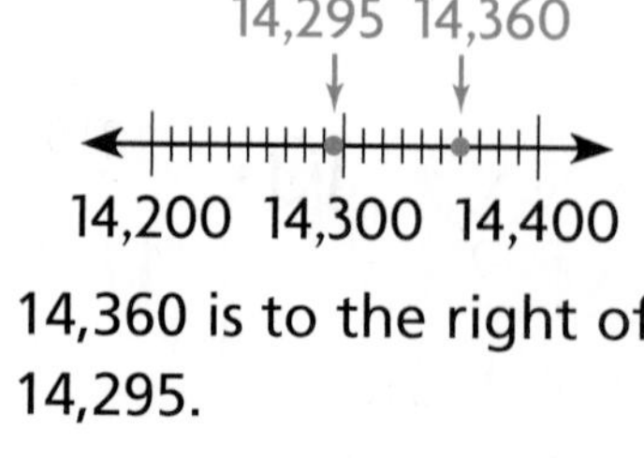

14,360 is to the right of 14,295.

14,360 > 14,295

C Compare.

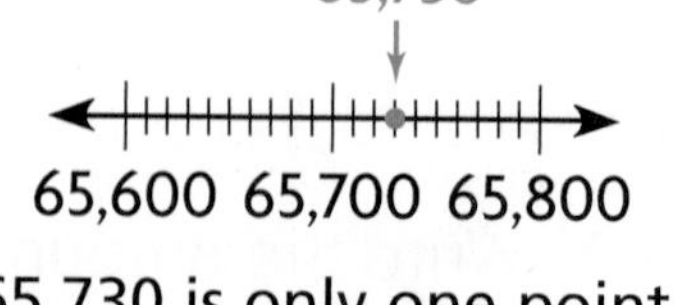

65,730 is only one point on the number line.

65,730 = 65,730

Use a Place-Value Chart

A place-value chart can help you compare greater numbers.

Compare 13,165 and 13,271, starting from the left.

TEN THOUSANDS	THOUSANDS	HUNDREDS	TENS	ONES
1	3,	1	6	5
1	3,	2	7	1
↑ Ten thousands are the same.	↑ Thousands are the same.	↑ 200 > 100		

So, 13,271 > 13,165 and 13,165 < 13,271.

Technology Link

More Practice: Harcourt Mega Math Country Countdown, *Harrison's Comparisons*, Levels G, L, and M; *Fraction Action*, Number Line Mine, Level B

MATH IDEA Compare numbers by using base-ten blocks, a number line, or a place-value chart.

Check

1. **Explain** how to use base-ten blocks to compare 341 and 300 + 40 + 1. What do you notice?

2. Use the number line in Example A on page 24 to compare 3,820 and 3,780. Which number is greater? Explain.

Compare the numbers. Write <, >, or = for each ●.

3. 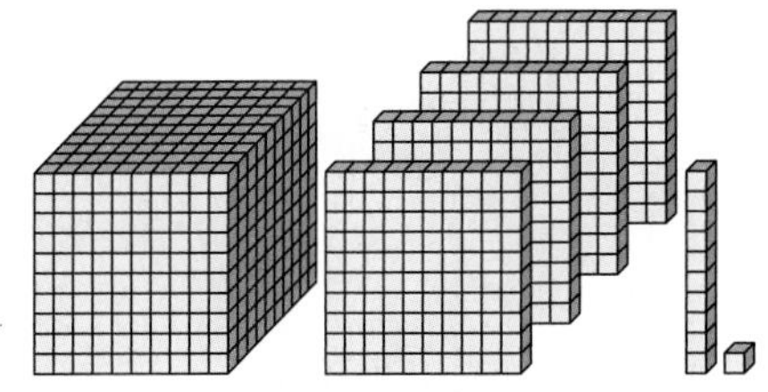 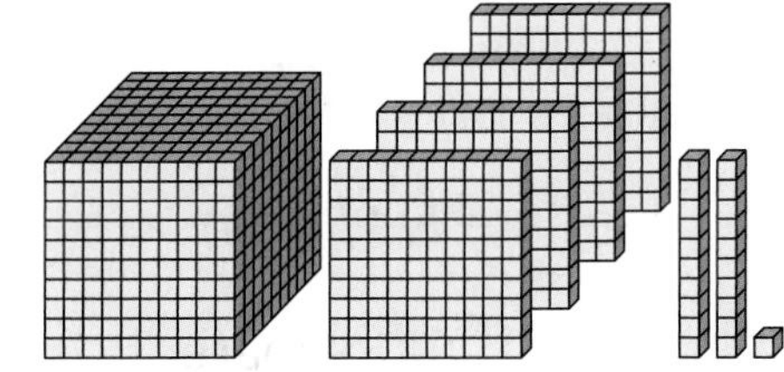

1,411 ● 1,421

4.

T	O
9	2
8	3

92 ● 83

5.

H	T	O
1	0	1
1	1	0

101 ● 110

6.

TH	H	T	O
2,	4	2	8
2,	4	3	8

2,428 ● 2,438

LESSON CONTINUES

Practice and Problem Solving

Extra Practice, page 36, Set B

Compare the numbers. Write <, >, or = for each ●.

7.

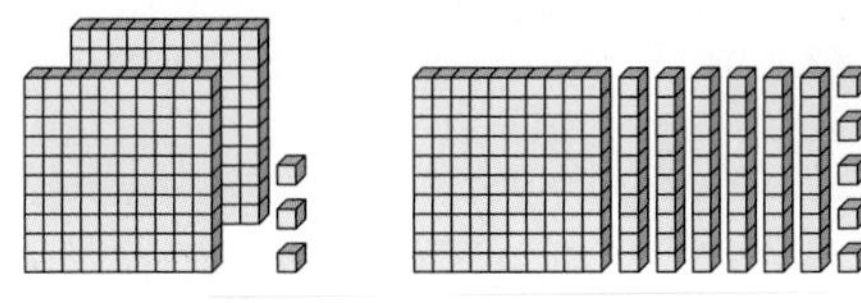

203 ● 165

8.

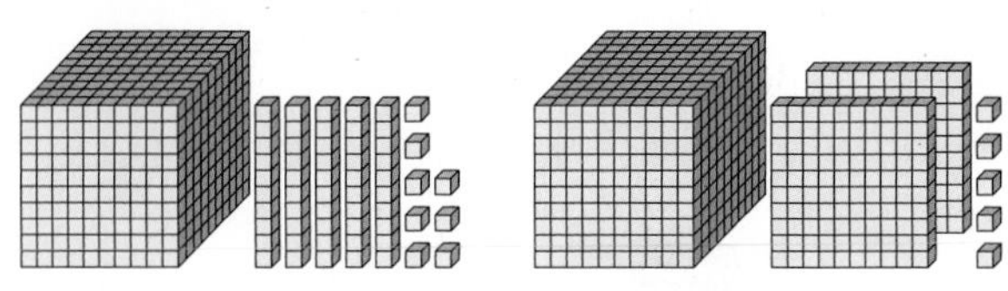

1,058 ● 1,205

9.

H	T	O
6	2	1
6	2	1

621 ● 621

10.

H	T	O
8	1	6
8	2	3

816 ● 823

11.

TH	H	T	O
4,	8	0	5
4,	8	1	9

4,805 ● 4,819

12. 629 ● 631

13. 5,712 ● 5,412

14. 2,412 ● 2,421

15. 1,894 ● 2,139

16. 10,348 ● 10,348

17. 37,393 ● 73,396

ALGEBRA Write the missing number that makes the number sentence true.

18. 341 = 34■

19. 887 < 8■4

20. 1,196 > 1,■98

21. What is the greatest place-value position in which the digits of 5,831 and 5,819 are different? Compare the numbers.

22. Compare the numbers 5,361 and 3,974. Which number is less? Draw a picture to show how you know.

For 23–25, use the numbers on the box.

23. List all the numbers that are less than 575.

24. List all the numbers that are greater than 830.

25. List all the numbers that are greater than 326 and less than 748.

26. **What's the Question?** Louis read 125 pages. Tom read 137 pages. The answer is 12.

27. **Write About It** You have 3 four-digit numbers. The digits in the thousands, hundreds, and ones places are the same. Which digits would you use to compare the numbers? Explain.

28. The numbers 456 and 564 have the same digits in a different order. Do they both have the same value? Explain.

29. **MULTISTEP** The sum of three addends is 24. One addend is 5. Another addend is 3 more than 7. What is the missing addend?

Maintain Skills

Write the time.

30. 

31. 

32. 

33. 

CRCT Test Prep

34. M3N1.b. Which shows 3 thousands, 6 hundreds, 7 tens, and 2 ones? (p. 6)

A. 3,072 C. 3,627
B. 3,602 D. 3,672

35. M3N1.a. What is the value of the digit 5 in 34,520? (p. 14)

A. 50 C. 5,000
B. 500 D. 50,000

Problem Solving Thinker's Corner

MANY USES OF NUMBERS Numbers tell how much or how many. They also tell the order of things. Numbers are even used to name things.

1. Give at least two examples for each.
   a. a number used to tell how much or how many
   b. a number used to tell the order of things
   c. a number used to name things
2. **REASONING** Give an example of numbers you would compare. Give an example of numbers that it wouldn't make sense to compare. Explain.

LESSON 

Order Numbers

Concepts/Skill to Maintain Comparison of numbers
also **M3P2.c., M3P3.a., M3P3.b., M3P3.c., M3P3.d.**

Learn

MOUNTAIN HIGH The table lists the heights of three mountains in the United States. Which is the tallest?

Use a number line to order the numbers.

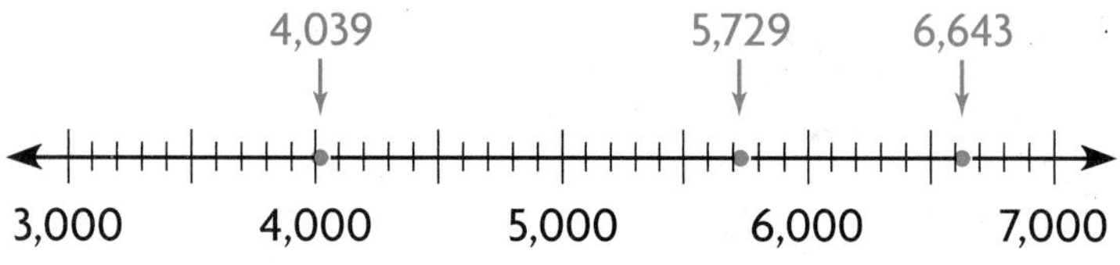

4,039 < 5,729 < 6,643

So, Clingmans Dome is the tallest.

You can order numbers by comparing the digits in the same place-value position from left to right.

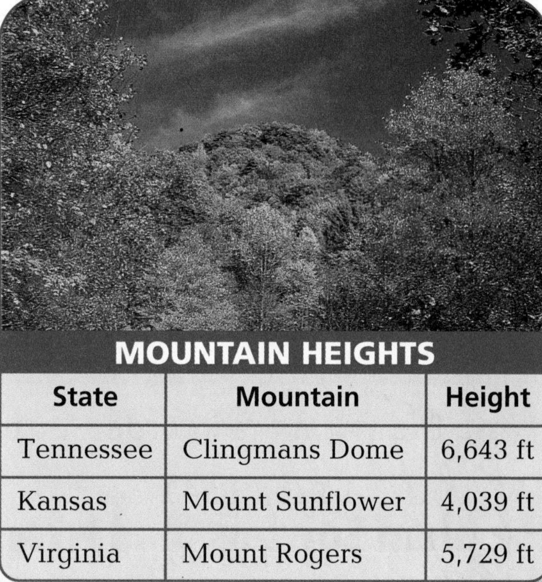

MOUNTAIN HEIGHTS

State	Mountain	Height
Tennessee	Clingmans Dome	6,643 ft
Kansas	Mount Sunflower	4,039 ft
Virginia	Mount Rogers	5,729 ft

Quick Review

Tell which number is greater.

1. 37 or 29
2. 21 or 32
3. 58 or 65
4. 120 or 99
5. 235 or 253

Example

Order 47,613; 45,435; and 46,551.

STEP 1

Compare ten thousands.

47,613
45,435
46,551

The digits are the same.

STEP 2

Compare thousands.

47,613
45,435
46,551

They are not the same.
7 > 6 > 5

STEP 3

Write the numbers in order from greatest to least.

47,613 > 46,551 > 45,435

Check

1. **Explain** how you can order the numbers 51,432; 51,438; and 51,463 from greatest to least.

Write the numbers in order from least to greatest.

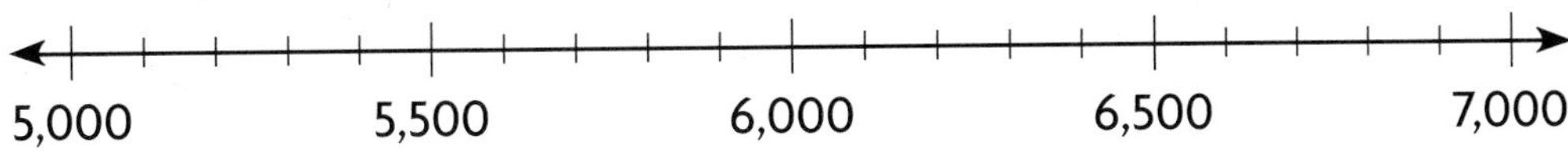

2. 5,200; 6,500; 5,900

3. 6,750; 6,125; 6,500

Practice and Problem Solving

Extra Practice, page 36, Set C

Write the numbers in order from least to greatest.

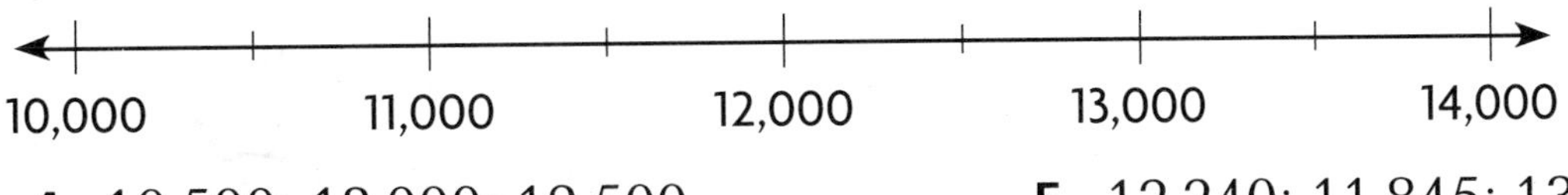

4. 10,500; 13,000; 12,500

5. 12,240; 11,845; 13,156

6.

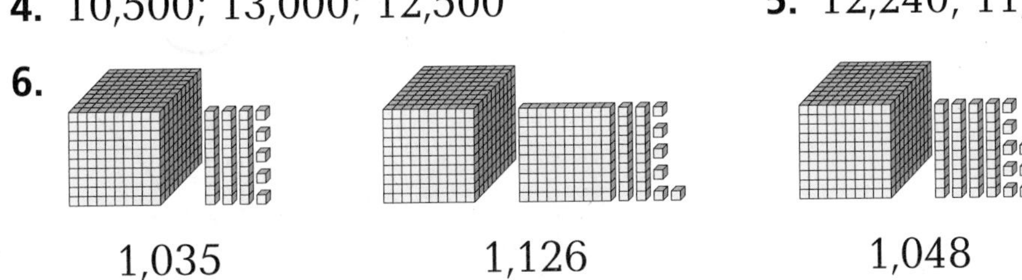

1,035 1,126 1,048

Write the numbers in order from greatest to least.

7. 7,837; 5,126; 3,541

8. 2,793; 2,728; 2,756

9. 32,603; 28,497; 90,050

10. 17,655; 22,600; 9,860

11. **REASONING** Write in order from least to greatest the six numbers whose digits are 2, 8, and 9.

12. Draw a picture that shows how to order 1,098; 1,126; and 973 from least to greatest.

13. **Vocabulary Power** The word *order* comes from the Latin word *ordo*, which means "a row or a line." How does this meaning relate to ordering numbers?

14. **What's the Error?** Jason said that the numbers 3,545; 3,556; and 3,554 were in order from least to greatest. What is his error?

Maintain Skills

Write the number of sides.

15.

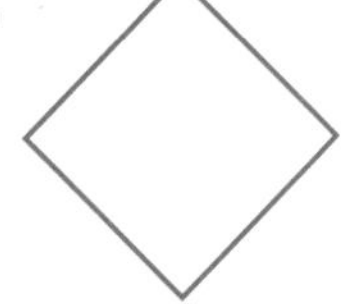

16.

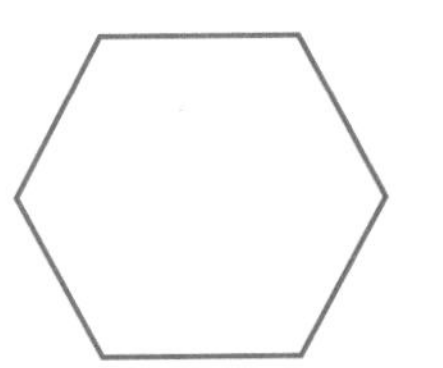

CRCT Test Prep

17. M3A1.a. Which is the next number in the pattern? (p. 12)

461, 561, 661, 761, □

A. 762
B. 771
C. 772
D. 861

Problem Solving Skill
Use a Bar Graph

M3D1.a. Solve problems by organizing and displaying data in bar graphs and tables. *also* M3P1.a., M3P1.b., M3P1.c., M3P1.d., M3P3., M3P3.a., M3P3.b., M3P3.c., M3P3.d., M3P4., M3P4.c., M3P5.b., M3P5.c.

UNDERSTAND | PLAN | SOLVE | CHECK

Quick Review

Compare. Write <, >, or = for each ●.

1. 124 ● 118
2. 229 ● 232
3. 244 ● 244
4. 3,156 ● 3,165
5. 4,371 ● 4,372

VOCABULARY

bar graph

FOLLOW THE TRAIL Nancy and Emilio are studying Georgia's state parks. They want to hike in the park that is larger than Fort Yargo but not as large as Fort Mountain. Which one should they choose?

A **bar graph** uses bars to show data. You can use a bar graph to solve problems.

Example

GEORGIA STATE PARKS

State Park	Size in Acres
Cloudland Canyon	3,485
Fort Yargo	1,814
Magnolia Springs	1,071
Fort Mountain	3,712

Size in Acres axis: 0, 500, 1,000, 1,500, 2,000, 2,500, 3,000, 3,500, 4,000

STEP 1

Look at the lengths of the bars in the graph. List the 4 parks from largest to smallest.

Fort Mountain, Cloudland Canyon, Fort Yargo, and Magnolia Springs

STEP 2

Find all the parks that are larger than Fort Yargo.

Cloudland Canyon and Fort Mountain

STEP 3

Find all the parks that are not as large as Fort Mountain.

Cloudland Canyon, Fort Yargo, and Magnolia Springs

STEP 4

Find the park that is listed in both Step 2 and Step 3.

Cloudland Canyon is the only state park listed in both steps.

So, Nancy and Emilio chose Cloudland Canyon.

Talk About It

- How does the size of Magnolia Springs compare to that of Fort Yargo?

Problem Solving Practice

1. **What if** Emilio and Nancy hiked in the park that is larger than Magnolia Springs but not as large as Cloudland Canyon? In which park did they hike?
2. What is the largest state park under 3,000 acres that Emilio and Nancy studied?
3. **What if** the parks were listed in order of size from least to greatest? What would be the order of the parks?

USE DATA For 4–5, use the bar graph at the right.

4. Which state is larger than Connecticut but smaller than New Jersey?

   A Hawaii **C** New Jersey
   B Rhode Island **D** Delaware

5. Name the three smallest states.

   F Delaware, Rhode Island, Hawaii
   G New Jersey, Hawaii, Connecticut
   H Hawaii, Rhode Island, New Jersey
   J Rhode Island, Delaware, Connecticut

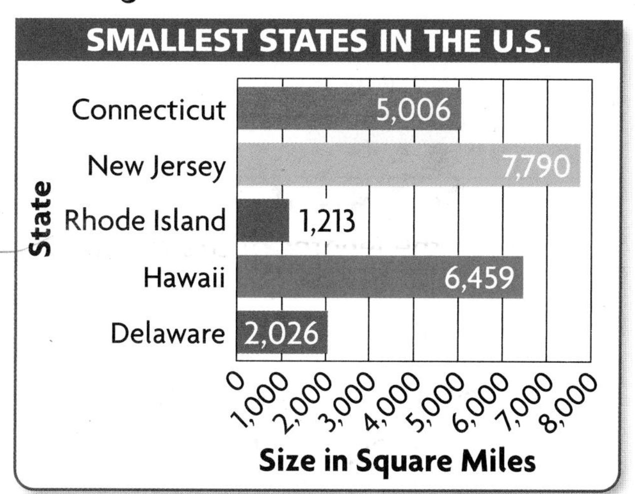

Mixed Applications

6. Louis had base-ten blocks that showed 6 hundreds, 7 tens, 3 ones. Tom gave him 2 hundreds, 1 ten, 5 ones. Using standard form, write the number that shows the value of Louis's blocks now.

7. Celia lives in a town with a population of 12,346. Last year there were 1,000 fewer people living in the town. How many people lived in the town last year?

8. Tony had 128 postcards. Arlo gave him some more postcards. Now Tony has 152 postcards. How many postcards did Arlo give to Tony?

9. There were 253 students that went to the Science Museum. Of them, 127 were girls. How many were boys?

10. **Write About It** Explain how you would compare 4,291; 4,921; and 4,129 to put them in order from greatest to least.

Problem Solving

LESSON 5

Nearest 10 and 100

M3N1.b. Understand the relative sizes of digits in place value notation (10 times, 100 times, 1/10 of a single digit whole number) and ways to represent them. *also* **M3P2.d., M3P3.a., M3P3.b., M3P3.d.**

Quick Review

Write the numbers in order from least to greatest.

1. 23, 19, 16 **2.** 37, 31, 23

3. 29, 33, 32 **4.** 59, 57, 58

5. 218, 287, 278

Learn

HOW CLOSE? There are 43 third graders and 47 fourth graders going on a field trip to the zoo. About how many students in each grade are going to the zoo?

You can estimate when you want to know *about how many*.

A number line can help you.

Example 1

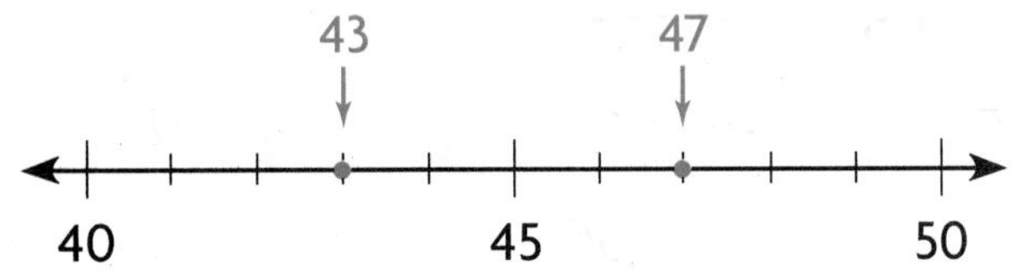

43 is closer to 40 than to 50.
40 is an estimate of 43.

47 is closer to 50 than to 40.
50 is an estimate of 47.

45 is halfway between 40 and 50.
If a number is halfway between two tens, estimate to the greater ten.
50 is an estimate of 45.

So, about 40 third graders and about 50 fourth graders are going to the zoo.

Example 2

Estimate 3-digit numbers to the nearest ten and the nearest hundred.

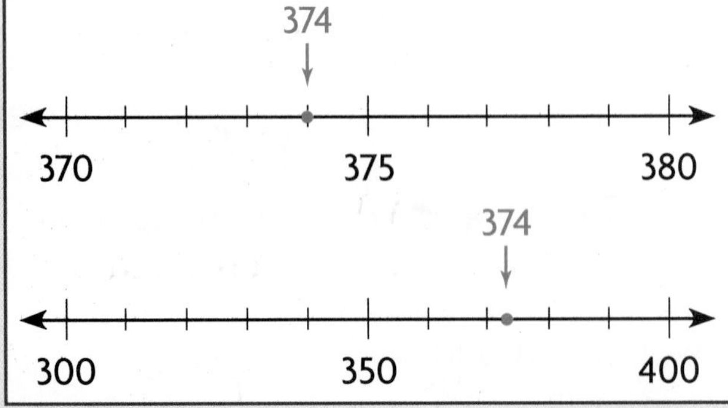

Estimate to the nearest ten.
374 is closer to 370 than to 380.
370 is an estimate of 374.

Round to the nearest hundred.
374 is closer to 400 than to 300.
400 is an estimate of 374.

Check

1. **Explain** how you can estimate 350 to the nearest hundred using the number line below.

Estimate to the nearest hundred and the nearest ten.

2. 643 **3.** 377 **4.** 445 **5.** 518 **6.** 750

Practice and Problem Solving

Extra Practice, page 36, Set D

Estimate to the nearest ten.

7. 16 **8.** 72 **9.** 53 **10.** 5 **11.** 78

12. 37 **13.** 44 **14.** 66 **15.** 94 **16.** 95

Estimate to the nearest hundred and the nearest ten.

17. 363 **18.** 405 **19.** 115 **20.** 165 **21.** 952

22. 698 **23.** 917 **24.** 385 **25.** 456 **26.** 883

USE DATA For 27–28, use the table.

ZOO ANIMALS

Type	Number
Mammals	214
Birds	428
Reptiles	174

27. To the nearest hundred, about how many kinds of birds does the zoo have?

28. **REASONING** The number of __?__ + the number of __?__ < the number of __?__ .

29. Kim estimated 348 to the nearest ten and said it was 350. She estimated 348 to the nearest hundred and said it was 400. Was this correct? Explain.

30. **Write a problem** about animals. Use estimating to the nearest ten or to the nearest hundred in your problem.

Maintain Skills

31. 63 + 20 = ■

32. 32 + 14 = ■

33. 57 – 30 = ■

34. 48 – 17 = ■

CRCT Test Prep

35. M3N1.b. Which shows 6 thousands, 4 tens, and 2 ones? (p. 6)

A. 640
B. 642
C. 6,042
D. 6,402

LESSON 

Nearest 1,000

M3N1.b. Understand the relative sizes of digits in place value notation (10 times, 100 times, 1/10 of a single digit whole number) and ways to represent them. *also* M3P3., M3P3.a-d., M3P4., M3P4.c.

Quick Review

Estimate to the nearest ten.

1. 52 **2.** 15 **3.** 27

4. 68 **5.** 76

Learn

ABOUT HOW MANY? When the Bronx Zoo in New York City first opened in 1899, it only had 843 animals. In a recent year, the Bronx Zoo had 4,405 animals.

To the nearest thousand, how many animals are in the zoo?

A number line can help you.

Example 1

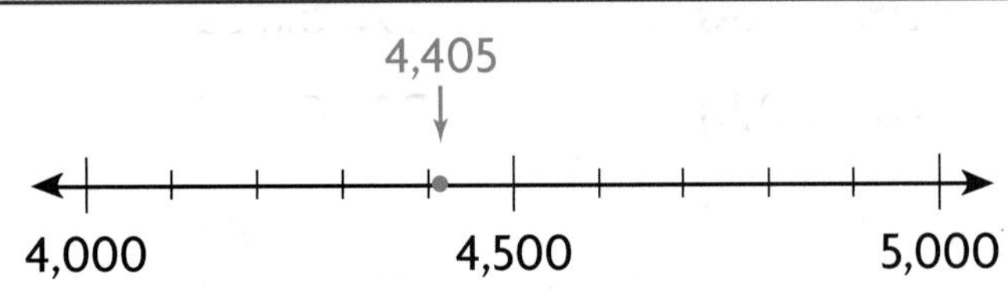

4,405 is closer to 4,000 than to 5,000.
4,000 is an estimate of 4,405.

4,500 is halfway between 4,000 and 5,000. If a number is halfway between two thousands, estimate to the greater thousand.
5,000 is an estimate of 4,500.

So, there are about 4,000 animals in the zoo.

Example 2

Estimate 4-digit numbers to the nearest thousand and the nearest hundred.

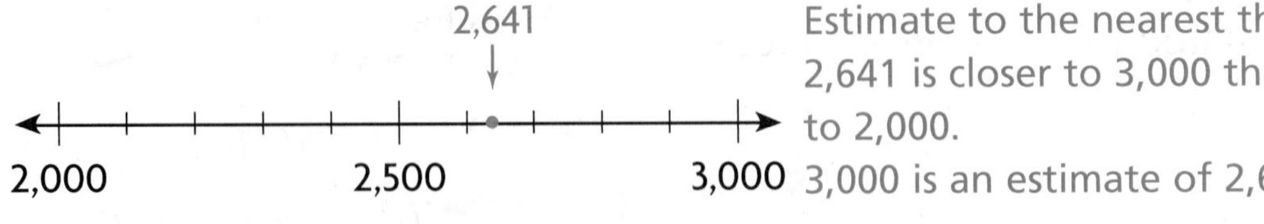

Estimate to the nearest thousand.
2,641 is closer to 3,000 than to 2,000.
3,000 is an estimate of 2,641.

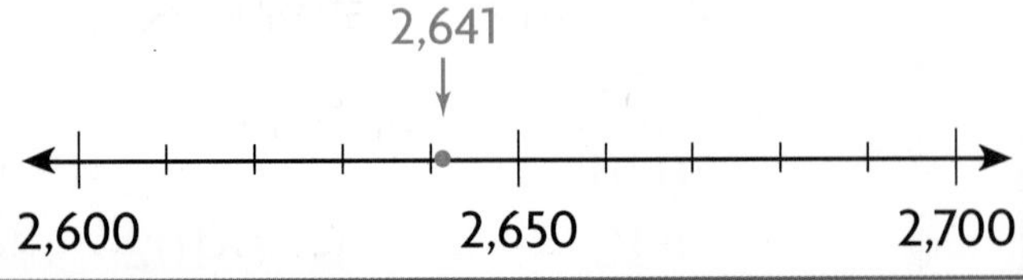

Estimate to the nearest hundred.
2,641 is closer to 2,600 than to 2,700.
2,600 is an estimate of 2,641.

Check

1. **Explain** how you would estimate 3,728 to the nearest thousand.

Estimate to the nearest thousand.

2. 6,427 3. 2,500 4. 4,526 5. 1,670

Practice and Problem Solving

Extra Practice, page 36, Set E

Estimate to the nearest thousand.

6. 8,312 7. 4,500 8. 674 9. 9,478
10. 1,611 11. 5,920 12. 2,543 13. 4,444

Estimate each to the nearest thousand, the nearest hundred, and the nearest ten.

14. 3,581 15. 6,318 16. 2,350 17. 8,914
18. 4,624 19. 5,337 20. 1,273 21. 2,845

USE DATA For 22–23, use the table.

22. Estimate the weights of the giraffe and rhinoceros to the nearest thousand pounds. About how many giraffes would it take to equal the weight of the rhinoceros?

23 **Write About It** Tell how to estimate the weight of the hippopotamus to the nearest thousand, hundred, and ten.

24. **FAST FACT** • SCIENCE Asian elephants weigh less than African elephants. One Asian elephant weighed 7,586 pounds. What is 7,586 estimated to the nearest thousand?

HEAVIEST LAND MAMMALS

Animal	Weight in Pounds
African elephant	11,023
Indian rhinoceros	8,818
Hippopotamus	4,409
Giraffe	2,646

Maintain Skills

Compare the numbers. Write <, >, or = for each ●.

25. 57 ● 87 26. 39 ● 15
27. 32 ● 23 28. 79 ● 82

CRCT Test Prep

29. M3A1.a. Which is the next number in the pattern? (p. 12)

23, 33, 43, 53, □

A. 54 B. 55 C. 60 D. 63

Extra Practice

Set A (pp. 22–23)

For 1–2, choose a benchmark of 10, 100, or 500 to estimate.

1. the number of pieces in a small bag of dog food
2. the number of teeth in your mouth
3. There are 25 students in Ken's third-grade class. There are 4 third-grade classes. About how many students are in the third grade?

Set B (pp. 24–27)

Compare the numbers. Write <, >, or = for each ●.

1. 400 ● 12
2. 646 ● 600
3. 741 ● 741
4. 57 ● 75
5. 4,701 ● 4,071
6. 10,313 ● 10,515

Set C (pp. 28–29)

Write the numbers in order from least to greatest.

1. 124; 562; 347
2. 102; 89; 157
3. 1,466; 1,365; 1,988

Write the numbers in order from greatest to least.

4. 42,218; 43,010; 42,115
5. 61,010; 61,501; 60,531

Set D (pp. 32–33)

Estimate to the nearest hundred and the nearest ten.

1. 414
2. 888
3. 502
4. 635
5. 157
6. 733
7. 374
8. 498

Set E (pp. 34–35)

Estimate to the nearest thousand.

1. 3,345
2. 8,866
3. 5,533
4. 6,500
5. 9,457
6. 1,168
7. 7,662
8. 2,220

Review/Test

✓ CHECK VOCABULARY AND CONCEPTS

Vocabulary
- benchmark numbers
- is less than (<)
- bar graph

Choose the best term from the box.

1. Numbers that help you estimate the number of objects without counting them are called __?__ . (p. 22)
2. A graph that uses bars to show data is a __?__ . (p. 30)

Suppose you want to estimate 371 to the nearest hundred. (pp. 32–33)

3. Which hundreds is 371 between?
4. Which hundred is 371 closer to?

✓ CHECK SKILLS

Compare the numbers. Write <, >, or = for each ●. (pp. 24–27)

5. 532 ● 523
6. 23,246 ● 32,325
7. 7,583 ● 7,583

Write the numbers in order from least to greatest. (pp. 28–29)

8. 143, 438, 92
9. 7,304; 7,890; 7,141
10. 23,256; 23,161; 23,470
11. Estimate 85 to the nearest ten. (pp. 32–33)
12. Estimate 824 to the nearest hundred. (pp. 32–33)
13. Estimate 3,721 to the nearest thousand and hundred. (pp. 34–35)

✓ CHECK PROBLEM SOLVING

USE DATA For 14–15, use the bar graph. (pp. 30–31)

14. On which night was the number of tickets sold greater than the number sold on Monday but less than the number sold on Wednesday?
15. On which night was the number of tickets sold less than the number sold on Friday but greater than the number sold on Wednesday?

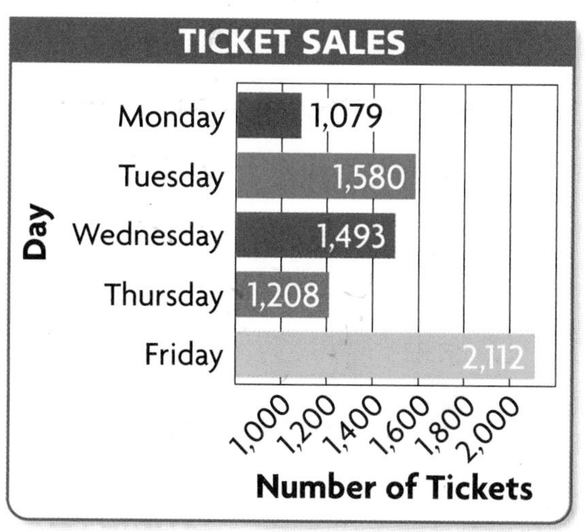

Chapter CRCT Test Prep

NUMBERS AND OPERATIONS

Use the table below to answer question 1.

Springfield School Students	
School	**Number of Students**
Central	824
Eastgate	931
Westville	796

1. M3N1.b. Springfield has three schools. The table shows how many students go to each school. What is the number of students that go to Westville estimated to the nearest hundred?

A. 700

B. 800

C. 900

D. 1,000

2. M3N1.b. Kelly collected 273 seashells at the beach. Which number shows how many seashells Kelly collected estimated to the nearest ten?

A. 200

B. 270

C. 300

D. 350

DATA ANALYSIS

Use the graph below to answer question 3.

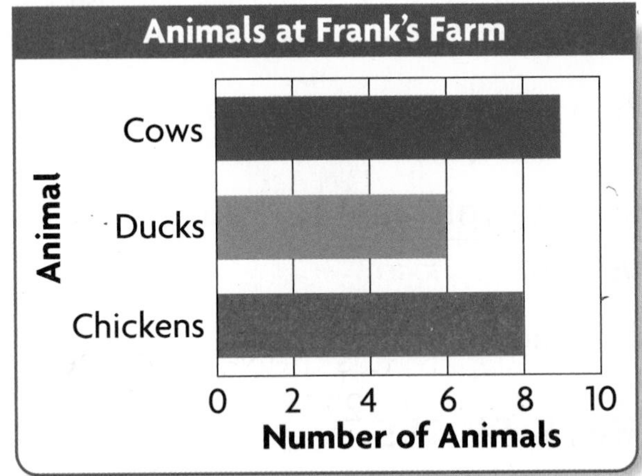

3. M3D1.b. The bar graph above shows the number of animals Frank has at his farm. How many cows are on Frank's farm?

A. 6

B. 8

C. 9

D. 10

Cumulative CRCT Test Prep

NUMBERS AND OPERATIONS

4. M3N1.a. What is 5,637 estimated to the nearest thousand?

A. 5,000

B. 5,500

C. 6,000

D. 6,500

5. M3N1.a. What is the value of the digit 9 in 89,427?

A. 90

B. 900

C. 9,000

D. 90,000

6. M3N1.a. What is 359 estimated to the nearest hundred?

A. 300

B. 350

C. 360

D. 400

7. M3N1.a. What number shows 3 thousands, 6 tens, 2 ones?

A. 3,062

B. 3,602

C. 3,620

D. 36,002

ALGEBRA

8. M3A1.a. What is the number next in the pattern?

576, 676, 776, □

A. 777

B. 786

C. 876

D. 976

9. M3A1.a. Gail is using a hundred chart to skip-count by threes. So far, she has shaded the chart as shown below.

1	2	3	4	5	6	7	8	9	10
11	12	13	14	15	16	17	18	19	20
21	22	23	24	25	26	27	28	29	30
31	32	33	34	35	36	37	38	39	40
41	42	43	44	45	46	47	48	49	50
51	52	53	54	55	56	57	58	59	60
61	62	63	64	65	66	67	68	69	70
71	72	73	74	75	76	77	78	79	80
81	82	83	84	85	86	87	88	89	90
91	92	93	94	95	96	97	98	99	100

When she finishes shading the chart, which of these numbers will be shaded?

A. 65

B. 74

C. 81

D. 97

GPS/CRCT Vocabulary

ELA3R2 The student acquires and uses grade-level words to communicate effectively. *also* **ELA3R3.b., ELA3R3.h., ELA3R3.r.**

VOCABULARY

- **whole number**
- **pattern**
- **benchmark numbers**
- **is greater than (>)**
- **is less than (<)**
- **is equal to (=)**
- **bar graph**

VOCABULARY MATCH

MATERIALS *For each pair* vocabulary cards, definition cards

- Shuffle the vocabulary cards and the definition cards together.
- Deal 4 cards to each player. Place the rest of the cards face down in a pile on the table.
- The players should match terms with their definitions to make pairs from their cards and set them aside.
- Take turns drawing a card from the pile. If it matches a card in your hand, keep it and set the pair aside. If not, return it to the bottom of the pile.

V	R	G	R	E	A	T	E	R	O
B	J	A	T	A	N	O	L	T	R
E	P	E	Q	U	A	L	I	T	Y
N	L	G	R	J	S	L	T	R	H
C	S	R	M	W	J	A	B	W	L
H	P	A	T	T	E	R	N	H	K
M	D	P	Z	T	L	M	T	O	P
A	T	H	E	B	Y	Q	O	L	N
R	F	E	S	T	L	W	M	E	U
K	M	D	X	O	P	S	L	F	Y

MATH WORD WORK

MATERIALS *For each student* Unit 1 *Math Word Work* puzzle

- Find and circle the terms listed below.

benchmark	**graph**
equality	**pattern**
greater	**whole**

WHAT'S IN THE BOX?

MATERIALS *For each pair* Unit 1 *What's in the Box?* puzzle

- With a partner, use the clues and the terms in the Vocabulary box on page 40 to help you fill in the blanks on your sheet.
- The letters in the boxes will spell one of the most important crops in Georgia.

1. ___ ___ ___ ☐ ___
2. ___ ___ ___ ___ ___ ☐
3. ___ ___ ___ ☐ ___ ___ ___
4. ___ ___ ☐ ___ ___ ___ ___ ___ ___ ___
5. ___ ___ ☐ ___ ___
6. ___ ___ ☐ ___ ___ ___ ___
7. ___ ___ ☐ ___

1. A **bar** _?_ uses bars to display data.
2. The numbers 0, 1, 2, 3, 4, ... are called _?_ **numbers**.
3. 376 **is** _?_ **than** 367.
4. Numbers that help you estimate without counting are _?_ **numbers**.
5. 820 **is** _?_ **to** 800 + 20.
6. A _?_ is an ordered set of numbers or objects.
7. 625 **is** _?_ **than** 652.

GRID GAME

MATERIALS *For each group* definition cards, counters, grid paper

- Look at the terms in the Vocabulary box on page 40. Write the terms randomly on your grid, one term to a box. Fill in all the boxes. You will use some terms more than once.
- Choose one player to be the "caller". The caller mixes up the definition cards, chooses one, and reads it aloud. Each player puts a counter on the term that matches the definition read. Each player can place one counter on his or her grid for each turn.
- The definition card goes back in the pile. Play until someone gets 4 counters in a row, either up and down, across, or diagonally.

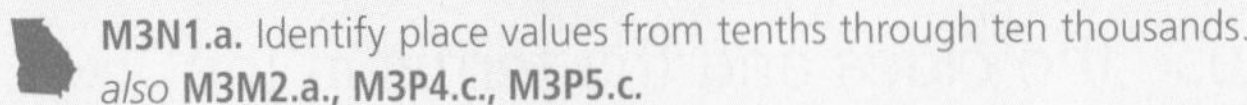

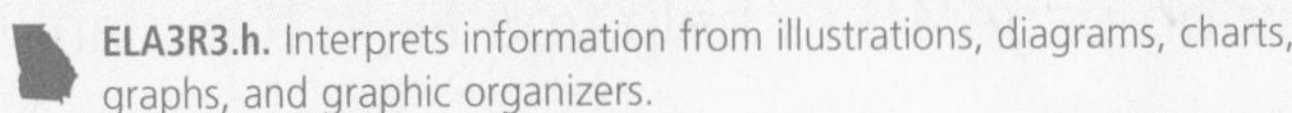

Task A

A FAMILY VACATION

Jeff's family is planning a vacation. The table shows the cities they might want to visit.

a. Jeff's father does not want to travel more than 1,500 miles. Which cities could they go to?

b. The city Jeff wants to visit is about 1,000 miles away when estimated to the nearest thousand. Which cities could Jeff want to visit?

Driving Distances From Atlanta

City, State	Distance (miles)
Albany, NY	1,010
Billings, MT	1,800
Boston, MA	1,110
Charleston, SC	290
Los Angeles, CA	2,190

Task B

MOUNTAIN MAYHEM!

The highest peak in Georgia, Brasstown Bald, is part of the Blue Ridge mountain range. The table shows the heights of some other peaks in Georgia's Blue Ridge mountains.

a. Suppose you wanted to climb the shortest peak. Which would you climb? Explain how the bar graph can help you order the peaks without comparing digits.

b. Suppose you climbed to 4,000 feet on Rocky Mountain. How many more feet would you have to climb to reach the top? Write the height of Rocky Mountain in expanded form to help.

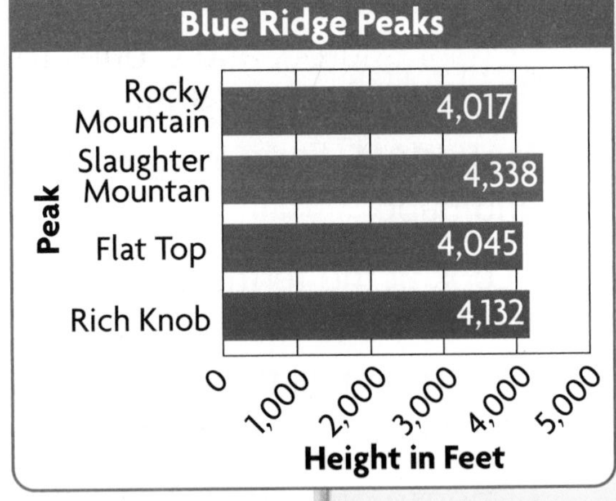

Maintain/Preview

Maintain

Write each number in standard form.

1. 4,000 + 300 + 20 + 6
2. 10,000 + 50 + 1
3. twenty-two thousand, nine hundred six
4. 8 hundreds 2 tens 7 ones

Predict the next number in each pattern.

5. 33, 36, 39, 42, ■
6. 85, 83, 81, 79, ■
7. 219, 215, 211, 207, ■
8. 401, 407, 413, 419, ■

Compare the numbers. Write <, >, or = for each ●.

9. 121 ● 112
10. 7,495 ● 7,945
11. 272 − 111 ● 88

Solve.

12. Marcus used 3 thousands, 1 hundred, and 6 ones to model a number. What number did he model?
13. Rabun Bald is the second highest mountain in Georgia. It has a height of 4,696 feet. What is this number estimated to the nearest hundred?

Preview

Find each sum or difference.

1. $\begin{array}{r} 25 \\ +23 \\ \hline \end{array}$
2. $\begin{array}{r} 38 \\ +47 \\ \hline \end{array}$
3. $\begin{array}{r} 67 \\ -21 \\ \hline \end{array}$
4. $\begin{array}{r} 71 \\ -18 \\ \hline \end{array}$

Write the amount.

5. 
6. 
7. 
8. 

CHAPTER 3 Addition

FAST FACT • SOCIAL STUDIES Dogs were first used as watchdogs, herding dogs, and hunting dogs. Now, more dogs are pets than workers. Some dogs are still trained to help disabled people.

INVESTIGATION Look at the chart. How can you find about how many dogs in all graduated during the four years?

CHECK WHAT YOU KNOW

Use this page to help you review and remember important skills needed for Chapter 3.

ADDITION FACTS

Add.

1. $\begin{array}{r} 2 \\ +7 \\ \hline \end{array}$
2. $\begin{array}{r} 9 \\ +4 \\ \hline \end{array}$
3. $\begin{array}{r} 7 \\ +9 \\ \hline \end{array}$
4. $\begin{array}{r} 3 \\ +8 \\ \hline \end{array}$
5. $\begin{array}{r} 8 \\ +7 \\ \hline \end{array}$

COLUMN ADDITION

Find the sum.

6. $\begin{array}{r} 1 \\ 4 \\ +6 \\ \hline \end{array}$
7. $\begin{array}{r} 2 \\ 1 \\ +9 \\ \hline \end{array}$
8. $\begin{array}{r} 6 \\ 6 \\ +6 \\ \hline \end{array}$
9. $\begin{array}{r} 5 \\ 4 \\ +7 \\ \hline \end{array}$
10. $\begin{array}{r} 8 \\ 5 \\ +2 \\ \hline \end{array}$

2-DIGIT ADDITION

Add.

11. $\begin{array}{r} 21 \\ +48 \\ \hline \end{array}$
12. $\begin{array}{r} 43 \\ +35 \\ \hline \end{array}$
13. $\begin{array}{r} 14 \\ +79 \\ \hline \end{array}$
14. $\begin{array}{r} 53 \\ +18 \\ \hline \end{array}$
15. $\begin{array}{r} 15 \\ +45 \\ \hline \end{array}$

VOCABULARY POWER

REVIEW

sum [sum] *noun*

The word *sum* comes from the Latin word *summus*, which means "highest." When early Romans added columns of numbers, they wrote the answer at the top. What word means the top of a mountain and comes from *summus*?

PREVIEW

Commutative Property of Addition
Identity Property of Addition
Associative Property of Addition
inverse operations
estimate
front-end estimation
expression
is not equal to (≠)

www.harcourtschool.com/mathglossary

LESSON 1

Algebra: Properties

M3N2.a. Use the properties of addition and subtraction to compute and verify the results of computation. *also* M3A1.c., M3P3.a., M3P3.b., M3P3.c., M3P3.d., M3P4.a., M3P4.b.

Quick Review

1. 4 + 9 = ■
2. 8 + 6 = ■
3. 8 + 7 = ■
4. 6 + 9 = ■
5. 9 + 7 = ■

VOCABULARY

Commutative Property of Addition
Identity Property of Addition
Associative Property of Addition

Learn

IN THE PARK Olivia saw 6 monarch butterflies and 7 swallowtails. Courtney saw 7 monarchs and 6 swallowtails. How many butterflies did each girl see in all?

Special rules, called properties, can help you add.

Commutative Property of Addition

You can add two or more numbers in any order and get the same sum.

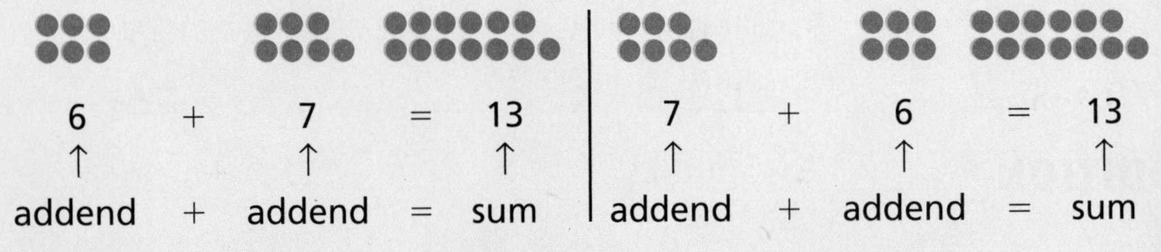

6	+	7	=	13	7	+	6	=	13
↑		↑		↑	↑		↑		↑
addend	+	addend	=	sum	addend	+	addend	=	sum

So, 6 + 7 = 7 + 6. Olivia and Courtney each saw 13 butterflies.

Identity Property of Addition

Courtney saw 12 tulips in a garden. Olivia didn't see any. How many tulips did the girls see in all?

When you add zero to a number, the sum is that number.

12 + 0 = 12

So, the girls saw 12 tulips in all.

Associative Property of Addition

Olivia saw 9 birds, 1 rabbit, and 4 squirrels in a meadow. How many animals did she see in all?

You can group addends in different ways and still get the same sum.

(9 + 1) + 4 = 9 + (1 + 4)
10 + 4 = 9 + 5
14 = 14

Hint: The ( ) symbols tell you which numbers to add first.

So, Olivia saw 14 animals in all.

Check

1. **Explain** how the Associative Property of Addition can help you find $2 + (8 + 4)$.

Find each sum.

2. $15 + 0 = ■$
3. $8 + 6 = ■$
   $6 + 8 = ■$
4. $4 + (6 + 5) = ■$
   $(4 + 6) + 5 = ■$

Practice and Problem Solving

Extra Practice, page 64, Set A

Find each sum.

5. $7 + 4 = ■$
   $4 + 7 = ■$
6. $(3 + 7) + 8 = ■$
   $3 + (7 + 8) = ■$
7. $8 + 9 = ■$
   $9 + 8 = ■$
8. $8 + (1 + 9) = ■$
   $(8 + 1) + 9 = ■$
9. $6 + 11 = ■$
   $11 + 6 = ■$
10. $8 + (5 + 6) = ■$
    $(8 + 5) + 6 = ■$
11. $13 + 0 = ■$
12. $(6 + 8) + 3 = ■$
    $6 + (8 + 3) = ■$
13. $8 + 5 = ■$
    $5 + 8 = ■$

14. Jake has 4 cats. Matthew has 5 birds and 2 dogs. Draw a picture to show how many pets they have in all.

15. The sum of two numbers is 14. One of the numbers is 5 less than the sum. What are the two numbers?

16. **REASONING** $3 + 9 = 12$ and $9 + 3 = 12$ shows the Commutative Property of Addition. Can you use the Commutative Property to subtract? Why or why not?

17. **MULTISTEP** Anna picked 7 roses, 7 tulips, and 3 daisies. Then she gave her mother 8 of the flowers. How many flowers did she have left?

Maintain Skills

Find the sum.

18. $24 + 22 = ■$
19. $18 + 27 = ■$

Find the difference.

20. $39 - 12 = ■$
21. $33 - 14 = ■$

CRCT Test Prep

22. M3N2.c. Josh saw 13 butterflies in his yard on Saturday. On Sunday he saw 8 more than he saw on Saturday. How many butterflies did he see in all?

A. 20 B. 21 C. 32 D. 34

LESSON 2

Algebra: Missing Addends

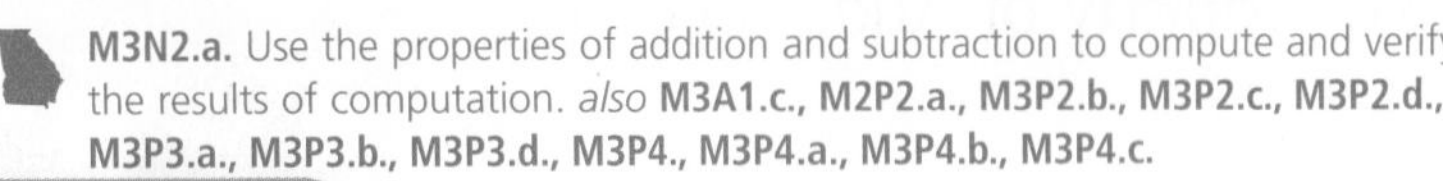

M3N2.a. Use the properties of addition and subtraction to compute and verify the results of computation. *also* M3A1.c., M2P2.a., M3P2.b., M3P2.c., M3P2.d., M3P3.a., M3P3.b., M3P3.d., M3P4., M3P4.a., M3P4.b., M3P4.c.

Learn

Quick Review

1. 5 + 6 = ■
2. 7 + 8 = ■
3. 6 + 9 = ■
4. 8 + 8 = ■
5. 5 + 7 = ■

VOCABULARY
inverse operations

HIKING Amy's family went hiking in the Chattahoochee National Forest in Georgia. They hiked on two trails that are a total of 28 miles long. The Bull Mountain trail is 15 miles long. How long is the Coosa Backcountry trail?

One Way Use addition to find the missing addend.

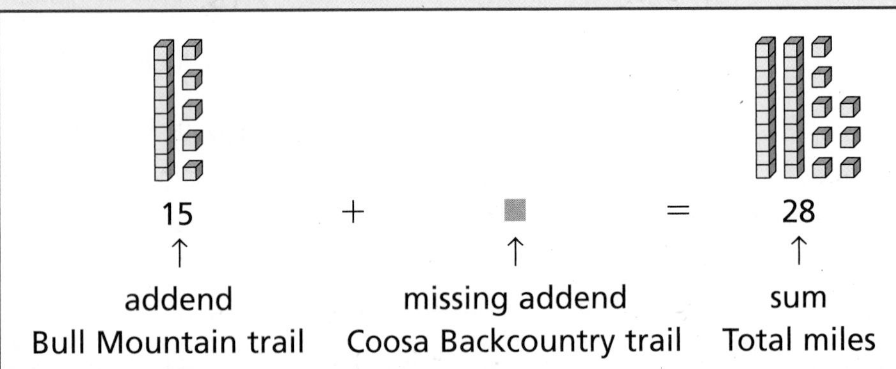

15 + 13 = 28

Another Way Use subtraction to find the missing addend.

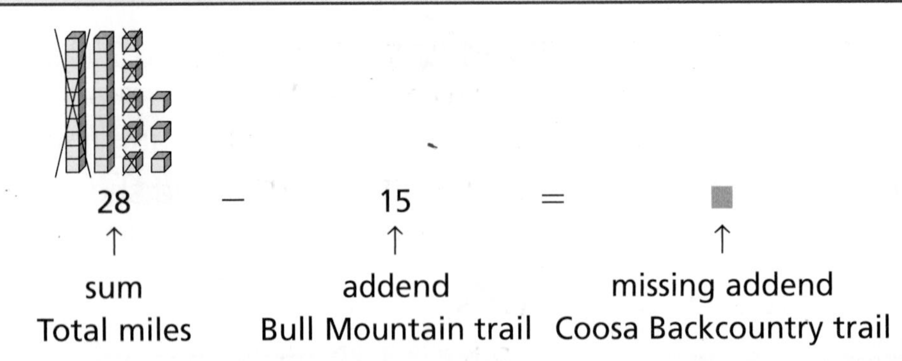

28 − 15 = 13

Since 15 + 13 = 28 and 28 − 15 = 13, the Coosa Backcountry trail is 13 miles long.

MATH IDEA Addition and subtraction are opposite or **inverse operations**. You can use inverse operations to find a missing addend.

Check

1. **Explain** how you can use subtraction to find ■ + 19 = 47.

Find the missing addend.

2. 25 + ■ = 61
3. ■ + 33 = 52
4. 44 + ■ = 60
5. ■ + 25 = 73

Practice and Problem Solving

Extra Practice, page 64, Set B

Find the missing addend.

6. 28 + ■ = 35
7. ■ + 43 = 61
8. ■ + 26 = 73
9. ■ + 36 = 84
10. ■ + 68 = 68
11. 35 + ■ = 43
12. 57 + ■ = 94
13. ■ + 29 = 75

14. James had 19 video games. He received more games as birthday gifts. Now James has 26 games. Use counters and an addition sentence to show how many games James received as gifts.

15. ***FAST FACT*** • SOCIAL STUDIES Indiana's Ghost Town Trail got its name from a railroad line running between old mining towns. The trail is 16 miles long. Four miles were added to the trail in 1993. How long was the trail in 1992?

16. **REASONING** How many pairs of missing addends are there for ■ + ■ = 8? List the pairs.

17. I am a number less than 50. My tens digit is 4. The sum of my digits is 4. What number am I?

18. I am a number less than 100. My tens digit is 7 more than my ones digit. My ones digit is 2. What number am I?

19. **What's the Error?** Jenna wrote 42 − 14 = 27 to help her find 14 + ■ = 42. Describe and correct her error.

Maintain Skills

Compare the numbers. Write <, >, or = for each ●.

20. 13 ● 18
21. 24 ● 16
22. 41 ● 29
23. 38 ● 56

CRCT Test Prep

24. M3N2.c. Jordan has a fish tank with 6 goldfish, 3 black mollies, and 4 guppies. How many fish does she have in all?

A. 10
B. 13
C. 14
D. 16

LESSON 3

Estimate Sums

M3N2.b. Use mental math and estimation strategies to add and subtract. *also* M3P1.b., M3P1.d., M3P3.a., M3P3.b., M3P3.c., M3P3.d., M3P4.b.

Quick Review

1. 5 + 25
2. 30 + 20
3. 70 + 20
4. \$4 + \$6
5. 20 + 55

VOCABULARY

estimate
front-end estimation

Learn

MANATEE SUMMER HOMES Wildlife officers counted 329 manatees living along Georgia's Atlantic Coast. They also counted 174 manatees off the coast of South Carolina. About how many manatees did the wildlife officers count in all?

To find *about* how many, you can **estimate**. One way to estimate is to use **front-end estimation**. Use the front digit of each number, and write zeros for the other digits.

Example

Use front-end estimation. Add the front digit of each addend. Write zeros for the other digits.

Think: Write 329 as 300.
Write 174 as 100.

$$\begin{array}{rcr} 329 & \rightarrow & 300 \\ +174 & \rightarrow & +100 \\ \hline & & 400 \end{array}$$

So, 400 is a reasonable estimate of how many manatees were counted.

▲ A manatee spends 5 to 8 hours per day feeding on plants in the water and along the shoreline.

More Examples

A Use front-end estimation.

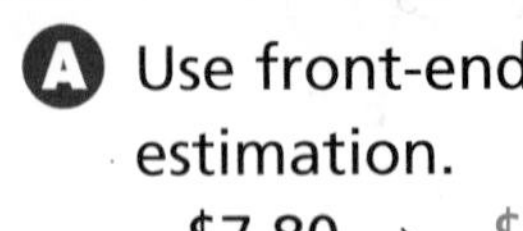

$$\begin{array}{rcr} \$7.80 & \rightarrow & \$7 \\ +\$4.35 & \rightarrow & +\$4 \\ \hline & & \$11 \end{array}$$

B Use front-end estimation.

$$\begin{array}{rcr} 3{,}260 & \rightarrow & 3{,}000 \\ +\ \ 755 & \rightarrow & +\ \ 700 \\ \hline & & 3{,}700 \end{array}$$

MATH IDEA When you do not need an exact answer, you can estimate by using front-end estimation.

- When you use front-end estimation, will your estimate be greater than or less than the actual sum? Explain.

Check

1. **Explain** whether you should use front-end estimation to decide if you have enough money. You want to buy books that cost $4.69 and $3.98.

Use front-end estimation to estimate the sum.

2. $410 + 380$ **3.** $\$5.30 + \$3.80$ **4.** $512 + 467$ **5.** $4,370 + 980$

Practice and Problem Solving

Extra Practice, page 64, Set C

Use front-end estimation to estimate the sum.

6. $206 + 668$ **7.** $\$6.38 + \$1.04$ **8.** $2,610 + 3,497$ **9.** $\$9.49 + \$4.67$

10. $319 + 543$ **11.** $279 + 325$ **12.** $805 + 79$ **13.** $6,278 + 7,913$

14. $1,489 + 6,243$ **15.** $\$6.61 + \$9.05$ **16.** $2,174 + 713$ **17.** $426 + 844$

18. One young manatee weighs 221 pounds. Another weighs 244 pounds. Explain how you would use front-end estimation to estimate their total weight.

19. **MULTISTEP** Erica earned $3.05 on Monday. If she earns about the same amount on Tuesday and Wednesday, can she buy a $13.00 CD? Explain.

For 20–22, use the numbers at the right.

23	289	3,470	17	66
51	4,890	2,880	231	

Choose two numbers whose sum is about:

20. 70. **21.** 500. **22.** 7,000.

Maintain Skills

Write <, >, or = for each ●.

23. 27 ● 38 **24.** 23 ● 26

25. 53 ● 43 **26.** 46 ● 64

27. 97 ● 35 **28.** 59 ● 85

CRCT Test Prep

29. M3N2.b. Ann has $32.03. Bill has $41.25. About how much money do they have in all? (p. 50)

A. $60.00 C. $80.00
B. $70.00 D. $90.00

LESSON 4

Mental Math: Addition

M3N2.b. Use mental math and estimation strategies to add and subtract. *also* M3N2.c., M3P1.c., M3P2.d., M3P3.a., M3P3.b., M3P3.c., M3P3.d., M3P4., M3P4.a.

Quick Review

1. 7 + ■ = 15
2. ■ + 4 = 12
3. 5 + ■ = 17
4. 9 + ■ = 18
5. ■ + 12 = 20

VOCABULARY

compensation

Learn

TURTLE TALK Last year, researchers found 412 leatherback turtle nests. This year, they found 385 nests. How many nests did the researchers find in all?

You can use mental math to help you add.

Example 1

Write each number in expanded form. Add the hundreds, then the tens, and then the ones. Add the sums.

Think: 412 = 400 + 10 + 2
385 = 300 + 80 + 5

$$\begin{array}{r} 400 \\ +300 \\ \hline 700 \end{array} + \begin{array}{r} 10 \\ +80 \\ \hline 90 \end{array} + \begin{array}{r} 2 \\ +5 \\ \hline 7 \end{array} = 797$$

So, the researchers found 797 nests in all.

▲ Leatherback Turtle

You can also use a mental math strategy called **compensation**. Change one addend to a multiple of ten and then adjust the other addend to keep the balance.

Example 2

Find 295 + 117 = ■

Add 5 to 295 to make 300. Subtract 5 from 117 to compensate for adding 5. Find the sum of 300 and 112.

$$\begin{aligned} 295 + 117 &= (295 + 5) + (117 - 5) \\ &= 300 + 112 \\ &= 412 \end{aligned}$$

Check

1. **Explain** how to use compensation to find 461 + 296.

Use mental math to find the sum.

2. $\begin{array}{r} 425 \\ +123 \\ \hline \end{array}$ **3.** $\begin{array}{r} 572 \\ +311 \\ \hline \end{array}$ **4.** $\begin{array}{r} 136 \\ +680 \\ \hline \end{array}$ **5.** $\begin{array}{r} 290 \\ +255 \\ \hline \end{array}$

Practice and Problem Solving

Extra Practice, Page 64, Set D

Use mental math to find the sum.

6. $\begin{array}{r} 134 \\ +234 \\ \hline \end{array}$ **7.** $\begin{array}{r} 644 \\ +199 \\ \hline \end{array}$ **8.** $\begin{array}{r} 218 \\ +386 \\ \hline \end{array}$ **9.** $\begin{array}{r} 317 \\ +452 \\ \hline \end{array}$ **10.** $\begin{array}{r} 521 \\ +375 \\ \hline \end{array}$

11. $\begin{array}{r} 263 \\ +425 \\ \hline \end{array}$ **12.** $\begin{array}{r} 285 \\ +304 \\ \hline \end{array}$ **13.** $\begin{array}{r} 460 \\ +228 \\ \hline \end{array}$ **14.** $\begin{array}{r} 724 \\ +198 \\ \hline \end{array}$ **15.** $\begin{array}{r} 462 \\ +247 \\ \hline \end{array}$

16. David had 125 baseball cards. He got 55 more for his birthday. How many baseball cards does he have now?

17. Jasmine earned $122 one summer and $140 another summer. How much money did she earn in all?

18. Marla found 114 seashells. Nathan found 199 seashells. How many seashells did they find in all?

19. **What's the Error?** Derek says the sum 185 + 65 is 240. Describe his error. Find the correct sum.

USE DATA Use the map.

20. **REASONING** Theo drove from Atlanta to Savannah. Kendra drove from Atlanta to Valdosta. Who drove farther? How much farther?

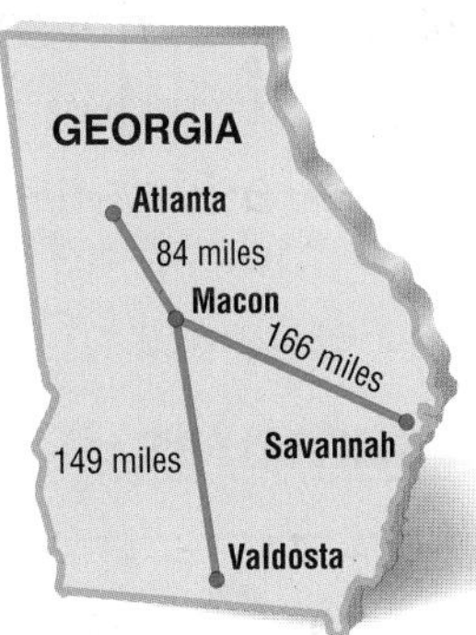

Maintain Skills

Write <, >, or = for each ●.

21. 48 ● 62 **22.** 97 ● 87

23. 44 ● 33 **24.** 58 ● 85

25. $\begin{array}{r} 27 \\ +39 \\ \hline \end{array}$ **26.** $\begin{array}{r} 46 \\ +15 \\ \hline \end{array}$ **27.** $\begin{array}{r} 82 \\ -26 \\ \hline \end{array}$

CRCT Test Prep

28. M3N2.b. Jason has 410 marbles in one jar and 231 marbles in another jar. About how many marbles does Jason have in all? (p. 50)

A. 400
B. 500
C. 600
D. 700

LESSON 5

Add 3- and 4-Digit Numbers

 M3N2.c. Solve problems requiring addition and subtraction. *also* M3P1.c., M3P3.a., M3P3.b., M3P3.c., M3P3.d.

Quick Review

1. 7 + ■ = 13
2. ■ + 9 = 18
3. 5 + 6
4. 8 + 7
5. 6 + 8

Learn

THOUSANDS OF BOOKS How many books did Grade 3 and Grade 4 read in all?

READ-A-THON RESULTS	
Grade 2	3,265 books
Grade 3	4,467 books
Grade 4	4,638 books

4,467 + 4,638 = ■

Estimate.

$$\begin{array}{r} 4{,}467 \\ +4{,}638 \\ \hline \end{array} \rightarrow \begin{array}{r} 4{,}000 \\ +4{,}000 \\ \hline 8{,}000 \end{array}$$

Example

STEP 1

Add the ones.
Regroup.
15 ones =
1 ten 5 ones

$$\begin{array}{r} {}^{1} \\ 4{,}467 \\ +4{,}638 \\ \hline 5 \end{array}$$

STEP 2

Add the tens.
Regroup.
10 tens =
1 hundred 0 tens

$$\begin{array}{r} {}^{1\,1} \\ 4{,}467 \\ +4{,}638 \\ \hline 05 \end{array}$$

STEP 3

Add the hundreds.
Regroup.
11 hundreds =
1 thousand
1 hundred

$$\begin{array}{r} {}^{1\;1\,1} \\ 4{,}467 \\ +4{,}638 \\ \hline 105 \end{array}$$

STEP 4

Add the thousands.

$$\begin{array}{r} {}^{1\;1\,1} \\ 4{,}467 \\ +4{,}638 \\ \hline 9{,}105 \end{array}$$

So, the two grades read 9,105 books in all. Since 9,105 is close to the estimate of 8,000, the answer is reasonable.

More Examples

A

$$\begin{array}{r} {}^{1\;\;1} \\ 4{,}325 \\ +\;\;867 \\ \hline 5{,}192 \end{array}$$

B

$$\begin{array}{r} {}^{2} \\ 591 \\ 173 \\ +290 \\ \hline 1{,}054 \end{array}$$

C

dollar sign ↓

$$\begin{array}{r} {}^{1\,1} \\ \$24.83 \\ +\$45.74 \\ \hline \$70.57 \end{array}$$

↑ decimal point

- Add money like whole numbers.
- Include a dollar sign, and use a decimal point to separate dollars and cents.

 **MATH IDEA** Estimate to see if your answer is reasonable.

Check

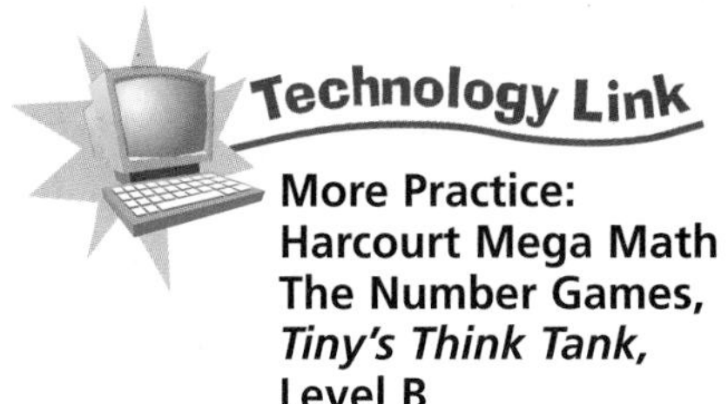

More Practice: Harcourt Mega Math The Number Games, *Tiny's Think Tank,* Level B

1. **Explain** whether you would regroup to find how many books Grades 2 and 3 read in all.

Solve. Estimate to check.

2. A music store sold 217 CDs one day and 112 CDs the next day. How many CDs did the store sell during those two days?
3. Beth had 462 seashells in her collection. Her aunt gave her 143 seashells. How many shells does she have in her collection now?
4. John bought one book for $14.25 and another book for $21.15. How much did he spend?
5. Sara read 274 pages last week and 394 pages this week. How many pages did she read in all?

Practice and Problem Solving

Extra Practice, page 64, Set E

Solve. Estimate to check.

6. Zoe's family drove 149 miles to Macon. Then they drove 166 miles to Savannah. How many miles did they drive in all?
7. Emily has 462 pennies in one jar and 589 pennies in another jar. How many pennies does she have?
8. Scott has $37.84. Ashley has $52.13. How much money do they have if they put their money together?
9. At the movie theater, Allan bought some popcorn for $4.15 and a drink for $3.65. How much money did he spend?
10. **What's the Question?** Eva read to page 112 in her book. There are 67 more pages in the book. The answer is 179 pages.
11. Sharon added 458 and 83. Was her answer greater than or less than 500? Explain how you know.
12. **ALGEBRA** Write the missing addend. 230 + ■ + 40 = 282
13. **ALGEBRA** Write the missing addend. 1,470 + 200 + ■ = 1,785

Maintain Skills

Find the sum or difference.

14. $\begin{array}{r} 19 \\ +24 \\ \hline \end{array}$

15. $\begin{array}{r} 30 \\ +62 \\ \hline \end{array}$

16. $\begin{array}{r} 83 \\ -37 \\ \hline \end{array}$

17. $\begin{array}{r} 45 \\ -18 \\ \hline \end{array}$

CRCT Test Prep

18. M3N2.c. In the morning, 274 people entered the park. In the afternoon, 329 people entered the park. How many people entered the park in all? (p. 54)

A. 503 B. 593 C. 603 D. 613

Problem Solving Strategy
Guess and Check

M3N2.c. Solve problems requiring addition and subtraction.
also **M3P1.a., M3P1.b., M3P1.c., M3P1.d., M3P3.a., M3P3.b., M3P3.c., M3P3.d., M3P4.a., M3P4.b.**

Quick Review

1. 21 + 6
2. 45 + 15
3. 9 + 36
4. 72 + 8
5. 12 + 13

PROBLEM The third-grade classes bought 75 containers of food for the animal shelter. They had 15 more cans than bags of food. How many bags and cans did the classes buy?

UNDERSTAND

- What are you asked to find?
- What information will you use?
- Is there any information you will not use?

PLAN

- What strategy can you use to solve the problem?

You can *guess and check* to find the number of bags and cans the classes bought.

SOLVE

- How can you use the strategy to solve the problem?

Guess the number of bags the classes bought. Add 15 to that number for the number of cans. Then check to see if the sum is 75.

BAGS	CANS	TOTAL	NOTES
20	20+15=35	20+35=55	too low
50	50+15=65	50+65=115	too high
30	30+15=45	30+45=75	just right

So, the classes bought 30 bags and 45 cans of food.

CHECK

- How can you use the first two guesses to make a better guess?

Problem Solving Practice

Use *guess and check* to solve.

1. **What if** the classes bought 120 containers and had 30 more cans than bags? How many bags and how many cans did they buy?

2. Pilar has 170 stamps in her collection. Her first book of stamps has 30 more stamps in it than her second book. How many stamps are in each book?

Strategies

- Act It Out or Use Objects
- Make a Picture or Diagram
- **Guess and Check**
- Use or Look for a Pattern
- Use Logical Reasoning

Problem Solving

Two numbers have a sum of 27. Their difference is 3. What are the two numbers?

3. Which is a reasonable guess for one of the numbers?

   A 3 **C** 27
   B 10 **D** 30

4. What solution answers the question?

   F 3 and 27 **H** 10 and 17
   G 10 and 13 **J** 12 and 15

Mixed Strategy Practice

USE DATA For 5–6, use the table.

5. The number of pounds used in Week 2 was greater than in Week 1, but less than in Week 3. The number of pounds used in Week 2 is an odd number that does not end in 5. How many pounds were used in Week 2?

6. **Write a problem** about the dog food used at the shelter in which the difference is greater than 5.

DOG FOOD USED AT SHELTER	
February	**Pounds**
Week 1	73
Week 2	■
Week 3	79
Week 4	81

7. The sum of two numbers is 55. Their difference is 7. What are the numbers?

8. There are 4 students in line. Max is before Keiko but after Liz. Adam is fourth. Who is first?

LESSON 7

Choose a Method

M3P1.d. Monitor and reflect on the process of mathematical problem solving. *also* M3N2.b., M3P1.b., M3P1.c., M3P2.a., M3P2.b., M3P2.d.

Quick Review

1. 350 + 40
2. 150 + 212
3. 560 + 161
4. 205 + 52
5. 90 + 215

Learn

You can find a sum by using paper and pencil, a calculator, or mental math.

PADDLE POWER Tom and Eli paddled from White Rock to Bear Corner to Raccoon Falls. How many yards did they paddle in all?

$$4,365 + 3,852 = \blacksquare$$

Use Paper and Pencil The numbers are large. The problem involves regrouping. So, paper and pencil is a good choice.

STEP 1

Add the ones.

$$\begin{array}{r} 4,365 \\ +3,852 \\ \hline 7 \end{array}$$

STEP 2

Add the tens. Regroup. 11 tens = 1 hundred 1 ten

$$\begin{array}{r} \scriptstyle 1 \quad \\ 4,365 \\ +3,852 \\ \hline 17 \end{array}$$

STEP 3

Add the hundreds. Regroup. 12 hundreds = 1 thousand 2 hundreds

$$\begin{array}{r} \scriptstyle 1\,1 \quad\;\; \\ 4,365 \\ +3,852 \\ \hline 217 \end{array}$$

STEP 4

Add the thousands.

$$\begin{array}{r} \scriptstyle 1\,1 \quad\;\; \\ 4,365 \\ +3,852 \\ \hline 8,217 \end{array}$$

So, Tom and Eli paddled 8,217 yards.

Use a Calculator $4,365 + 3,852 + 3,978 = \blacksquare$

The numbers are large. The problem involves regrouping. So, a calculator is a good choice.

REASONING How can you estimate to check?

Use Mental Math

$9.30 + $5.60 = ■

There is no regrouping. You can add the dollar and cents amounts in your head. So, mental math is a good choice.

Think: Add the dollar amounts. $9.00 + $5.00 = $14.00
Then add the cents. $0.30 + $0.60 = $0.90
Find the sum. $14.00 + $0.90 = $14.90

So, $9.30 + $5.60 = $14.90.

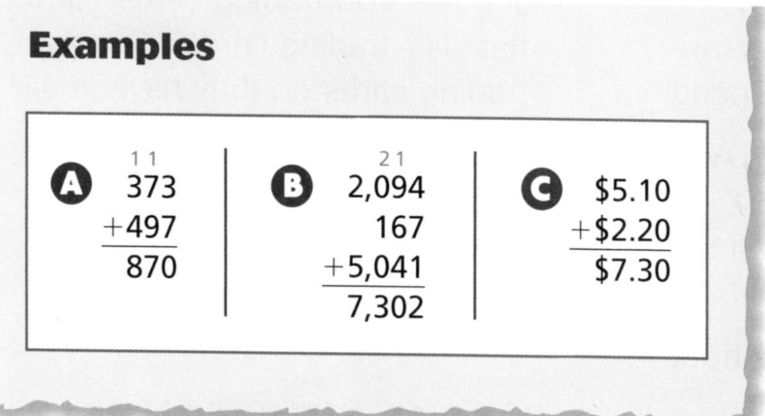

Examples

A	**B**	**C**
11 373 +497 870	21 2,094 167 +5,041 7,302	$5.10 +$2.20 $7.30

- Which example can you solve by using mental math? Explain.

MATH IDEA You can find a sum by using paper and pencil, a calculator, or mental math. Choose the method that works best with the numbers in the problem.

Check

1. **Explain** how you can use mental math to add 747 and 242.

Tell whether each problem can be solved by using mental math, paper and pencil, or calculator. Then solve each problem using the method you chose.

2. Gary and Brandon paddled 1,348 yards. Then they paddled 1,231 yards. How many yards did they paddle in all?

3. On Friday, 919 people went to see a play. On Saturday, 489 people went to the play. How many people went to the play in all?

4. Look back at problems 2 and 3. Did you choose the best method? Could you solve the problem another way? Explain.

LESSON CONTINUES ▶

Practice and Problem Solving

Tell whether each problem can be solved by using mental math, paper and pencil, or calculator. Then solve each problem using the method you chose.

5. There were 821 third-graders and 709 fourth-graders on a school trip. What is the total number of students that went on the trip?

6. On Monday, 458 tickets were sold to a concert. On Tuesday, 221 tickets were sold. How many tickets were sold in the two days?

7. Megan bought some notebooks for \$4.11 and some stickers for \$3.48. How much did she spend?

8. Jeff has 469 trading cards. April has 347 trading cards. How many trading cards do they have in all?

9. Mary spent \$15.00 on one DVD and \$22.50 on another DVD. How much did she spend on the two DVDs?

10. Look back at Problems 5–9. Did you choose the best method? Could you solve the problem another way? Explain.

Find the sum. Explain your method.

11. $429 + 640 = ■$

12. $565 + 424 = ■$

13. $\$14.40 + \$10.20 = ■$

14. **NUMBER SENSE** Write a number less than 3,425 + 8,630 but greater than 7,614 + 4,429.

15. ALGEBRA Write the missing addend. 4,020 + ■ = 4,222

16. **ESTIMATION** Allie estimates that 5,109 + 5,231 is about 1,000. Do you agree or disagree? Explain.

17. **What's the Error?** Sergio used paper and pencil to find this sum. Describe his error. Find the sum.

```
 1 11
 8,235
+  986
 -----
 9,211
```

18. **USE DATA** Use the price list. If Craig mows and rakes 2 lawns, has he earned more than \$20? Explain how you know.

CRAIG'S PRICE LIST	
Weed Garden	\$5.00
Mow Lawn	\$7.50
Rake Lawn	\$4.50

19. **Vocabulary Power** The root of the word *calculator* is the Greek word *kalyx*, which means "pebble or small stone." Small stones were once counted to find sums. When do you use a calculator to find sums?

20. **FAST FACT** • SOCIAL STUDIES Volunteers raise Canine Companion puppies until they are about 18 months old. Use a calculator to find how many weeks this is.

21. Can you add two 3-digit numbers and get a sum greater than 2,000? Explain.

Maintain Skills

Find the sum or difference.

22. $\begin{array}{r} 53 \\ +37 \\ \hline \end{array}$ **23.** $\begin{array}{r} 24 \\ +36 \\ \hline \end{array}$ **24.** $\begin{array}{r} 45 \\ +47 \\ \hline \end{array}$

25. $\begin{array}{r} 70 \\ -26 \\ \hline \end{array}$ **26.** $\begin{array}{r} 54 \\ -37 \\ \hline \end{array}$ **27.** $\begin{array}{r} 84 \\ -39 \\ \hline \end{array}$

Write <, >, or = for each ●.

28. 45 ● 54 **29.** 30 ● 28

30. 16 ● 96 **31.** 23 ● 20

32. Write the amount.

CRCT Test Prep

Use the graph below to answer question 33.

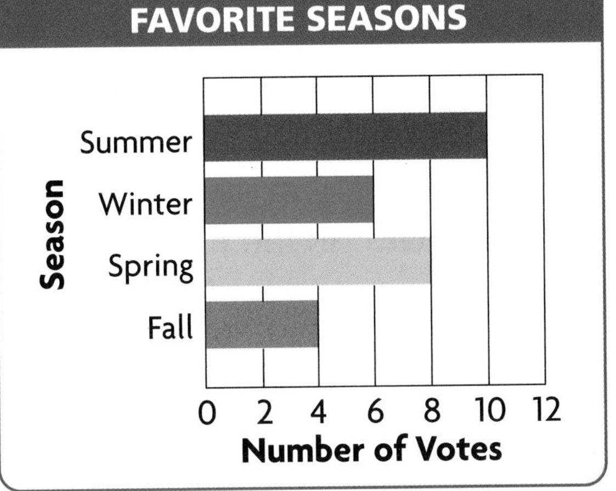

33. M3D1.b. How many students did NOT vote for summer? (p. 30)

A. 12 B. 18 C. 20 D. 24

Problem Solving Thinker's Corner

Try to make a greater sum than your partner's.

MATERIALS: index cards numbered 0–9

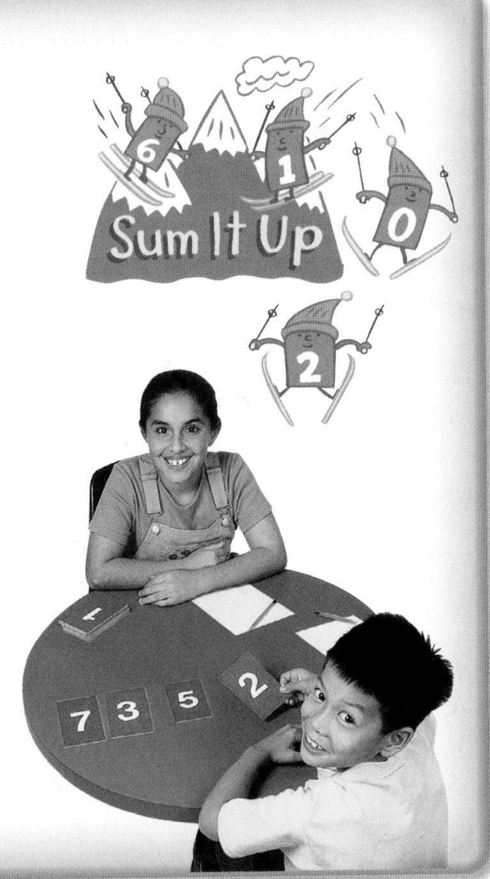

- Player 1 chooses 4 cards and uses the digits to write two different 4-digit addends. Each digit should be used twice. Player 1 replaces the cards.
- Player 2 repeats the first step.
- Both players find the sum. The player with the greater sum wins. Play this game several times. See if you can find a winning strategy.
- Repeat this game. Try to make the lesser sum.

1. When making the greater sum, where is the best place to put a 9?
2. When making the lesser sum, where is the best place to put a 9?

LESSON 8

Algebra: Expressions and Number Sentences

M3A1. Students will use mathematical expressions to represent relationships between quantities and interpret given expressions. *also* M3A1.c., M3P2.a., M3P2.b., M3P2.c., M3P2.d., M3P4.a., M3P4.b., M3P5.

Quick Review

1. 14 + 14
2. 12 + 21
3. 42 + 25
4. 90 + 18
5. 25 + 49

VOCABULARY

expression
is not equal to (≠)

Learn

LUNCH LINE In the morning, visitors bought 34 packets of food for the animals in the petting zoo. In the afternoon, visitors bought 58 packets. How many food packets were bought in all?

You can write an expression for this problem. An **expression** is part of a number sentence. It combines numbers and operation signs. It does not have an equal sign.

$34 + 58$ is the expression that models the problem.

$34 + 58 = 92$ is a number sentence.

Visitors bought 92 food packets in all.

MATH IDEA A number sentence can be true or false.

$4 + 3 = 7$ is true. $4 - 3 = 7$ is false.

Another way to show that $4 - 3$ does not equal 7 is to write $4 - 3 \neq 7$.

The ≠ is a symbol of inequality that means "**is not equal to**."

Mike spent $12 for a cap and $18 for a shirt at the petting zoo. How much more did the shirt cost?

$18 ● $12 = $6

Which symbol will make the sentence *true*?

Try +. $18 + $12 = $6 False or $18 + $12 ≠ $6.
Try −. $18 − $12 = $6 **True**.

So, the correct symbol is −.

Check

Write an expression to solve.

1. Takeo had 273 cards. He gave away 35. Write an expression to show the number of cards he has left.

2. Mia had 13 apples. She bought 7 more. Write an expression to show the number of apples she has in all.

Write + or − to complete the number sentence.

3. $12 \bullet 2 = 10$ 4. $37 \bullet 11 \neq 40$ 5. $126 \bullet 79 = 47$ 6. $367 \bullet 43 = 410$

Practice and Problem Solving

Extra Practice, page 64, Set F

Write an expression to solve.

7. Gwen bought 12 red pencils and 2 blue pencils. Write an expression to show the number of pencils she bought.

8. Ned had 17 crayons. He gave away 5. Write an expression to show the number of crayons he has left.

Write + or − to complete the number sentence.

9. $4 \bullet 3 = 1$
10. $28 \bullet 9 = 37$
11. $329 \bullet 87 = 222 + 20$
12. $559 \bullet 50 = 609$
13. $74 \bullet 47 = 17 + 10$
14. $444 \bullet 6 \neq 460 - 10$

Write the missing number.

15. $\blacksquare + 3 = 14$
16. $140 + 5 = \blacksquare$
17. $45 - \blacksquare = 25$
18. $30 - \blacksquare = 20$
19. $21 - \blacksquare = 12$
20. $\blacksquare - 25 = 18$

21. **REASONING** Blair says, "12 + 3 + 1 = 19 − 3 is a true number sentence." Do you agree or disagree? Explain.

22. **REASONING** Use the numbers 5, 9, and 14. Write two true number sentences—one using the equal sign and one using the not equal sign.

Maintain Skills

Find each sum or difference.

23. $91 + 26$
24. $73 + 22$
25. $66 + 19$
26. $85 - 37$
27. $77 - 24$
28. $62 - 43$

CRCT Test Prep

29. M3A1.a. Which is the next number in the pattern? (p. 2)

33, 36, 39, 42, □

A. 43
B. 44
C. 45
D. 46

Extra Practice

Set A (pp. 46–47)

Find each sum.

1. $8 + 9 = ■$
   $9 + 8 = ■$
2. $9 + 5 = ■$
   $5 + 9 = ■$
3. $8 + (3 + 7) = ■$
   $(8 + 3) + 7 = ■$
4. $7 + 8 = ■$
   $8 + 7 = ■$

Set B (pp. 48–49)

Find the missing addend.

1. $15 + ■ = 23$
2. $■ + 6 = 35$
3. $16 + ■ = 34$
4. $■ + 25 = 44$

Set C (pp. 50–51)

Use front-end estimation to estimate the sum.

1. $645 + 594$
2. $584 + 248$
3. $560 + 439$
4. $2,375 + 4,082$
5. $6,757 + 4,446$

Set D (pp. 52–53)

Use mental math to find the sum.

1. $276 + 322$
2. $492 + 466$
3. $325 + 204$
4. $372 + 615$
5. $682 + 290$

Set E (pp. 54–55)

Solve. Estimate to check.

1. Susie read 214 pages in one book and 222 pages in another book. How many pages did she read?
2. Brett bought a jigsaw puzzle for $31.25 and a board game for $18.25. How much did he spend?

Set F (pp. 62–63)

Write an expression to solve.

1. Alana made 34 bracelets. She gave away 15. Write an expression to show the number of bracelets she has left.
2. Robyn had 47 marbles. Then, she bought 20 more. Write an expression to show the number of marbles she has in all.

Review/Test

CHECK VOCABULARY

Choose the best term from the box.

Vocabulary
estimate
front-end estimation
inverse operations

1. To find *about* how many, you can ? . (p. 50)
2. When you estimate a sum by adding the front digit of each addend, you are using ? . (p. 50)

CHECK SKILLS

Find the missing addend. (pp. 48–49)

3. $16 + \blacksquare = 53$
4. $\blacksquare + 29 = 46$
5. $7 + \blacksquare = 25$

Use front-end estimation to estimate the sum. (pp. 50–51)

6. $\begin{array}{r} 267 \\ +193 \\ \hline \end{array}$
7. $\begin{array}{r} 6{,}528 \\ +1{,}347 \\ \hline \end{array}$

Use mental math to find the sum. (pp. 52–53)

8. $\begin{array}{r} 341 \\ +327 \\ \hline \end{array}$
9. $\begin{array}{r} 382 \\ +495 \\ \hline \end{array}$

Tell whether each problem can be solved by using mental math, paper and pencil, or a calculator. Then solve each problem using the method you chose. (pp. 58–61)

10. Katie's family drove 291 miles to visit her grandparents. Then, they drove 132 miles to visit her aunt. How many miles did they drive in all?
11. Kevin spent $18.32 on a present for his sister and $15.62 on a present for his brother. How much did he spend in all?

Write an expression to solve. (pp. 62–63)

12. Shelby had 24 seashells. Then, she found 19 seashells. Write an expression that shows the number of seashells she has now.
13. Rick had 32 balloons. He tied 8 balloons to the mailbox. Write an expression that shows the number of balloons he has left.

CHECK PROBLEM SOLVING

14. Mr. Samuel has 150 pennies in two jars. There are 40 more pennies in one jar than in the other. How many pennies are in each jar? (pp. 56–57)
15. Two numbers have a sum of 47. Their difference is 5. What are the two numbers? (pp. 56–57)

Chapter CRCT Test Prep

NUMBERS AND OPERATIONS

1. M3N2.b. Use front-end estimation to estimate the sum.

$$\begin{array}{r} 295 \\ +537 \\ \hline \end{array}$$

A. 600

B. 700

C. 800

D. 900

2. M3N2.c. An ice cream shop sold 3,462 vanilla ice cream cones and 4,978 chocolate ice cream cones one summer. How many ice cream cones were sold in all?

A. 7,440

B. 8,430

C. 8,440

D. 8,540

3. M3N2.b. Use front-end estimation to estimate the sum.

$$819 + 397 = \square$$

A. 800

B. 900

C. 1,000

D. 1,100

ALGEBRA

4. M3A1.c. Which number goes in the □ to make the number sentence true?

$$28 + \square = 40$$

A. 12

B. 18

C. 22

D. 28

5. M3A1.c. Maggie and Jason picked 25 peaches in all. Jason picked 17 peaches. Which number sentence can you use to find the number of peaches Maggie picked?

A. $25 + \square = 17$

B. $\square + 17 = 25$

C. $17 + 25 = \square$

D. $\square - 17 = 25$

6. M3A1.c. Which number goes in the □ to make the number sentence true?

$$\square + 31 = 73$$

A. 22

B. 32

C. 42

D. 52

Check

1. **Explain** how you would use front-end estimation to estimate 767 − 422.

Use front-end estimation to estimate the difference.

2. $\begin{array}{r} 87 \\ -32 \\ \hline \end{array}$

3. $\begin{array}{r} 478 \\ -115 \\ \hline \end{array}$

4. $\begin{array}{r} \$9.01 \\ -\$2.60 \\ \hline \end{array}$

5. $\begin{array}{r} 813 \\ -491 \\ \hline \end{array}$

6. $\begin{array}{r} 5{,}020 \\ -1{,}750 \\ \hline \end{array}$

Practice and Problem Solving

Extra Practice, page 82, Set A

Use front-end estimation to estimate the difference.

7. $\begin{array}{r} 42 \\ -19 \\ \hline \end{array}$

8. $\begin{array}{r} 613 \\ -371 \\ \hline \end{array}$

9. $\begin{array}{r} \$7.08 \\ -\$3.80 \\ \hline \end{array}$

10. $\begin{array}{r} 625 \\ -489 \\ \hline \end{array}$

11. $\begin{array}{r} 4{,}819 \\ -1{,}966 \\ \hline \end{array}$

12. $\begin{array}{r} 84 \\ -23 \\ \hline \end{array}$

13. $\begin{array}{r} 880 \\ -114 \\ \hline \end{array}$

14. $\begin{array}{r} 322 \\ -199 \\ \hline \end{array}$

15. $\begin{array}{r} \$5.17 \\ -\$1.01 \\ \hline \end{array}$

16. $\begin{array}{r} 3{,}288 \\ -1{,}255 \\ \hline \end{array}$

USE DATA For 17–20, use the table.

17. About how many more pounds does a leatherback turtle weigh than a hawksbill turtle?

18. About how much do two hawksbill turtles weigh?

19. How many loggerhead turtles weigh about the same as one leatherback turtle? Explain.

20. **Write a problem** about sea turtle weights using estimation and subtraction.

ADULT SEA TURTLE WEIGHTS

Sea Turtle	Weight in Pounds
Loggerhead	185
Hawksbill	125
Leatherback	779

Maintain Skills

Write the amount.

21.    

CRCT Test Prep

22. M3N2.c. Carlos found 115 soda cans and 129 plastic cups. How many cups and cans did he find? (p. 54)

A. 227
B. 241
C. 244
D. 256

LESSON 2

Mental Math: Subtraction

M3N2.b. Use mental math and estimation strategies to add and subtract. *also* M3N2.c., M3P1.c., M3P3.a., M3P3.b., M3P3.c., M3P3.d.

Quick Review

1. 40 − 20 = ■
2. 800 − 100 = ■
3. 600 − 300 = ■
4. 70 − 20 = ■
5. 500 − 100 = ■

Learn

FAMILY VACATION The Franklin family is trying to decide where to go for their vacation. The beach is 277 miles from their house. The lake is 150 miles from their house. How much farther from their house is the beach than the lake?

You can use mental math to help you subtract.

Example 1

Write each number in expanded form. Subtract the hundreds, then the tens, and then the ones. Add the sums together.

Think: 277 = 200 + 70 + 7
150 = 100 + 50 + 0

$$\begin{array}{r} 200 \\ -100 \\ \hline 100 \end{array} + \begin{array}{r} 70 \\ -50 \\ \hline 20 \end{array} + \begin{array}{r} 7 \\ -0 \\ \hline 7 \end{array} = 127$$

So, the beach is 127 miles farther from their house than the lake.

When there is regrouping, you can use compensation to help you subtract mentally.

Example 2

Find 467 − 195 = ■
Add 5 and 195 to make 200. Add 5 to 467 to compensate for subtracting an extra 5. Find the difference of 472 and 200.

$$\begin{aligned} 467 - 195 &= (467 + 5) - (195 + 5) \\ &= 472 - 200 \\ &= 272 \end{aligned}$$

Check

1. **Explain** how to use compensation to find 874 − 347.

Use mental math to find the difference.

2. $\begin{array}{r} 846 \\ -722 \\ \hline \end{array}$

3. $\begin{array}{r} 649 \\ -125 \\ \hline \end{array}$

4. $\begin{array}{r} 542 \\ -299 \\ \hline \end{array}$

5. $\begin{array}{r} 934 \\ -480 \\ \hline \end{array}$

Practice and Problem Solving

Extra Practice, page 82, Set B

Use mental math to find the difference.

6. $\begin{array}{r} 465 \\ -123 \\ \hline \end{array}$

7. $\begin{array}{r} 833 \\ -475 \\ \hline \end{array}$

8. $\begin{array}{r} 526 \\ -360 \\ \hline \end{array}$

9. $\begin{array}{r} 957 \\ -553 \\ \hline \end{array}$

10. $\begin{array}{r} 584 \\ -362 \\ \hline \end{array}$

11. $\begin{array}{r} 726 \\ -455 \\ \hline \end{array}$

12. $\begin{array}{r} 704 \\ -692 \\ \hline \end{array}$

13. $\begin{array}{r} 827 \\ -306 \\ \hline \end{array}$

14. $\begin{array}{r} 637 \\ -114 \\ \hline \end{array}$

15. $\begin{array}{r} 713 \\ -270 \\ \hline \end{array}$

16. $\begin{array}{r} 872 \\ -521 \\ \hline \end{array}$

17. $\begin{array}{r} 716 \\ -488 \\ \hline \end{array}$

18. Cathy had 525 beads. She used 290 beads to make a necklace and 40 beads to make a bracelet. How many beads does she have left?

19. **MULTISTEP** Jose had 216 trading cards. He got 57 more for his birthday. Then, he gave 23 to his little brother. How many trading cards does he have now?

20. **What's the Error?** Martin used compensation to find 422 − 195 and got 217. What is his error? What is the correct answer?

Maintain Skills

Write <, >, or = for each ●.

21. 16 ● 61

22. 92 ● 99

23. 23 ● 63

24. 47 ● 41

25. $\begin{array}{r} 65 \\ +28 \\ \hline \end{array}$

26. $\begin{array}{r} 92 \\ -47 \\ \hline \end{array}$

27. $\begin{array}{r} 73 \\ -18 \\ \hline \end{array}$

CRCT Test Prep

28. M3A1.a. What is the next number in the pattern? (p. 12)

457, 467, 477, 487, ■

A. 488
B. 490
C. 497
D. 587

LESSON 3

Subtract 3- and 4-Digit Numbers

M3N2.c. Solve problems requiring addition and subtraction.
also M3P3.a., M3P3.b., M3P3.c., M3P3.d., M3P4., M3P4.c.

Quick Review

Estimate the difference.

1. 363 − 140 **2.** 515 − 272

3. 704 − 451 **4.** 281 − 165

5. 492 − 384

Learn

WALK OR RIDE? If you hiked the Appalachian National Scenic Trail, you would hike 2,167 miles. The driving distance from one end to the other along roads and highways is 1,377 miles. How many more miles is it to hike than to drive?

Subtract. 2,167 − 1,377 = ■

Estimate. 2,167 → 2,000
−1,377 → −1,000
1,000

Example

STEP 1

Subtract the ones.

$$\begin{array}{r} 2{,}167 \\ -1{,}377 \\ \hline 0 \end{array}$$

STEP 2

Subtract the tens. Regroup.
1 hundred 6 tens =
0 hundreds 16 tens

$$\begin{array}{r} {\scriptstyle 0\ 16} \\ 2{,}\not{1}\not{6}7 \\ -1{,}377 \\ \hline 90 \end{array}$$

STEP 3

Subtract the hundreds. Regroup.
2 thousands 0 hundreds =
1 thousand 10 hundreds

$$\begin{array}{r} {\scriptstyle 10} \\ {\scriptstyle 1\ \not{0}\ 16} \\ \not{2}{,}\not{1}\not{6}7 \\ -1{,}377 \\ \hline 790 \end{array}$$

STEP 4

Subtract the thousands.

$$\begin{array}{r} {\scriptstyle 10} \\ {\scriptstyle 1\ \not{0}\ 16} \\ \not{2}{,}\not{1}\not{6}7 \\ -1{,}377 \\ \hline 790 \end{array}$$

So, it is 790 more miles to hike the Appalachian Trail than to drive. Since 790 is close to the estimate of 1,000, the answer is reasonable.

More Examples

A

$$\begin{array}{r} {\scriptstyle 13\ 15} \\ {\scriptstyle 2\ \not{3}\ \not{5}\ 13} \\ \not{3}{,}\not{4}\not{6}\not{3} \\ -1{,}867 \\ \hline 1{,}596 \end{array}$$

B

$$\begin{array}{r} {\scriptstyle 9\ 11} \\ {\scriptstyle 3\ \not{10}\ \not{1}\ 17} \\ \not{4}{,}\not{0}\not{2}\not{7} \\ -\ 598 \\ \hline 3{,}429 \end{array}$$

C

$$\begin{array}{r} {\scriptstyle 11\ 10} \\ {\scriptstyle 3\ \not{1}\ \not{0}\ 15} \\ \$\not{4}\not{2}.\not{1}\not{5} \\ -\$27.36 \\ \hline \$14.79 \end{array}$$

D

$$\begin{array}{r} {\scriptstyle 9\ 9} \\ {\scriptstyle 4\ \not{10}\ \not{10}\ 10} \\ \not{5}{,}\not{0}\not{0}\not{0} \\ -3{,}574 \\ \hline 1{,}426 \end{array}$$

Check

1. **Explain** how subtracting 4-digit numbers is like subtracting 3-digit numbers. How is it different?

Solve. Estimate to check.

2. Jon has 255 trading cards. Mandy has 197 trading cards. How many more trading cards does Jon have than Mandy?

3. Lucy hiked 1,674 yards. Kevin hiked 2,142 yards. How many more yards did Kevin hike than Lucy?

Practice and Problem Solving

Extra Practice, page 82, Set C

Solve. Estimate to check.

4. Suzie lives 628 miles from Savannah and 685 miles from Altanta. How much further does she live from Atlanta than Savannah?

5. Andy collected 1,416 pennies. Marci collected 1,603 pennies. How many more pennies did Marci collect than Andy?

6. Sandy has $24.94. Catherine has $31.29. How much more money does Catherine have?

7. Emily read 486 pages. Bill read 519 pages. How many more pages did Bill read than Emily?

8. Elise subtracted 1,754 from 1,800. Was her answer greater than 100? How do you know?

9. The Appalachian Trail opened in 1937. Write a number sentence that shows how long the trail has been open.

10. **What's the Error?** Jada says that the difference between 4,152 and 3,861 is greater than the sum of 196 and 95. Explain her error and find the correct difference.

11. ***FAST FACT*** • SOCIAL STUDIES Mount Katahdin, in Maine, is 5,267 feet high. Springer Mountain, in Georgia, is 3,782 feet high. How much higher is Mount Katahdin?

Maintain Skills

Write the time.

12. 

13. 

CRCT Test Prep

14. M3N1.a. What is the value of the hundreds digit in 42,865? (p. 14)

A. 200
B. 600
C. 800
D. 8,000

LESSON 4

Choose a Method

 M3N2.b. Use mental math and estimation strategies to add and subtract.

Quick Review

1. 135 − 20
2. 500 − 50
3. 395 − 30
4. 671 − 421
5. 105 − 95

Learn

You can find a difference by using paper and pencil, a calculator, or mental math.

UP, UP AND AWAY A hot-air balloon rose to 1,025 feet above the ground. Then it rose to 1,920 feet above the ground. How much higher was it then?

Subtract. 1,920 − 1,025 = ■

Use Paper and Pencil The numbers are large. The problem involves regrouping. So, paper and pencil is a good choice.

STEP 1

Subtract the ones. 5 > 0
Regroup.
2 tens 0 ones =
1 ten 10 ones

```
      1 10
  1, 9 2 0
 −1, 0 2 5
 ---------
         5
```

STEP 2

Subtract the tens. 2 > 1
Regroup.
9 hundreds 1 ten =
8 hundreds 11 tens

```
       11
     8 1 10
  1, 9 2 0
 −1, 0 2 5
 ---------
       9 5
```

STEP 3

Subtract the hundreds.
Subtract the thousands.

```
       11
     8 1 10
  1, 9 2 0
 −1, 0 2 5
 ---------
     8 9 5
```

So, the hot-air balloon was 895 feet higher.

REASONING How can you add to check your answer?

Use a Calculator 3,894 − 2,596 = ■

The amounts are large. The problem involves regrouping. So, a calculator is a good choice.

1298

REASONING How can you estimate to check your answer?

Use Mental Math

$6.80 – $3.10 = ■

There is no regrouping. You can subtract the dollar and cents amounts in your head. So, using mental math is a good choice.

Think: Subtract the dollar amounts. $6.00 – $3.00 = $3.00
Subtract the cents amounts. $0.80 – $0.10 = $0.70
The difference is $3.00 + $0.70, or $3.70.

Examples

A	B	C
8 17 8 9̸ 7̸ – 6 8 9 2 0 8	11 12 1̸ 2̸ 16 1̸, 2̸ 3̸ 6̸ – 8 4 7 3 8 9	790 –240 550

- Which problem can you solve using mental math? Explain.
- Which method would you use to solve Example A? Explain.

MATH IDEA You can find a difference by using paper and pencil, a calculator, or mental math. Choose the method that works best with the numbers in the problem.

Check

1. **Explain** how you can use mental math to subtract 656 from 987.

Tell whether each problem can be solved by using mental math, paper and pencil, or a calculator. Then solve each problem using the method you chose.

2. On Friday, 2,815 people went to the park. On Saturday, 6,219 people went to the park. How many more people went to the park on Saturday?

3. Meghan has 524 stickers. Steve has 388 stickers. How many more stickers does Meghan have than Steve?

4. Look back at problems 2 and 3. Did you choose the best method? Could you solve the problem another way? Explain.

LESSON CONTINUES

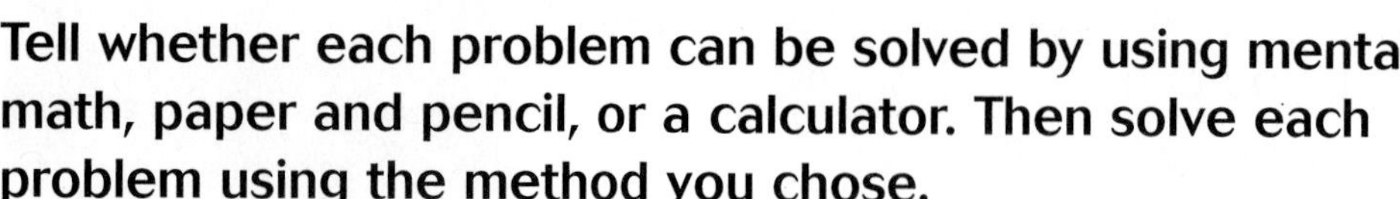

Tell whether each problem can be solved by using mental math, paper and pencil, or a calculator. Then solve each problem using the method you chose.

5. One male horse weighs 853 pounds. One female horse weighs 722 pounds. How much more does the male horse weigh?

6. At the beginning of the month, a store had 6,334 pencils. At the end of the month, the store had 4,213 pencils. How many pencils were sold?

7. Kurt had $34.22 when he went to the book store. He spent $18.34 on an art book. How much money does he have left?

8. Jack has 731 trading cards. Melanie has 594 trading cards. How many more trading cards does Jack have?

9. There are 529 third-graders. 344 of the third-graders are boys. How many are girls?

10. Look back at Problems 5–9. Did you choose the best method? Could you solve the problem another way? Explain.

USE DATA For 11–16, use the table.

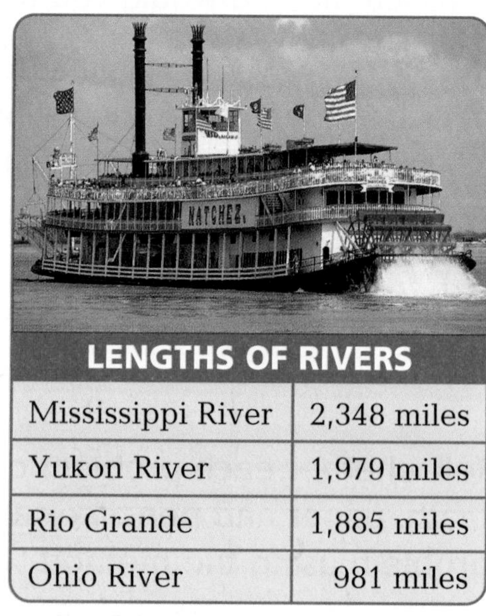

LENGTHS OF RIVERS	
Mississippi River	2,348 miles
Yukon River	1,979 miles
Rio Grande	1,885 miles
Ohio River	981 miles

11. What is the difference between the lengths of the Ohio River and the Rio Grande?

12. The Ohio River is 998 miles shorter than which one of these rivers?

13. How much longer is the Mississippi River than the Ohio River?

14. The Savannah River is 314 miles long. What is the difference between the lengths of the Savannah River and the Mississippi River?

15. How much longer is the Yukon River than the Rio Grande?

16. **Write a problem** about the difference between river lengths. Exchange with a partner. Solve.

17. **Vocabulary Power** When you add the suffix *-or* to a word, it can mean "someone or something that does." How does adding this suffix change the meaning of the word *calculate?*

18. **MULTISTEP** Sheli's mother was born 25 years before 1987. How old was Sheli's mother in 2004?

19. Write a 3-digit number you could subtract from 274 without regrouping.

Maintain Skills

Write the letters of the shapes that answer the questions.

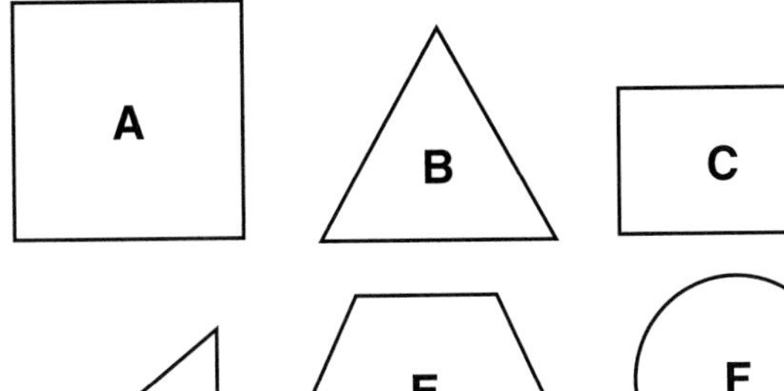

20. Which are triangles?

21. Which are quadrilaterals?

22. Which are polygons?

CRCT Test Prep

23. M3N2.c. Mrs. Jimenez baked 175 cookies and sold 158 of them at the bake sale. How many cookies were left? (p. 74)

A. 17 C. 27
B. 23 D. 133

24. M3N2.c. Kelly bought a DVD for $15.15 and another DVD for $20.55. How much did Kelly spend? (p. 54)

A. $30.60 C. $35.70
B. $35.65 D. $35.75

Problem Solving Thinker's Corner

SOLVE IT!

Find the sum or difference.

51 − 23 O	36 + 49 N	70 − 53 H		
64 − 15 y	91 + 59 P	647 + 178 A	313 + 448 U	500 − 195 E
200 − 77 C	464 + 446 T	384 + 165 J	675 − 179 S	853 − 194 M

To answer the riddle, match the letters from the sums and differences above to the numbers below.

Who can jump higher than a house? ___ ___ ___ ___ ___ ___.
825 85 49 28 85 305

___   ___ ___ ___ ___ ___   ___ ___ ___ ' ___   ___ ___ ___ ___!
825   17 28 761 496 305   123 825 85 910   549 761 659 150

LESSON 5

Problem Solving Skill
Estimate or Exact Answer

M3N2.b. Use mental math and estimation strategies to add and subtract. *also* **M3P1.a., M3P1.b., M3P1.c., M3P1.d., M3P2.d., M3P3., M3P3.a., M3P3.b., M3P3.c., M3P3.d., M3P4.**

UNDERSTAND ▶ PLAN ▶ SOLVE ▶ CHECK

Quick Review

1. $(3 + 2) + 1 = ■$
2. $4 + (5 + 5) = ■$
3. $7 + (3 + 4) = ■$
4. $(12 + 8) + 5 = ■$
5. $32 + (6 + 14) = ■$

VIEW FROM THE TOP The table shows some of the highest points along the Appalachian Trail, which stretches from Maine to Georgia.

HIGH POINTS ALONG THE APPALACHIAN TRAIL

High Point	State	Height in Feet
Mount Katahdin	Maine	5,267
Mount Washington	New Hampshire	6,288
Springer Mountain	Georgia	3,782
Mount Rogers	Virginia	5,729
Clingmans Dome	Tennessee	6,643

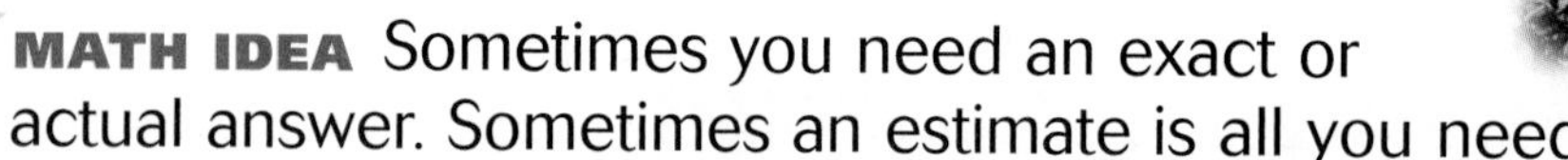

MATH IDEA Sometimes you need an exact or actual answer. Sometimes an estimate is all you need.

Examples

A How many feet higher is Clingmans Dome than Springer Mountain?

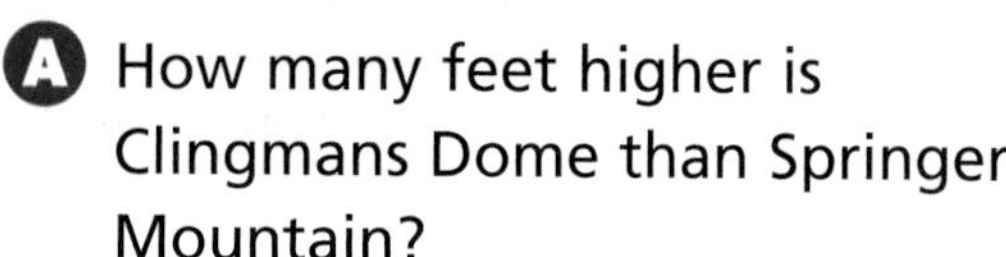

Since the problem asks *how many feet higher,* subtract to find the actual answer.

$$\begin{array}{r} 6,643 \\ -3,782 \\ \hline 2,861 \end{array}$$

So, Clingmans Dome is 2,861 feet higher than Springer Mountain.

B Suppose an airplane is flying 2,098 feet above Mount Katahdin. Estimate the height of the airplane.

Since the problem asks for an *estimate,* you can use front-end estimation to find the height.

$$\begin{array}{rcr} 2,098 & \rightarrow & 2,000 \\ +5,267 & \rightarrow & +5,000 \\ \hline & & 7,000 \end{array}$$

So, the height of the airplane is about 7,000 feet.

Problem Solving Practice

Tell whether you need an exact answer or an estimate. Then solve.

1. Kayla's class went to a water park. Kayla took $35.00. She paid $24.95 for the ticket and $7.39 for a T-shirt. Does she have enough money to buy a bottle of juice that costs $2.50?

2. Records showed there were 783 students at the water park. There were 496 girls. About how many students were boys?

Eve has 439 stickers in her collection. Her sister Ellen has 674 stickers. How many stickers do the sisters have in all?

3. Which number sentence can you use to solve the problem?
   - **A** 439 + 439 = ▒
   - **B** 439 + 674 = ▒
   - **C** 674 − 439 = ▒
   - **D** 674 + 674 = ▒

4. How many stickers do Eve and Ellen have in all?
   - **F** 235
   - **G** 439
   - **H** 1,113
   - **J** 1,348

Mixed Applications

For 5–6, use the table.

5. **Write About It** Explain how you would compare the building heights, and put them in order from greatest to least.

6. How much taller is the Bank of America Plaza than One Atlantic Center?

TALLEST BUILDINGS IN ATLANTA, GEORGIA

Name	Height in Feet
Bank of America Plaza	1,023
SunTrust Plaza	871
One Atlantic Center	820

7. I am a 2-digit number. My tens digit is two more than my ones digit. My ones digit is between 4 and 6. What number am I?

8. Wesley has 4 more hockey cards than baseball cards. If he has 28 cards in all, how many hockey cards does he have?

9. **What's the Question?** Last week Luann ran 50 miles and Patrick ran 15 miles. The answer is 35 miles.

10. **REASONING** Joel had 48 inches of rope. He cut 15 inches off each end of the rope. What is the length of the rope he has left?

Extra Practice

Set A (pp. 70–71)

Use front-end estimation to estimate the difference.

1. $\begin{array}{r} 63 \\ -49 \\ \hline \end{array}$

2. $\begin{array}{r} 547 \\ -164 \\ \hline \end{array}$

3. $\begin{array}{r} \$9.65 \\ -\$5.48 \\ \hline \end{array}$

4. $\begin{array}{r} 595 \\ -227 \\ \hline \end{array}$

5. $\begin{array}{r} 8{,}732 \\ -4{,}759 \\ \hline \end{array}$

6. $\begin{array}{r} 795 \\ -309 \\ \hline \end{array}$

7. $\begin{array}{r} 7{,}850 \\ -2{,}187 \\ \hline \end{array}$

8. $\begin{array}{r} 8{,}026 \\ -4{,}826 \\ \hline \end{array}$

9. $\begin{array}{r} \$55.75 \\ -\$47.46 \\ \hline \end{array}$

10. $\begin{array}{r} 2{,}521 \\ -1{,}779 \\ \hline \end{array}$

Set B (pp. 72–73)

Use mental math to find the difference.

1. $\begin{array}{r} 622 \\ -294 \\ \hline \end{array}$

2. $\begin{array}{r} 713 \\ -401 \\ \hline \end{array}$

3. $\begin{array}{r} 924 \\ -598 \\ \hline \end{array}$

4. $\begin{array}{r} 623 \\ -380 \\ \hline \end{array}$

5. $\begin{array}{r} 849 \\ -355 \\ \hline \end{array}$

6. $\begin{array}{r} 534 \\ -321 \\ \hline \end{array}$

7. $\begin{array}{r} 736 \\ -414 \\ \hline \end{array}$

8. $\begin{array}{r} 952 \\ -295 \\ \hline \end{array}$

9. $\begin{array}{r} 573 \\ -212 \\ \hline \end{array}$

10. $\begin{array}{r} 379 \\ -116 \\ \hline \end{array}$

Set C (pp. 74–75)

Solve. Estimate to check.

1. Katy has 814 stickers in her collection. Jake has 517 stickers in his collection. How many more stickers does Katy have?

2. Lily had $25.31. She spent $13.66 at the shoe store. How much money does Lily have left?

Set D (pp. 76–79)

Tell whether each problem can be solved by using mental math, paper and pencil, or a calculator. Then solve each problem using the method you chose.

1. Lindsey paddled 4,033 feet in her canoe. Ronald paddled 2,077 feet in his. How much farther did Lindsey paddle than Ronald?

2. The library was built 6 years before the post office was built. The post office was built in 1971. How old was the library in 1988?

Review/Test

CHECK VOCABULARY AND CONCEPTS

Choose the correct term from the box.

Vocabulary
estimate
regroup

1. To find *about* how many more, you can ? . (p. 70)

Use mental math to find the difference. (pp. 72–73)

2. $\begin{array}{r} 637 \\ -499 \\ \hline \end{array}$

3. $\begin{array}{r} 512 \\ -380 \\ \hline \end{array}$

4. $\begin{array}{r} 860 \\ -375 \\ \hline \end{array}$

CHECK SKILLS

Use front-end estimation to estimate the difference. (pp. 70–71)

5. $\begin{array}{r} 67 \\ -29 \\ \hline \end{array}$

6. $\begin{array}{r} 967 \\ -283 \\ \hline \end{array}$

7. $\begin{array}{r} 748 \\ -599 \\ \hline \end{array}$

8. $\begin{array}{r} 4,175 \\ -1,832 \\ \hline \end{array}$

9. $\begin{array}{r} 8,596 \\ -3,714 \\ \hline \end{array}$

Solve. Estimate to check. (pp. 74–75)

10. Heather lives 367 miles from her grandparents' house and 521 miles from her aunt's house. How much closer does she live to her grandparents?

11. Maya is reading a book with 466 pages. She has already read 274 pages. How many pages does she have left to read?

12. Matt has $35.96. Ally has $24.29. How much more money does Matt have than Ally?

13. Casey had 622 marbles. She gave some marbles to her brother. Now she has 326 marbles. How many marbles did she give to her brother?

CHECK PROBLEM SOLVING

14. Abe wants each person at his party to have about 1 cup of punch. If he invites 18 children and 9 adults, about how many cups of punch should he make? (pp. 80–81)

15. Danielle wants to buy a favor for each child who attends her birthday party. She invited 16 girls and 15 boys. How many favors should she buy? (pp. 80–81)

Chapter CRCT Test Prep

NUMBERS AND OPERATIONS

1. M3N2.b. Use front-end estimation to estimate the difference.

$$\begin{array}{r} 595 \\ -239 \\ \hline \end{array}$$

A. 100

B. 200

C. 300

D. 400

2. M3N2.c. Kara bought a book that cost $3.35. She paid with a $5 bill. How much change did she get?

A. $1.35

B. $1.65

C. $1.75

D. $2.35

3. M3N2.c. Matt has 871 marbles. Janine has 623 marbles. How many more marbles does Matt have than Janine?

A. 258 marbles

B. 252 marbles

C. 248 marbles

D. 242 marbles

NUMBERS AND OPERATIONS

Use the table below to answer question 4.

Mountain Heights	
Mountain	**Height**
Brasstown Bald	4,784 feet
Stone	1,683 feet

4. M3N2.b. The table shows the heights of two mountains in Georgia. Use front-end estimation to find about how much taller Brasstown Bald Mountain is than Stone Mountain.

A. 2,000 feet

B. 3,000 feet

C. 4,000 feet

D. 5,000 feet

5. M3N2.c. A music store sold 4,356 CDs in all during June and July. 2,472 of those CDs were sold in June. How many CDs were sold in July?

A. 2,824

B. 2,184

C. 2,124

D. 1,884

Cumulative CRCT Test Prep

ALGEBRA

6. M3A1.a. Emily wrote the number pattern below. What is the missing number?

8, 16, 24, □, 40

A. 28

B. 30

C. 32

D. 36

7. M3A1.c. Which number belongs in the □ to make this number sentence true?

117 + □ = 125

A. 7

B. 8

C. 9

D. 10

8. M3A1.c. Anna baked 36 cookies in the morning. In the afternoon, she baked more cookies. When Anna finished baking, she had a total of 60 cookies. Which number sentence shows how many cookies Anna baked?

A. □ − 36 = 60

B. 36 + □ = 60

C. 60 + 36 = □

D. 6 + □ = 36

DATA ANALYSIS

Use the graph below to answer question 9.

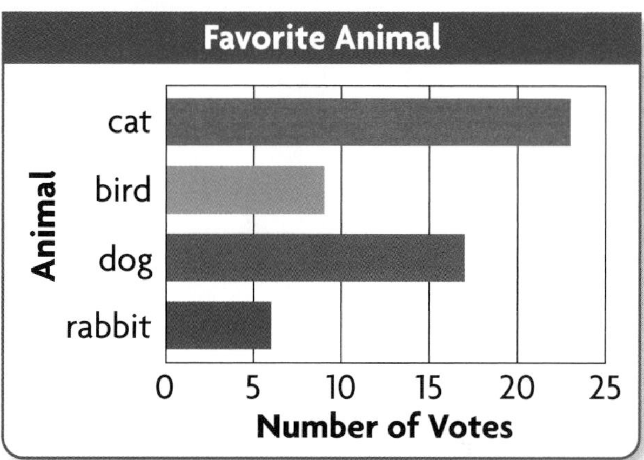

9. M3D1.b. Kevin asked students at his school to name their favorite animal. He made the bar graph above to show the results. Which animal got more votes than birds, but fewer votes than cats?

A. cat

B. bird

C. dog

D. rabbit

CHAPTER 5

Use Money

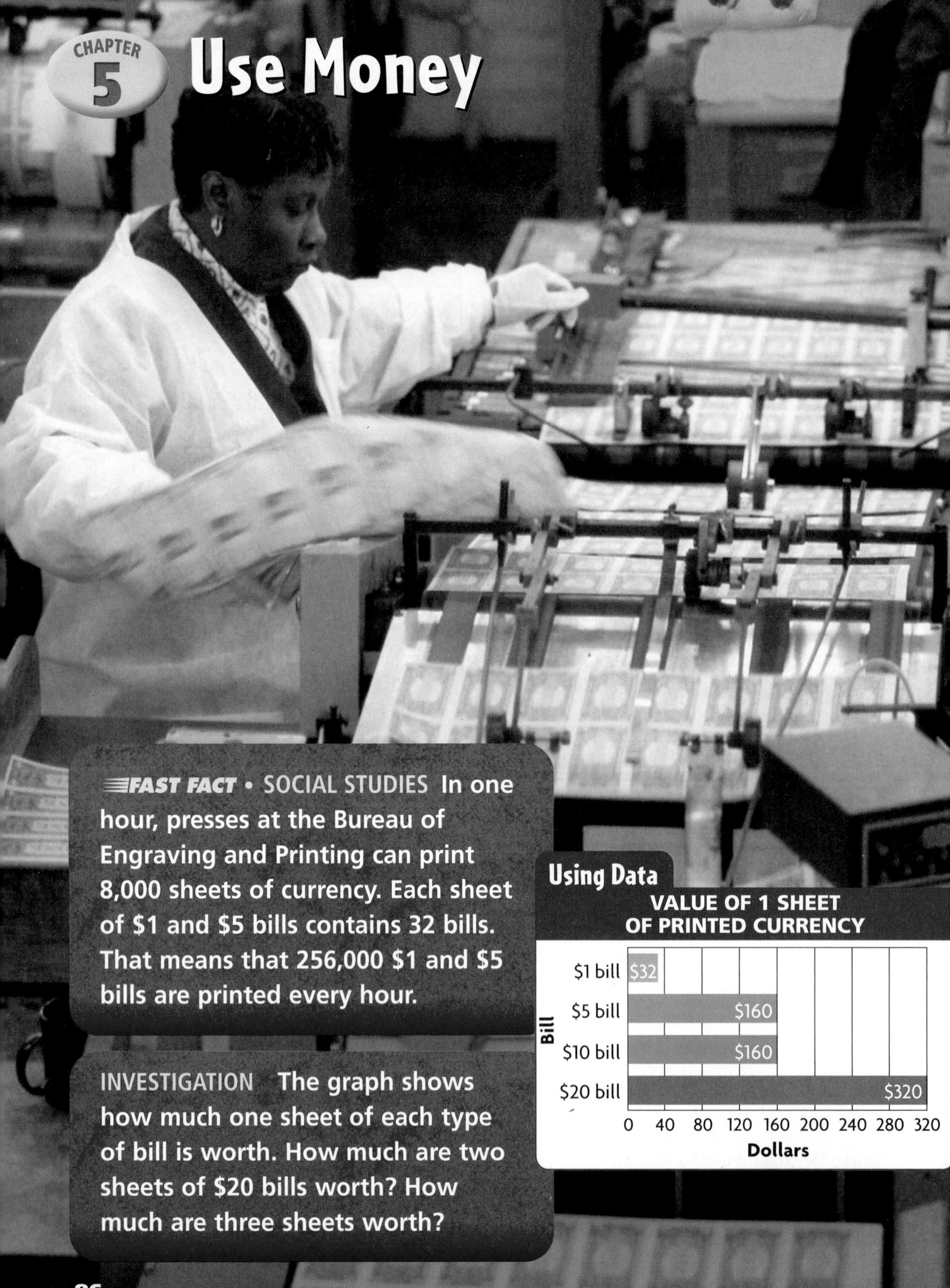

FAST FACT • SOCIAL STUDIES In one hour, presses at the Bureau of Engraving and Printing can print 8,000 sheets of currency. Each sheet of $1 and $5 bills contains 32 bills. That means that 256,000 $1 and $5 bills are printed every hour.

INVESTIGATION The graph shows how much one sheet of each type of bill is worth. How much are two sheets of $20 bills worth? How much are three sheets worth?

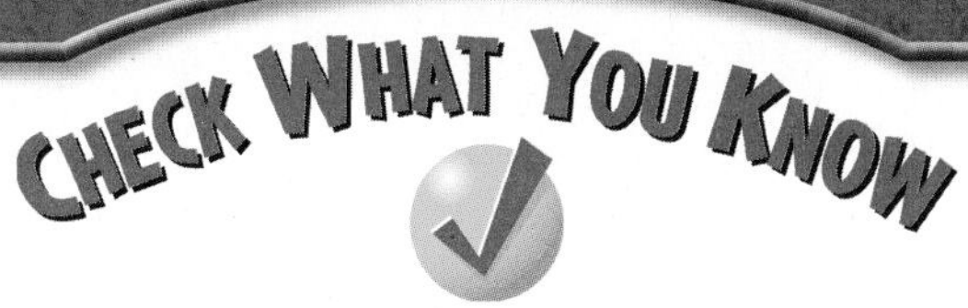

Use this page to help you review and remember important skills needed for Chapter 5.

COUNT COINS

Count and write the amount.

1. 

2. 

3. 

4. 

SAME AMOUNTS

Show the amount of money in two ways. Draw and label each coin.

5. 

6. 

7. 

8. 

VOCABULARY POWER

REVIEW

dollar sign [dä′lər sīn] *noun*

The dollar sign was being used before the first United States dollar was printed in 1785. What other sign is used to show amounts of United States money less than $1?

PREVIEW

decimal point

equivalent

www.harcourtschool.com/mathglossary

LESSON 1

Count Bills and Coins

Concepts/Skill to Maintain Money
also M3A1.c.

Learn

EVERY CENT COUNTS Jolene has some coins. Andrew has some bills and coins. How much money does each person have?

Quick Review

Add 5 to each number.

1. 15 **2.** 30 **3.** 55

4. 25 **5.** 95

VOCABULARY

decimal point
equivalent

Examples

Jolene's Money

A Start with the coin of greatest value. Count on to find the total.

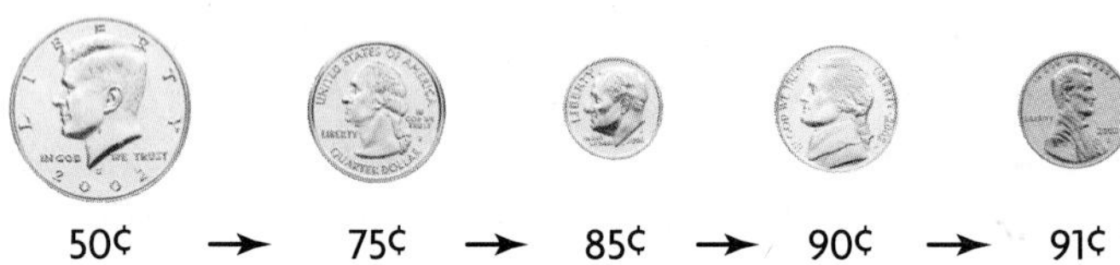

50¢ → 75¢ → 85¢ → 90¢ → 91¢

Read: 91 cents. Write: 91¢ or $0.91
dollar sign ↑ ↑ **decimal point**

So, Jolene has 91¢.

Remember

half dollar
50¢

quarter
25¢

dime
10¢

nickel
5¢

penny
1¢

Andrew's Money

B Start with the bills. Then count on the coins.

$1.00 → $2.00 → $2.25 → $2.50 → $2.60 → $2.61 → $2.62

Read: 2 dollars and 62 cents. Write: $2.62

So, Andrew has $2.62.

- Would the total amount be the same if you counted the coins and bills in a different order? Explain.
- **What if** Jolene found 4 more pennies and another nickel? How much money would she then have in all?

Equivalent Sets

Sets of money that have the same value are **equivalent**. You can make two equivalent sets of money with a value of $6.13 by using different combinations of bills and coins.

One Way

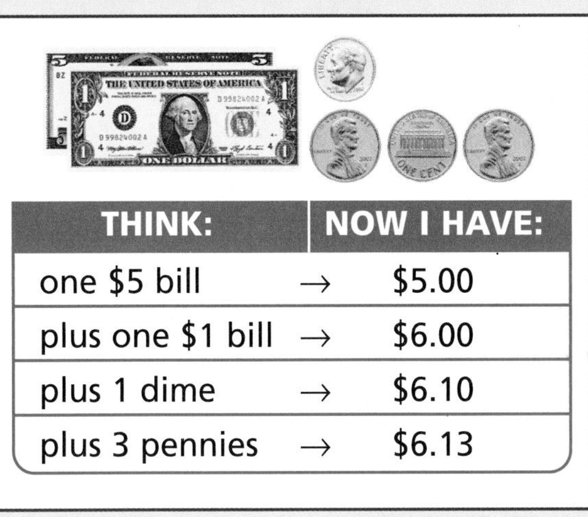

THINK:		NOW I HAVE:
one $5 bill	→	$5.00
plus one $1 bill	→	$6.00
plus 1 dime	→	$6.10
plus 3 pennies	→	$6.13

Another Way

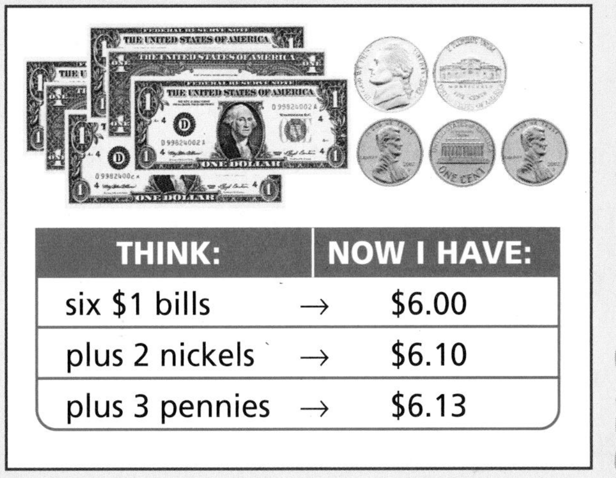

THINK:		NOW I HAVE:
six $1 bills	→	$6.00
plus 2 nickels	→	$6.10
plus 3 pennies	→	$6.13

- Which set uses the fewest bills and coins?
- Name two sets of coins that are equivalent to one dollar.
- What are three ways to show 50¢?

Technology Link

More Practice: Harcourt Mega Math The Number Games, *Buggy Bargains,* Levels A, B

Check

1. Explain three different ways to make $2.26.

Write the amount.

2. 

3. 

4. 

5.  

Find two equivalent sets for each. List the coins and bills.

6. $0.35 **7.** $5.50 **8.** $2.46 **9.** $6.92

LESSON CONTINUES

Practice and Problem Solving

Extra Practice, page 100, Set A

Write the amount.

10. 

11. 

Find two equivalent sets for each. List the coins and bills.

12. $0.67 **13.** $5.03 **14.** $2.25 **15.** $3.75

16. $1.40 **17.** $2.15 **18.** $4.35 **19.** $8.04

Write the missing number.

20. 1 dime = ■ nickels

21. 5 pennies = ■ nickel

22. 2 quarters = ■ dimes

23. 1 quarter = ■ nickels

24. 1 half dollar = ■ quarters

25. 1 dollar = ■ quarters

For 26–29, list the fewest bills and coins you can use to make each amount.

26. $0.48 **27.** $1.79 **28.** $2.37 **29.** $8.86

30. Tom had $0.43 in his pocket. Three coins fell out of a hole in the pocket. Tom still has the coins shown at the right. What coins fell out of his pocket?

31. **Vocabulary Power** Colonial Americans used Spanish silver dollar coins. The dollar was cut into 8 bits called pieces of eight. If 2 bits equaled 25¢, what did 4 bits equal?

32. **REASONING** Fiona has 2 quarters and 1 nickel. Jake has an equivalent set using dimes and nickels. Jake has 8 coins. How many dimes and nickels does Jake have?

33. **MULTISTEP** How can you show 40¢ with 8 coins? with 5 coins? with 4 coins? Can you show 40¢ with 3 coins? Explain.

34. **What's the Error?** Brett said he could show 25¢ with 5 coins, with 3 coins, and with 2 coins. What is his error? Explain.

35. **FAST FACT • SOCIAL STUDIES** The United States Mint was established in 1792. How many years ago was this?

36. Abraham Lincoln's likeness was first used on the penny in 1909. This was 100 years after Lincoln's birth. In what year was Abraham Lincoln born?

Maintain Skills

Compare the numbers. Write <, >, or = for each ●.

37. 60 ● 64

38. 43 ● 79

39. Write the product.

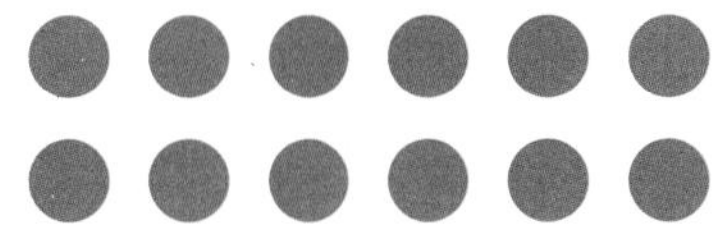

$2 \times 6 = ■$

CRCT Test Prep

40. M3A1.a. Which number comes next in the pattern? (p. 12)
3, 7, 11, 15, 19, □

A. 22
B. 23
C. 24
D. 25

41. M3N1.a. Which digit is in the ten thousands place of 62,950? (p. 14)

A. 2
B. 5
C. 6
D. 9

Problem Solving LINKUP . . . to Social Studies

NEW GOLDEN COIN In 2000 the golden dollar coin took the place of the Susan B. Anthony dollar coin. On the front of the golden coin is Sacagawea and her infant son. A Shoshone Indian, Sacagawea helped explorers Lewis and Clark on their expedition to the West.

Write the amount.

1.

2.

3.

4.

LESSON 2

Problem Solving Strategy
Act It Out

M3P5. Students will represent mathematics in multiple ways. *also* M3P1.a., M3P1.c., M3P1.d., M3P3., M3P3.a., M3P3.b., M3P3.c., M3P3.d.

PROBLEM Patty has four $1 bills, 3 quarters, 5 dimes, 1 nickel, and 5 pennies. How many different equivalent sets of bills and coins can she use to pay for a magazine that costs $4.75?

Quick Review

1. 2 quarters = ■ pennies
2. 10 dimes = ■ quarters
3. 4 nickels = ■ dimes
4. 1 quarter = ■ nickels
5. 10 pennies = ■ nickels

UNDERSTAND

- What are you asked to find?
- What information will you use?

PLAN

- What strategy can you use?

Act it out to model sets of bills and coins with a value of $4.75.

SOLVE

- How can you use the strategy to solve the problem?

Use the correct amount of play money to model different ways to make $4.75.

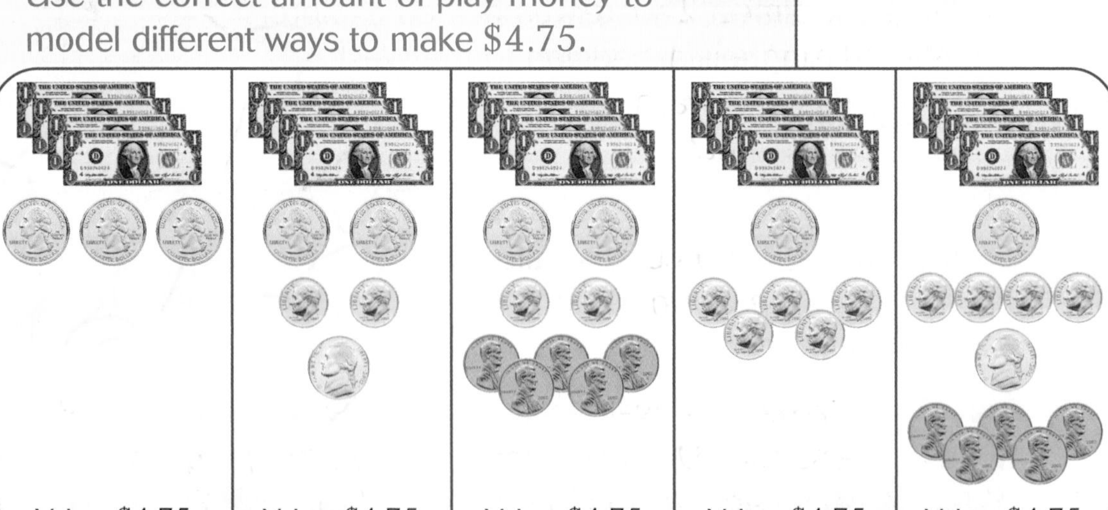

Value: $4.75	Value: $4.75	Value: $4.75	Value: $4.75	Value: $4.75

So, there are 5 equivalent sets.

CHECK

- How can you decide if your answer is correct?

Problem Solving Practice

Act it out to solve.

1. **What if** Patty's magazine costs $5.25? What equivalent sets of bills and coins can she use?

2. Tyler has one $1 bill, 5 quarters, 1 dime, and 2 nickels. What equivalent sets of bills and coins can he use to pay for a goldfish that costs $1.35?

Strategies

- **Act It Out or Use Objects**
- Make a Picture or Diagram
- Guess and Check
- Use or Look for a Pattern
- Use Logical Reasoning

Problem Solving

Kevin has 7 quarters, 4 dimes, and 1 nickel. He wants to buy a bookmark that costs $1.80.

3. Kevin wants to keep 1 quarter. Which set of coins should he use?
   - **A** 6 quarters, 2 dimes, 1 nickel
   - **B** 6 quarters, 3 dimes
   - **C** 7 quarters, 1 dime
   - **D** 6 quarters, 3 dimes, 1 nickel

4. If Kevin uses the fewest coins, which type of coin will he NOT use?
   - **F** quarters
   - **G** dimes
   - **H** nickels
   - **J** none of the above

Mixed Strategy Practice

USE DATA For 5–7, use the table.

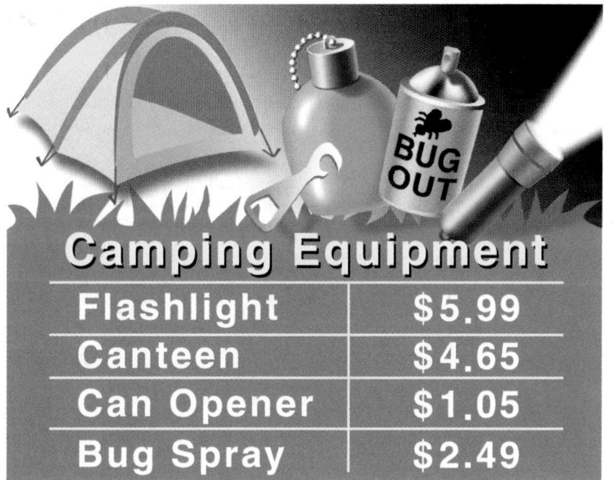

Camping Equipment	
Flashlight	$5.99
Canteen	$4.65
Can Opener	$1.05
Bug Spray	$2.49

5. Laura has one $5 bill, four $1 bills, 7 quarters, 2 dimes, 2 nickels, and 4 pennies. Using exact change, how many different ways can she pay for the flashlight?

6. Paco has only quarters and nickels in his pocket. What 9 coins would he use to buy the can opener, using exact change?

7. Fran, Geri, Harold, and Ivan each buy a different item. Use the clues to decide what each person buys. Fran pays with one $1 bill and 1 nickel. Ivan pays with one $5 bill. Geri pays with three $1 bills.

8. **Write About It** Betty has three $1 bills, 5 quarters, 7 dimes, and 2 nickels. Explain how Betty can trade some of her bills and coins for a $5 bill.

LESSON 3

Compare Money Amounts

Concepts/Skill to Maintain Money *also* M3P2.a., M3P2.b., M3P2.c., M3P2.d., M3P4.b.

Quick Review

Write <, >, or = for each ●.

1. 463 ● 643
2. 510 ● 105
3. 874 ● 748
4. 296 ● 926
5. 713 ● 713

Learn

MONEY MATTERS Ming and Ben have the sets of bills and coins pictured below. Who has more money?

Count each amount and compare.

Ming has $5.75.
Ben has $5.50.
$5.75 > $5.50.
So, Ming has more money.

Ming's money

Ben's money

Examples Compare. Which amount is greater?

A

Since $2.73 = $2.73, the amounts are equal.

B

Since $3.54 < $4.12, then $4.12 is the greater amount.

- **REASONING** Is a set of bills and coins always worth more than a set that has fewer bills and coins? Explain.

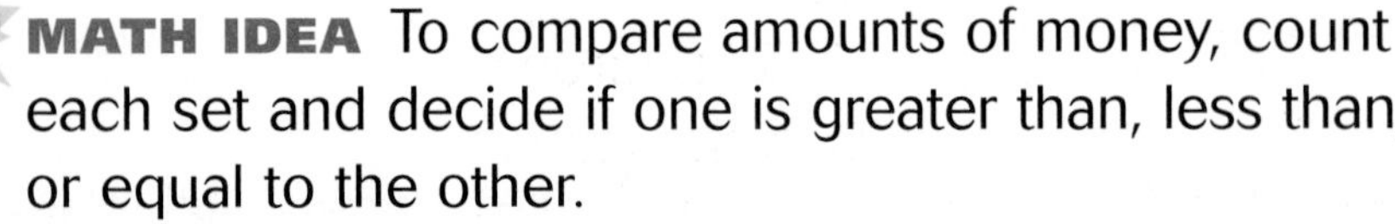

MATH IDEA To compare amounts of money, count each set and decide if one is greater than, less than, or equal to the other.

Check

1. **Explain** how you can use what you know about comparing whole numbers to compare amounts of money.

Use < or > to compare the amounts of money.

2. a. 

b.   

Practice and Problem Solving

Extra Practice, page 100, Set B

Use < or > to compare the amounts of money.

3. a. 

b. 

4. a. 

b. 

5. Sandra has 2 \$1 bills and 5 dimes. Jason has 10 quarters and 2 pennies. Who has more money? Explain.

6. Kim spent 1 \$5 bill and a nickel. Ben spent 4 \$1 bills, 3 quarters, and 2 dimes. Who spent more money? Explain.

7. Setsuo sells lemonade for 25¢ a glass. He has 9 quarters, 6 dimes, and 3 nickels. How many glasses of lemonade did he sell? Draw a picture to explain.

8. **What's the Error?** Janice says that \$4.87 is greater than \$6.21 because 87 cents is greater than 21 cents. Describe her error. Explain which is greater.

Maintain Skills

9. $21 + 98$

10. $18 + 42$

11. $256 + 148$

12. $49 - 33$

13. $82 - 57$

14. $621 - 444$

CRCT Test Prep

15. M3N1.a. What is the value of the blue digit? 15,271 (p. 14)

A. 5 ones
B. 5 tens
C. 5 hundreds
D. 5 thousands

LESSON 4

Make Change

Concepts/Skill to Maintain Money *also* M3P2., M3P2.a., M3P2.b., M3P2.d., M3P3.a., M3P3.b., M3P3.c., M3P3.d., M3P5.

Quick Review

Add 10¢ to each amount.

1. 55¢ **2.** 70¢ **3.** 83¢
4. 29¢ **5.** 41¢

Explore

MATERIALS
play bills and coins

Jessica buys a kitty toy at Pal's Pet Store. She pays with a $5 bill. How much change will she get?

Activity

Start with $2.89, the cost of the kitty toy. Count on coins and bills to $5.00, the amount Jessica paid.

$2.90 → $3.00 → $4.00 → $5.00

Count the coins and bills she received to find the change.

1 penny, 1 dime, and two $1 bills equal $2.11.

PAL'S PET STORE

Dog Leash	$5.99
Dog Shampoo	$3.68
Kitty Toy	$2.89
Fish Food	$1.29
Chew Bone	$3.59
Bird Seed Bell	$2.63

So, Jessica will get $2.11 in change.

- Why do people start with the coin of least value when making change?

Try It

Each person pays with a $5 bill. Use play money to make change. Draw a picture to show the change each person will get.

a. Tony buys a bird seed bell.

b. Marian buys fish food. Show her change, using the fewest coins.

c. Emma buys a chew bone. Show at least two different ways to make change.

Connect

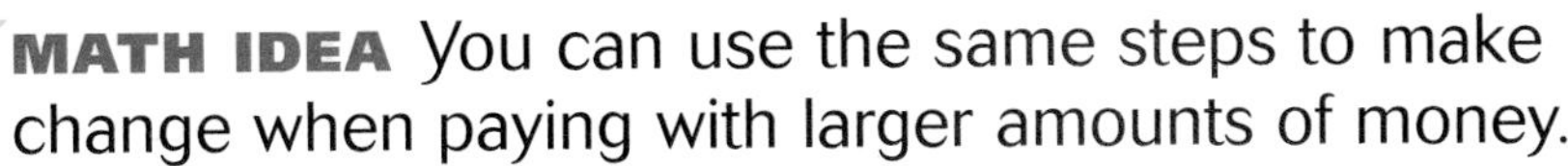

MATH IDEA You can use the same steps to make change when paying with larger amounts of money.

Dog shampoo costs $3.68. Anton pays with a $10 bill. Show the change Anton will get.

Count on from the cost of the dog shampoo to the amount paid.

$3.69 → $3.70 → $3.75 → $4.00 → $5.00 → $10.00

Count the coins and bills. 2 pennies, 1 nickel, 1 quarter, one $1 bill, and one $5 bill equal $6.32.

So, Anton will get $6.32 in change.

Technology Link

More Practice: Harcourt Mega Math The Number Games, *Buggy Bargains,* Levels D, H

Practice and Problem Solving

Copy and complete the table. Use play money.

	COST OF ITEM	AMOUNT PAID	CHANGE IN COINS AND BILLS	TOTAL AMOUNT OF CHANGE
1.	$0.54	$1.00	■	■
2.	$3.23	$10.00	■	■
3.	$2.69	$5.00	■	■

4. **REASONING** Dana buys rocks for her fish tank for $0.65. She pays with a $1 bill. The clerk has run out of quarters. What is the least number of coins Dana can get? List the coins.

5. **What's the Question?** Evan bought a dog bowl for $2.85 and a chewbone for $3.59. He paid with a $10 bill. The answer is $3.56.

Maintain Skills

6. 375 + 499 **7.** 800 − 274 **8.** 359 − 276

9. 420 + 292 = ■

CRCT Test Prep

10. M3N1.a. What is the value of the digit 2 in 7,293? (p. 6)

A. 2 C. 200
B. 20 D. 2,000

LESSON 5

Add and Subtract Money Amounts

 **M3N2.c.** Solve problems requiring addition and subtraction. *also* **M3P3.c., M3P3.d.**

Quick Review

1. 863 + 219
2. 673 − 482
3. 457 + 361
4. 1,073 − 845
5. 920 + 549

Learn

CHECK YOUR CHANGE Matthew bought a dog collar for $3.95 and a leash for $4.64. How much money did Matthew spend?

Example 1

Add. $3.95 + $4.64 = ■

STEP 1

Add money like whole numbers.

$$\begin{array}{r} \$3.95 \\ +\$4.64 \\ \hline \end{array} \rightarrow \begin{array}{r} {}^{1} \\ 395 \\ +464 \\ \hline 859 \end{array}$$

STEP 2

Write the sum in dollars and cents.

$$\begin{array}{r} \$3.95 \\ +\$4.64 \\ \hline \$8.59 \end{array}$$

So, Matthew spent $8.59.

Julia bought a dog bed for $28.98. She paid for it with a $50 bill. How much change should she get?

Example 2

Subtract. $50.00 − $28.98 = ■

STEP 1

Subtract money like whole numbers.

$$\begin{array}{r} \$50.00 \\ -\$28.98 \\ \hline \end{array} \rightarrow \begin{array}{r} {}^{4\ \ 9\ \ 9\ \ 10} \\ \not{5},\not{0}\ \not{0}\ \not{0} \\ -2,8\ 9\ 8 \\ \hline 2,1\ 0\ 2 \end{array}$$

STEP 2

Write the difference in dollars and cents.

$$\begin{array}{r} \$50.00 \\ -\$28.98 \\ \hline \$21.02 \end{array}$$

So, Julia should get $21.02 in change.

Check

1. **Explain** how you can check the subtraction to be sure Julia got the correct change.

Solve.

2. Katie bought a soft pretzel for \$1.19. She paid for it with a \$5 bill. How much change did she get?

3. Kevin bought one DVD for \$14.89 and another DVD for \$22.51. How much did he spend in all?

Practice and Problem Solving

Extra Practice, page 100, Set C

Solve.

4. Megan bought a present for her brother for \$24.87 and a present for her mother for \$38.26. How much did she spend on their presents?

5. Rodrigo bought a sketch book for \$15.25. He gave the cashier a \$20 bill. What was his change?

Write <, >, or = for each ●.

6. \$5.00 ● \$3.94 + \$1.06

7. \$4.57 − \$1.14 ● \$5.71

USE DATA For 8–9, use Justin's money at the right.

8. **MULTISTEP** A cat bed costs \$8.59. Does Justin have enough money to buy it? Explain.

9. **MULTISTEP** Does Justin have enough money to buy the cat bed and a cat collar that costs \$2.99? Explain.

10. **Write a problem** using two money amounts greater than \$5. Solve.

Maintain Skills

Write <, >, or = for each ●.

11. 127 ● 171

12. 682 ● 659

13. $\begin{array}{r} 723 \\ -581 \\ \hline \end{array}$

14. $\begin{array}{r} 308 \\ -156 \\ \hline \end{array}$

15. $\begin{array}{r} 428 \\ -134 \\ \hline \end{array}$

CRCT Test Prep

16. M3A1.c. What number goes in the □ to make the number sentence true? (p. 48)

$$42 + \square = 54$$

A. 4
B. 12
C. 16
D. 20

Extra Practice

Set A (pp. 88–91)

Write the amount.

1. 

2.

Find two equivalent sets for each. List the coins and bills.

3. $0.47
4. $4.38
5. $2.81
6. $6.76

Set B (pp. 94–95)

Use < or > to compare the amounts of money.

1. a. 

   b. 

2. Maria has 3 quarters, 3 dimes, and 1 nickel. She wants to buy a slice of pie for $1.10. Does she have enough money? Explain.

3. Ronnie has 1 quarter, 4 dimes, and 3 nickels. Lydia has 3 quarters. Who has more money? Explain.

Set C (pp. 98–99)

Solve.

1. Ryan bought a CD for $15.99 and a book for $26.45. He paid with a $50 bill. What was Ryan's change?

2. Kelly bought a sweater for $21.75 and a skirt for $37.99. How much did she spend?

USE DATA For 3–4, use the table.

FREIDA'S FRUIT STAND	
Fruit	**Price**
Bananas	$0.65 each pound
Plums	$0.45 each
Grapes	$1.33 each pound
Apples	$0.24 each
Blueberries	$1.79 each pint

3. How much more does a pint of blueberries cost than an apple?

4. Ezra buys 2 plums and a pound of grapes and pays with a $5 bill. How much change does Ezra get?

Review/Test

CHECK VOCABULARY AND CONCEPTS

Vocabulary
- decimal point
- equivalent
- change

Choose the best term from the box.

1. Sets of money that have the same value are ___?___ . (p. 89)

Copy and complete the table. (pp. 96–97)

	COST OF ITEM	AMOUNT PAID	CHANGE IN COINS AND BILLS	AMOUNT OF CHANGE
2.	$4.62	$10.00	■	■
3.	$3.49	$5.00	■	■

CHECK SKILLS

Write the amount. (pp. 88–91)

4. 

5. 

Use $<$ or $>$ to compare the amounts of money. (pp. 94–95)

6. a.  

b. 

Solve. (pp. 98–99)

7. Jon bought a pair of shoes for $41.23. He paid with a $50 bill. How much change did Jon get?

8. Erin bought some yarn for $4.50 and a pair of scissors for $1.50. How much did she spend in all?

CHECK PROBLEM SOLVING

Act it out to solve. (pp. 92–93)

9. Michelle has two $1 bills, 5 quarters, 3 dimes, and 4 nickels. How many different ways can she make $3.50?

10. Brian has one $5 bill, one $1 bill, 5 quarters, 3 dimes, and 3 nickels. How many different ways can he make $7.35?

Chapter CRCT Test Prep

NUMBERS AND OPERATIONS

1. M3N2.c. Lorenzo has 4 quarters and 7 nickels. Mary has 6 quarters and 3 dimes. How much more money does Mary have?

A. $0.15

B. $0.25

C. $0.35

D. $0.45

2. M3N2.c. Ethan bought a fish tank for $18, rocks for $5.34, and some fish for $4.50. How much money did Ethan spend in all?

A. $10.02

B. $17.84

C. $27.84

D. $28.24

3. M3N2.c. Sasha bought a pencil for $0.85 and a notebook for $2.35. She paid with a $5 bill. How much change did Sasha receive?

A. $1.80

B. $1.90

C. $2.10

D. $2.20

NUMBERS AND OPERATIONS

4. M3N2.c. Jason wants to buy a sketch book that costs $5.35. He has one $5 bill and one dime. How much more money does Jason need?

A. $0.10

B. $0.15

C. $0.20

D. $0.25

Use the table below to answer question 5.

Pocket Money

Student	Amount of Money
Sue	$2.45
Harry	$6.40
Justin	$3.85
Gina	$6.75

5. M3N2.c. The table shows the amount of money each student has in his or her pocket. How much more money does Gina have than Sue?

A. $0.35

B. $2.90

C. $4.30

D. $9.20

Cumulative CRCT Test Prep

NUMBERS AND OPERATIONS

6. M3N2.b. Use front-end estimation to estimate the difference.

$$\begin{array}{r} 881 \\ -642 \\ \hline \end{array}$$

A. 200

B. 300

C. 400

D. 500

7. M3N2.c. One summer, David made \$344 for mowing lawns and \$375 for walking dogs. How much money did David make that summer?

A. \$619

B. \$639

C. \$711

D. \$719

8. M3N1.a. In 2000, the population of Macon, Georgia, was 97,255. What is the value of the digit 2 in the number 97,255?

A. 2 ten thousands

B. 2 thousands

C. 2 hundreds

D. 2 tens

ALGEBRA

9. M3A1.c. Mr. Timmins wrote the number sentence below on the board.

$$\square + 43 = 83$$

Which number belongs in the □ to make the number sentence true?

A. 20

B. 30

C. 40

D. 50

10. M3A1.a. What is the next number in the pattern?

100, 120, 140, 160, □

A. 180

B. 186

C. 200

D. 260

11. M3A1.c. Which number sentence can you use to find the missing addend?

$$21 + \square = 94$$

A. $94 + 21 = \square$

B. $21 + 94 = \square$

C. $21 - 94 = \square$

D. $94 - 21 = \square$

CHAPTER 6

Understand Time

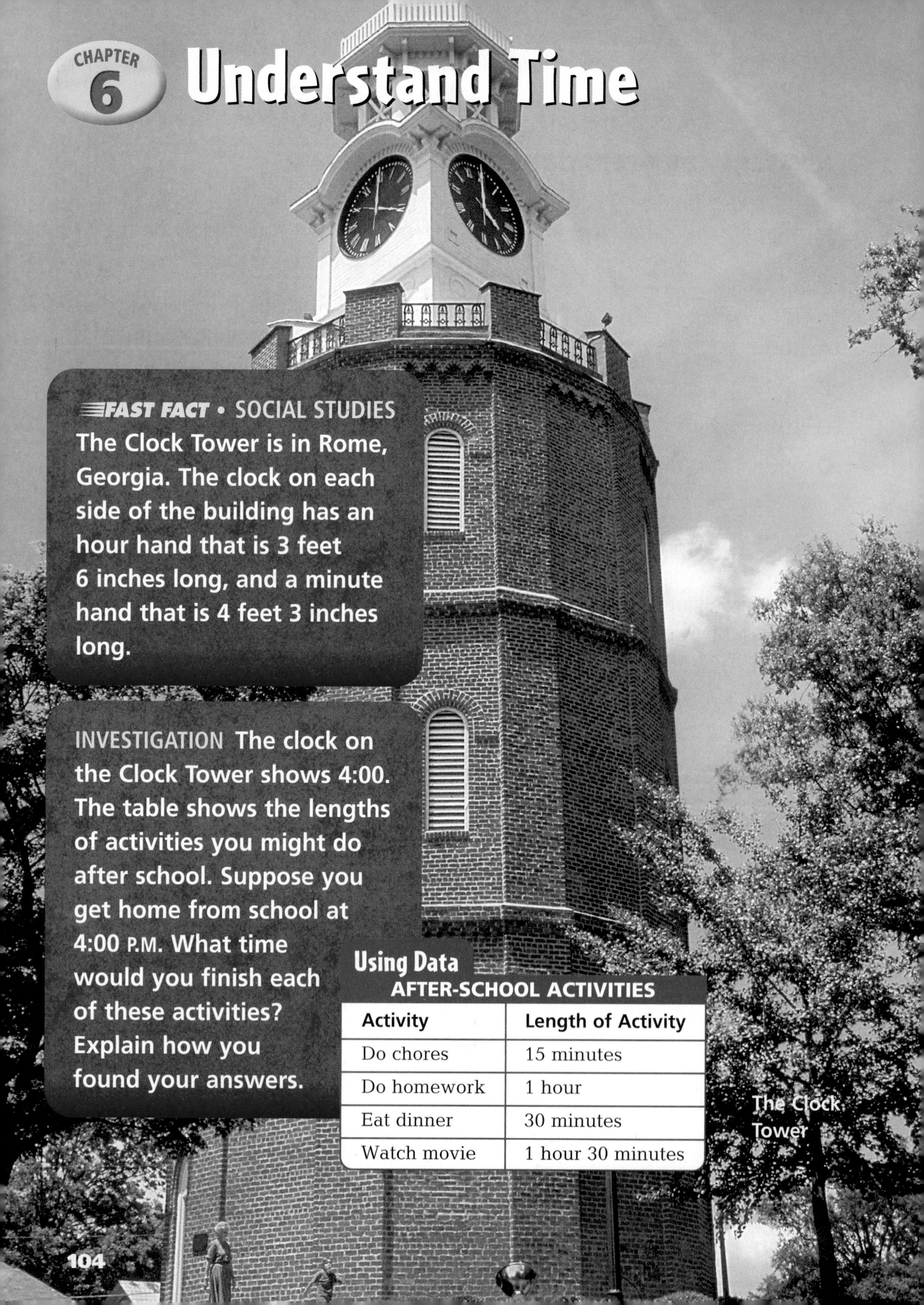

FAST FACT • SOCIAL STUDIES
The Clock Tower is in Rome, Georgia. The clock on each side of the building has an hour hand that is 3 feet 6 inches long, and a minute hand that is 4 feet 3 inches long.

INVESTIGATION The clock on the Clock Tower shows 4:00. The table shows the lengths of activities you might do after school. Suppose you get home from school at 4:00 P.M. What time would you finish each of these activities? Explain how you found your answers.

Using Data

AFTER-SCHOOL ACTIVITIES

Activity	Length of Activity
Do chores	15 minutes
Do homework	1 hour
Eat dinner	30 minutes
Watch movie	1 hour 30 minutes

The Clock Tower

CHECK WHAT YOU KNOW

Use this page to help you review and remember important skills needed for Chapter 6.

TELL TIME

Read and write the time.

1. 
2. 
3. 
4. 
5. 
6. 
7. 
8. 
9. 

VOCABULARY POWER

REVIEW

minute [min′it] *noun*

Minute has meanings other than "small amount of time." When pronounced as [mī•n(y)o͞ot′], it is an adjective that means "very small." Can you think of other words that mean "very small"?

PREVIEW

A.M.	midnight
P.M.	elapsed time
noon	schedule

www.harcourtschool.com/mathglossary

LESSON 1 Tell Time

Concepts/Skill to Maintain Time

Quick Review

Add 5 to each number.

1. 25 **2.** 10

3. 15 **4.** 5

5. 30

VOCABULARY

clockwise

counterclockwise

Learn

WHAT TIME IS IT? The hands, numbers, and marks on a clock help you tell what time it is. In one minute, the minute hand moves from one mark to the next.

To find the number of minutes after the hour, count by fives and ones to where the minute hand is pointing.

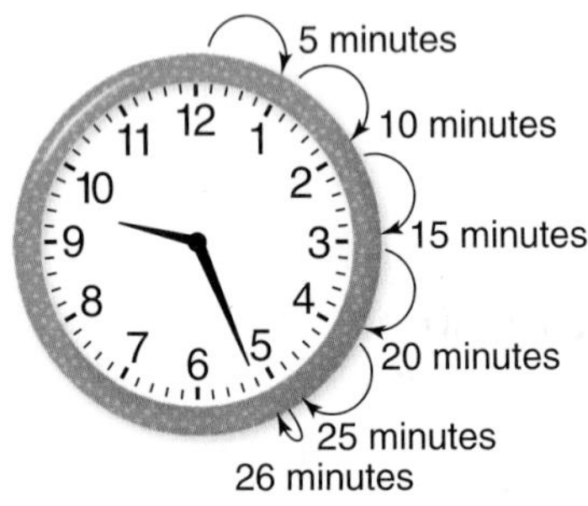

Read: nine twenty-six, or 26 minutes after nine

Write: 9:26

When a clock shows 31 or more minutes *after* the hour, you can read the time as a number of minutes *before* the next hour.

Count back by fives and ones to where the minute hand is pointing.

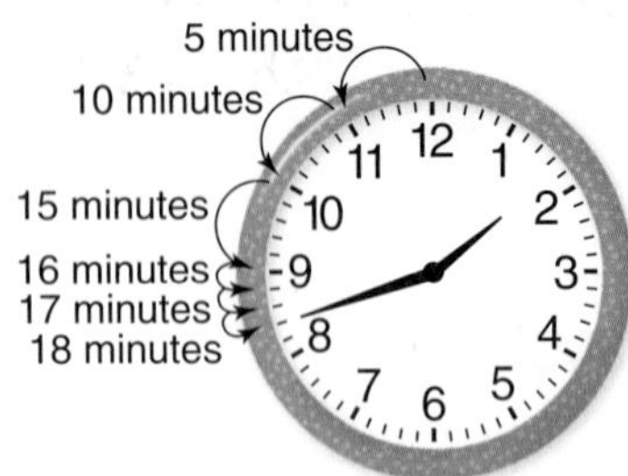

Read: 18 minutes before two

Write: 1:42

A digital clock uses numbers to show the hour and the number of minutes after the hour.

Read: seven fifty-two, or 8 minutes before eight

Write: 7:52

1:20

Read: one twenty, or 20 minutes after one

Write: 1:20

Remember

In five minutes, the minute hand moves from one number to the next.

Half Hour and Quarter Hour

You can also tell time by parts of an hour. On the clocks below, you can see how one hour can be divided into 2 equal parts, or half hours, or into 4 equal parts, or quarter hours. A half hour has 30 minutes, and a quarter hour has 15 minutes.

Read: half past seven

Write: 7:30

Read: quarter past ten

Write: 10:15

Read: quarter to three

Write: 2:45

ESTIMATION Sometimes an estimate of the time is asked for. Look at where the minute hand is pointing to estimate the time to the nearest half hour.

Is the time closer to 8:00 or 8:30?

The minute hand is closer to the hour mark, so the estimated time is about 8:00.

Is the time closer to 3:30 or 4:00?

The minute hand is closer to the half hour mark, so the estimated time is about 3:30.

Check

1. **Explain** why 30 minutes is called a half hour.

Write each time. Then write two ways you can read each time.

2. 

3. 

4. 

5. 

LESSON CONTINUES 

Practice and Problem Solving

Extra Practice, page 116, Set A

Write each time. Then write two ways you can read each time.

6. 

7. 

8. 

9. 

Write two ways you can read each time.

10. 

11. 

12. 

13. 

For 14–19, write the letter of the clock that matches each time.

a. 

b. 

c. 

d. 

14. 13 minutes before six

15. 10:28

16. twelve thirty-five

17. quarter past six

18. 5:47

19. 25 minutes before one

Estimate each time to the nearest half hour.

20. 

21. 

22. 

23. 

24. It takes Ann 28 minutes to walk to school. It takes Rob a half hour to walk to school. Who has the longer walk? Explain.

25. **Reasoning** Look at the clock below. Is the time closer to 5:10 or 5:15? Explain.

26. **Reasoning** Does it take about 1 minute or about 5 minutes to tie your shoe? to make your lunch?

27. Joni needs to leave at about 5:30. If the minute hand is on the 2, is it closer to 5:00 or 5:30?

28. Mr. Olsen bought 8 copies of the newspaper for his class. He spent $16. How much did each newspaper cost?

Maintain Skills

Find each sum or difference.

29. $\begin{array}{r} 191 \\ +980 \\ \hline \end{array}$

30. $\begin{array}{r} 744 \\ +309 \\ \hline \end{array}$

31. $\begin{array}{r} 600 \\ -343 \\ \hline \end{array}$

32. $\begin{array}{r} 163 \\ +572 \\ \hline \end{array}$

33. $\begin{array}{r} 703 \\ -425 \\ \hline \end{array}$

34. $\begin{array}{r} 800 \\ -326 \\ \hline \end{array}$

CRCT Test Prep

35. M3N1.a. What is the value of the 2 in 56,297? (p. 14)

A. 2
B. 20
C. 200
D. 2,000

36. M3A1.a. Which number comes next in the pattern? (p. 12)

300, 303, 306, 309, □

A. 312
B. 311
C. 310
D. 306

Problem Solving Thinker's Corner

VISUAL THINKING You can describe the direction of turns by knowing how the hands of a clock move.

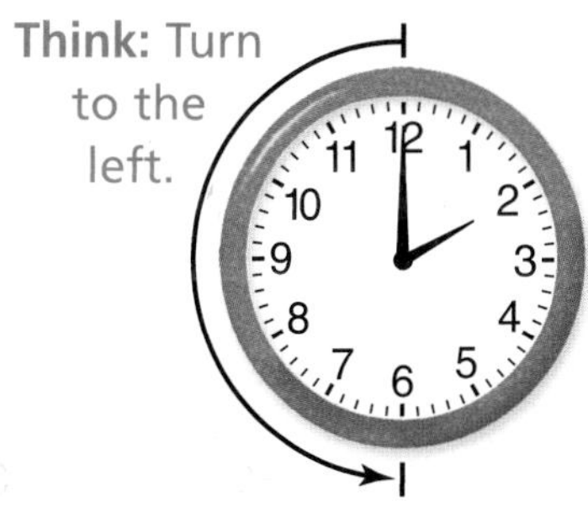

The turns that the hands of a clock make are called **clockwise** turns.

Turns in the opposite direction are called **counterclockwise** turns.

Describe each turn. Write *clockwise* or *counterclockwise*.

1. 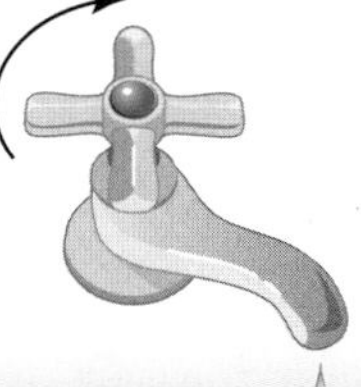

2. 

3. 

LESSON 2

A.M. and P.M.

Concepts/Skill to Maintain Time *also* M3P2.a., M3P2.d., M3P3.a., M3P3.b., M3P3.c., M3P3.d.

Quick Review

Write one way to read each time.

1. 3:22 **2.** 12:34

3. 9:45 **4.** 5:10

5. 11:55

VOCABULARY

A.M. **noon**

P.M. **midnight**

Learn

IT'S ABOUT TIME Using A.M. and P.M. helps you know what time of the day or night it is. **A.M.** is used for the hours from 12 midnight to 12 noon. **P.M.** is used for the hours from 12 noon to 12 midnight.

12:00 in the day is **noon**.
12:00 at night is **midnight**.

Here are some ways to read and write times.

quarter to midnight
eleven forty-five P.M.
11:45 P.M.

quarter past seven
seven fifteen A.M.
7:15 A.M.

half past three
three thirty P.M.
3:30 P.M.

MATH IDEA The hours between midnight and noon are A.M. hours. The hours between noon and midnight are P.M. hours.

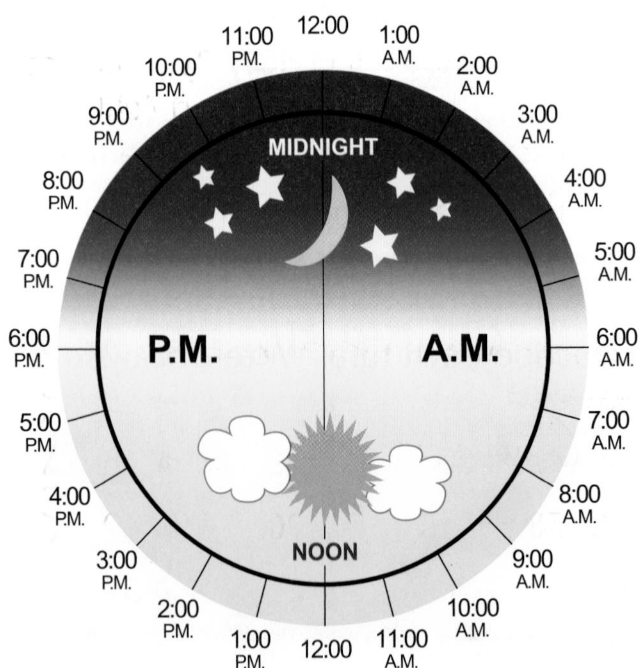

Check

1. **List** three things that you do in the A.M. hours.
2. **Name** something you do at 9:00 A.M. and something you do at 9:00 P.M. Explain how these times are different.

Write the time, using A.M. or P.M.

3. 
school starts

4. 
eat lunch

5. 
do homework

6. 

library closes

Practice and Problem Solving

Extra Practice, page 116, Set B

Write the time, using A.M. or P.M.

7. 
get ready for school

8. 
go to the store

9. 
recess

10. 

go to bed

Write two ways you can read each time. Then write the time, using A.M. or P.M.

11. 
play softball

12. 
moon shines

13. 
sun rises

14. 

eat dinner

15. **What's the Error?** Ty says that 11:45 A.M. is close to midnight. Explain his error. Then give a time that is close to midnight.

16. **REASONING** Are you awake during more A.M. or P.M. hours? Explain.

Maintain Skills

Compare. Write <, >, or = for each ●.

17. 42 ● 83

18. 36 ● 46

19. 78 ● 87

20. 51 ● 49

21. 24 ● 28

22. 62 ● 57

CRCT Test Prep

23. M3N2.c. Katie has 412 seashells. Marcos has 396 seashells. How many seashells do they have in all? (p. 54)

A. 708
B. 784
C. 788
D. 808

LESSON 3

Elapsed Time

M3M1. Students will further develop their understanding of the concept of time by determining elapsed time of a full, half, and quarter-hour. *also* M3P2., M3P3., M3P3.a., M3P3.b., M3P3.c., M3P3.d., M3P5.

Quick Review

Skip-count by fives.

1. 5, 10, 15, ■
2. 15, 20, 25, ■
3. 30, 35, 40, ■
4. 10, 15, 20, ■
5. 40, 45, 50, ■

VOCABULARY

elapsed time

Learn

GAME TIME Abby and her father played basketball from 8:15 P.M. to 8:45 P.M. How long did they play basketball?

The amount of time that passes from the start of an activity to the end of that activity is called the **elapsed time.** Find the elapsed time from 8:15 P.M. to 8:45 P.M.

Activity

Materials: clocks with movable hands

Move the minute hand on your clock to find the elapsed time.

Start: 8:15

Count the minutes: 30 minutes

So, they played basketball for 30 minutes.

If you know the start time and elapsed time of an activity, you can find the end time.

Example

Soccer practice starts at 11:00 A.M. It lasts 2 hours 15 minutes. Use your clock to find the time that practice ends.

Start: 11:00

Count the hours.

Count the minutes.

So, practice ends at 1:15 P.M.

Check

1. **Explain** how to find the elapsed time from 1:15 P.M. to 1:45 P.M.

Use a clock to find the elapsed time.

2. start: 9:15 A.M.
   end: 10:00 A.M.
3. start: 3:45 P.M.
   end: 5:45 P.M.
4. start: 10:00 A.M.
   end: 11:15 A.M.

Use a clock to find the end time.

5. start: 3:30 P.M.
   elapsed time: 1 hour 30 minutes
6. start: 11:30 A.M.
   elapsed time: 45 minutes

Practice and Problem Solving

Extra Practice, page 116, Set C

Use a clock to find the elapsed time.

7. start: 7:00 A.M.
   end: 10:00 A.M.
8. start: 5:15 P.M.
   end: 7:20 P.M.
9. start: 1:30 P.M.
   end: 2:15 P.M.

Use a clock to find the end time.

10. start: 4:15 P.M.
    elapsed time: 1 hour 15 minutes
11. start: 11:45 A.M.
    elapsed time: 65 minutes
12. **What's the Question?** The basketball game started at 11:30 A.M. It ended at 1:15 P.M. The answer is 1 hour 45 minutes.
13. **Write About It** Explain how you can use a clock to find the elapsed time from 10:30 A.M. to 1:15 P.M.

Maintain Skills

Write the amount.

14.

CRCT Test Prep

15. M3N2.c. Matt has 461 pennies. Kathy has 100 fewer pennies than Matt. How many pennies does Kathy have? (p. 74)

A. 361
B. 451
C. 460
D. 561

LESSON 4

Problem Solving Skill
Use a Schedule

M3M1. Students will further develop their understanding of the concept of time by determining elapsed time of a full, half, and quarter-hour. *also* M3D1.a., M3P1.a., M3P1.b., M3P1.c., M3P1.d., M3P2.a., M3P2.b., M3P2.c., M3P2.d., M3P3.b., M3P3.c., M3P3.d.

UNDERSTAND → PLAN → SOLVE → CHECK

Quick Review

1. 15 + 5 = ■
2. 15 + ■ = 25
3. ■ + 15 = 30
4. 15 + 30 = ■
5. 30 + ■ = 45

VOCABULARY
schedule

RIGHT ON TIME A **schedule** is a table that lists activities or events and the times they happen.

Stacy makes a schedule to plan her activities from the time she gets home until she eats dinner. You can use what you know about elapsed time to finish Stacy's schedule.

STACY'S SCHEDULE		
Activity	Time	Elapsed Time
Eat snack	3:45 P.M.–4:05 P.M.	20 minutes
Do homework	4:05 P.M.–5:10 P.M.	■
Walk dog	5:10 P.M.–■	25 minutes

How long will Stacy do homework?

Think: Find the elapsed time.
4:05 P.M. to 5:05 P.M. — 1 hour
5:05 P.M. to 5:10 P.M. — 5 minutes

So, Stacy will do homework for 1 hour 5 minutes.

When will Stacy walk her dog?

Think: Find the end time.
Start: 5:10 P.M.
Count on 25 minutes to 5:35 P.M.

So, Stacy will walk her dog from 5:10 P.M. to 5:35 P.M.

Talk About It

- **REASONING** You can use a schedule to find elapsed times of events. If you know the elapsed times, how can you find start or end times on a schedule?
- How long does it take Stacy to do her homework and walk her dog?
- Stacy starts eating dinner at 6:00 P.M. It takes her 30 minutes to eat her dinner. What time does she finish eating dinner?

Problem Solving Practice

USE DATA For 1–3, use the class schedule.

MORNING CLASS SCHEDULE	
Activity	**Time**
Reading	8:30 A.M. – 9:15 A.M.
Math	9:15 A.M. – 10:15 A.M.
Recess	10:15 A.M. – 10:35 A.M.
Music	10:35 A.M. – 11:20 A.M.
Art	11:20 A.M. – 12:05 P.M.

1. Which activities last 45 minutes each?
2. Which activity is the longest?
3. **ESTIMATION** About how long are the reading and math activities altogether?

Copy and complete the schedule.

	THE SCIENCE CHANNEL SCHEDULE		
	Program	**Time**	**Elapsed Time**
4.	Animals Around Us	■ – 7:00 P.M.	1 hour
5.	Wonderful Space	7:00 P.M. – ■	25 minutes
6.	Weather in Your Town	7:25 P.M. – 7:30 P.M.	■
7.	Earthly Treasures	7:30 P.M. – ■	30 minutes

For 8–9, use the schedule you completed.

8. What time does *Earthly Treasures* end?

   A 7:00 P.M.
   B 7:30 P.M.
   C 8:00 P.M.
   D 8:30 P.M.

9. What time does *Animals Around Us* begin?

   F 5:00 P.M.
   G 6:00 P.M.
   H 7:00 P.M.
   J 8:00 P.M.

Mixed Applications

10. Mr. Brooks will need chairs for 8 adults and 14 children for a party. Should Mr. Brooks estimate to decide how many chairs to rent? Explain.

11. **MULTISTEP** There were 438 people on a train. At the station, 113 people got off and 256 people got on. How many people are on the train now?

12. **MULTISTEP** The sum of two numbers is 72. Their difference is 24. What are the numbers?

13. **Write a problem** you can solve by using a time line. Trade problems with a partner and solve.

Extra Practice

Set A (pp. 106–109)

Write two ways you can read each time.

1. 

2. 

3. 

4. 2:30

Set B (pp. 110–111)

Write the time, using A.M. or P.M.

1. 
recess

2. 
play at park

3. 
plant flowers

4. 

go to library

Set C (pp. 112–113)

Use a clock to find the elapsed time.

1. start: 7:00 P.M.
   end: 9:45 P.M.
2. start: 11:15 A.M.
   end: 12:30 P.M.
3. start: 9:30 P.M.
   end: 11:00 P.M.
4. start: 6:45 P.M.
   end: 8:00 P.M.
5. start: 11:30 A.M.
   end: 2:00 P.M.
6. start: 9:30 A.M.
   end: 10:45 A.M.

Use a clock to find the end time.

7. start: 3:45 P.M.
   elapsed time: 1 hour 30 minutes
8. start: 9:30 A.M.
   elapsed time: 2 hours 45 minutes
9. start: 10:15 A.M.
   elapsed time: 1 hour 15 minutes
10. start: 9:45 P.M.
    elapsed time: 1 hour 15 minutes

Review/Test

CHECK VOCABULARY

Choose the best term from the box.

Vocabulary
midnight
noon
schedule
elapsed time

1. 12:00 at night is ? . (p. 110)
2. The amount of time that passes from the start of an activity to the end of that activity is ? . (p. 112)
3. A ? is a table that lists activities or events and the times they happen. (p. 114)

CHECK SKILLS

Write two ways you can read each time.
Then write the time, using A.M. or P.M. (pp. 106–109, 110–111)

4. 
dance class

5. 
bedtime

6. 
eat lunch

7. 7:38
eat breakfast

Use a clock to find the elapsed time. (pp. 112–113)

8. start: 8:00 A.M.
end: 9:30 A.M.

9. start: 3:15 P.M.
end: 4:30 P.M.

10. start: 8:15 P.M.
end: 9:00 P.M.

11. start: 1:45 P.M.
end: 4:15 P.M.

12. start: 6:45 A.M.
end: 9:30 A.M.

13. start: 11:00 A.M.
end: 1:15 P.M.

CHECK PROBLEM SOLVING

USE DATA For 14–15, use the schedule. (pp. 114–115)

14. At what time does Bob start to read?
15. Which activity is the shortest?

BOB'S SATURDAY SCHEDULE	
Activity	**Time**
Breakfast	7:30 A.M. – 8:00 A.M.
Read book	8:00 A.M. – 8:45 A.M.
Play baseball	8:45 A.M.–10:15 A.M.

Chapter CRCT Test Prep

MEASUREMENT

Use the schedule below to answer question 1.

Vince's Schedule	
Activity	**Time**
Homework	3:00 P.M.–4:15 P.M.
Soccer Practice	4:15 P.M.–5:45 P.M.
Chores	5:45 P.M.–7:30 P.M.

1. M3M1. How long does Vince spend at soccer practice?

   A. 1 hour

   B. 1 hour 15 minutes

   C. 1 hour 30 minutes

   D. 1 hour 45 minutes

2. M3M1. Juan has been reading for 1 hour. It is now 4:45. At what time did Juan start reading?

   A. 3:15

   B. 4:00

   C. 3:45

   D. 5:45

MEASUREMENT

3. M3M1. Joshua worked on a jigsaw puzzle from 1:15 P.M. to 3:30 P.M. How long did he spend working on the puzzle?

   A. 1 hour 45 minutes

   B. 2 hours 15 minutes

   C. 2 hours 45 minutes

   D. 3 hours 30 minutes

4. M3M1. Jerry started playing basketball at 12:30 P.M. He played for 2 hours 30 minutes. What time did he finish playing basketball?

   A. 1:00 P.M.

   B. 2:00 P.M.

   C. 3:00 P.M.

   D. 4:00 P.M.

5. M3M1. Mark finished working on his science project at 1:15. He had been working on it for two hours. At what time did Mark start his project?

   A. 3:15

   B. 2:30

   C. 1:15

   D. 11:15

Cumulative CRCT Test Prep

NUMBERS AND OPERATIONS

6. M3N2.b. Use front-end estimation to estimate the sum.

$$\begin{array}{r} 658 \\ +495 \\ \hline \end{array}$$

A. 900

B. 1,000

C. 1,100

D. 1,200

7. M3N1.a. Which of these numbers has a 7 in the thousands place?

A. 70,246

B. 62,074

C. 46,702

D. 27,640

8. M3N2.c. Christopher had $10.50. He spent $6.45 on a movie ticket. How much money does Christopher have left?

A. $3.05

B. $4.00

C. $4.05

D. $4.55

ALGEBRA

9. M3A1.c. Together, Karen and Shelly have 31 postcards. Karen has 17 postcards. Which number sentence tells you how many postcards Shelly has?

A. 17 + □ = 31

B. 31 + □ = 17

C. 17 + 31 = □

D. □ + 31 = 17

10. M3A1.c. Which number belongs in the □ to make the number sentence true?

46 + 81 = 81 + □

A. 18

B. 46

C. 64

D. 127

11. M3A1.a. Rico wrote the number pattern below. What is the next number in the pattern?

500, 503, 506, 509, □

A. 509

B. 510

C. 512

D. 513

GPS/CRCT Vocabulary

ELA3R2 The student acquires and uses grade-level words to communicate effectively. *also* **ELA3R3.b., ELA3R3.h., ELA3R3.r.**

VOCABULARY

- inverse operations
- is not equal to (≠)
- decimal point
- equivalent
- clockwise
- counterclockwise
- elapsed time
- expression
- estimate
- A.M.
- P.M.
- noon
- midnight
- schedule

VOCABULARY CROSSWORD

MATERIALS *For each student* Unit 2 *Vocabulary Crossword* puzzle

Use the clues to fill in the squares of the crossword puzzle.

- DOWN

1. The amount of time that passes from the the start of an activity to the end of the activity is the __?__ **time**.
2. 12:00 at night is called __?__.
4. 12:00 in the day is called __?__.

- ACROSS

3. A __?__ **point** separates dollars from cents.
5. The hands on a clock move __?__.
6. To __?__ is to find *about* how many.

MATH WORD WORK (MEMORY)

MATERIALS *For each group* vocabulary cards

- Mix up the cards and place them face down. Arrange them in 5 rows and 4 columns.
- Take turns turning over a pair of cards. If the cards are a match, the player must give the definition of the term on the cards. If the definition is correct, the player takes the cards. The player with the greatest number of pairs wins!

PROPERTY POPCORN

MATERIALS *For each pair* 6 small bowls, Unit 2 *Property Popcorn* cards, 2 handfuls of popcorn

- Use the bowls, cards, and pieces of popcorn to show you know the properties of addition.
  - **a.** Use 3 bowls, 1 plus sign, 1 equals sign, and pieces of popcorn to show the **Identity Property of Addition**.
  - **b.** Use 4 bowls, 2 plus signs, 1 equals sign, and pieces of popcorn to show the **Commutative Property of Addition**.
  - **c.** Use 6 bowls, 4 plus signs, 4 parentheses, 1 equals sign, and pieces of popcorn to show the **Associative Property of Addition**. You can see the photo to help.
- After you have shown all 3 properties, enjoy your popcorn!

CLUES

- Each partner should come up with an example or a clue for each vocabulary term shown at the right. For example, a clue for *A.M.* could be "morning." A clue for *equivalent* could be "2 quarters or 5 dimes."
- Take turns giving your partner clues. The partner that correctly names the most vocabulary terms wins!

Word List
decimal point
equivalent
elapsed time
expression
perimeter
A.M.
P.M.

Georgia Tasks

M3N2.c. Solve problems requiring addition and subtraction. *also* M3D1., M3N2.b., M3M1., M3P4.c., M3P5.b., M3P5.c.

ELA3R3.h. Interprets information from illustrations, diagrams, charts, graphs, and graphic organizers.

Task A

CAPITAL CITIES

Atlanta has not always been the capital of Georgia. The table shows the years that cities were named the state capital of Georgia.

a. What missing addend sentence can you write to show how many years Savannah was capital?

b. Suppose you had to write a report on 50 years of Georgia's history. You want to write about when Augusta was capital. Which fifty-year period could you choose?

Cities in Georgia Named Capital

City	Year
Savannah	1777
Augusta	1781
Louisville	1796
Milledgeville	1807
Atlanta	1868

Task B

THE GREAT OUTDOORS

Amy is going to a festival at a state park. She uses the schedule of activities to see what she wants to do while at the festival.

a. Amy must leave the park by 1:00 P.M. Find three activities she can do.

b. Amy's brother wants to participate in all four activities. Which times should he go to each activity?

Schedule of Activities

Activity	Time
Biking	10:00 A.M.–11:00 A.M. 1:00 P.M.–2:00 P.M.
Bird Watching	9:00 A.M.–9:45 A.M. 11:15 A.M.–12:00 P.M. 1:30 P.M.–2:15 P.M.
Leaf Printing	9:00 A.M.–9:30 A.M. 12:15 P.M.–12:45 P.M. 2:00 P.M.–2:30 P.M.
Hiking	10:00 A.M.–11:30 A.M. 1:00 P.M.–2:30 P.M.

Maintain/Preview

Maintain

Use front-end estimation to estimate each sum or difference.

1. $\begin{array}{r} 3{,}048 \\ +4{,}122 \\ \hline \end{array}$ **2.** $\begin{array}{r} \$3.35 \\ +\$6.12 \\ \hline \end{array}$ **3.** $\begin{array}{r} 632 \\ -215 \\ \hline \end{array}$ **4.** $\begin{array}{r} \$23.25 \\ -\$12.87 \\ \hline \end{array}$

Solve. Estimate to check.

5. Josh bought a shirt for $15.09 and a DVD for $22.58. How much did he spend?

6. Tia paddled 7,829 feet down a river. Jeff paddled 4,581 feet. How many more feet did Tia paddle?

Write <, >, or = for each ●.

7. 14 + 287 ● 305 − 4

8. 4,084 − 2,925 ● 1,215 + 276

9. There are 185 students on a field trip. There are 25 more girls than boys. How many boys and how many girls are on the trip?

10. **Write About It** How do you know when a question is asking for an estimate and not an exact answer?

Preview

Skip-count to find the missing numbers.

1. 4, 8, ■, ■, 20, ■

2. 5, ■, 15, 20, ■, 30, ■

3. 2, 4, ■, 8, ■, ■

4. 3, 6, ■, ■, ■, 18, 21

5. 6, ■, 18, 24, ■, ■

6. 10, ■, 30, ■, ■, 60, 70

Find how many in all. You may draw a picture to help.

7. 6 + 6 + 6 + 6

8. 2 + 2 + 2 + 2 + 2

9. 4 groups of 3

10. 2 groups of 4

11. 8 + 8 + 8

12. 3 groups of 5

Understand Multiplication

FAST FACT • SOCIAL STUDIES There are more than 350,000 apple trees in the state of Georgia. They produce over 20 million pounds of apples each year! Farmers in Georgia also grow other fruits, such as blueberries, grapes, peaches, and strawberries.

INVESTIGATION The pictograph shows the weights of different fruits at a market. There are 16 ounces in a pound. How many of each fruit would you get in a pound?

Using Data

WEIGHT OF FRUITS

Apple	🛍 🛍 🛍 🛍 🛍 🛍
Orange	🛍 🛍 🛍 🛍 🛍
Peach	🛍 🛍 🛍
Banana	🛍 🛍 🛍 🛍
Kiwi	🛍 🛍 🛍
Plum	🛍 🛍
Pear	🛍 🛍 🛍 🛍 🛍 🛍

Key: Each 🛍 = 1 ounce.

CHECK WHAT YOU KNOW

Use this page to help you review and remember important skills needed for Chapter 7.

SKIP-COUNT

Skip-count to find the missing numbers.

1. 2, 4, 6, ■, ■, ■, 14, 16, ■, ■

2. 3, 6, ■, 12, ■, ■, 21

3. 5, 10, ■, ■, 25, ■, ■, ■, ■, 50

4. 10, 20, ■, ■, 50, ■, ■, ■, 90

EQUAL GROUPS

Write how many there are in all.

5.

3 groups of 3 = ■

6.

5 groups of 2 = ■

7.

3 groups of 4 = ■

Find how many in all. You may wish to draw a picture.

8. 2 groups of 6

9. 3 groups of 5

10. 4 groups of 2

VOCABULARY POWER

REVIEW

equal [ē′kwəl] *adjective*

When two things are *equal,* they have the same measure or amount. Name two amounts that are equal. Use an equal sign (=) to show that two amounts are equal.

PREVIEW

- multiply (×)
- product
- Commutative Property of Multiplication
- factors
- array

www.harcourtschool.com/mathglossary

LESSON 1

Algebra: Addition and Multiplication

M3N3.a. Describe the relationship between addition and multiplication, i.e., multiplication is defined as repeated addition. *also* M3P3.a., M3P3.b., M3P3.c., M3P3.d., M3P4., M3P4.a., M3P4.b.

Learn

SLURP! There are 3 juice boxes in a package. If Cara buys 5 packages, how many juice boxes will she have?

You can add to find how many in all.

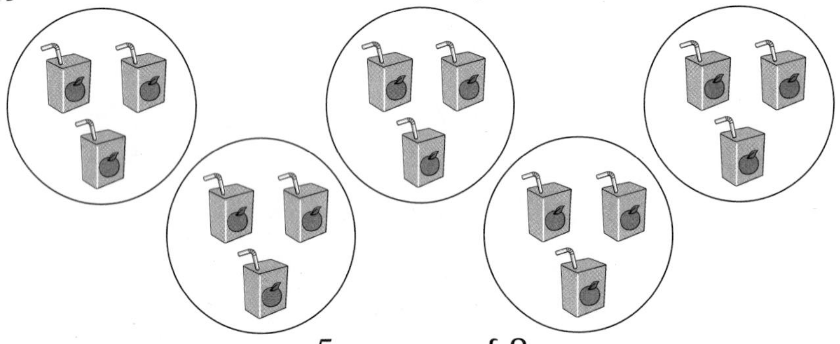

5 groups of 3

Write: $3 + 3 + 3 + 3 + 3 = 15$

Say: 5 threes equal 15.

You can multiply to find how many in all.

Write: $5 \times 3 = 15$

Say: 5 times 3 equals 15.

So, Cara will have 15 juice boxes.

MATH IDEA When you combine equal groups, you can **multiply** ($\times$) to find how many in all.

REASONING Can you use multiplication to find $2 + 3 + 2$? Why or why not?

Check

1. **Explain** two ways to find the total if the juice boxes come in packages of 4, and Cara buys 3 packages.

Quick Review

1. $3 + 3 + 3$
2. $5 + 5 + 5$
3. $2 + 2 + 2$
4. $2 + 2 + 2 + 2$
5. $4 + 4 + 4$

VOCABULARY

multiply ($\times$)

Remember

You can use a number sentence to show addition.
$2 + 2 + 2 = 6$

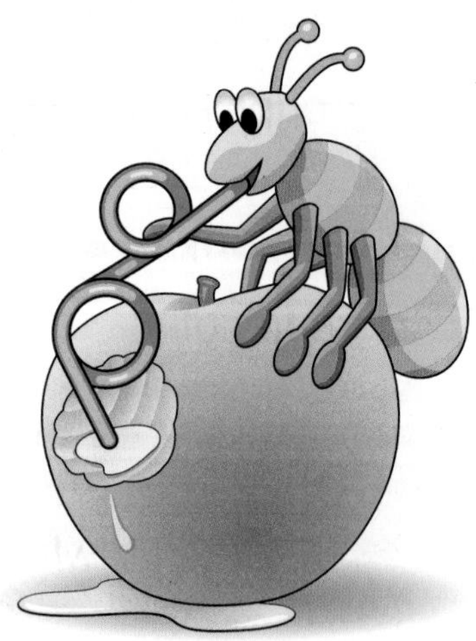

Technology Link

More Practice: Harcourt Mega Math Country Countdown, *Counting Critters,* Level V

Copy and complete.

2.  

a. ■ groups of ■ = ■
b. ■ + ■ + ■ = ■
c. ■ × ■ = ■

3. 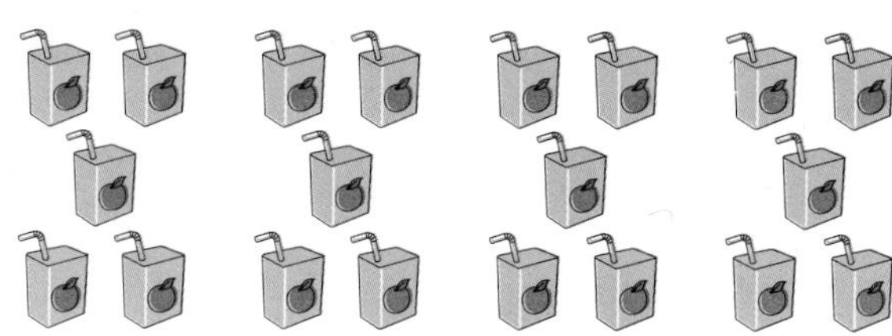

a. ■ groups of ■ = ■
b. ■ + ■ + ■ + ■ = ■
c. ■ × ■ = ■

Practice and Problem Solving

Extra Practice, page 138, Set A

Copy and complete.

4.  

a. ■ groups of ■ = ■
b. ■ + ■ + ■ = ■
c. ■ × ■ = ■

5.  

a. ■ groups of ■ = ■
b. ■ + ■ = ■
c. ■ × ■ = ■

For 6–9, choose the letter of the number sentence that matches. Draw a picture that shows the multiplication sentence.

a. $6 \times 2 = 12$	**b.** $3 \times 8 = 24$	**c.** $3 \times 4 = 12$	**d.** $6 \times 4 = 24$

6. $4 + 4 + 4$

7. $2 + 2 + 2 + 2 + 2 + 2$

8. $8 + 8 + 8$

9. $4 + 4 + 4 + 4 + 4 + 4$

10. Can you write a multiplication sentence about this picture? Explain why or why not.

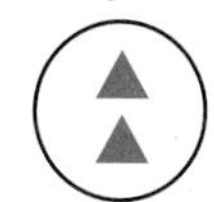 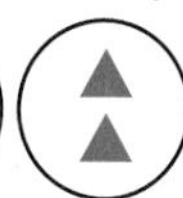 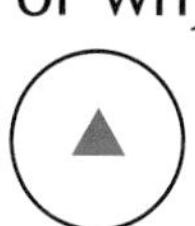 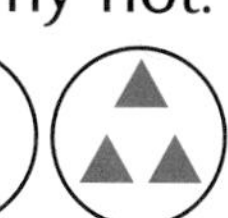 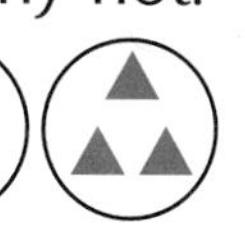

11. **Write a problem** that could be solved by using this multiplication sentence.

$$6 \times 2 = 12$$

Maintain Skills

12. $437 - 229$

13. $684 + 321$

14. $239 + 605$

15. $830 - 723$

CRCT Test Prep

16. M3N2.c. Ian has 127 marbles and Carla has 215 marbles. How many more marbles does Carla have than Ian? (p. 74)

A. 88
B. 98
C. 108
D. 118

LESSON 2

Multiply with 2 and 5

M3N3.b. Know the multiplication facts with understanding and fluency to 10×10. *also* **M3A1.c., M3P3.a., M3P3.b., M3P3.c., M3P3.d., M3P4., M3P4.c.**

Quick Review

How many are in all?

1. 1 group of 8
2. 3 groups of 2
3. 2 groups of 5
4. 4 groups of 2
5. 3 groups of 3

VOCABULARY

factors
product

Learn

SMART ROCKS The chips that run computers are made from a mineral found in rocks. Mrs. Frank asked 5 students to bring in 2 rocks each for a science project. How many rocks does she need?

Use counters.

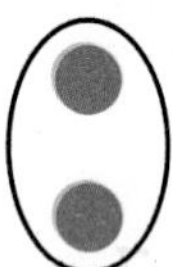 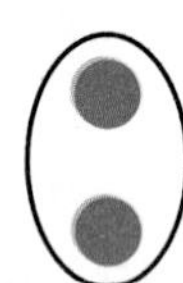 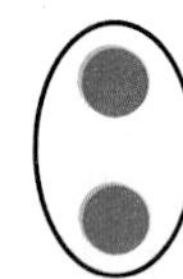 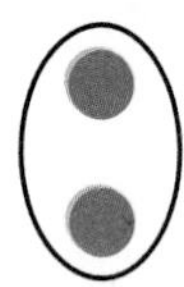 

There are 5 groups, with 2 in each group.

Since each group has the same number, you can multiply to find how many in all.

$5 \times 2 = 10$
↑ factor ↑ factor ↑ product

$$\begin{array}{r} 2 \\ \times 5 \\ \hline 10 \end{array}$$
← factor
← factor
← product

So, Mrs. Frank needs 10 rocks in all.

Computer chip
Crystal

 **MATH IDEA** The numbers that you multiply are **factors**. The answer is the **product**.

- Name the factors and product in $3 \times 2 = 6$.

Check

1. Find the products 1×2 through 9×2. What do you notice about the products? What skip-counting pattern do they show?

Find the product.

2.  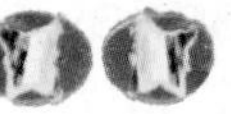 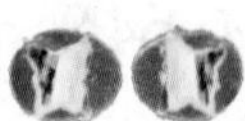    
$4 \times 2 = ■$

3. 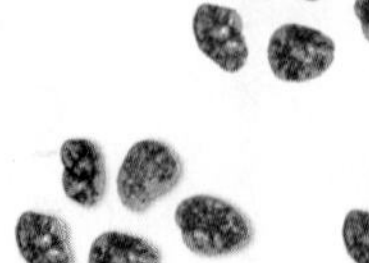
$3 \times 5 = ■$

4. 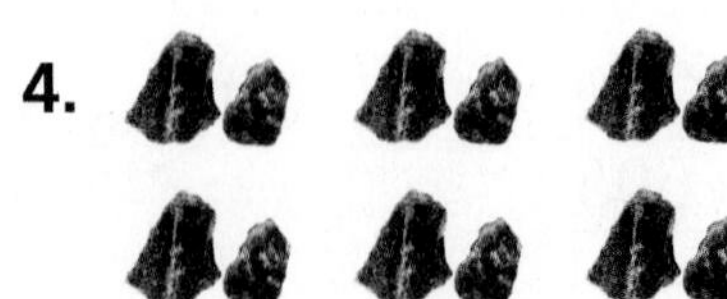
$6 \times 2 = ■$

Practice and Problem Solving

Extra Practice, page 138, Set B

Find the product.

5. 

$2 \times 2 = ■$

6.  

$5 \times 5 = ■$

7. 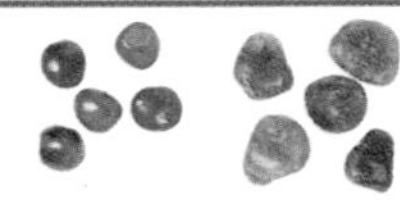 

$4 \times 5 = ■$

Copy and complete.

	×	1	2	3	4	5	6	7	8	9
8.	2	■	■	■	■	■	■	■	■	■
9.	5	■	■	■	■	■	■	■	■	■

Complete.

10. $8 \times 2 = ■$

11. $■ = 4 \times 5$

12. $6 \times 2 = ■$

13. $■ = 7 \times 5$

14. $■ = 9 \times 5$

15. $8 \times 5 = ■$

16. $■ = 7 \times 2$

17. $6 \times 5 = ■$

18. $\begin{array}{r} 2 \\ \times 8 \\ \hline \end{array}$

19. $\begin{array}{r} 5 \\ \times 8 \\ \hline \end{array}$

20. $\begin{array}{r} 2 \\ \times 9 \\ \hline \end{array}$

21. $\begin{array}{r} 5 \\ \times 9 \\ \hline \end{array}$

22. $3 + 3 = 2 \times ■$

23. $4 \times ■ = 4 + 4 + 4$

24. $2 \times 5 = ■ + 5$

25. Write a multiplication problem about the rocks below. Then solve.

26. **REASONING** Drew has 5 pairs of white socks and 2 pairs of black socks. How many more white socks than black socks does Drew have?

27. ***FAST FACT*** • SOCIAL STUDIES In 2003, there were 9,939 people working in the Georgia mining industry. What is the value of the 3 in 9,939?

Maintain Skills

28. Write the amount.

CRCT Test Prep

29. M3A1.a. Tony wrote this number pattern. Predict the next number. (p. 12)

869, 759, 649, 539, ___

A. 549
B. 459
C. 449
D. 429

LESSON 3

HANDS ON

Arrays

M3N3.c. Use arrays and area models to develop understanding of the distributive property.... *also* M3N3.e., M3P1.c., M3P1.d., M3P2., M3P3., M3P4.a., M3P4.b., M3P5., M3P5.b.

Quick Review

Find how many in all.

1. 2 groups of 2
2. 3 groups of 3
3. 4 groups of 2
4. 5 groups of 5
5. 2 groups of 3

VOCABULARY

array

Commutative Property of Multiplication

MATERIALS

square tiles

Explore

An **array** shows objects in rows and columns.

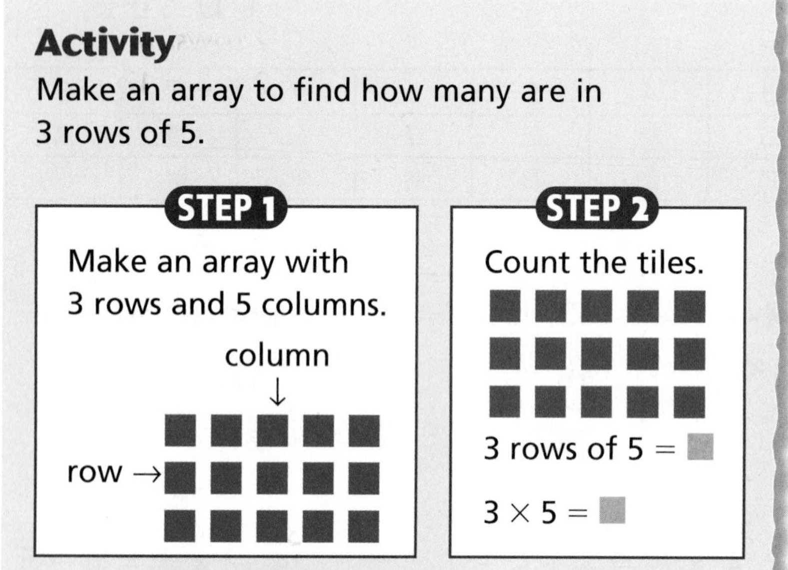

Activity

Make an array to find how many are in 3 rows of 5.

STEP 1

Make an array with 3 rows and 5 columns.

STEP 2

Count the tiles.

3 rows of 5 = ■

$3 \times 5 =$ ■

- How many tiles are in the 3 rows of 5?
- What multiplication sentence can you write to find the number of tiles?
- Make an array with 3 rows of 3. What shape is formed by this array? What multiplication sentence can you write to find the number of tiles?

Technology Link

More Practice: Harcourt Mega Math Country Countdown, *Counting Critters*, Level W; The Number Games, *Up, Up, and Array*, Level A

Try It

Copy and complete.

a. 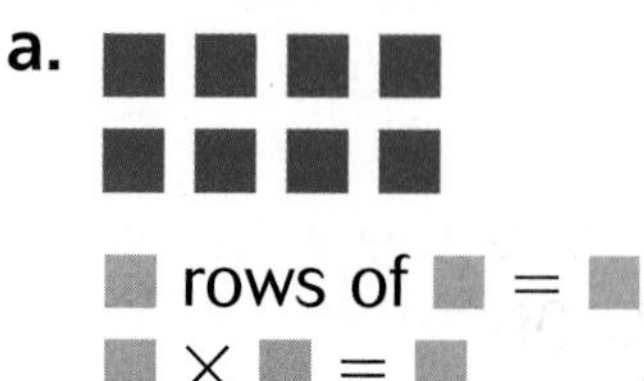

■ rows of ■ = ■

■ × ■ = ■

b. 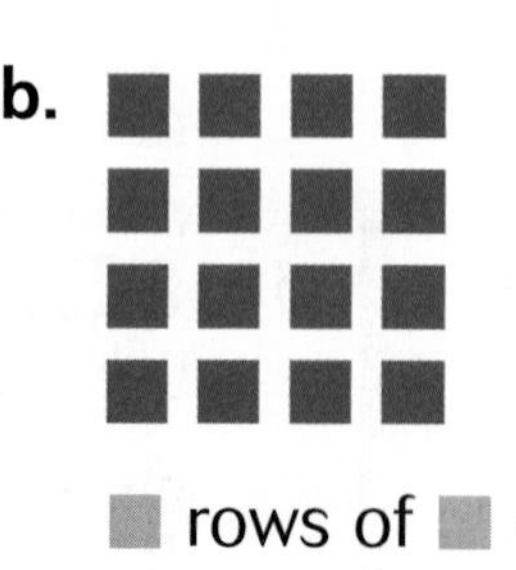

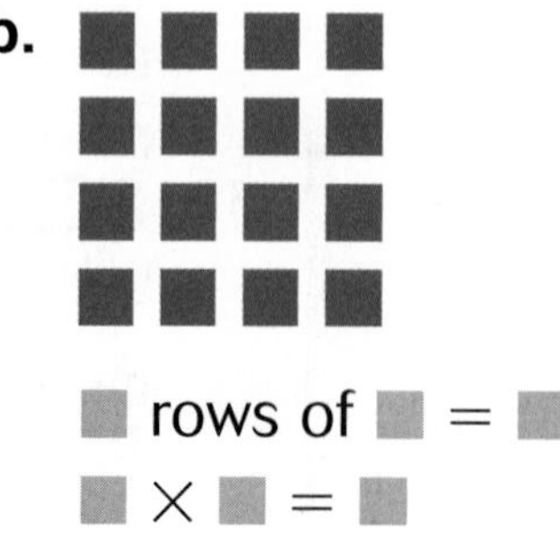

■ rows of ■ = ■

■ × ■ = ■

Connect

The **Commutative Property of Multiplication** states that two factors can be multiplied in any order. The product is the same.

Use arrays to show the Commutative Property of Multiplication.

Examples

A

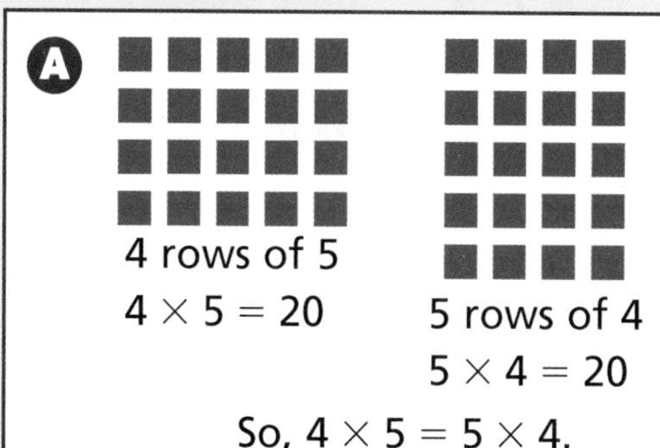

4 rows of 5
$4 \times 5 = 20$

5 rows of 4
$5 \times 4 = 20$

So, $4 \times 5 = 5 \times 4$.

B

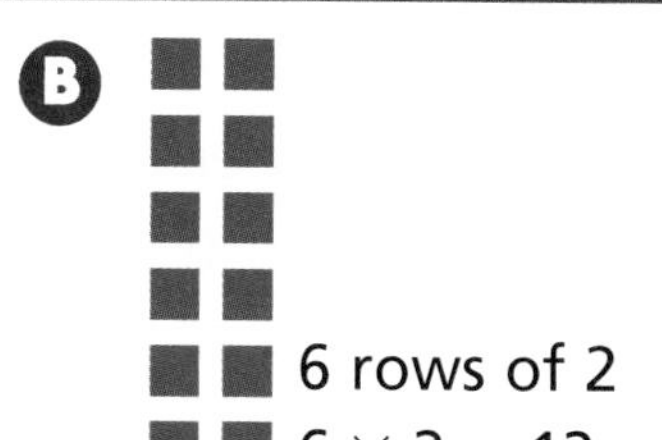

6 rows of 2
$6 \times 2 = 12$

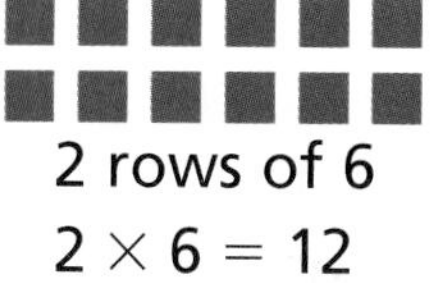

2 rows of 6
$2 \times 6 = 12$

So, $6 \times 2 = 2 \times 6$.

Practice and Problem Solving

Copy and complete.

1. 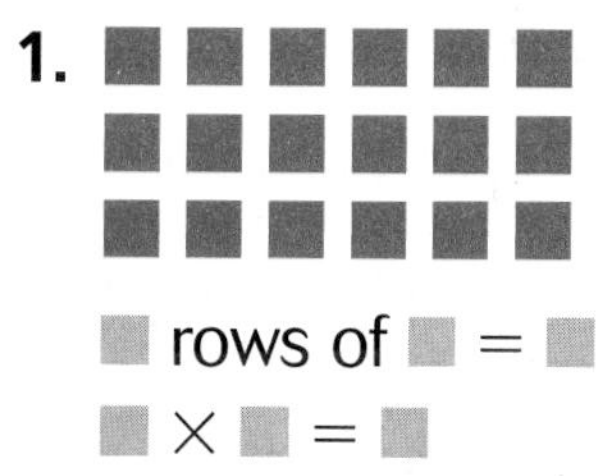

■ rows of ■ = ■
■ × ■ = ■

2. 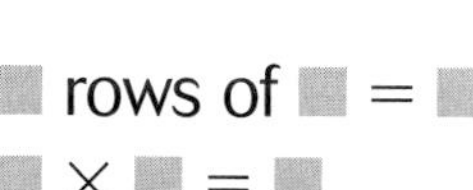

■ rows of ■ = ■
■ × ■ = ■

3. 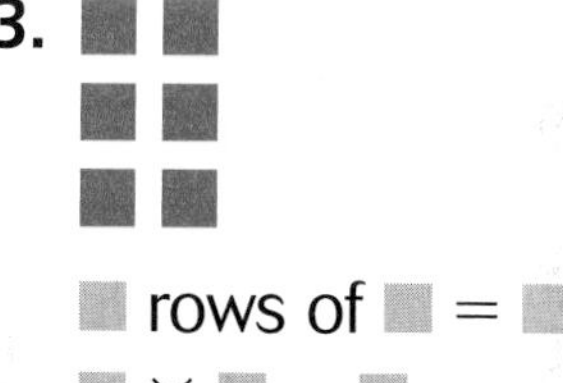

■ rows of ■ = ■
■ × ■ = ■

Find the product. You may wish to draw an array.

4. $2 \times 5 =$ ■
5. $6 \times 4 =$ ■
6. $8 \times 3 =$ ■
7. $3 \times 5 =$ ■

8. **Write About It** Miguel needs a book cover that costs \$1.99 and a package of markers that costs \$2.79. He has \$5.00. Does he have enough money to buy both items?

9. **REASONING** The sum of Jarrod's age and Kayla's age is 21. Kayla is 5 years older than Jarrod. How old are Kayla and Jarrod?

Maintain Skills

Use a ruler to measure to the nearest centimeter.

10.
11.

CRCT Test Prep

12. M3N1.a. What is the value of the 7 in 67,409? (p. 14)

A. 70,000
B. 7,000
C. 700
D. 70

LESSON 4

Multiply with 3

M3N3.b. Know the multiplication facts with understanding and fluency to 10 × 10. *also* M3N3.e., M3A1.c., M3D1.b.

Quick Review

1. $2 + 2 = 2 \times ■$
2. $3 \times ■ = 5 + 5 + 5$
3. $2 \times 6 = 6 + ■$
4. $■ \times 5 = 10$
5. $2 \times 4 = ■$

Learn

PRACTICE, PRACTICE, PRACTICE

Pat practiced soccer 2 hours each day for 3 days. How many hours did he practice in all?

For 2 hours, move 2 spaces. For 3 days, make 3 jumps of 2 spaces.

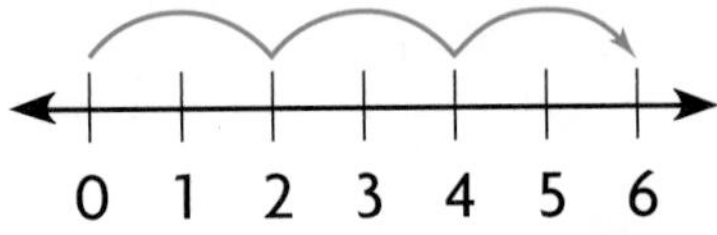

Multiply: $3 \times 2 = 6$

Val practiced soccer 3 hours each day for 2 days. How many hours did she practice in all?

For 3 hours, move 3 spaces. For 2 days, make 2 jumps of 3 spaces.

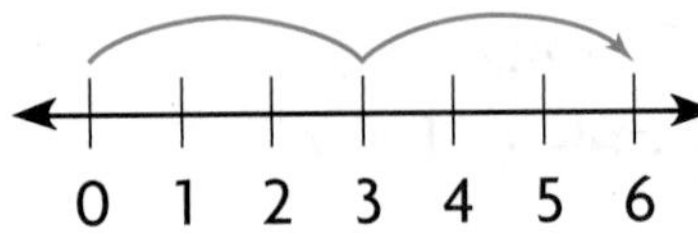

Multiply: $2 \times 3 = 6$

So, both Pat and Val practiced for 6 hours.

A number line can help you understand the Commutative Property of Multiplication.

One Way Use a number line.

Multiply. $3 \times 5 = 15$

0 1 2 3 4 5 6 7 8 9 10 11 12 13 14 15

Multiply. $5 \times 3 = 15$

0 1 2 3 4 5 6 7 8 9 10 11 12 13 14 15

So, $3 \times 5 = 5 \times 3$.

- **REASONING** Use the factors 3 and 6 to explain the Commutative Property of Multiplication.

Multiplication Practice

What if Pat scored 4 goals in each of 3 games and Val scored 3 goals in each of 4 games? Which example shows Pat's goals? Val's goals? How many goals did each player score?

Another Way Draw a picture.

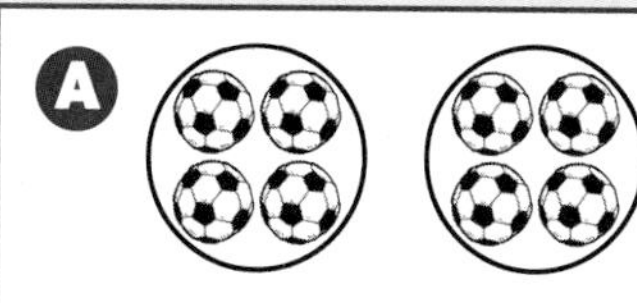

$3 \times 4 = 12$

$4 \times 3 = 12$

Example A shows Pat's goals.

Example B shows Val's goals.

Each player scored 12 goals.

- **What if** Val scored 8 goals in each of 3 games and Pat scored 3 goals in each of 8 games? How many goals did each player score?

Check

1. **Explain** how knowing the product 7×3 can help you find the product 3×7.

2. Find the products 3×1 through 3×9. Add the digits of each product together. What do you notice about each sum?

Use the number line or draw a picture to find the product.

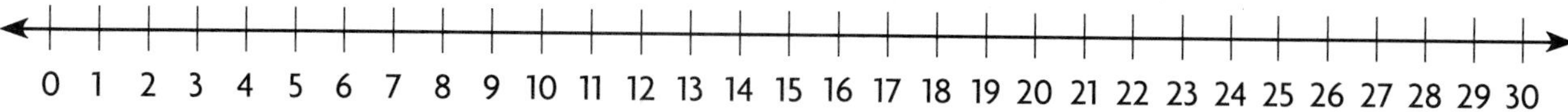

3. $4 \times 3 = ■$ **4.** $■ = 3 \times 4$ **5.** $7 \times 3 = ■$ **6.** $■ = 3 \times 7$

7. $■ = 6 \times 3$ **8.** $■ = 3 \times 6$ **9.** $3 \times 8 = ■$ **10.** $■ = 8 \times 3$

11. $\begin{array}{r} 5 \\ \times 3 \\ \hline \end{array}$ **12.** $\begin{array}{r} 3 \\ \times 5 \\ \hline \end{array}$ **13.** $\begin{array}{r} 3 \\ \times 9 \\ \hline \end{array}$ **14.** $\begin{array}{r} 9 \\ \times 3 \\ \hline \end{array}$

LESSON CONTINUES

Practice and Problem Solving

Extra Practice, page 138, Set C

Use the number line or draw a picture to find the product.

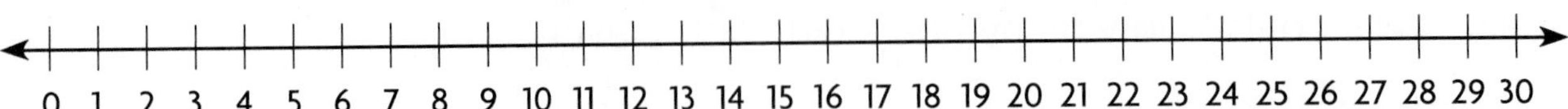

15. $3 \times 6 = \blacksquare$

16. $\blacksquare = 5 \times 5$

17. $3 \times 9 = \blacksquare$

18. $\blacksquare = 9 \times 3$

19. $\blacksquare = 9 \times 2$

20. $7 \times 3 = \blacksquare$

21. $\blacksquare = 4 \times 5$

22. $2 \times 8 = \blacksquare$

23. $7 \times 2 = \blacksquare$

24. $\begin{array}{r} 3 \\ \times 8 \\ \hline \end{array}$

25. $\begin{array}{r} 1 \\ \times 5 \\ \hline \end{array}$

26. $\begin{array}{r} 3 \\ \times 9 \\ \hline \end{array}$

Copy and complete.

27.

×	1	2	3	4	5	6	7	8	9
3	■	■	■	■	■	■	■	■	■

Write the missing factor.

28. $2 \times 3 = \blacksquare \times 2$

29. $3 \times \blacksquare = 7 \times 3$

30. $5 \times 3 = \blacksquare \times 5$

31. $6 \times 3 = \blacksquare \times 2$

32. $4 \times 3 = 6 \times \blacksquare$

33. $8 \times 3 = \blacksquare \times 8$

34. **What's the Error?** Sam played soccer for 2 hours a day, 3 days a week, for 4 weeks. Sam said he played soccer for a total of 6 hours during the month. What is Sam's error?

35. **MULTISTEP** Alice builds 3 tables with 3 legs and 2 tables with 4 legs. How many legs does she use in all?

USE DATA For 36–39, use the bar graph.

36. How many more goals did Matt's soccer team score in Game 4 than in Game 1?

37. How many goals did Matt's team score in the four games?

38. If Matt's team scores twice as many goals in Game 5 as in Game 3, how many goals will it score?

39. **Write a problem** using the bar graph.

40. **Vocabulary Power** One number *times* another means that you multiply. Write a multiplication sentence. Circle the "times" sign, ×. Then draw a picture to show your sentence.

41. **MULTISTEP** Matt needs 25 tennis balls. There are 5 balls in 1 package. If he buys 4 packages, will he have enough tennis balls? Draw a picture to show your answer.

Maintain Skills

Write *A.M.* or *P.M.* for each.

42. see the sun: 10:00 _?_

43. play at the park: 4:30 _?_

44. Which two shapes can you put together to make a hexagon?

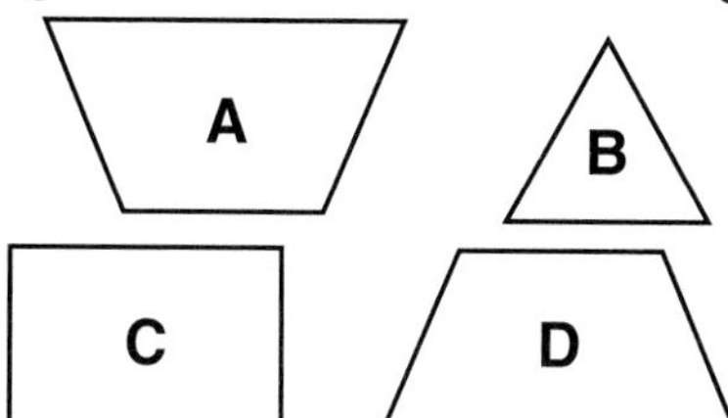

CRCT Test Prep

45. M3N1.a. Which digit is in the hundreds place in the number 3,401? (p. 6)

A. 0 B. 1 C. 3 D. 4

46. M3N2.c. Brett has 435 marbles. Luz has 167 marbles. How many more marbles does Brett have than Luz? (p. 74)

A. 602 B. 378 C. 332 D. 268

Problem Solving Thinker's Corner

SOLVE THE RIDDLE! **Find the product. To answer the riddle, match the letters to the products below.**

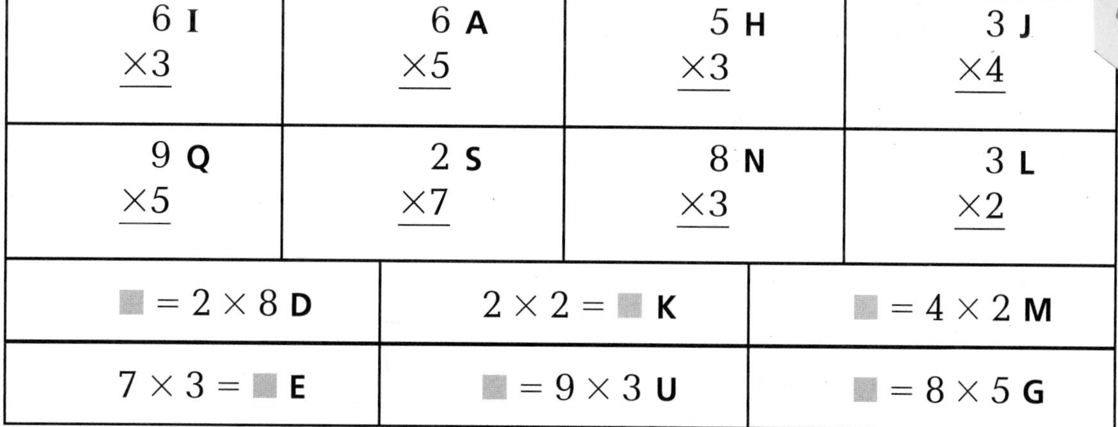

6 I ×3	6 A ×5	5 H ×3	3 J ×4
9 Q ×5	2 S ×7	8 N ×3	3 L ×2

■ = 2 × 8 D	2 × 2 = ■ K	■ = 4 × 2 M
7 × 3 = ■ E	■ = 9 × 3 U	■ = 8 × 5 G

What is a mouse's favorite game?

?	?	?	?		?	?	?		?	?	?	?	?	?
15	18	16	21		30	24	16		14	45	27	21	30	4

LESSON 5

Problem Solving Skill
Too Much/Too Little Information

M3N3.g. Solve problems requiring multiplication. *also* M3P1.a., M3P1.b., M3P1.c., M3P1.d., M3P3.a., M3P3.b., M3P3.c., M3P3.d., M3P4.b.

Quick Review

1. 3×5
2. 4×3
3. 3×3
4. 9×3
5. 3×6

UNDERSTAND → PLAN → SOLVE → CHECK

FIND THE FACTS Three students walked 6 blocks to the craft store. Each one bought 5 pieces of poster board to make posters for the school book fair. They stayed at the store for 45 minutes. How many pieces of poster board did the students buy in all?

Example

STEP 1

Find what the problem asks.

- How many pieces of poster board did the students buy in all?

STEP 2

Find what facts are needed to solve the problem.

- the number of students
- the number of pieces of poster board each one buys

STEP 3

Look for extra information.

- how far they walked
- how long they were at the store

Do you need this information to solve the problem?

STEP 4

Solve the problem.

- multiply

  3 students $\times$ 5 pieces $=$ 15 pieces

So, the students bought 15 pieces of poster board in all.

Talk About It

- Is there too much or too little information in the problem above?
- Three students went to a restaurant. They each bought a sandwich. How much did they spend in all? Does this problem have too much, too little, or the right amount of information? What information is missing from the problem?

Problem Solving Practice

USE DATA For 1–4, use the table. Write *a*, *b*, or *c* to tell whether the problem has

a. too much information. **b.** too little information. **c.** the right amount of information.

Solve those with too much or the right amount of information. Tell what is missing for those with too little information.

SCHOOL SUPPLIES	
Pack of Paper	$1
Backpack	$9
Pack of Pencils	$3
Lunch Box	$4

1. Felix wants to buy a backpack and a box of crayons. How much will he spend?
2. Marisa bought 2 packs of pencils. She was second in line to pay for her supplies. How much did Marisa spend?
3. Sam bought 2 backpacks and a lunch box. He received $3 change. How much money had he given the clerk?
4. Sally had $15. She bought 5 packs of paper and a lunch box. How much did she spend?

Mixed Applications

USE DATA For 5–6, use the table above.

You have $15 to spend on school supplies.

5. Which items can you buy?
   - **A** a backpack, 3 packs of pencils
   - **B** a backpack, a pack of pencils, a lunch box
   - **C** a lunch box, 2 packs of paper, a backpack
   - **D** 4 packs of pencils, a backpack
6. **MULTISTEP** How much more money do you need if you choose to buy 2 packs of pencils, a lunch box, and a backpack?
   - **F** $1
   - **G** $2
   - **H** $3
   - **J** $4
7. **MULTISTEP** Joe bought two tapes at the music store. They cost $7.28 and $7.71. How much change did he receive from $20.00?
8. **What's the Question?** There are 4 people in the Tamura family. Movie tickets cost $6 each. The answer is $24.

Problem Solving

Extra Practice

Set A (pp. 126–127)

Copy and complete.

1. 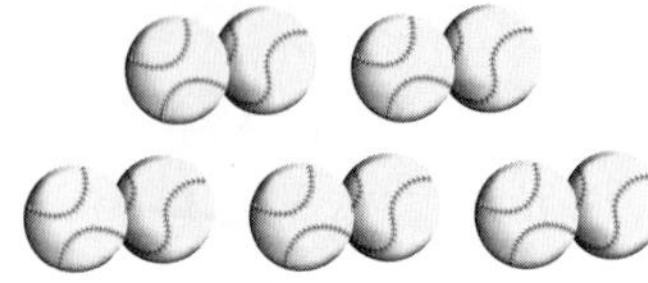

   a. ■ groups of ■ = ■

   b. ■ + ■ + ■ + ■ + ■ = ■

   c. ■ × ■ = ■

2. 

   a. ■ groups of ■ = ■

   b. ■ + ■ + ■ + ■ = ■

   c. ■ × ■ = ■

For 3–8, find how many in all.

3. 5 groups of 3
4. $4 + 4 + 4 + 4$
5. $7 + 7 + 7$
6. 5×4
7. 4 groups of 5
8. 5×5
9. Ana bought 6 packages of 5 cards each. How many cards did she buy?

Set B (pp. 128–129)

Find the product.

1. $7 \times 2 =$ ■
2. $5 \times 2 =$ ■
3. $7 \times 5 =$ ■
4. $8 \times 2 =$ ■
5. $4 \times 5 =$ ■
6. $9 \times 5 =$ ■
7. ■ $= 6 \times 5$
8. ■ $= 2 \times 2$
9. ■ $= 5 \times 5$
10. Keith bought 5 packages of 3 toy cars each. David has 16 toy cars. Who has more cars? How do you know?

Set C (pp. 132–135)

Find the product.

1. $7 \times 3 =$ ■
2. $5 \times 3 =$ ■
3. ■ $= 3 \times 9$
4. $\begin{array}{r} 6 \\ \times 3 \\ \hline \end{array}$
5. $\begin{array}{r} 5 \\ \times 6 \\ \hline \end{array}$
6. $\begin{array}{r} 3 \\ \times 8 \\ \hline \end{array}$
7. $\begin{array}{r} 3 \\ \times 9 \\ \hline \end{array}$
8. $\begin{array}{r} 5 \\ \times 9 \\ \hline \end{array}$

Find the missing factor.

9. $4 \times 3 =$ ■ $\times 4$
10. $5 \times$ ■ $= 9 \times 5$
11. ■ $\times 8 = 8 \times 3$

Review/Test

✓ CHECK VOCABULARY AND CONCEPTS

Choose the best term from the box.

Vocabulary
- array
- factors
- multiply (×)
- product

1. When groups have the same number, you can __?__ to find how many in all. (p. 126)
2. The numbers you multiply are __?__. (p. 128)
3. The answer to a multiplication problem is the __?__. (p. 128)

Find the product. You may wish to draw an array. (pp. 130–131)

4. $4 \times 5 =$ ■
5. $3 \times 2 =$ ■
6. $3 \times 6 =$ ■
7. $7 \times 3 =$ ■

CHECK SKILLS

For 8–9, choose the letter of the number sentence that matches. (pp. 126–127)

8. $3 + 3 + 3 + 3$
9. $4 + 4 + 4 + 4 + 4$

a. $5 \times 4 = 20$
b. $6 \times 2 = 12$
c. $4 \times 3 = 12$

Find the product. (pp. 128–129; 132–135)

10. $3 \times 8 =$ ■
11. $3 \times 7 =$ ■
12. ■ $= 5 \times 6$
13. $4 \times 2 =$ ■
14. $\begin{array}{r} 3 \\ \times 9 \\ \hline \end{array}$
15. $\begin{array}{r} 6 \\ \times 3 \\ \hline \end{array}$
16. $\begin{array}{r} 8 \\ \times 5 \\ \hline \end{array}$
17. $\begin{array}{r} 7 \\ \times 5 \\ \hline \end{array}$
18. $\begin{array}{r} 5 \\ \times 9 \\ \hline \end{array}$

✓ CHECK PROBLEM SOLVING

Write *a*, *b*, or *c* to tell whether the problem has

a. too much information.
b. too little information.
c. the right amount of information.

Solve those with too much or the right amount of information. Tell what is missing for those with too little information. (pp. 136–137)

19. Pete practices 3 hours a day, Monday through Friday. How many hours does he practice each week?

20. Ramiro worked on his science project 3 hours longer than Sue. How much time did each of them spend on the project?

Chapter CRCT Test Prep

NUMBERS AND OPERATIONS

1. M3N3.c. What multiplication sentence does the array show?

A. $5 \times 5 = 25$

B. $2 \times 5 = 10$

C. $4 \times 5 = 20$

D. $4 \times 4 = 16$

2. M3N3.a. What multiplication sentence matches the addition sentence?

$$3 + 3 + 3 + 3 = 12$$

A. $4 \times 4 = 16$

B. $3 \times 3 = 9$

C. $4 \times 3 = 12$

D. $3 \times 2 = 6$

3. M3N3.g. Katie has 2 bags of marbles. Each bag has 8 marbles in it. How many marbles does Katie have?

A. 10

B. 12

C. 14

D. 16

ALGEBRA

4. M3A1.c. Which number belongs in the □ to make the number sentence true?

$$8 \times 5 = \square$$

A. 20

B. 30

C. 40

D. 50

5. M3A1.c. Sanjay has 7 packs of trading cards. There are 5 cards in each pack. Which number sentence could he use to find the total number of cards?

A. $7 + 5 = \square$

B. $7 - 5 = \square$

C. $7 \times 5 = \square$

D. $5 + \square = 7$

6. M3A1.c. Which number belongs in the □ to make the number sentence true?

$$5 + 5 + 5 = \square \times 5$$

A. 3

B. 4

C. 5

D. 6

Cumulative CRCT Test Prep

NUMBERS AND OPERATIONS

7. M3N3.g. Tony has 4 pairs of sneakers in his closet. How many sneakers does he have in all?

   A. 4

   B. 6

   C. 8

   D. 10

8. M3N2.b. Use front-end estimation to estimate the sum.

$$\begin{array}{r} 749 \\ +422 \\ \hline \end{array}$$

   A. 900

   B. 1,000

   C. 1,100

   D. 1,200

9. M3N2.c. Josephine had 673 marbles in her collection. She gave away 289 marbles. How many marbles does Josephine have left?

   A. 396

   B. 384

   C. 416

   D. 424

DATA ANALYSIS

Use the graph below to answer question 10.

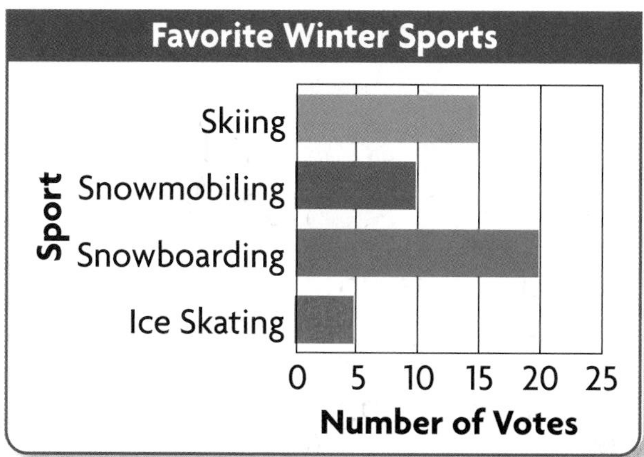

10. M3D1.b. The bar graph shows the results of a survey about students' favorite winter sports. How many more students voted for snowboarding than skiing?

   A. 1

   B. 5

   C. 10

   D. 20

CHAPTER 8

Multiplication Facts Through 5

The Georgia Scorcher is a roller coaster in Austell, Georgia. Each train has eight rows of four seats.

FAST FACT • SOCIAL STUDIES There are more than 600 roller coasters in North America today. Some can reach speeds greater than 70 miles per hour!

INVESTIGATION Compare the number of seats on the roller coasters in the pictograph with the coaster in the photo. How many riders can a train on each roller coaster hold? Which roller coasters have the same number of seats per train as the Georgia Scorcher?

Using Data

ROLLER COASTER SEATS PER TRAIN

Roller Coaster	Seats
Hercules (Pennsylvania)	
Wicked Twister (Ohio)	
Alpengeist (Virginia)	
Mamba (Missouri)	

Key: Each = 4 seats.

Use this page to help you review and remember important skills needed for Chapter 8.

MODEL MULTIPLICATION

Copy and complete.

1. 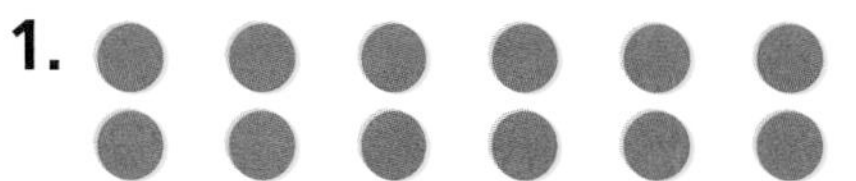

   $6 \times 2 = ■$

2. $3 \times 4 = ■$

3. $5 \times 3 = ■$

4. $4 \times 2 = ■$

COMMUTATIVE PROPERTY OF MULTIPLICATION

Complete.

5. $4 \times 5 = ■ \times 4$
6. $3 \times 6 = ■ \times 3$
7. $2 \times 7 = ■ \times 2$
8. $5 \times 8 = ■ \times 5$
9. $4 \times 7 = ■ \times 4$
10. $3 \times 9 = ■ \times 3$

VOCABULARY POWER

REVIEW

factor [fak′tər] *noun*

A factory is a place where parts are put together to make something. A *factor* is one of the numbers that is put together to make a product. How are the meanings of *factory* and *factor* alike? What are the factors in $4 \times 6 = 24$?

PREVIEW

multiple

www.harcourtschool.com/mathglossary

LESSON 1

Multiply with 1 and 0

M3N3.b. Know the multiplication facts with understanding and fluency to 10 × 10.
also **M3A1.c., M3P2.a., M3P2.b., M3P2.c., M3P2.d., M3P3., M3P3.a., M3P3.b., M3P3.c., M3P3.d.**

Quick Review

1. $2 \times 5 = ■$
2. $3 \times 4 = 4 + 4 + ■$
3. $6 \times 2 = ■$
4. $5 + 5 + 5 = ■ \times 5$
5. $3 \times 2 = ■$

Learn

ALL OR NOTHING Tina saw 5 cars. One clown sat in each car. How many clowns were there in all?

Example

STEP 1

Count the cars.

STEP 2

Count the clowns in the cars.

STEP 3

Write the multiplication sentence.

5	×	1	=	5
↑		↑		↑
number of groups		number in each group		number in all

So, there were 5 clowns in all.

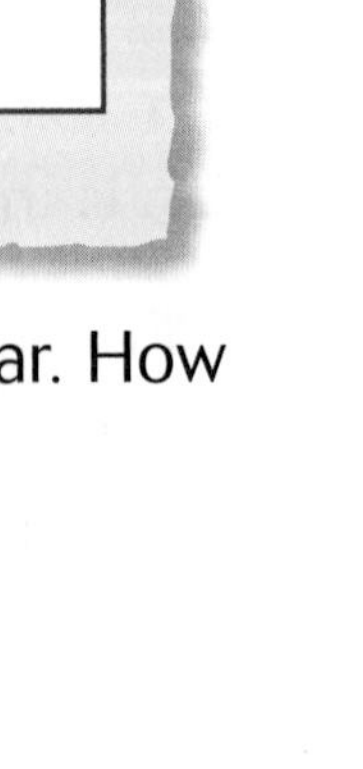

Suppose Tina saw 3 cars with 0 clowns in each car. How many clowns were there in all?

3	×	0	=	0
↑		↑		↑
number of groups		number in each group		number in all

So, there were 0 clowns in all.

MATH IDEA The product of 1 and any number equals that number. The product of 0 and any number equals 0.

REASONING What is 498 × 1? 498 × 0? How do you know?

Check

1. **Explain** what happens when you multiply by 1. What happens when you multiply by 0?

Find the product.

2. $4 \times 1 = ■$
3. $5 \times 0 = ■$
4. $1 \times 3 = ■$

Practice and Problem Solving

Extra Practice, page 156, Set A

Find the product.

5. $2 \times 1 = ■$
6. $4 \times 0 = ■$
7. $0 \times 5 = ■$
8. $■ = 9 \times 1$
9. $■ = 0 \times 7$
10. $3 \times 3 = ■$
11. $■ = 1 \times 8$
12. $0 \times 0 = ■$
13. $\begin{array}{r} 9 \\ \times 0 \\ \hline \end{array}$
14. $\begin{array}{r} 1 \\ \times 3 \\ \hline \end{array}$
15. $\begin{array}{r} 5 \\ \times 4 \\ \hline \end{array}$
16. $\begin{array}{r} 8 \\ \times 5 \\ \hline \end{array}$
17. Multiply 4 by 1.
18. Find the product of 0 and 8.

Complete.

19. $■ = 9 \times 5$
20. $3 + 9 = 3 \times ■$
21. $3 \times 6 = ■ \times 9$
22. $8 + 7 = ■ \times 5$
23. $0 \times 8 = ■ \times 9$
24. $9 \times ■ = 3 \times 3$
25. **REASONING** Ann is younger than Rick. Rick is older than Tracy. Tracy is older than Ann. Who is the oldest?
26. **Write About It** Which is less, the product of your age and 1 or the product of your age and 0? Explain.
27. **Vocabulary Power** The word *zero* comes from an old Arabic word that means "empty." Explain what it means for a group to have zero items.

Maintain Skills

Compare. Write $<$, $>$ or $=$ for each ●.

28. 86 ● 28
29. 51 ● 55
30. 73 ● 37
31. 30 ● 29
32. 42 ● 24
33. 64 ● 94

CRCT Test Prep

34. M3N2.c. Carol bought a pencil for \$0.32. She paid with a \$1 bill. How much change did she get? (p. 96)

A. \$0.32
B. \$0.68
C. \$0.78
D. \$1.32

LESSON 2

Multiply on a Multiplication Table

M3N3.b. Know the multiplication facts with understanding and fluency to 10 × 10. *also* M3P2.a., M3P2.b., M3P2.c., M3P2.d., M3P3.a., M3P3.b., M3P3.c., M3P3.d., M3P4., M3P4.c.

Quick Review

1. 0×3
2. 4×2
3. 1×9
4. 8×1
5. 2×5

VOCABULARY

multiple

Learn

TWISTS AND TURNS There are 6 cars in the Twister ride at the amusement park. Each car holds 4 people. How many people does the Twister ride hold?

$$6 \times 4 = \blacksquare$$

- How could you use an array to find 6×4?

You can use a multiplication table to find the product. The product is found where row 6 and column 4 meet.

Multiplication Table

(column ↓ 4; row → 6)

×	0	1	2	3	4	5	6	7	8	9
0	0	0	0	0	0	0	0	0	0	0
1	0	1	2	3	4	5	6	7	8	9
2	0	2	4	6	8	10	12	14	16	18
3	0	3	6	9	12	15	18	21	24	27
4	0	4	8	12	16	20	24	28	32	36
5	0	5	10	15	20	25	30	35	40	45
6	0	6	12	18	24	30	36	42	48	54
7	0	7	14	21	28	35	42	49	56	63
8	0	8	16	24	32	40	48	56	64	72
9	0	9	18	27	36	45	54	63	72	81

$6 \times 4 = 24$ (6 ↑ factor, 4 ↑ factor, 24 ↑ product)

$\begin{array}{r} 4 \\ \times 6 \\ \hline 24 \end{array}$ ← factor, ← factor, ← product

So, the Twister ride holds 24 people.

MATH IDEA A **multiple** of 4 is any product that has 4 as a factor. 4, 8, 12, 16, and so on are all multiples of 4.

REASONING How can you use the multiplication table to find other multiples of 4?

- Name the multiples of 3 in the multiplication table.
- Are the multiples of 5 all even numbers? Explain.

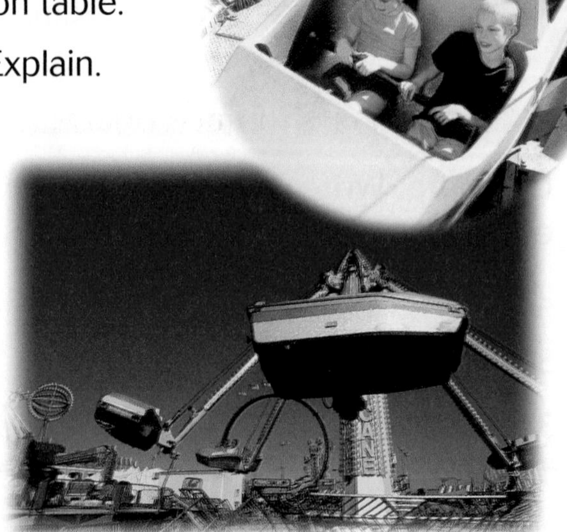

Check

1. **Explain** how you can use the multiplication table to find 4×8.

Find the product.

2. $2 \times 4 = \blacksquare$
3. $9 \times 4 = \blacksquare$
4. $\blacksquare = 4 \times 5$
5. $4 \times 3 = \blacksquare$

Practice and Problem Solving

Extra Practice, page 156, Set B

Find the product.

6. $4 \times 2 = ■$
7. $9 \times 0 = ■$
8. $4 \times 5 = ■$
9. $■ = 5 \times 8$
10. $4 \times 4 = ■$
11. $1 \times 9 = ■$
12. $■ = 4 \times 7$
13. $3 \times 0 = ■$
14. $■ = 8 \times 4$

15. $\begin{array}{r} 2 \\ \times 3 \\ \hline \end{array}$
16. $\begin{array}{r} 5 \\ \times 1 \\ \hline \end{array}$
17. $\begin{array}{r} 4 \\ \times 6 \\ \hline \end{array}$
18. $\begin{array}{r} 0 \\ \times 4 \\ \hline \end{array}$
19. $\begin{array}{r} 7 \\ \times 4 \\ \hline \end{array}$
20. $\begin{array}{r} 5 \\ \times 5 \\ \hline \end{array}$
21. $\begin{array}{r} 3 \\ \times 6 \\ \hline \end{array}$
22. $\begin{array}{r} 4 \\ \times 9 \\ \hline \end{array}$
23. $\begin{array}{r} 8 \\ \times 2 \\ \hline \end{array}$
24. $\begin{array}{r} 7 \\ \times 5 \\ \hline \end{array}$
25. $\begin{array}{r} 4 \\ \times 8 \\ \hline \end{array}$
26. $\begin{array}{r} 9 \\ \times 4 \\ \hline \end{array}$

Copy and complete.

27.

×	0	1	2	3	4	5	6	7	8	9
4	■	■	■	■	■	■	■	■	■	■

28. $9 \times 0 = ■ \times 4$
29. $2 \times 9 = ■ \times 3$
30. $4 \times 4 = ■ \times 2$
31. Name some multiples of 2. Explain.
32. Find the product of 4 and 9.
33. Find the product of 7 and 0.
34. Is 12 a multiple of 6? Explain.
35. Each ride costs 4 tickets. If Tonya went on 7 different rides, how many tickets did she use? Draw a picture to show your answer.
36. **FAST FACT** • SOCIAL STUDIES There are 617 steel roller coasters and 131 wooden roller coasters in North America. How many more steel than wooden ones are there?
37. **MULTISTEP** Ahmed has 3 packs of 8 baseball cards and 11 extra cards. How many cards does he have in all?
38. Since $9 \times 4 = 36$ and $10 \times 4 = 40$, what is 11×4? How do you know?

Maintain Skills

Write the name of each figure.

39. 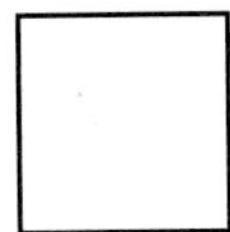

40. 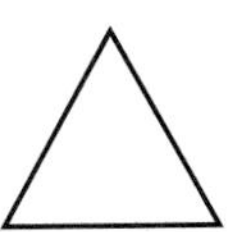
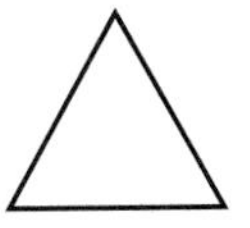

41. 

42. 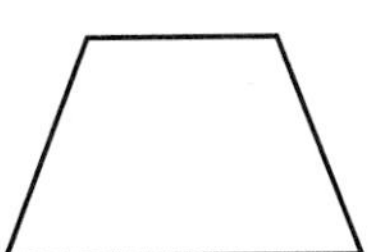

CRCT Test Prep

43. M3A1.c. Which number belongs in the □ to make the number sentence true? (p. 144)

$$4 \times \square = 0$$

A. 0
B. 1
C. 4
D. 8

LESSON 3

Problem Solving Strategy
Look for a Pattern

M3A1.a. Describe and extend numeric and geometric patterns. *also* M3P1.a., M3P1.b., M3P1.c., M3P1.d., M3P2.a., M3P2.b., M3P2.c., M3P2.d., M3P3.c., M3P4.a.

Quick Review

1. $3 \times ■ = 6$
2. $3 + ■ = 9$
3. $■ \times 2 = 12$
4. $12 + ■ = 15$
5. $14 + ■ = 18$

PROBLEM Emily is playing a number pattern game. She says the numbers 3, 5, 8, 10, 13, 15, 18, 20, and 23. What is a rule for her pattern? What are the next four numbers she will say?

UNDERSTAND

- What are you asked to find?
- What information will you use?
- Is there information you will not use? If so, what?

PLAN

- What strategy can you use to solve the problem?

You can *look for a pattern.*

SOLVE

- How can you use the strategy to solve the problem?

Use a number line to look for the pattern. Then write a rule and the next four numbers.

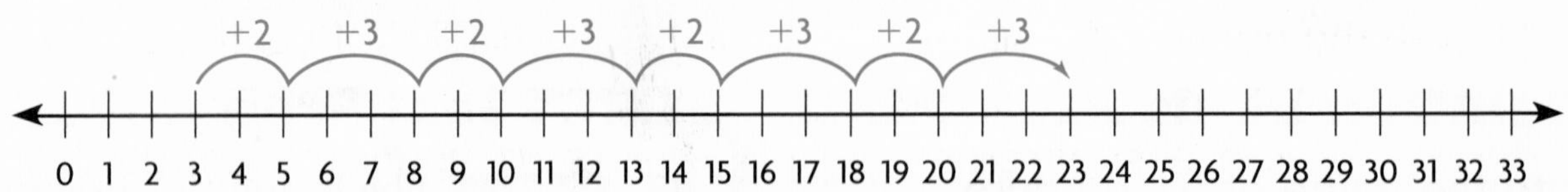

So, a rule is *add 2 and then add 3*. The next four numbers in Emily's pattern will be 25, 28, 30, and 33.

CHECK

- How do you know if your answer is correct?

Problem Solving Practice

Use *look for a pattern* to solve.

1. **What if** the first number in Emily's pattern is 3 and the rule is *multiply by 2 and then subtract 2*? What are the first five numbers in her pattern?
2. Albert's pattern is 3, 6, 9, and 12. What is a rule for his pattern? What are the next four numbers?

Strategies

Act It Out or Use Objects
Make a Picture or Diagram
Guess and Check
Use or Look for a Pattern
Use Logical Reasoning

Karen is thinking of a number pattern. The first four numbers are 4, 8, 12, and 16.

3. What are the next three numbers in Karen's pattern?

   A 16, 20, 24 **C** 18, 20, 22
   B 17, 19, 21 **D** 20, 24, 28

4. Which number doesn't fit in Karen's pattern?

   F 20 **H** 32
   G 28 **J** 35

Mixed Strategy Practice

5. Bo bicycled 4 miles a day last week. He did not bicycle on Saturday or Sunday. How far did he bicycle last week?
6. **What's the Error?** Look at this pattern. Which number doesn't fit this pattern? Explain.
   11, 21, 31, 41, 51, 60, 71
7. **REASONING** Use the digits 0–9 to write the greatest possible 4-digit number using 4 different digits. Write the least possible 4-digit number using 4 different digits.
8. If this is the time now, what time will it be in 2 hours 15 minutes?

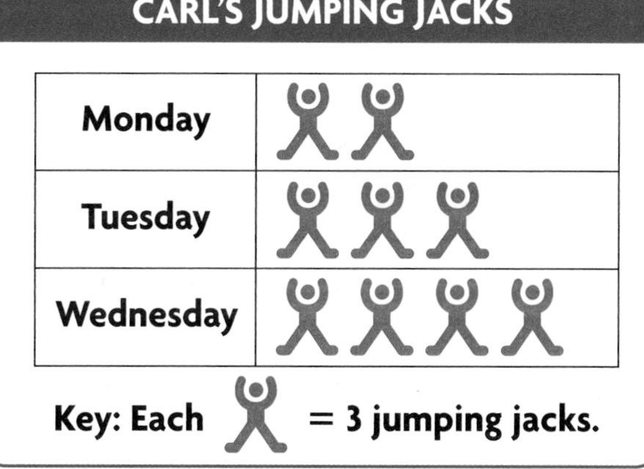

9. **USE DATA** If Carl continues the pattern above, how many jumping jacks will he do on Saturday?
10. **Write a problem** about a number pattern. Tell how you would explain to a second grader how to find the next number in your pattern.

LESSON 4

Practice Multiplication

M3N3.b. Know the multiplication facts with understanding and fluency to 10×10. *also* M3N3.e., M3A1.c.

Quick Review

1. $3 \times \blacksquare = 12$
2. $2 \times 6 = \blacksquare$
3. $0 \times 8 = \blacksquare$
4. $4 \times 5 = \blacksquare$
5. $9 \times \blacksquare = 9$

Learn

FACTS IN FLIGHT At the airport, Nicole saw 6 jets waiting to take off. Each jet had 3 engines. How many engines were there in all?

$$6 \times 3 = \blacksquare$$

There are many ways to find a product.

A. You can make equal groups or arrays.

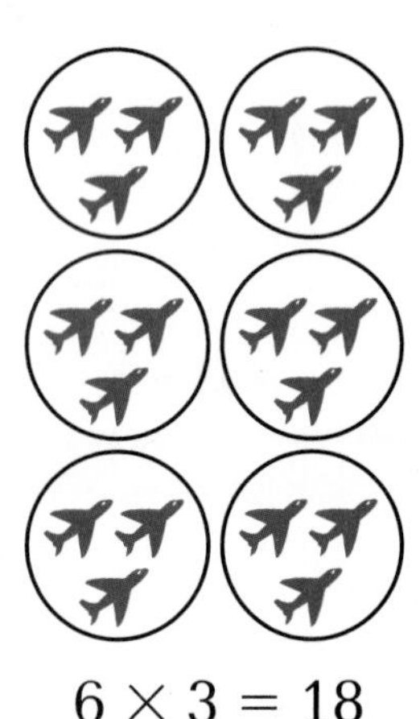

$6 \times 3 = 18$

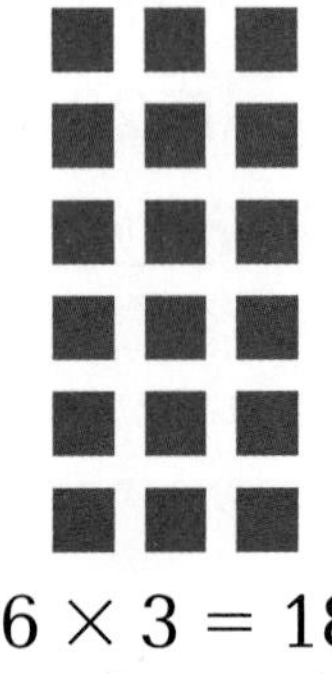

$6 \times 3 = 18$

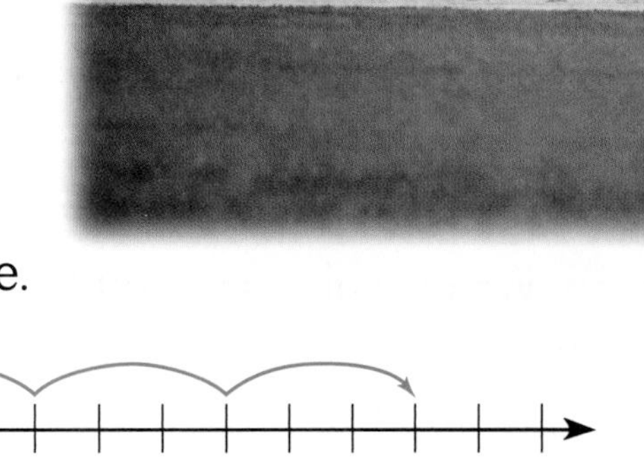

B. You can skip-count on a number line.

0 1 2 3 4 5 6 7 8 9 10 11 12 13 14 15 16 17 18 19 20

$6 \times 3 = 18$

C. You can double a fact that you already know.

Think: $3 \times 3 = 9$ and $9 + 9 = 18$, so $6 \times 3 = 18$.

D. You can use the Commutative Property of Multiplication.

Think: $3 \times 6 = 6 \times 3 = 18$.

Technology Link

More Practice: Harcourt Mega Math The Number Games, *Up, Up, and Array,* Level A

Another Way to Find a Product

E. You can use a multiplication table.

×	0	1	2	3	4	5	6	7	8	9
0	0	0	0	0	0	0	0	0	0	0
1	0	1	2	3	4	5	6	7	8	9
2	0	2	4	6	8	10	12	14	16	18
3	0	3	6	9	12	15	18	21	24	27
4	0	4	8	12	16	20	24	28	32	36
5	0	5	10	15	20	25	30	35	40	45
row→ 6	0	6	12	18	24	30	36	42	48	54
7	0	7	14	21	28	35	42	49	56	63
8	0	8	16	24	32	40	48	56	64	72
9	0	9	18	27	36	45	54	63	72	81

(column ↓ 3)

Think: The product is found where row 6 and column 3 meet.

$$6 \times 3 = 18$$

So, there are 18 engines in all.

MATH IDEA You can use equal groups, arrays, skip-counting, doubles, the Commutative Property of Multiplication, or a multiplication table to help you find products or multiples.

- Are the multiples of 6 always even numbers? Explain why or why not.

Check

1. **Explain** two ways to find 4×8.

Write a multiplication sentence for each.

2. 

3. 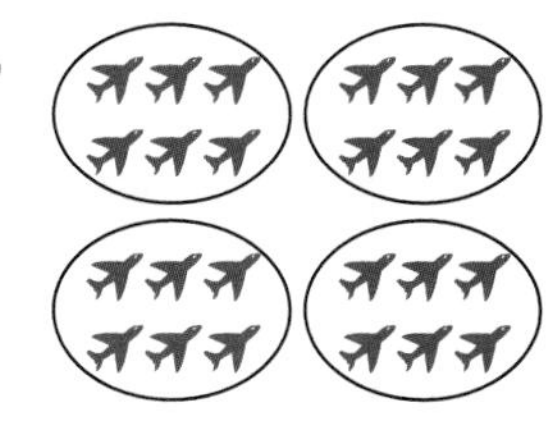

4. 

Find the product.

5. $2 \times 6 = ■$

6. $5 \times 3 = ■$

7. $■ = 1 \times 7$

8. $■ = 7 \times 3$

LESSON CONTINUES

Practice and Problem Solving

Extra Practice, page 156, Set C

Find the product.

9. $7 \times 4 =$ ■
10. $2 \times 8 =$ ■
11. $7 \times 5 =$ ■
12. $4 \times 2 =$ ■
13. ■ $= 5 \times 4$
14. $9 \times 4 =$ ■
15. ■ $= 2 \times 5$
16. $9 \times 1 =$ ■
17. ■ $= 1 \times 9$
18. $6 \times 2 =$ ■
19. $5 \times 6 =$ ■
20. ■ $= 8 \times 4$
21. $5 \times 1 =$ ■
22. $3 \times 0 =$ ■
23. $2 \times 9 =$ ■
24. $6 \times 5 =$ ■
25. $2 \times 4 =$ ■
26. ■ $= 3 \times 7$
27. $8 \times 5 =$ ■
28. ■ $= 9 \times 3$
29. $\begin{array}{r} 9 \\ \times 3 \\ \hline \end{array}$
30. $\begin{array}{r} 0 \\ \times 6 \\ \hline \end{array}$
31. $\begin{array}{r} 5 \\ \times 7 \\ \hline \end{array}$
32. $\begin{array}{r} 8 \\ \times 3 \\ \hline \end{array}$
33. $\begin{array}{r} 4 \\ \times 9 \\ \hline \end{array}$
34. $\begin{array}{r} 4 \\ \times 4 \\ \hline \end{array}$

Copy and complete.

35.

×	2	4	7	8	9
2	■	■	■	■	■

36.

×	3	5	7	8	9
3	■	■	■	■	■

37.

×	2	7	5	3	8
4	■	■	■	■	■

38.

×	1	6	9	7	8
5	■	■	■	■	■

Compare. Write <, >, or = for each ●.

39. 3×2 ● 4×1
40. 7×4 ● 4×8
41. 5×8 ● $35 + 6$
42. 4×6 ● 8×3
43. 3×6 ● 5×4
44. 7×5 ● 8×3

45. **REASONING** Jenny baked some cookies. She put 4 chocolate chips and 2 pecans on each cookie. If she used 24 chocolate chips in all, how many pecans did she use?

46. **MULTISTEP** Pedro and Jon have 20 toy cars altogether. If Jon buys another toy car, he will have twice as many toy cars as Pedro. How many toy cars does Pedro have?

47. 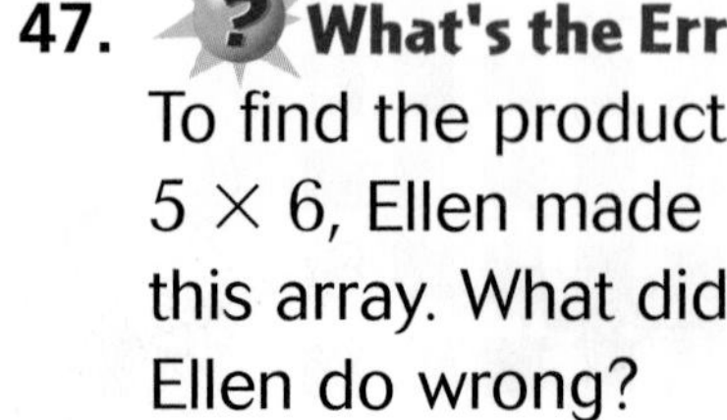
What's the Error? To find the product 5×6, Ellen made this array. What did Ellen do wrong?

48. **REASONING** Look at this number pattern. What is a rule? What are the missing numbers?

8, 11, 14, ■, ■, ■, 26

49. Three vans are going to the airport. There are 9 people in each van. How many people are going to the airport?

50. **MULTISTEP** Marie has 4 loose stamps and 5 sheets of 8 stamps each. How many stamps does she have in all?

Maintain Skills

51. Write the time.

52. $\begin{array}{r} 109 \\ +737 \\ \hline \end{array}$

53. $\begin{array}{r} 324 \\ -195 \\ \hline \end{array}$

54. $\begin{array}{r} 170 \\ +480 \\ \hline \end{array}$

55. $\begin{array}{r} 608 \\ -372 \\ \hline \end{array}$

CRCT Test Prep

56. M3N2.c. Jordan has a fish tank with 6 goldfish, 3 black mollies, and 4 guppies. How many fish does she have in all? (p. 46)

A. 10 B. 13 C. 14 D. 16

57. M3A1.c. Which number belongs in the □ to make the number sentence true? (p. 54)

$$420 + \square = 480$$

A. 20 B. 40 C. 60 D. 80

Problem Solving Thinker's Corner

FINDING MULTIPLES

You can use a hundred chart to show multiples.

MATERIALS: hundred chart, crayons

a. Start at 2. Shade all of the multiples of 2 with a yellow crayon.

b. Start at 3. Shade all of the multiples of 3 with a blue crayon.

c. What numbers are now shaded both yellow and blue (green)?

d. Look at the green numbers. These numbers are multiples of which number?

1	2	3	4	5	6	7	8	9	10
11	12	13	14	15	16	17	18	19	20
21	22	23	24	25	26	27	28	29	30
31	32	33	34	35	36	37	38	39	40
41	42	43	44	45	46	47	48	49	50
51	52	53	54	55	56	57	58	59	60
61	62	63	64	65	66	67	68	69	70
71	72	73	74	75	76	77	78	79	80
81	82	83	84	85	86	87	88	89	90
91	92	93	94	95	96	97	98	99	100

LESSON 5

Algebra: Missing Factors

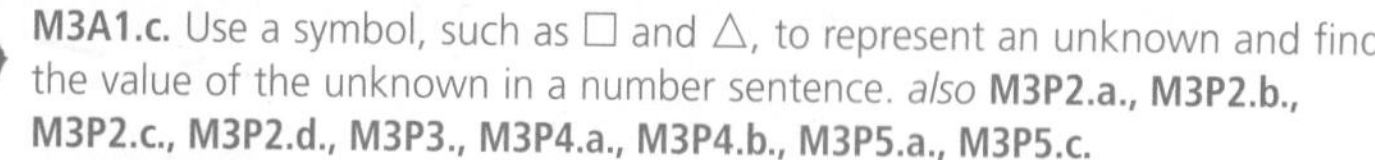

M3A1.c. Use a symbol, such as □ and △, to represent an unknown and find the value of the unknown in a number sentence. *also* M3P2.a., M3P2.b., M3P2.c., M3P2.d., M3P3., M3P4.a., M3P4.b., M3P5.a., M3P5.c.

Quick Review

1. 4×6
2. 2×7
3. 3×0
4. 6×1
5. 3×6

Learn

BLUE RIBBON BAKING Mike's muffins won first prize at the county fair. Each plate held 5 muffins. He made 35 muffins. How many plates did he use?

■ × 5 = 35   How can you find the missing factor?

One Way Use square tiles.

Make an array with 35 tiles.
Use 5 tiles in a row.
Count how many rows of 5 tiles.
There are 7 rows of 5 tiles.
The missing factor is 7.

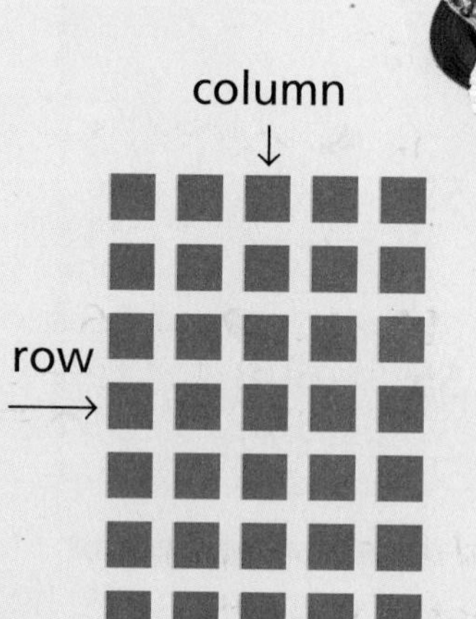

■ × 5 = 35
7 × 5 = 35
↑ ↑ ↑
factor (*rows*) factor (*columns*) product (*total number of tiles*)

Another Way Use a multiplication table.

Start at the column for 5.
Look down to the product, 35.
Look left across the row from 35.
The missing factor is 7.

×	0	1	2	3	4	5	6	7	8	9
0	0	0	0	0	0	0	0	0	0	0
1	0	1	2	3	4	5	6	7	8	9
2	0	2	4	6	8	10	12	14	16	18
3	0	3	6	9	12	15	18	21	24	27
4	0	4	8	12	16	20	24	28	32	36
5	0	5	10	15	20	25	30	35	40	45
6	0	6	12	18	24	30	36	42	48	54
7	0	7	14	21	28	35	42	49	56	63
8	0	8	16	24	32	40	48	56	64	72
9	0	9	18	27	36	45	54	63	72	81

■ × 5 = 35
7 × 5 = 35
↑ ↑ ↑
factor (*row*) factor (*column*) product (*row 7 column 5*)

So, Mike used 7 plates.

MATH IDEA When you know the product and one factor, square tiles or a multiplication table can help you find the missing factor.

REASONING How can you use square tiles or a multiplication table to find factors for 24?

Check

1. **Explain** how to use the table to find the missing factor in ■ × 6 = 18.

Find the missing factor.

2. ■ × 2 = 8
3. 3 × ■ = 9
4. 5 × ■ = 20

Practice and Problem Solving

Extra Practice, page 156, Set D

Find the missing factor.

5. ■ × 4 = 12
6. ■ × 3 = 21
7. 5 × ■ = 0
8. 2 × ■ = 12
9. 1 × ■ = 9
10. 8 × ■ = 24
11. ■ × 6 = 30
12. ■ × 4 = 32
13. ■ × 2 = 18
14. 4 × ■ = 16
15. 5 × ■ = 15
16. ■ × 6 = 24
17. 4 × 6 = ■ × 3
18. 9 × ■ = 50 − 5
19. 7 × ■ = 32 − 4

20. The product of 4 and another factor is 28. What is the other factor?

21. If you multiply 9 by a number, the product is 27. What is the number?

22. There are 2 chairs at each table. If there are 14 chairs, how many tables are there? Write a multiplication sentence to solve.

23. **MULTISTEP** There are 4 oatmeal cookies and 3 sugar cookies on each plate. How many cookies are on 5 plates?

24. **Write About It** How can you use a multiplication table to find the multiples of 6?

25. **What's the Question?** Pies are on sale for $3 each. Carly spent $12 on pies. The answer is 4 pies.

Maintain Skills

Write the amount.

26. 

27.
$$\begin{array}{r} 400 \\ -137 \\ \hline \end{array}$$

28.
$$\begin{array}{r} 453 \\ +487 \\ \hline \end{array}$$

CRCT Test Prep

29. M3N1.b. Which number means 10,000 + 1,000 + 10 + 1? (p. 14)

A. 10,111
B. 11,011
C. 11,101
D. 11,110

Extra Practice

Set A (pp. 144–145)

Find the product.

1. $0 \times 5 = ■$ **2.** $3 \times 7 = ■$ **3.** $1 \times 7 = ■$ **4.** $4 \times 3 = ■$

5. $■ = 6 \times 3$ **6.** $■ = 8 \times 5$ **7.** $■ = 0 \times 9$ **8.** $■ = 1 \times 1$

9. Is the product of 3 and 0 *greater than, less than,* or *equal to* the product of 0 and 6? Explain.

Set B (pp. 146–147)

Find the product.

1. $\begin{array}{r} 8 \\ \times 4 \\ \hline \end{array}$ **2.** $\begin{array}{r} 4 \\ \times 0 \\ \hline \end{array}$ **3.** $\begin{array}{r} 4 \\ \times 6 \\ \hline \end{array}$ **4.** $\begin{array}{r} 4 \\ \times 4 \\ \hline \end{array}$ **5.** $\begin{array}{r} 4 \\ \times 9 \\ \hline \end{array}$

6. $3 \times 4 = ■$ **7.** $■ = 2 \times 4$ **8.** $■ = 4 \times 7$ **9.** $5 \times 4 = ■$

10. Mario has 4 packs of 8 stickers. He also has 19 loose stickers. How many stickers does he have in all?

Set C (pp. 150–153)

Find the product.

1. $4 \times 6 = ■$ **2.** $5 \times 3 = ■$ **3.** $8 \times 0 = ■$ **4.** $9 \times 5 = ■$

5. $5 \times 8 = ■$ **6.** $3 \times 6 = ■$ **7.** $7 \times 4 = ■$ **8.** $3 \times 9 = ■$

9. $8 \times 2 = ■$ **10.** $3 \times 7 = ■$ **11.** $6 \times 5 = ■$ **12.** $4 \times 8 = ■$

13. A movie is shown 5 times each day. How many times is that movie shown in one week?

Set D (pp. 154–155)

Find the missing factor.

1. $■ \times 9 = 18$ **2.** $5 \times ■ = 20$ **3.** $■ \times 1 = 8$ **4.** $■ \times 9 = 9$

5. $2 \times ■ = 14$ **6.** $4 \times ■ = 16$ **7.** $3 \times ■ = 21$ **8.** $■ \times 8 = 32$

9. Jill has 9 baskets with an equal number of eggs in each. If she has 36 eggs in all, how many are in each basket?

Review/Test

✓ CHECK VOCABULARY

Choose the best term from the box.

Vocabulary
array
zero
multiple
one
factor

1. The product of _?_ and any number equals that number. (p. 144)
2. The product of _?_ and any number equals zero. (p. 144)
3. A _?_ of 5 is any product that has 5 as a factor, such as 5, 10, 15, and so on. (p. 146)

✓ CHECK SKILLS

Find the product. (pp. 144–145)

4. $5 \times 1 = \blacksquare$ **5.** $0 \times 6 = \blacksquare$ **6.** $\blacksquare = 1 \times 8$ **7.** $\blacksquare = 9 \times 0$

Find the product. (pp. 146–147)

8. $\blacksquare = 4 \times 3$ **9.** $2 \times 4 = \blacksquare$ **10.** $5 \times 4 = \blacksquare$ **11.** $\blacksquare = 8 \times 4$

12. $4 \times 9 = \blacksquare$ **13.** $4 \times 4 = \blacksquare$ **14.** $\blacksquare = 6 \times 4$ **15.** $4 \times 0 = \blacksquare$

Find the missing factor. (pp. 154–155)

16. $2 \times \blacksquare = 8$ **17.** $\blacksquare \times 5 = 30$ **18.** $1 \times \blacksquare = 9$ **19.** $\blacksquare \times 6 = 18$

20. $\blacksquare \times 1 = 9$ **21.** $4 \times \blacksquare = 32$ **22.** $\blacksquare \times 3 = 18$ **23.** $7 \times \blacksquare = 0$

✓ CHECK PROBLEM SOLVING

Solve. (pp. 148–149)

24. The first four numbers in the pattern are 4, 8, 12, 16. What is a rule? What are the next three numbers?

25. Lin saw this number pattern: 10, 13, 16, 19, 22, 25, and 28. What is a rule? What are the next three numbers?

Chapter CRCT Test Prep

NUMBERS AND OPERATIONS

1. M3N3.b. Find the product.

$$\begin{array}{r} 4 \\ \times 7 \\ \hline \end{array}$$

A. 11

B. 24

C. 28

D. 32

2. M3N3.g. Mikal has 9 boxes of toy cars. There are 5 toy cars in each box. Which number sentence could he use to find the total number of toy cars?

A. $9 \times 5 = 45$

B. $5 + 9 = 14$

C. $9 - 5 = 4$

D. $9 \times 9 = 81$

3. M3N3.b. Find the product.

$$\begin{array}{r} 1 \\ \times 9 \\ \hline \end{array}$$

A. 0

B. 1

C. 9

D. 19

ALGEBRA

4. M3A1.c. What is the missing factor in the multiplication sentence below?

$$5 \times \square = 35$$

A. 3

B. 5

C. 7

D. 9

5. M3A1.c. What is the missing number in the table?

×	2	4	5
4	8	□	20

A. 4

B. 12

C. 16

D. 18

6. M3A1.c. Which number belongs in the □ to make the number sentence true?

$$3 \times \square = 24$$

A. 4

B. 5

C. 6

D. 8

Cumulative CRCT Test Prep

NUMBERS AND OPERATIONS

7. M3N3.c. What multiplication sentence does the array show?

A. $4 \times 6 = 24$

B. $5 \times 6 = 30$

C. $4 \times 4 = 16$

D. $6 \times 6 = 36$

Use the table below to answer question 8.

Three Sisters Volcanoes, Oregon	
Volcano	**Height (in feet)**
North Sister	10,085
Middle Sister	10,047
South Sister	10,358

8. M3N1.a. The table shows the heights of volcanoes in the Three Sisters area of Oregon. What is the value of the digit 3 in the height of the South Sister?

A. 30,000

B. 3,000

C. 300

D. 30

ALGEBRA

Use the table below to answer question 9.

Fall Festival Tickets	
Number of Tickets	**Cost**
1	$7.00
2	$14.00
3	$21.00
4	☐

9. M3A1.a. Laura wants to buy four tickets to the fall festival. How much will it cost to her to buy 4 tickets?

A. $25.00

B. $28.00

C. $32.00

D. $36.00

10. M3A1.c. Which number belongs in the ☐ to make the number sentence true?

1,000 + 800 + ☐ + 2 = 1,862

A. 6

B. 60

C. 600

D. 6,000

CHAPTER 9

Multiplication Facts and Strategies

FAST FACT • MUSIC
A marching band plays music and moves in formation. Marching bands are popular at parades and football games. Many bands compete in state and national marching band contests.

INVESTIGATION **The pictograph shows the number of musicians in different high school marching bands. Draw an array that each band could use as a formation for its musicians. Then break apart each array into two smaller arrays to find the total number of musicians in each marching band.**

Using Data

GEORGIA MARCHING BANDS

High School	Musicians
Duluth	🎺 🎺 🎺
Peachtree Ridge	🎺 🎺 🎺 🎺 🎺 🎺 🎺 🎺
Parkview	🎺 🎺 🎺 🎺 🎺 🎺 🎺

Key: Each 🎺 = 8 Musicians.

CHECK WHAT YOU KNOW

Use this page to help you review and remember important skills needed for Chapter 9.

ARRAYS

Find the product.

1. $2 \times 4 = ■$
2. $3 \times 6 = ■$
3. $4 \times 5 = ■$
4. $5 \times 6 = ■$
5. $4 \times 4 = ■$
6. $3 \times 7 = ■$

MULTIPLICATION FACTS THROUGH 5

Find the product.

7. $7 \times 3 = ■$
8. $5 \times 5 = ■$
9. $■ = 7 \times 4$
10. $1 \times 2 = ■$
11. $4 \times 1 = ■$
12. $6 \times 3 = ■$
13. $9 \times 5 = ■$
14. $■ = 6 \times 1$
15. $\begin{array}{r} 6 \\ \times 4 \\ \hline \end{array}$
16. $\begin{array}{r} 4 \\ \times 2 \\ \hline \end{array}$
17. $\begin{array}{r} 2 \\ \times 3 \\ \hline \end{array}$
18. $\begin{array}{r} 8 \\ \times 4 \\ \hline \end{array}$
19. $\begin{array}{r} 3 \\ \times 1 \\ \hline \end{array}$

VOCABULARY POWER

REVIEW

array [ə•rā′] *noun*

An array is an orderly arrangement of objects, pictures, or numbers in rows and columns. Why can you use an array to show 4×6 but not $4 + 6$?

www.harcourtschool.com/mathglossary

LESSON 1

Multiply with 6

M3N3.b. Know the multiplication facts with understanding and fluency to 10 × 10. *also* M3A1.c., M3P3., M3P4.

Quick Review

1. 5 × 3 = ■
2. 5 × ■ = 25
3. 5 × 9 = ■
4. ■ × 5 = 30
5. 40 = 5 × ■

Learn

MARCHING MULTIPLES The school band has 6 rows, with 6 students in each row. How many students are in the band?

Example

Find 6 × 6 = ■.

One Way Break apart an array to find the product.

STEP 1

Make an array that shows 6 rows of 6.

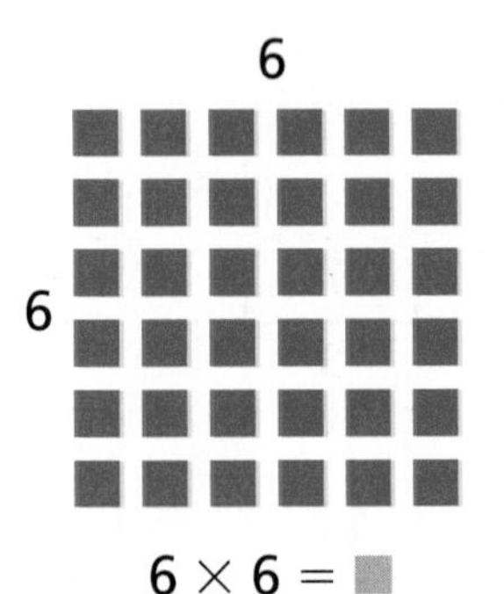

6 × 6 = ■

STEP 2

Break the array into two smaller arrays.

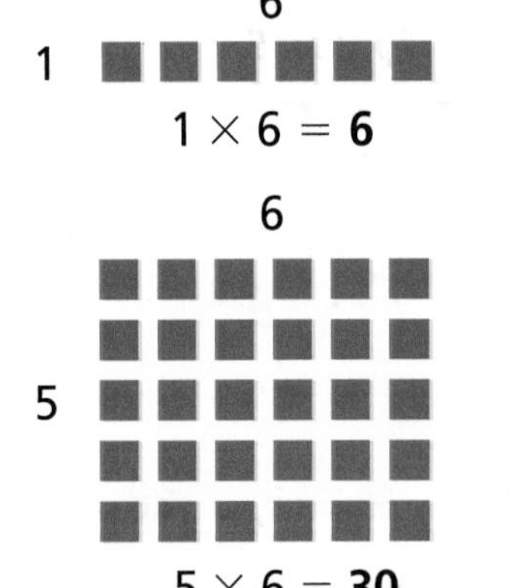

5 × 6 = **30**

STEP 3

Add the products of the two arrays.

$$\begin{array}{r} 6 \\ +30 \\ \hline 36 \end{array}$$

6 × 6 = 36

So, there are 36 students in the band.

- What are two other ways to break apart the 6 × 6 array?

Another Way When you multiply with 6, you can use doubles. The product of each 6's fact is double the product of each 3's fact.

To find 6 × 6
- First find the 3's fact. **Think:** 6 × 3 = 18
- Double the product. 18 + 18 = 36
- So, 6 × 6 = 36.

3's facts	6's facts
0 × 3 = 0	0 × 6 = 0
1 × 3 = 3	1 × 6 = 6
2 × 3 = 6	2 × 6 = 12
3 × 3 = 9	3 × 6 = 18
4 × 3 = 12	4 × 6 = 24
5 × 3 = 15	5 × 6 = 30
6 × 3 = 18	6 × 6 = ■
7 × 3 = 21	7 × 6 = 42
8 × 3 = 24	8 × 6 = 48
9 × 3 = 27	9 × 6 = 54

Check

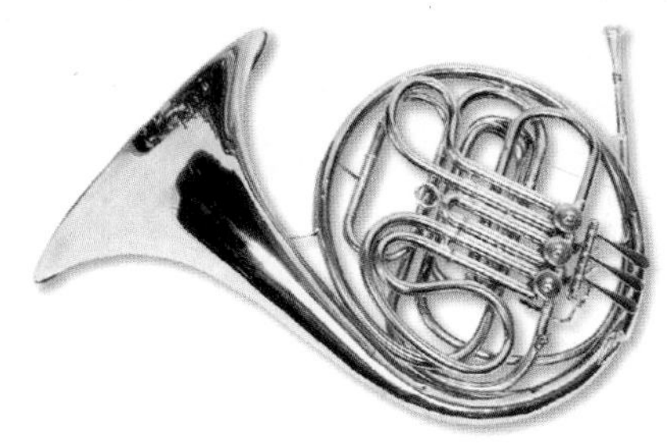

1. **Explain** how you can use 8×3 to find 8×6.

Find each product.

2. $7 \times 6 = \blacksquare$ 3. $4 \times 6 = \blacksquare$ 4. $5 \times 6 = \blacksquare$

Practice and Problem Solving

Extra Practice, page 174, Set A

Find each product.

5. $3 \times 6 = \blacksquare$ 6. $6 \times 5 = \blacksquare$ 7. $5 \times 9 = \blacksquare$ 8. $\blacksquare = 8 \times 6$

9. $4 \times 7 = \blacksquare$ 10. $\blacksquare = 3 \times 4$ 11. $4 \times 9 = \blacksquare$ 12. $6 \times 0 = \blacksquare$

13. $\begin{array}{r} 5 \\ \times 7 \\ \hline \end{array}$ 14. $\begin{array}{r} 6 \\ \times 7 \\ \hline \end{array}$ 15. $\begin{array}{r} 8 \\ \times 3 \\ \hline \end{array}$ 16. $\begin{array}{r} 6 \\ \times 1 \\ \hline \end{array}$ 17. $\begin{array}{r} 5 \\ \times 8 \\ \hline \end{array}$ 18. $\begin{array}{r} 6 \\ \times 6 \\ \hline \end{array}$

Copy and complete each table.

	Multiply by 3.	
19.	4	■
20.	6	■
21.	9	■

	Multiply by 5.	
22.	6	■
23.	3	■
24.	8	■

	Multiply by 6.	
25.	4	■
26.	7	■
27.	9	■

Complete.

28. $\blacksquare \times 4 = 12$ 29. $\blacksquare \times 6 = 42$ 30. $48 = 8 \times \blacksquare$

31. $\blacksquare \times 4 = 4 \times 3$ 32. $3 \times 6 = \blacksquare \times 2$ 33. $\blacksquare \times 6 = 40 + 8$

34. ***FAST FACT*** • MUSIC A guitar has 6 strings. A banjo has 5 strings. How many strings are on 4 guitars and 2 banjos?

35. **Write About It** Draw arrays to show that 6×4 is the same as 1×4 plus 5×4.

Maintain Skills

36. $\begin{array}{r} 327 \\ -\ 82 \\ \hline \end{array}$ 37. $\begin{array}{r} 600 \\ -346 \\ \hline \end{array}$

38. $\begin{array}{r} 103 \\ +731 \\ \hline \end{array}$ 39. $\begin{array}{r} 228 \\ +632 \\ \hline \end{array}$

CRCT Test Prep

40. M3N3.b. Find the product. (p. 162)

$\begin{array}{r} 6 \\ \times 8 \\ \hline \end{array}$

A. 14
B. 24
C. 32
D. 48

LESSON 2

Multiply with 8

M3N3.b. Know the multiplication facts with understanding and fluency to 10 × 10. *also* M3A1.c., M3P3.a., M3P3.b., M3P3.c., M3P3.d.

Quick Review

1. 30 = ■ × 6
2. 2 × 6 = ■
3. 6 × 3 = ■
4. 6 × ■ = 42
5. 7 × 6 = ■

Learn

BAKE-OFF Mr. Lee baked 6 peach pies for the state fair. He used 8 peaches in each pie. How many peaches did he use in all?

Example

Find 6 × 8 = ■.

One Way Break apart an array to find the product.

STEP 1

Make an array that shows 6 rows of 8.

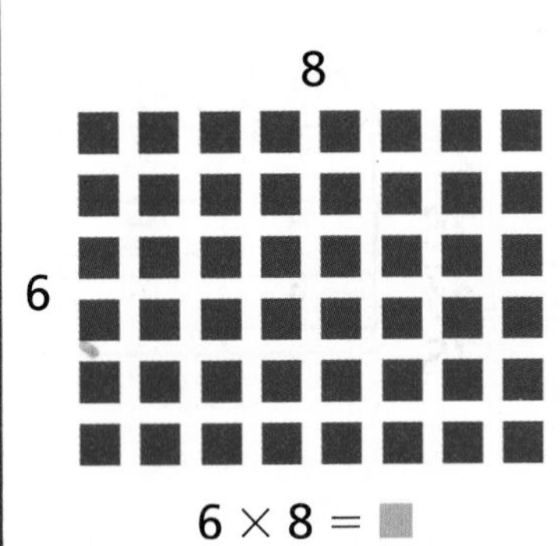

6 × 8 = ■

STEP 2

Break the array into two smaller arrays.

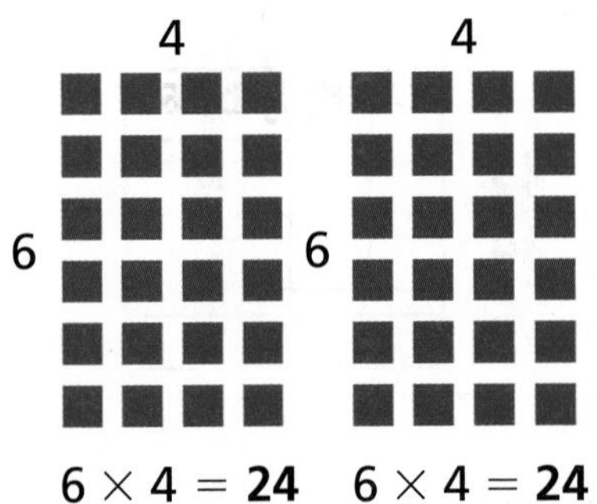

6 × 4 = **24** 6 × 4 = **24**

STEP 3

Add the products of the two arrays.

$$\begin{array}{r} 24 \\ +24 \\ \hline 48 \end{array}$$

6 × 8 = 48

So, Mr. Lee used 48 peaches in all.

- What are two other ways to break apart the 6 × 8 array?

Another Way When you multiply with 8, you can use doubles. The product of each 8's fact is double the product of each 4's fact.

the product of each 4's fact.	
0 × 4 = 0	7 × 4 = 28
1 × 4 = 4	8 × 4 = 32
2 × 4 = 8	9 × 4 = 36
3 × 4 = 12	0 × 8 = 0
4 × 4 = 16	1 × 8 = 8
5 × 4 = 20	2 × 8 = 16
6 × 4 = 24	3 × 8 = 24
	4 × 8 = 32
	5 × 8 = 40
	6 × 8 = ■

To find 6 × 8

- First find the 4's fact. **Think:** 6 × 4 = 24
- Double the product. 24 + 24 = 48
- So, 6 × 8 = 48.

Check

1. **Explain** how you can use $4 \times 5 = 20$ to find 8×5.

Find each product.

2. $4 \times 8 = ■$ 3. $7 \times 8 = ■$ 4. $6 \times 8 = ■$ 5. $8 \times 8 = ■$

Practice and Problem Solving

Extra Practice, page 174, Set B

Find each product.

6. $5 \times 4 = ■$ 7. $8 \times 3 = ■$ 8. $9 \times 8 = ■$ 9. $7 \times 4 = ■$

10. $8 \times 6 = ■$ 11. $3 \times 4 = ■$ 12. $7 \times 5 = ■$ 13. $8 \times 8 = ■$

14. $\begin{array}{r} 4 \\ \times 8 \\ \hline \end{array}$ 15. $\begin{array}{r} 6 \\ \times 7 \\ \hline \end{array}$ 16. $\begin{array}{r} 9 \\ \times 6 \\ \hline \end{array}$ 17. $\begin{array}{r} 4 \\ \times 9 \\ \hline \end{array}$ 18. $\begin{array}{r} 3 \\ \times 7 \\ \hline \end{array}$ 19. $\begin{array}{r} 6 \\ \times 8 \\ \hline \end{array}$

Copy and complete each table.

	Multiply by 4.	
20.	5	■
21.	6	■
22.	8	■

	Multiply by 6.	
23.	7	■
24.	9	■
25.	8	■

	Multiply by 8.	
26.	9	■
27.	6	■
28.	8	■

Compare. Write $<$, $>$, or $=$ for each ●.

29. 2×3 ● 2×4 30. 5×8 ● 8×5 31. 5×5 ● 4×6

32. **ALGEBRA** Hal has 7 bags of 8 green apples and 1 bag of red apples. He has 60 apples in all. How many red apples does he have?

33. **What's the Error?** Robin says, "I can find 8×6 by thinking of $3 \times 6 = 18$ and doubling it."

Maintain Skills

34. $\begin{array}{r} 172 \\ +781 \\ \hline \end{array}$ 35. $\begin{array}{r} 399 \\ +421 \\ \hline \end{array}$

36. $\begin{array}{r} 900 \\ -713 \\ \hline \end{array}$ 37. $\begin{array}{r} 662 \\ -122 \\ \hline \end{array}$

CRCT Test Prep

38. M3N3.a. Which multiplication sentence can be written for $2 + 2 + 2 + 2$? (p. 126)

A. 2×2 C. 2×8
B. 4×2 D. 8×4

LESSON 3

Problem Solving Skill
Use a Bar Graph

M3D1. Students will create and interpret simple tables and graphs. *also* M3P1.a., M3P1.b., M3P1.d., M3P2.a., M3P2.b., M3P2.c., M3P2.d., M3P3.a., M3P3.b., M3P3.c., M3P3.d., M3P4.b.

UNDERSTAND › PLAN › SOLVE › CHECK

Quick Review

1. 6 × 4 = ■
2. ■ = 9 × 2
3. 7 × 2 = ■
4. 8 × 4 = ■
5. 7 × ■ = 28

FACE PAINTING The art club went on a field trip to the arts and crafts fair. It takes 5 tickets to get your face painted at the fair. How many tickets will it take for all the third grade students to get their faces painted?

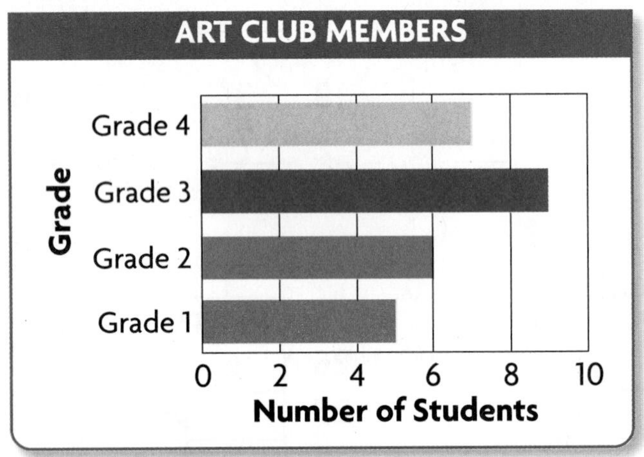

Look at the bar graph. There are 9 students in Grade 3.

You can use multiplication to find the number of tickets needed.

9	×	5	=	45
factor		factor		product
number of students		each student needs 5 tickets		total number of tickets needed

Talk About It

- How many tickets would it take for all the second grade students to get their faces painted?
- How would you use the bar graph to find the total number of tickets needed for the fourth grade students to get their faces painted?

REASONING If the fifth grade students needed a total of 15 tickets to get their faces painted, how can you use missing factors to find how many fifth grade students there are?

Problem Solving Practice

USE DATA For 1–2, use the bar graph.

1. Explain how to use this bar graph to find which juice had the most bottles sold. How many bottles of it were sold?

2. Each bottle of grape juice costs \$2. How much money was spent on the bottles of grape juice?

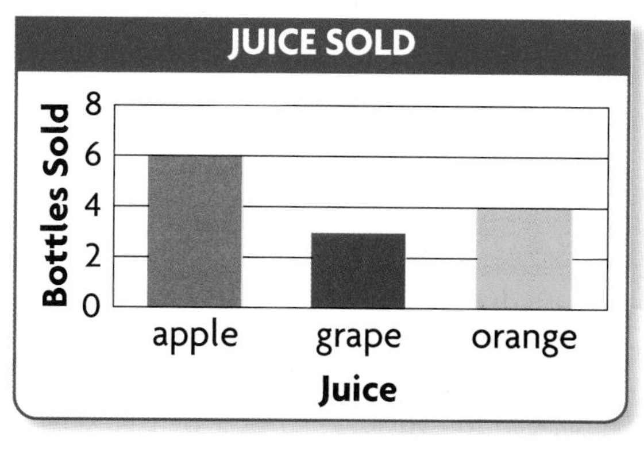

USE DATA For 3–4, use the bar graph.

3. What is the total number of books these four students read this month?
   - **A** 7
   - **B** 16
   - **C** 22
   - **D** 28

4. Students earn 4 stickers for each book read. How many stickers did Paul earn?
   - **F** 6
   - **G** 10
   - **H** 20
   - **J** 24

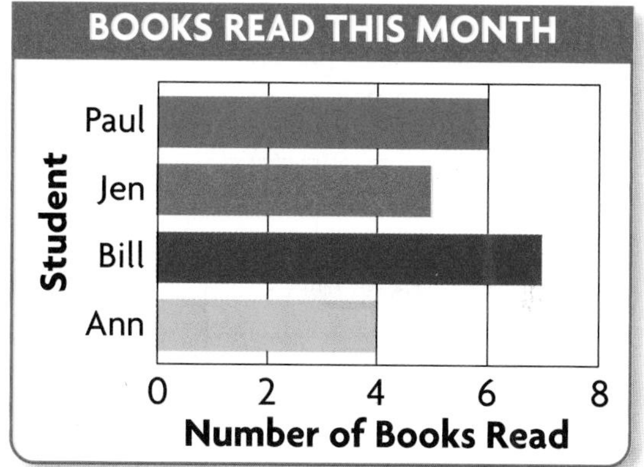

Mixed Applications

USE DATA For 5–8, use the table.

5. How many tickets do Brandon and his 3 friends need in all for admission to the Science Center?

6. **MULTISTEP** Brandon and his 3 friends used 28 tickets. They used 4 more tickets for dinosaur exhibits than for space exhibits. How many tickets did they use for each?

7. **MULTISTEP** Abigail's father gave her 14 tickets. She used tickets for admission and the space exhibits. How many tickets did she have left?

SCIENCE CENTER

Activity	Tickets
Admission	5
Space exhibits	3
Dinosaur exhibits	4
Animal exhibits	2

8. **Write a problem** about tickets used at the Science Center in which the product is greater than 15 and is a multiple of 3.

LESSON 4

Multiply with 7

M3N3.b. Know the multiplication facts with understanding and fluency to 10 × 10. *also* M3A1.c., M3P2.d.

Quick Review

1. $8 \times 5 = \blacksquare$
2. $6 \times 4 = \blacksquare$
3. $3 \times 8 = \blacksquare$
4. $2 \times 6 = \blacksquare$
5. $5 \times 6 = \blacksquare$

Learn

PARADE! PARADE! Students built a float for a parade. They worked on the float for 8 weeks. How many days did they work on the float?

Example

Find $8 \times 7 = \blacksquare$.

Break apart an array to find the product.

STEP 1

Make an array that shows 8 rows of 7.

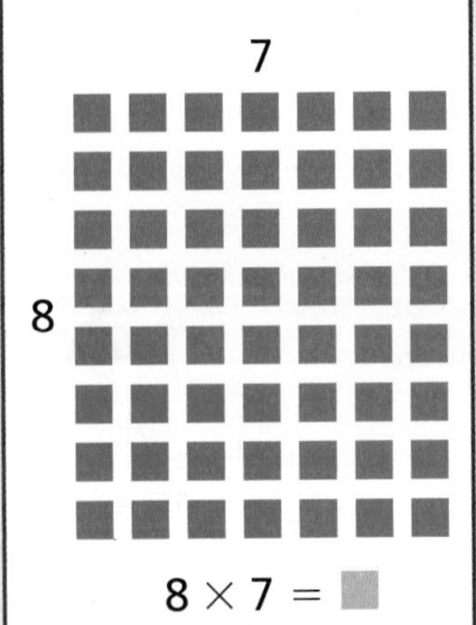

$8 \times 7 = \blacksquare$

STEP 2

Break the array into two smaller arrays.

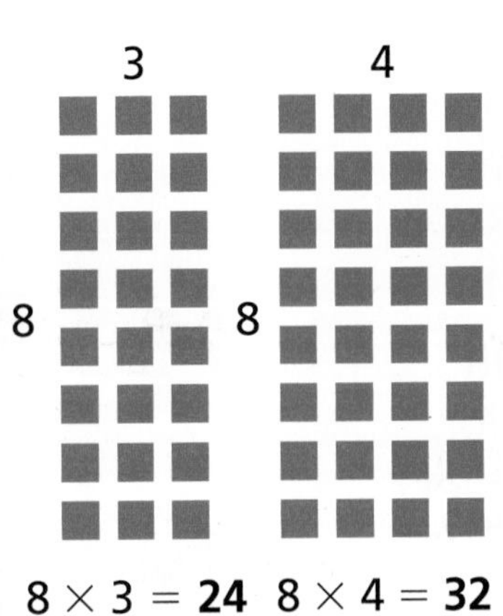

$8 \times 3 = $ **24** $\quad 8 \times 4 = $ **32**

STEP 3

Add the products of the two arrays.

$$\begin{array}{r} 24 \\ +32 \\ \hline 56 \end{array}$$

$8 \times 7 = 56$

So, the students worked on the float for 56 days.

- What are two other ways to break apart the 8×7 array?

Check

1. **Explain** how you could break apart 7×5 into two arrays to help you find the product.

Technology Link

More Practice: Harcourt Mega Math The Number Games, *Up, Up, and Array,* Level B

Find each product.

2. $4 \times 7 = \blacksquare$
3. $0 \times 7 = \blacksquare$
4. $8 \times 7 = \blacksquare$
5. $6 \times 7 = \blacksquare$

Practice and Problem Solving

Extra Practice, page 174, Set C

Find each product.

6. $2 \times 7 = ■$ **7.** $2 \times 9 = ■$ **8.** $3 \times 7 = ■$

9. $6 \times 6 = ■$ **10.** $7 \times 6 = ■$ **11.** $■ = 6 \times 9$

12. $■ = 5 \times 9$ **13.** $7 \times 7 = ■$ **14.** $4 \times 7 = ■$

15. $3 \times 6 = ■$ **16.** $■ = 4 \times 9$ **17.** $■ = 5 \times 5$

18. $\begin{array}{r} 1 \\ \times 7 \\ \hline \end{array}$ **19.** $\begin{array}{r} 7 \\ \times 9 \\ \hline \end{array}$ **20.** $\begin{array}{r} 6 \\ \times 8 \\ \hline \end{array}$ **21.** $\begin{array}{r} 8 \\ \times 8 \\ \hline \end{array}$ **22.** $\begin{array}{r} 4 \\ \times 5 \\ \hline \end{array}$ **23.** $\begin{array}{r} 8 \\ \times 7 \\ \hline \end{array}$

Copy and complete each table.

	Multiply by 6.	
24.	4	■
25.	6	■
26.	9	■

	Multiply by 7.	
27.	6	■
28.	5	■
29.	8	■

	Multiply by 8.	
30.	6	■
31.	7	■
32.	9	■

Complete.

33. $7 \times 6 = ■ + 21$ **34.** $■ \times 4 = 30 - 2$ **35.** $8 + 6 = 7 \times ■$

36. **REASONING** How can you tell without multiplying that 7×9 is less than 9×8?

37. **? What's the Question?** Joanna has 9 boxes of pears. She has 72 pears in all. The answer is 8 pears.

38. **MULTISTEP** Shayla was on vacation for 7 weeks. She spent 3 weeks at band camp and the rest of the time at home. How many days did she spend at home?

39. Break apart the array. Then write the multiplication fact.

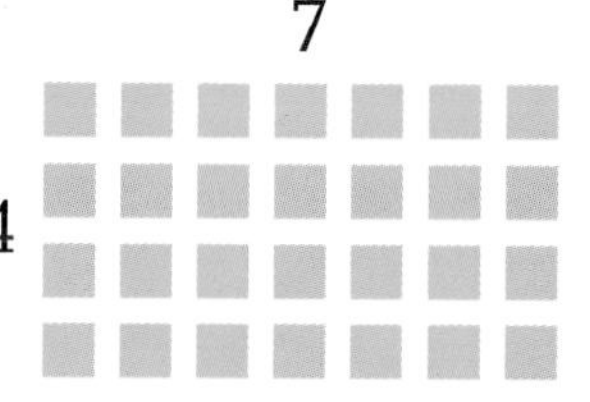

40. **ALGEBRA** Find a one-digit number to make this number sentence true. $■ \times 7 + 10 > 67 - 9$

Maintain Skills

41. Write the product.

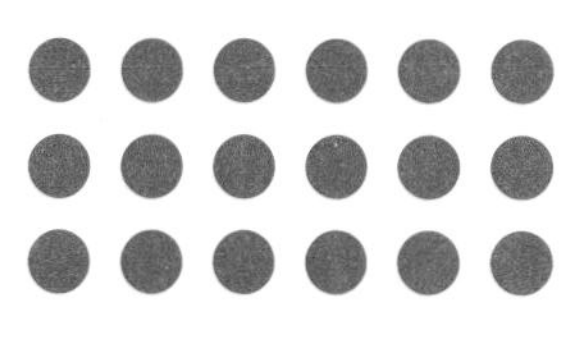

$3 \times 6 = ■$

CRCT Test Prep

42. M3N3.b. Which number belongs in the □ to make the number sentence true? (p. 164)

$$7 \times 8 = \square$$

A. 56 B. 49 C. 35 D. 21

LESSON 5

Algebra: Practice the Facts

M3N3.b. Know the multiplication facts with understanding and fluency to 10×10. *also* M3A1.c., M3P2.a., M3P2.b., M3P2.c., M3P2.d., M3P4.b.

Quick Review

1. $6 \times 3 = ■$
2. $5 \times 4 = ■$
3. $2 \times 8 = ■$
4. $4 \times 9 = ■$
5. $7 \times 8 = ■$

Learn

SPLASH! Each instructor teaches a group of 6 children. If there are 7 instructors, how many children are taking swimming lessons?

$$7 \times 6 = ■$$

You have learned many ways to find 7×6.

A. Break an array into known facts.

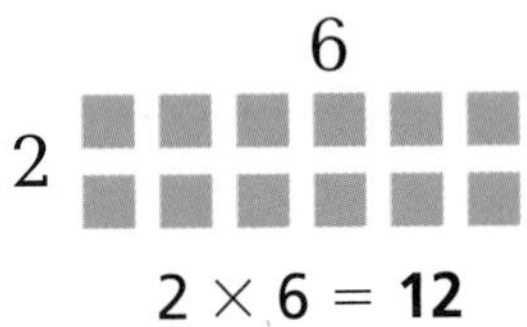

$2 \times 6 = \mathbf{12}$

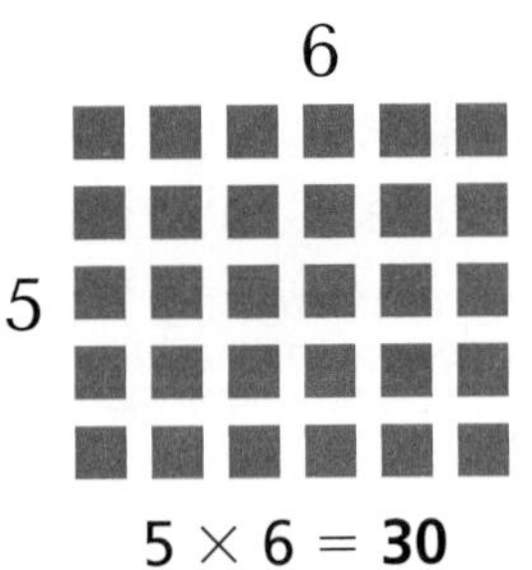

$5 \times 6 = \mathbf{30}$

$12 + 30 = 42$, so $7 \times 6 = 42$.

B. Use a multiplication table.

×	0	1	2	3	4	5	6	7	8	9
0	0	0	0	0	0	0	0	0	0	0
1	0	1	2	3	4	5	6	7	8	9
2	0	2	4	6	8	10	12	14	16	18
3	0	3	6	9	12	15	18	21	24	27
4	0	4	8	12	16	20	24	28	32	36
5	0	5	10	15	20	25	30	35	40	45
6	0	6	12	18	24	30	36	42	48	54
7	0	7	14	21	28	35	42	49	56	63
8	0	8	16	24	32	40	48	56	64	72
9	0	9	18	27	36	45	54	63	72	81

$7 \times 6 = 42$

C. Use the Commutative Property of Multiplication.

Try changing the order of the factors:

Think: If $6 \times 7 = 42$, then $7 \times 6 = 42$.

D. When you multiply with 6, you can use doubles.

To find a 6's fact, you can double a 3's fact.

- First find the 3's fact.
  Think: $7 \times 3 = 21$
- Double the product. $21 + 21 = 42$
  $7 \times 6 = 42$

So, 42 children are taking lessons.

Ways to Find a Product

What if there are 8 instructors with 5 swimmers each? How many children are taking lessons?

$$8 \times 5 = \blacksquare$$

David and Niam use different ways to find 8×5.

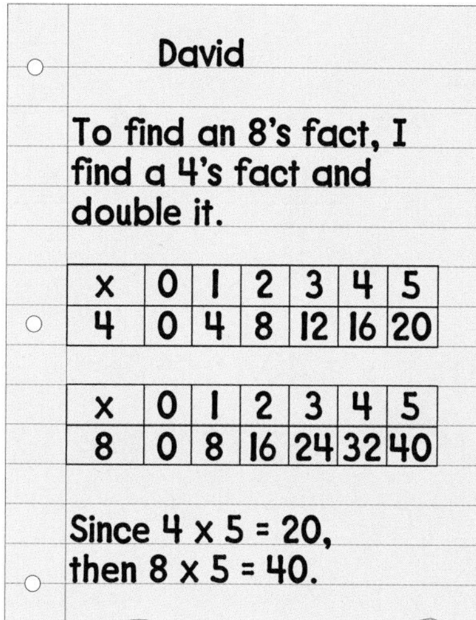

David

To find an 8's fact, I find a 4's fact and double it.

x	0	1	2	3	4	5
4	0	4	8	12	16	20

x	0	1	2	3	4	5
8	0	8	16	24	32	40

Since 4 x 5 = 20, then 8 x 5 = 40.

Niam

I can use the Commutative Property of Multiplication.

I know that 8 x 5 is the same as 5 x 8.

5 x 8 = 8 x 5 = 40

- What is another way that David or Niam could find 8×5?

REASONING As you multiply two whole number factors, when is the product *less than* the greater factor? *equal to* the greater factor? *greater than* either of the factors? Explain.

Check

1. **Explain** how you could use $9 \times 5 = 45$ to find 8×5.
2. **Describe** how you could use doubles to find 6×9.

Find each product.

3. $4 \times 5 = \blacksquare$
4. $3 \times 7 = \blacksquare$
5. $6 \times 4 = \blacksquare$
6. $7 \times 6 = \blacksquare$
7. $2 \times 5 = \blacksquare$
8. $6 \times 6 = \blacksquare$
9. $\blacksquare = 4 \times 3$
10. $2 \times 2 = \blacksquare$
11. $1 \times 8 = \blacksquare$
12. $\blacksquare = 5 \times 3$
13. $9 \times 2 = \blacksquare$
14. $5 \times 5 = \blacksquare$
15. 5×9
16. 6×3
17. 7×7
18. 4×8
19. 0×4
20. 3×3

Practice and Problem Solving

Extra Practice, page 174, Set D

Find each product.

21. $8 \times 5 = \blacksquare$
22. $0 \times 6 = \blacksquare$
23. $9 \times 3 = \blacksquare$
24. $5 \times 6 = \blacksquare$
25. $9 \times 8 = \blacksquare$
26. $8 \times 3 = \blacksquare$
27. $\blacksquare = 1 \times 8$
28. $8 \times 8 = \blacksquare$
29. $6 \times 8 = \blacksquare$
30. $\blacksquare = 4 \times 9$
31. $\blacksquare = 2 \times 8$
32. $8 \times 7 = \blacksquare$
33. $\begin{array}{r} 2 \\ \times 6 \\ \hline \end{array}$
34. $\begin{array}{r} 6 \\ \times 7 \\ \hline \end{array}$
35. $\begin{array}{r} 8 \\ \times 9 \\ \hline \end{array}$
36. $\begin{array}{r} 5 \\ \times 7 \\ \hline \end{array}$
37. $\begin{array}{r} 5 \\ \times 1 \\ \hline \end{array}$
38. $\begin{array}{r} 4 \\ \times 4 \\ \hline \end{array}$
39. $\begin{array}{r} 2 \\ \times 9 \\ \hline \end{array}$
40. $\begin{array}{r} 0 \\ \times 3 \\ \hline \end{array}$
41. $\begin{array}{r} 2 \\ \times 4 \\ \hline \end{array}$
42. $\begin{array}{r} 4 \\ \times 7 \\ \hline \end{array}$
43. $\begin{array}{r} 9 \\ \times 6 \\ \hline \end{array}$
44. $\begin{array}{r} 7 \\ \times 9 \\ \hline \end{array}$

Find each missing factor.

45. $\blacksquare \times 4 = 20$
46. $8 \times \blacksquare = 56$
47. $\blacksquare \times 6 = 0$
48. $6 \times \blacksquare = 42$
49. $8 \times \blacksquare = 24$
50. $\blacksquare \times 5 = 40$
51. $4 \times \blacksquare = 16$
52. $3 \times \blacksquare = 12$

Write $<$, $>$, or $=$ for each ●.

53. 3×2 ● 6
54. 4×2 ● $5 + 2$
55. 6×3 ● 7×2
56. 4×9 ● 6×6
57. 3×4 ● 18
58. 5×9 ● 6×8
59. 7×4 ● $30 - 4$
60. 3×8 ● 6×4
61. 5×7 ● 6×6
62. $8 + 9$ ● 8×9
63. 7×7 ● 50
64. 9×3 ● $9 + 9$

65. **Vocabulary Power** The word *double* means "twice as many." A double scoop is two scoops of ice cream. What number is the double of 8?

66. **ALGEBRA** Write *true* or *false* for each.

 a. $1 \times 8 = 9$
 b. $0 \times 7 = 0$
 c. $0 \times 0 = 0$
 d. $1 \times 9 = 1$

USE DATA For 67–68, use the table.

67. **MULTISTEP** Sara buys 4 cakes and 1 loaf of bread at the bake sale. How much does she pay?

68. **MULTISTEP** Greg buys 2 cakes and one cupcake. How much change does he get from a $10 bill?

69. **REASONING** List as many factors as you can for each of the following numbers: 12, 18, and 24.

70. **MULTISTEP** Mr. Wu taught 3 lessons each day for 6 days. Then he taught 2 lessons each day for 3 days. How many lessons did he teach?

71. **MULTISTEP** Ed arranged 5 rows of 6 pennies each. He had one more coin in his pocket. If he had a total of \$0.35, what coin was in his pocket?

Maintain Skills

Choose <, >, or = for each ●.

72. 67 ● 76 **73.** 25 ● 41

74. 71 ● 17 **75.** 25 ● 52

76. 33 ● 48 **77.** 94 ● 59

Find the sum or difference.

78. 39 + 14 = ■ **79.** 47 − 7 = ■

CRCT Test Prep

80. M3N2.c. Tameo bought some tape for \$1.39 and a sheet of stickers for \$1.53. How much did he spend in all? (p. 98)

A. \$0.14
B. \$1.81
C. \$2.92
D. \$3.51

Problem Solving Thinker's Corner

MULTIPLICATION CONCENTRATION
MATERIALS: 40 index cards
PLAYERS: 2

Using index cards, record all of the multiplication facts for 7's and 8's. Write a fact on one card and the product on another card.

Shuffle cards and place cards in 5 rows with numbers face down.

a. Player One turns over two cards and tries to match a multiplication sentence and a product.

b. If there is a match, Player One keeps the two cards. If there is no match, the cards are turned face down again.

c. Players take turns turning over cards. When all of the pairs have been matched, the player with the greater number of cards wins.

Extra Practice

Set A (pp. 162–163)

Find each product.

1. $5 \times 6 = \blacksquare$ **2.** $6 \times 2 = \blacksquare$ **3.** $0 \times 6 = \blacksquare$ **4.** $6 \times 7 = \blacksquare$

5. $6 \times 4 = \blacksquare$ **6.** $6 \times 3 = \blacksquare$ **7.** $\blacksquare = 8 \times 6$ **8.** $4 \times 7 = \blacksquare$

9. $8 \times 2 = \blacksquare$ **10.** $\blacksquare = 6 \times 6$ **11.** $6 \times 1 = \blacksquare$ **12.** $6 \times 9 = \blacksquare$

Complete.

13. $\blacksquare \times 4 = 16$ **14.** $\blacksquare \times 5 = 35$ **15.** $2 \times \blacksquare = 8$ **16.** $8 \times \blacksquare = 24$

Set B (pp. 164–165)

Find each product.

1. $7 \times 8 = \blacksquare$ **2.** $8 \times 0 = \blacksquare$ **3.** $8 \times 3 = \blacksquare$ **4.** $6 \times 8 = \blacksquare$

5. $\blacksquare = 8 \times 4$ **6.** $\blacksquare = 2 \times 5$ **7.** $8 \times 1 = \blacksquare$ **8.** $8 \times 8 = \blacksquare$

9. $8 \times 2 = \blacksquare$ **10.** $5 \times 8 = \blacksquare$ **11.** $2 \times 2 = \blacksquare$ **12.** $8 \times 9 = \blacksquare$

13. Dolores has 8 bags of 4 apples. Ruth has 3 bags of 8 apples. How many more apples does Dolores have?

Set C (pp. 168–169)

Find each product.

1. $1 \times 7 = \blacksquare$ **2.** $\blacksquare = 7 \times 5$ **3.** $6 \times 7 = \blacksquare$ **4.** $3 \times 7 = \blacksquare$

5. $2 \times 7 = \blacksquare$ **6.** $3 \times 3 = \blacksquare$ **7.** $7 \times 7 = \blacksquare$ **8.** $4 \times 7 = \blacksquare$

9. $8 \times 1 = \blacksquare$ **10.** $0 \times 7 = \blacksquare$ **11.** $\blacksquare = 7 \times 8$ **12.** $9 \times 7 = \blacksquare$

13. Alex has 8 bags of rocks. Each bag has 7 rocks. Vera takes 3 bags. How many rocks does Alex have left?

Set D (pp. 170–173)

Find each product.

1. $8 \times 7 = \blacksquare$ **2.** $6 \times 7 = \blacksquare$ **3.** $\blacksquare = 6 \times 4$ **4.** $7 \times 3 = \blacksquare$

5. $9 \times 8 = \blacksquare$ **6.** $8 \times 6 = \blacksquare$ **7.** $7 \times 7 = \blacksquare$ **8.** $3 \times 5 = \blacksquare$

9. $9 \times 7 = \blacksquare$ **10.** $\blacksquare = 6 \times 5$ **11.** $8 \times 8 = \blacksquare$ **12.** $9 \times 6 = \blacksquare$

13. List the factors for 16.

Review/Test

CHECK CONCEPTS

Name a way to break apart each array. Then write the product. (pp. 162–163, 168–169)

1. 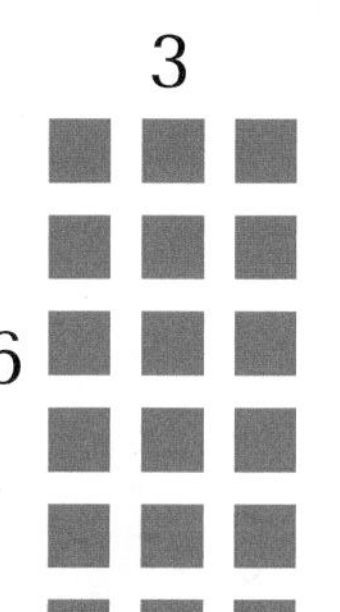

2. 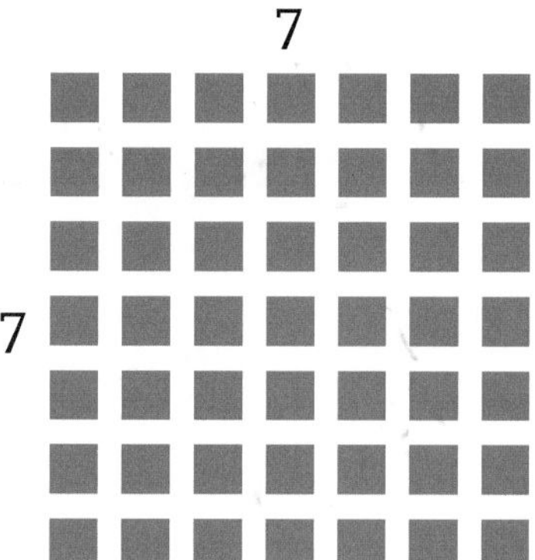

3. 

CHECK SKILLS

Find each product. (pp. 162–163, 164–165, 168–169, 170–172)

4. $6 \times 7 = \blacksquare$ **5.** $\blacksquare = 8 \times 7$ **6.** $4 \times 6 = \blacksquare$ **7.** $9 \times 7 = \blacksquare$

8. $\blacksquare = 5 \times 8$ **9.** $6 \times 0 = \blacksquare$ **10.** $3 \times 8 = \blacksquare$ **11.** $5 \times 7 = \blacksquare$

12. $6 \times 6 = \blacksquare$ **13.** $8 \times 9 = \blacksquare$ **14.** $8 \times 6 = \blacksquare$ **15.** $6 \times 9 = \blacksquare$

16. $\begin{array}{r} 8 \\ \times 8 \\ \hline \end{array}$ **17.** $\begin{array}{r} 8 \\ \times 4 \\ \hline \end{array}$ **18.** $\begin{array}{r} 2 \\ \times 7 \\ \hline \end{array}$ **19.** $\begin{array}{r} 7 \\ \times 3 \\ \hline \end{array}$ **20.** $\begin{array}{r} 6 \\ \times 2 \\ \hline \end{array}$ **21.** $\begin{array}{r} 7 \\ \times 4 \\ \hline \end{array}$

CHECK PROBLEM SOLVING

Solve. (pp. 166–167)

For 22–25, use the bar graph.

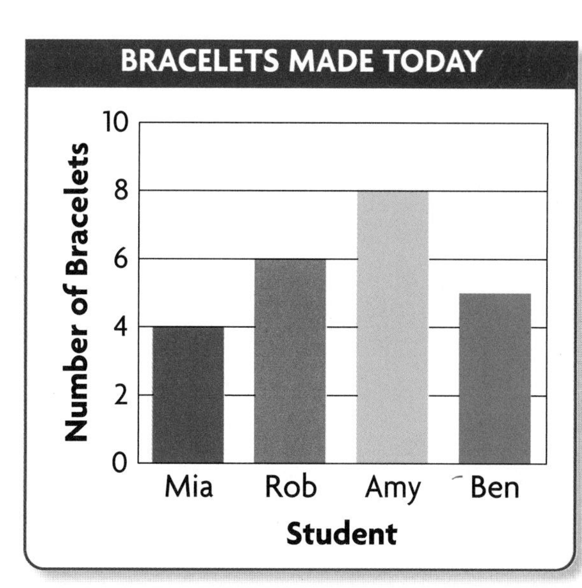

22. Who made the least number of bracelets?

23. How many bracelets will Ben make in 5 days if he makes the same number of bracelets each day?

24. How many more bracelets did Rob make than Mia?

25. How many bracelets were made in all?

Chapter CRCT Test Prep

NUMBERS AND OPERATIONS

1. M3N3.g. Desi bought 7 boxes of crayons. There are 8 crayons in each box. How many crayons did Desi buy?

A. 15

B. 28

C. 32

D. 56

2. M3N3.c. What multiplication fact does the array show?

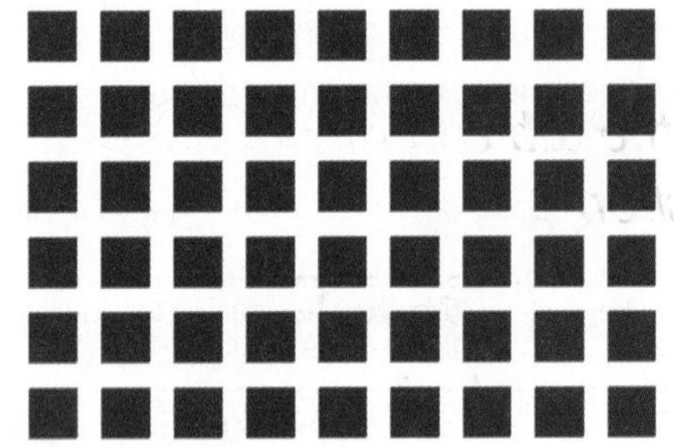

A. $6 \times 9 = 54$

B. $6 \times 6 = 36$

C. $5 \times 9 = 45$

D. $6 \times 8 = 48$

3. M3N3.b. Find the product.

$$\begin{array}{r} 8 \\ \times 4 \\ \hline \end{array}$$

A. 12

B. 24

C. 32

D. 36

DATA ANALYSIS

Use the graph below to answer question 4.

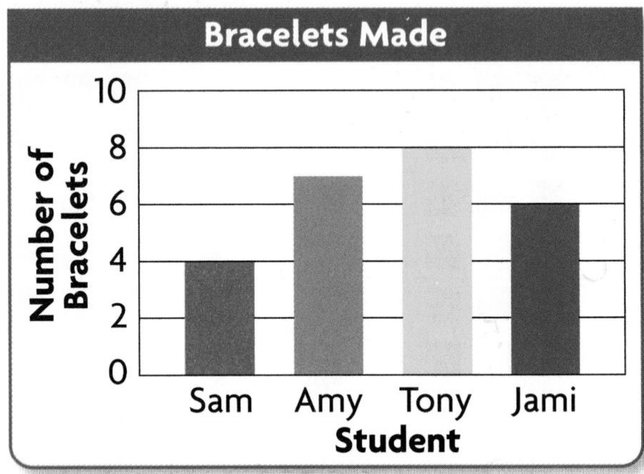

4. M3D1.a. The bar graph shows the number of bracelets that 4 students made. They used 7 inches of string to make each bracelet. How many inches of string did Amy use?

A. 7 in.

B. 42 in.

C. 49 in.

D. 58 in.

Cumulative CRCT Test Prep

MEASUREMENT

5. M3M1. Rob got to the park at 5:15 P.M. He stayed there for 45 minutes. At what time did Rob leave the park?

   A. 5:30 P.M.

   B. 5:45 P.M.

   C. 6:00 P.M.

   D. 6:15 P.M.

6. M3M1. Mila started getting ready for school at 7:25. It took her a half hour to get ready. At what time was Mila ready to go to school?

   A. 7:25

   B. 7:40

   C. 7:55

   D. 8:00

7. M3M1. Meghann started watching a movie at 3:30 P.M. The movie was 2 hours long. At what time did the movie end?

   A. 4:30 P.M.

   B. 4:45 P.M.

   C. 5:15 P.M.

   D. 5:30 P.M.

ALGEBRA

8. M3A1.a. Jon made the number pattern below. Then he covered up one of the numbers so his classmates could guess the number. What is the missing number in Jon's pattern?

   115, 125, 135, □, 155, 165

   A. 130

   B. 145

   C. 185

   D. 205

Use the table below to answer question 9.

Multiply by 7.	
1	7
3	21
5	35
7	□
9	63

9. M3A1.c. Which number belongs in the □?

   A. 49

   B. 47

   C. 45

   D. 42

CHAPTER 10

Multiplication Facts and Patterns

FAST FACT • SOCIAL STUDIES
Dogsled teams were used to deliver mail in places such as Michigan, Minnesota, Wisconsin, and Alaska. Large teams of dogs could pull 400 to 500 pounds of mail.

INVESTIGATION A full-grown Samoyed sled dog weighs about 50 pounds. A team of 10 Samoyeds weighs about 500 pounds. The pictograph shows the weights of different newborn puppies. What would 10 newborn Samoyed puppies weigh? Find how much 10 newborn puppies would weigh for each of the other types of puppies shown in the pictograph.

Using Data

WEIGHT OF A NEWBORN PUPPY

Siberian Husky	🐶🐶🐶🐶🐶🐶
Alaskan Malamute	🐶🐶🐶🐶🐶🐶🐶🐶
American Eskimo	🐶🐶🐶🐶🐶
Samoyed	🐶🐶🐶🐶🐶

Key: Each 🐶 = 2 ounces.

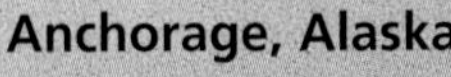
Anchorage, Alaska

CHECK WHAT YOU KNOW

Use this page to help you review and remember important skills needed for Chapter 10.

SKIP-COUNT BY TENS

Continue the pattern.

1. 10, 20, 30, 40, ■, ■
2. 30, 40, 50, 60, 70, ■, ■

Skip-count by tens to find the missing numbers.

3. 3, 13, 23, ■, ■, 53, ■, ■, 83, ■
4. 7, 17, 27, ■, ■, 57, ■, 77, ■, ■
5. 5, 15, 25, ■, ■, 55, ■, ■, ■
6. 64, 54, 44, ■, ■, ■, ■

FIND MISSING FACTORS

Find the missing factor.

7. ■ × 4 = 32
8. 5 × ■ = 35
9. ■ × 6 = 36
10. 2 × ■ = 18
11. 7 × ■ = 28
12. ■ × 8 = 16
13. 5 × ■ = 45
14. ■ × 4 = 36
15. ■ × 4 = 24
16. 6 × ■ = 54
17. 3 × ■ = 24
18. ■ × 8 = 64
19. 5 × ■ = 40
20. 9 × ■ = 9
21. ■ × 4 = 0
22. 7 × ■ = 56

VOCABULARY POWER

REVIEW

product [prä′dəkt] *noun*

A product in mathematics is the answer to a multiplication problem. Tell another meaning for *product* that you find in your social studies book.

PREVIEW

Associative Property
Identity Property
Zero Property
Distributive Property
multistep problem

www.harcourtschool.com/mathglossary

LESSON 1

Multiply with 9 and 10

M3N3.b. Know the multiplication facts with understanding and fluency to 10 × 10. *also* M3N1.b., M3P1.a., M3P1.b., M3P1.c.

Quick Review

1. $4 \times 8 = ■$
2. $7 \times 5 = ■$
3. $8 \times 0 = ■$
4. $3 \times 6 = ■$
5. $6 \times 7 = ■$

Learn

TIMBER! Beavers cut down trees with their large front teeth. If 5 beavers each cut down 10 trees, how many trees did they cut down in all?

$5 \times 10 = ■$

One Way You can skip-count by tens 5 times.

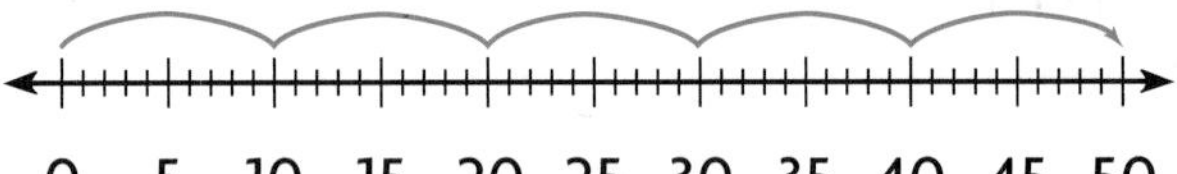

Think: 10, 20, 30, 40, 50

So, $5 \times 10 = 50$.

Another Way Use a pattern to multiply by 10.

The product of 1 and any number equals that number.

$0 \times 1 = 0$
$1 \times 1 = 1$
$2 \times 1 = 2$
$3 \times 1 = 3$
$4 \times 1 = 4$
$5 \times 1 = 5$
$6 \times 1 = 6$
$7 \times 1 = 7$
$8 \times 1 = 8$
$9 \times 1 = 9$

When you multiply a number by 10, that number "moves" to the tens place.

$0 \times 10 = 0$
$1 \times 10 = 10$
$2 \times 10 = 20$
$3 \times 10 = 30$
$4 \times 10 = 40$
$5 \times 10 = ■$
$6 \times 10 = 60$
$7 \times 10 = 70$
$8 \times 10 = 80$
$9 \times 10 = 90$

So, $5 \times 10 = 50$. The beavers cut down 50 trees in all.

▲ When beavers cut down trees, they eat the bark and use the branches to build homes in the water.

×	0	1	2	3	4	5	6	7	8	9	10
0	0	0	0	0	0	0	0	0	0	0	0
1	0	1	2	3	4	5	6	7	8	9	10
2	0	2	4	6	8	10	12	14	16	18	20
3	0	3	6	9	12	15	18	21	24	27	30
4	0	4	8	12	16	20	24	28	32	36	40
5	0	5	10	15	20	25	30	35	40	45	50
6	0	6	12	18	24	30	36	42	48	54	60
7	0	7	14	21	28	35	42	49	56	63	70
8	0	8	16	24	32	40	48	56	64	72	80
9	0	9	18	27	36	45	54	63	72	81	90
10	0	10	20	30	40	50	60	70	80	90	100

Reasoning

- How can you use skip-counting to find 6×10?

Multiply with 9

Lynn's class made 7 animal posters. The students drew 9 animals on each poster. How many animals did they draw in all?

$$7 \times 9 = ■$$

Lynn and Jeff use different ways to find 7×9.

Lynn

I'll think of the 10's fact first.

7 x 10 = 70

Next, I'll subtract the first factor, 7.

70 - 7 = 63

Since 70 - 7 = 63,
7 x 9 = 63.

Jeff

I'll use a pattern in the products of the 9's facts.

7 x 9 = ■

- The tens digit will be 1 less than the factor 7.
- The sum of the digits in the product will be 9.

So, 7 x 9 = 63.

$0 \times 9 = 0$
$1 \times 9 = 9$
$2 \times 9 = 18$
$3 \times 9 = 27$
$4 \times 9 = 36$
$5 \times 9 = 45$
$6 \times 9 = 54$
$7 \times 9 = ■$
$8 \times 9 = 72$
$9 \times 9 = 81$

So, Lynn's class drew 63 animals.

MATH IDEA You can use facts you already know or a pattern to find 9's facts.

Technology Link
More Practice:
Harcourt Mega Math
The Number Games,
Up, Up, and Array,
Level C

Check

1. **Explain** how to use a 10's fact to find 3×9.
2. **Explain** how to use a pattern to find 6×9.

Find the product.

3. $3 \times 10 = ■$
4. $10 \times 6 = ■$
5. $■ = 7 \times 9$
6. $1 \times 9 = ■$
7. $8 \times 9 = ■$
8. $■ = 9 \times 2$
9. $4 \times 10 = ■$
10. $2 \times 10 = ■$

Find the missing factor.

11. $■ \times 7 = 63$
12. $5 \times ■ = 30$
13. $10 \times ■ = 60$
14. $■ \times 6 = 48$
15. $■ \times 9 = 90$
16. $6 \times ■ = 24$
17. $■ \times 8 = 64$
18. $9 \times ■ = 45$

LESSON CONTINUES

Practice and Problem Solving

Extra Practice, page 192, Set A

Find the product.

19. ■ $= 10 \times 4$ **20.** $4 \times 8 =$ ■ **21.** $9 \times 8 =$ ■ **22.** ■ $= 8 \times 6$

23. $9 \times 9 =$ ■ **24.** ■ $= 7 \times 10$ **25.** $10 \times 10 =$ ■ **26.** $2 \times 8 =$ ■

27. $\begin{array}{r} 10 \\ \times\ 8 \\ \hline \end{array}$ **28.** $\begin{array}{r} 9 \\ \times 4 \\ \hline \end{array}$ **29.** $\begin{array}{r} 5 \\ \times 10 \\ \hline \end{array}$ **30.** $\begin{array}{r} 8 \\ \times 8 \\ \hline \end{array}$ **31.** $\begin{array}{r} 9 \\ \times 3 \\ \hline \end{array}$ **32.** $\begin{array}{r} 7 \\ \times 8 \\ \hline \end{array}$

33. $\begin{array}{r} 4 \\ \times 3 \\ \hline \end{array}$ **34.** $\begin{array}{r} 10 \\ \times\ 1 \\ \hline \end{array}$ **35.** $\begin{array}{r} 8 \\ \times 3 \\ \hline \end{array}$ **36.** $\begin{array}{r} 6 \\ \times 9 \\ \hline \end{array}$ **37.** $\begin{array}{r} 9 \\ \times 7 \\ \hline \end{array}$ **38.** $\begin{array}{r} 10 \\ \times\ 6 \\ \hline \end{array}$

Find the missing factor.

39. ■ $\times 6 = 0$ **40.** $10 \times$ ■ $= 20$ **41.** ■ $\times 7 = 28$

42. $5 \times$ ■ $= 4 \times 10$ **43.** ■ $\times 2 = 12 + 8$ **44.** $6 \times 6 =$ ■ $\times 4$

Copy and complete each table.

	Multiply by 10.	
45.	6	■
46.	8	■

	Multiply by 8.	
47.	5	■
48.	7	■

	Multiply by 9.	
49.	8	■
50.	9	■

Compare. Write <, >, or = for each ●.

51. 10×6 ● $75 - 15$ **52.** 9×9 ● 10×8 **53.** 7×9 ● 10×7

54. 8×9 ● 9×8 **55.** $16 + 40$ ● 9×6 **56.** 10×10 ● $50 + 50$

57. ***FAST FACT*** • SOCIAL STUDIES The beaver was adopted as the New York state animal in 1975. How many years ago was that?

58. **MULTISTEP** Malcolm cut 3 pies into 10 pieces each and 2 pies into 8 pieces each. How many pieces of pie did he have in all?

59. **What's the Error?** Describe Mike's error. Then solve the problem correctly.

Mike

9 x 4 = ■

Think: 10 x 4 = 40
40 - 9 = 31
So, 9 x 4 = 31.

60. **MULTISTEP** Emiko had 4 sheets with 10 animal stickers on each. After she gave some stickers away, she had 37 left. How many stickers did she give away?

Maintain Skills

Compare. Write <, >, or = for each ●.

61. 28 ● 52 **62.** 43 ● 36

63. 82 ● 29 **64.** 90 ● 66

Find each sum or difference.

65. $164 + 288$ **66.** $534 - 261$ **67.** $191 + 386$

68. $924 - 639$ **69.** $566 + 241$ **70.** $443 - 325$

CRCT Test Prep

71. M3M1. Meg went to the store at 11:15 A.M. She got home 2 hours later. At what time did she get home? (pp. 112)

A. 9:15 A.M. C. 1:15 P.M.
B. 12:15 P.M. D. 2:15 P.M.

72. M3N3.b. Jesse has 3 rows of 9 stamps. Lou has 2 rows of 6 stamps. How many stamps do they have in all? (p. 170)

A. 27 C. 56
B. 39 D. 60

Problem Solving LINKUP . . . to Reading

STRATEGY • CLASSIFY AND CATEGORIZE When you *classify* information, you group similar information. When you *categorize,* you name the groups that you have classified.

MATERIALS: hundred charts, colored pencils

Shade the multiples of 2, 3, 4, 5, 6, and 7 on your charts.

1	2	3	4	5	6	7	8	9	10
11	12	13	14	15	16	17	18	19	20
21	22	23	24	25	26	27	28	29	30
31	32	33	34	35	36	37	38	39	40
41	42	43	44	45	46	47	48	49	50
51	52	53	54	55	56	57	58	59	60
61	62	63	64	65	66	67	68	69	70
71	72	73	74	75	76	77	78	79	80
81	82	83	84	85	86	87	88	89	90
91	92	93	94	95	96	97	98	99	100

For 1–6, use your hundred charts. Tell if the statement is *true* or *false*. If the statement is false, tell why.

1. Even numbers have even multiples.
2. Odd numbers have odd and even multiples.
3. The product of any number and an odd number is an odd number.
4. The product of any number and an even number is an even number.
5. The product of any number and 6 can be even or odd.
6. The product of 9 and 6 is an even number.

LESSON 2

Algebra: Find a Rule

M3A1.a. Describe and extend numeric and geometric patterns. *also* M3P2.a., M3P2.b., M3P2.c., M3P2.d., M3P3.a., M3P3.b., M3P3.c., M3P3.d.

Quick Review

1. $5 \times 4 = ■$
2. $7 \times 5 = ■$
3. $6 \times 8 = ■$
4. $7 \times 2 = ■$
5. $8 \times 6 = ■$

Learn

CLIP CLOP Horses wear a horseshoe on each of their 4 hooves. How many horseshoes are needed for 6 horses?

Think: 1 horse needs 4 horseshoes.
2 horses need 8 horseshoes.
3 horses need 12 horseshoes, and so on.

Look for a pattern. Write a rule.

Horses	1	2	3	4	5	6
Horseshoes	4	8	12	16	20	■

Pattern: The number of horseshoes equals the number of horses times 4.

Rule: Multiply the number of horses by 4.

Since $6 \times 4 = 24$, then 24 horseshoes are needed for 6 horses.

MATH IDEA You can write a rule to describe a number pattern in a table.

Technology Link
More Practice: Harcourt Mega Math Ice Station Exploration, *Arctic Algebra*, Level D

Example

Write a rule to find the cost of the bread.

Loaves of bread	1	2	4	5	7	9
Cost	\$3	\$6	\$12	\$15	\$21	\$27

Rule: Multiply the number of loaves of bread by \$3.

- How can you use the rule to find the cost of 3 loaves of bread?

Check

1. **Explain** how you could use a rule to find the number of horseshoes on 8 horses.

2. Write a rule for the table. Then copy and complete the table.

Nickels	1	2	3	4	5	6	7	8	9	10
Pennies	5	10	15	■	■	■	■	■	■	■

Practice and Problem Solving

Extra Practice, page 192, Set B

Write a rule for each table. Then copy and complete the table.

3.

Spiders	1	2	3	4	5	6
Legs	8	16	24	■	■	■

4.

Toy cars	1	2	3	4	5	6
Cost	$2	$4	$6	■	■	■

5.

Tables	3	4	5	7	8	9
Legs	12	16	20	■	■	■

6.

Guitars	2	3	5	6	7	8
Strings	12	18	30	■	■	■

For 7–8, use the table below.

Dimes	1	2	3	4	5	6	7	8	9	10
Nickels	2	4	6	■	■	■	■	■	■	■

7. Write a rule to find the number of nickels. Copy and complete the table.

8. **REASONING** How many dimes can you trade for 18 nickels? How many nickels can you trade for 8 dimes?

9. **REASONING** Yogurt comes in packages of 6 cups. How many packages are needed to serve 23 students each a cup of yogurt?

10. Each pudding pack costs $4. How much do 5 packs cost? Make a table and write a rule to find your answer.

Maintain Skills

Write the time.

11. 

12. 

CRCT Test Prep

13. M3N2.c. Nieta had 314 stickers. She gave 54 away and collected 32 more. How many does she have now? (p. 74)

A. 400
B. 292
C. 260
D. 228

LESSON 3

Algebra: Multiply with 3 Factors

M3N3.e. Apply the identity, commutative, and associative properties of multiplication and verify the results. *also* **M3A1.c., M3P3.a., M3P3.b., M3P3.c., M3P3.d.**

Quick Review

1. $2 \times 2 = ■$
2. $4 \times 7 = ■$
3. $3 \times 2 = ■$
4. $6 \times 5 = ■$
5. $9 \times 4 = ■$

VOCABULARY

Associative Property of Multiplication

Learn

PRACTICE, PRACTICE . . . Julia has been taking horseback riding lessons for 3 months. At each lesson she rides for 2 hours. If she has 4 lessons each month, for how many hours has she ridden?

$$3 \times 2 \times 4 = ■$$

MATH IDEA The **Associative Property of Multiplication**, or Grouping Property, states that when the grouping of factors is changed, the product remains the same.

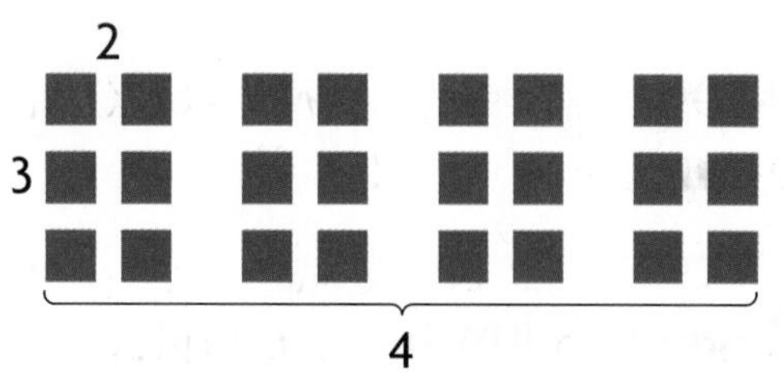

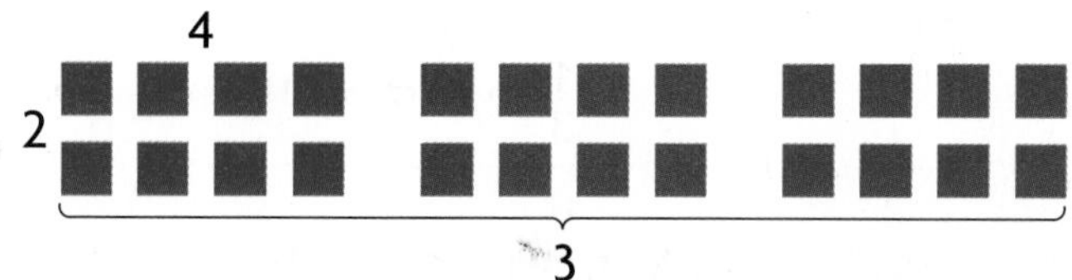

$(3 \times 2) \times 4 = ■$

↓

$6 \quad \times 4 = 24$

$3 \times (2 \times 4) = ■$

↓

$3 \times \quad 8 \quad = 24$

Multiply the numbers in parentheses ( ) first.

So, Julia has ridden for 24 hours.

Check

1. **Tell** which numbers you would multiply first to find $7 \times 2 \times 3$ mentally.

Find each product.

2. $(2 \times 4) \times 1 = ■$
3. $2 \times (1 \times 3) = ■$
4. $2 \times (4 \times 2) = ■$
5. $(3 \times 3) \times 2 = ■$

Practice and Problem Solving

Extra Practice, page 192, Set C

Find each product.

6. $(4 \times 2) \times 5 = ■$ **7.** $(3 \times 3) \times 6 = ■$ **8.** $8 \times (2 \times 2) = ■$

9. $(6 \times 1) \times 2 = ■$ **10.** $■ = 5 \times (7 \times 1)$ **11.** $■ = 3 \times (3 \times 3)$

12. $■ = (2 \times 3) \times 5$ **13.** $■ = (5 \times 2) \times 7$ **14.** $(4 \times 2) \times 4 = ■$

Use parentheses. Find the product.

15. $6 \times 1 \times 8 = ■$ **16.** $9 \times 2 \times 1 = ■$ **17.** $■ = 7 \times 4 \times 2$

18. $■ = 9 \times 8 \times 0$ **19.** $6 \times 5 \times 2 = ■$ **20.** $4 \times 2 \times 9 = ■$

Find the missing factor.

21. $(1 \times ■) \times 8 = 64$ **22.** $(2 \times 4) \times ■ = 24$ **23.** $42 = 7 \times (■ \times 2)$

24. $2 \times 4 \times ■ = 8$ **25.** $2 \times 4 \times ■ = 40$ **26.** $14 = ■ \times 2 \times 7$

27. Show that $(6 \times 2) \times 1$ is the same as $6 \times (2 \times 1)$.

28. **REASONING** Explain why 18×2 is the same as $9 \times (2 \times 2)$.

29. Ross made 2 cakes for each of 3 friends. In each cake he used 3 apples. How many apples did he use?

30. **ALGEBRA** Darla had 2 singing lessons a month for 2 months. She learned the same number of songs at each lesson. She learned 12 songs in all. How many songs did she learn at each lesson?

31. **Vocabulary Power** One meaning for the word *property* is "any of the special features that belong to something." Use the numbers 2, 3, and 4 to explain the Associative Property of Multiplication.

Maintain Skills

32. Write the amount.

CRCT Test Prep

33. M3N3.g Irene bought 100 apples. She made 7 pies. Each pie had 8 apples in it. How many apples were left over? (p. 164)

A. 56 B. 44 C. 34 D. 16

LESSON 4

Algebra: Multiplication Properties

M3N3.e. Apply the identity, commutative, and associative properties of multiplication and verify the results. *also* M3N3.c., M3A1.c., M3P2.a., M3P2.b., M3P2.c., M3P2.d., M3P3., M3P4.a., M3P4.b.

Quick Review

1. 6 × 3
2. 9 × 1
3. 2 × 8
4. 4 × 4
5. 3 × 5

VOCABULARY

Identity Property
Zero Property
Distributive Property

Learn

You can use multiplication properties to help you find products.

Identity Property The product of 1 and any number equals that number.

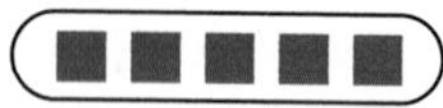

1 × 5 = 5

Zero Property The product of 0 and any number equals 0.

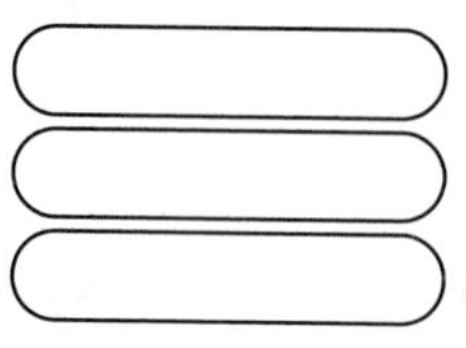

3 × 0 = 0

Commutative Property You can multiply two factors in any order and get the same product.

2 × 4 = 8 4 × 2 = 8

Associative Property You can group factors in different ways and get the same product.

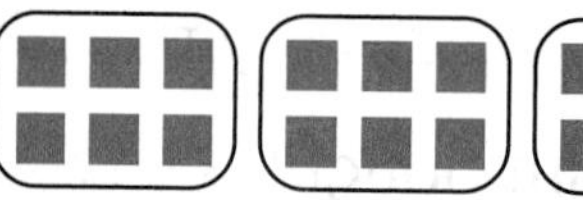

(2 × 3) × 3 = ■
6 × 3 = 18

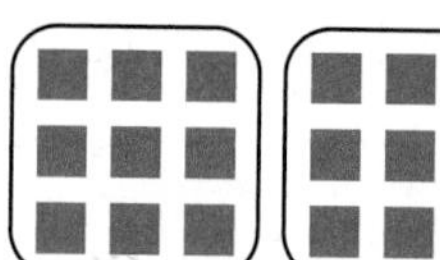

2 × (3 × 3) = ■
2 × 9 = 18

Distributive Property You can think of one factor as the sum of two addends. Then multiply each addend by the other factor and add the products.

Find 5 × 7.

Think: 5 × 7 = 5 × (3 + 4)
= (5 × 3) + (5 × 4)
= 15 + 20

So, 5 × 7 = 35.

Make an array.

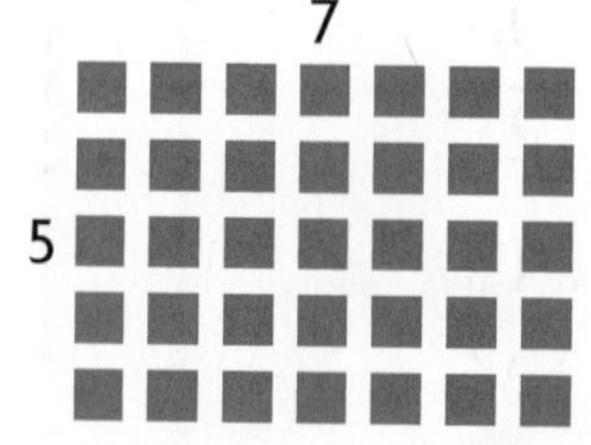

5 × 7 = ■

Break the array into two smaller arrays.

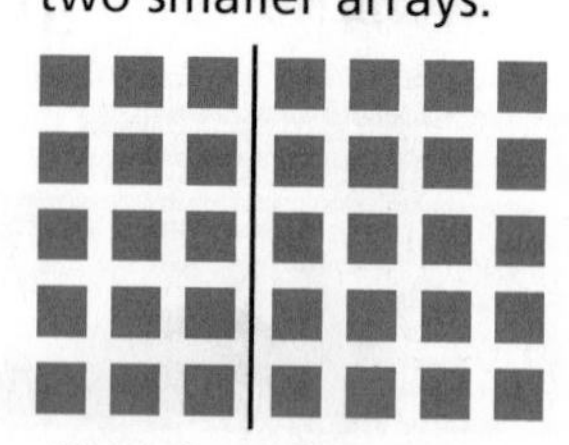

5 × 3 + 5 × 4

Check

1. **Explain** how the Commutative Property helps you find 8×5 when you know that $5 \times 8 = 40$.

Find the product. Tell which property you used to help you.

2. 9×0
3. 1×7
4. 3×8
5. 6×9
6. $(2 \times 3) \times 5$
7. $(4 \times 4) \times 2$
8. $3 \times (2 \times 7)$
9. $2 \times (3 \times 8)$

Practice and Problem Solving

Extra Practice, page 192, Set D

Find the product. Tell which property you used to help you.

10. 0×6
11. 9×4
12. 8×1
13. 8×9
14. 5×9
15. 6×6
16. 7×4
17. 8×8
18. $(4 \times 2) \times 3$
19. $2 \times (4 \times 5)$
20. $5 \times (2 \times 3)$
21. $(3 \times 3) \times 9$

Write the missing number for each ■.

22. $6 \times 7 =$ ■ $\times 6$
23. $2 \times (3 \times 5) = ($■ $\times 3) \times 5$
24. $5 \times$ ■ $= 1 \times 5$
25. $9 \times 5 =$ ■ $\times 9$
26. $3 \times 5 = (3 \times$ ■$) + (3 \times 2)$
27. ■ $\times 7 = 7 \times 4$
28. **Write About It** Explain how you can use the Distributive Property to find 7×8. Draw an array to show your answer.
29. **REASONING** On Tuesday Kim bought 4 shirts for $8 each. On Friday she bought more of the same shirts. In the two days, she spent $48. How many shirts did she buy on Friday? Explain.

Maintain Skills

Find the sum or difference.

30. $583 + 258$
31. $208 + 257$
32. $826 - 419$
33. $648 - 452$

CRCT Test Prep

34. M3M1. Gordon leaves his house at 7:45 A.M. School starts at 8:15 A.M. How much time does Gordon have to get to school? (p. 112)

A. 15 min
B. 20 min
C. 25 min
D. 30 min

LESSON 5

Problem Solving Skill
Multistep Problems

M3N3.g. Solve problems requiring multiplication. *also* M3P1.a., M3P1.b., M3P1.c., M3P1.d., M3P3.a., M3P3.b., M3P3.c., M3P3.d.

UNDERSTAND | PLAN | SOLVE | CHECK

Quick Review

1. $(2 \times 3) \times 4 = \blacksquare$
2. $(5 \times 1) \times 7 = \blacksquare$
3. $4 + 16 + 5 = \blacksquare$
4. $7 + 8 + 2 = \blacksquare$
5. $3 \times (4 \times 2) = \blacksquare$

VOCABULARY
multistep problem

KNOW THE SCORE Jeff's football team scored 6 points for a touchdown but missed the extra point. Then they scored 3 points for each of 4 field goals. How many points did they score in all?

To find how many points in all, you must solve a **multistep problem**, or a problem with more than one step.

Example

STEP 1

Find how many points were scored by touchdowns.	1 touchdown was scored. Each touchdown = 6 points. $1 \times 6 = 6$ 6 points were scored in touchdowns.

STEP 2

Find how many points were scored by field goals.	4 field goals were scored. Each field goal = 3 points. $4 \times 3 = 12$ 12 points were scored in field goals.

STEP 3

Find how many points were scored in all.	Add the points scored by touchdowns and field goals. $6 + 12 = 18$ So, 18 points were scored in all.

Talk About It

- Does it matter if you find the points scored in touchdowns first or the points scored in field goals first? Explain.

Problem Solving Practice

Solve.

1. To raise money for the school, Lucia sold 9 boxes of cards. Ginger sold 7 boxes. Each box cost $3. How much money did they raise in all?

2. The Wilsons drove 598 miles in 3 days. They drove 230 miles the first day and 175 miles the second day. How far did they go the third day?

Kelsey bought 3 boxes of tacos. Each box had 6 tacos. Then she gave 4 tacos away.

3. Which shows the first step you take to find how many tacos Kelsey had left?
   A $3 + 6 = 9$
   B $6 - 3 = 3$
   C $3 \times 6 = 18$
   D $3 \times 4 = 12$

4. How many tacos did Kelsey have left?
   F 12
   G 14
   H 18
   J 22

Mixed Applications

USE DATA For 5–7, use the graph.

5. **MULTISTEP** How many students did NOT vote for hot dogs?

6. **MULTISTEP** How many students voted in all?

7. **Write a problem** about the graph. Exchange with a partner and solve.

8. **What's the Question?** Rob spent $30 for 4 tickets. He bought 3 children's tickets for $7 each and 1 adult ticket. The answer is $9.

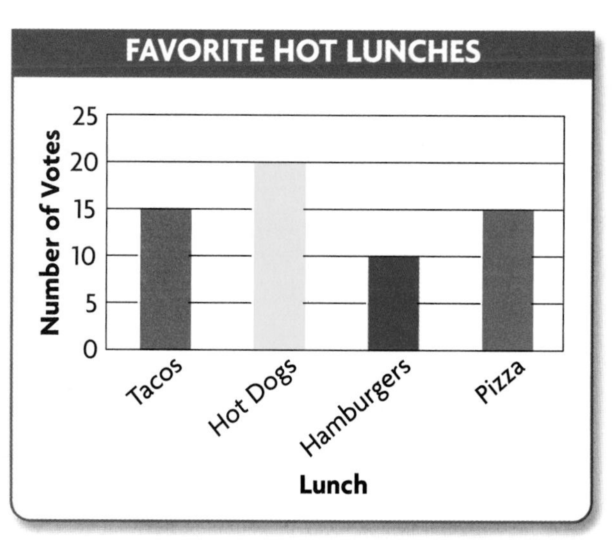

Extra Practice

Set A (pp. 180–183)

Find the product.

1. $9 \times 7 = ■$
2. $6 \times 9 = ■$
3. $6 \times 10 = ■$
4. $10 \times 3 = ■$
5. $3 \times 9 = ■$
6. $8 \times 9 = ■$
7. $10 \times 7 = ■$
8. $9 \times 5 = ■$

Find the missing factor.

9. $■ \times 9 = 36$
10. $90 = 9 \times ■$
11. $7 \times ■ = 56$
12. $21 = ■ \times 7$

Set B (pp. 184–185)

Write a rule for each table. Then copy and complete the table.

1.

Packs	1	2	3	4	5	6
Cards	4	8	12	■	■	■

2.

Bags	1	2	3	4	5	6
Oranges	6	12	18	■	■	■

3.

Cans	1	2	3	4	5	6
Tennis Balls	3	6	9	■	■	■

4.

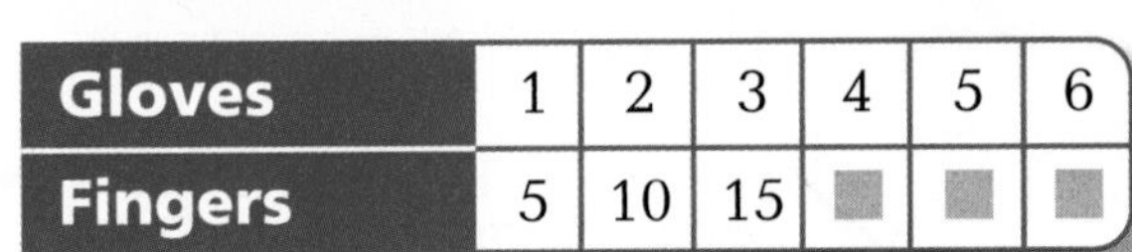

Gloves	1	2	3	4	5	6
Fingers	5	10	15	■	■	■

Set C (pp. 186–187)

Find each product.

1. $(4 \times 1) \times 3 = ■$
2. $(3 \times 2) \times 3 = ■$
3. $(5 \times 1) \times 5 = ■$
4. $4 \times (2 \times 2) = ■$
5. $10 \times (3 \times 3) = ■$
6. $(6 \times 1) \times 7 = ■$

Find the missing factor.

7. $(4 \times ■) \times 1 = 16$
8. $5 \times (2 \times ■) = 20$
9. $■ \times (7 \times 1) = 49$

Set D (pp. 188–189)

Find the product. Tell which property you used to help you.

1. 0×7
2. 9×2
3. 1×8
4. 3×8
5. 5×9
6. 5×0
7. 4×8
8. 9×9
9. $(6 \times 2) \times 2$
10. $(4 \times 5) \times 2$
11. $2 \times (3 \times 5)$
12. $(3 \times 8) \times 3$

Review/Test

CHECK VOCABULARY AND CONCEPTS

Choose the best term from the box.

1. A problem with more than one step is a _?_. (p. 190)
2. The _?_ of Multiplication states that when the grouping of factors is changed, the product remains the same. (p. 186)

Vocabulary
- factor
- Associative Property
- multistep problem

CHECK SKILLS

Find the product. (pp. 180–183)

3. $9 \times 7 = ■$
4. $■ = 9 \times 4$
5. $6 \times 9 = ■$
6. $8 \times 9 = ■$
7. $10 \times 5 = ■$
8. $3 \times 10 = ■$
9. $■ = 9 \times 9$
10. $10 \times 7 = ■$

Write a rule for the table. Then copy and complete the table. (pp. 184–185)

11.

Insects	1	2	3	4	5	6	7
Legs	6	12	18	■	■	■	■

Find each product. (pp. 186–187)

12. $(3 \times 1) \times 6 = ■$
13. $■ = 5 \times (2 \times 2)$
14. $(3 \times 3) \times 9 = ■$
15. $4 \times (2 \times 5) = ■$
16. $■ = (2 \times 4) \times 8$
17. $9 \times (4 \times 1) = ■$

Find the product. Tell which property you used to help you. (pp. 188–189)

18. 1×6
19. 2×9
20. 8×0
21. 7×8
22. 4×6
23. 5×9

CHECK PROBLEM SOLVING

Solve. (pp. 190–191)

24. In March, Mr. Holly's class raised \$176. In April, the students raised \$209. How much do they still need in order to raise \$500?

25. Joe bought 5 guppies for \$3 each and 8 goldfish for \$2 each. How much did he spend?

Chapter CRCT Test Prep

NUMBERS AND OPERATIONS

1. M3N3.d. Mrs. Walsh bought 6 bags of oranges. Each bag contains 10 oranges. How many oranges did she buy?

A. 4

B. 16

C. 30

D. 60

2. M3N3.e. Which number should Karen write to make the equation true?

$$(8 \times \square) \times 1 = 8 \times (9 \times 1)$$

A. 4

B. 7

C. 8

D. 9

3. M3N3.b. Find the product.

$$\begin{array}{r} 9 \\ \times 3 \\ \hline \end{array}$$

A. 12

B. 18

C. 27

D. 36

ALGEBRA

4. M3A1.a. What rule was used to make this table?

Squares	1	2	3	4
Sides	4	8	12	16

A. Add 8 to the number of squares.

B. Multiply the number of squares by 2.

C. Multiply the number of squares by 4.

D. Multiply the number of squares by 8.

5. M3A1.c. Which number belongs in the □ to make the number sentence true?

$$6 \times 4 = \square \times 6$$

A. 1

B. 4

C. 6

D. 24

6. M3A1.c. What is the missing factor?

$$3 \times \square = 0$$

A. 0

B. 1

C. 3

D. 10

Cumulative CRCT Test Prep

ALGEBRA

7. M3A1.c. Which number belongs in the □ to make the number sentence true?

$$\square + 14 = 53$$

A. 39

B. 49

C. 57

D. 67

8. M3A1.c. Sheila bought 8 boxes of cookies. Each box has the same number of cookies. She has 64 cookies in all. Which number sentence can Sheila use to find the number of cookies in each box?

A. $64 + 8 = \square$

B. $\square + 64 = 8$

C. $8 \times \square = 64$

D. $64 - \square = 8$

9. M3A1.c. Write the missing addend.

$$210 + \square + 3 = 243$$

A. 30

B. 40

C. 43

D. 50

DATA ANALYSIS

Use the graph below to answer question 10.

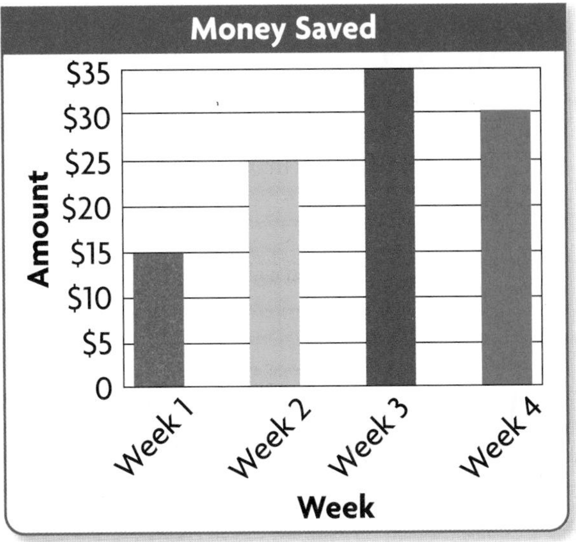

10. M3D1.b. Leo made this bar graph to show how much money he saved. How much more money did Leo save during Week 3 than he saved in Week 1?

A. \$5

B. \$10

C. \$20

D. \$35

GPS/CRCT Vocabulary

ELA3R2 The student acquires and uses grade-level words to communicate effectively. *also* **ELA3R3.b., ELA3R3.h., ELA3R3.r.**

VOCABULARY

- **multiply (×)**
- **factors**
- **multiple**
- **array**
- **product**
- **Commutative Property**
- **Associative Property**
- **Identity Property**
- **Zero Property**
- **Distributive Property**
- **multistep problem**

VOCABULARY MATCH

MATERIALS *For each pair* 20 vocabulary cards, definition cards

- Shuffle the vocabulary cards and the definition cards together.
- Deal 4 cards to each player. Place the rest of the cards face down in a pile on the table.
- The players should match terms with their definitions to make pairs from their cards and set them aside.
- Take turns drawing a card from the pile. If it matches a card in your hand, keep it and set the pair aside. If not, return it to the bottom of the pile.

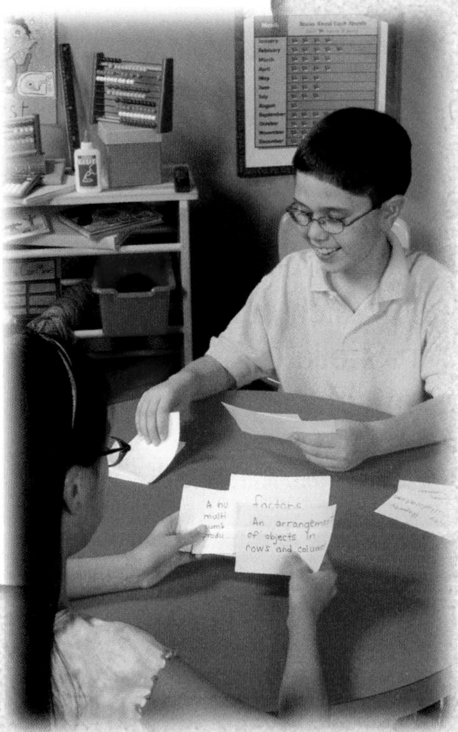

MATH WORD WORK

MATERIALS *For each student* Unit 3 *Math Word Work* puzzle

- Use the five properties of multiplication to fill in the boxes.

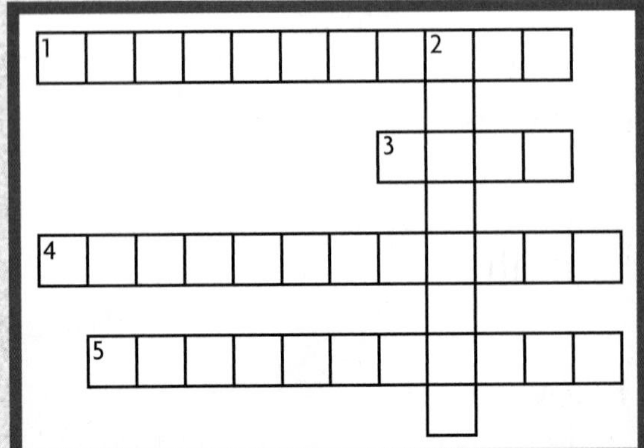

WHAT'S IN THE BOX?

MATERIALS *For each pair* Unit 3 *What's in the Box?* puzzle

- With a partner, use the clues and the terms in the Vocabulary box on page 196 to help you fill in the blanks on your sheet.
- The letters in the boxes will spell a city in Georgia.

1. A _?_ of 3 is any product that has 3 as a factor.
2. The numbers you multiply together to get a product are called _?_.
3. In $3 \times 2 = 6$, 6 is called the _?_.
4. $6 \times 0 = 0$ is an example of the _?_ **Property**.
5. The _?_ **Property** says the product of 1 and any number equals that number.

1.	☐ _ _ _ _ _ _ _ _
2.	_ ☐ _ _ _ _ _ _
3.	_ _ _ _ _ _ ☐ _
4.	_ _ _ ☐
5.	_ _ _ ☐ _ _ _ _

PROPERTY POPCORN

MATERIALS *For each pair* 6 small bowls, 2 handfuls of popcorn

- Place 4 pieces of popcorn in each bowl to represent 6×4.
- Separate the bowls into 2 groups. Write down the multiplication expressions you need to find the total number of pieces of popcorn in each group.
- Use what you know about the Distributive Property to fill in the missing numbers below.

$$6 \times 4 = (\blacksquare \times 4) + (\blacksquare \times 4)$$

- See how many ways you can "distribute" the bowls of popcorn.
- After you have shown all the ways, enjoy your popcorn!

M3N3.g. Solve problems requiring multiplication. *also* **M3N2.c., M3D1., M3P2.a., M3P2.b., M3P2.c., M3P2.d., M3P5.c.**

S3CS2.a. Add, subtract, multiply, and divide whole numbers mentally, on paper, and with a calculator.

Task A

ART

The High Museum of Art in Atlanta, Georgia, displays several different types of art, such as African, American, European, folk, and modern. The table to the right shows the different admission prices for the museum.

Ticket Prices	
Type of ticket	**Price**
Adult	\$10
Senior	\$8
Child	\$6

a. Suppose you had \$40. How many children, adults, and seniors could you buy tickets for? Explain.

b. Groups of 10 or more can buy tickets for \$8 each. Katie's family has 4 adults, 3 children, and 3 seniors. Is it less expensive for Katie's family to buy a group of 10 tickets? Explain how you found your answer.

Task B

RAIN, RAIN, RAIN!

Atlanta, Georgia, receives lots of rain! The pictograph shows the average rainfall each year in several cities.

Average Rain Each Year	
Los Angeles, CA	💧💧💧
Atlanta, GA	💧💧💧💧💧💧💧💧💧💧
Honolulu, HI	💧💧💧💧💧
Baltimore, MD	💧💧💧💧💧💧💧💧
Omaha, NE	💧💧💧💧💧💧

Key: Each 💧 = 5 inches.

a. How many inches of rainfall does Atlanta receive on average each year?

b. Richmond, Virginia receives an average of 45 inches of rain each year. How many 💧 should you use to show Richmond on the pictograph? Explain.

Maintain/Preview

Maintain

Copy and complete.

1\.

■ rows of ■ = ■

■ × ■ = ■

2\. 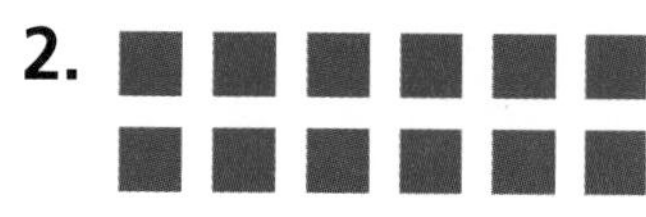

■ rows of ■ = ■

■ × ■ = ■

3\. 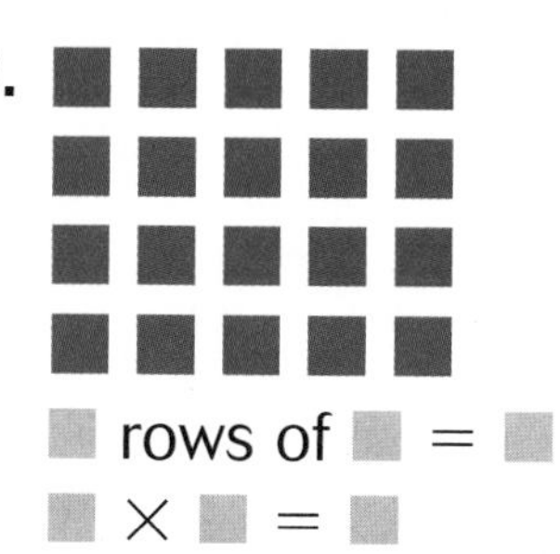

■ rows of ■ = ■

■ × ■ = ■

Find each product.

4\. $\begin{array}{r} 5 \\ \times 5 \\ \hline \end{array}$

5\. $\begin{array}{r} 7 \\ \times 3 \\ \hline \end{array}$

6\. $\begin{array}{r} 2 \\ \times 8 \\ \hline \end{array}$

7\. $\begin{array}{r} 10 \\ \times\ 3 \\ \hline \end{array}$

8\. $\begin{array}{r} 6 \\ \times 1 \\ \hline \end{array}$

9\. Charlotte is thinking of a number pattern. The first four numbers are 6, 12, 18, and 24. What are the next three numbers?

10\. **MULTISTEP** Henry baked 6 pans of muffins. Each pan holds 6 muffins. His family has eaten 8 of the muffins. How many muffins are left?

Preview

Complete.

1\. 

■ groups

■ in each group

2\. 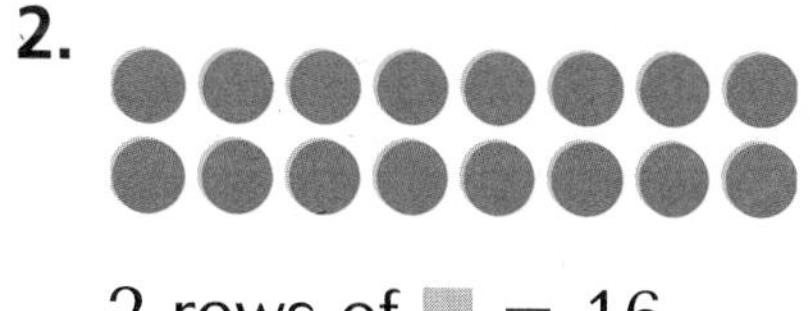

2 rows of ■ = 16

3\. 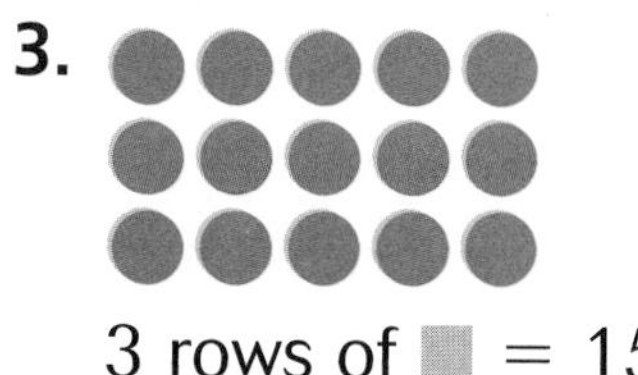

3 rows of ■ = 15

4\. 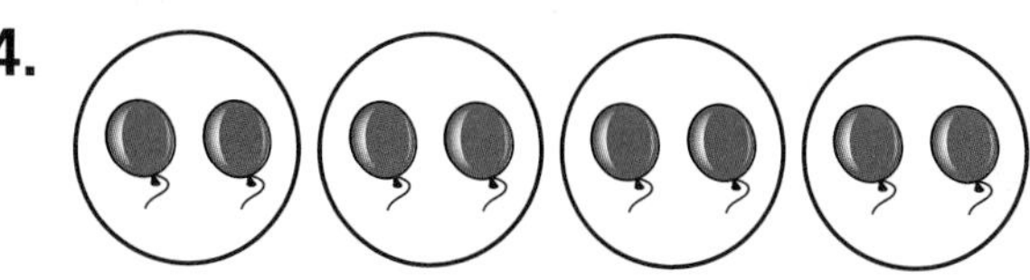

■ groups

■ in each group

Find the missing factor.

5\. 4 × ■ = 36

6\. 9 × ■ = 27

7\. 35 = ■ × 5

8\. 56 = 7 × ■

Understand Division

FAST FACT • SOCIAL STUDIES In the sport of white-water rafting, people use paddles to move boats along rivers through shallow, fast-moving water called rapids. Georgia's Chattooga River offers some of the country's best white-water rafting courses.

INVESTIGATION The graph shows different kinds of white-water boats and the number of people each boat can hold. There are 24 people who want to go rafting. It costs $10 to rent a large raft, $8 to rent a small raft, $6 to rent a canoe, and $5 to rent a kayak. If they will rent only one type of boat, which boat should they rent to spend the least amount of money?

Using Data

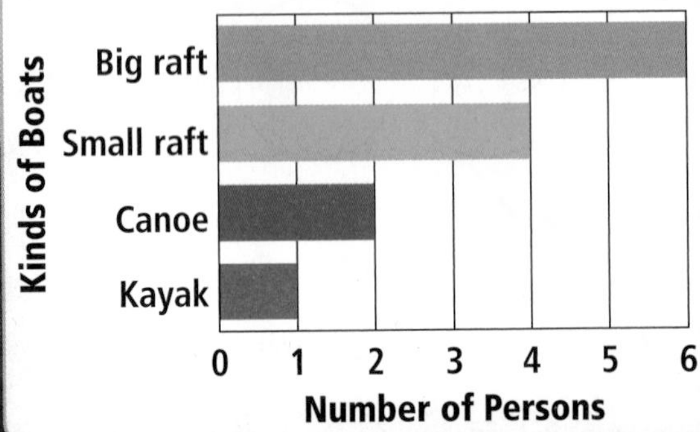

CHECK WHAT YOU KNOW

Use this page to help you review and remember important skills needed for Chapter 11.

MULTIPLICATION FACTS THROUGH 10

Find the product.

1. $6 \times 7 = \blacksquare$ **2.** $3 \times 8 = \blacksquare$ **3.** $\blacksquare = 8 \times 9$ **4.** $9 \times 0 = \blacksquare$

5. $5 \times 7 = \blacksquare$ **6.** $\blacksquare = 10 \times 4$ **7.** $4 \times 4 = \blacksquare$ **8.** $2 \times 4 = \blacksquare$

9. $\blacksquare = 9 \times 9$ **10.** $\blacksquare = 6 \times 8$ **11.** $8 \times 7 = \blacksquare$ **12.** $4 \times 3 = \blacksquare$

MAKE EQUAL GROUPS

Complete.

13.

■ groups
■ in each group

14.

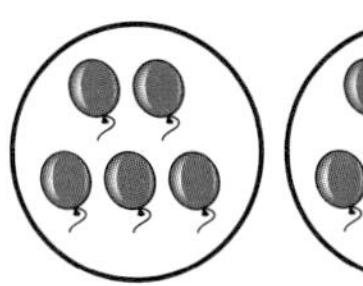

■ groups
■ in each group

15.

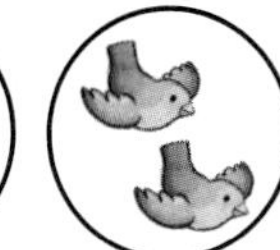

■ groups
■ in each group

16.

■ groups
■ in each group

17.

■ groups
■ in each group

18.

■ groups
■ in each group

VOCABULARY POWER

REVIEW

group [gro͞op] *noun*

Group means "a number of persons or things that are collected." Suppose you have 20 marbles. How many groups of 5 marbles do you have?

PREVIEW

divide (÷) quotient
dividend inverse operations
divisor fact family

GO ON-LINE www.harcourtschool.com/mathglossary

LESSON 1

The Meaning of Division

M3N4.b. Recognize that division . . . is determining the size of the parts when the whole is separated into a given number of equal parts as in a sharing model. *also* M3P2., M3P2.d., M3P3., M3P3.a., M3P3.b., M3P3.c., M3P3.d., M3P5., M3P5.a., M3P5.b., M3P5.c.

Quick Review

1. 6×4
2. 3×5
3. 2×6
4. 7×3
5. 4×3

VOCABULARY

divide (÷)

MATERIALS

counters

Explore

When you multiply, you put equal groups together. When you **divide**, you separate into equal groups.

Activity 1 Divide 14 counters into 2 equal groups. How many counters are in each group?

STEP 1

Use 14 counters.

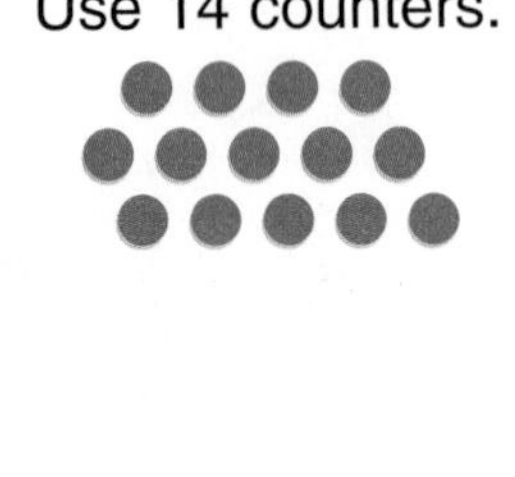

STEP 2

Show 2 groups. Place a counter in each group

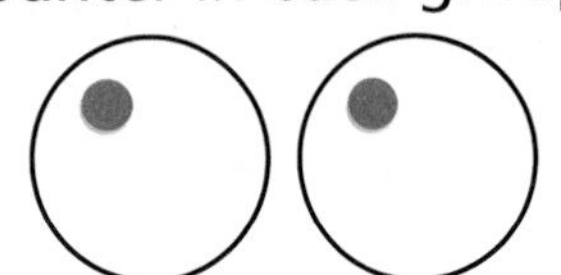

STEP 3

Continue until all counters are used.

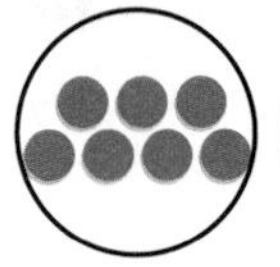
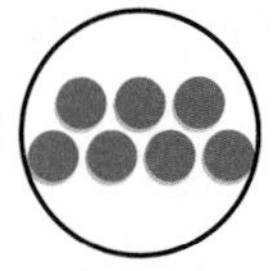

So, there are 7 counters in each of 2 groups.

Activity 2 Divide 14 counters into groups of 2. How many groups of 2 counters can you make?

STEP 1

Use 14 counters.

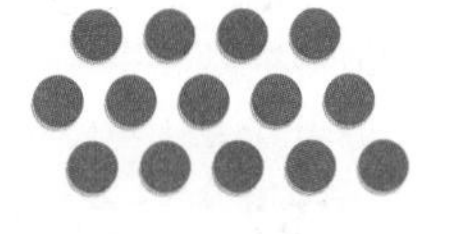

STEP 2

Make groups of 2.

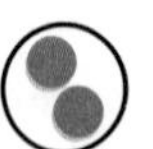

STEP 3

Continue making groups of 2 until all counters are used.

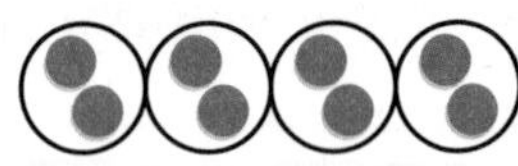

So, there are 7 groups of 2 counters.

Try It

Use counters to make equal groups. Draw a picture to show how you divided.

a. Divide 15 counters into 5 equal groups. How many are in each group?

b. Divide 15 counters into groups of 5. How many groups of 5 counters can you make?

We are putting 15 counters in 5 equal groups. How many should be in each group?

Connect

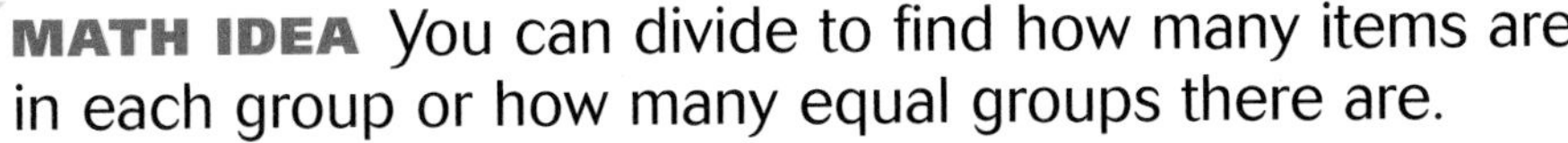

MATH IDEA You can divide to find how many items are in each group or how many equal groups there are.

Four friends share 20 marbles equally. How many marbles will each person get?

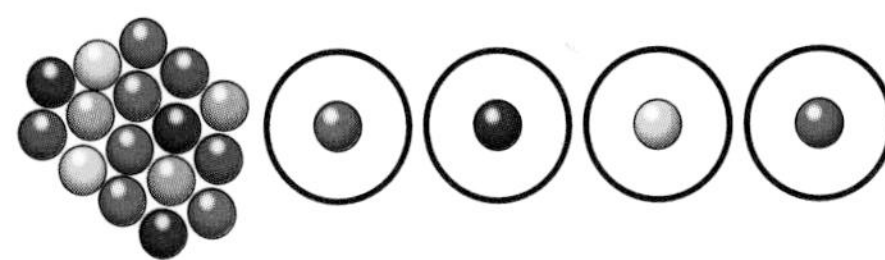

Put one marble in each group until all marbles are used.

Each person will get 5 marbles.

Each person wants 4 marbles. How many people can share 20 marbles?

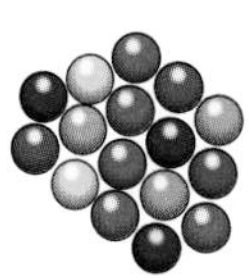

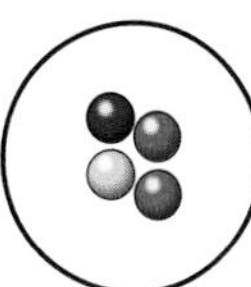

Make equal groups of 4 marbles until all marbles are used.

Five people can share 20 marbles.

Practice and Problem Solving

Copy and complete the table. Use counters to help.

	COUNTERS	NUMBER OF EQUAL GROUPS	NUMBER IN EACH GROUP
1.	15	5	■
2.	21	■	3
3.	24	3	■
4.	28	■	7

For 5–8, use counters and draw a picture.

5. Five friends share 30 stickers equally. How many will each person get?

6. Elijah has 18 books that he wants to put into equal groups. List three different ways that he could do this.

7. **REASONING** Three friends share some grapes equally. If each gets 9 grapes, how many grapes are there altogether?

8. **Write About It** Explain how to divide 32 counters into 4 equal groups.

Maintain Skills

9. Write the product.

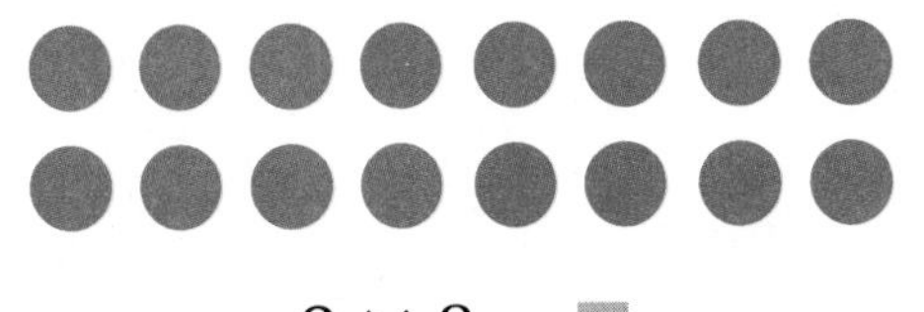

$2 \times 8 = ■$

CRCT Test Prep

10. M3N3.g. The sixth graders charged $4 to wash each car. How much money did they make for washing 8 cars? (p. 146)

A. $2 B. $4 C. $12 D. $32

LESSON 2

Subtraction and Division

M3N4.b. Recognize that division may be . . . determining how many equal parts of a given size or amount may be taken away from the whole as in repeated subtraction. . . . *also* **M3N4.a., M3P2.a., M3P2.b., M3P2.d., M3P3.a., M3P3.b., M3P3.c., M3P3.d., M3P4., M3P4.a., M3P4.b.**

Quick Review

How many are there in all?

1. 2 groups of 3
2. 4 groups of 4
3. 5 groups of 2
4. 3 groups of 9
5. 1 group of 8

Learn

GET IN THE GAME Ana has 12 game pieces for a game. Each player gets 4 pieces. How many people can play?

$12 \div 4 = \blacksquare$

12 ↑ number of pieces; 4 ↑ number for each player; ■ ↑ number of players

One Way Use a number line. Start at 12. Count back by 4s until you reach 0. Count the number of times you subtract 4.

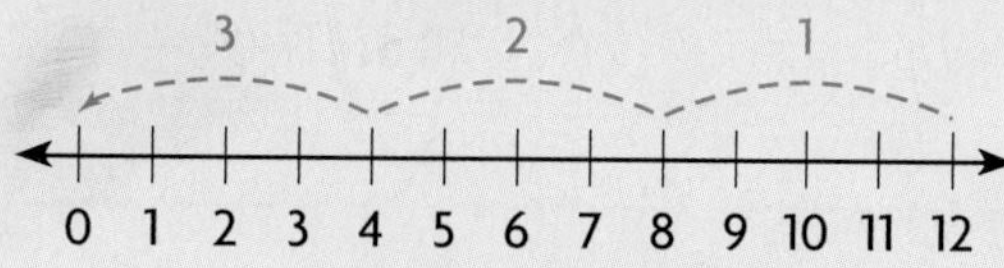

You subtract 4 three times.

Another Way Start with 12. Take away groups of 4 until you reach 0. Count the number of times you subtract 4.

$$\begin{array}{r} 12 \\ -\ 4 \\ \hline 8 \end{array} \quad \begin{array}{r} 8 \\ -4 \\ \hline 4 \end{array} \quad \begin{array}{r} 4 \\ -4 \\ \hline 0 \end{array}$$

Number of times you subtract 4: **1** **2** **3**

Since you subtract 4 from 12 three times, there are 3 groups of 4 in 12.

So, 3 people can play.

Write: $12 \div 4 = 3$ or $4\overline{)12}$ with quotient 3

Read: Twelve divided by four equals three.

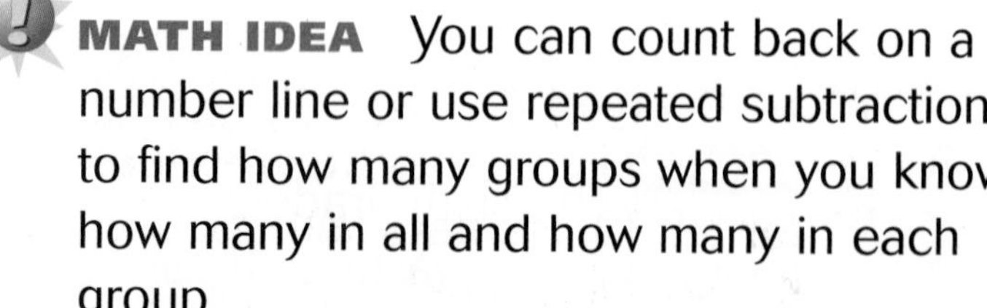

MATH IDEA You can count back on a number line or use repeated subtraction to find how many groups when you know how many in all and how many in each group.

- **Discuss** how to count back to find $15 \div 5$.

Check

1. **Explain** how to use repeated subtraction to prove that $18 \div 6 = 3$.

Write the division sentence for each.

2. 

3. $$\begin{array}{r} 8 \\ -2 \\ \hline 6 \end{array} \quad \begin{array}{r} 6 \\ -2 \\ \hline 4 \end{array} \quad \begin{array}{r} 4 \\ -2 \\ \hline 2 \end{array} \quad \begin{array}{r} 2 \\ -2 \\ \hline 0 \end{array}$$

Practice and Problem Solving

Extra Practice, page 216, Set A

Write a division sentence for each.

4. 0 5 10 15 20

5. $$\begin{array}{r} 24 \\ -\ 8 \\ \hline 16 \end{array} \quad \begin{array}{r} 16 \\ -\ 8 \\ \hline 8 \end{array} \quad \begin{array}{r} 8 \\ -8 \\ \hline 0 \end{array}$$

Use a number line or subtraction to solve.

6. $15 \div 3 = \blacksquare$
7. $21 \div 7 = \blacksquare$
8. $30 \div 5 = \blacksquare$
9. $36 \div 6 = \blacksquare$
10. $2\overline{)10}$
11. $8\overline{)16}$
12. $7\overline{)35}$
13. $5\overline{)25}$

ALGEBRA Complete. Write +, −, ×, or ÷ for each ●.

14. $20 - 5 = 5 \bullet 3$
15. $24 \div 6 = 18 \bullet 14$
16. $32 \bullet 8 = 4 \times 10$
17. $8 \bullet 2 = 2 + 2$

18. **MULTISTEP** Scott buys 22 baseball cards. He keeps 10 cards and divides the rest equally between 2 friends. How many cards will each friend get?

19. **REASONING** Nora says that $8 \div 4 = 0$ because $8 - 4 = 4$ and $4 - 4 = 0$. Is Nora correct? Explain.

20. Explain how to use repeated subtraction to find $100 \div 10$.

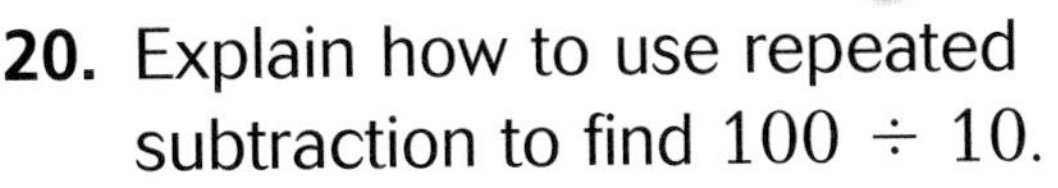

Maintain Skills

Name each polygon.

21. 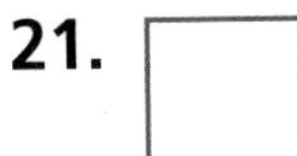

22.  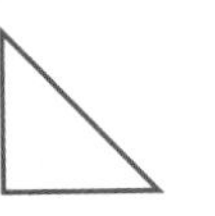

23. 

24. 

CRCT Test Prep

25. M3N2.c. Felipe buys a notebook for \$1.39. He pays with a \$5 bill. How much change should he get? (p. 96)

A. \$3.61
B. \$3.71
C. \$4.61
D. \$6.39

LESSON 3

Algebra: Multiplication and Division

M3N4.a. Understand the relationship between division and multiplication and between division and subtraction. *also* M3A1.c., M3P4., M3P4.a.

Quick Review

1. 2×7
2. 4×2
3. 2×9
4. 6×3
5. 3×8

VOCABULARY

dividend divisor quotient inverse operations

Learn

STICK WITH STAMPS Use what you know about arrays and multiplication to understand division.

Mark is putting stamps into his stamp album. Each page holds 18 stamps in 3 equal rows. How many stamps are in each row?

$18 \div 3 = \blacksquare$

18 ↑ number of stamps; 3 ↑ number of rows; ■ ↑ number in each row

Show an array with 18 in 3 equal rows. Find how many are in each row.

Since $3 \times 6 = 18$, then $18 \div 3 = 6$.

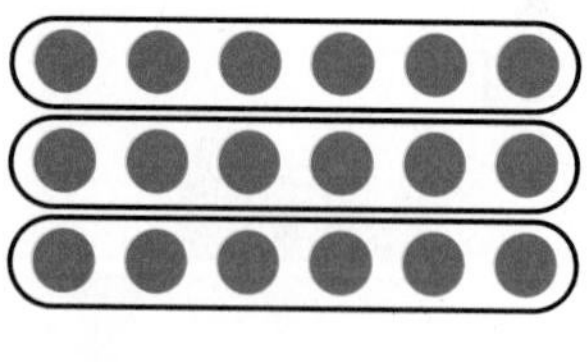

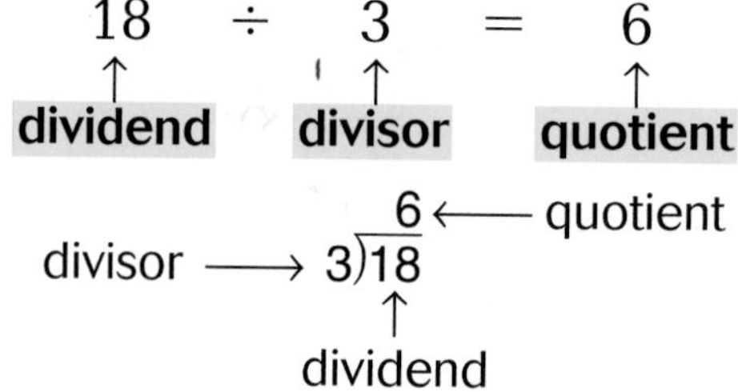

So, there are 6 stamps in each row.

Technology Link

More Practice: Harcourt Mega Math Ice Station Exploration, *Arctic Algebra,* Level E

MATH IDEA Multiplication and division are opposite or **inverse operations**. The divisor and quotient in a division sentence are the factors in the related multiplication sentence.

Examples

A

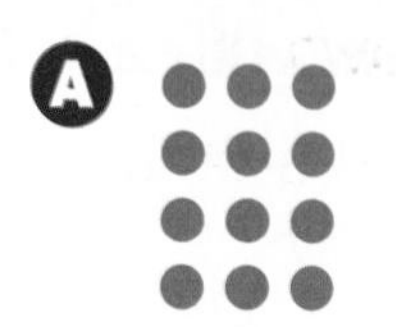

4 rows of 3 = 12

$12 \div 4 = 3$

B

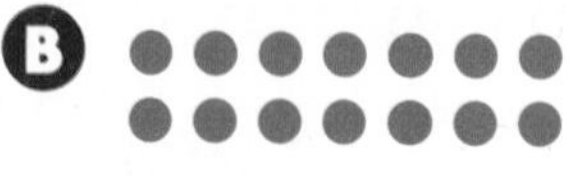

2 rows of 7 = 14

$14 \div 2 = 7$

C

3 rows of 5 = 15

$15 \div 3 = 5$

Use Variables

A variable is a symbol that stands for an unknown number. A box, ■, can be a variable.

16 ÷ 2 = ■

Think: 2 × ■ = 16
2 × 8 = 16

So, 16 ÷ 2 = 8.

2 rows of ■ = 16

A triangle, △, or a square, □, can also be a variable.

24 ÷ 4 = △

Think: 4 × △ = 24
4 × 6 = 24

So, 24 ÷ 4 = 6.

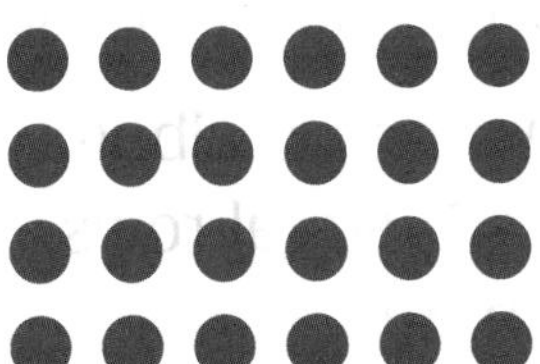

4 rows of △ = 24

Examples

 12 ÷ 2 = □

Think: 2 × □ = 12
2 × 6 = 12, so, □ = 6.

So, 12 ÷ 2 = 6.

 15 ÷ 5 = ■

Think: 5 × ■ = 15
5 × 3 = 15, so, ■ = 3.

So, 15 ÷ 5 = 3.

MATH IDEA You can use a variable to stand for an unknown number.

Check

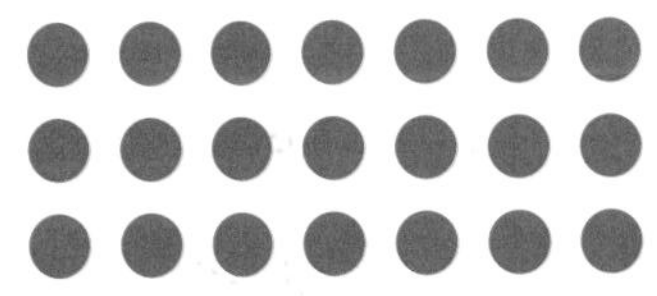

1. Explain how to use this array to multiply and divide.

Copy and complete.

2. 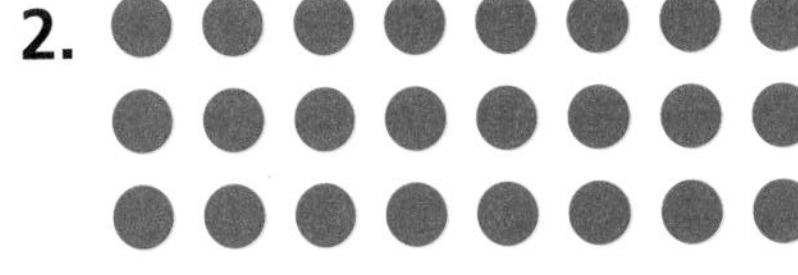

3 rows of ■ = 24

24 ÷ 3 = ■

3. 2 rows of ■ = 18

18 ÷ 2 = ■

4. 

3 rows of ■ = 18

18 ÷ 3 = ■

Find the number that the variable stands for.

5. 12 ÷ 3 = △
△ = ?

6. 16 ÷ 4 = ■
■ = ?

7. 20 ÷ 4 = □
□ = ?

Practice and Problem Solving

Extra Practice, page 216, Set B

Copy and complete.

8. 3 rows of ■ = 21

21 ÷ 3 = ■

9. 5 rows of ■ = 30

30 ÷ 5 = ■

10. 5 rows of ■ = 40

40 ÷ 5 = ■

Complete each number sentence. Draw an array to help.

11. 3 × ■ = 18   18 ÷ 3 = ■

12. 5 × ■ = 25   25 ÷ 5 = ■

13. 6 × ■ = 24   24 ÷ 6 = ■

14. 3 × ■ = 24   24 ÷ 3 = ■

Find the number that the variable stands for.

15. 12 ÷ 2 = △
△ = ?

16. 15 ÷ 3 = ■
■ = ?

17. 18 ÷ 6 = □
□ = ?

18. 14 ÷ 7 = ■
■ = ?

19. 25 ÷ 5 = △
△ = ?

20. 24 ÷ 8 = □
□ = ?

21. 5 × □ = 20
□ = ?

22. 6 × ■ = 18
■ = ?

23. 3 × △ = 21
△ = ?

ALGEBRA **Complete.**

24. 4 × 2 = 24 ÷ ■
■ = ?

25. △ × 3 = 30 ÷ 5
△ = ?

26. 4 × 1 = □ ÷ 4
□ = ?

27. Tory arranged 28 stamps so that 7 were in each row. How many rows did she make?

28. **What's the Question?** Christy puts 36 pennies into 4 equal piles. The answer is 9 pennies.

29. **Vocabulary Power** One definition of *array* is "a number of objects arranged in equal rows and equal columns." Tell the number of rows and columns shown in the array in Exercise 10.

30. **REASONING** Mark bakes 14 muffins. He eats 2 muffins and divides the rest equally among 6 friends. What division sentence shows how many muffins each friend gets?

31. **FAST FACT** • SCIENCE Frogs lay many eggs which hatch into tadpoles. In about 12 to 16 weeks, the tadpoles become frogs. About how many months does it take for a tadpole to become a frog?

32. **MULTISTEP** Colin has 24 toy cars. He puts an equal number of cars into each of 3 boxes. How many cars will be in 2 of the boxes?

Maintain Skills

Write <, >, or = for each ●.

33. 16 ● 13

34. 98 ● 89

35. 46 ● 64

Find the sum or difference.

36. $\begin{array}{r} 248 \\ +119 \\ \hline \end{array}$ **37.** $\begin{array}{r} 629 \\ -354 \\ \hline \end{array}$ **38.** $\begin{array}{r} 825 \\ -238 \\ \hline \end{array}$

CRCT Test Prep

39. M3N3.g Zach puts 1 ice cube in each of 7 cups. How many ice cubes are there in all? (p. 144)

A. 1 B. 6 C. 7 D. 8

40. M3A1.a Predict which numbers continue this pattern. (p. 148)

14, 21, 28, 35

A. 40, 47, 54
B. 42, 49, 56
C. 32, 39, 46
D. 42, 50, 59

Problem Solving Thinker's Corner

THE HOBBY STORE

VISUAL THINKING Mr. Burns wrote number sentences to help him remember how to place the shells in the display cases at the Hobby Store.

For 1–3, draw a picture to show how the shells will be displayed.

1. $5 \times 8 = 40$
$40 \div 5 = 8$

2. $4 \times 7 = 28$
$28 \div 4 = 7$

3. $4 \times 9 = 36$
$36 \div 4 = 9$

4. Write a problem using division to find how many equal groups. Write a number sentence to solve.

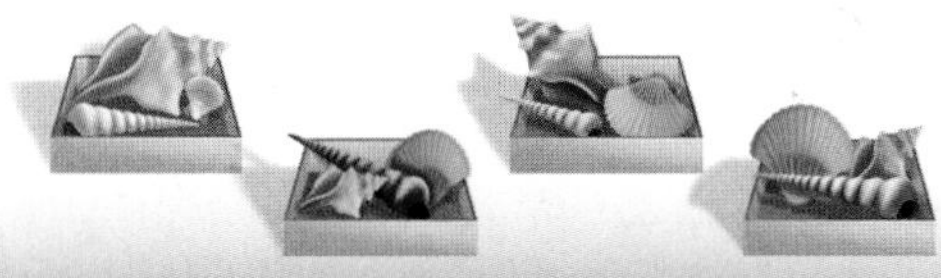

5. Mr. Burns has 16 new shells. He wants to put them into 8 equal groups. Write a problem using division to find how many shells are in each group. Write a number sentence to solve.

LESSON 4

Algebra: Fact Families

M3N4.a. Understand the relationship between division and multiplication and between division and subtraction. *also* M3P2.a., M3P2.b., M3P2.c., M3P2.d., M3P4., M3P4.a., M3P4.b., M3P4.d.

Quick Review

1. 3 × ■ = 18
2. ■ × 6 = 18
3. 18 ÷ 6 = ■
4. 5 × ■ = 25
5. 25 ÷ 5 = ■

VOCABULARY

fact family

Learn

FUN FACTS A set of related multiplication and division number sentences is called a **fact family**.

Fact Family for 3, 5, and 15

factor		factor		product	dividend		divisor		quotient
3	×	5	=	15	15	÷	5	=	3
5	×	3	=	15	15	÷	3	=	5

Activity

Materials: square pieces of paper, scissors

Use this triangle fact card to think of the fact family for 3, 5, and 15.

Make a set of triangle fact cards. Use them to write fact families.

Product 15

Factor 3 5 Factor

A Fold each paper in half three times. Open up the paper and cut along the folds to make triangle cards.

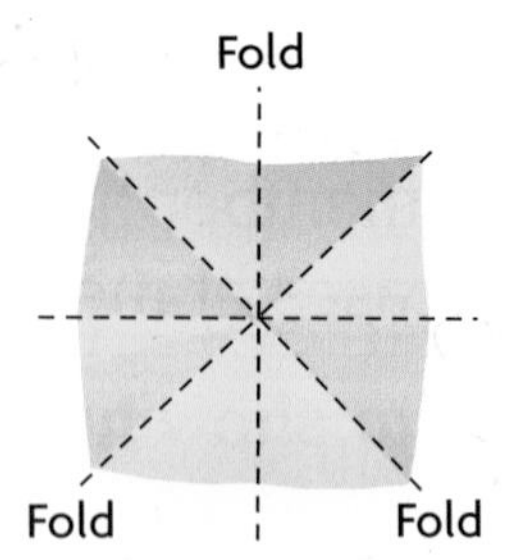

B Make triangle fact cards for each of these products: 12, 15, 18, 20, 24, 25, and 30.

C Write fact families for at least 3 triangle fact cards.

- **REASONING** How many triangle fact cards can you make for the product 12? Explain.

Using a Multiplication Table

MATH IDEA Use related multiplication facts to find quotients or missing divisors in division sentences.

Examples

A Find the quotient.
12 ÷ 3 = ■

Think: 3 × ■ = 12

Find the row for the factor 3. Look across to find the product 12.
Look up to find the missing factor, 4.
3 × 4 = 12

So, 12 ÷ 3 = 4.

B Find the missing divisor.
30 ÷ ■ = 5

Think: ■ × 5 = 30

Find the factor 5 in the top row. Look down to find the product 30. Look left to find the missing factor, 6.
6 × 5 = 30

So, 30 ÷ 6 = 5.

Remember

3 × 4 = 12
↑ factor ↑ factor ↑ product

×	0	1	2	3	4	5	6
0	0	0	0	0	0	0	0
1	0	1	2	3	4	5	6
2	0	2	4	6	8	10	12
3	0	3	6	9	12	15	18
4	0	4	8	12	16	20	24
5	0	5	10	15	20	25	30
6	0	6	12	18	24	30	36

• **REASONING** How can you use multiplication to check $20 \div 5 = 4$?

Check

1. **Explain** how you can use a multiplication table to show how $5 \times 2 = 10$ and $10 \div 2 = 5$ are related.

Write the missing number for each triangle fact card.

2. 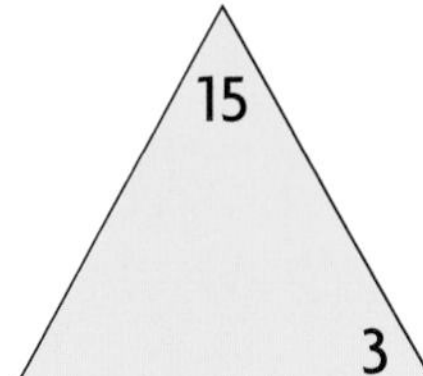

3. 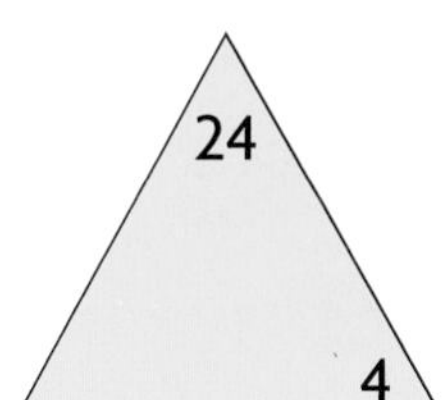

4. 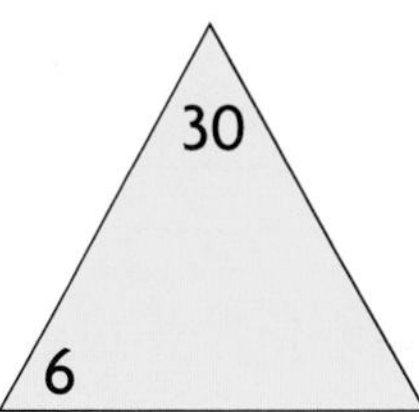

5. 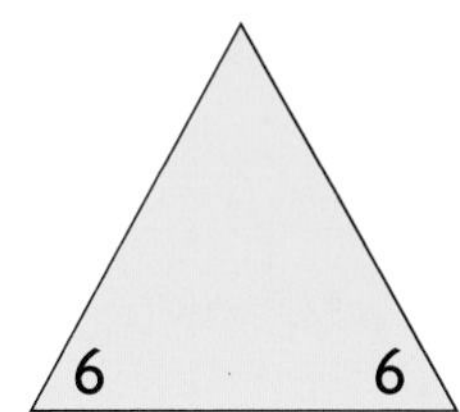

Write the fact family.

6. 3, 6, 18 7. 4, 4, 16 8. 4, 5, 20 9. 3, 7, 21

LESSON CONTINUES

Practice and Problem Solving

Extra Practice, page 216, Set C

Write the missing number for each triangle fact card.

10. 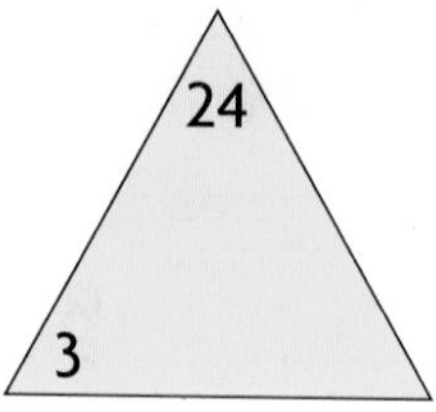

11. 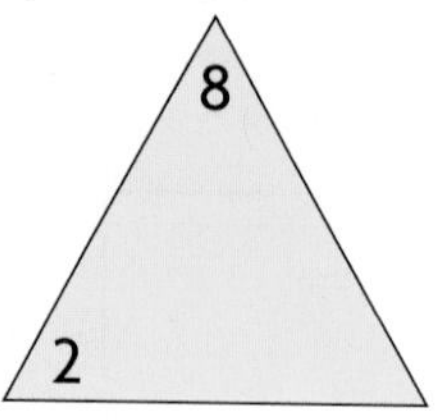

12. 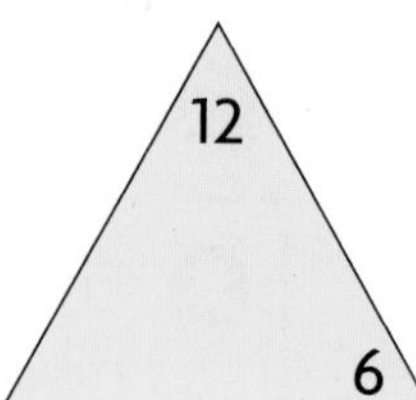

13. 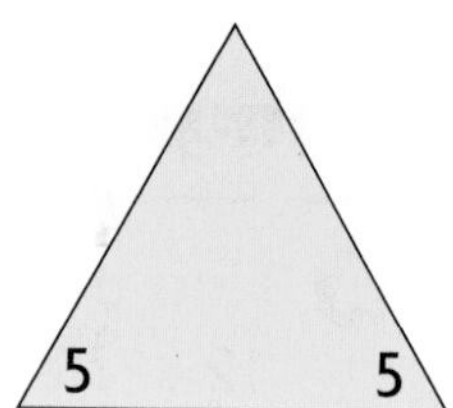

Write the fact family.

14. 5, 6, 30 **15.** 2, 8, 16 **16.** 4, 7, 28 **17.** 5, 5, 25

Find the quotient or product.

18. $3 \times 6 = \blacksquare$ **19.** $6 \times 3 = \blacksquare$ **20.** $18 \div 3 = \blacksquare$ **21.** $18 \div 6 = \blacksquare$

22. $4 \times 9 = \blacksquare$ **23.** $9 \times 4 = \blacksquare$ **24.** $36 \div 4 = \blacksquare$ **25.** $36 \div 9 = \blacksquare$

26. $8 \times 5 = \blacksquare$ **27.** $5 \times 8 = \blacksquare$ **28.** $40 \div 8 = \blacksquare$ **29.** $40 \div 5 = \blacksquare$

Write the other three sentences in the fact family.

30. $3 \times 7 = 21$ **31.** $1 \times 5 = 5$ **32.** $4 \times 3 = 12$

33. $5 \times 3 = 15$ **34.** $6 \times 4 = 24$ **35.** $9 \times 2 = 18$

Find the quotient or the missing divisor or dividend.

36. $8 \div 4 = \blacksquare$ **37.** $16 \div 2 = \blacksquare$ **38.** $7 = \blacksquare \div 3$ **39.** $2 = 12 \div \blacksquare$

40. $\blacksquare \div 8 = 3$ **41.** $10 \div \blacksquare = 2$ **42.** $30 \div \blacksquare = 6$ **43.** $28 \div 4 = \blacksquare$

ALGEBRA Complete.

44. $\blacksquare \div 5 = 6 + 3$ **45.** $6 \times \blacksquare = 54 \div 9$ **46.** $42 - 6 = \blacksquare \times 9$

47. What do you notice about the fact family for 6, 6, and 36?

48. **REASONING** How are $20 \div 5 = 4$ and $20 \div 4 = 5$ alike? How are they different?

49. **MULTISTEP** Geri made 20 bookmarks. She kept 2 and then put an equal number in each of 3 gift boxes. How many bookmarks are in each box?

50. **REASONING** Kendra says, "There are 3 teaspoons in 1 tablespoon, so there are 15 teaspoons in 5 tablespoons." Do you agree or disagree? Explain.

51. **MULTISTEP** Mr. Tapia has 6 toys for each cat and dog in his pet store. He has 7 dogs and 9 cats. How many toys does Mr. Tapia have?

52. **What's the Error?** John says that since $4 + 4 = 8$, then $8 \div 4 = 4$. Describe his error and give the correct quotient.

Maintain Skills

Write the time.

53.

54.

55. Write the amount.

CRCT Test Prep

56. M3N3.b. Denise spent 3 hours at math camp each day for 1 week. How many hours did she spend at math camp? (p. 132)

A. 3 hours
B. 4 hours
C. 14 hours
D. 21 hours

57. M3A1.c. What number goes in the □ to make the sentence true? (p. 154)

$$3 \times \square = 18$$

A. 5 B. 6 C. 7 D. 8

Problem Solving Thinker's Corner

MATERIALS: triangle fact cards, paper

Players: 2

a. One player chooses a triangle fact card and holds it so that one number is hidden.

b. The other player names the hidden number and writes the fact family.

c. Players take turns until all cards are used. The player with the most correct number sentences wins.

1. How can you make sure your fact families are complete?

2. What card did you hope to choose for your opponent? Explain.

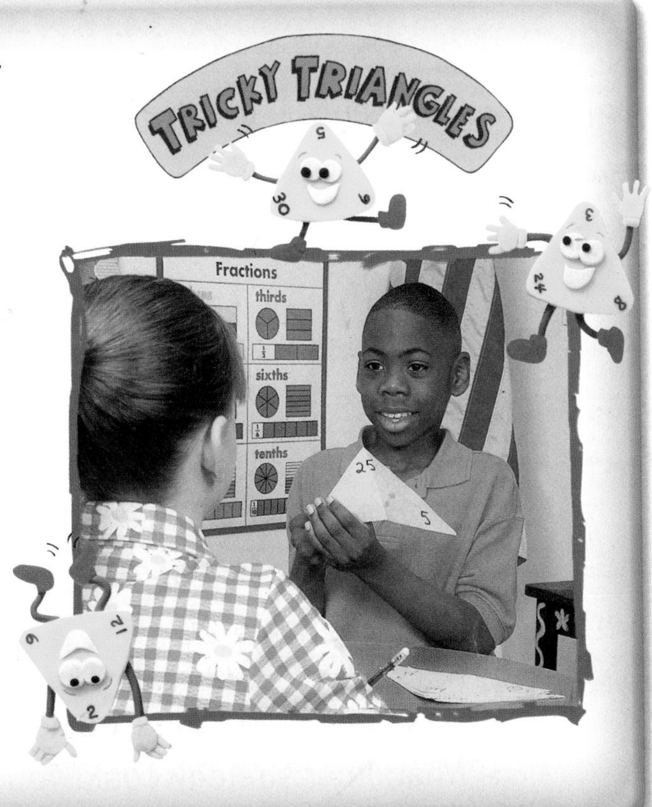

LESSON 5

Problem Solving Strategy
Make a Picture

M3N4.f. Solve problems requiring division. *also* M3P1.a., M3P1.b., M3P1.c., M3P3.a., M3P3.b., M3P3.c., M3P3.d., M3P5., M3P5.a., M3P5.b., M3P5.c.

PROBLEM Megan puts 36 animal trading cards in her binder. She puts 9 cards on each page. How many pages will Megan need for her cards?

Quick Review

1. $8 \times 4 = ■$
2. $30 = 6 \times ■$
3. $10 \times 5 = ■$
4. $18 = ■ \times 6$
5. $27 = 9 \times ■$

UNDERSTAND

- What are you asked to find?
- What information will you use?
- Is there information you will not use? If so, what?

PLAN

- What strategy can you use?

Make a picture to help you find the number of pages Megan will need.

SOLVE

- How can you use the strategy to solve the problem?

Make a picture to show pages that hold 9 cards each. Count the number of pages needed to hold 36 cards.

1	2	3
4	5	6
7	8	9

10	11	12
13	14	15
16	17	18

19	20	21
22	23	24
25	26	27

28	29	30
31	32	33
34	35	36

So, Megan needs 4 pages for her cards.

CHECK

- How can you decide if your answer is correct?
- What other strategy could you use?

Problem Solving Practice

Make a picture to solve.

1. **What if** Megan buys 27 trading cards to add to her collection? How many pages will she need for the new cards?
2. Rosita has 28 cards. She wants to keep 4 cards and divide the rest equally among 4 friends. How many cards will each friend get?

Jorge has 45 trading cards in his collection. His binder holds 10 pages. Each page holds 9 trading cards.

3. How many pages will Jorge use for the cards he has?
   - **A** 5
   - **B** 10
   - **C** 45
   - **D** 90
4. Which number sentence shows how to find how many trading cards fit in Jorge's binder?
   - **F** $45 + 10 = 55$
   - **G** $9 \times 10 = 90$
   - **H** $10 + 9 = 19$
   - **J** $45 \div 9 = 5$

Strategies

- Act It Out or Use Objects
- **Make a Picture or Diagram**
- Guess and Check
- Use or Look for a Pattern
- Use Logical Reasoning

Problem Solving

Mixed Strategy Practice

USE DATA For 5–8, use the graph.

5. **MULTISTEP** Sebastian collects coins. How many coins in all are in Sebastian's coin collection?
6. Tim has 4 times as many quarters in his collection as Sebastian has. How many quarters are in Tim's collection?
7. **MULTISTEP** Sebastian added some half dollars to his collection. There are 5 more pennies than half dollars in his collection. How many half dollars did Sebastian add to his collection?

SEBASTIAN'S COIN COLLECTION

pennies	●●●
nickels	●●●●
dimes	●●
quarters	●

Key: Each ● = 5 coins.

8. **Write a problem** using the data in the pictograph.

Extra Practice

Set A (pp. 204–205)

Write a division sentence for each.

1. 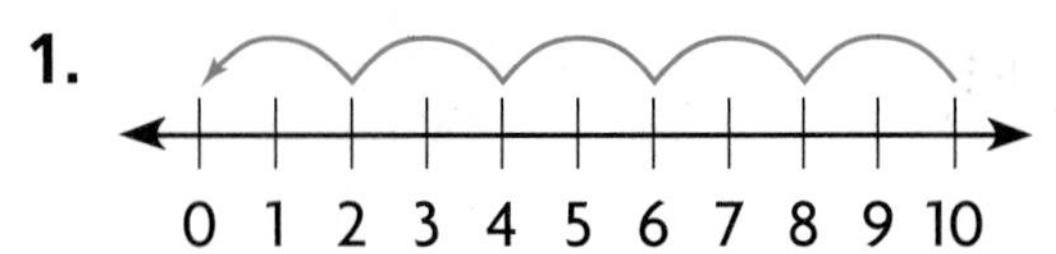

2.

$$\begin{array}{r} 36 \\ -\ 9 \\ \hline 27 \end{array} \quad \begin{array}{r} 27 \\ -\ 9 \\ \hline 18 \end{array} \quad \begin{array}{r} 18 \\ -\ 9 \\ \hline 9 \end{array} \quad \begin{array}{r} 9 \\ -9 \\ \hline 0 \end{array}$$

Use a number line or subtraction to solve.

3. $15 \div 5 = ■$ **4.** $18 \div 3 = ■$ **5.** $12 \div 4 = ■$ **6.** $16 \div 4 = ■$

7. $7\overline{)14}$ **8.** $5\overline{)20}$ **9.** $3\overline{)24}$ **10.** $8\overline{)40}$

Set B (pp. 206–209)

Complete each number sentence. Draw an array to help.

1. $4 \times ■ = 8$ $8 \div 4 = ■$ **2.** $6 \times ■ = 30$ $30 \div 6 = ■$

3. $8 \times ■ = 32$ $32 \div 8 = ■$ **4.** $4 \times ■ = 12$ $12 \div 4 = ■$

5. What division sentence could you write for an array that shows $5 \times 8 = 40$?

6. How can you use $5 + 5 + 5 + 5 = 20$ to help you find $20 \div 5$?

Find the number that the variable stands for.

7. $2 \times ■ = 12$
■ = ?

8. $\triangle \times 4 = 36$
$\triangle$ = ?

9. $20 \div 4 = \square$
$\square$ = ?

Set C (pp. 210–213)

Write the fact family.

1. 2, 3, 6 **2.** 3, 7, 21 **3.** 3, 9, 27 **4.** 3, 6, 18

5. 4, 6, 24 **6.** 4, 8, 32 **7.** 5, 5, 25 **8.** 3, 8, 24

Find the quotient or the missing divisor.

9. $6 \div ■ = 3$ **10.** $18 \div 6 = ■$ **11.** $■ = 12 \div 3$ **12.** $20 \div ■ = 4$

13. $30 \div 6 = ■$ **14.** $3 = 15 \div ■$ **15.** $9 \div ■ = 3$ **16.** $16 \div 4 = ■$

17. Jerome made 30 cookies. He ate 3 and divided the rest equally among 3 friends. How many cookies did each friend get?

Review/Test

CHECK VOCABULARY AND CONCEPTS

Choose the best term from the box.

Vocabulary
- divide (÷)
- dividend
- divisor
- quotient
- inverse operations

1. Multiplication and division are opposite operations, or _?_. (p. 206)
2. In $18 \div 6 = 3$, the number 3 is called the _?_. (p. 206)
3. When you separate into equal groups, you _?_. (p. 202)
4. In $32 \div 8 = 4$, the number 8 is called the _?_. (p. 206)

Use a number line or subtraction to solve. (pp. 204–205)

5. $10 \div 5 = ■$
6. $27 \div 9 = ■$
7. $4\overline{)20}$
8. $8\overline{)32}$

CHECK SKILLS

Complete each number sentence.
Draw an array to help. (pp. 206–209)

9. $2 \times ■ = 6$ $6 \div 2 = ■$
10. $3 \times ■ = 15$ $15 \div 3 = ■$
11. $4 \times ■ = 4$ $4 \div 4 = ■$
12. $5 \times ■ = 30$ $30 \div 5 = ■$

Find the number that the variable stands for. (pp. 206–209)

13. $14 \div 2 = \square$
    $\square = $ _?_
14. $■ \times 5 = 20$
    $■ = $ _?_
15. $18 \div 9 = \triangle$
    $\triangle = $ _?_

Write the fact family. (pp. 210–213)

16. 4, 5, 20
17. 2, 7, 14
18. 4, 9, 36

CHECK PROBLEM SOLVING

Make a picture to solve. (pp. 214–215)

19. Ms. Kraft has 20 pencils to divide equally among 5 groups of students. How many pencils does each group get?
20. Fernando has 24 rocks in his collection. If a box holds 6 rocks, how many boxes will Fernando need for his collection?

Chapter CRCT Test Prep

NUMBERS AND OPERATIONS

1. M3N4.b. How many groups of 5 are in 15?

   A. 2

   B. 3

   C. 4

   D. 5

2. M3N4.f. Scott had 20 juice boxes. He gave 4 juice boxes to each friend. How many friends received juice boxes?

   A. 2

   B. 4

   C. 5

   D. 8

3. M3N4.a. Which division sentence represents these subtractions?

$$\begin{array}{r} 18 \\ -\ 6 \\ \hline 12 \end{array} \quad \begin{array}{r} 12 \\ -\ 6 \\ \hline 6 \end{array} \quad \begin{array}{r} 6 \\ -\ 6 \\ \hline 0 \end{array}$$

   A. $18 \div 2 = 9$

   B. $12 \div 2 = 6$

   C. $18 \div 6 = 3$

   D. $6 \div 6 = 1$

NUMBERS AND OPERATIONS

4. M3N4.a. What division fact belongs to the same fact family as these multiplication facts?

$$4 \times 6 = 24 \qquad 6 \times 4 = 24$$

   A. $24 \div 2 = 12$

   B. $24 \div 3 = 8$

   C. $24 \div 8 = 3$

   D. $24 \div 6 = 4$

5. M3N4.b. Which division fact does the picture show?

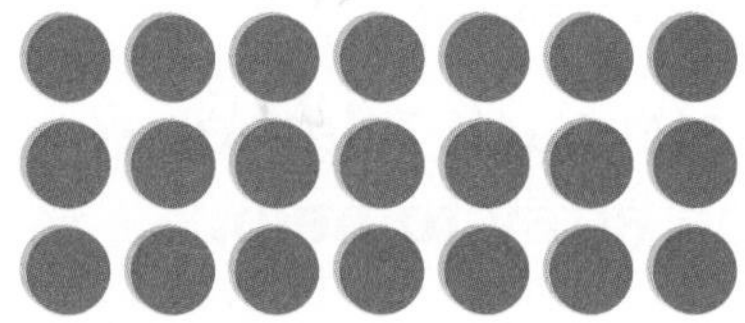

3 rows of 7 = 21

   A. $24 \div 3 = 8$

   B. $21 \div 3 = 7$

   C. $12 \div 3 = 4$

   D. $12 \div 6 = 2$

6. M3N4.f. Ella bakes 18 muffins. She puts 3 muffins in each bag. How many bags does Ella use?

   A. 9

   B. 6

   C. 4

   D. 3

Cumulative CRCT Test Prep

NUMBERS AND OPERATIONS

7. M3N3.e. Which expression should Marcus write in the □ to make the number sentence true?

$$(3 \times 2) \times 7 = \square$$

A. 5×7

B. 3×9

C. $(2 \times 3) \times 7$

D. $(2 + 3) + 7$

8. M3N2.b. Use front-end estimation to estimate the difference.

$$\begin{array}{r} 652 \\ -147 \\ \hline \end{array}$$

A. 200

B. 300

C. 400

D. 500

9. M3N2.c. Sara's lunch cost \$2.65. She paid with a \$5 bill. How much change did Sara receive?

A. \$2.25

B. \$2.35

C. \$3.35

D. \$3.65

ALGEBRA

10. M3A1.a. Rebecca went to art class on June 1, June 5, June 9, and June 13. If this pattern continues, what is the next date when Rebecca will go to art class?

A. June 14

B. June 15

C. June 17

D. June 19

11. M3A1.a. What is the next number in this number pattern?

150, 200, 250, 300, □

A. 350

B. 400

C. 450

D. 500

12. M3A1.c. What number belongs in the □ to make all the number sentences true?

$$5 \times \square = 35 \quad \square \times 5 = 35$$

$$35 \div \square = 5 \quad 35 \div 5 = \square$$

A. 5

B. 6

C. 7

D. 8

Division Facts Through 5

FAST FACT • SCIENCE A pelican is a large seabird. Under its long bill, a pelican has a pouch for catching and storing food. Some kinds of pelicans fly over the water and dive for fish.

INVESTIGATION The pictograph shows the number of fish that some pelicans caught by diving. Suppose each pelican caught 4 fish on each dive. Use counters to find the number of dives it takes for each pelican to catch the fish shown in the pictograph.

Using Data

FISH CAUGHT

Pelican 1	🐟 🐟 🐟 🐟 🐟 🐟
Pelican 2	🐟 🐟 🐟 🐟 🐟 🐟 🐟 🐟
Pelican 3	🐟 🐟 🐟 🐟

Key: Each 🐟 = 2 fish.

CHECK WHAT YOU KNOW

Use this page to help you review and remember important skills needed for Chapter 12.

MULTIPLICATION FACTS THROUGH 5

Find each product.

1. $6 \times 3 =$ ■ **2.** $3 \times 5 =$ ■ **3.** ■ $= 9 \times 2$ **4.** $7 \times 4 =$ ■

5. ■ $= 1 \times 7$ **6.** ■ $= 3 \times 1$ **7.** $5 \times 8 =$ ■ **8.** $3 \times 9 =$ ■

9. $1 \times 1 =$ ■ **10.** $6 \times 5 =$ ■ **11.** $4 \times 6 =$ ■ **12.** ■ $= 2 \times 8$

MODEL DIVISION

Copy and complete.

13.

3 rows of ■ = 18

$18 \div 3 =$ ■

14.

2 rows of ■ = 14

$14 \div 2 =$ ■

15. 

4 rows of ■ = 20

$20 \div 4 =$ ■

FACT FAMILIES

Write the fact family.

16. 3, 7, 21 **17.** 2, 4, 8 **18.** 5, 3, 15 **19.** 4, 4, 16

VOCABULARY POWER

REVIEW

divide [di•vīd′] *verb*

When you *multiply*, you use *multiplication*. When you *divide*, what operation do you use? Use *multiply* and *divide* in a sentence.

www.harcourtschool.com/mathglossary

LESSON 1

Divide by 2 and 5

M3N4.a. Understand the relationship between division and multiplication and between division and subtraction. *also* M3N4.f., M3P2.a., M3P2.b., M3P2.d., M3P3.a., M3P3.b., M3P3.c., M3P3.d.

Quick Review

1. $2 \times \blacksquare = 10$
2. $4 \times \blacksquare = 8$
3. $5 \times \blacksquare = 20$
4. $\blacksquare \times 5 = 35$
5. $\blacksquare \times 2 = 18$

Learn

CRAFTY MATH Mrs. Jackson knit 12 hats. She put an equal number of hats on each of 2 shelves in the craft shop. How many hats are on each shelf?

$12 \div 2 = \blacksquare$

Use a related multiplication fact to find the quotient.

Think: $2 \times \blacksquare = 12$

$2 \times 6 = 12$

$12 \div 2 = 6$, or $2\overline{)12}$ with quotient 6

So, there are 6 hats on each shelf.

Remember

16 ÷ 2 = 8

16 ↑ dividend, 2 ↑ divisor, 8 ↑ quotient

×	0	1	2	3	4	5
0	0	0	0	0	0	0
1	0	1	2	3	4	5
2	0	2	4	6	8	10
3	0	3	6	9	12	15
4	0	4	8	12	16	20
5	0	5	10	15	20	25
6	0	6	12	18	24	30

What if Mrs. Jackson knits 15 hats and puts an equal number of hats on each of 5 shelves? How many hats are on each shelf?

$15 \div 5 = \blacksquare$

Use the multiplication table to find the quotient.

Think: $5 \times \blacksquare = 15$ $\quad 5 \times 3 = 15$

$15 \div 5 = 3$, or $5\overline{)15}$ with quotient 3

So, there are 3 hats on each shelf.

MATH IDEA You can find missing factors in related multiplication facts to help you divide.

- How can you use $3 \times 2 = 6$ to help you find $6 \div 2$?

Check

1. **Explain** how you can use multiplication to check $20 \div 5 = 4$.

Copy and complete each table.

2.

÷	2	4	6	8
2	■	■	■	■

3.

÷	10	15	20	25
5	■	■	■	■

Practice and Problem Solving

Extra Practice, page 232, Set A

Copy and complete each table.

4.

÷	10	12	14	16
2	■	■	■	■

5.

÷	30	35	40	45
5	■	■	■	■

Find each missing factor and quotient.

6. $2 \times ■ = 4$ $\quad 4 \div 2 = ■$

7. $5 \times ■ = 20$ $\quad 20 \div 5 = ■$

8. $5 \times ■ = 35$ $\quad 35 \div 5 = ■$

9. $2 \times ■ = 16$ $\quad 16 \div 2 = ■$

Find each quotient.

10. $6 \div 2 = ■$

11. $10 \div 2 = ■$

12. $■ = 10 \div 5$

13. $5 \div 5 = ■$

14. $2\overline{)2}$

15. $5\overline{)15}$

16. $5\overline{)35}$

17. $2\overline{)16}$

Complete.

18. $10 \div 2 = ■ \times 1$

19. $40 \div 5 = 4 \times ■$

20. $■ \div 2 = 3 + 4$

21. **REASONING** What do you notice about the numbers that can be equally divided by 2?

22. **MULTISTEP** Mrs. Jackson sells hats for \$5. She has \$15. How many more hats must she sell to have \$35 in all?

23. **What's the Error?** Philip used the multiplication fact $2 \times 8 = 16$ to find $8 \div 2 = ■$. Describe his error. What is the correct quotient?

Maintain Skills

Write the time.

24. 

25. 

CRCT Test Prep

26. M3N3.g. James made an array with 3 rows of 9 tiles. Choose the number sentence that shows how many tiles are in the array. (p. 180)

A. $9 - 3 = 6$

B. $3 + 9 = 12$

C. $9 \div 3 = 3$

D. $3 \times 9 = 27$

LESSON 2

Divide by 3 and 4

M3N4.a. Understand the relationship between division and multiplication and between division and subtraction. *also* M3N4.f., M3P2.a., M3P2.b., M3P2.d., M3P3., M3P3.a., M3P3.b., M3P3.c., M3P3.d.

Quick Review

1. ■ × 3 = 18
2. 4 × ■ = 12
3. ■ × 4 = 16
4. 4 × ■ = 32
5. 3 × ■ = 21

Learn

PADDLE POWER The Traveler Scouts want to rent canoes. There are 24 people in the group. A canoe can hold 3 people. How many canoes should the group rent?

24 ÷ 3 = ■

Use the multiplication table to find a related multiplication fact.

×	0	1	2	3	4	5	6	7	8	9
0	0	0	0	0	0	0	0	0	0	0
1	0	1	2	3	4	5	6	7	8	9
2	0	2	4	6	8	10	12	14	16	18
3	0	3	6	9	12	15	18	21	24	27
4	0	4	8	12	16	20	24	28	32	36
5	0	5	10	15	20	25	30	35	40	45

Think: 3 × ■ = 24
3 × 8 = 24 24 ÷ 3 = 8, or $3\overline{)24}$ = 8

So, the group should rent 8 canoes.

What if the group wants to rent rowboats instead? If each rowboat holds 4 people, how many rowboats should they rent?

24 ÷ 4 = ■

Think: 4 × ■ = 24
4 × 6 = 24 24 ÷ 4 = 6, or $4\overline{)24}$ = 6

So, the group should rent 6 rowboats.

- **REASONING** How can you use 21 ÷ 3 = 7 to find 24 ÷ 3?

Check

1. **Explain** how you can use multiplication to find 12 ÷ 4.

Write the multiplication fact you can use to find the quotient. Then write the quotient.

2. 12 ÷ 3 = ■
3. 8 ÷ 4 = ■
4. 15 ÷ 3 = ■
5. 28 ÷ 4 = ■

Practice and Problem Solving

Extra Practice, page 232, Set B

Write the multiplication fact you can use to find the quotient. Then write the quotient.

Technology Link

More Practice: Harcourt Mega Math The Number Games, *Up, Up, and Array,* Level E

6. $27 \div 3 = \blacksquare$ **7.** $\blacksquare = 4 \div 4$ **8.** $30 \div 3 = \blacksquare$

9. $16 \div 4 = \blacksquare$ **10.** $18 \div 3 = \blacksquare$ **11.** $\blacksquare = 20 \div 4$

Copy and complete each table.

12.

÷	9	12	15	18
3	■	■	■	■

13.

÷	16	20	24	28
4	■	■	■	■

Find each quotient.

14. $12 \div 4 = \blacksquare$ **15.** $\blacksquare = 6 \div 3$ **16.** $\blacksquare = 14 \div 2$ **17.** $12 \div 2 = \blacksquare$

18. $\blacksquare = 18 \div 2$ **19.** $32 \div 4 = \blacksquare$ **20.** $\blacksquare = 9 \div 3$ **21.** $30 \div 5 = \blacksquare$

22. $3\overline{)3}$ **23.** $3\overline{)18}$ **24.** $4\overline{)36}$ **25.** $5\overline{)20}$

Complete.

26. $20 \div 4 = 8 - \blacksquare$ **27.** $24 \div 3 = \blacksquare \times 2$ **28.** $36 \div \blacksquare = 18 \div 2$

29. **MULTISTEP** Yusef collected 38 pinecones. He kept 11 pinecones for himself and divided the rest equally among 3 friends. How many pinecones did each friend get?

30. **MULTISTEP** The scouts saw squirrels and birds. If there were 4 animals and 12 legs, how many squirrels and birds were there? Draw a picture to show your answer.

31. **REASONING** Two numbers have a product of 16 and a quotient of 4. What are they?

32. **Write About It** Explain how to solve $32 \div 4$ in 2 different ways.

Maintain Skills

33. Write the product.

$4 \times 6 = \blacksquare$

CRCT Test Prep

34. M3N2.c. Paula had $1.36. Her aunt gave her $5.25 for her birthday. How much money does Paula have now? (p. 98)

A. $3.89 C. $6.51
B. $5.61 D. $6.61

LESSON 3

Use 1 and 0 in Division

M3N4.a. Understand the relationship between division and multiplication and between division and subtraction. *also* M3P2.a., M3P2.b., M3P2.c., M3P2.d., M3P3.a., M3P3.b., M3P3.c., M3P3.d.

Quick Review

1. $8 \times \blacksquare = 8$
2. $3 \times 0 = \blacksquare$
3. $\blacksquare \times 1 = 4$
4. $0 \times 10 = \blacksquare$
5. $1 \times \blacksquare = 7$

Learn

MOO . . . VE OVER Here are some rules for dividing with 1 and 0.

RULE A

Any number divided by 1 equals that number.

3	÷	1	=	3
↑		↑		↑
number of cows		number of stalls		number in each stall

If there is only 1 stall, then all of the cows must be in that stall.

RULE B

Any number (except 0) divided by itself equals 1.

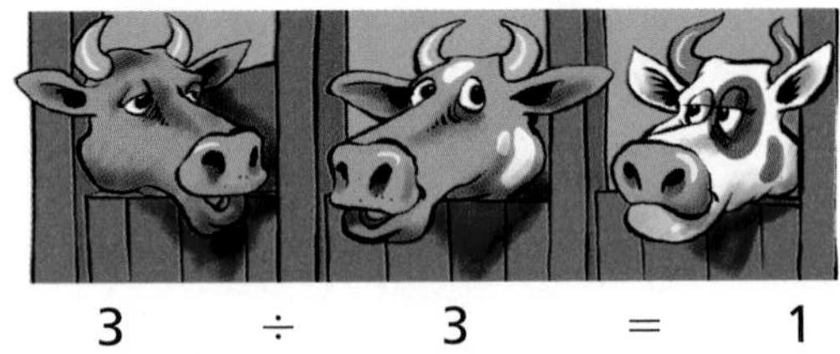

3	÷	3	=	1
↑		↑		↑
number of cows		number of stalls		number in each stall

If there are the same number of cows and stalls, then one cow goes in each stall.

RULE C

Zero divided by any number (except 0) equals 0.

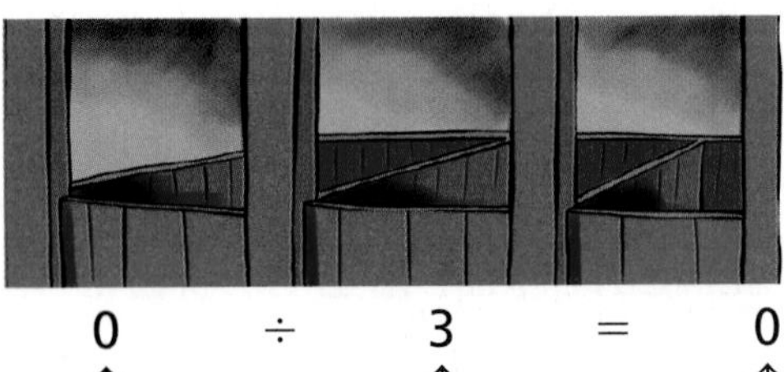

0	÷	3	=	0
↑		↑		↑
number of cows		number of stalls		number in each stall

If there are no cows, then no matter how many stalls you have, there won't be any cows in the stalls.

RULE D

You cannot divide by 0.

If there are no stalls, then you aren't separating cows into equal groups. So, using division doesn't make sense.

- **REASONING** How can you use multiplication to show that $3 \div 0 = \blacksquare$ doesn't make sense?

Check

1. **Explain** how you can use multiplication to check $0 \div 9 = 0$.

Find each quotient.

2. $3 \div 3 =$ ■ **3.** ■ $= 5 \div 1$ **4.** $0 \div 2 =$ ■ **5.** ■ $= 6 \div 6$

6. $7 \div 1 =$ ■ **7.** $0 \div 6 =$ ■ **8.** ■ $= 4 \div 4$ **9.** $10 \div 1 =$ ■

Practice and Problem Solving

Extra Practice, page 232, Set C

Find each quotient.

10. $2 \div 1 =$ ■ **11.** $8 \div 8 =$ ■ **12.** ■ $= 6 \div 3$ **13.** $1 \div 1 =$ ■

14. $20 \div 5 =$ ■ **15.** ■ $= 0 \div 4$ **16.** ■ $= 5 \div 5$ **17.** $10 \div 2 =$ ■

18. $3 \div 1 =$ ■ **19.** $21 \div 3 =$ ■ **20.** $32 \div 4 =$ ■ **21.** ■ $= 0 \div 7$

22. Divide 2 by 2. **23.** Divide 4 by 1. **24.** Divide 0 by 3. **25.** Divide 14 by 2.

26. $5\overline{)35}$ **27.** $9\overline{)9}$ **28.** $2\overline{)16}$ **29.** $5\overline{)0}$ **30.** $2\overline{)14}$

31. $3\overline{)18}$ **32.** $1\overline{)8}$ **33.** $4\overline{)36}$ **34.** $7\overline{)7}$ **35.** $1\overline{)0}$

Compare. Write <, >, or = for each ●.

36. $4 \div 1$ ● $4 \div 4$ **37.** $0 \div 9$ ● $9 \div 1$ **38.** $6 + 4$ ● $5 \div 1$

39. **MULTISTEP** A farmer has 6 bales of hay. He feeds 2 bales to his cows. He divides the rest equally among 4 stalls. How many bales are in each stall?

40. **REASONING** Chelsea says, "Ask me to divide any number by 1, and I'll give you the quotient." What is her strategy?

41. Use what you know about 0 and 1 to find each quotient.
a. $398 \div 398 =$ ■ **b.** $971 \div 1 =$ ■ **c.** $0 \div 426 =$ ■

Maintain Skills

42. $22 + 38$

43. $54 - 17$

44. $93 - 28$

45. $62 + 29$

CRCT Test Prep

46. M3N3.g. Akiko bought 3 sandwiches. Each sandwich cost \$4. How much did she spend for the sandwiches? (p. 132)

A. \$4 B. \$7 C. \$12 D. \$15

LESSON 

Algebra: Expressions

M3N4.c. Recognize problem-solving situations in which division may be applied and write corresponding mathematical expressions. *also* **M3P3.a., M3P3.b., M3P3.c., M3P3.d., M3P4., M3P5.**

Learn

HAPPY CAMPERS The 21 campers were divided into 3 equal groups. How many campers are in each group?

Write an expression to show how many campers are in each group.

21 campers	divided into	3 groups
↓	↓	↓
21	÷	3

You can use the expression to write a number sentence. A number sentence uses an equal sign to show that two amounts are equal. Use the number sentence to solve the problem.

21 campers	divided into	3 groups	is equal to	7 campers in each group.
↓	↓	↓	↓	↓
21	÷	3	=	7

So, there are 7 campers in each group.

Mr. Gonzales is lining up 20 campers in 4 rows for relay races. There are 5 campers in each row.

$$20 \bullet 4 = 5$$

Which symbol will complete the number sentence?

Try + $20 + 4 \neq 5$

Try − $20 - 4 \neq 5$

Try × $20 \times 4 \neq 5$

Try ÷ $20 \div 4 = 5$

So, the correct symbol is ÷.

Quick Review

1. $20 \div 4 = \blacksquare$
2. $0 \div 7 = \blacksquare$
3. $10 \div 10 = \blacksquare$
4. $36 \div 4 = \blacksquare$
5. $16 \div 2 = \blacksquare$

Remember

An *expression* is part of a number sentence.

Examples:

3 + 4   4 × 2

25 − 12   12 ÷ 6

Check

1. Write a number sentence using multiplication to describe the relay race problem above.

Write an expression to describe each problem.

2. Seven campers shared 63 carrot sticks equally. How many carrot sticks did each camper eat?

3. Amy used 72 beads to make bracelets. Each bracelet has 9 beads. How many bracelets did Amy make?

Practice and Problem Solving

Extra Practice, page 232, Set D

For 4–6, write an expression to describe each problem.

4. On the nature hike, Beth picked up two pinecones. There were 48 seeds in one and 55 seeds in the other. How many seeds were in the two pinecones in all?

5. **FAST FACT** • SCIENCE About 65 species of pine trees grow in North America. Thirty-six of them grow in the United States. How many do not grow in the United States?

6. **MULTISTEP** Matt and 7 other campers made bird feeders from pinecones and peanut butter. They shared 40 pinecones equally. How many pinecones did each camper use?

7. **Vocabulary Power** A *symbol* can be used to show something easily and quickly. A stop sign is a symbol that tells drivers to stop. Name other symbols that you see every day.

Write +, −, ×, or ÷ to complete the number sentence.

8. $13 \bullet 7 = 2 \times 3$

9. $12 + 5 = 9 \bullet 8$

10. $6 \times 4 = 8 \bullet 3$

11. **Write a problem** for each expression.

a. $35 \div 5$ b. 7×3 c. $15 - 3$

Maintain Skills

12. $48 + 21$

13. $125 + 592$

14. $86 - 13$

15. $622 - 404$

16. $673 + 235 = \blacksquare$

17. $429 - 391 = \blacksquare$

CRCT Test Prep

18. M3N2.c. Josh bought a pair of scissors for \$2.25, a pack of paper for \$1.95, and markers for \$3.75. He gave the clerk a \$10 bill. How much change should Josh get? (p. 98)

A. \$1.05
B. \$2.05
C. \$3.05
D. \$4.05

LESSON 5

Problem Solving Skill
Choose the Operation

M3P1.c. Apply and adapt a variety of appropriate strategies to solve problems *also* **M3P1.a., M3P1.b., M3P2.d., M3P3.a., M3P3.b., M3P3.c., M3P3.d.**

UNDERSTAND | **PLAN** | **SOLVE** | **CHECK**

NATURE WALK On a hike, the campers saw 6 chipmunks, 4 deer, and 8 butterflies. They also saw 3 turtles on each of 4 large rocks. How many turtles did they see in all?

This chart can help you decide when to use each operation.

ADD	• Join groups of different sizes.
SUBTRACT	• Take away. • Compare amounts.
MULTIPLY	• Join equal groups.
DIVIDE	• Separate into equal groups. • Find the number in each group.

MATH IDEA Before you solve a problem, decide what operation to use. Write an expression to solve the problem.

Since you are joining equal groups, multiply.

4	×	3	=	12
↓		↓		↓
number of rocks		number of turtles on each rock		total number of turtles

So, they saw 12 turtles in all.

- **REASONING** When would you use division to solve a problem?
- Write an expression you could use to find how many animals they saw in all.

Quick Review

Choose +, −, ×, or ÷ for each ●.

1. 18 ● 5 = 13
2. 16 ● 8 = 2
3. 3 ● 2 = 6
4. 4 ● 4 = 16
5. 15 − 7 = 4 ● 4

Problem Solving Practice

Choose the operation. Then solve.

1. David collected 8 acorns and 16 wildflowers. He put the same number of wildflowers in each of 8 vases. How many wildflowers were in each vase?
2. **MULTISTEP** The camp counselor put 4 pears, 5 apples, and 7 bananas in a basket. If 3 pieces of fruit were eaten, how many pieces of fruit were left?
3. Beth has a scrapbook. Each page can hold 8 small postcards or 6 large postcards. How many small postcards fit on 4 pages?
4. Shawn took 8 photos of birds, 9 photos of wildflowers, and 15 photos of campers. How many photos did he take?

Thirty students went on a camp cookout. Six students sat at each picnic table. How many tables did they fill?

5. Which number sentence can you use to solve the problem?

   A $30 + 6 = ■$ **C** $30 \div 6 = ■$
   B $30 - 6 = ■$ **D** $30 \times 6 = ■$

6. What is the answer to the question?

   F 24 students
   G 5 tables
   H 5 students
   J 1 table

Mixed Applications

USE DATA For 7–9, use the graph.

7. **MULTISTEP** Gina took 5 packs of soda to the cookout. Were there enough bottles of soda for 28 people? Explain.
8. **MULTISTEP** Khar bought 3 packs of water. He gave 4 bottles to friends. How many bottles of water did he have left?
9. **What's the Question?** The answer is 30 bottles of juice.

Extra Practice

Set A (pp. 222–223)

Find each missing factor and quotient.

1. $2 \times ■ = 10$ $\quad 10 \div 2 = ■$ **2.** $5 \times ■ = 30$ $\quad 30 \div 5 = ■$

Find each quotient.

3. $15 \div 5 = ■$ **4.** $■ = 16 \div 2$ **5.** $■ = 45 \div 5$ **6.** $10 \div 5 = ■$

7. $2\overline{)2}$ **8.** $5\overline{)20}$ **9.** $2\overline{)18}$ **10.** $5\overline{)25}$ **11.** $2\overline{)12}$

12. Divide 20 by 2. **13.** Divide 35 by 5. **14.** Divide 6 by 2.

Set B (pp. 224–225)

Write the multiplication fact you can use to find the quotient. Then write the quotient.

1. $18 \div 3 = ■$ **2.** $32 \div 4 = ■$ **3.** $9 \div 3 = ■$

Find each quotient.

4. $28 \div 4 = ■$ **5.** $12 \div 3 = ■$ **6.** $■ = 27 \div 3$ **7.** $■ = 8 \div 4$

8. $4\overline{)16}$ **9.** $3\overline{)15}$ **10.** $4\overline{)24}$ **11.** $3\overline{)21}$ **12.** $4\overline{)12}$

13. Divide 30 by 3. **14.** Divide 20 by 4. **15.** Divide 36 by 4.

Set C (pp. 226–227)

Find each quotient.

1. $0 \div 4 = ■$ **2.** $■ = 3 \div 3$ **3.** $■ = 8 \div 1$ **4.** $10 \div 10 = ■$

5. $7\overline{)7}$ **6.** $8\overline{)0}$ **7.** $1\overline{)4}$ **8.** $3\overline{)0}$ **9.** $9\overline{)9}$

Set D (pp. 228–229)

Write an expression to describe each problem.

1. Four friends share 28 stickers equally. How many stickers does each friend get?

2. Melinda had \$15. She buys slippers for \$8. How much money does she have now?

Write +, −, ×, or ÷ to complete the number sentence.

3. $6 \times 3 = 12 \; ■ \; 6$ **4.** $5 \times 7 = 38 \; ■ \; 3$ **5.** $24 \div 3 = 4 \; ■ \; 2$

CHAPTER 12

Review/Test

CHECK VOCABULARY

Choose the best term from the box.

Vocabulary
divided
multiplied
zero

1. You cannot divide by _?_. (p. 226)
2. Any number (except 0) _?_ by itself equals 1. (p. 226)

CHECK SKILLS

Find each quotient. (pp. 222–227)

3. $16 \div 4 = \blacksquare$
4. $\blacksquare = 21 \div 3$
5. $6 \div 1 = \blacksquare$
6. $\blacksquare = 25 \div 5$
7. $8 \div 2 = \blacksquare$
8. $0 \div 5 = \blacksquare$
9. $\blacksquare = 9 \div 3$
10. $\blacksquare = 8 \div 1$
11. $4\overline{)32}$
12. $1\overline{)10}$
13. $2\overline{)18}$
14. $3\overline{)0}$
15. $5\overline{)15}$
16. $2\overline{)14}$
17. $3\overline{)15}$
18. $5\overline{)0}$
19. $4\overline{)24}$
20. $5\overline{)40}$

Write an expression to describe each problem. (pp. 228–229)

21. Lila made 18 muffins. She put 3 muffins in each bag. How many bags did Lila fill?
22. Kyle had 32 shells. He gave 8 to his friend. How many shells does Kyle have now?
23. Marcy planted 24 flowers in 4 rows. Each row had the same number of flowers. How many flowers did Marcy plant in each row?

CHECK PROBLEM SOLVING

Choose the operation. Then solve. (pp. 230–231)

24. Chiang has 24 trading cards. She puts the cards into piles of 6. How many piles does she make?
25. Casey has 5 packs of stickers. Each pack has 8 stickers. How many stickers does he have?

Chapter CRCT Test Prep

NUMBERS AND OPERATIONS

1. M3N4.f. Katie had 10 cookies. She gave the same number of cookies to each of 5 friends. How many cookies did each person get?

A. 2

B. 3

C. 4

D. 5

2. M3N4.c. A group of 12 people want to ride a Ferris wheel. Two people will sit in each car. Which expression tells how many cars they need?

A. $12 - 2$

B. $12 + 2$

C. 12×2

D. $12 \div 2$

3. M3N4.f. A farmer bought 16 carrots. He gave 4 carrots to each of his horses. How many horses does the farmer have?

A. 4

B. 5

C. 12

D. 20

ALGEBRA

4. M3A1.c. Which numbers complete the table?

÷	20	25	30	35	40
5	4	5	□	□	□

A. 4, 5, 6

B. 5, 6, 7

C. 6, 7, 8

D. 7, 8, 9

5. M3A1.c. Which number belongs in the □ to make the number sentence true?

$$14 \div 2 = \square$$

A. 1

B. 4

C. 6

D. 7

6. M3A1.c. Colin has 24 toy cars. He wants to put the same number of cars into each of 3 boxes. Which number sentence can he use to find the number of cars he should put in each box?

A. $24 - 3 = \square$

B. $24 \div 3 = \square$

C. $24 \times 3 = \square$

D. $24 + 3 = \square$

Cumulative CRCT Test Prep

ALGEBRA

7. M3A1.a. Pam read 8 pages of a book on Monday, 16 pages on Tuesday, and 24 pages on Wednesday. If the pattern continues, how many pages will Pam read on Friday?

A. 8

B. 32

C. 34

D. 40

8. M3A1.c. Jay bought 48 marbles. He wants to put 6 marbles in each bag. Which number sentence can he use to find the number of bags he will need?

A. $6 - \square = 48$

B. $6 + \square = 48$

C. $6 \times \square = 48$

D. $6 \div \square = 48$

9. M3A1.c. Which number belongs in the $\square$ to make the number sentence true?

$$45 + \square = 71$$

A. 24

B. 26

C. 34

D. 116

DATA ANALYSIS

Use the graph below to answer question 10.

10. M3D1.b. Geri's class took a survey to find out their favorite ice cream flavors. How many more students chose chocolate than butter pecan?

A. 6

B. 8

C. 10

D. 12

Division Facts Through 10

FAST FACT • SOCIAL STUDIES The first pizzeria in the United States was opened in 1905 in New York City. America's favorite pizza topping is pepperoni.

Using Data

PEPPERONI PIZZA	
Restaurant	**Pieces of Pepperoni**
Mario's Pizza	32
Broadway Pizza	56
Mamma Mia's	40
Lorenzo's Pizza	48

INVESTIGATION The table shows the number of pieces of pepperoni on each pizza at different restaurants. Suppose each pizza is cut into 8 slices and the pieces of pepperoni are divided equally among the 8 slices. Use counters to find the number of pieces of pepperoni there would be on 1 slice of pizza from each restaurant.

Use this page to help you review and remember important skills needed for Chapter 13.

COMMUTATIVE PROPERTY OF MULTIPLICATION

Use the Commutative Property of Multiplication to help you find each product.

1. $7 \times 8 = ■$ $8 \times 7 = ■$
2. $6 \times 8 = ■$ $8 \times 6 = ■$
3. $7 \times 9 = ■$ $9 \times 7 = ■$
4. $6 \times 10 = ■$ $10 \times 6 = ■$

DIVISION FACTS THROUGH 5

Find each quotient.

5. $35 \div 5 = ■$
6. $8 \div 2 = ■$
7. $20 \div 4 = ■$
8. $0 \div 5 = ■$
9. $■ = 18 \div 3$
10. $12 \div 4 = ■$
11. $■ = 9 \div 1$
12. $16 \div 2 = ■$

MISSING FACTORS

Find the missing factor.

13. $3 \times ■ = 27$
14. $25 = ■ \times 5$
15. $■ \times 6 = 12$
16. $45 = 9 \times ■$
17. $6 \times ■ = 48$
18. $■ \times 8 = 32$
19. $35 = 5 \times ■$
20. $20 = ■ \times 4$

REVIEW

quotient [kwō′shənt] *noun*

The word *quotient* comes from the Latin root *quot*, which means "how many." Write a word problem that could be solved by finding a quotient. Use the words *how many* in your problem.

www.harcourtschool.com/mathglossary

LESSON 1

Divide by 6, 7, and 8

M3N4.a. Understand the relationship between division and multiplication and between division and subtraction. *also* **M3A1.c., M3P2.b., M3P4.a.**

Quick Review

1. $6 \times 3 = \blacksquare$
2. $6 \times 7 = \blacksquare$
3. $7 \times 4 = \blacksquare$
4. $7 \times 8 = \blacksquare$
5. $8 \times 4 = \blacksquare$

Learn

IT'S IN THE BAG The Bagel Stop sells bagels in bags of 6. Ramona has 24 fresh bagels to put in bags. How many bags does she need?

$24 \div 6 = \blacksquare$

Use a related multiplication fact to find the quotient.

Think: $6 \times \blacksquare = 24$

$6 \times 4 = 24$

$24 \div 6 = 4$, or $6\overline{)24}$ with quotient 4

So, Ramona needs 4 bags.

Examples

A $63 \div 7 = \blacksquare$

Think: $7 \times \blacksquare = 63$

$7 \times 9 = 63$

$63 \div 7 = 9$, or $7\overline{)63}$ with quotient 9

B $56 \div 8 = \blacksquare$

Think: $8 \times \blacksquare = 56$

$8 \times 7 = 56$

$56 \div 8 = 7$, or $8\overline{)56}$ with quotient 7

MATH IDEA Think of related multiplication facts to help you divide.

- What multiplication fact can you use to find $42 \div 7$? What is the quotient?

Technology Link

More Practice:
Harcourt Mega Math The Number Games, *Up Up and Array,* Levels F and G

Equal Groups

Remember, you can also use equal groups and arrays to help you find a quotient.

Here are two different ways to find 28 ÷ 7.

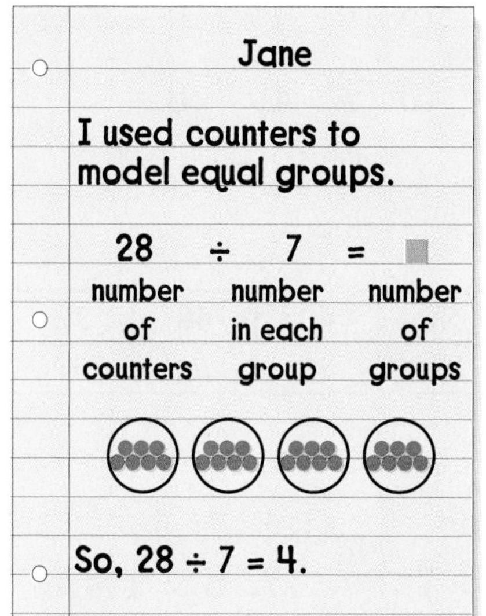

Kevin

I modeled the problem with an array.

28 ÷ 7 = ■

number in array | number in each row | number of rows

So, 28 ÷ 7 = 4.

- **REASONING** You have used equal groups and arrays to help you find products. Why can you also use them to help you find quotients?

Check

1. **Explain** how you would use a related multiplication fact to find 18 ÷ 6.

Find the missing factor and quotient.

2. $8 \times ■ = 16$ $\quad 16 \div 8 = ■$
3. $7 \times ■ = 35$ $\quad 35 \div 7 = ■$
4. $6 \times ■ = 36$ $\quad 36 \div 6 = ■$
5. $6 \times ■ = 30$ $\quad 30 \div 6 = ■$

Copy and complete each table.

6.

÷	14	21	28	35
7	■	■	■	■

7.

÷	6	12	18	24
6	■	■	■	■

Find the quotient.

8. $21 \div 7 = ■$
9. $42 \div 6 = ■$
10. $■ = 56 \div 7$
11. $32 \div 8 = ■$
12. $8\overline{)40}$
13. $7\overline{)42}$
14. $8\overline{)24}$
15. $6\overline{)24}$

LESSON CONTINUES

Practice and Problem Solving

Extra Practice, page 252, Set A

Find the missing factor and quotient.

16. $7 \times ■ = 14$ $14 \div 7 = ■$
17. $6 \times ■ = 60$ $60 \div 6 = ■$
18. $6 \times ■ = 48$ $48 \div 6 = ■$
19. $8 \times ■ = 72$ $72 \div 8 = ■$
20. $7 \times ■ = 42$ $42 \div 7 = ■$
21. $8 \times ■ = 40$ $40 \div 8 = ■$

Copy and complete each table.

22.

÷	42	63	56	49
7	■	■	■	■

23.

÷	56	40	48	32
8	■	■	■	■

Find the quotient.

24. $36 \div 6 = ■$
25. $80 \div 8 = ■$
26. $■ = 0 \div 7$
27. $8 \div 1 = ■$
28. $■ = 15 \div 3$
29. $■ = 18 \div 6$
30. $45 \div 5 = ■$
31. $24 \div 8 = ■$
32. $8\overline{)64}$
33. $2\overline{)14}$
34. $7\overline{)28}$
35. $6\overline{)0}$
36. Divide 42 by 6.
37. Divide 8 by 8.
38. Divide 35 by 5.

Write a division sentence for each.

39.

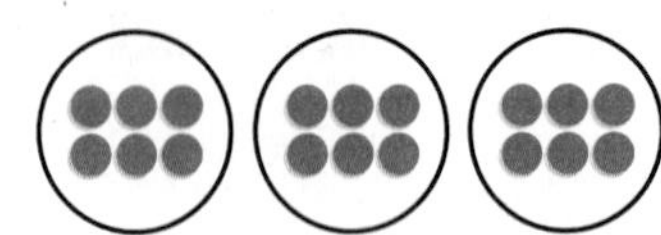

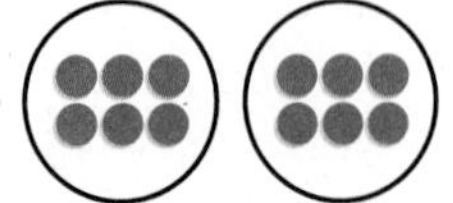

40.

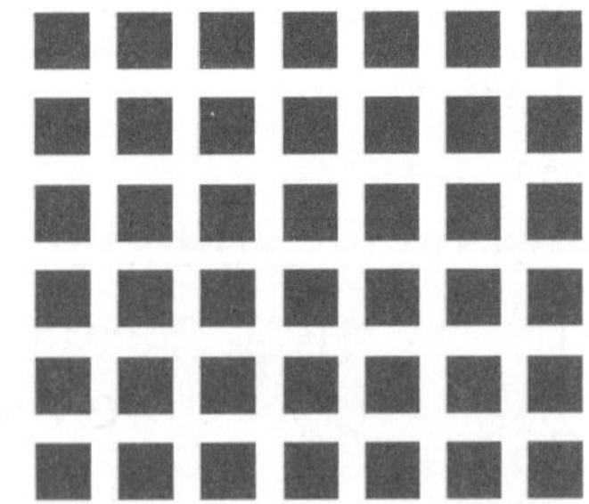

ALGEBRA **Complete.**

41. $3 + ■ = 49 \div 7$
42. $8 \times 5 = ■ \times 10$
43. $■ - 4 = 24 \div 6$
44. $■ \times 4 = 8 \times 3$
45. $6 \div 6 = 0 + ■$
46. $5 + 3 = 16 \div ■$

47. **REASONING** Is the quotient $24 \div 6$ greater than or less than the quotient $24 \div 4$? How do you know?

48. **? What's the Question?** Hikara bought 35 fruit chews. Fruit chews come in packs of 5. The answer is 7 packs.

49. **FAST FACT** • SOCIAL STUDIES The bagel is the only bread product that is boiled before it is baked. A baker made 48 bagels and placed an equal number in each of 6 bags. How many bagels are in 2 bags?

50. **MULTISTEP** Asha had 24 pictures of her friends. She put 8 pictures on each page in a photo album. Her album has 20 pages. How many album pages do not have pictures?

Maintain Skills

Write the time.

51.

52.

53. Write the amount.

CRCT Test Prep

54. M3N2.c. Luther read 154 pages of his book on Saturday. He read 139 pages on Sunday. How many pages did he read in all? (p. 54)

A. 215 B. 283 C. 293 D. 294

55. M3N2.c. Patricia collected 205 stickers. She gave 28 stickers to her sister. How many stickers does Patricia have left? (p. 74)

A. 177 B. 187 C. 233 D. 277

Problem Solving LINKUP . . . to Reading

STRATEGY • CHOOSE IMPORTANT INFORMATION

Some word problems have more information than you need. Before you solve a problem, find the facts you need to solve the problem.

Mrs. Taylor baked 8 batches of muffins. She had a total of 48 muffins. She also baked 2 cakes. How many muffins were in each batch?

Facts You Need: baked 8 batches of muffins, total of 48 muffins

Fact You Don't Need: baked 2 cakes

$$48 \div 8 = 6$$

So, there were 6 muffins in each batch.

Write the important facts. Solve the problem.

1. Bonnie made 4 batches of cookies and 3 pies in the morning. She made 3 batches of cookies in the afternoon. She made 63 cookies in all. How many cookies were in each batch?

LESSON 2

Divide by 9 and 10

M3N4.a. Understand the relationship between division and multiplication and between division and subtraction. *also* M3A1.c., M3P2.b., M3P2.d., M3P3., M3P3.a., M3P3.b., M3P3.c., M3P3.d., M3P5.a., M3P5.c.

Quick Review

1. 9 × 3 = ■
2. 9 × 5 = ■
3. 10 × 4 = ■
4. 8 × 10 = ■
5. 9 × 10 = ■

Learn

PLENTY OF PINS Katie collects different kinds of pins. She has boxes that hold 9 or 10 pins. Help Katie organize her collection.

Examples

A Katie puts her 45 state flag pins in boxes that hold 9 pins each. How many boxes does she need?

45 ÷ 9 = ■

Think: 9 × ■ = 45

9 × 5 = 45

45 ÷ 9 = 5, or $9\overline{)45}$ with quotient 5

So, Katie needs 5 boxes for her state flag pins.

B Katie puts her 60 flower pins in boxes that hold 10 pins each. How many boxes does she need?

60 ÷ 10 = ■

Think: 10 × ■ = 60

10 × 6 = 60

60 ÷ 10 = 6, or $10\overline{)60}$ with quotient 6

So, Katie needs 6 boxes for her flower pins.

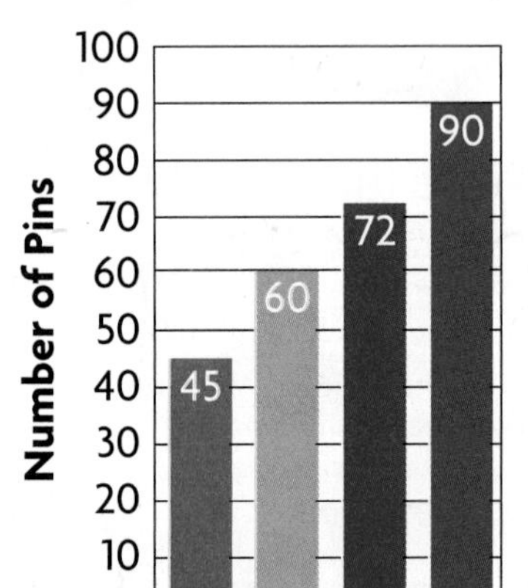

Check

1. **Explain** how to use a related multiplication fact to find 36 ÷ 9. What is the quotient?

Copy and complete each table.

2.

÷	9	18	27	36
9	■	■	■	■

3.

÷	20	30	40	50
10	■	■	■	■

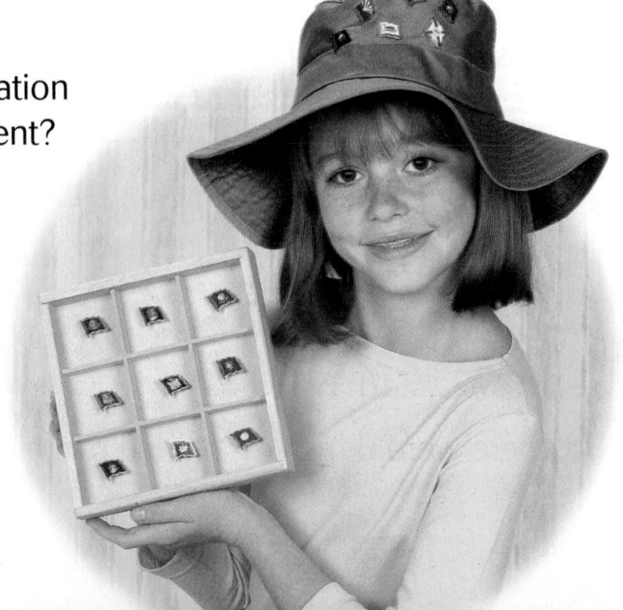

Practice and Problem Solving

Extra Practice, page 252, Set B

Copy and complete each table.

4.

÷	54	72	63	81
9	■	■	■	■

5.

÷	70	90	80	100
10	■	■	■	■

Find the quotient.

6. $45 \div 9 = $ ■ **7.** ■ $= 10 \div 10$ **8.** ■ $= 0 \div 9$ **9.** $60 \div 10 = $ ■

10. $9 \div 1 = $ ■ **11.** $12 \div 6 = $ ■ **12.** $18 \div 3 = $ ■ **13.** ■ $= 36 \div 9$

14. ■ $= 50 \div 10$ **15.** $14 \div 2 = $ ■ **16.** ■ $= 12 \div 4$ **17.** $40 \div 5 = $ ■

18. $8\overline{)64}$ **19.** $5\overline{)25}$ **20.** $7\overline{)28}$ **21.** $3\overline{)24}$

22. Divide 72 by 8. **23.** Divide 42 by 7. **24.** Divide 70 by 10.

ALGEBRA Write +, −, ×, or ÷ for each ●.

25. 10 ● $10 = 2 - 1$ **26.** $8 \times 3 = 20$ ● 4 **27.** 12 ● $7 = 50 \div 10$

28. $3 \times 6 = 2$ ● 9 **29.** 81 ● $9 = 3 \times 3$ **30.** $6 \times 7 = 35$ ● 7

31. **REASONING** Ken has 89 patches in his collection. He puts 8 patches on his vest and puts the rest in boxes of 9 patches each. How many boxes does Ken need?

32. **REASONING** Boxes for 9 pins cost \$4 each. Boxes for 10 pins cost \$5 each. Janine has 90 pins. If she wants to spend the least amount of money, what type of boxes should she buy?

33. **Vocabulary Power** The words *division, dividend,* and *divisor* come from a Latin word that means "to take apart." How is division like taking something apart?

34. **Write About It** Make a table showing the 9's division facts. Describe any patterns you see in your table.

Maintain Skills

Compare. Write <, >, or = for each ●.

35. 39 ● 56 **36.** 74 ● 47

37. 63 ● 69 **38.** 22 ● 11

CRCT Test Prep

39. M3N3.b. Which expression has the same product as $2 \times 3 \times 9$? (p. 186)

A. 2×6 C. 3×9

B. 6×6 D. 6×9

LESSON 3

Practice Division Facts

M3N4.a. Understand the relationship between division and multiplication and between division and subtraction. *also* M3A1.c., M3P3.a., M3P3.b., M3P3.c., M3P3.d., M3P4.a., M3P4.b., M3P5.c.

Quick Review

1. $7 \times \blacksquare = 56$
2. $\blacksquare \times 3 = 27$
3. $6 \times \blacksquare = 30$
4. $\blacksquare \times 4 = 16$
5. $5 \times \blacksquare = 40$

Learn

BOXED CARS Bobby has 36 toy cars that he wants to put in display boxes. Each display box holds 9 cars. How many display boxes will Bobby need?

$36 \div 9 = \blacksquare$

There are many ways to find the quotient.

A. Use counters.

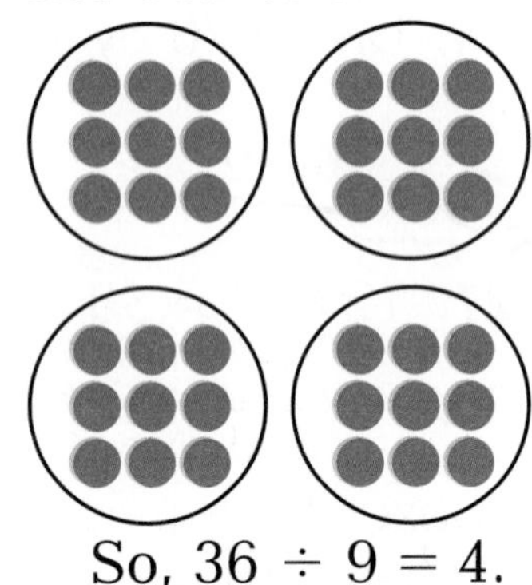

So, $36 \div 9 = 4$.

B. Use repeated subtraction.

$$\begin{array}{r}36\\-\;9\\\hline 27\end{array}\quad\begin{array}{r}27\\-\;9\\\hline 18\end{array}\quad\begin{array}{r}18\\-\;9\\\hline 9\end{array}\quad\begin{array}{r}9\\-9\\\hline 0\end{array}$$

Number of times you subtract 9: 1 2 3 4

So, $36 \div 9 = 4$.

C. Use fact families.

Fact Family for 4, 9, and 36

factor		factor		product	dividend		divisor		quotient
4	×	9	=	36	36	÷	9	=	4
9	×	4	=	36	36	÷	4	=	9

So, $36 \div 9 = 4$.

D. Use an array.

Make an array with 36 tiles.
Count the rows of 9 tiles each.
There are 4 rows of 9 tiles.

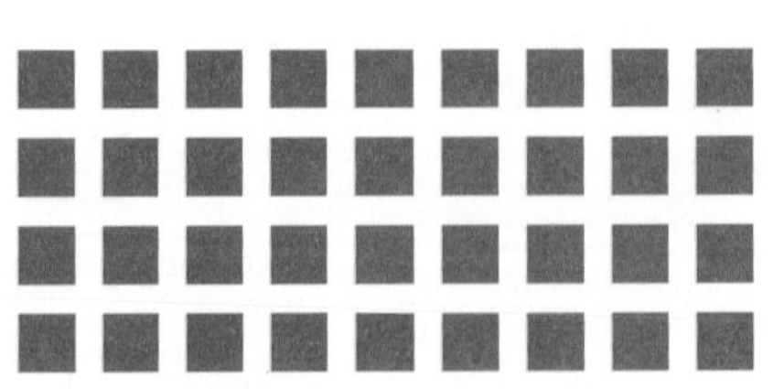

Since $4 \times 9 = 36$, then $36 \div 9 = 4$.

Find Missing Factors

E. Use a multiplication table.

Think: ■ × 9 = 36

- Find the given factor 9 in the top row.
- Look down the column to find the product, 36.
- Look left across the row to find the missing factor, 4.

$4 \times 9 = 36 \quad 36 \div 9 = 4$

So, Bobby needs 4 display boxes.

×	0	1	2	3	4	5	6	7	8	9	10
0	0	0	0	0	0	0	0	0	0	0	0
1	0	1	2	3	4	5	6	7	8	9	10
2	0	2	4	6	8	10	12	14	16	18	20
3	0	3	6	9	12	15	18	21	24	27	30
4	0	4	8	12	16	20	24	28	32	36	40
5	0	5	10	15	20	25	30	35	40	45	50
6	0	6	12	18	24	30	36	42	48	54	60
7	0	7	14	21	28	35	42	49	56	63	70
8	0	8	16	24	32	40	48	56	64	72	80
9	0	9	18	27	36	45	54	63	72	81	90
10	0	10	20	30	40	50	60	70	80	90	100

MATH IDEA Use equal groups, repeated subtraction, fact families, arrays, and multiplication tables to help you find quotients.

Technology Link

More Practice:
Harcourt Mega Math The Number Games, *Up, Up, and Array,* Levels F and G

Check

1. **Explain** how to find $56 \div 8$ in two different ways.

Write a division sentence for each.

2. 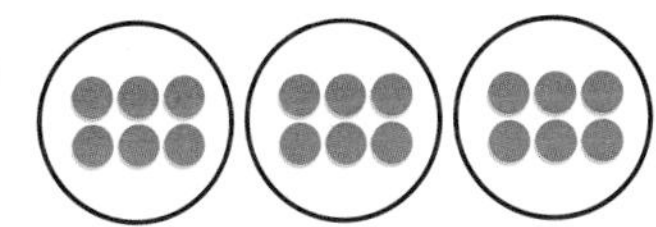

3.  

4.
$$\begin{array}{r} 21 \\ -\ 7 \\ \hline 14 \end{array} \quad \begin{array}{r} 14 \\ -\ 7 \\ \hline 7 \end{array} \quad \begin{array}{r} 7 \\ -7 \\ \hline 0 \end{array}$$

Find the missing factor and quotient.

5. $3 \times$ ■ $= 15 \quad 15 \div 3 =$ ■
6. $8 \times$ ■ $= 32 \quad 32 \div 8 =$ ■
7. $4 \times$ ■ $= 40 \quad 40 \div 4 =$ ■
8. $7 \times$ ■ $= 56 \quad 56 \div 7 =$ ■

Find the quotient.

9. $10 \div 2 =$ ■
10. $18 \div 9 =$ ■
11. ■ $= 49 \div 7$
12. $80 \div 10 =$ ■
13. $6\overline{)0}$
14. $9\overline{)9}$
15. $8\overline{)40}$
16. $5\overline{)20}$

LESSON CONTINUES

Practice and Problem Solving

Extra Practice, page 252, Set C

Write a division sentence for each.

17. 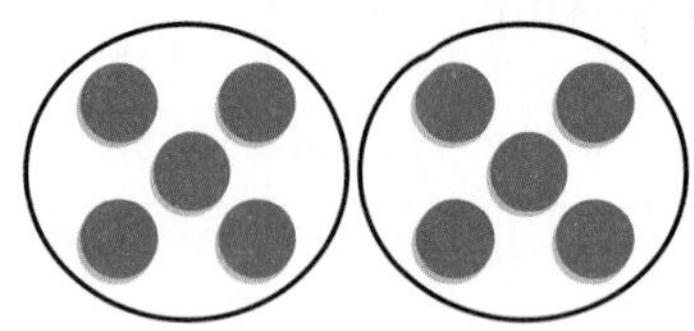

18. 

19.
$$\begin{array}{r} 27 \\ -\ 9 \\ \hline 18 \end{array} \nearrow \begin{array}{r} 18 \\ -\ 9 \\ \hline 9 \end{array} \nearrow \begin{array}{r} 9 \\ -9 \\ \hline 0 \end{array}$$

Find the missing factor and quotient.

20. $10 \times$ ■ $= 90$ $\quad 90 \div 10 =$ ■

21. $7 \times$ ■ $= 35$ $\quad 35 \div 7 =$ ■

22. $4 \times$ ■ $= 16$ $\quad 16 \div 4 =$ ■

23. $9 \times$ ■ $= 63$ $\quad 63 \div 9 =$ ■

Find the quotient.

24. $10 \div 1 =$ ■

25. ■ $= 35 \div 5$

26. $50 \div 10 =$ ■

27. ■ $= 16 \div 2$

28. ■ $= 81 \div 9$

29. ■ $= 20 \div 10$

30. $60 \div 6 =$ ■

31. $24 \div 3 =$ ■

32. $9\overline{)54}$

33. $7\overline{)28}$

34. $8\overline{)72}$

35. $10\overline{)100}$

36. Divide 63 by 7.

37. Divide 30 by 5.

38. Divide 0 by 9.

Choose the letter of the division sentence that matches each.

a. $42 \div 6 = 7$ b. $32 \div 8 = 4$ c. $56 \div 7 = 8$ d. $24 \div 8 = 3$

39. 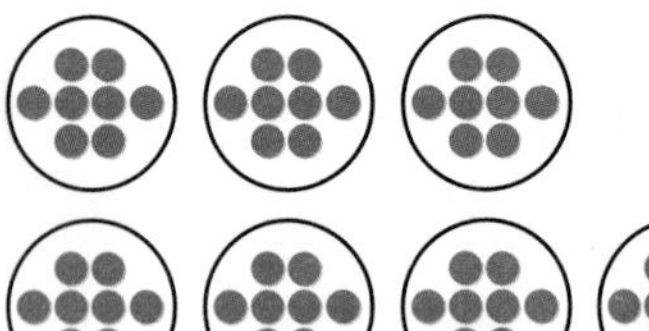

40. 

Compare. Write <, >, or = for each ●.

41. 9×6 ● 9×5

42. $24 \div 6$ ● $16 \div 4$

43. $4 + 4$ ● $72 \div 8$

44. 8×5 ● 10×4

45. $23 - 18$ ● $45 \div 5$

46. 3×3 ● $70 \div 10$

47. **REASONING** Roberta has some boxes that hold 8 cars in each. Could the full boxes hold 20 cars in all? Explain.

48. **Write a problem** about Jonah buying several toy cars that cost \$3 each. Use division in your problem.

49. MULTISTEP Chi has 2 sheets of stickers. Each sheet has 9 rows of 7 stickers. If Chi uses 2 rows of stickers, how many stickers will Chi have left?

50. MULTISTEP Carla put 24 toy animals in 4 boxes. Each box has the same number of animals. How many animals are in 3 boxes?

Maintain Skills

51. $\begin{array}{r} 35 \\ +22 \\ \hline \end{array}$

52. $\begin{array}{r} 137 \\ +353 \\ \hline \end{array}$

53. $\begin{array}{r} 78 \\ -21 \\ \hline \end{array}$

54. $\begin{array}{r} 348 \\ -162 \\ \hline \end{array}$

Compare. Write <, >, or = for each ●.

55. 58 ● 34

56. 18 ● 21

57. 60 ● 59

58. 44 ● 37

59. 83 ● 88

60. 97 ● 79

CRCT Test Prep

61. M3N2.c. Maria buys pencils for \$1.39, a notebook for \$1.79, and a marker for \$0.85. If she pays with a \$5 bill, how much change will she get? (p. 98)

A. \$4.03 C. \$1.82
B. \$1.97 D. \$0.97

62. M3A1.c. What number goes in the □ to make the sentence true? (p. 240)

28 ÷ 7 = □

A. 3 B. 4 C. 6 D. 7

Problem Solving Thinker's Corner

MAKE A PREDICTION Using what you know about multiplication and division, make a prediction to complete each statement. Choose from the terms below.

greater than less than equal to

1. The quotient will be __?__ the dividend in the division problems below.
2. The product will be __?__ each factor in the multiplication problems below.

Check your predictions by completing the number sentences below. Use each number in the box only once.

48	6	4
30	63	8
9	5	36

3. ■ ÷ 6 = ■

4. 9 × ■ = ■

5. ■ ÷ 7 = ■

6. ■ × ■ = ■

LESSON 4

Algebra: Find the Cost

M3N4.a. Understand the relationship between division and multiplication and between division and subtraction.
also M3N4.f., M3N3.g., M3A1.c., M3P2.d., M3P3.a., M3P3.b., M3P3.c., M3P3.d.

Quick Review

1. 2 × 9 = ■
2. 4 × 4 = ■
3. 6 × 2 = ■
4. 3 × 5 = ■
5. 10 × 2 = ■

Learn

WHAT'S FOR LUNCH? Mrs. Hugo buys 3 pizzas for her family. How much does Mrs. Hugo spend?

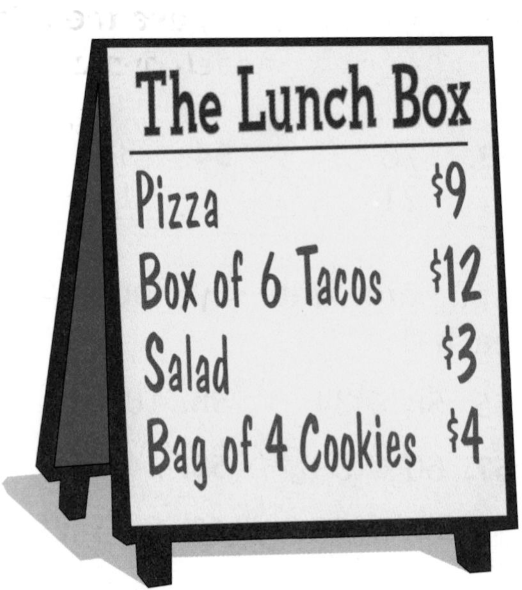

To find the total amount spent, multiply the number of pizzas by the cost of one pizza.

3	×	$9	=	$27
↑		↑		↑
number of pizzas		cost of one		total spent

So, Mrs. Hugo spends $27 for 3 pizzas.

Nicolas buys a box of 6 tacos. How much does each taco cost?

To find the cost of one taco, divide the total amount spent by the number of tacos bought.

$12	÷	6	=	$2
↑		↑		↑
total spent		number of tacos		cost of one

So, each taco costs $2.

MATH IDEA Multiply to find the cost of multiple items. Divide to find the cost of one item.

Check

1. **Explain** how you can find the cost of one cookie.

For 2–3, write a number sentence. Then solve.

2. Alan bought 4 salads. Each salad cost $3. How much did Alan spend?
3. Kim spent $12 on bags of cookies. How many cookies did she buy?

Practice and Problem Solving

Extra Practice, page 252, Set D

For 4–5, write a number sentence. Then solve.

4. Sherry bought 4 hot dogs. Each hot dog cost $4. How much did Sherry spend?

5. Mr. Hess spends $18 for an order of 6 sandwiches. How much does each sandwich cost?

USE DATA For 6–16, use the price list at the right to find the cost of each number of items.

Read-n-Rock

PRICE LIST	
Books	$4 each
CDs	$7 each
DVDs	$9 each

6. 4 DVDs
7. 6 CDs
8. 8 CDs
9. 7 books
10. 2 CDs
11. 5 DVDs
12. 3 books
13. 9 CDs
14. 5 books
15. 2 DVDs and 6 books
16. 4 books and 5 CDs

Find the cost of one of each item.

17. 9 markers cost $27.
18. 6 notepads cost $18.
19. 3 stamps cost $15.
20. 7 toy cars cost $28.
21. 10 pens cost $20.
22. 2 T-shirts cost $12.

23. **REASONING** Ako has $20. She wants to buy rubber stamps that cost $6 each. How many rubber stamps can she buy? Explain.

24. **MULTISTEP** Heidi buys 3 puzzle books for $24. She gives the clerk $30. How much does each book cost? How much change does she get?

Maintain Skills

25. Which shapes have more than 3 sides?

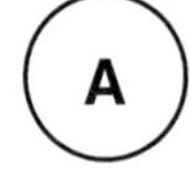

CRCT Test Prep

26. M3N3.g. Latasha makes 2 sandwiches for each of her 4 friends. She puts 2 slices of ham in each sandwich. How many slices of ham does she use? (p. 186)

A. 2
B. 4
C. 8
D. 16

LESSON 5

Problem Solving Strategy
Use Logical Reasoning

M3N4.f. Solve problems requiring division. *also* **M3P1.a., M3P1.b., M3P1.c., M3P1.d., M3P3.a., M3P3.b., M3P3.c., M3P3.d.**

Quick Review

1. $18 \div 3 = ■$
2. $12 \div 4 = ■$
3. $24 \div 6 = ■$
4. $20 \div 2 = ■$
5. $10 \div 5 = ■$

PROBLEM Mike baked 3 batches of popovers. The extra batter made 4 more popovers. He made 31 popovers in all. How many popovers does the tin hold?

UNDERSTAND

- What are you asked to find?
- What information will you use?

PLAN

- What strategy can you use to solve the problem?

You can *use logical reasoning* to find how many popovers the tin holds.

SOLVE

- How can you use the strategy to solve the problem?

Begin with the total number of popovers. Subtract the number of extra popovers from the total.

31	−	4	=	27
↑		↑		↑
total popovers		extra popovers		popovers in 3 batches

Divide to find the number of popovers in each batch.

27	÷	3	=	9
↑		↑		↑
popovers in 3 batches		number of batches		number in each batch

So, Mike's tin holds 9 popovers.

CHECK

- Look back. Does your answer make sense?

Problem Solving Practice

Use logical reasoning to solve.

1. **What if** Mike used a different tin to bake 4 batches of popovers? Then he used the extra batter to make 3 more popovers. He made 27 popovers in all. How many popovers does this tin hold?

2. **MULTISTEP** Mr. Jones spent $30 at the sports shop. He bought a mitt for $10 and 4 baseballs. How much did each baseball cost?

Strategies

- Act It Out or Use Objects
- Make a Picture or Diagram
- Guess and Check
- Use or Look for a Pattern
- **Use Logical Reasoning**

Problem Solving

Mr. Lo bought 2 books that cost the same amount. He gave the cashier $20 and received $6 in change. How much money did each book cost?

3. Which number sentence shows how to find the total cost of the 2 books?

   A $\$20 + \$6 = \$26$
   B $2 \times \$6 = \$12$
   C $\$20 - \$6 = \$14$
   D $\$20 \div 2 = \$10$

4. How much money did each book cost?

   F $6
   G $7
   H $10
   J $14

Mixed Strategy Practice

USE DATA For 5–7, use the price list.

5. **MULTISTEP** Zach pays for an apple pie and a bag of cookies with a $10 bill. He gets his change in quarters and dimes. There are 13 coins in all. How many of each coin does Zach get?

6. **What's the Error?** Lara says a lemon tart and 2 boxes of muffins cost $11.65. Describe Lara's error and give the correct cost of the items.

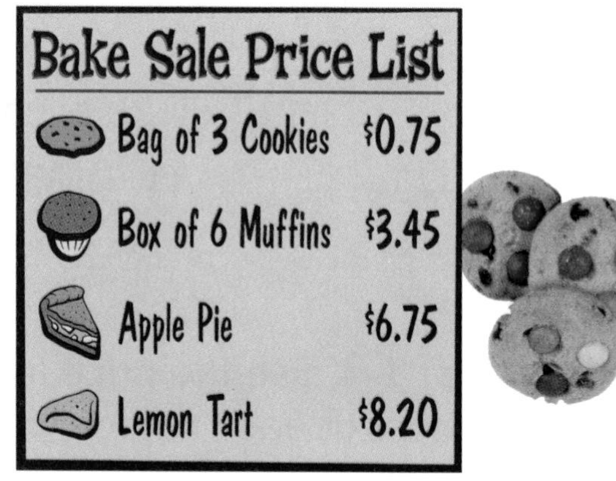

7. Tim has 3 quarters, 2 dimes, 2 nickels, and 5 pennies. List all the ways he can pay for a bag of cookies.

Extra Practice

Set A (pp. 238–241)

Find the missing factor and quotient.

1. $8 \times ■ = 32$ $32 \div 8 = ■$
2. $7 \times ■ = 35$ $35 \div 7 = ■$

Find the quotient.

3. $42 \div 6 = ■$
4. $■ = 24 \div 4$
5. $64 \div 8 = ■$
6. $■ = 21 \div 7$
7. $7\overline{)49}$
8. $2\overline{)2}$
9. $6\overline{)36}$
10. $5\overline{)40}$
11. $8\overline{)48}$
12. Divide 63 by 7.
13. Divide 80 by 8.
14. Divide 15 by 3.

Set B (pp. 242–243)

Find the quotient.

1. $■ = 36 \div 9$
2. $20 \div 10 = ■$
3. $■ = 20 \div 5$
4. $54 \div 6 = ■$
5. $3\overline{)12}$
6. $10\overline{)70}$
7. $9\overline{)72}$
8. $4\overline{)16}$
9. $9\overline{)27}$
10. Divide 56 by 8.
11. Divide 60 by 6.
12. Divide 100 by 10.

Set C (pp. 244–247)

Find the quotient.

1. $6 \div 6 = ■$
2. $■ = 7 \div 1$
3. $■ = 0 \div 5$
4. $28 \div 7 = ■$
5. $9\overline{)81}$
6. $3\overline{)18}$
7. $6\overline{)24}$
8. $2\overline{)20}$
9. $7\overline{)0}$
10. Divide 32 by 4.
11. Divide 40 by 10.
12. Divide 16 by 8.

Set D (pp. 248–249)

PRICE LIST	
Mugs	$4
Aprons	$8

USE DATA For 1–4, use the price list at the right to find the cost of each number of items.

1. 3 aprons
2. 5 mugs
3. 6 aprons
4. 8 mugs

Find the cost of one of each item.

5. 2 pizzas cost $14.
6. 4 tapes cost $32.
7. 5 books cost $25.
8. 6 pens cost $12.
9. 7 balls cost $21.
10. 3 shirts cost $27.

Review/Test

CHECK CONCEPTS

Write a division sentence for each. (pp. 244–247)

1. 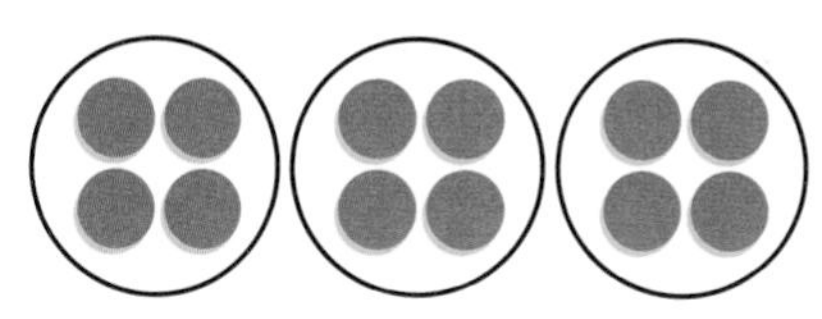

2. 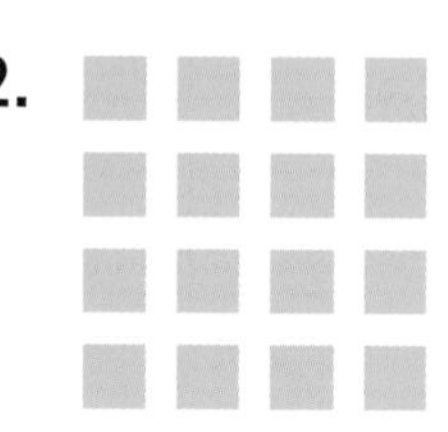

3. $\begin{array}{r} 24 \\ -\ 8 \\ \hline 16 \end{array} \nearrow \begin{array}{r} 16 \\ -\ 8 \\ \hline 8 \end{array} \nearrow \begin{array}{r} 8 \\ -8 \\ \hline 0 \end{array}$

CHECK SKILLS

Find the missing factor and quotient. (pp. 238–241)

4. $8 \times \blacksquare = 40$ $\quad 40 \div 8 = \blacksquare$

5. $6 \times \blacksquare = 42$ $\quad 42 \div 6 = \blacksquare$

6. $7 \times \blacksquare = 56$ $\quad 56 \div 7 = \blacksquare$

7. $8 \times \blacksquare = 32$ $\quad 32 \div 8 = \blacksquare$

Find the quotient. (pp. 238–247)

8. $14 \div 7 = \blacksquare$

9. $\blacksquare = 30 \div 5$

10. $40 \div 4 = \blacksquare$

11. $\blacksquare = 63 \div 9$

12. $8\overline{)24}$

13. $10\overline{)90}$

14. $2\overline{)14}$

15. $9\overline{)18}$

16. $3\overline{)27}$

For 17–20, use the price list at the right to find the cost of each number of items. (pp. 248–249)

17. 4 balloons

18. 7 noisemakers

19. 3 noisemakers

20. 9 balloons

PARTY SUPPLIES PRICE LIST	
Balloons	\$3 each
Noisemakers	\$2 each

Find the cost of one of each item. (pp. 248–249)

21. 5 notebooks cost \$10.

22. 6 markers cost \$18.

23. 5 caps cost \$35.

CHECK PROBLEM SOLVING

Use logical reasoning to solve. (pp. 250–251)

24. Nikki used a tin to make 3 batches of popovers. Then she made 2 extra popovers. She made 26 popovers in all. How many popovers does the tin hold?

25. Roger earned \$35. He made \$15 from a paper route. He also walked 4 dogs after school. How much did Roger charge to walk each dog?

Chapter CRCT Test Prep

NUMBERS AND OPERATIONS

1. M3N4.f. Ramona baked 36 muffins. She put 9 muffins in each bag. How many bags did Ramona use?

   A. 24

   B. 18

   C. 9

   D. 4

2. M3N4.b. Which of the following number sentences does the drawing show?

   A. $40 \div 5 = 8$

   B. $80 \div 10 = 8$

   C. $10 \div 2 = 5$

   D. $50 \div 5 = 10$

3. M3N4.a. Which of the following multiplication facts belongs to the same fact family as these division facts?

   $56 \div 8 = 7$ $56 \div 7 = 8$

   A. $8 \times 8 = 64$

   B. $7 \times 8 = 56$

   C. $7 \times 7 = 49$

   D. $5 \times 6 = 30$

NUMBERS AND OPERATIONS

4. M3N4.c. Kevin bought 8 pies at the farmer's market. He paid a total of $48 for the pies. Which of the following expressions could he use to find the cost of each pie?

   A. $48 \div 8$

   B. $48 + 8$

   C. $48 - 8$

   D. 48×8

Use the table below to answer question 5.

Price List	
Item	**Price**
Ice Cream Cone	$4
Waffle Cone	$5
Ice Cream Cup	$3

5. M3N4.f. The table shows the prices of different ice creams at Camille's Ice Cream Shop. Henry has $9. How many ice cream cups can he buy?

   A. 1

   B. 3

   C. 5

   D. 9

Cumulative CRCT Test Prep

ALGEBRA

Use the table below to answer question 6.

Lee's Division Table	
56	8
49	7
42	6
35	5
28	4

6. M3A1.a. Lee made the division table above. What is the rule for Lee's pattern?

A. Divide by 6.

B. Subtract 8.

C. Divide by 7.

D. Divide by 9.

7. M3A1.c. What number belongs in the □ to make the number sentence true?

$$5 \times \square = 45$$

A. 6 C. 8

B. 7 D. 9

8. M3A1.a. What is the next number in the pattern?

24, 26, 28, 30, □

A. 31 C. 33

B. 32 D. 34

DATA ANALYSIS

Use the graph below to answer question 9.

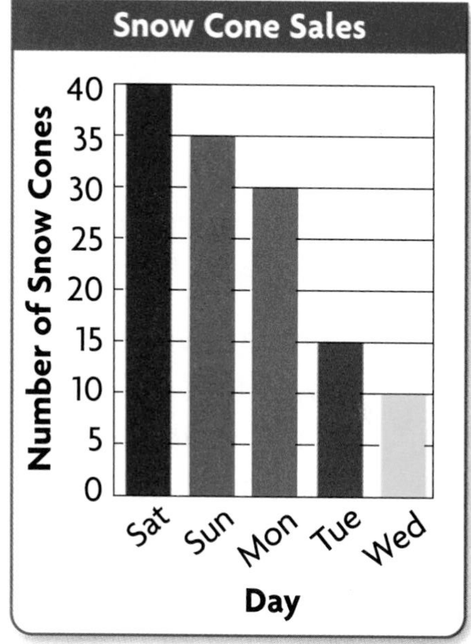

9. M3D1.b. The bar graph shows the number of snow cones sold in 5 days. How many more snow cones were sold on Sunday than on Tuesday?

A. 10

B. 20

C. 30

D. 40

ELA3R2 The student acquires and uses grade-level words to communicate effectively. *also* **ELA3R3.b., ELA3R3.h., ELA3R3.r.**

VOCABULARY

divide (÷)
quotient
inverse operations
dividend
divisor
fact family

VOCABULARY CONCENTRATION

MATERIALS *For each group* vocabulary cards, definition cards

- Mix up the vocabulary cards and definition cards, and place them face down in 4 rows and 3 columns.
- Take turns turning over two cards at a time. The player that matches a term with the correct definition removes the cards. If a term does not match the definition, turn both cards face down, and continue playing.
- Play the game until all the terms and definitions have been matched.
- The player with the most matched cards wins the game.

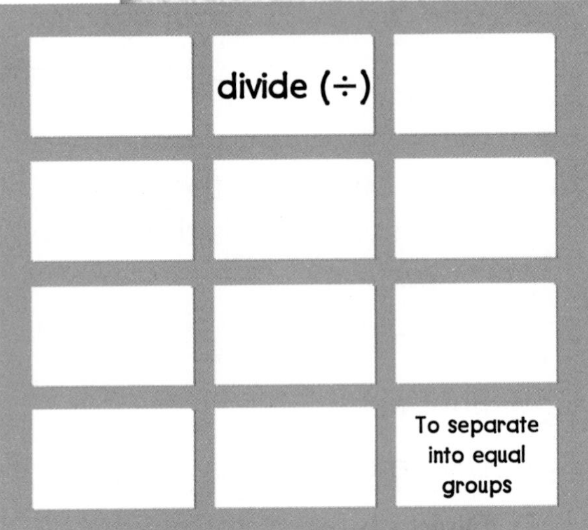

A	I	T	V	E	A	I	M	B	F
I	T	A	K	Q	S	R	V	P	A
N	B	J	R	L	A	D	B	E	C
V	M	Q	U	O	T	I	E	N	T
E	C	I	E	P	Z	V	E	I	S
R	V	B	D	I	V	I	S	O	R
S	N	M	T	B	T	D	I	T	N
E	D	I	V	I	D	E	P	A	V
L	O	S	T	N	S	N	M	L	O
V	A	C	I	A	J	D	K	B	I

MATH WORD WORK

MATERIALS *For each student* Unit 4 *Math Word Work* puzzle

- Find and circle the terms listed below.

divide **dividend**
quotient **divisor**
inverse **fact**

WORDS IN ACTION

MATERIALS *For each pair* 3 index cards, markers

- Work with a partner to make a set of cards for the terms shown at the right. Write each term on an index card. Place the cards face down on a table.
- Write a division problem like this one on a sheet of paper.

$$32 \div 4 = 8$$

- One partner turns over a card, and the other tells which part of the division problem matches the vocabulary term.
- Continue until all the parts of the division problem have been identified. Write a new problem, trade roles with your partner, and play again.

GRID GAME

MATERIALS *For each group* definition cards, grid paper, counters

- Look at the terms in the Vocabulary box on page 256. Write the terms randomly on your grid, one term in each box. Fill in all the boxes. Use two of the terms 2 times each and four of the words 3 times each.
- Choose one player to be the "caller". The caller mixes up the definition cards, chooses one, and reads it aloud. Each player puts a counter on the term that matches the definition read. Each player can place one counter on his or her grid for each turn.
- The definition card goes back in the pile. Play until someone gets 4 counters in a row, either up and down, across, or diagonally.

M3N4.c. Recognize problem-solving situations in which division may be applied and write corresponding mathematical expressions. *also* M3N4.e., M3N4.f., M3D1.

ELA3R3.h. Interprets information from illustrations, diagrams, charts, graphs, and graphic organizers.

Task A

A GARDEN

Evan bought tomato plants for his vegetable garden. He bought a pack that had 24 plants.

a. Make an array to show one way that Evan could arrange the plants. Write a multiplication sentence and a division sentence for your picture.

b. Explain how your array shows that multiplication and division are inverse operations.

Task B

BASEBALL BARGAINS

Kade and Lydia are going to a baseball game. The table shows the prices of different items that they can buy.

Kade has $3 and Lydia has $4.

a. What is one item that Kade can buy? Write a division sentence to show how much ithe item costs.

b. Suppose Kade and Lydia put their money together. Write at least two items they could buy. Explain.

Maintain/Preview

Maintain

Copy and complete the table. Use counters to help.

	Counters	Number of Equal Groups	Number in Each Group
1.	24	■	6
2.	56	7	■
3.	30	■	6

Write the fact family.

4. 3, 7, 21 **5.** 5, 8, 40 **6.** 2, 8, 16 **7.** 4, 9, 36

Find each quotient.

8. $15 \div 3 =$ ■ **9.** $10\overline{)70}$ **10.** $7\overline{)28}$ **11.** $16 \div 4 =$ ■

12. Joanne has 42 marbles. She put the same number of marbles into each of 6 bags. How many marbles did she put in each bag?

13. Terry bought 3 bags of chocolate for a party. He spent $15. How much did each bag of chocolate cost?

Preview

USE DATA For 1–3, use the table.

1. How many people chose basketball?

2. Which sport did most people choose?

3. Did more people choose football or soccer? How many more?

Favorite Sports	
Sport	**Tally**
Baseball	卌 ||||
Basketball	卌 ||
Football	卌 |
Soccer	||||

Choose the better estimate.

4. A marker is about 6 __?__ long.

A inches **B** feet

5. A bus is about 20 __?__ long.

A inches **B** feet

6. The teacher's desk is about 3 __?__ long.

A inches **B** feet

7. A glass is about 8 __?__ high.

A inches **B** feet

Collect and Graph Data

Sue Hendrickson

◀ Sue is the largest, most complete Tyrannosaurus rex fossil skeleton ever found.

FAST FACT • SCIENCE Dinosaurs lived on Earth many years ago. This Tyrannosaurus rex skeleton, named Sue, was found in South Dakota in 1990 by Sue Hendrickson. It is 41 feet long.

INVESTIGATION The chart shows the lengths of different dinosaurs. Organize the data in a table or graph. What conclusion can you make from the way you organized the data?

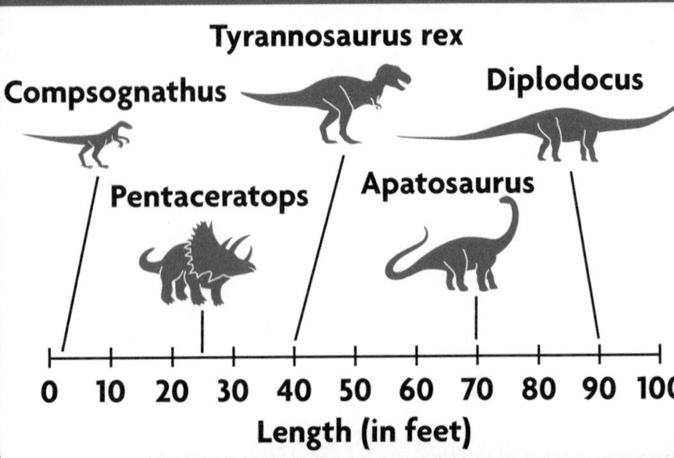

CHECK WHAT YOU KNOW

Use this page to help you review and remember important skills needed for Chapter 14.

COLUMN ADDITION

Find the sum.

1.	2.	3.	4.	5.
8	9	8	5	9
3	3	6	4	5
4	1	4	7	9
+7	+6	+2	+3	+3

READ A TABLE

For 6–9, use the information in this table.

6. What is the title of the table?
7. How many students like snowy weather best?
8. What kind of weather had the fewest votes?
9. How many students were asked?

OUR FAVORITE WEATHER	
Type	**Students**
Sunny	7
Rainy	4
Snowy	8
Cloudy	3

VOCABULARY POWER

REVIEW

table [tā'bəl] *noun*

Table comes from the French word for *tablet,* which means "a slab of metal, stone, or wood used for writing." In mathematics, the meaning of *table* is "an arrangement of data in rows and columns." What is another meaning of *table*?

PREVIEW

data
tally table
frequency table
survey
results
scale
horizontal bar graph
vertical bar graph

www.harcourtschool.com/mathglossary

LESSON 1

HANDS ON

Collect Data

M3D1.a. Solve problems by organizing and displaying data in bar graphs and tables. *also* M3P2., M3P2.a., M3P2.b., M3P2.c., M3P2.d., M3P3.a., M3P3.b., M3P3.c., M3P3.d., M3P5., M3P5.b., M3P5.c.

Quick Review

Write numbers for the tally marks.

1. |||
2. ||
3. ||||̸
4. ||||̸ ||||̸ |
5. ||||̸ ||

VOCABULARY

data **tally table** **frequency table**

MATERIALS

pencils, paper

Explore

Information collected about people or things is called **data**.

The students in Kelly's class voted for their favorite dinosaurs and made tables to show the results.

A **tally table** uses tally marks to record data.

A **frequency table** uses numbers to record data.

FAVORITE DINOSAUR	
Name	**Tally**
Apatosaurus	||||̸	
Brachiosaurus	||||̸ ||
Tyrannosaurus	||||̸ ||||̸ ||
Stegosaurus	|||

FAVORITE DINOSAUR	
Name	**Number**
Apatosaurus	6
Brachiosaurus	7
Tyrannosaurus	12
Stegosaurus	3

Collect data about your classmates' favorite dinosaurs. Organize the data in a tally table.

Activity 1

STEP 1

Write the title and headings. List four answer choices.

STEP 2

Ask classmates *What's your favorite dinosaur?* Make a tally mark for each answer.

Favorite Dinosaur

Name	Tally

- Why is a tally table good for recording data?

Try It

Decide on a question to ask your classmates.

a. Write four answer choices in a tally table.

b. Ask your classmates the question. Complete the tally table.

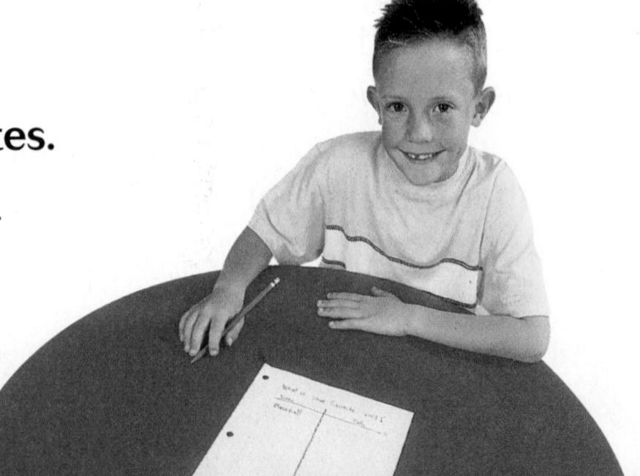

Connect

Use the data you organized in the tally table on page 262 to make a frequency table.

Activity 2

STEP 1

Write the title and headings. List the four answer choices.

STEP 2

Count the number of tally marks in each row. Write each number in the frequency table.

Favorite Dinosaur

Name	Number

• Why is a frequency table a good way to show data?

Practice and Problem Solving

1. Make a tally table about three after-school activities. Ask your classmates which activity they like best. For each answer, make a tally mark beside the activity.

2. Use the data from your tally table to make a frequency table. Which activity was chosen by the greatest number of classmates? the least number?

3. Which table is better for reading results? Which table is better for collecting data?

4. **MULTISTEP** How many more students chose oranges and apples than chose bananas?

5. **Write a problem** using the information in the Favorite Fruit tally table.

FAVORITE FRUIT	
Name	**Tally**
Grapes	卌 卌 卌 |
Oranges	||||
Apples	卌
Bananas	卌 |||

Maintain Skills

6. Write the product.

$4 \times 5 = \blacksquare$

CRCT Test Prep

7. M3N2.c. Ebony buys a sandwich for \$3.49. She has a coupon for \$0.50 off. She pays with a \$5 bill. How much change will she receive? (p. 98)

A. \$1.01
B. \$1.51
C. \$2.01
D. \$3.99

LESSON 2

Use Data from a Survey

M3D1.a. Solve problems by organizing and displaying data in bar graphs and tables. *also* **M3P3., M3P3.a., M3P3.b., M3P3.c., M3P3.d., M3P4.c., M3P5.b., M3P5.c.**

Quick Review

1. 17 + 21 + 12
2. 13 + 9 + 6
3. 24 + 5 + 7
4. 8 + 14 + 7
5. 19 + 13 + 21 + 5

VOCABULARY

survey
results

Learn

SURVEY SAYS . . . A **survey** is a method of gathering information or data. The answers from a survey are called the **results** of the survey.

Jillian and Ted took a survey to find their classmates' favorite snacks. The tally table shows the choices and votes of their classmates.

What are the favorite snacks of their classmates?

Since cookies got the greatest number of votes, 12, cookies are the favorite snack.

FAVORITE SNACK	
Snack	**Tally**
Popcorn	||||
Cookies	𝍸 𝍸 ||
Granola bars	𝍸
Apples	𝍸 ||
Pretzels	||

Check

1. **Explain** how you can find the number of students who answered Jillian and Ted's survey.
2. List the snacks at the right in order from the most votes to the fewest votes.

For 3–4, use the tally table below.

DO YOU HAVE AN OLDER BROTHER OR SISTER?	
Answer	**Tally**
Yes	𝍸 𝍸 ||
No	𝍸 𝍸 𝍸 ||

3. How many people were surveyed?
4. Write a statement that describes the survey results.

Practice and Problem Solving

Extra Practice, page 272, Set A

For 5–7, use the tally table.

5. List the subjects in order from the most votes to the fewest votes.

6. How many students answered the survey?

7. How many more students chose math than chose social studies?

FAVORITE SCHOOL SUBJECT	
Subject	**Tally**
Math	𝍸 𝍸 |||
Science	𝍸 ||||
Reading	𝍸 𝍸 𝍸
Social Studies	𝍸	
Art	𝍸 ||

For 8–10, use the frequency table.

8. How many more students chose basketball than chose baseball?

9. How many students answered this survey?

10. **What if** 5 more students chose basketball? How would that change the results of the survey?

11. **What's the Error?** Lily wrote the following number sentence: $24 \times 0 = 24$. What's her error?

FAVORITE SPORT	
Sport	**Number**
Basketball	26
Football	15
Baseball	17
Hockey	21
Swimming	30

12. **Write About It** Think of a survey question. Write four possible answers. Survey your classmates. Make a tally table and a frequency table to record your classmates' choices. Explain the results.

13. **MULTISTEP** Jamie has 48 stickers. They are arranged on 6 sheets so that each sheet has the same number of stickers. How many stickers do 3 sheets contain?

Maintain Skills

Write *true* or *false* for each sentence.

14. A trapezoid has 4 sides and 3 vertices.

15. A triangle has 3 sides and 3 angles.

16. A quadrilateral has 5 sides.

CRCT Test Prep

17. M3N3.b. Toshio had 4 packages of 6 bagels. He gave one package away. How many bagels in all does he have now? (p. 132)

A. 10
B. 18
C. 24
D. 28

LESSON 3

Problem Solving Skill
Draw Conclusions

M3D1.b. Construct and interpret bar graphs using scale increments of 1, 2, 5, and 10. *also* M3P1.a., M3P1.b., M3P1.c., M3P1.d., M3P3.a., M3P3.b., M3P3.d.

UNDERSTAND PLAN SOLVE CHECK

Quick Review

1. $6 + 2 + 3 = \blacksquare$
2. $5 + 7 + 6 = \blacksquare$
3. $9 + 1 + 4 = \blacksquare$
4. $3 + 8 + 5 = \blacksquare$
5. $13 + 4 + 8 = \blacksquare$

DOWN UNDER The United States is in the Northern Hemisphere. Australia is in the Southern Hemisphere. Places in the Southern Hemisphere have the same seasons as the Northern Hemisphere, but they happen at different times of the year. Which 3 months of the year do you think make up winter in Australia?

A bar graph can be used to display data. You can draw conclusions by using the data and what you know.

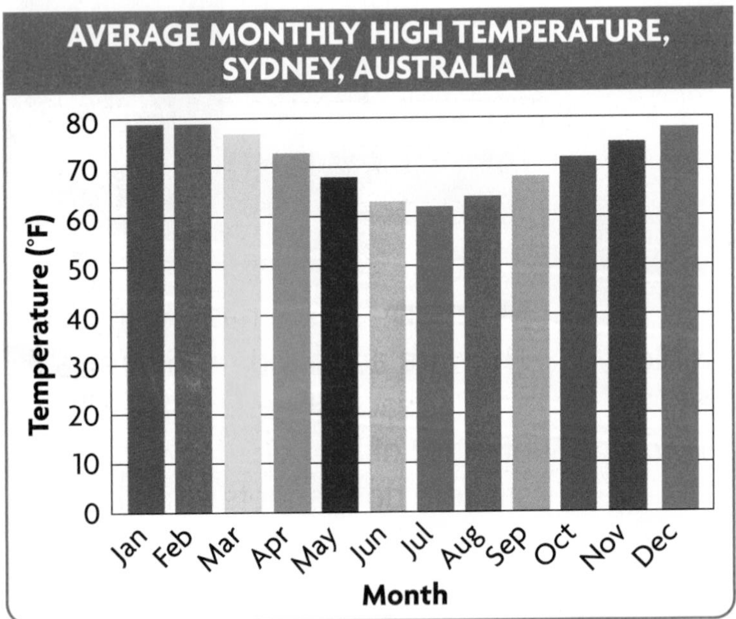

Winter is the season when it is the coldest. Using the bar graph, the coldest temperatures are in June, July, and August.

So, June, July, and August are probably the winter months in Australia.

Talk About It

- The order of the seasons is the same in both the Northern and Southern Hemispheres. What season is it in Australia in October? How do you know?

Problem Solving Practice

For 1–4, use the graph on page 266.

1. Joe's family is planning a visit to Sydney, Australia, in the fall. During which months of the year could they plan to go?

2. January 26 is a national holiday, called Australia Day. It celebrates the founding of the country. In what season is Australia Day?

3. In how many months is the average high temperature in Sydney above 70 degrees?

4. About how much warmer is it in Sydney during the summer than it is during the winter? Explain your answer.

For 5–6, use the graph.

5. Which conclusion can you make about the data?
   - **A** More rain fell in June than August.
   - **B** Two more inches of rain fell in July than in May.
   - **C** The rainfall decreased from May to August.
   - **D** Four inches of rain fell in July.

6. How many total inches of rain fell from May to August?
   - **F** 17 inches
   - **G** 18 inches
   - **H** 19 inches
   - **J** 20 inches

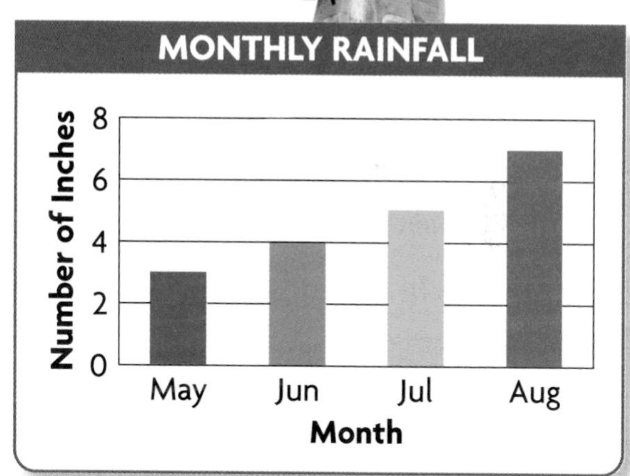

Mixed Applications

7. **MULTISTEP** Lloyd spent \$3.59, \$4.50, and \$9.75 for games. He gave the clerk \$20.00. How much change did he receive?

8. In the library, there are 3 shelves with 9 new books on each shelf. How many new books are on the shelves?

9. Anna's team scored 89 points, 96 points, 98 points, and 107 points. How many points did the team score in all?

10. **? What's the Question?** Look at the Monthly Rainfall graph above. The answer is 4 more inches.

LESSON 4

Bar Graphs

M3D1.b. Construct and interpret bar graphs using scale increments of 1, 2, 5, and 10. *also* M3P1.b., M3P1.d., M3P3.a., M3P3.b., M3P3.c., M3P3.d., M3P4.

Quick Review

1. $4 \times 10 = \blacksquare$
2. $7 \times 7 = \blacksquare$
3. $8 \times 3 = \blacksquare$
4. $\blacksquare \times 6 = 36$
5. $9 \times \blacksquare = 81$

VOCABULARY

scale
horizontal bar graph
vertical bar graph

Learn

SLEEPY ANIMALS A bar graph uses bars to show data. A **scale** of numbers helps you read the number each bar shows.

These bar graphs show the same data.

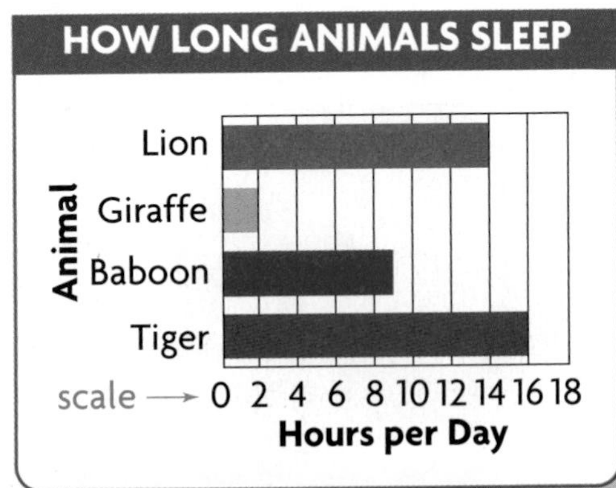

In a **horizontal bar graph**, the bars go across from left to right.

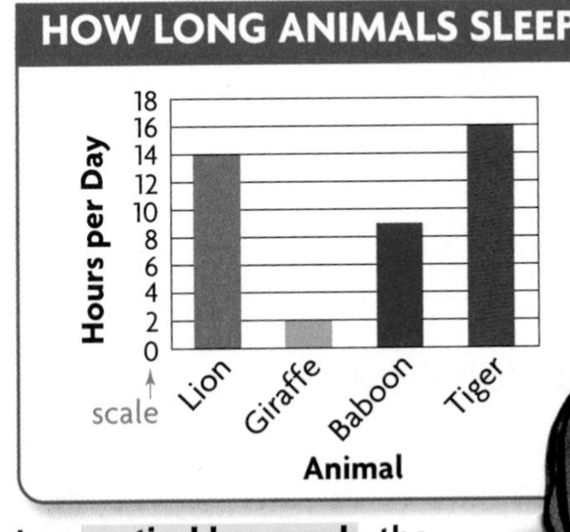

In a **vertical bar graph**, the bars go up from the bottom.

- What scale is used in the bar graphs? Why is this a good scale?
- How do you read the bar for the baboon, which ends halfway between two lines?

Examples

A

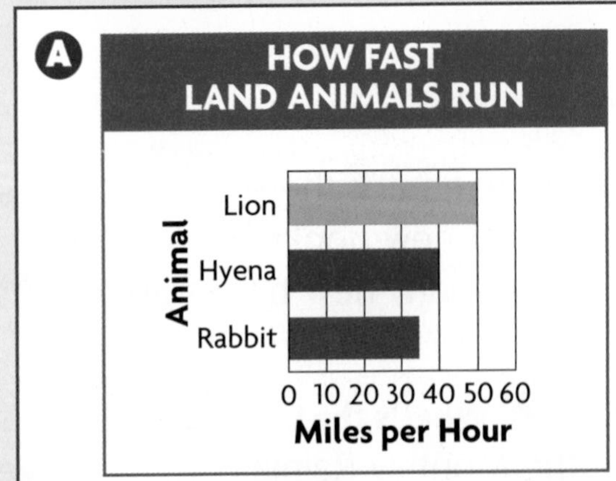

B

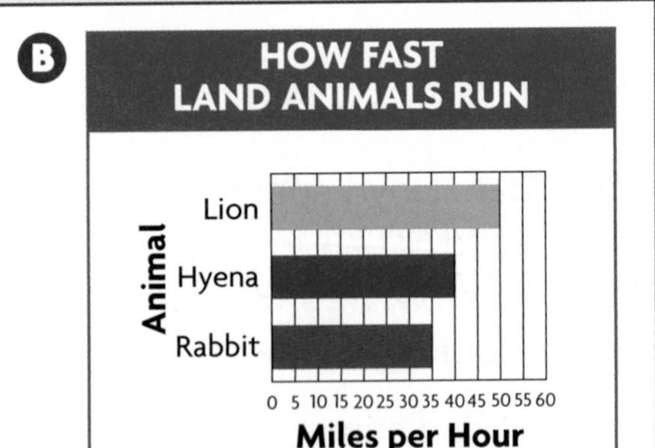

- How are these graphs alike? How are they different?

Check

1. **Explain** how you would use the graph in Example A to tell how fast a rabbit runs.

For 2–3, use the bar graphs in Examples A and B.

2. How fast can a lion run?
3. How fast can a hyena run?

Practice and Problem Solving

Extra Practice, page 272, Set B

For 4–6, use the Length of Sea Animals bar graph.

4. Is this a vertical or horizontal bar graph?
5. How long is a giant squid?
6. How much longer is a gray whale than a bottlenose dolphin?

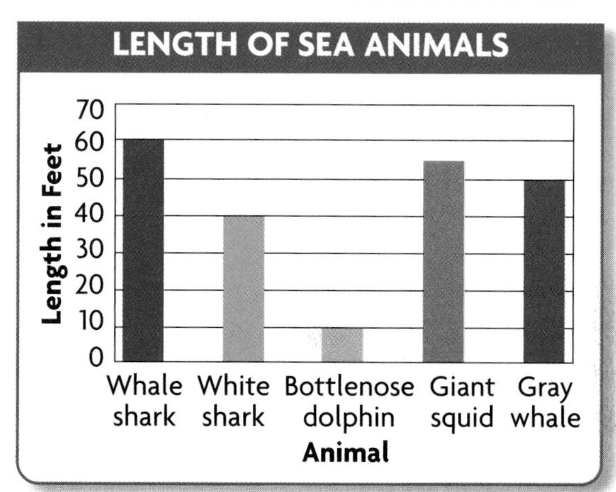

For 7–8, use the Favorite Wild Animals bar graph.

7. Which animal received the most votes?
8. **MULTISTEP** Were there more votes in all for crocodile and lion, or for giraffe and elephant? Explain.
9. **Vocabulary Power** The word *scale* has more than one meaning. What meaning is found in your math book? What is another meaning for *scale*?

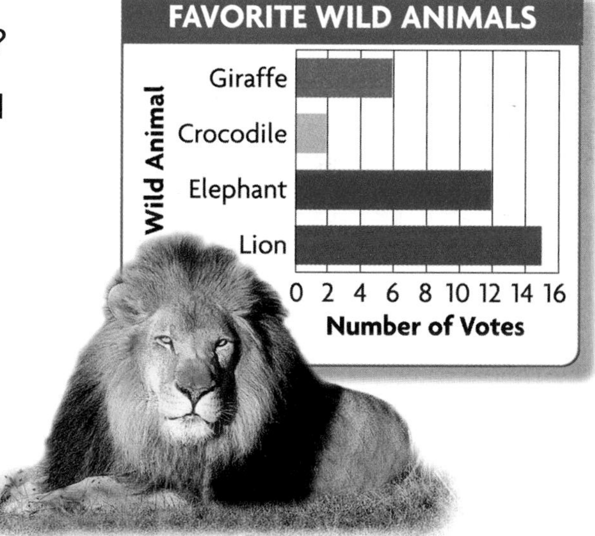

Maintain Skills

Compare. Write <, >, or = for each ●.

10. 63 ● 49
11. 18 ● 81
12. 23 ● 32

CRCT Test Prep

13. M3N4.f. Meg put 24 counters in 4 equal piles. How many counters are in each pile? (p. 224)

A. 4
B. 6
C. 7
D. 20

LESSON 5

Make Bar Graphs

M3D1.b. Construct and interpret bar graphs using scale increments of 1, 2, 5, and 10. *also* M3P2., M3P2.a., M3P2.b., M3P2.c., M3P2.d., M3P3.d., M3P5.

Quick Review

1. 3×2 2. 4×5 3. 6×3
4. 8×10 5. 7×4

MATERIALS
bar graph pattern, crayons

Explore

You can make a bar graph to show the number of each type of animal at the Oglebay Zoo in West Virginia. Use the data in the table to make a horizontal bar graph.

OGLEBAY ZOO	
Animal	**Number**
Snakes	6
Goats	10
Owls	4
Turtles	3

Activity

STEP 1

Write a title and labels. Decide on the best scale to use, and write the numbers.

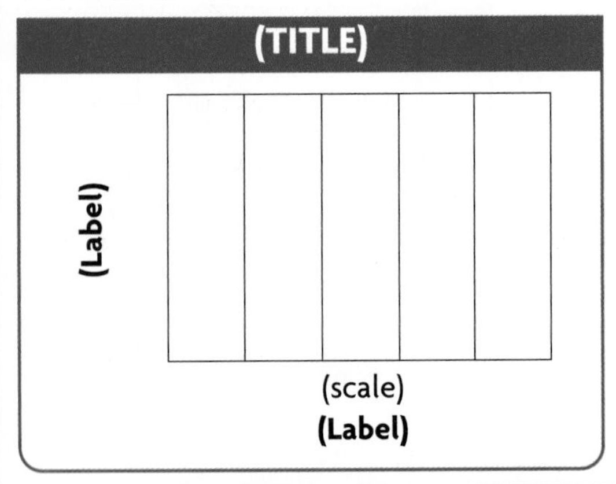

STEP 2

Complete the bar graph. Make the length of each bar equal to the number of each type of animal.

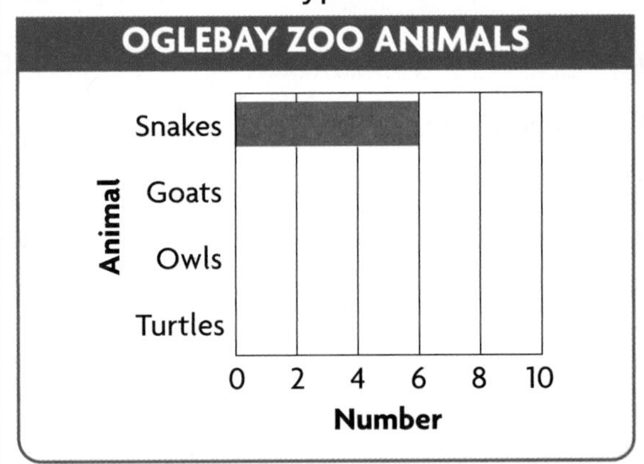

- Name the parts of a bar graph.
- Explain where you would draw the bar for turtles.

Try It

Use your bar graph.

a. There are 5 tortoises at the Oglebay Zoo. Make a bar for the tortoises.

b. There are 6 deer at the Oglebay Zoo. Make a bar for the deer.

Connect

You can make a bar graph of data you collect from a survey.

- Take a survey in your classroom. Decide on a question. Give your classmates four possible choices. Record the choices in a table. Make a bar graph of the data in the table.
- How many classmates answered your survey?
- What scale did you use?
- What is the title of your graph?
- What did you find from your survey?

Practice and Problem Solving

1. Copy and complete the Wildlife Center bar graph. Use the data in the table at the right.
2. Why is 2 a good scale to use?

WILDLIFE CENTER	
Animal	**Number**
Monkeys	3
Zebras	8
Polar bears	2

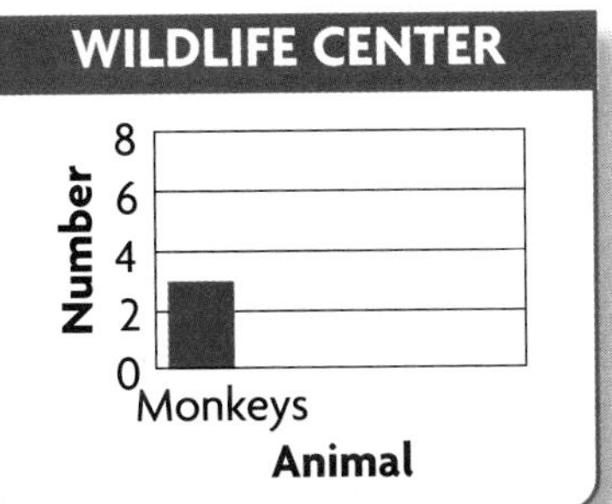

For 3–5, use the Favorite Pets table.

3. Make a bar graph. Why is 1 a good scale to use?
4. For which pet is the bar the longest?
5. **MULTISTEP** Are there more birds and cats, or more dogs and fish? Explain.

FAVORITE PETS	
Animal	**Number**
Birds	3
Fish	1
Dogs	5
Cats	4

Maintain Skills

Find each sum or difference.

6. $\begin{array}{r} 432 \\ +169 \\ \hline \end{array}$ 7. $\begin{array}{r} 821 \\ -274 \\ \hline \end{array}$ 8. $\begin{array}{r} 344 \\ +626 \\ \hline \end{array}$

9. $521 + 352 = \blacksquare$

CRCT Test Prep

10. M3M1. What is the elapsed time from 10:45 A.M. to 1:15 P.M.? (p. 112)

A. 2 hr 5 min
B. 2 hr 20 min
C. 2 hr 30 min
D. 2 hr 45 min

Extra Practice

Set A (pp. 264–265)

For 1–3, use the tally table.

FAVORITE HOBBY	
Hobby	**Tally**
Collecting stamps	𝍷𝍷𝍷𝍷
Collecting sports cards	𝍸 𝍸
Collecting coins	𝍷𝍷
Reading	𝍸 𝍷𝍷𝍷

1. How many people answered the survey?
2. What is the most popular hobby?
3. How many fewer people chose collecting coins than chose reading?

For 4–6, use the frequency table.

4. How many people answered the survey?
5. Did more people choose peas or carrots?
6. How many more people chose corn than chose beans?

FAVORITE VEGETABLE	
Type	**Number**
Carrots	6
Peas	6
Beans	3
Corn	12

Set B (pp. 268–269)

For 1–3, use the Plant Height bar graph.

1. How tall is the tomato plant?
2. How much taller is the green bean plant than the cucumber plant?
3. Which plant is 8 inches tall?

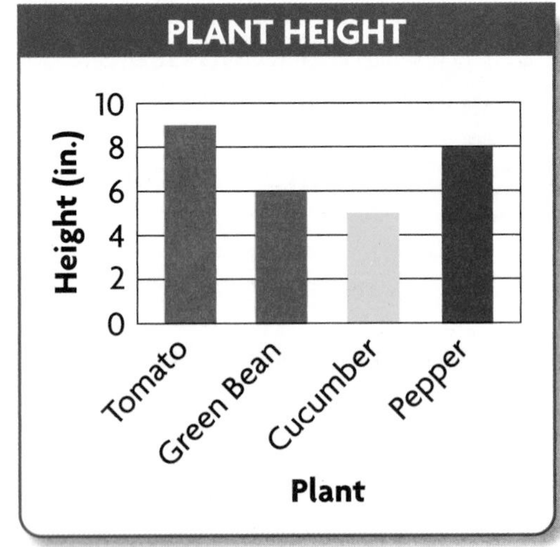

For 4–6, use the Favorite Sports bar graph.

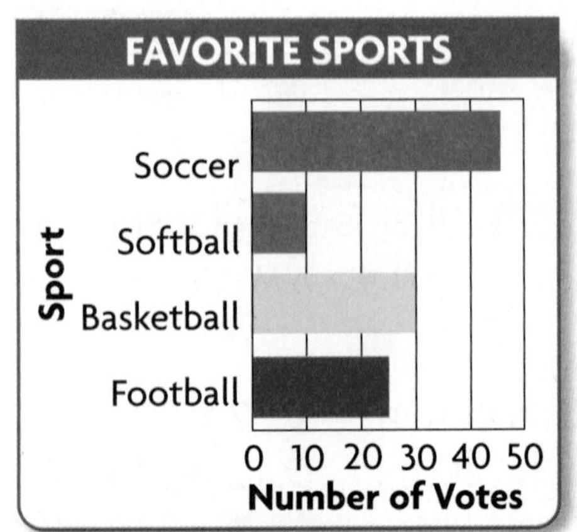

4. Which sport got the least votes?
5. How many more votes did soccer get than basketball?
6. How many people voted in all?

Review/Test

CHECK VOCABULARY

Choose the best term from the box.

Vocabulary
data
survey
tally table
frequency table
scale

1. A method of gathering information is a __?__. (p. 264)
2. Information collected about people or things is called __?__. (p. 262)
3. A table that uses numbers to record data is a __?__. (p. 262)

CHECK SKILLS

For 4–6, use the tally table. (pp. 262–263)

4. List the instruments in order from the most votes to the fewest votes.
5. How many people answered the survey?
6. How many more people voted for the guitar than for the flute?

FAVORITE MUSICAL INSTRUMENT	
Musical Instrument	**Tally**
Guitar	|||| |||| ||||
Flute	|||| ||||
Drums	|||| |||| |||| |||
Piano	|||| |||| |||

For 7–9, use the bar graph. (pp. 268–269)

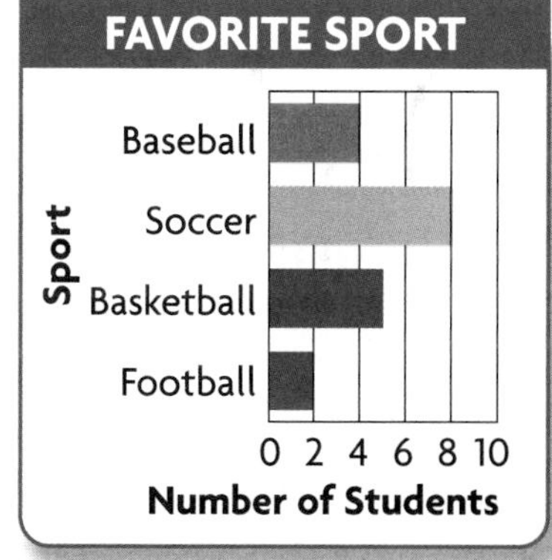

7. How many students chose soccer?
8. How many students answered the survey?
9. How many more students chose basketball than football?

CHECK PROBLEM SOLVING

Solve. (pp. 266–267)

10. Can you conclude that there was more rain February and March than in April and May? Explain.

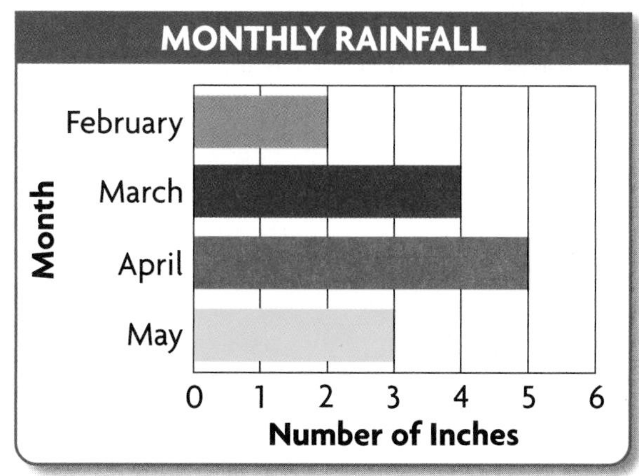

Chapter CRCT Test Prep

DATA ANALYSIS

Use the table below to answer question 1.

Favorite Breakfast Foods	
Type of Food	**Tally**
Cereal	𝍸 𝍸 |||
Eggs	𝍸 ||
Oatmeal	|||
Pancakes	𝍸 𝍸 |

1. M3D1.a. Which types of food each received at least 10 votes?

   A. pancakes and eggs

   B. eggs and oatmeal

   C. cereal and pancakes

   D. cereal and eggs

Use the table below to answer question 2.

Field Trip Votes	
Place	**Number of Students**
Farm	𝍸 𝍸 𝍸
Factory	𝍸 𝍸 𝍸 𝍸 𝍸
Library	𝍸 𝍸 |||
Park	𝍸 𝍸 𝍸 𝍸 |

2. M3D1.a. How many students voted for a field trip?

   A. 25

   B. 55

   C. 74

   D. 84

DATA ANALYSIS

Use the graph below to answer question 3.

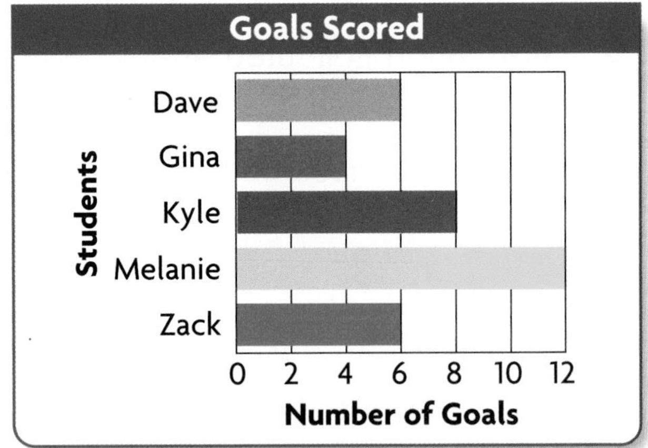

3. M3D1.b. The bar graph shows the number of goals that five students scored during their soccer games. How many goals did Gina and Melanie score in all?

   A. 20

   B. 16

   C. 12

   D. 4

Cumulative CRCT Test Prep

NUMBERS AND OPERATIONS

4. M3N4.f. Lisa has 21 stuffed animals. She wants to put an equal number on each of 3 shelves in her room. How many animals will she put on each shelf?

A. 24

B. 18

C. 14

D. 7

5. M3N3.g. Crystal has 6 packages of stickers. Each package has 8 stickers. How many stickers does she have?

A. 42

B. 46

C. 48

D. 54

6. M3N2.c. Lance bought a pen for \$1.09 and a notebook for \$1.89. He gave the clerk a \$5 bill. How much change did Lance receive?

A. \$2.02

B. \$2.98

C. \$3.11

D. \$3.91

ALGEBRA

7. M3A1.c. Which of the following will help you find the missing addend in this number sentence?

$$\square + 29 = 53$$

A. $53 + 29 = 82$

B. $53 - 29 = 24$

C. $50 - 30 = 20$

D. $50 + 30 = 80$

8. M3A1.c. Rosa had 43 stickers. She bought a new pack of stickers. Now she has 55 stickers. Which number sentence can be used to find the number of stickers in the new pack?

A. $43 - \square = 55$

B. $43 + \square = 55$

C. $43 \times \square = 55$

D. $43 \div \square = 55$

9. M3A1.a. What are the next two numbers in the pattern?

11, 18, 25, 32, □, □

A. 33 and 34

B. 34 and 36

C. 37 and 42

D. 39 and 46

15 Customary and Metric Length

FAST FACT • SCIENCE The Saturn V rocket that took astronauts to the moon was made at the Marshall Space Flight Center in Huntsville, Alabama. This rocket had more than 3 million parts! Many people collect models of spacecraft.

INVESTIGATION The graph shows the length of different models of spacecraft. How can you figure out how much longer the model of the Saturn V rocket is than the model of the space shuttle?

Using Data

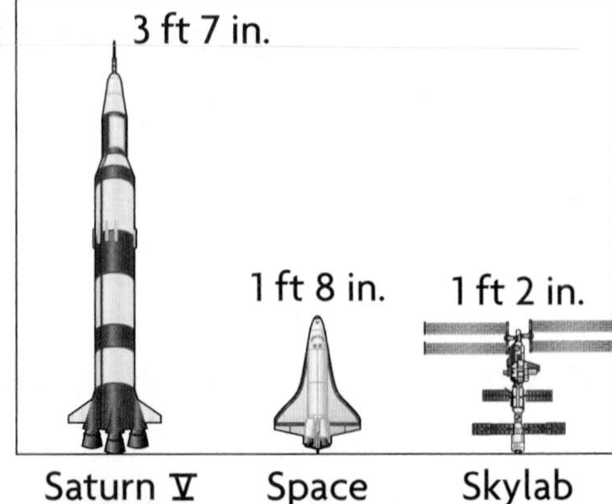

CHECK WHAT YOU KNOW

Use this page to help you review and remember important skills needed for Chapter 15.

MEASURE TO THE NEAREST INCH

Write the length to the nearest inch.

1. 

2. 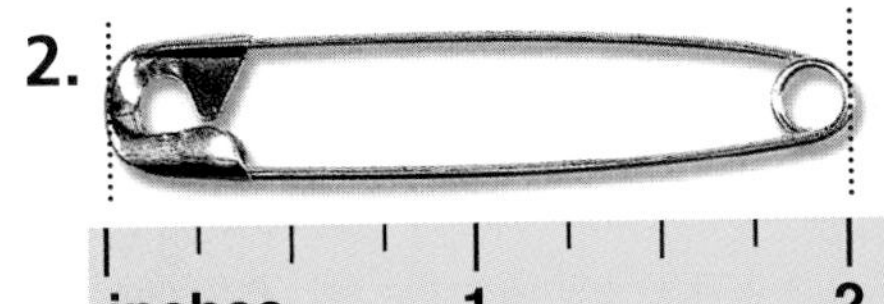

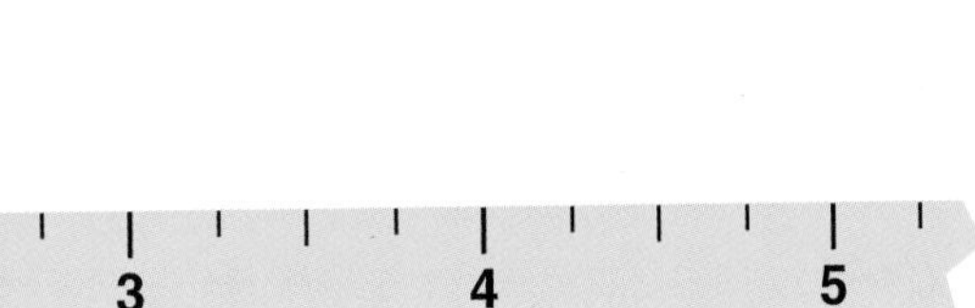

inches 1 2 3 4 5

MEASURE TO THE NEAREST CENTIMETER

Write the length to the nearest centimeter.

3. 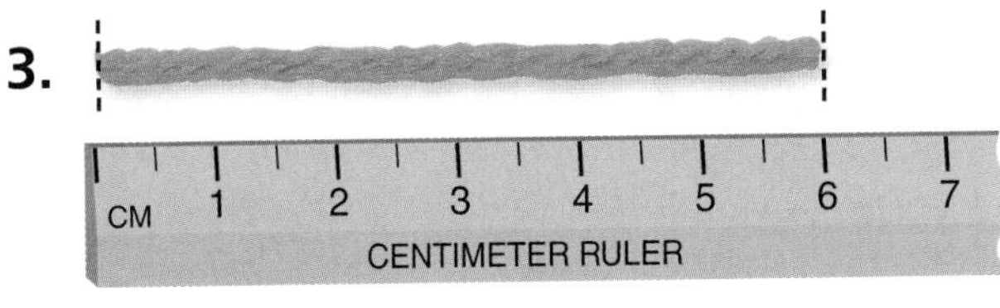

4. 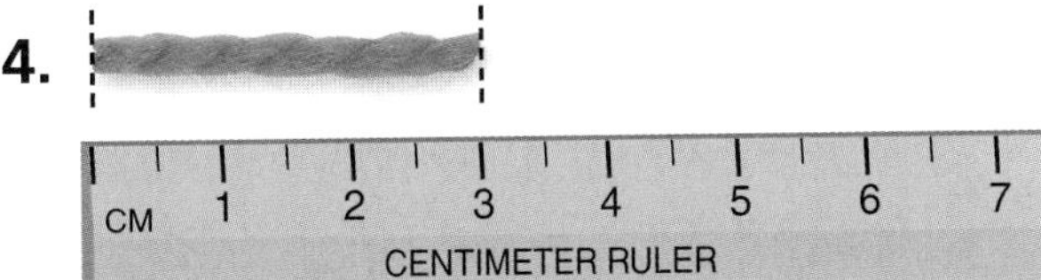

5. 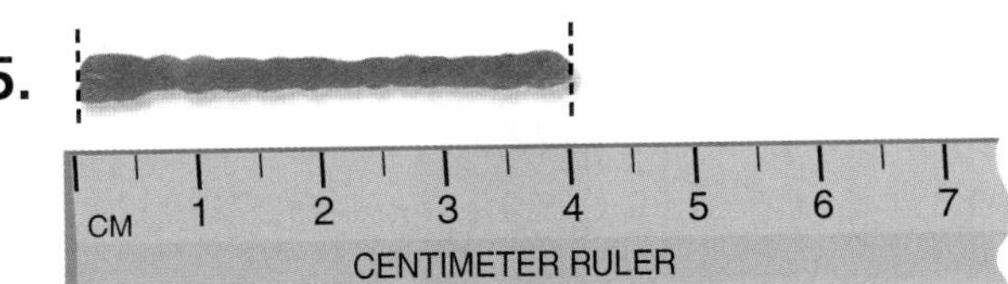

6. 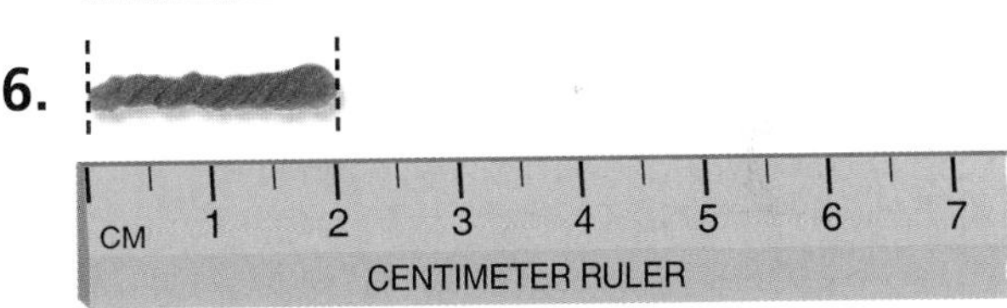

VOCABULARY POWER

REVIEW

inch [inch] *noun*

When used as a noun, an *inch* is a customary unit used to measure length. When used as a verb, *inch* means "to move by small amounts" or "to move slowly." Write one sentence using *inch* as a noun and one sentence using *inch* as a verb.

PREVIEW

foot (ft)
yard (yd)
mile (mi)
millimeter (mm)
centimeter (cm)
meter (m)
kilometer (km)

www.harcourtschool.com/mathglossary

LESSON 1

Measure to the Nearest $\frac{1}{2}$ and $\frac{1}{4}$ Inch

M3M2.b. Measure to the nearest $\frac{1}{4}$ inch, $\frac{1}{2}$ inch, and . . . inch . . . . *also* M3M2.c., M3P2., M3P2.a., M3P2.b., M3P2.c., M3P2.d.

Quick Review

1. $7 \times ■ = 42$
2. $■ \times 5 = 45$
3. $■ \times 8 = 32$
4. $6 \times ■ = 48$
5. $9 \times ■ = 63$

Learn

HOW LONG? An estimate is an answer that is close to the actual answer. You can estimate length by using an item close to 1 inch, like a small paper clip or your knuckle.

You can measure objects to the nearest inch or $\frac{1}{2}$ inch.

HANDS ON

Activity

MATERIALS: small paper clips, ruler

Copy the table. Use paper clips to estimate the length of each ribbon. Then measure to the nearest inch and $\frac{1}{2}$ inch.

LENGTHS OF RIBBONS

Color	Estimate	Nearest Inch	Nearest $\frac{1}{2}$ Inch
green	about 1 inch		
yellow			
red			

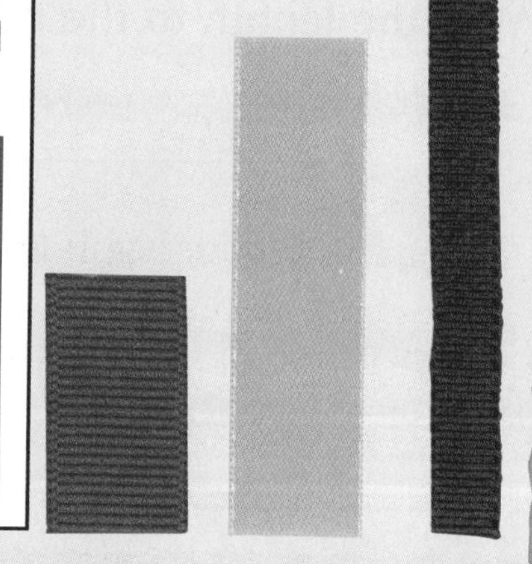

Example

What is the length of this crayon to the nearest $\frac{1}{2}$ inch?

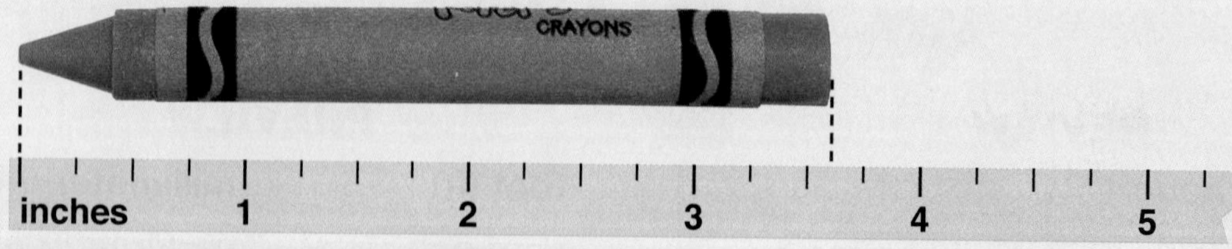

To measure to the nearest $\frac{1}{2}$ inch:

STEP 1

Line up one end of the crayon with the zero mark on the ruler.

STEP 2

Find the $\frac{1}{2}$-inch mark that is closest to the other end of the crayon.

So, the length of the crayon to the nearest $\frac{1}{2}$ inch is $3\frac{1}{2}$ inches.

Measuring to the Nearest $\frac{1}{4}$ Inch

You can also measure to the nearest $\frac{1}{4}$ inch.

Example

What is the length of this pencil to the nearest $\frac{1}{4}$ inch?

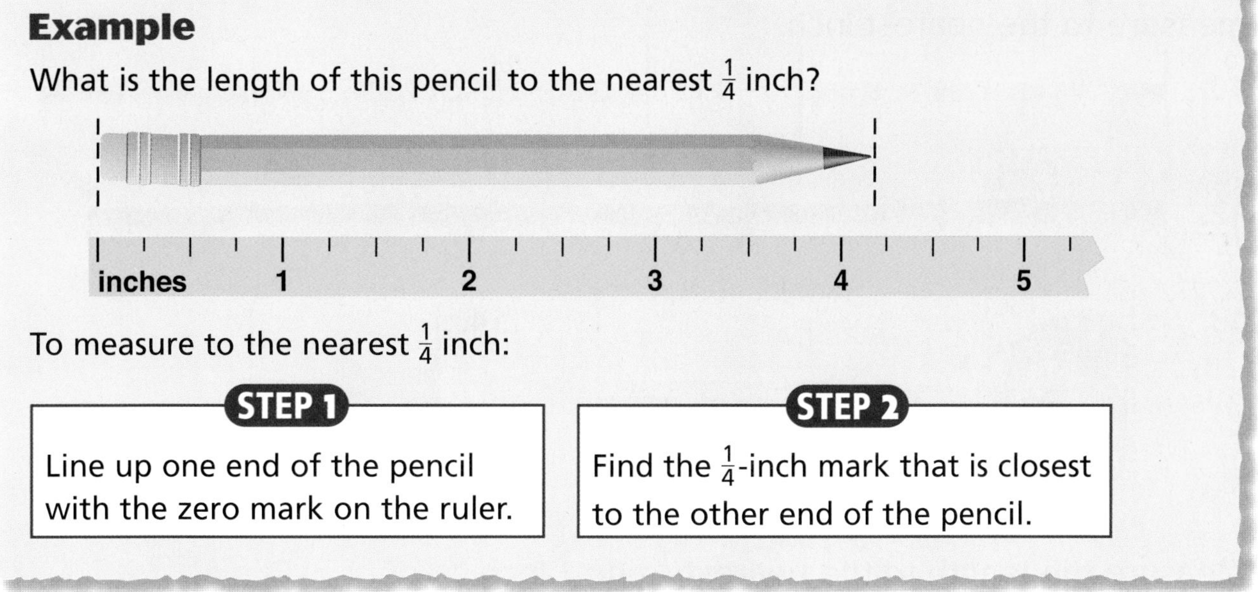

To measure to the nearest $\frac{1}{4}$ inch:

STEP 1

Line up one end of the pencil with the zero mark on the ruler.

STEP 2

Find the $\frac{1}{4}$-inch mark that is closest to the other end of the pencil.

So, the length of the pencil to the nearest $\frac{1}{4}$ inch is $4\frac{1}{4}$ inches.

Check

1. **Describe** where you find $\frac{1}{2}$-inch marks on a ruler.

Estimate the length in inches. Then use a ruler to measure to the nearest inch.

Measure the length to the nearest $\frac{1}{2}$ and $\frac{1}{4}$ inch.

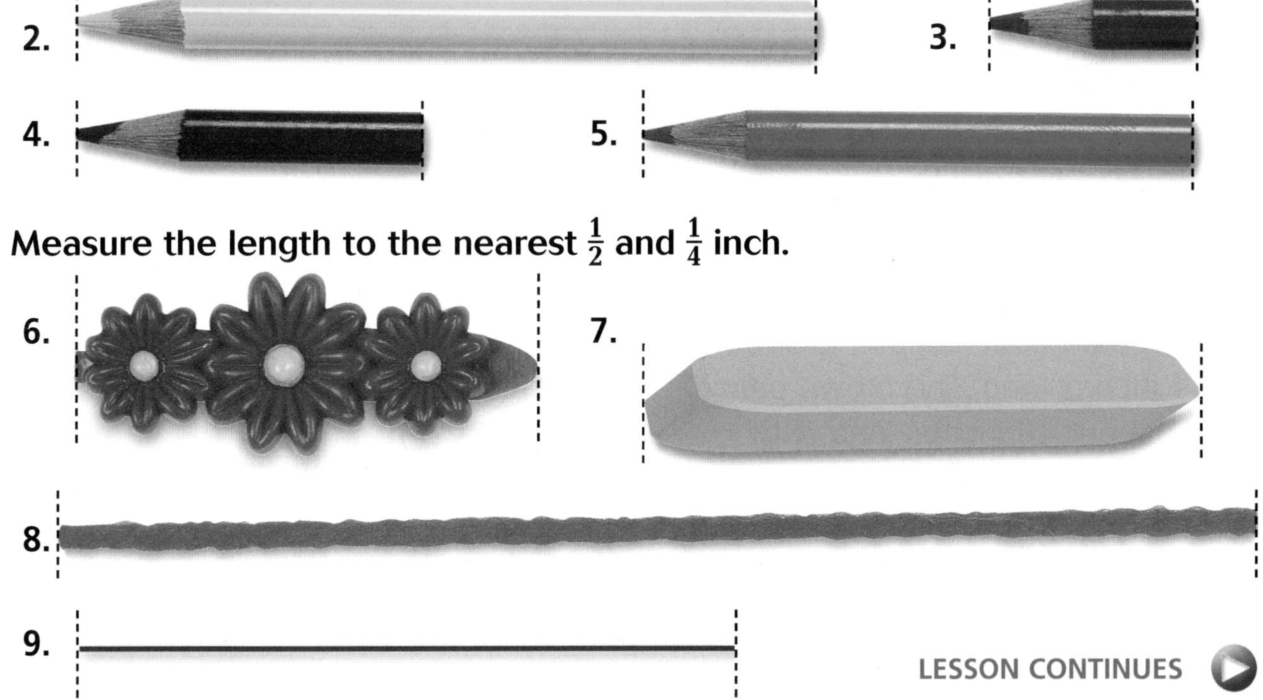

LESSON CONTINUES

Practice and Problem Solving

Extra Practice, page 294, Set A

Estimate the length in inches. Then use a ruler to measure to the nearest inch.

10.

11.

12.

13.

14.

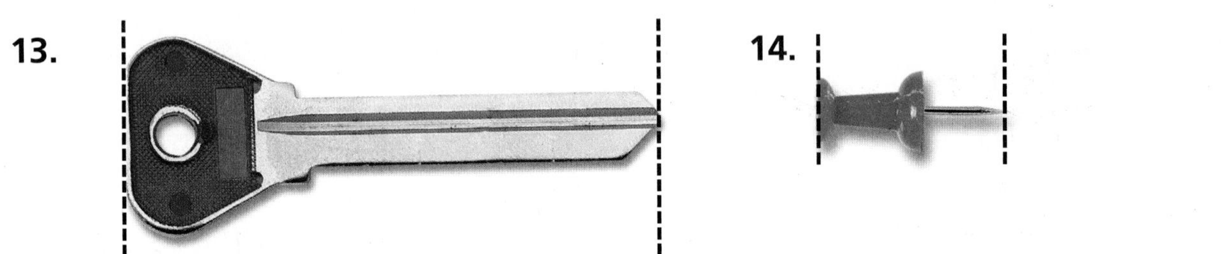

Measure the length to the nearest $\frac{1}{2}$ and $\frac{1}{4}$ inch.

15.

16.

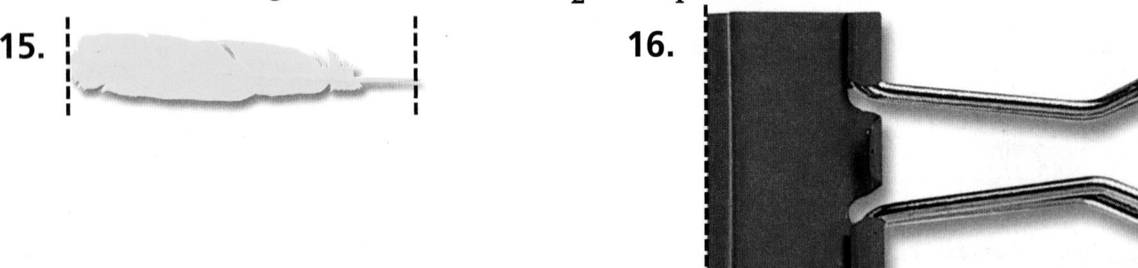

17.

18.

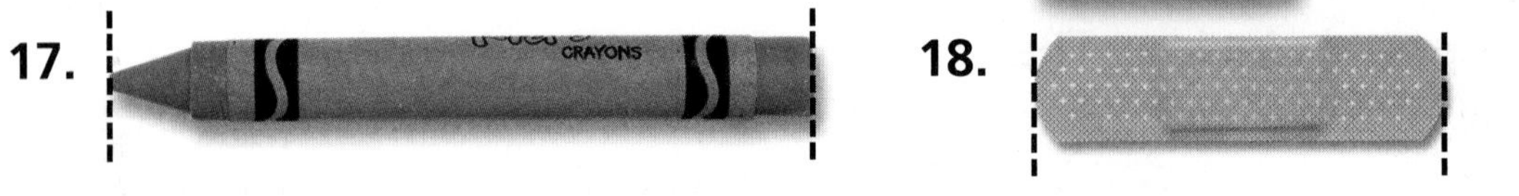

19.

Use a ruler. Draw a line for each length.

20. 1 inch

21. $2\frac{1}{2}$ inches

22. $4\frac{3}{4}$ inches

23. $5\frac{1}{4}$ inches

24. **FAST FACT** • SCIENCE The ruby-throated hummingbird is about 4 inches long. The brown pelican is about 40 inches long. The pelican is about how many times as long as the hummingbird?

25. **Vocabulary Power** The word *rule* comes from the Latin word *regula*, which means "straight stick." What math word is related to *rule* and could be described as a straight stick?

26. Measure the classroom door from side to side to the nearest inch. Then measure a door at home in the same way. Which door has the greater measure?

27. **MULTISTEP** Joyce used 72 beads to make 9 necklaces with an equal number of beads on each. How many beads were on 2 necklaces?

28. A brush measures $6\frac{1}{2}$ inches. Between which two inch marks does the end of the brush lie? Explain.

29. Find two different sized books. Measure the length of each cover to the nearest half inch and quarter inch.

30. Suppose you need at least 5 inches of yarn for an art project. Is this blue piece of yarn long enough? Explain.

Maintain Skills

Write <, >, or = for each ●.

31. 26 ● 31 **32.** 19 ● 16

33. 49 ● 75 **34.** 89 ● 98

35. $\begin{array}{r} 437 \\ +291 \\ \hline \end{array}$ **36.** $\begin{array}{r} 600 \\ -491 \\ \hline \end{array}$ **37.** $\begin{array}{r} 821 \\ -199 \\ \hline \end{array}$

CRCT Test Prep

38. M3N3.g. Noah had 8 rows of 6 toy cars. He gave 5 cars to his brother. How many cars does Noah have left? (p. 190)

A. 58
B. 53
C. 43
D. 19

Problem Solving Thinker's Corner

You can measure lengths in more than one way. For example, use string to measure the line drawings.

MATERIALS: 2 pieces of string, each 1 ft long
2 different-colored markers

a. Start with one end of string on one end of line drawing A. Cover the line drawing with the string.

b. Make a mark on the string for the end of the line drawing.

c. Repeat for line drawing B.

1. Measure the lengths marked on the pieces of string. Record the measurements.

2. Which line drawing has the greater length?

LESSON 2

Inch, Foot, Yard, and Mile

 M3M2.b. Measure to the nearest $\frac{1}{4}$ inch, $\frac{1}{2}$ inch, and millimeter (mm) in addition to the previously learned inch, foot, yard, centimeter, and meter. *also* M3M2.c., M3P3., M3P3.a., M3P3.b., M3P3.c., M3P3.d.

Quick Review

1. 41 + 52
2. 36 + 36
3. 12 + 34
4. 27 + 63
5. 12 + 12 + 12

VOCABULARY

foot (ft)
yard (yd)
mile (mi)

Learn

CHOOSING UNITS You know that an inch (in.) is used to measure length and distance. Other customary units used to measure length and distance are the **foot (ft)**, **yard (yd)**, and **mile (mi)**.

Examples

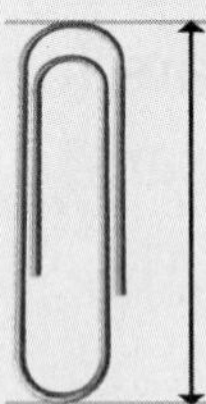

A paper clip is about 1 inch long.

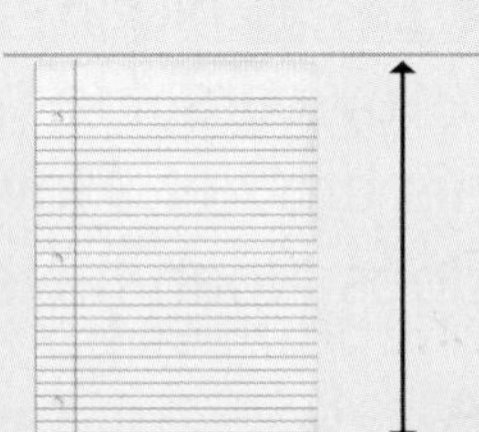

A sheet of notebook paper is about 1 foot long.

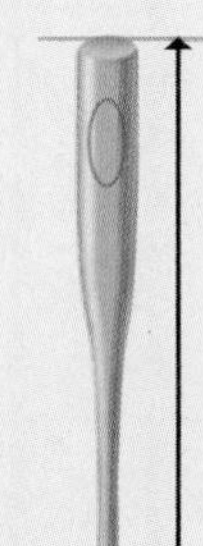

A baseball bat is about 1 yard long.

You can walk 1 mile in about 20 minutes.

TABLE OF MEASURES
1 foot = 12 inches
1 yard = 3 feet = 36 inches
1 mile = 5,280 feet

- Explain which unit you would use to estimate the length of your hand.

A yardstick is 3 times as long as a 1-foot ruler.

Check

1. **Build** a 1-foot "ruler" using 1-inch square tiles. Use it to measure one side of a sheet of paper.

Choose the better estimate.

2. The pencil is 6 _?_ long.
   A feet B inches
3. The car is 2 _?_ long.
   A miles B yards
4. The book is 1 _?_ wide.
   A foot B yard
5. The park is 3 _?_ wide.
   A miles B inches

Practice and Problem Solving

Extra Practice, page 294, Set B

Choose the better estimate.

6. Sal rides the bus 3 __?__ to school.

   A miles **B** feet

7. A football is about 1 __?__ long.

   A mile **B** foot

8. The distance between the floor and the doorknob is about 3 __?__.

   A feet **B** inches

9. Sarah's math book is 11 __?__ long.

   A yards **B** inches

Choose the tool you would use to measure each. Write *ruler* or *yardstick*.

10. the length of a playground
11. the width of a binder
12. the width of a book
13. the height of a giraffe
14. Cut a sheet of 1-inch grid paper into 6-inch strips. Use the strips and tape to make a 1-foot strip and a 1-yard strip. How many strips were needed for each?
15. **MULTISTEP** Mitchell got 5 stickers from each of 6 friends. He bought 13 more stickers. How many stickers does Mitchell have in all?
16. Angie thinks this grasshopper is about 4 inches long. Do you agree with her estimate? Measure to check and record the length.

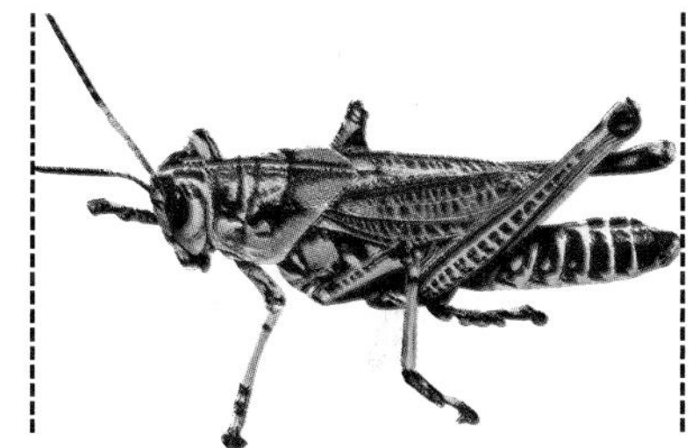

17. **Write About It** Estimate the distance from your desk to the classroom door in feet and in yards. Then measure the distance. Record your estimates and the actual measurement.

Maintain Skills

Write the amount.

18. 

19.    

CRCT Test Prep

20. M3M2.c Which unit would you use to measure the length of a spoon? (p. 282)

    A. inches
    B. feet
    C. yards
    D. miles

LESSON 3

Compare Customary Units

 **M3M2.d.** Compare one unit to another within a single system of measurement. *also* **M3P2.a., M3P2.b., M3P2.c., M3P2.d., M3P3.a., M3P3.b., M3P3.c., M3P3.d., M3P4.a., M3P4.b.**

Learn

CHANGE IT The students in Mrs. Lopez's class need fabric that is 12 feet long for a banner. How many yards of fabric should they buy?

To change feet into yards, they must know how these units are related.

- A yard is longer than a foot.
- 3 feet = 1 yard

1 ft **1 ft** **1 ft**

1 yd

Jake and Theresa used different ways to change feet into yards.

Jake
I'll draw 12 lines to show feet. I'll circle groups of 3 to show yards.

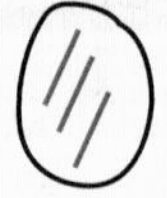 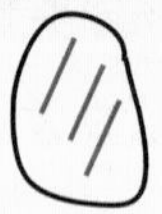  

There are 4 groups of 3 feet.
So, 12 feet equals 4 yards.

Theresa
I'll make a table.

Yards	1	2	3	4
Feet	3	6	9	12

The table shows that 4 yards equals 12 feet.

So, they should buy 4 yards of fabric.

 **MATH IDEA** To compare one unit to another, first decide how the units are related.

- Explain why Jake circled groups of 3 feet.

Check

1. Write how many inches are in 4 feet. Use the Table of Measures to help.

Quick Review

Choose the smaller unit of measure in each.

1. foot, inch

2. mile, yard

3. inch, yard

4. yard, foot

5. foot, mile

Remember

Table of Measures

Length
12 inches = 1 foot
3 feet = 1 yard
36 inches = 1 yard
5,280 feet = 1 mile

Technology Link

More Practice:
Harcourt Mega Math The Number Games, *Tiny's Think Tank,* Level M

Copy and complete. Use the Table of Measures to help.

2. Change miles to feet.
larger unit: ?

1 mile = ■ feet

3. Change feet to inches.
larger unit: ?

1 foot = ■ inches

Practice and Problem Solving

Extra Practice, page 294, Set C

Copy and complete. Use the Table of Measures to help.

4. Change yards to feet.
larger unit: ?

1 yard = ■ feet

5. Change inches to yards.
larger unit: ?

■ inches = 1 yard

Change the units. Use the Table of Measures to help.

6. ■ feet = 1 yard

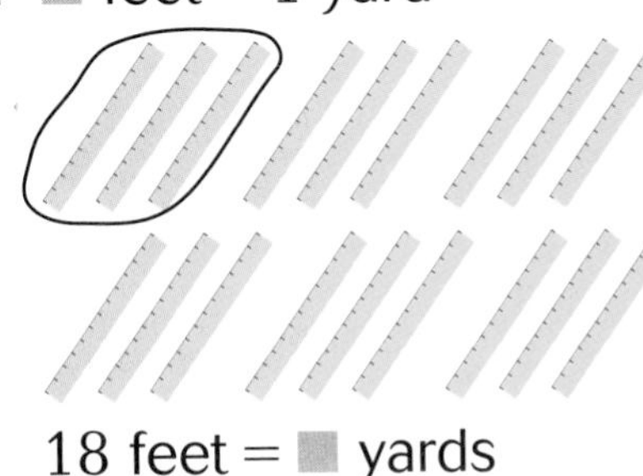

18 feet = ■ yards

7. ■ inches = 1 foot

feet	1	2
inches	12	■

■ inches = 2 feet

Compare. Write <, >, or = for each ●.

8. 5 yards ● 10 feet

9. 1 yard ● 36 inches

10. 1 mile ● 6,000 feet

11. **MULTISTEP** Neil bought 2 sandwiches. He paid with a $10 bill. He received $4 in change. How much did each sandwich cost?

12. Callie has 23 inches of yarn. Is this more than or less than 2 feet? Explain.

13. **What's the Error?** Dylan said that 60 inches equal 6 feet. Describe his error. Draw a model to show your answer.

Maintain Skills

14. Write the product.

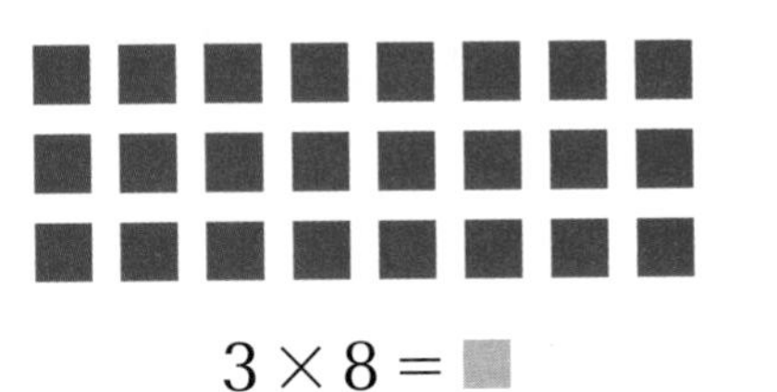

$3 \times 8 = ■$

CRCT Test Prep

15. M3N2.c. Yolanda had $2.19. She lost a quarter. She wants to buy a book for $2.15. How much more does she need? (p. 98)

A. $0.24
B. $0.21
C. $0.11
D. $0.04

LESSON 4

Metric Length

M3M2.b. Measure to the nearest $\frac{1}{4}$ inch, $\frac{1}{2}$ inch, and millimeter (mm) in addition to the previously learned inch, foot, yard, centimeter, and meter. *also* **M3M2.a., M3M2.c., M3P2., M3P2.b., M3P2.c., M3P5.**

Quick Review

1. 5 × 10
2. 10 × 7
3. 10 × 10
4. 10 × 1
5. 9 × 10

VOCABULARY

millimeter (mm)
centimeter (cm)
meter (m)
kilometer (km)

Learn

MAKE IT METRIC In the metric system, **millimeter (mm)**, **centimeter (cm)**, **meter (m)**, and **kilometer (km)** are units used to measure length and distance.

A *millimeter* is about the thickness of a dime.

A *centimeter* is about the width of your index finger.

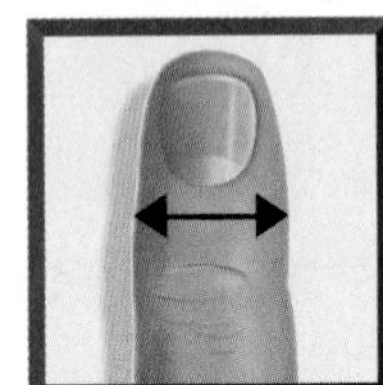

Your armspan is about 1 *meter* long.

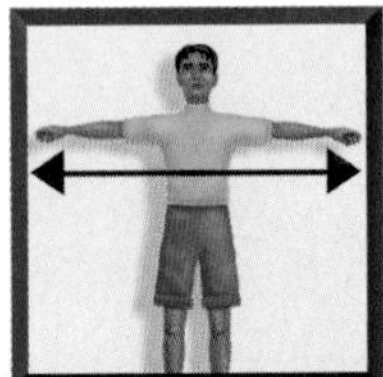

A *kilometer* is a little more than half a mile.

Activity

Materials: centimeter ruler

STEP 1

Copy the table.

LENGTH IN CENTIMETERS		
Object	**Estimate**	**Measure**

STEP 2

Write four objects that you would measure using centimeters.

STEP 3

Estimate the length of each object in centimeters. Record your estimates.

STEP 4

Use a centimeter ruler. Measure the length of each object to the nearest centimeter. Record your measurements.

Measuring to the Nearest Millimeter

You can also measure to the nearest millimeter.

Example

What is the length of this toy car to the nearest millimeter?

STEP 1

Line up one end of the car with the zero mark on the ruler.

STEP 2

Find the millimeter mark that is closest to the other end of the car.

So, the length of the toy car to the nearest millimeter is 53 millimeters.

Check

1. **Explain** how to find the length in centimeters of objects that do not line up exactly with a centimeter mark.

Estimate the length in centimeters. Then use a ruler to measure to the nearest millimeter and centimeter.

2.

3.

4.

5.

Technology Link

More Practice: Harcourt Mega Math Ice Station Exploration, *Linear Lab*, Levels H and I

Choose the unit you would use to measure each. Write *mm*, *cm*, *m*, or *km*.

6. the length of a crayon
7. the length of a chalkboard
8. the length of a carrot
9. the length of a playground
10. the length of a highway
11. the length of an ant

LESSON CONTINUES 

Practice and Problem Solving

Extra Practice, page 294, Set D

Estimate the length in centimeters. Then use a ruler to measure to the nearest millimeter and centimeter.

12.

13. 

14. 

15. 

Choose the unit you would use to measure each. Write *mm, cm, m,* or *km*.

16. the distance you can ride a bike in 30 minutes

17. the length of a ladybug

18. the length of a pencil

19. the length of your classroom

Choose the better estimate.

20. Ali walked 4 __?__ in one hour.

A kilometers **B** millimeters

21. Carole's ponytail is 10 __?__ long.

A centimeters **B** millimeters

22. The wall is 3 __?__ high.

A centimeters **B** meters

23. The paper clip is 3 __?__ long.

A kilometers **B** centimeters

Use a ruler. Draw a line for each length.

24. 2 centimeters

25. 45 millimeters

26. 14 centimeters

27. **Write About It** Choose 3 objects inside your classroom and 3 outside. Estimate and measure the lengths. Record the results. Tell what tool you used to measure each.

28. ***FAST FACT*** • **GEOGRAPHY** Snake River Canyon in Idaho has a maximum depth of 2,400 meters. Write this number in word form and expanded form.

29. **REASONING** Chad says 203 centimeters is the same as 2 meters plus 3 centimeters. Do you agree? Explain.

30. **MULTISTEP** Adam was second in line. Susan stood behind Adam and in front of Jean. Tim was first in line. Who was fourth in line?

31. **What's the Error?** Nick said that the line below measures about 2 cm. Describe his error. Give the correct measure.

32. Sarah drew this poster for her science project. What is the length of the bottom edge of her poster in centimeters?

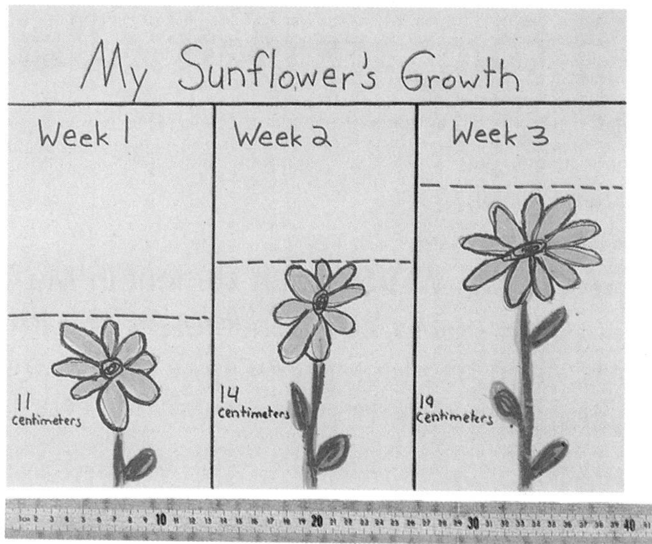

Maintain Skills

Write the sum or difference.

33. $\begin{array}{r} 799 \\ +110 \\ \hline \end{array}$

34. $\begin{array}{r} 486 \\ +145 \\ \hline \end{array}$

35. $\begin{array}{r} 673 \\ -125 \\ \hline \end{array}$

36. $\begin{array}{r} 926 \\ -418 \\ \hline \end{array}$

CRCT Test Prep

37. M3M2.c Choose the best estimate. (p. 286)

The length of Pam's bedroom is 3 __?__.

A. millimeters
B. centimeters
C. meters
D. kilometers

Problem Solving Thinker's Corner

Measure the pieces of yarn and break the code! To find the correct letter for each blank, match the measurement and the color of the yarn.

W
T
T
H

S
E
C

R
A
E

What did the mother bird call the baby bird?

?	?	?	?	?	?	?	?	?	?
3 cm	5 cm	2 cm	2 cm	4 cm	5 cm	2 cm	1 cm	1 cm	3 cm

LESSON 5

Compare Metric Units

M3M2.d. Compare one unit to another within a single system of measurement. *also* M3P3.a., M3P3.b., M3P3.c., M3P3.d.

Learn

BALLS OF YARN Each student in Ms. Tahn's art class needs 200 centimeters of yarn. If Ms. Tahn has 8 students, how many meters of yarn are needed?

Quick Review

1. 10×2
2. $200 + 200$
3. $100 + 100$
4. $400 + 400$
5. $1,000 + 1,000$

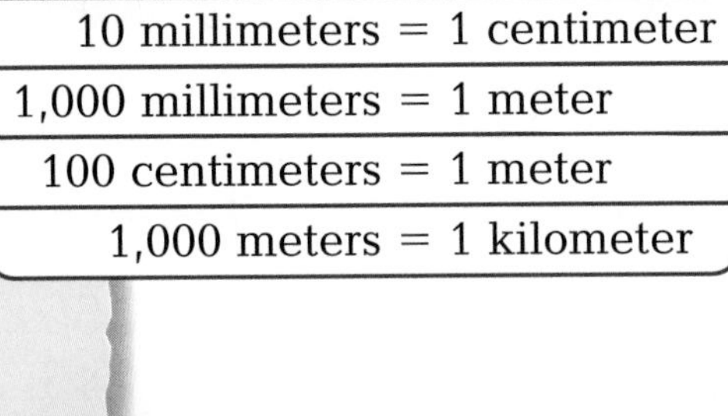

TABLE OF MEASURES
10 millimeters = 1 centimeter
1,000 millimeters = 1 meter
100 centimeters = 1 meter
1,000 meters = 1 kilometer

Example

To change centimeters into meters, you must know how these units are related. Use the Table of Measures.

- A meter is longer than a centimeter.
- 100 centimeters = 1 meter

Make a table and to find the answer.

Students	Centimeters	Meters
1	200	2
2	400	4
3	600	6
4	800	8
5	1,000	10
6	1,200	12
7	1,400	14
8	1,600	16

The 8 students need 1,600 centimeters of yarn.

1,600 centimeters = 16 meters

So, 16 meters of yarn are needed.

- If Ms. Tahn had 20 meters of yarn, how many more students could get 200 centimeters of yarn?

Check

1. **Write** how many millimeters are in 6 centimeters. Use the Table of Measures to help.

Copy and complete. Use the Table of Measures to help.

2. Change centimeters to millimeters.
   larger unit: ?

   1 centimeter = ▪ millimeters

3. Change kilometers to meters.
   larger unit: ?

   1 kilometer = ▪ meters

Practice and Problem Solving

Extra Practice, page 294, Set E

Copy and complete. Use the Table of Measures to help.

4. Change meters to millimeters.
   larger unit: ?

   1 meter = ▪ millimeters

5. Change meters to centimeters.
   larger unit: ?

   ▪ centimeters = 1 meter

Change the units. Use the Table of Measures to help.

6. ▪ millimeters = 1 centimeter

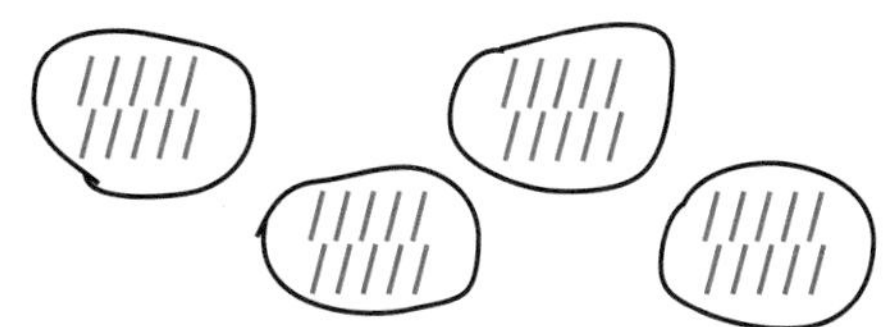

40 millimeters = ▪ centimeters

7. ▪ centimeters = 1 meter

cm	100	200	▪
m	1	2	3

▪ centimeters = 3 meters

Compare. Write <, >, or = for each ●.

8. 5 mm ● 1 cm

9. 1 m ● 50 cm

10. 100 m ● 1 km

11. Mrs. Wallace's house key measures 50 millimeters long. How many centimeters long is her key?

12. **What's the Error?** Benito said that 8 centimeters equal 40 millimeters. Describe his error.

13. **MULTISTEP** Katie had a ribbon that measured 35 centimeters. She used 28 centimeters of ribbon for an art project. How many millimeters does she have left?

Maintain Skills

14. 22 + 73

15. 94 − 82

16. 62 + 19

17. 51 − 28

18. 39 + 39

19. 67 − 39

CRCT Test Prep

20. M3N3.g. Jackie put 8 beads on each of 4 bracelets, and 20 beads on a necklace. How many beads did she use in all? (p. 190)

A. 12 B. 32 C. 40 D. 52

LESSON 6

Problem Solving Strategy
Use Logical Reasoning

M3M2.c. Estimate length and represent it using appropriate units. *also* M3P1.a., M3P1.b., M3P1.c., M3P4.

PROBLEM Four students are comparing their heights. Their heights, in centimeters, are 133, 132, 131, and 130. Ali is 132 cm tall. Deb is not the shortest or the tallest. Ben is taller than Carl. Who is the tallest?

Quick Review

1. 300 + 400
2. 800 + 100
3. 2,000 + 2,000
4. 250 + 250
5. 900 + 200

UNDERSTAND

- What are you asked to find?

PLAN

- What strategy can you use to solve the problem?

You can *use logical reasoning.*

SOLVE

- How can you use the strategy to solve the problem?

Make a table like the one shown.

Fill in the information for Ali and Deb.

	130	131	132	133
Ali	no	no	yes	no
Ben			no	
Carl			no	
Deb	no		no	no

Look at the table. There is one box left in Deb's row. She must be 131 cm tall.

Since Ben is taller than Carl, Ben must be 133 cm tall and Carl must be 130 cm tall.

So, Ben is the tallest.

	130	131	132	133
Ali	no	no	yes	no
Ben	no	no	no	yes
Carl	yes	no	no	no
Deb	no	yes	no	no

CHECK

- How can you check your answer?

Problem Solving Practice

Use logical reasoning to solve.

1. **What if** Ali had been 131 cm tall? How tall would Deb be?
2. Erin, Frank, Greg, and Holly measured the lengths of different rooms in their houses. The lengths, in meters, are 3, 4, 5, and 6. Erin's room was not the longest. Frank's room was 4 meters long. Both Greg and Holly's rooms were longer than Erin's. Whose room had the shortest length?

Strategies

- Act It Out or Use Objects
- Make a Picture or Diagram
- Guess and Check
- Use or Look for a Pattern
- **Use Logical Reasoning**

Problem Solving

Jacob used 4 pieces of yarn for an art project. The pieces were 40, 60, 80, and 100 centimeters long. The red piece was 60 cm. The green piece was not the shortest. The yellow piece was 40 cm shorter than the blue piece.

3. How long was the blue piece?

   A 40 centimeters
   B 60 centimeters
   C 80 centimeters
   D 100 centimeters

4. What color was the longest piece?

   F red
   G yellow
   H blue
   J green

Mixed Strategy Practice

USE DATA For 5–6, use the table.

5. Compare the heights of the mountain peaks. List them in order from the least to the greatest heights.
6. Which two mountain peaks have a difference in height of 128 meters?
7. **Write a problem** that uses kilometers, meters, centimeters, or millimeters.

GEORGIA MOUNTAIN PEAKS	
Peak	**Height**
Blue Mountain	1,219 meters
Powell Mountain	1,170 meters
Eagle Mountain	1,298 meters

8. Reese had some peanuts. He ate 3 peanuts. Then he gave 4 friends 5 peanuts each. He had 1 peanut left. How many peanuts did he start with?

Extra Practice

Set A (pp. 278–281)

Measure the length to the nearest $\frac{1}{2}$ and $\frac{1}{4}$ inch.

1. 

2.

Set B (pp. 282–283)

Choose the better estimate.

1. A pen is 6 __?__ long.
   A inches **B** feet

2. A car is 6 __?__ long.
   A miles **B** feet

Set C (pp. 284–285)

Copy and complete. Use the Table of Measures on page 284 to help.

1. Change feet to yards.
   larger unit: __?__
   ■ feet = 1 yard

2. Change inches to yards.
   larger unit: __?__
   ■ inches = 1 yard

Set D (pp. 286–289)

Estimate the length in centimeters. Then use a ruler to measure to the nearest millimeter and centimeter.

1. 

2.

3. 

4. 

Set E (pp. 290–291)

Copy and complete. Use the Table of Measures on page 290 to help.

1. Change millimeters to meters.
   larger unit: __?__
   1 meter = ■ millimeters

2. Change meters to kilometers.
   larger unit: __?__
   1 kilometer = ■ meters

Review/Test

CHECK VOCABULARY

Choose the best term from the box.

Vocabulary
foot
meter

1. A door is about 1 __?__ wide. (p. 286)

CHECK SKILLS

Measure the length to the nearest $\frac{1}{2}$ and $\frac{1}{4}$ inch. (pp. 278–281)

2.

Choose the better estimate. (pp. 282–283)

3. The wall is 3 __?__ high.
   A miles B yards

4. The marker is 6 __?__ long.
   A inches B feet

Copy and complete. Use the Table of Measures on page 284 to help. (pp. 284–285)

5. Change feet to miles.
   larger unit: __?__
   ■ feet = 1 mile

6. Change inches to feet.
   larger unit: __?__
   ■ inches = 1 foot

Measure the length to the nearest millimeter and centimeter. (pp. 286–289)

7.

Copy and complete. Use the Table of Measures on page 290 to help. (pp. 290–291)

8. Change millimeters to centimeters.
   larger unit: __?__
   ■ millimeters = 1 centimeter

9. Change centimeters to meters.
   larger unit: __?__
   ■ centimeters = 1 meter

CHECK PROBLEM SOLVING

Use logical reasoning to solve. (pp. 318–319)

10. Rod has 4 model cars. Their lengths are 10, 12, 14, and 16 centimeters. The blue car is the shortest. The green car is 4 centimeters longer than the red car. What is the length of the white car?

Chapter CRCT Test Prep

MEASUREMENT

1. M3M2.a. Which unit of measure would be the most appropriate to find the distance from Atlanta, Georgia, to Washington, DC?

   A. inches

   B. feet

   C. yards

   D. miles

2. M3M2.b. To the nearest $\frac{1}{2}$ inch, what is the length of Julia's hair clip?

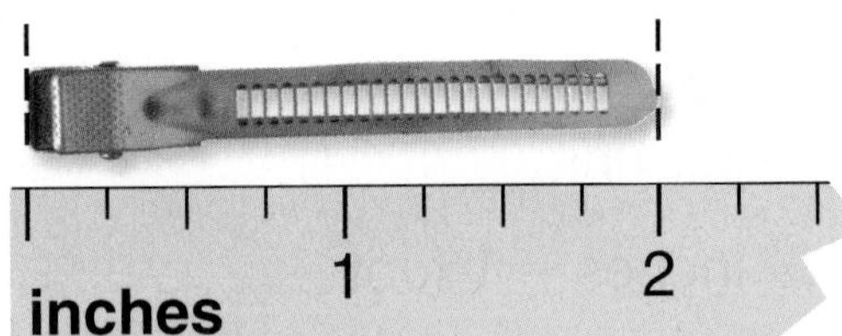

   A. $1\frac{1}{2}$ inches

   B. 2 inches

   C. $2\frac{1}{2}$ inches

   D. 3 inches

3. M3M2.d. Which of the following is shorter than 1 foot?

   A. 1 inch

   B. 1 yard

   C. 1 mile

   D. 1 kilometer

MEASUREMENT

4. M3M2.c. Which of the following is about 3 meters long?

   A. car

   B. pencil

   C. shoe

   D. bicycle

5. M3M2.c. Which is the best estimate of your height?

   A. 4 inches

   B. 4 feet

   C. 4 meters

   D. 4 yards

6. M3M2.b. To the nearest millimeter, what is the length of the ribbon below?

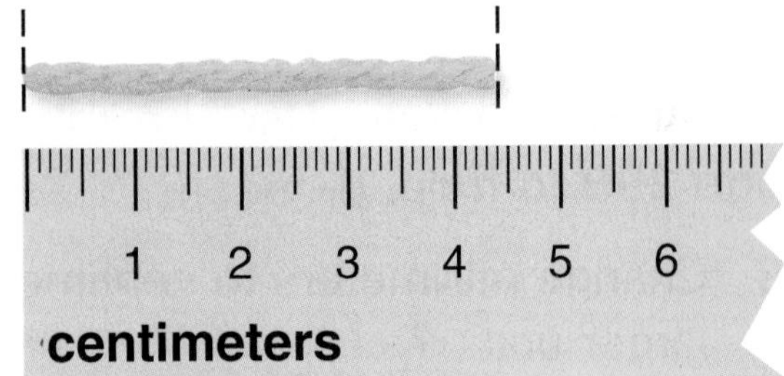

   A. 4 millimeters

   B. 5 millimeters

   C. 44 millimeters

   D. 54 millimeters

Cumulative CRCT Test Prep

NUMBERS AND OPERATIONS

7. M3N2.c. The Oakdale Band members are selling raffle tickets. Last week, they sold 768 tickets. They sold 632 tickets this week. How many tickets did they sell during these two weeks?

A. 1,100

B. 1,200

C. 1,300

D. 1,400

8. M3N3.e. What number should Zoe write to make the number sentence true?

$$2 \times (9 \times 3) = (2 \times \square) \times 3$$

A. 2

B. 3

C. 5

D. 9

9. M3N4.c. Ken has 35 seashells. He wants to put the same number of shells into each of 5 buckets. Which expression shows the number of shells he should put in each bucket?

A. 35 − 5

B. 35 + 5

C. 35 × 5

D. 35 ÷ 5

ALGEBRA

10. M3A1.a. Kendra wrote the number pattern below. What is rule for her pattern?

40, 36, 32, 28

A. Divide by 3.

B. Add 3.

C. Multiply by 4.

D. Subtract 4.

Use the table below to answer question 11.

Yards	1	2	3	4
Feet	3	6	9	□

11. M3A1.c. How many feet are in 4 yards?

A. 3 feet

B. 9 feet

C. 12 feet

D. 15 feet

12. M3A1.c. Which number belongs in the □ to make the number sentence true?

$$\square \times 5 = 5 + 5 + 5 + 5$$

A. 4

B. 5

C. 10

D. 20

ELA3R2 The student acquires and uses grade-level words to communicate effectively. *also* ELA3R3.b., ELA3R3.h., ELA3R3.r.

VOCABULARY
- data
- tally table
- horizontal bar graph
- foot
- mile
- meter
- frequency table
- survey
- scale
- yard
- millimeter
- kilometer

VOCABULARY CONCENTRATION

MATERIALS *For each group* vocabulary cards, definition cards

- Mix up the vocabulary cards and definition cards, and place them face down in 4 rows and 3 columns.
- Take turns turning over two cards at a time. The player that matches a term with the correct definition removes the cards. If a term does not match the definition, turn both cards face down, and continue playing.
- Play the game until all the terms and definitions have been matched.
- The player with the most matched cards wins the game.

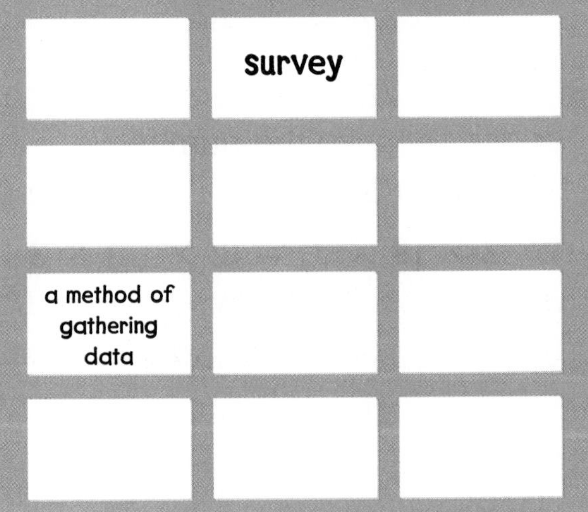

MATH WORD WORK (MEMORY)

MATERIALS *For each group* vocabulary cards

- Mix up the cards and place them face down. Arrange them in 3 rows and 4 columns.
- Take turns turning over a pair of cards. If the cards are a match, the player must give the definition of the term on the cards. If the definition is correct, the player takes the cards. The player with the greatest number of pairs wins!

CLUES

Word List
- foot
- yard
- mile
- millimeter
- meter
- kilometer

- Each partner should come up with an example or a clue for each vocabulary term shown at the right. For example, a clue for *foot* could be "the length of a book." A clue for *meter* could be "the width of a door."
- Take turns giving your partner your clues. The partner that correctly names the most vocabulary words wins!

TREEMENDOUS!

MATERIALS *For each pair* Unit 5 *Treemendous!* puzzle

- With your partner, use the clues and the terms in the Vocabulary box on page 298 to help you fill in the blanks on your sheet.
- The letters in the boxes will spell the state tree of Georgia.

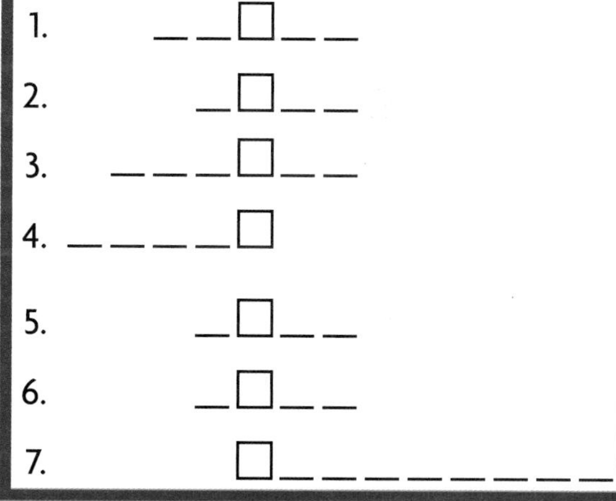

1. A __?__ **table** uses marks to record data.
2. 1 __?__ is equal to 5,280 feet.
3. A __?__ is a method of gathering information or data.
4. The numbers on a graph that help you read the number each bar shows is called the __?__.
5. There are 12 inches in 1 __?__.
6. Information that is collected about people or things is __?__.
7. The metric unit you would use to measure the distance an airplane flies is the __?__.

Georgia Tasks

M3D1.a. Solve problems by organizing and displaying data in bar graphs and tables. *also* **M3M2.c., M3M2.d., M3D1.b., M3P5.c.**

ELA3R3.h. Interprets information from illustrations, diagrams, charts, graphs, and graphic organizers. *also* **SS3G1**

Task A

OUTDOOR FUN

The third grade classes are going to Fort Mountain State Park in the Chattahoochee National Forest. They took a survey to see how many students wanted to do each activity. The tally table shows the results.

a. Make a bar graph to display the information in the table.

b. Write a question your classmates could answer by looking at your graph.

Activities Survey

Activity	Tally
Fishing	𝍸 𝍸 𝍸 𝍸
Hiking	𝍸 |||
Horseback Riding	𝍸 𝍸 ||
Miniature Golf	𝍸 𝍸 𝍸
Mountain Biking	||||

Task B

YARN DOLLS

Natalie is making yarn dolls. These pictures show the lengths of some of the pieces of yarn Natalie needs.

Yarn Measurement

Estimate	Actual
1.	
2.	
3.	

1.

2.

3.

a. Copy and complete the table. Estimate the length of each piece of yarn to the nearest inch. Use a ruler to measure each piece of yarn to the nearest inch.

b. Compare each estimate to the measured length. Write *is greater than, is less than*, or *is equal to*.

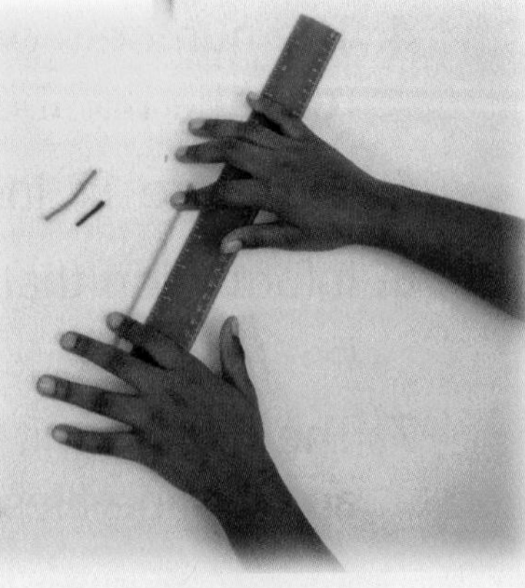

Maintain/Preview

Maintain

For 1–2, use the tally table.

1. How many students were surveyed?
2. How many more students chose apple juice than chose grape juice?

Favorite Juice	
Juice	**Tally**
Apple	卌 卌 卌 |||
Grape	卌 ||||
Grapefruit	卌 卌	
Orange	卌 卌 卌 |||

For 3–4, use the bar graph.

3. How many more students play soccer than play baseball?
4. How many students play football?

After-School Activities

Number of Students

0 2 4 6 8

Football Baseball Piano Soccer

Activity

Compare. Write $<$, $>$, or $=$ for each ●.

5. 8 yd ● 20 ft
6. 30 mm ● 3 cm
7. 4 km ● 5,000 m
8. An American black bear is about 6 feet tall. About how many yards tall is an American black bear?
9. Julia needs 2 feet of ribbon to make a pillow. If she wants to make 3 pillows, how many yards of ribbon does she need?

Preview

Choose the best term from the box.

1. 
2. 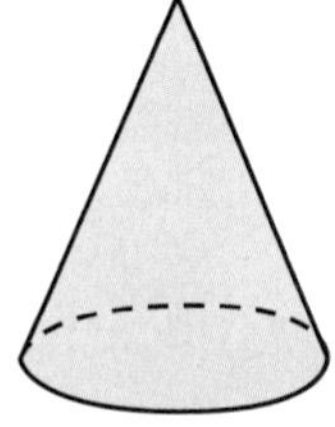
3. 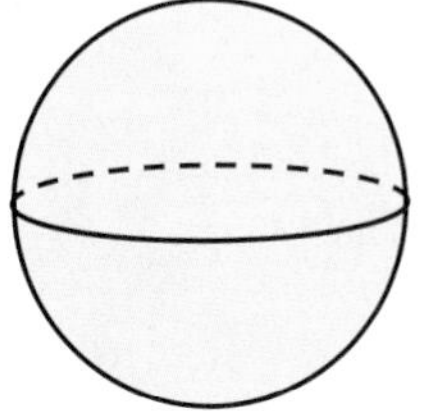
4. 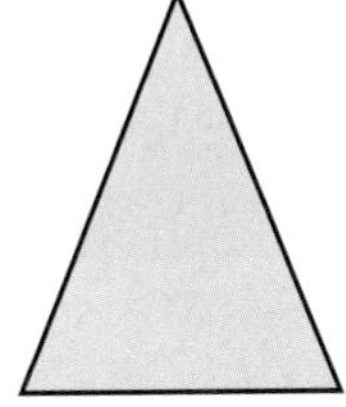

circle	square
rectangle	triangle
cone	sphere
cylinder	prism

CHAPTER 16

Plane Figures

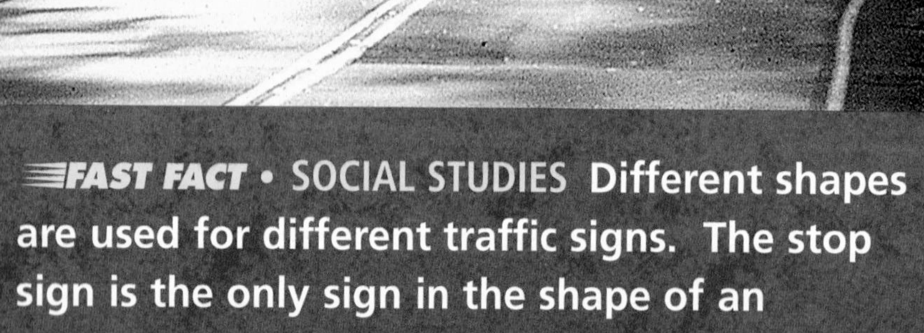

FAST FACT • SOCIAL STUDIES **Different shapes are used for different traffic signs. The stop sign is the only sign in the shape of an octagon. Signs for school zones are in the shape of a pentagon. Yield signs are triangles.**

INVESTIGATION **Make a list of the traffic signs you see on your way to school. Tell what geometric shapes are used for each sign. Describe each shape.**

CHECK WHAT YOU KNOW

Use this page to help you review and remember important skills needed for Chapter 16.

IDENTIFY PLANE FIGURES

Choose the best term from the box.

circle
rectangle
square
triangle

1. 2. 3.

4. 5. 6.

SIDES AND VERTICES

Tell the number of sides and vertices in each figure.

7. 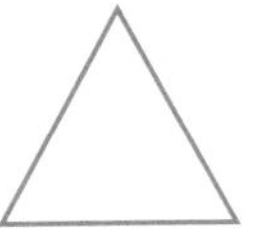
8. 
9. 
10. 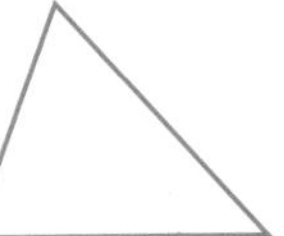
11. 
12. 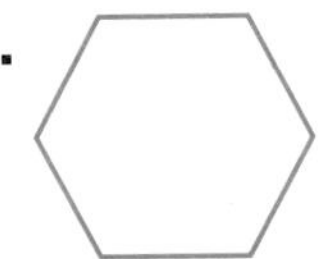
13. 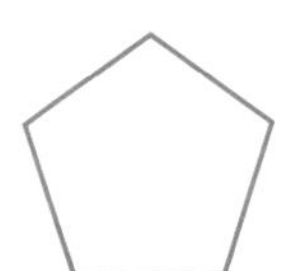
14. 

VOCABULARY POWER

REVIEW

triangle [trī′ang′gəl] *noun*

Tri- at the beginning of *triangle* means "three." List some other words that begin with *tri-*, and tell how *three* is part of their meanings.

PREVIEW

- right angle
- acute angle
- obtuse angle
- polygon
- quadrilateral
- equilateral triangle
- isosceles triangle
- scalene triangle

www.harcourtschool.com/mathglossary

Line Segments and Angles

M3G1.c. Examine and compare angles of fundamental geometric figures. *also* M3P2.a., M3P2.b., M3P2.c.

Quick Review

Write the number of sides each figure has.

1. ▭ 2. □ 3. △

4. ⏢ 5. ◺

VOCABULARY

line	**angle**
point	**right angle**
line segment	**acute angle**
ray	**obtuse angle**

Learn

POINT TO POINT Victor drew this plane figure by connecting points on grid paper. The sides of his figure are line segments. The terms below can help you describe figures in geometry.

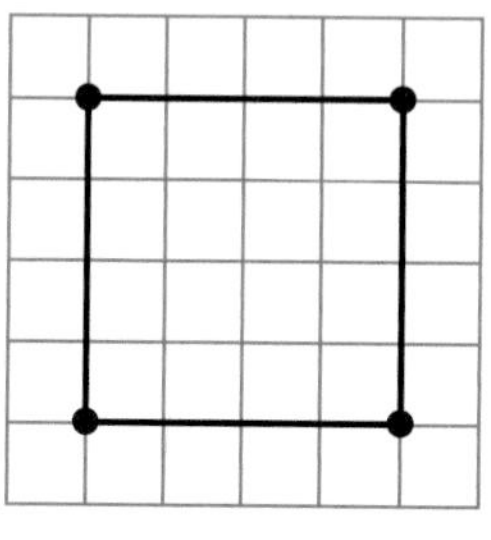

Term

A **line** is straight. It continues in both directions. It does not end.	
A **point** is an exact position or location.	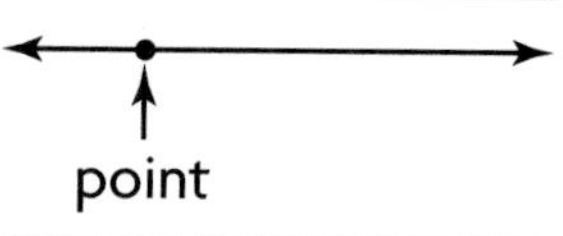
A **line segment** is straight. It is part of a line, and it has two endpoints.	
A **ray** is part of a line. It has one endpoint. It is straight and continues in one direction.	
An **angle** is formed by two rays or line segments that share an endpoint.	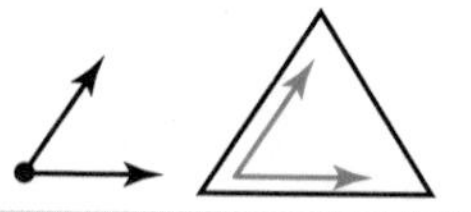 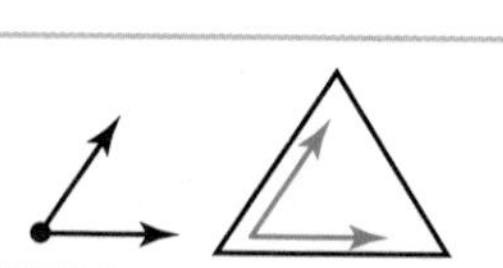

- How many line segments did Victor draw?
- **REASONING** How are lines and line segments alike? How are they different?

Look at the angles in the plane figure that Victor drew. These four angles are right angles. A **right angle** is a special angle that forms a square corner. Use the corner of a sheet of paper to tell whether an angle is a right angle.

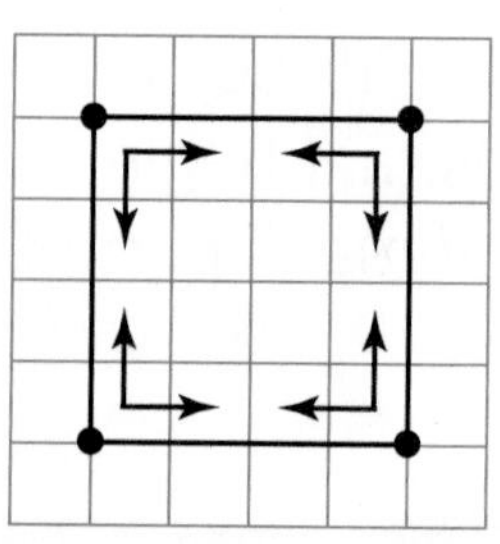

Naming Angles

You can think of a right angle as $\frac{1}{4}$ of a turn around a circle.

You can name angles by the size of the opening between the rays.

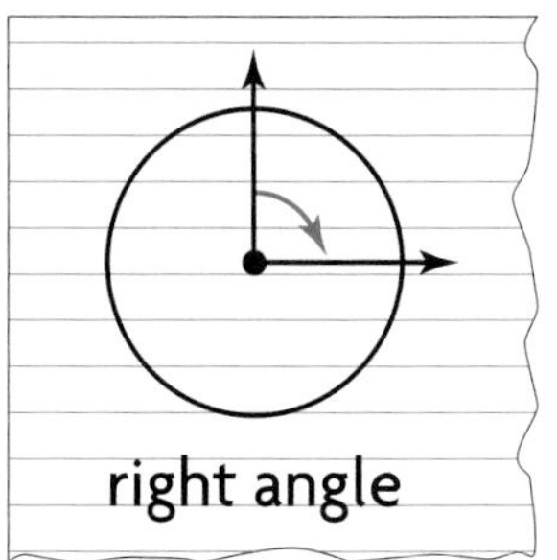

Some angles are smaller than a right angle. These are **acute angles**.

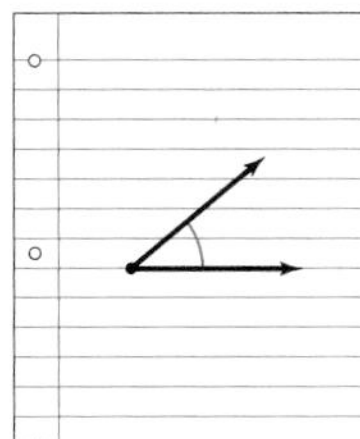
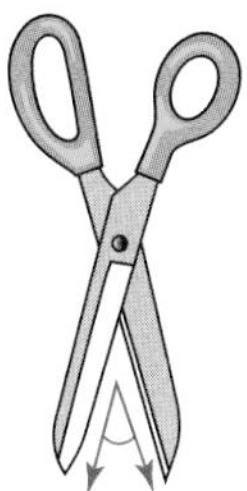

Some angles are larger than a right angle. These are **obtuse angles**.

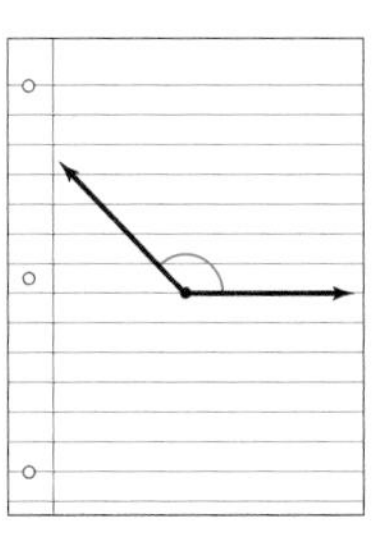
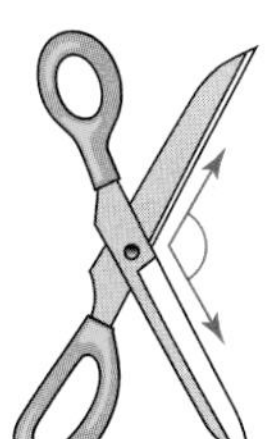

- **REASONING** The angle shown at the right is made up of two $\frac{1}{4}$ turns around the circle. What do the two rays form in this diagram?

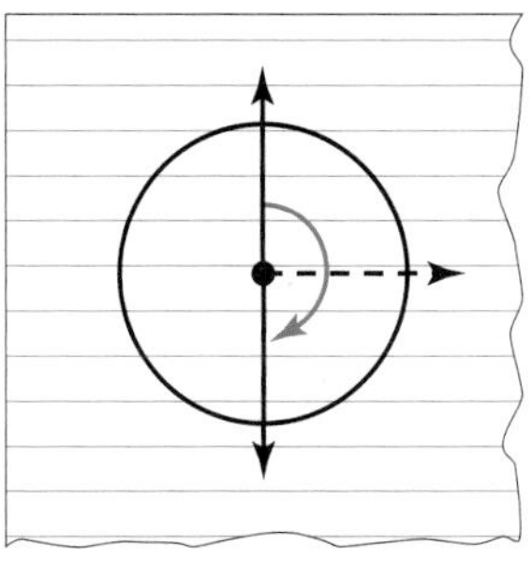

MATH IDEA You can identify angles in plane figures. You can tell if an angle is a right angle, an acute angle, or an obtuse angle.

Check

1. **Draw** a triangle on grid paper like the one shown at the right. What kinds of angles does this triangle have?

Name each figure.

2. 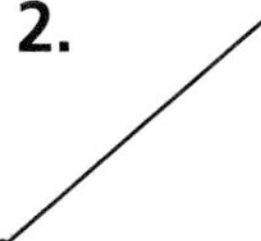

3. 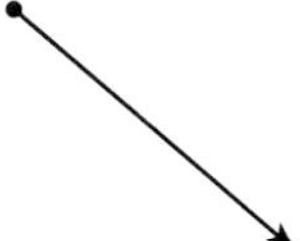

4. 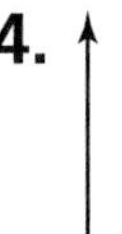

5. •

LESSON CONTINUES

Practice and Problem Solving

Extra Practice, page 326, Set A

Name each figure.

6. 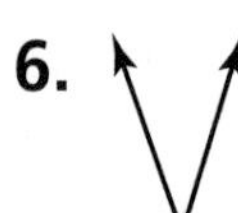

7. 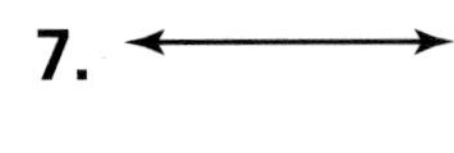

8. 

9. 

Use a corner of a sheet of paper to tell whether each angle is a *right angle*, an *acute angle*, or an *obtuse angle*.

10. 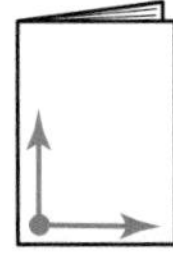

11. 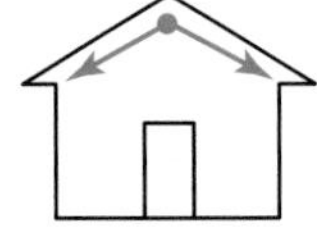

12. 

13. 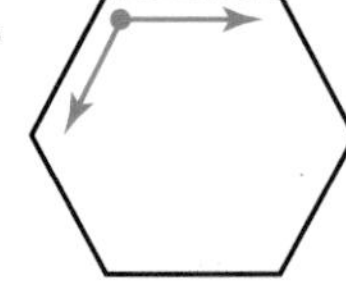

Draw and label each figure. You may wish to use a ruler or straightedge.

14. line segment **15.** ray **16.** line **17.** acute angle

Copy and complete the table.

	Figure	Number of Line Segments	Number of Angles	Types of Angles	Number of Right Angles
18.		■	■	■	■
19.		■	■	■	■
20.		■	■	■	■
21.		■	■	■	■
22.		■	■	■	■

23. **MULTISTEP** Blanca bought 3 packs of stickers. Each pack has 10 stickers. If she gives 4 stickers to a friend, how many will she have left?

24. **Write About It** Use a ruler or a straightedge to draw a triangle and a right angle. Describe the parts of each figure.

25. **FAST FACT** • SCIENCE Geese fly in a "V" formation to save energy so that they can fly farther. What kind of angle describes this formation?

26. List at least 3 objects in the room that contain right angles. How can you be sure the angles are right angles?

Maintain Skills

Write <, >, or = for each ●.

27. 43 ● 29

28. 42 ● 68

29. 93 ● 36

30. 61 ● 27

31. $\begin{array}{r} 164 \\ +321 \\ \hline \end{array}$

32. $\begin{array}{r} 294 \\ +498 \\ \hline \end{array}$

33. $\begin{array}{r} 789 \\ -167 \\ \hline \end{array}$

34. $\begin{array}{r} 672 \\ -385 \\ \hline \end{array}$

CRCT Test Prep

35. M3N1.a. What is the value of the blue digit in 3,495? (p. 6)

A. 4,000
B. 400
C. 40
D. 4

36. M3N2.c. Will bought a magazine for $2.79 and 3 pieces of candy for 9¢ each. How much money did he spend? (p. 98)

A. $2.88
B. $2.96
C. $3.06
D. $5.49

Problem Solving Thinker's Corner

CLOCKS AND ANGLES Use what you learned in this lesson to describe the angles made by the hands of a clock.

Write whether each angle is a *right angle,* an *acute angle,* or an *obtuse angle*.

1.

7:45

2.

11:15

3.

9:00

4.

3:30

5. **REASONING** The hour hand is between the 3 and 4. The minute hand is pointing to the 5. What time is it? Describe the angle made by the hands.

6. Joy left for school at 7:50 A.M. It took her 15 minutes to walk to school. What time is it? Describe the angle made by the hands.

LESSON 2

Types of Lines

M3G1.b. Identify and explain the properties of fundamental geometric figures. *also* M3P2.a., M3P2.b., M3P2.c., M3P2.d., M3P3., M3P3.a., M3P3.b., M3P3.c., M3P3.d.

Learn

GET IN LINE Here are some ways to describe the relationships between lines.

Lines that cross are **intersecting lines**. Intersecting lines form angles.

Some intersecting lines cross to form right angles.

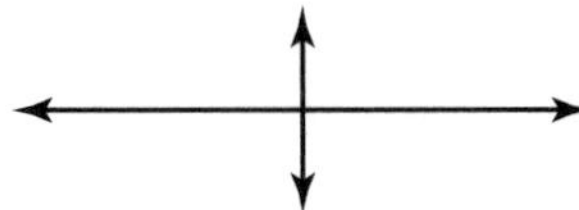

Some lines never cross. They do not form angles and are always the same distance apart.

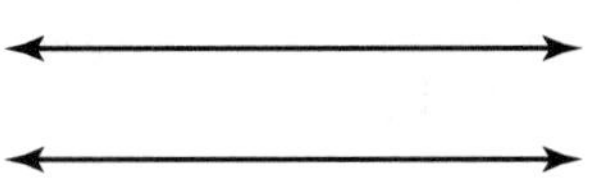

Quick Review

Write *right angle*, *obtuse angle*, or *acute angle*.

1.

2.

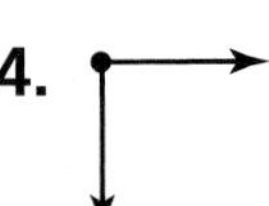

3.

4.

5.

VOCABULARY

intersecting lines

You may see models of lines that intersect and lines that do not intersect in the world around you.

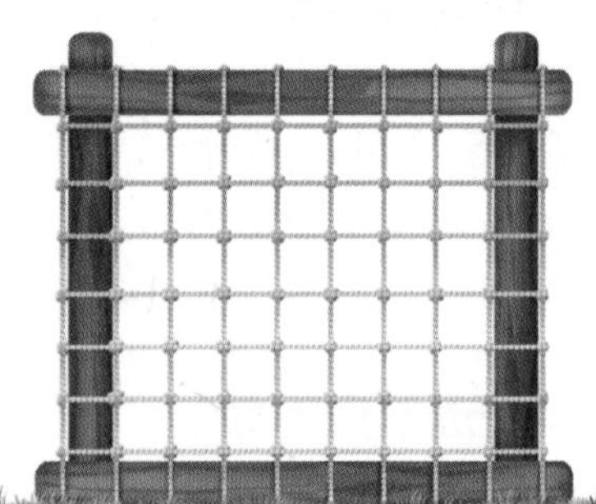

- Are the angles in the climbing net right angles? How can you check?
- **REASONING** Do intersecting lines always form right angles? Explain.

Check

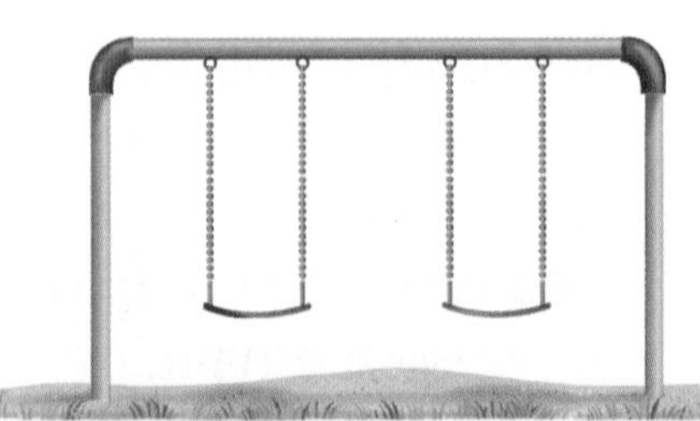

1. **Explain** how to tell whether the swing chains are intersecting or not intersecting.

Describe the lines. Write *intersecting* or *not intersecting*.

2. 

3.

4. 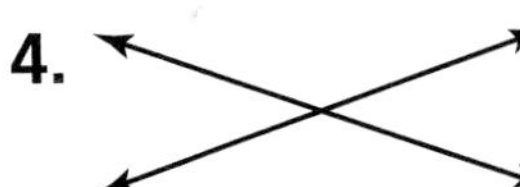

Practice and Problem Solving

Extra Practice, page 326, Set B

Describe the lines. Write *intersecting* or *not intersecting*.

5. 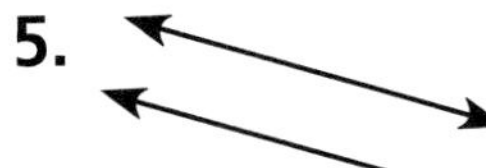

6. 

7.  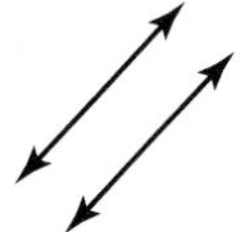

Describe the intersecting lines. Write *with right angles* or *without right angles*.

8. 

9.  

10. 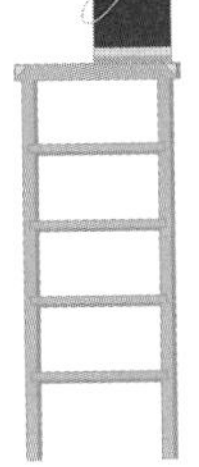

USE DATA For 11–13, use the map at the right.

11. Which street does not intersect Oak Street?

12. Does Oak Street form right angles with Pine Street or Maple Street? Explain.

13. **What's the Question?** The answer is obtuse angle.

14. **REASONING** Use what you know about line relationships to describe the sides of a rectangle.

15. **Write About It** Draw and label sets of lines that intersect and lines that do not intersect. Use a ruler to help. Describe the angles in each of your drawings.

Maintain Skills

16. Write the amount.

CRCT Test Prep

17. M3N3.g. Talia is paid $5 to baby-sit for 1 hour. How much will she earn in 4 hours? (p. 128)

A. $9 B. $20 C. $25 D. $30

LESSON 3

Plane Figures

M3G1.b. Identify and explain the properties of fundamental geometric figures. *also* M3G1.c., M3P2.a., M3P2.b., M3P2.c., M3P2.d., M3P3.

Learn

SHAPE UP! A closed figure begins and ends at the same point. An open figure has ends that do not meet. A **polygon** is a closed plane figure with straight sides that are line segments. A circle is an example of a plane figure that has no straight sides.

polygons

A
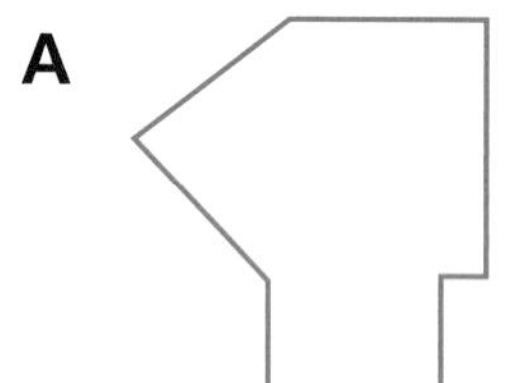

B

not polygons

C
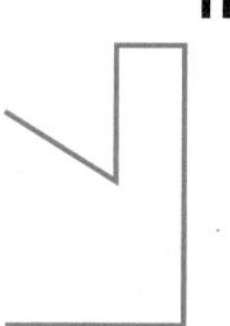

D
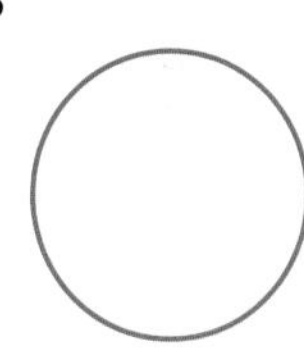

REASONING Why do you think the sides of a polygon are sometimes called *edges*?

MATH IDEA You can count the number of *sides* and *angles* for any polygon.

Quick Review

Write the number of sides each figure has.

1.  2.

3.  4. 5.

VOCABULARY

polygon
quadrilateral
pentagon
hexagon
octagon

Examples

Find the number of sides and angles for each polygon.

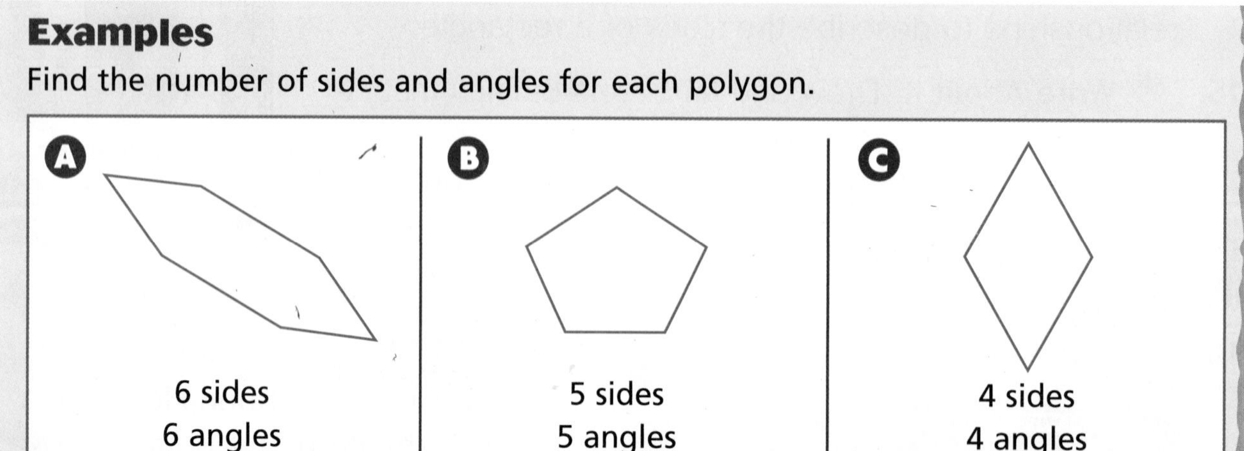

A	B	C
6 sides 6 angles	5 sides 5 angles	4 sides 4 angles

• Explain why a circle is not a polygon.

MATH IDEA You can name and sort polygons by the number of *sides* or *angles* they have.

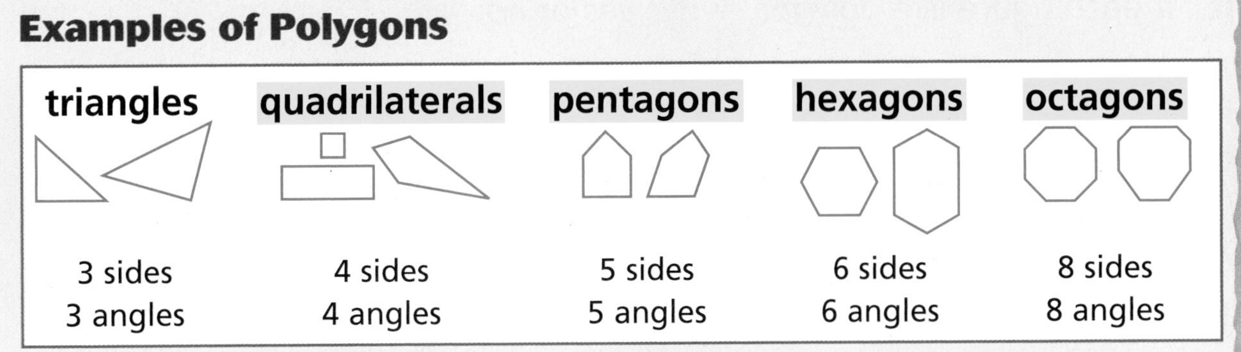

- What do you notice about the number of sides and the number of angles in polygons?

Check

1. Draw a polygon that has 10 sides and 10 angles.

Tell if each figure is a polygon. Write *yes* or *no*.

2. 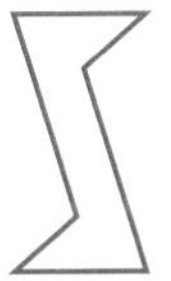

3. 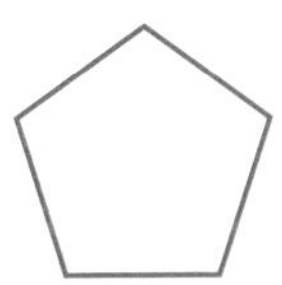

4. 

5. 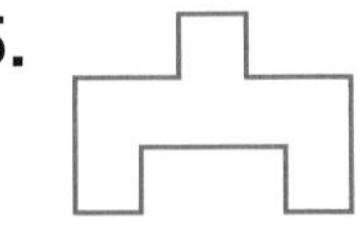

6. 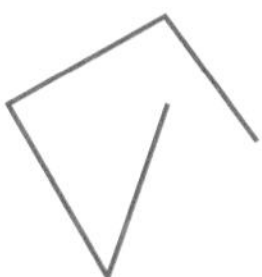

Write the number of sides and angles each polygon has. Then name the polygon.

7. 

8. 

9. 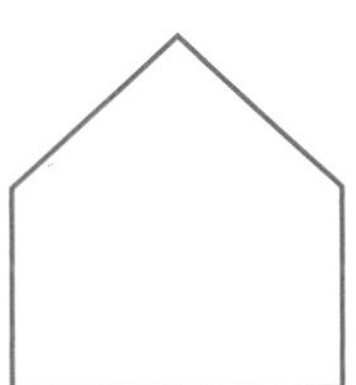

10. 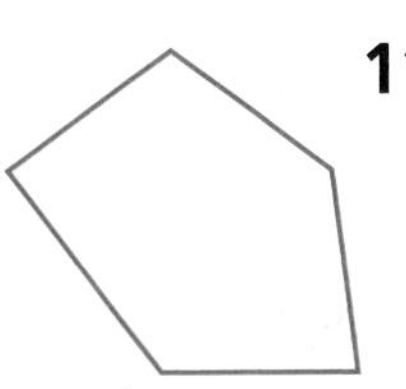

11. 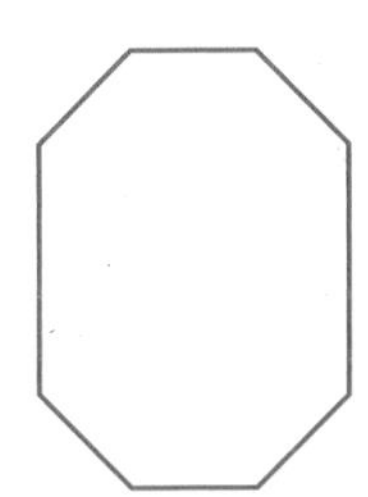

Draw an example of each figure.

12. octagon

13. pentagon

14. hexagon

15. quadrilateral

LESSON CONTINUES

Practice and Problem Solving

Extra Practice, page 326, Set C

Tell if each figure is a polygon. Write *yes* or *no*.

16. 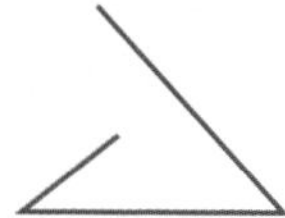

17. 

18. 

19. 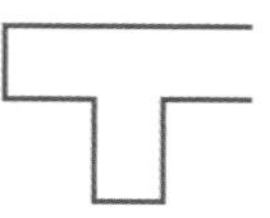

20. 

Write the number of sides and angles each polygon has. Then name the polygon.

21. 

22. 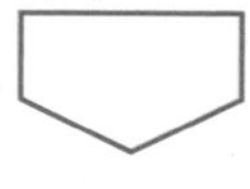

23. 

24. 

25. 

For 26–30, write the letters of the figures that answer the questions.

A B C D E

26. Which are polygons?

27. Which is a quadrilateral?

28. Which figures have some angles that are acute angles?

29. Which figures are closed figures?

30. Which figures have some sides that are always the same distance apart?

For 31–36, draw each figure.

31. a polygon with 4 sides

32. a pentagon with 1 right angle

33. a triangle with 3 acute angles

34. a quadrilateral with an obtuse angle

35. a circle

36. a triangle with 3 equal sides

37. **REASONING** Shawna says she can draw a triangle with 2 right angles. Do you think this is possible or impossible? Explain.

38. **Vocabulary Power** In the word *polygon, poly-* means "many" and *-gon* means "angles." Explain how this helps you understand why a circle is not a polygon.

39. Mr. Gomez delivered 3 cases of pasta to each of 3 stores. Each case had 8 boxes. How many boxes of pasta did he deliver?

40. **Write About It** Draw polygons with 3, 4, 5, 6, and 8 sides. Then label each polygon.

41. Look at each figure at the right. What happens to the size of the angles as the number of sides increases?

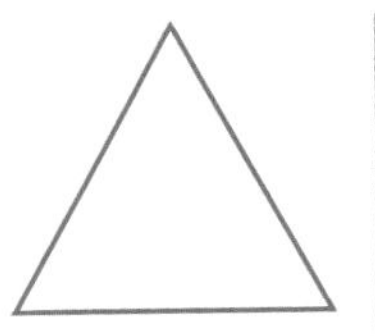
3 sides

4 sides

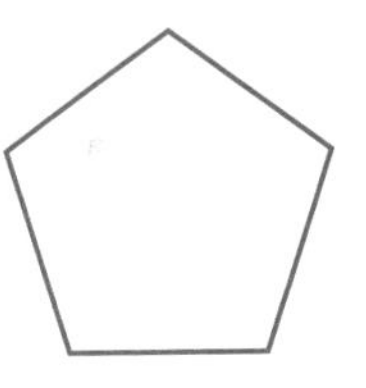
5 sides

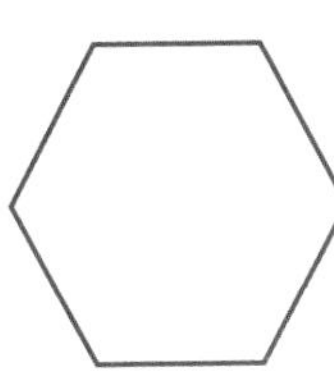
6 sides

Maintain Skills

42. $\begin{array}{r} 466 \\ +527 \\ \hline \end{array}$

43. $\begin{array}{r} 684 \\ +359 \\ \hline \end{array}$

44. $\begin{array}{r} 700 \\ -293 \\ \hline \end{array}$

45. $\begin{array}{r} 900 \\ -564 \\ \hline \end{array}$

46. $\begin{array}{r} 432 \\ +391 \\ \hline \end{array}$

47. $\begin{array}{r} 832 \\ -566 \\ \hline \end{array}$

CRCT Test Prep

48. M3M1. Dawson got to the soccer field at 3:15 P.M. The game started 45 minutes later. What time did the game start? (p. 112)

A. 4:00 A.M.
B. 4:00 P.M.
C. 4:15 A.M.
D. 4:15 P.M.

Problem Solving Thinker's Corner

VISUAL THINKING You can put together polygons to make other plane figures.

MATERIALS: pattern blocks

Look at a hexagon and a trapezoid.

The trapezoid has side lengths and angles that match the hexagon.

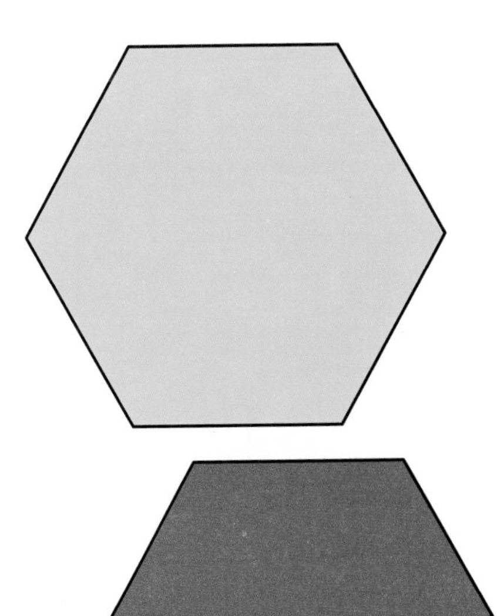

1. Can you make a hexagon by putting together trapezoids? Explain.
2. Try the same thing with triangles. Which triangles did you use? Explain.
3. See if you can make other polygons by combining pattern blocks.

LESSON 4

Triangles

M3G1.a. Draw and classify previously learned fundamental geometric figures as well as scalene, isosceles, and equilateral triangles. *also* M3G1.b., M3G1.c.

Learn

TIME FOR TRIANGLES Beverly and Armando sorted these triangles in different ways.

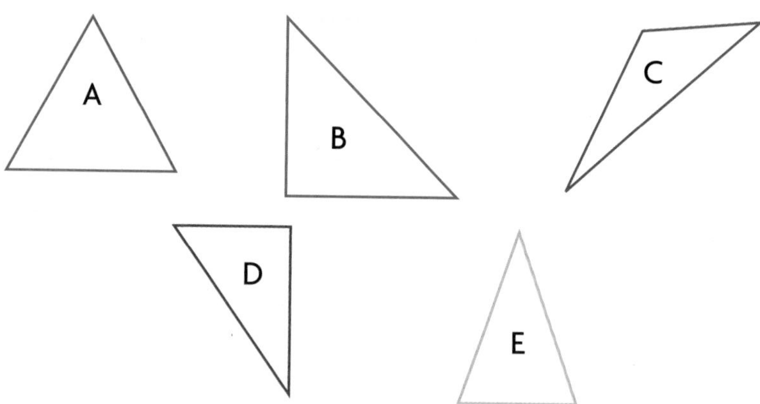

Quick Review

Write if each angle is a *right angle, obtuse angle*, or *acute angle*.

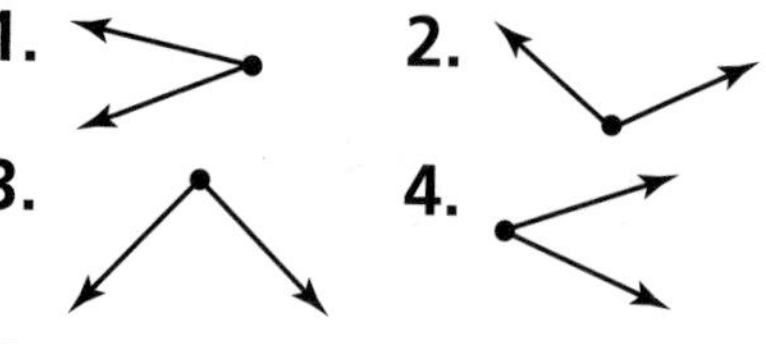

VOCABULARY

- **equilateral triangle**
- **isosceles triangle**
- **scalene triangle**
- **right triangle**
- **obtuse triangle**
- **acute triangle**

This is how Beverly sorted the triangles.

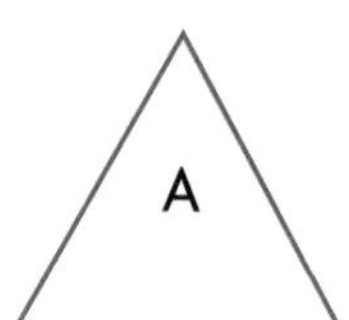

All sides are equal.

Two sides are equal.

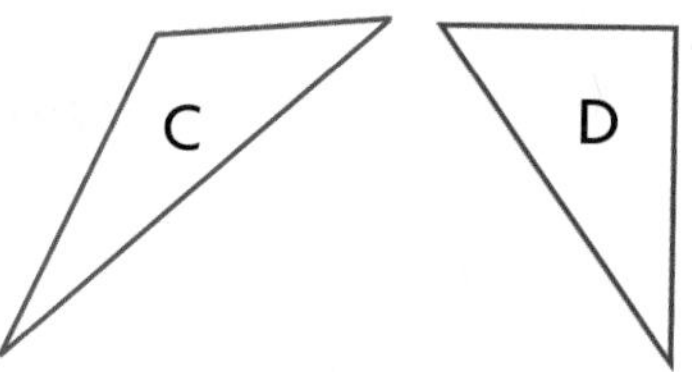

No sides are equal.

This is how Armando sorted the triangles.

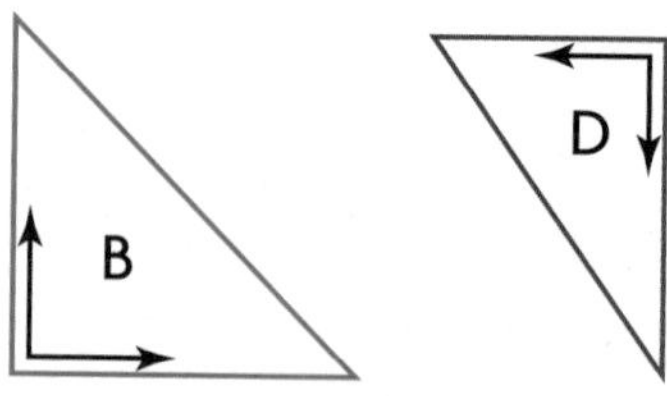

One angle is a right angle.

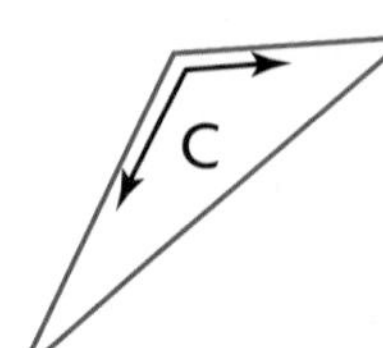

One angle is an obtuse angle.

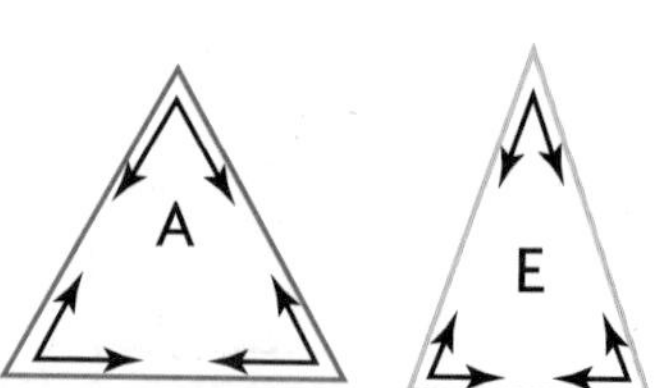

All angles are acute angles.

- How did Beverly sort the triangles? How did Armando sort the triangles?
- How can you check if an angle is an obtuse angle or an acute angle?

Name Triangles

You can name triangles by their equal sides.

equilateral triangle

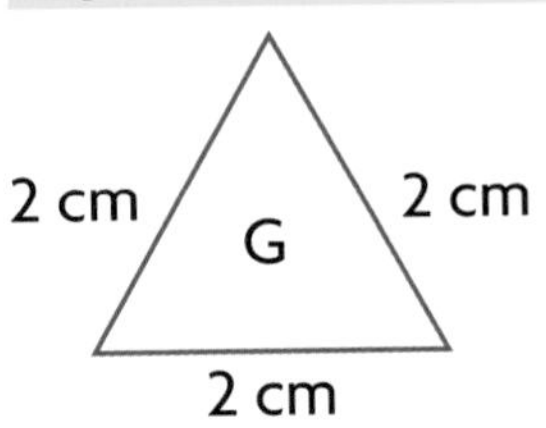

3 equal sides

isosceles triangle

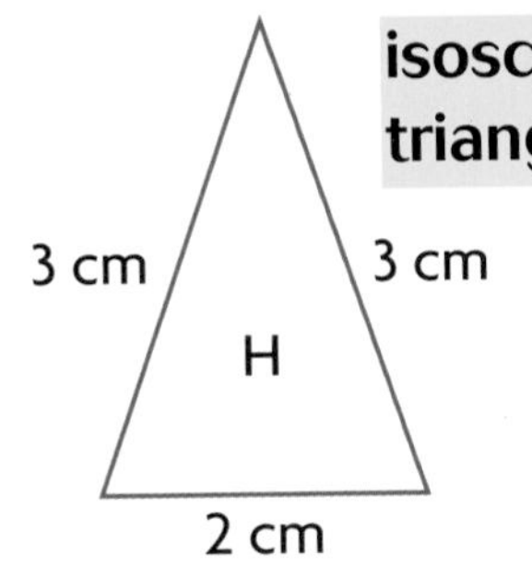

2 equal sides

scalene triangle

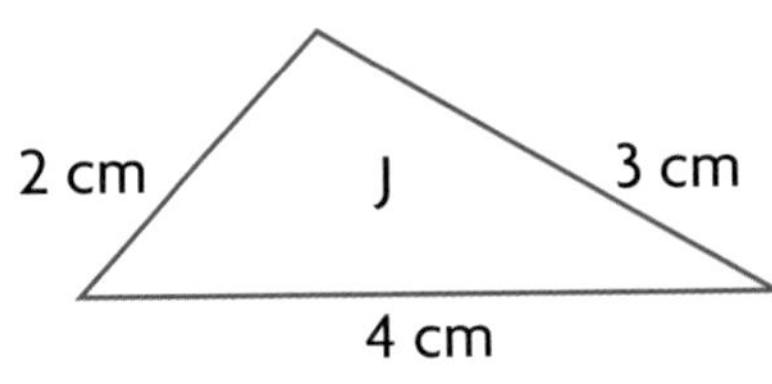

0 equal sides

You can name triangles by their angles.

right triangle

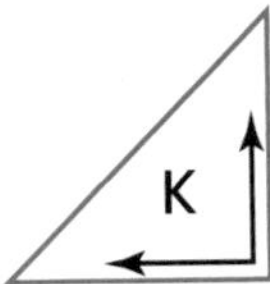

1 right angle

obtuse triangle

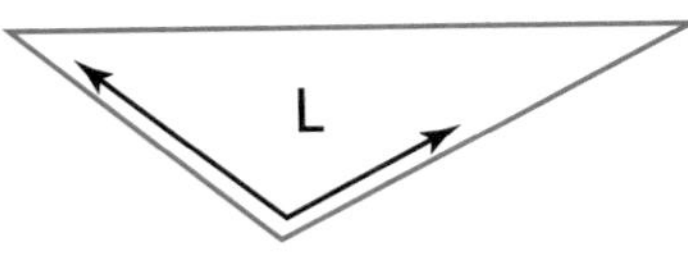

1 obtuse angle

acute triangle

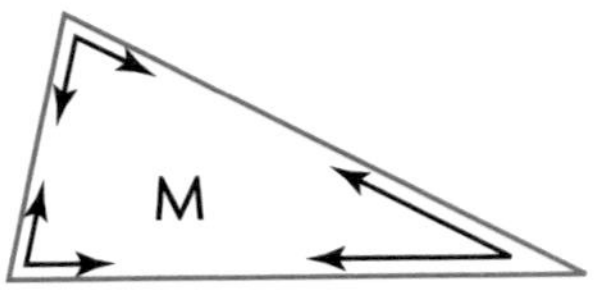

3 acute angles

- How are triangles J and M alike? How are they different?

MATH IDEA You can name and sort triangles by their sides or their angles.

Check

1. **Describe** triangle N by its sides. Then describe it by its angles.

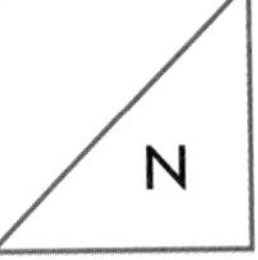

For 2–5, use the triangles at the right. Write *O, P, Q,* or *R*.

2. Which triangles have 0 equal sides?
3. Which triangle is an equilateral triangle?
4. Which triangles have 3 acute angles?
5. Which triangle is obtuse?

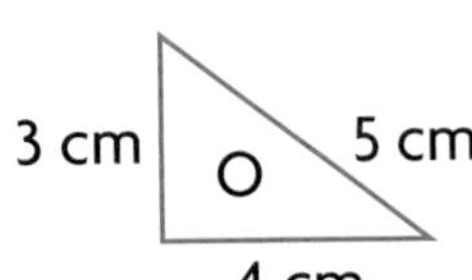

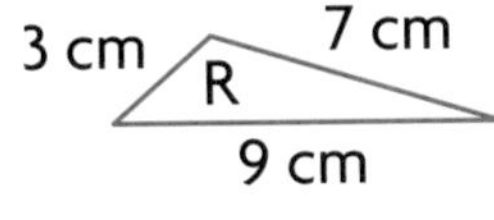

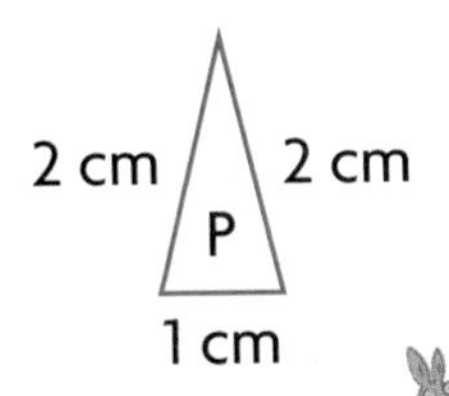

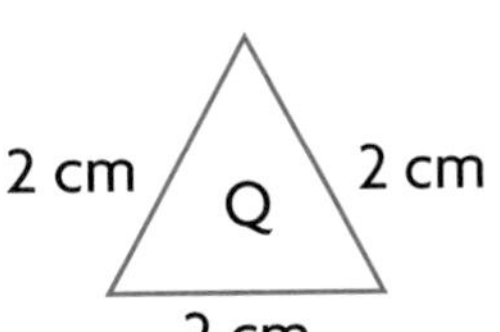

LESSON CONTINUES

Practice and Problem Solving

Extra Practice, page 326, Set D

For 6–9, use the triangles at the right. Write *A, B,* or *C*.

6. Which triangle is scalene?
7. Which triangles have at least 2 equal sides?
8. Which triangle has 1 obtuse angle? Which triangle has 3 acute angles?
9. Which triangle has the greatest angle measure?

Name each triangle. Write *equilateral, isosceles,* or *scalene*.

10. 4 cm, 4 cm, 4 cm

11. 4 cm, 6 cm, 8 cm

12. 2 cm, 2 cm, 3 cm

13. 2 cm, 2 cm, 2 cm

14. 3 cm, 5 cm, 4 cm

15. 2 cm, 2 cm, 1 cm

Name each triangle. Write *right, obtuse,* or *acute*.

16.

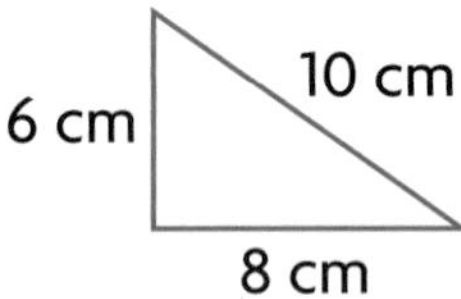

17.

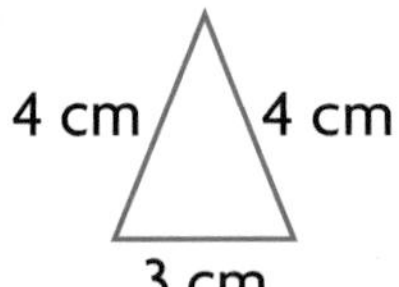

18.

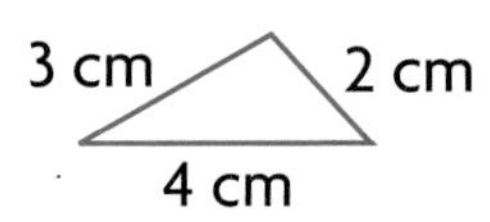

Draw each type of triangle. Use grid paper.

19. obtuse

20. scalene

21. right isoceles

22. acute equilateral

USE DATA For 23–24, use the diagram at the right.

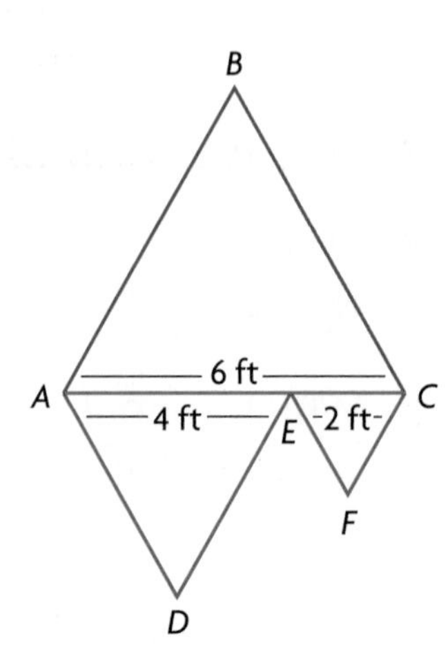

23. MULTISTEP Mrs. Liu has a garden with paths that are equilateral triangles. The shortest path from *A* to *C* is the green path. Which path is longer: the blue path or the red path? Explain.

24. **What's the Question?** The answer is 4 feet longer.

25. **REASONING** Brett says he can draw a triangle with 2 obtuse angles. Do you think this is possible? Explain.

26. Draw a triangle with 2 equal sides and one right angle. You may use grid paper to help. Name the triangle.

Maintain Skills

Measure the length of each object to the nearest centimeter.

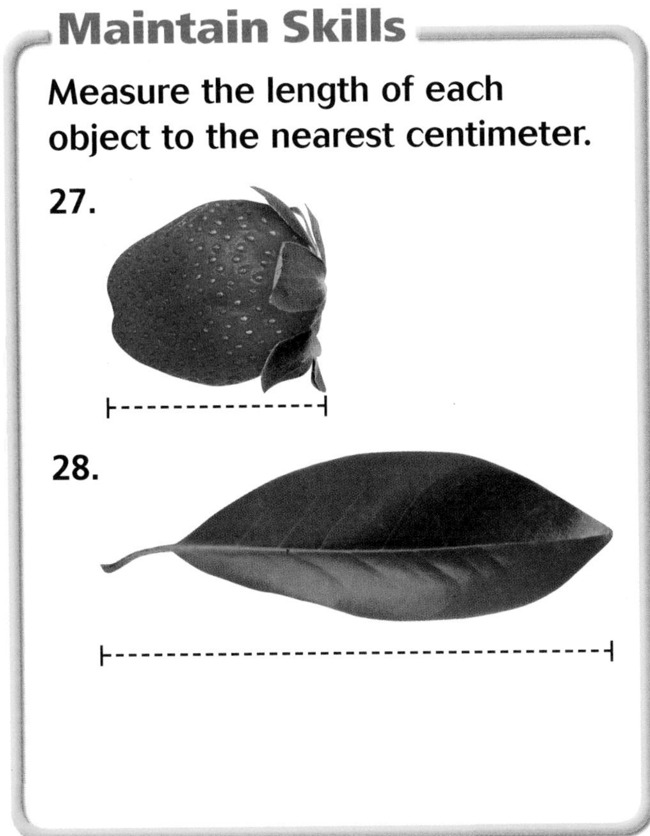

CRCT Test Prep

Use the graph below to answer question 29.

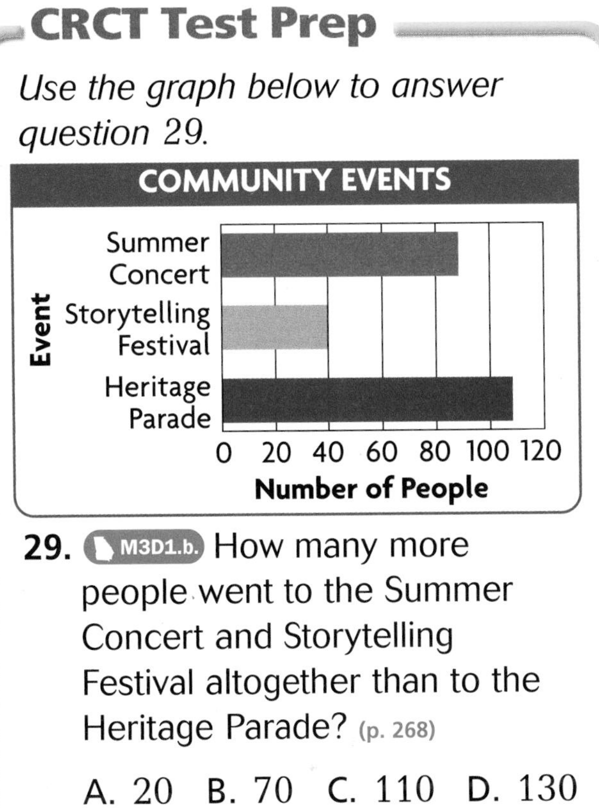

29. M3D1.b. How many more people went to the Summer Concert and Storytelling Festival altogether than to the Heritage Parade? (p. 268)

A. 20 B. 70 C. 110 D. 130

Problem Solving LINKUP . . . to Art

Many artists use triangles in their works. The Native American blanket at the right uses different kinds of triangles. Find and name as many triangles on the blanket as you can.

MATERIALS: grid paper, pencil, crayons

1. Draw and color a blanket design on grid paper. Use different kinds of triangles in your design.
2. Trade designs with a classmate and describe the triangles you see.

LESSON

5 Quadrilaterals

M3G1.b. Identify and explain the properties of fundamental geometric figures. *also* M3G1.c.

Learn

LIMIT OF FOUR Polygons with 4 sides and 4 angles are quadrilaterals.

quadrilaterals

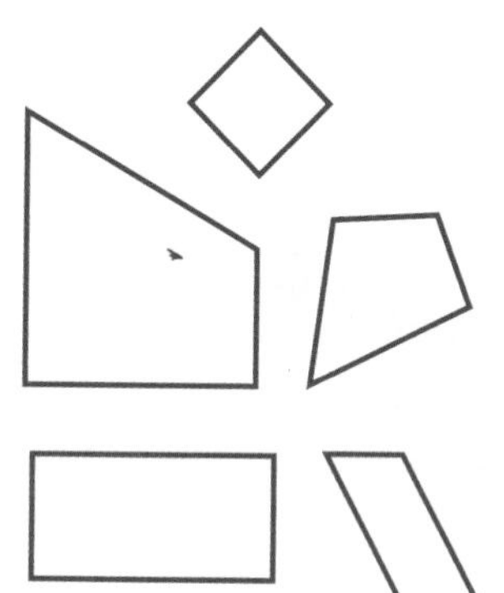

not quadrilaterals

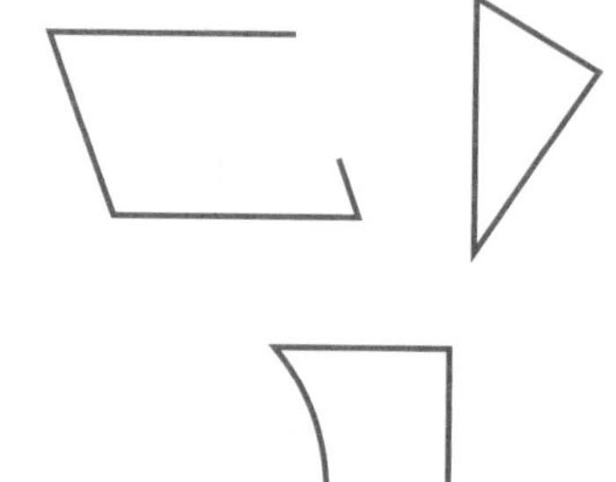

Quick Review

Describe the lines. Write *intersecting* or *not intersecting.*

1. 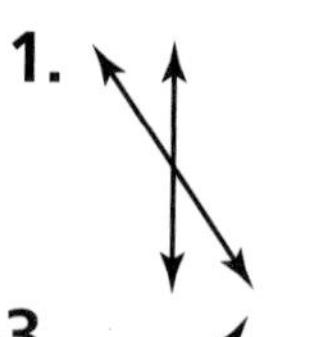
2. 
3.
4. 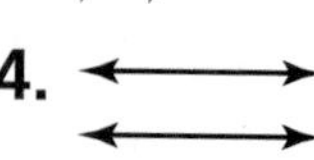
5.

VOCABULARY

trapezoid

A **trapezoid** is a special kind of quadrilateral. Trapezoids always have one pair of sides that are the same distance apart, but the sizes of the angles are not always the same.

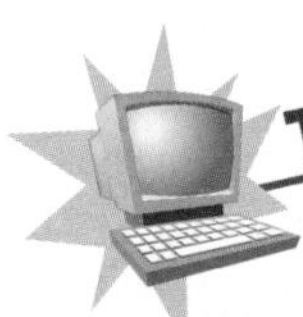

Technology Link

More Practice: Harcourt Mega Math Ice Station Exploration, *Polar Planes,* Level G

Examples of Trapezoids

A

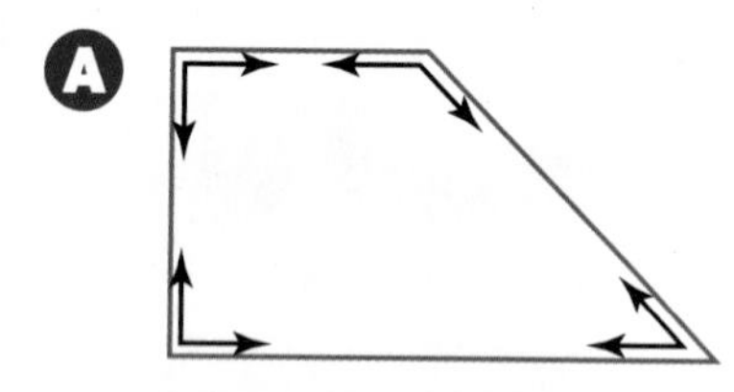

2 right angles
1 acute angle
1 obtuse angle
1 pair of sides that are the same distance apart

B

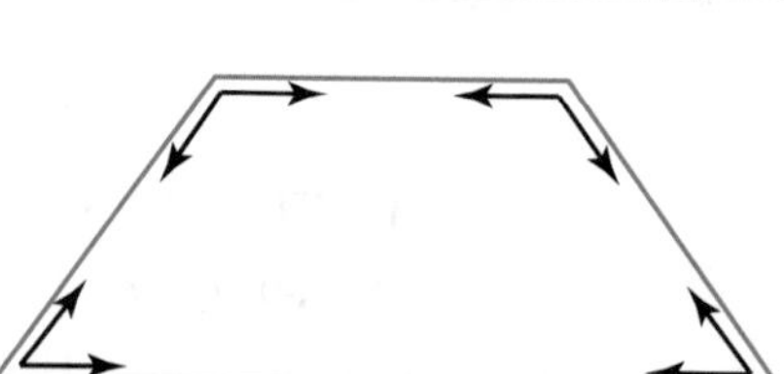

2 acute angles
2 obtuse angles
1 pair of sides that are the same distance apart

- How is a trapezoid like a rectangle? How is it different?

Other Names for Quadrilaterals

Here are some quadrilaterals with pairs of equal sides and 4 right angles.

rectangles

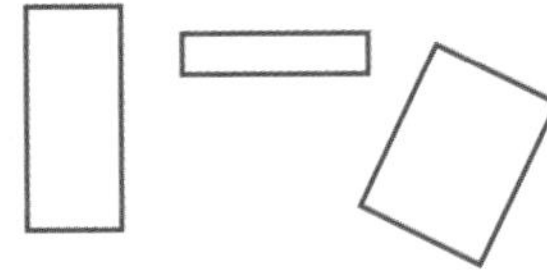

2 pairs of sides that are always the same distance apart
2 pairs of equal sides
4 right angles

squares

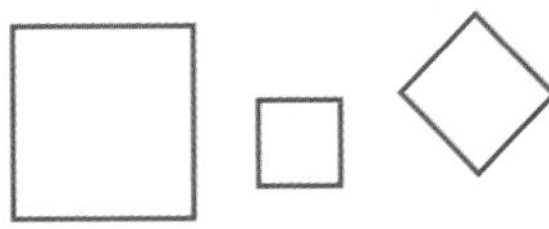

2 pairs of sides that are always the same distance apart
4 pairs of equal sides
4 right angles

- Why is a square a rectangle?

MATH IDEA You can name and sort quadrilaterals by looking at their sides and angles.

Check

1. **Describe** the sides and angles of this quadrilateral. What is another name for it?

For 2–4, use the quadrilaterals at the right.

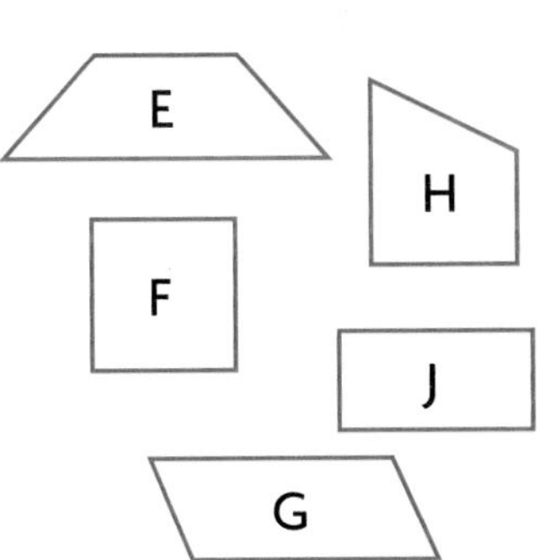

2. Which quadrilaterals have 2 pairs of sides that are always the same distance apart?
3. Which quadrilaterals have 2 or more right angles?
4. How are quadrilateral E and quadrilateral G alike? How are they different?

Write as many names for each quadrilateral as you can.

5. 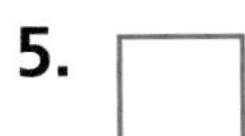
6.
7.
8. 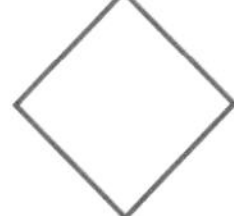
9. 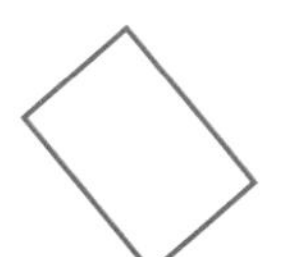
10. 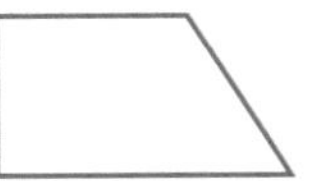

LESSON CONTINUES

Practice and Problem Solving

Extra Practice, page 326, Set E

For 11–13, use the quadrilaterals at the right. Write *A, B, C, D,* and *E*.

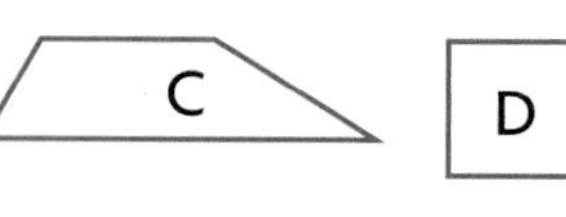

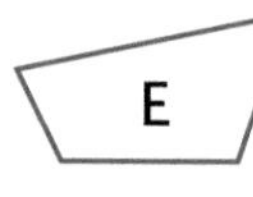

11. Which quadrilaterals have 2 pairs of equal sides?

12. Which quadrilaterals have no right angles?

13. How are quadrilateral A and quadrilateral D alike? How are they different?

For 14–19, write as many names for each quadrilateral as you can.

14. 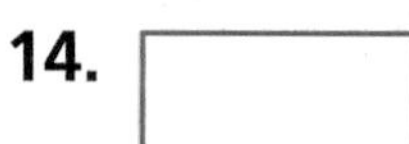

15.

16. 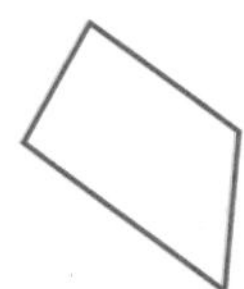

17.

18.

19. 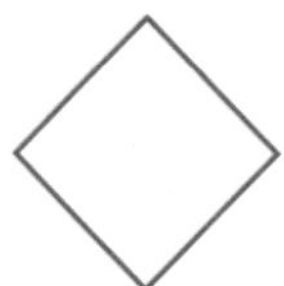

For 20–23, write *all* the letters that describe each quadrilateral.

20.

21. 

22.

23. 

a. It has 4 equal sides.
b. It has 2 pairs of sides that are the same distance apart.
c. It has 4 right angles.
d. It has 2 pairs of equal sides.

24. REASONING How is figure G like the figures to its right?

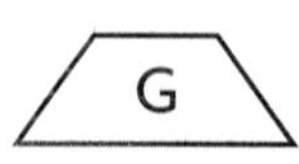

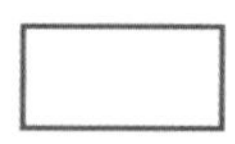

25. I have 4 equal sides and 4 right angles. What am I?

26. I have 5 sides and 5 angles. What am I?

27. **What's the Error?** Colin said that a square is not a quadrilateral. Explain his error.

28. **Write About It** Draw and label 4 different quadrilaterals on grid paper. Explain how each is different from the others.

29. Akemi sees a tile with 4 right angles. She says it must be a square. Do you agree or disagree? Explain.

30. Dante drew a quadrilateral with 2 acute angles and two obtuse angles. What could he have drawn?

Maintain Skills

Write $<$, $>$, or $=$ for each ●.

31. 67 ● 12

32. 45 ● 90

33. 82 ● 29

34. 53 ● 35

Write the amount.

35. 

36. Write the time.

CRCT Test Prep

37. M3N2.c. Donato gave away 23 marbles. He bought 16 more. Then he had 361 marbles. How many marbles did he have to begin with? (p. 250)

A. 368 B. 345 C. 322 D. 300

38. M3N4.f. Lino had 15 photos. He put an equal number of photos on each of 3 album pages. How many photos are on each page? (p. 224)

A. 45
B. 12
C. 5
D. 3

Problem Solving LINKUP . . . to Reading

STRATEGY • USE GRAPHIC AIDS Graphic aids, such as charts, diagrams, and maps, display information. Drawings and diagrams can be used to show how to build things, such as houses and bridges.

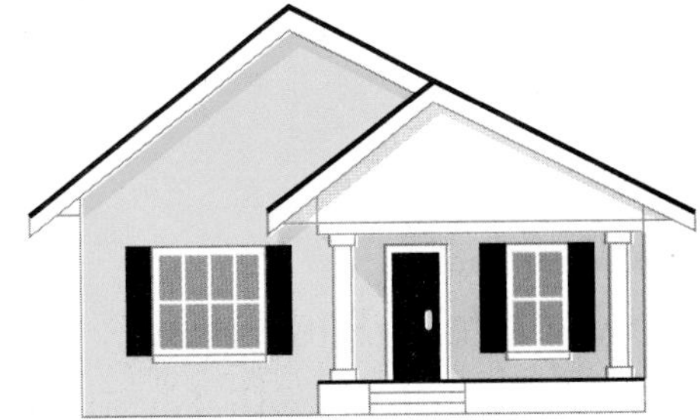

1. Look at the drawing of the bridge. What kinds of angles do you see? What plane figures were used in the drawing?

2. Look at the drawing of the house. What kind of angle was used for the roof? What other angles do you see in the drawing?

Circles

M3G1.d. Identify the center, diameter, and radius of a circle.
also M3P2.a., M3P2.b., M3P2.c., M3P2.d., M3P3.d.

Quick Review

Name each figure.

1. 2. 3. 4. 5.

VOCABULARY
circle
center
radius
diameter

Learn

ROUND AND ROUND A **circle** is a plane figure in which each point is the same distance from a certain point, called the **center**.

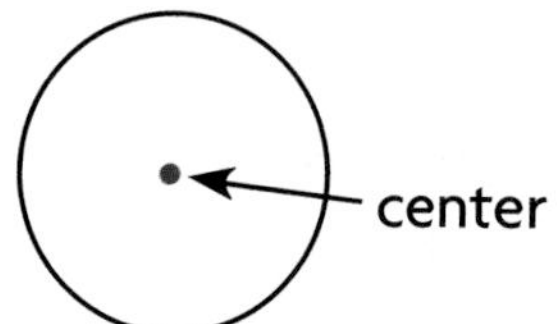

MATH IDEA All circles have the same shape, but not the same size.

You can describe the size of a circle by the length of its radius and diameter.

A **radius** of a circle is a line segment that connects the center to a point on the circle.

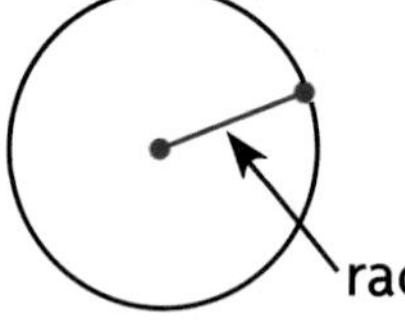

A **diameter** of a circle is a line segment that connects two points on the circle and passes through the center.

- How are all circles alike?
- **REASONING** How are the radius and diameter of a circle alike? How are they different?

Check

1. Draw a circle. Then draw a radius and diameter of the circle. Label your radius and diameter.

Name the part of the circle shown in blue.

2. 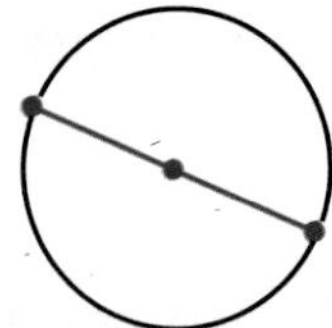

3. 

4. 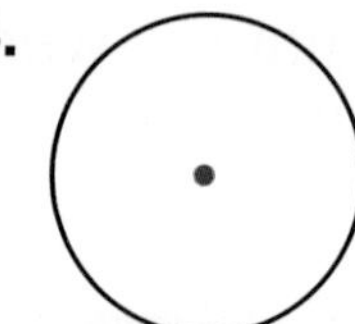

Practice and Problem Solving

Extra Practice, page 326, Set F

Name the part of the circle shown in red.

5. 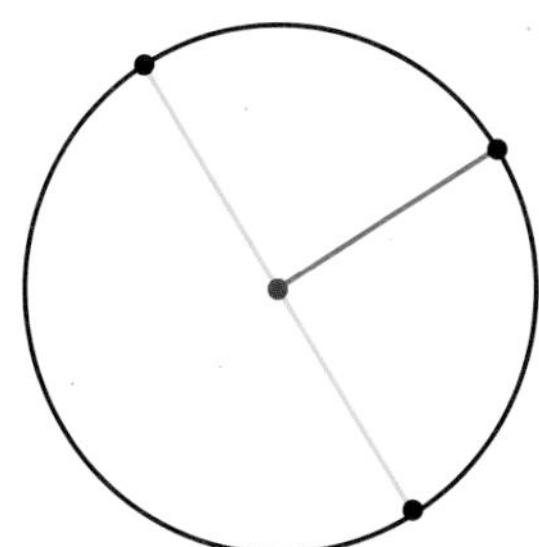

6. 

7. 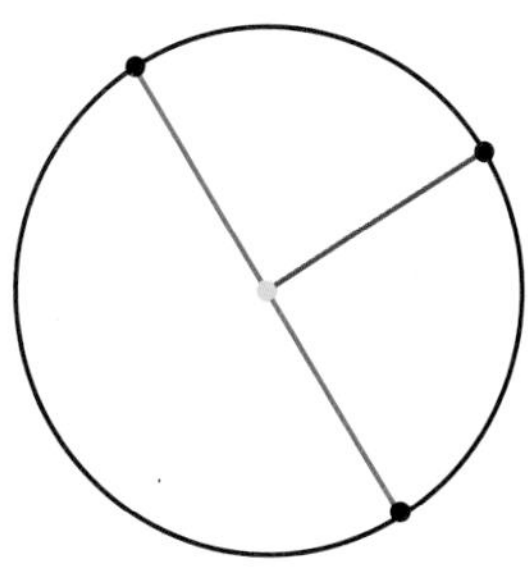

8. Draw a circle and its radius. Then draw a radius that forms a right angle with the first radius.

9. **REASONING** Carl drew a circle with a radius that was 3 inches long. How long is the diameter of Carl's circle? Explain.

10. **What's the Error?** Trent says that the line segment in the figure at the right is a diameter of the circle because it connects two points on the circle. What is his error?

11. Describe the relationship between the radius of a circle and its diameter.

12. **MULTISTEP** Alan had 6 boxes of cookies. Each box had 8 cookies. He sold 2 boxes. How many cookies does he have left?

13. **Vocabulary Power** The word *radius* comes from a Latin word that means "the spoke of a wheel." How does this help you remember what a radius is?

Maintain Skills

Write the amount.

14. 

15.     

CRCT Test Prep

16. M3N3.g. Kori planted 8 rows of seeds in his garden. Each row has 4 seeds. Which of these sentences shows the number of seeds Kori planted? (p. 230)

A. $8 \div 4 = 2$
B. $8 - 4 = 4$
C. $8 + 4 = 12$
D. $8 \times 4 = 32$

LESSON 7

Problem Solving Strategy
Make a Diagram

M3G1.a. Draw and classify previously learned fundamental geometric figures as well as scalene, isosceles, and equilateral triangles. *also* **M3P1.a., M3P1.b., M3P1.c., M3P1.d., M3P2.a., M3P2.b., M3P2.c., M3P2.d., M3P3.a., M3P3.b., M3P3.c., M3P3.d., M3P5.**

PROBLEM Mr. Carter drew some plane figures on a chalkboard. He asked his students to show how the figures were alike, and how they were different.

Quick Review

Tell how many sides each figure has.

1. △
2. ⬠
3. ▭
4. □
5. ⬡

VOCABULARY

Venn diagram

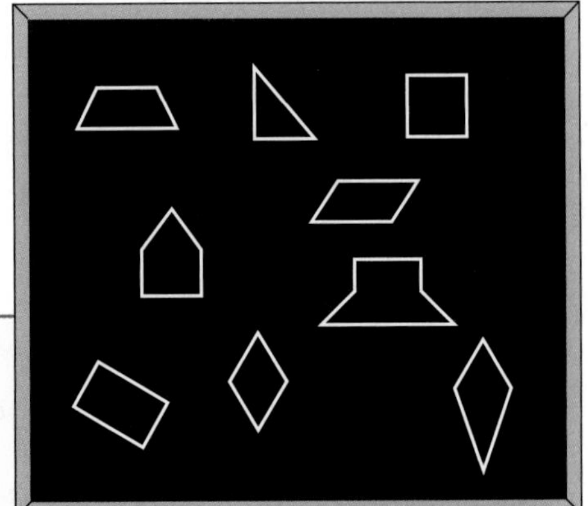

UNDERSTAND

- What are you asked to find?
- What information will you use?

PLAN

- What strategy can you use?

You can *make a diagram.*

SOLVE

- How can you show how the figures are alike and how they are different?

You can *make a Venn diagram.*

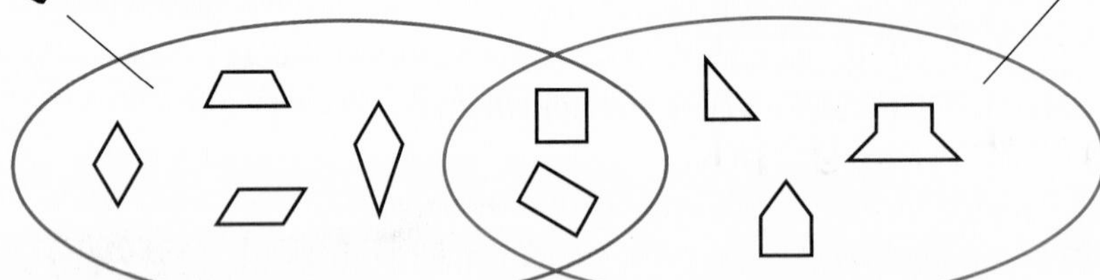

A **Venn diagram** shows relationships among sets of things. Each set in the diagram above has plane figures in it that are described by its label. The figures inside the area where the sets overlap are described by both labels.

CHECK

- What other strategy could you use?

Problem Solving Practice

1. **What if** the plane figure shown below was one of the figures on the chalkboard? Describe where it would be in the Venn diagram on page 324.

2. Some Venn diagrams have sets that do not overlap. Explain why the sets in the diagram below do not overlap.

Strategies

- Act It Out or Use Objects
- **Make a Picture or Diagram**
- Guess and Check
- Use or Look for a Pattern
- Use Logical Reasoning

Problem Solving

Marisa used the labels *multiples of 4* and *multiples of 6* for the sets in her Venn diagram.

3. Which number could be in the area where the sets overlap?

   A 36 **C** 28
   B 32 **D** 26

4. Which number would *not* be in the area where the sets overlap?

   F 12 **H** 30
   G 24 **J** 36

Mixed Strategy Practice

USE DATA For 5–7, use the bar graph.

5. Ms. Colmery's class filled 5 rows and 2 extra chairs in the museum auditorium. How many chairs were in each row?

6. **REASONING** Describe at least two ways chairs can be arranged in equal rows for Mr. Leong's class.

7. How many students visited the museum in all? Write a number sentence and solve.

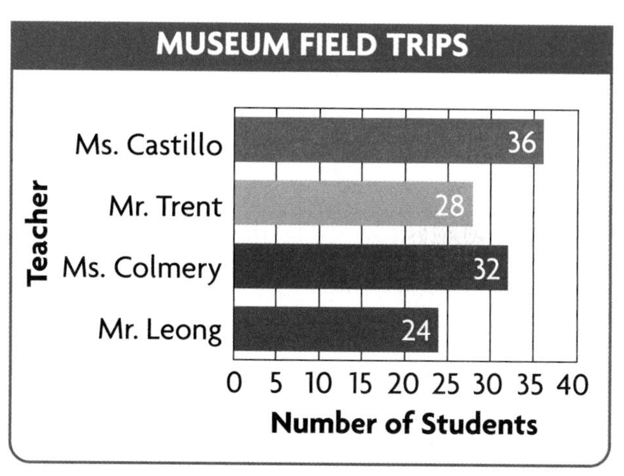

Extra Practice

Set A (pp. 304–307)

Name each figure.

1. 2. 3. 4.

Set B (pp. 308–309)

Describe the lines. Write *intersecting* or *not intersecting*. Tell whether the intersecting lines form right angles.

1. 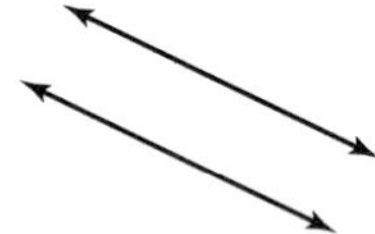
2.
3.
4.

Set C (pp. 310–313)

Write the number of sides and angles each polygon has. Then name the polygon.

1.
2. 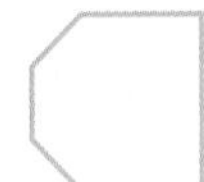
3. 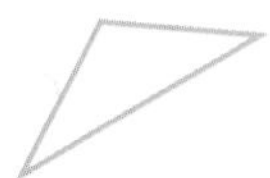
4. 
5. 

Set D (pp. 314–317)

Name each triangle. Write *equilateral, isosceles,* or *scalene.*

1. 1 cm, 4 cm, 3 cm
2. 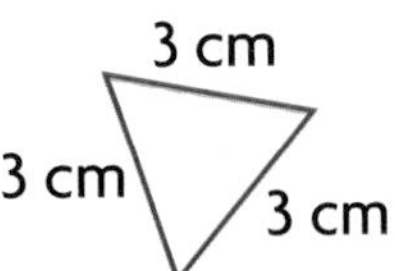

3. 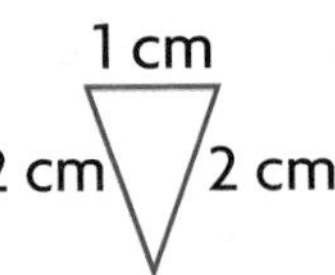

4. 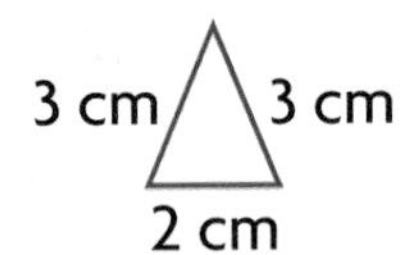

5. 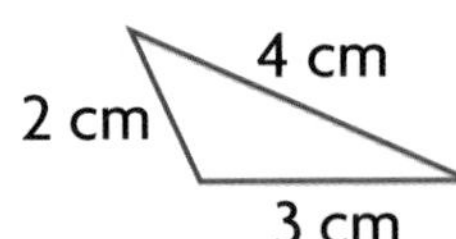

Set E (pp. 318–321)

Write as many names for each quadrilateral as you can.

1. 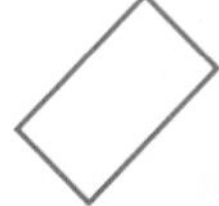
2. 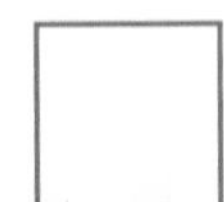
3. 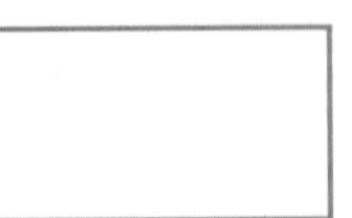
4. 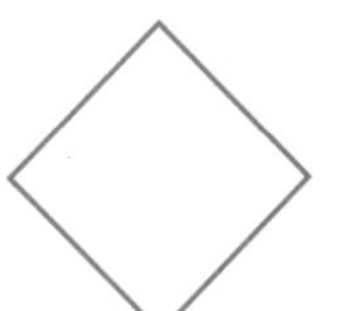
5. 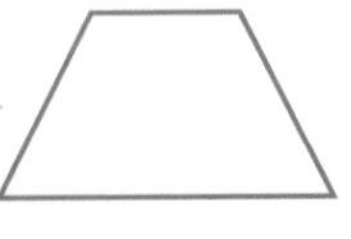

Set F (pp. 322–323)

Name the part of each figure shown in red.

1. 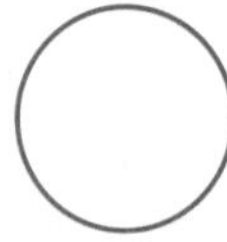
2. 
3. 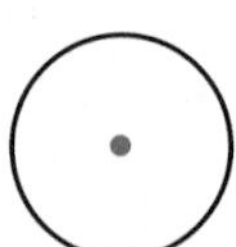
4. 

Review/Test

CHECK VOCABULARY

Choose the best term from the box.

1. An __?__ is formed by two rays with the same endpoint. (p. 304)
2. A __?__ is a triangle that has 3 equal sides. (p. 315)
3. A __?__ is a line segment that connects the center of a circle to a point on the circle. (p. 322)

Vocabulary
- line segment
- radius
- diameter
- angle
- equilateral triangle
- right triangle

CHECK SKILLS

Write whether each angle is a *right angle*, an *acute angle*, or an *obtuse angle*. (pp. 304–307)

4. 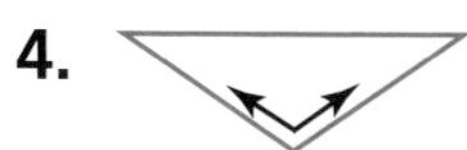
5. 
6. 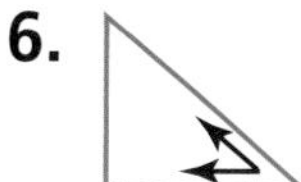
7. 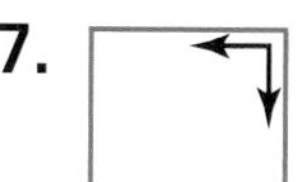

Write the number of sides and angles each polygon has. Then name the polygon. (pp. 310–313)

8. 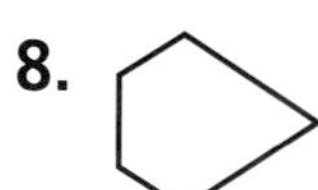
9. 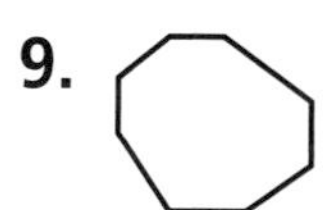
10.
11.

Name each triangle. Write *equilateral, isosceles,* or *scalene*. (pp. 314–317)

12. 3 cm, 3 cm, 2 cm
13. 3 cm, 3 cm, 3 cm
14. 3 cm, 4 cm, 2 cm
15. 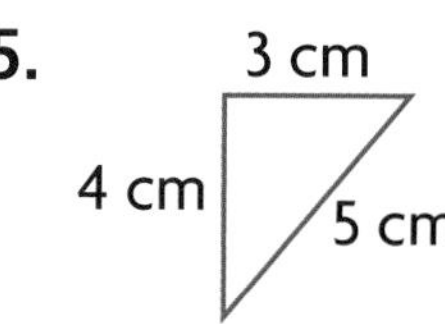

Name each quadrilateral. (pp. 318–321)

16.
17. 

Name the part of each circle. (pp. 322–323)

18. 
19. 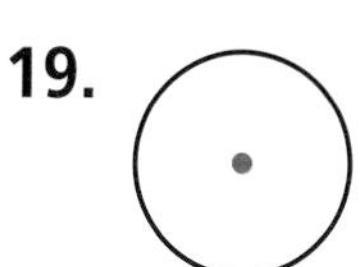

CHECK PROBLEM SOLVING

20. Describe where the figure below should be in the Venn diagram. Explain. (pp. 324–325)

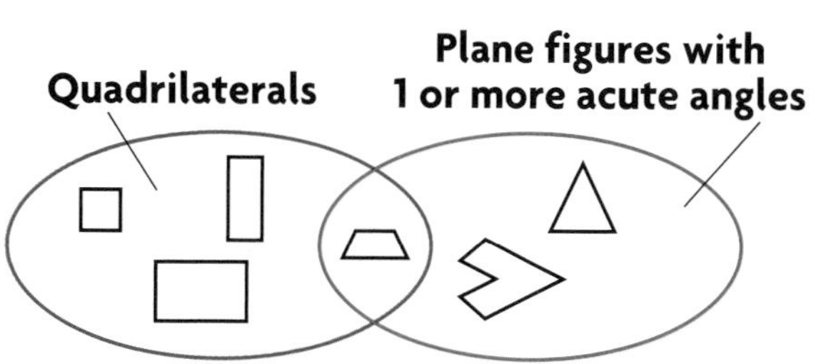

Chapter CRCT Test Prep

GEOMETRY

1. M3G1.a. Which figure is NOT a triangle?

A. 

B. 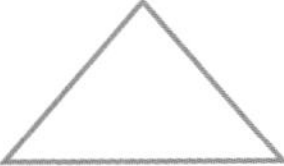

C. 

D. 

2. M3G1.a. Lynn has a baseball pennant that is shaped like the triangle below.

What type of triangle is Lynn's pennant?

A. obtuse

B. right

C. isosceles

D. equilateral

GEOMETRY

3. M3G1.d. Which shows the diameter of the circle?

A. 

B. 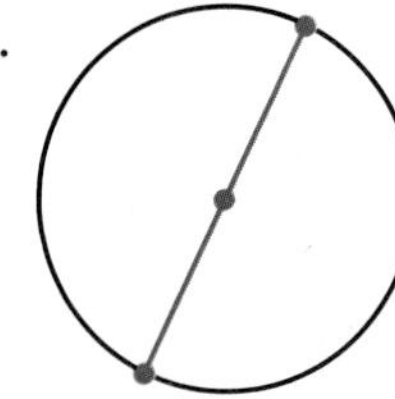

C. 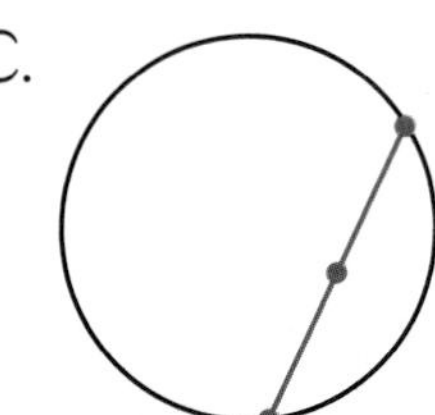

D. 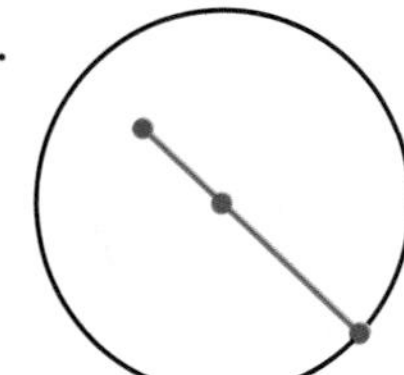

4. M3G1.b. Helen drew a polygon with 5 equal sides. What is the name of the figure Helen drew?

A. circle

B. square

C. hexagon

D. pentagon

Cumulative CRCT Test Prep

MEASUREMENT

5. M3M1. The schedule shows the activities for field day at Arthur's school.

Field Day Schedule	
Activity	**Time**
Relay Races	9:00 A.M. to 10:15 A.M.
Scavenger Hunt	10:30 A.M. to 11:45 A.M.
Lunch	Noon to 12:45 P.M.
Softball Game	1:00 P.M. to 4:00 P.M.
Team Awards	4:15 P.M. to 4:45 P.M.

How long is the scavenger hunt?

A. 1 hour

B. 1 hour 15 minutes

C. 1 hour 30 minutes

D. 2 hours

6. M3M2.c. Which is the best estimate of the length of your math book?

A. 10 inches

B. 10 feet

C. 10 yards

D. 10 miles

7. M3M2.c. Which is the best unit to use to measure the length of a house?

A. millimeters

B. centimeters

C. meters

D. kilometers

ALGEBRA

8. M3A1.c. There are 6 chairs at each table in a restaurant. If there are 42 chairs, which number sentence can you use to find the number of tables?

A. $6 + \square = 42$

B. $\square - 6 = 42$

C. $6 \times \square = 42$

D. $\square \div 6 = 42$

9. M3A1.a. Jamal wrote this number pattern. What number is missing?

235, 242, 249, 256, □

A. 260

B. 263

C. 270

D. 277

10. M3A1.c. Which of the following will help you find the missing factor in this number sentence?

$$7 \times \square = 28$$

A. $28 - 7 = 21$

B. $28 \div 7 = 4$

C. $28 + 7 = 35$

D. $7 + 4 = 11$

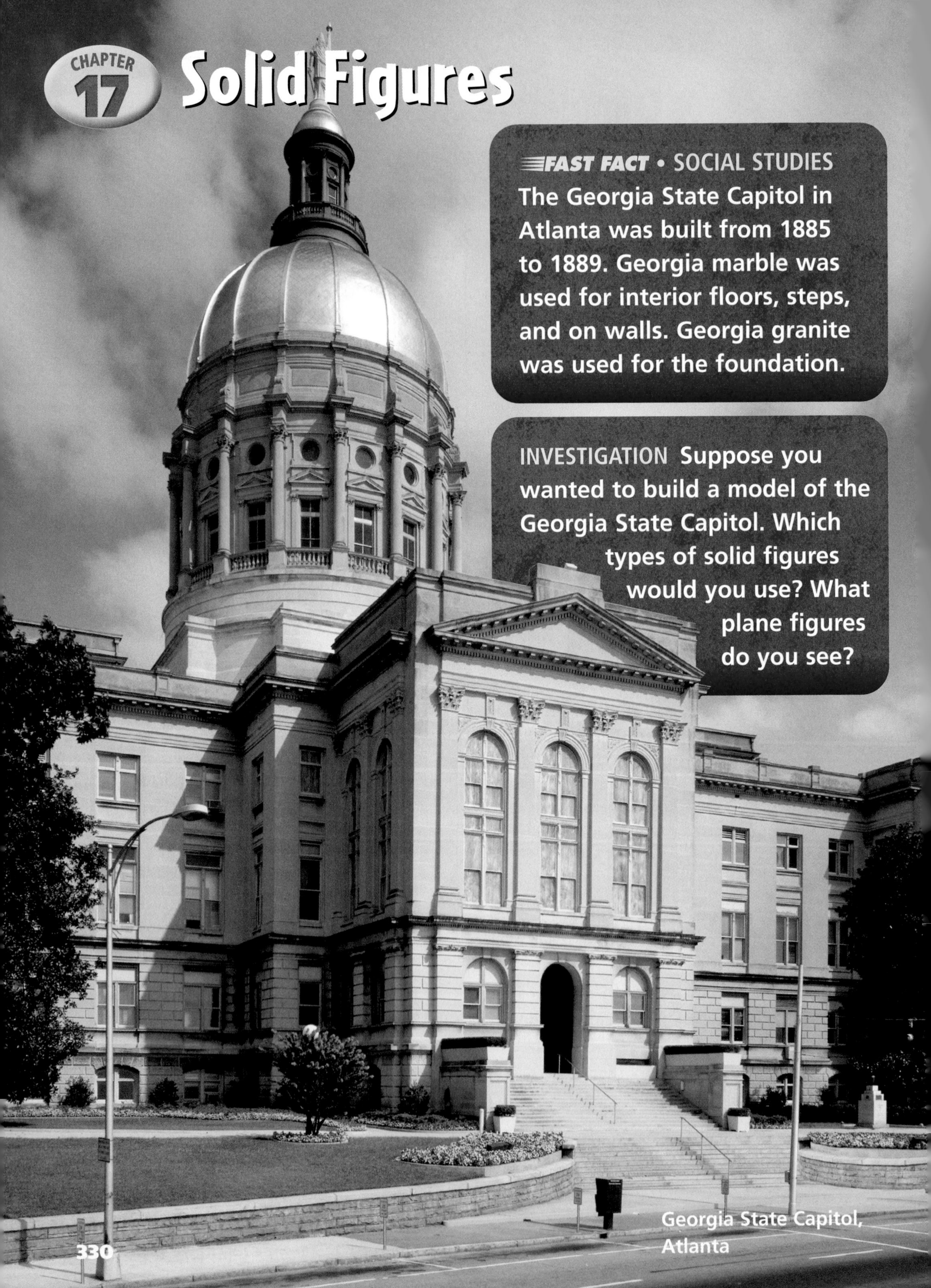

CHAPTER 17 Solid Figures

FAST FACT • SOCIAL STUDIES
The Georgia State Capitol in Atlanta was built from 1885 to 1889. Georgia marble was used for interior floors, steps, and on walls. Georgia granite was used for the foundation.

INVESTIGATION **Suppose you wanted to build a model of the Georgia State Capitol. Which types of solid figures would you use? What plane figures do you see?**

Georgia State Capitol, Atlanta

Use this page to help you review and remember important skills needed for Chapter 17.

IDENTIFY SOLID FIGURES

Choose the best term from the box.

cone
cube
cylinder
rectangular prism
sphere

1. 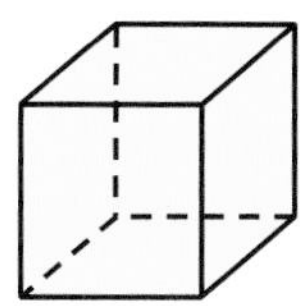
2. 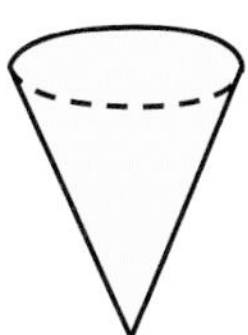
3. 
4. 
5. 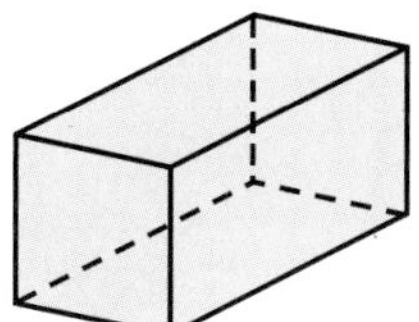
6. 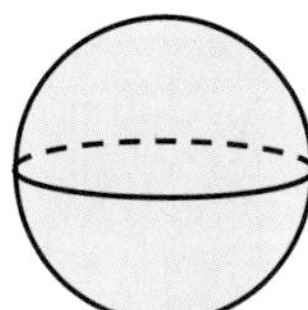
7. 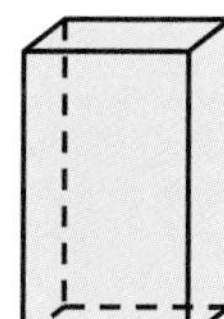
8. 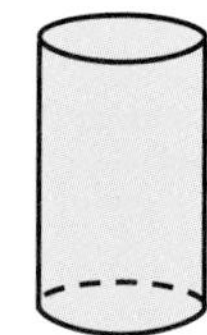
9. 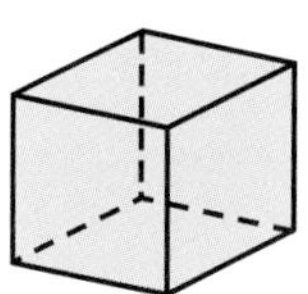

VOCABULARY POWER

REVIEW

quadrilateral [kwä•drə•lat′ər•əl] *noun*

A quadrilateral is a polygon that has four sides. Look in a dictionary for *quadruple*. Is *four* part of its definition? Explain.

PREVIEW

face

edge

vertex

www.harcourtschool.com/mathglossary

LESSON 1

Solid Figures

M3G1.b. Identify and explain the properties of fundamental geometric figures. *also* M3P2.a., M3P2.b., M3P2.c., M3P2.d.

Learn

FIGURE IT OUT Use names of solid figures to describe objects around you.

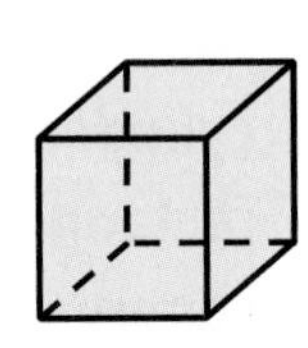

cube

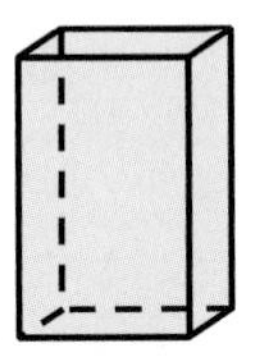

rectangular prism

sphere

cylinder

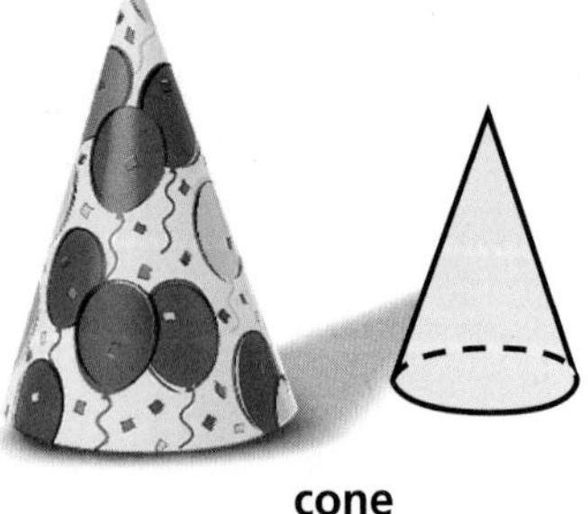

cone

Quick Review

Name each plane figure.

1. ◯
2. ◺
3. □
4. ▭
5. △

VOCABULARY

face edge vertex

Technology Link

More Practice: Harcourt Mega Math Ice Station Exploration, *Frozen Solids,* Level A

A **face** is a flat surface of a solid figure.

An **edge** is the line segment formed where two faces meet.

A **vertex** is a point where three or more edges meet. Two or more are called vertices.

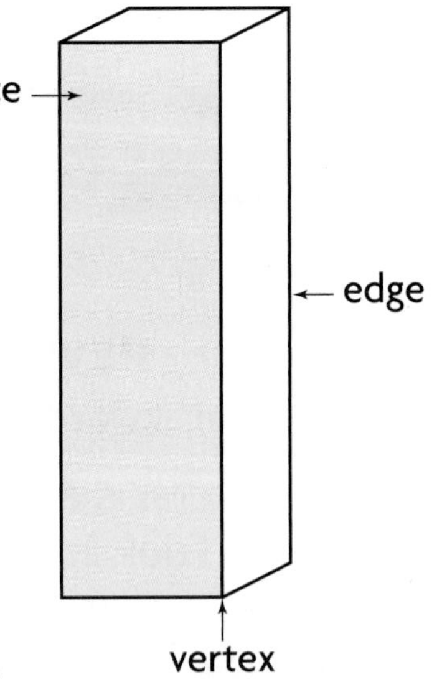

A rectangular prism has 6 faces, 12 edges, and 8 vertices.

- How many edges does a cube have?
- **REASONING** Which solid figures will roll? Explain how you know.

Tracing Faces

Use names of plane figures to describe the faces of solid figures.

Activity

MATERIALS: solid figures, paper, crayons

Trace the faces of several solid figures. Then name the faces that make up each solid figure.

STEP 1

On a large sheet of paper, make a chart like the one below. Trace the faces of each solid figure.

Name of Figure	Faces	Names and Number of Faces
rectangular prism	▯ ▭ ▭ ▯ ▭ ▭	

STEP 2

Record the names and number of faces for each solid figure.

Name of Figure	Faces	Names and Number of Faces
rectangular prism	▯ ▭ ▭ ▯ ▭ ▭	6 rectangles

- **REASONING** Use the words *all, some,* or *none* to describe the faces of the solid figures you traced.

MATH IDEA Some solid figures have faces, edges, and vertices. Faces of solid figures are plane figures such as squares and rectangles.

Check

1. **Describe** the faces of a cube.

Name the solid figure that each object looks like.

2. 

3. 

4. 

5. 

LESSON CONTINUES 

Practice and Problem Solving

Extra Practice, page 344, Set A

Name the solid figure that each object looks like.

6. 

7. 

8. 

9. 

Which solid figure has the faces shown?

10. 

11. 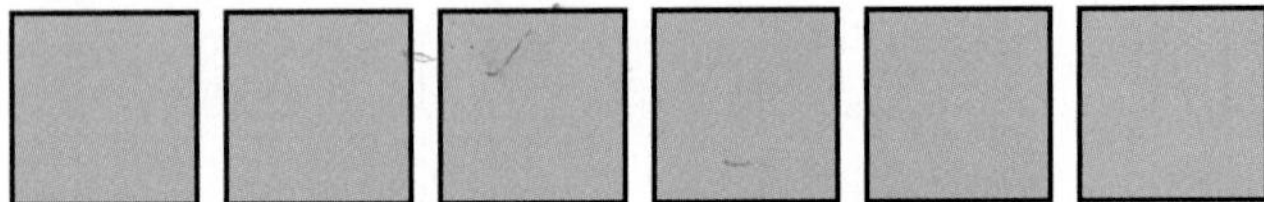

Copy and complete the table.

	FIGURE	FACES	EDGES	VERTICES
12.	Rectangular prism	■	■	■
13.	Cube	■	■	■

14. **REASONING** An analogy is a comparison of similar features of objects. For example, *day* is to *light* as *night* is to *darkness*. Complete each analogy.

    a. A cereal *box* is to a *rectangular prism* as a *ball* is to a __?__.

    b. A *square* is to a *cube* as a *rectangle* is to a __?__.

15. **Write About It** List objects you might find at a grocery store that look like each of the following solid figures. Think of at least two objects for each figure.

    a. sphere

    b. rectangular prism

    c. cylinder

16. Josh painted a box shaped like a rectangular prism. Each face was a different color. How many colors did Josh use?

17. **MULTISTEP** Cindy has 19 large shells and 17 small shells. How many groups of 4 shells can she make?

18. **Write a problem** about a solid figure. Give clues about the figure. Exchange with a classmate and decide what the figure is.

Maintain Skills

Write the product.

19. 

$4 \times 7 = ■$

20. 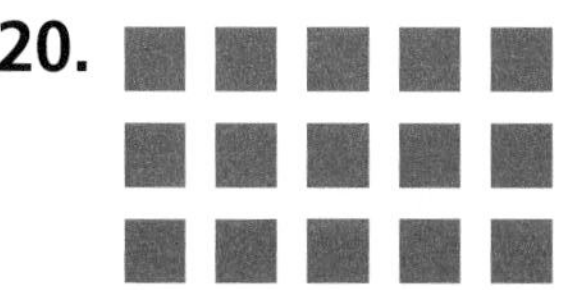

$3 \times 5 = ■$

CRCT Test Prep

21. M3N4.f. Tom put 42 dimes into 6 equal piles. How many dimes were in two piles? (p. 190)

A. 14 B. 10 C. 8 D. 6

22. M3N1.b. Which of these numbers has a 3 in the thousands place? (p. 14)

A. 352
B. 3,502
C. 30,502
D. 35,002

Problem Solving Thinker's Corner

VISUAL THINKING You can use connecting cubes or other blocks to model solid figures.

For 1–4, build and name the figure.

1. 

2. 

3. 

4. 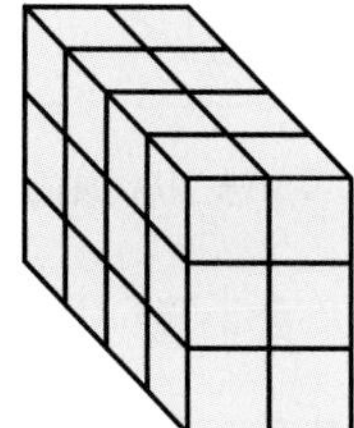

5. Use 27 blocks to build a cube. Then use the same number of blocks to build a rectangular prism.

LESSON 2

Combine Solid Figures

Concepts/Skill to Maintain Geometric shapes. *also* M3P3.a., M3P3.b., M3P3.c., M3P3.d., M3P4.

Quick Review

Name each solid figure.

1. 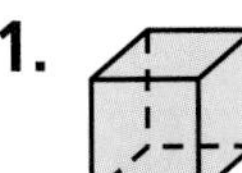  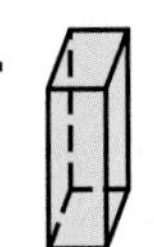
2.  
3.  
4.
5. 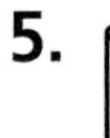

Learn

PUT IT ALL TOGETHER Some objects are made up of two or more solid figures put together. Look at the castle on the right. What solid figures make up the shape of the castle?

Look at each part of the castle separately. Think about the solid figures you know.

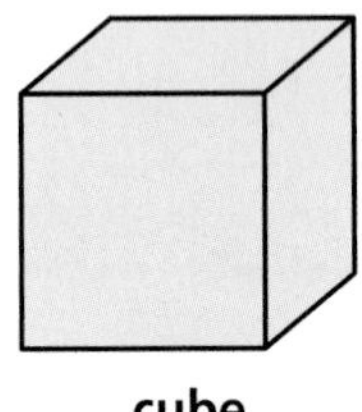

cube

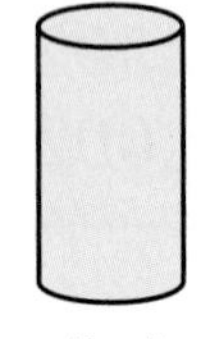

cylinder

cone

So, the castle is made up of a cube, two cylinders, and two cones.

▲ Craigievar Castle, near Alford, Scotland

MATH IDEA Solid figures can be combined to make different solid objects.

Examples

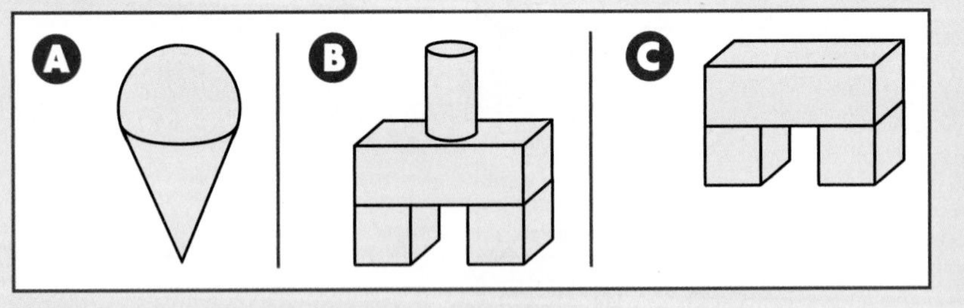

- What solid figures are used to make Object A?
- What solid figures are used to make Object B?

Technology Link

More Practice: Harcourt Mega Math Ice Station Exploration, *Frozen Solids,* Level B

Check

1. **Explain** how you can make Object B look like Object C.

Name the solid figures used to make each object.

2. 

3. 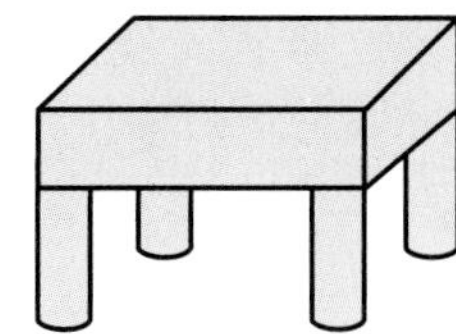

4. 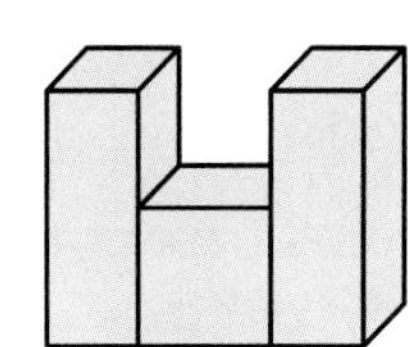

Practice and Problem Solving

Extra Practice, page 344, Set B

Name the solid figures used to make each object.

5. 

6. 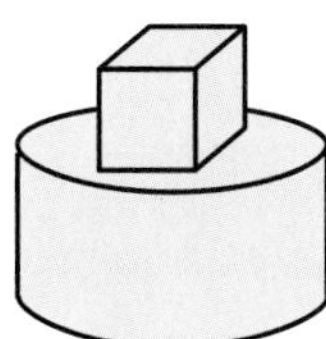

7. 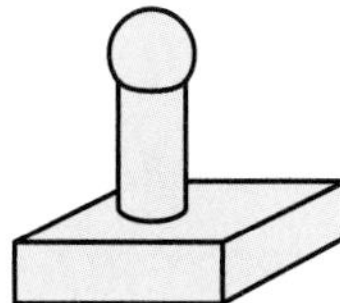

Each pair of objects should be the same. Name the solid figure that is missing.

8. 

9. 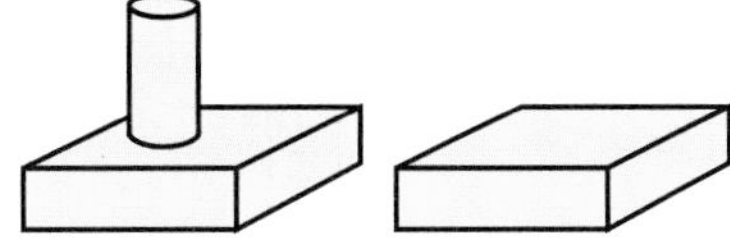

10. 

11. 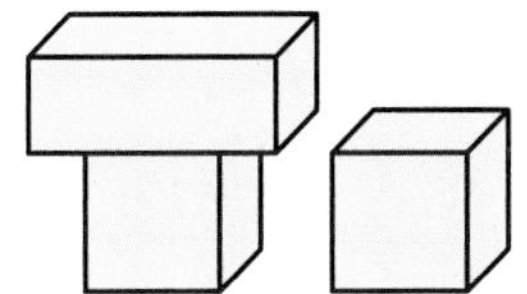

12. 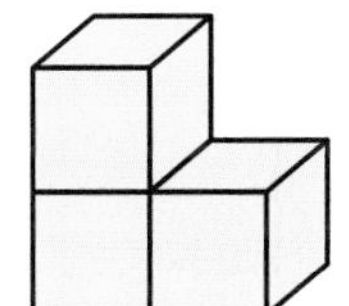

13. 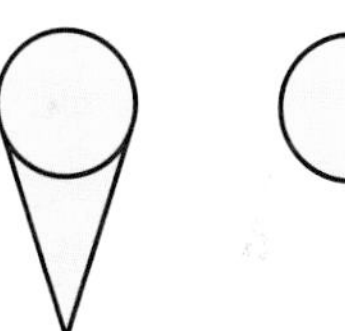

14. **MULTISTEP** Gwen had three $1 bills and 4 dimes. She paid $0.75 for a pen and $1.20 for a snack. How much money does she have left?

15. ***FAST FACT*** • SOCIAL STUDIES Georgia was one of the 13 original colonies. It became a state in 1788. How many years ago is this?

Maintain Skills

16. Write the amount.

17. $\begin{array}{r} 343 \\ +239 \\ \hline \end{array}$

18. $\begin{array}{r} 751 \\ -390 \\ \hline \end{array}$

CRCT Test Prep

19. M3N4.b. Four friends shared 32 crackers equally. How many crackers did each friend get? (p. 224)

A. 4
B. 7
C. 8
D. 28

LESSON 3

Draw Figures

M3G1.a. Draw and classify previously learned fundamental geometric figures as well as scalene, isosceles, and equilateral triangles. *also* M3P2.a., M3P2.b., M3P2.c., M3P2.d., M3P4.c.

Learn

DRAW IT You can draw polygons using line segments. Since a polygon is a closed figure, it will begin and end at the same point.

Quick Review

Write the number of sides each figure has.

1. 2. 3. 4. 5.

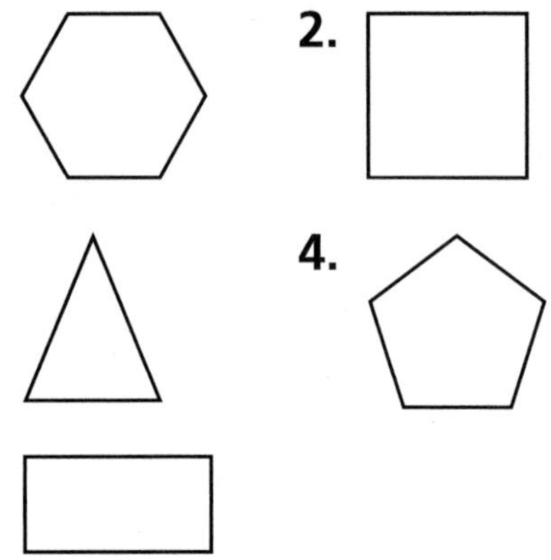

Activity 1 Draw plane figures.

MATERIALS: polygon worksheet, pencil, ruler

STEP 1

On your worksheet, use a ruler to draw line segments from *A* to *B*, from *B* to *C*, and from *C* to *A*.

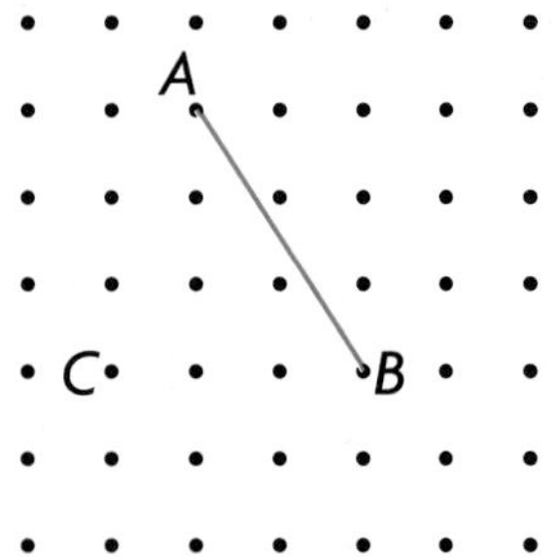

STEP 2

Use a ruler to draw line segments from *D* to *E*, *E* to *F*, *F* to *G*, *G* to *H*, *H* to *I*, and *I* to *D*.

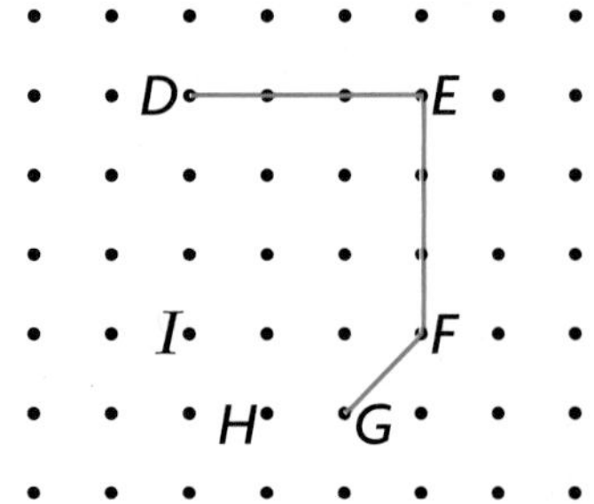

STEP 3

Use a ruler to draw line segments from *J* to *K*, *K* to *L*, *L* to *M*, and *M* to *J*.

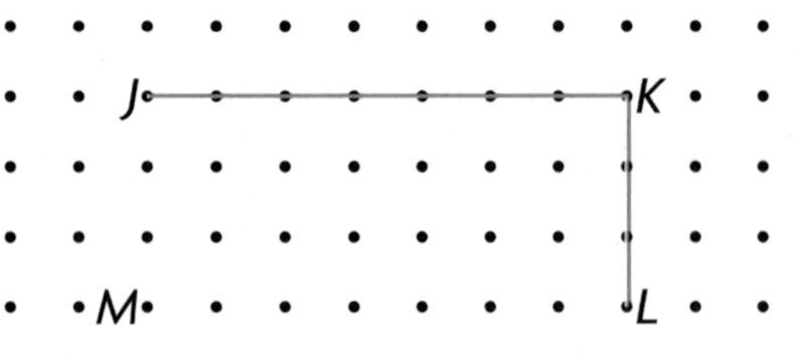

- What polygons did you draw? How many sides and angles does each polygon have?
- Describe the angles in each polygon that you drew.
- **REASONING** Can a line segment be drawn on a rectangle to form 2 triangles that are the same size and shape? Draw pictures on dot paper to explain.

Draw a Solid Figure

The faces of solid figures are polygons. Look to see where these faces meet to find edges and vertices.

HANDS ON

Activity 2

MATERIALS: dot paper, pencil, ruler

STEP 1

Use a ruler to draw a square. Make each line segment 4 units long.

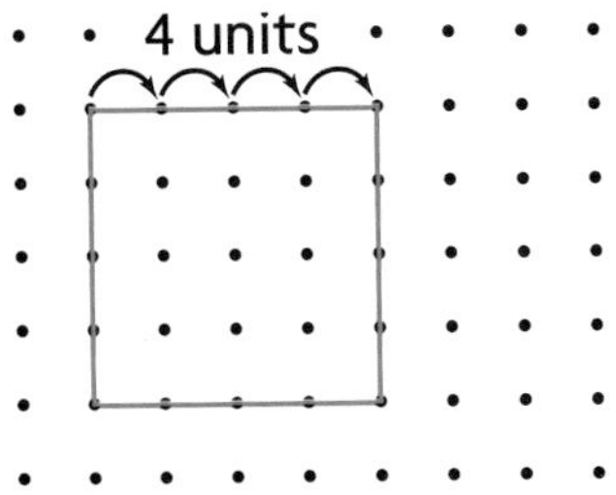

4 units

STEP 2

Draw slanted line segments from 3 of the corners, as shown.

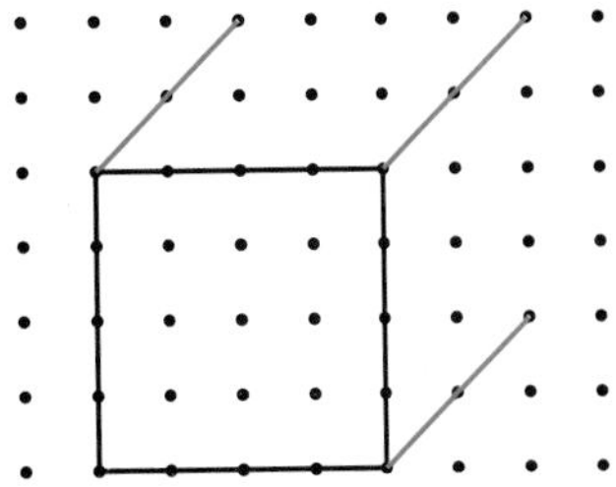

STEP 3

Draw line segments to connect the endpoints of the slanted line segments, as shown.

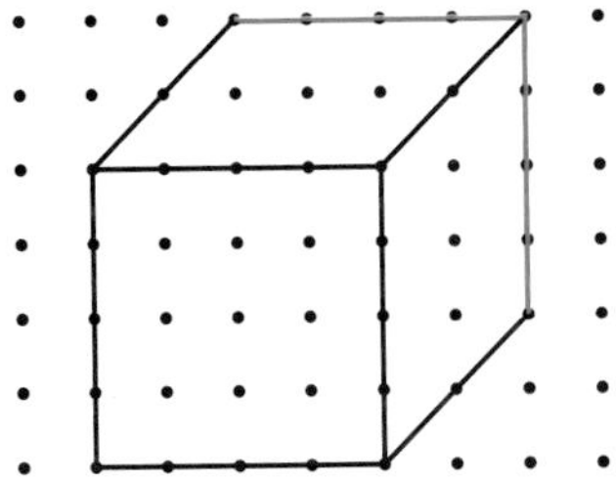

STEP 4

Draw dashed line segments to show the faces that cannot be seen.

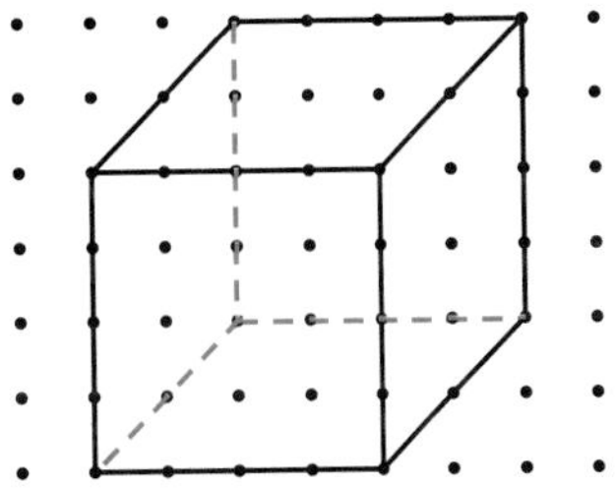

- How many faces does a cube have? How many edges and vertices does a cube have?

Check

1. **Explain** what a vertex is. Compare the number of vertices of a cube and a rectangular prism.

For 2–4, draw each figure on dot paper. Then, write the number of line segments needed to draw each figure.

2. pentagon
3. rectangle
4. hexagon

Practice and Problem Solving

Extra Practice, page 344, Set C

For 5–7, draw each figure on dot paper. Then, write the number of line segments needed to draw each figure.

5. trapezoid **6.** octagon **7.** triangle

For 8, copy the solid figure on dot paper. Name the figure.

8.

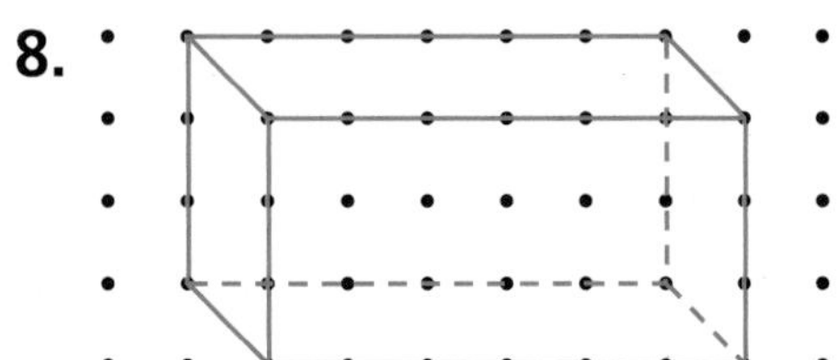

For 9–14, copy each figure on dot paper. Draw the missing line segments so that the figure matches its label.

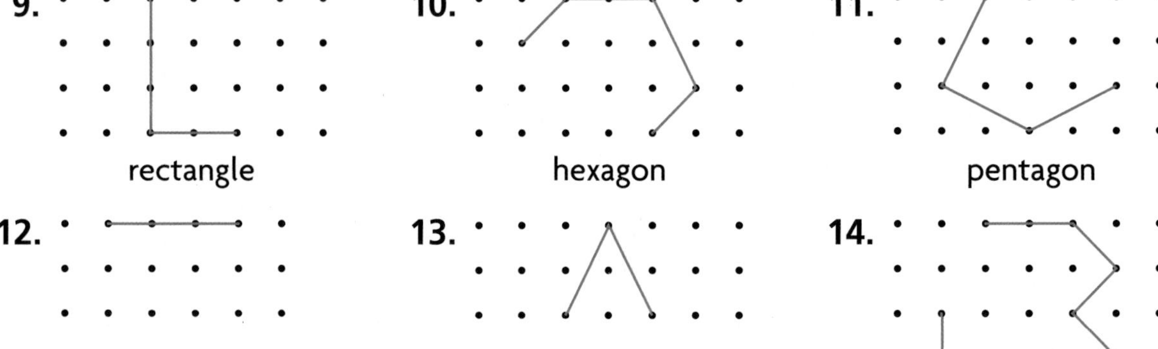

15. **FAST FACT • SOCIAL STUDIES** The Olympic flag was first used at the 1920 Summer Olympics. There were 2,669 athletes taking part. At the 1992 Summer Olympics, there were 9,367 athletes. Which Olympics had more athletes? How many more?

16. Trace the figure shown at the right. Cut out the figure along the solid lines. Then fold along the 5 dotted lines. Tape the edges of the figure together. What solid figure do you have?

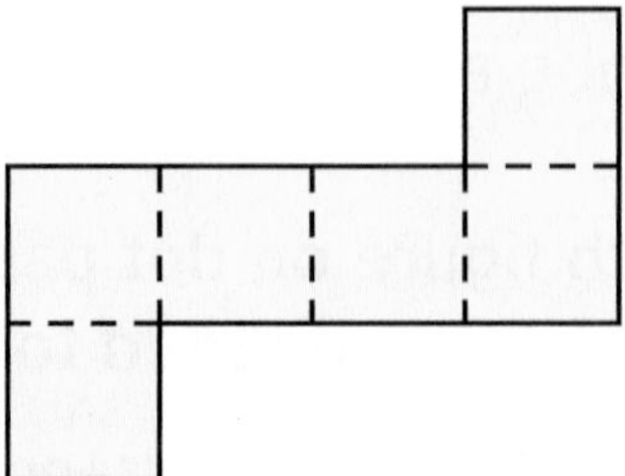

17. **MULTISTEP** Rex drew 2 quadrilaterals and 2 hexagons. Ali drew an octagon, 2 pentagons, and a triangle. Who drew more angles? Explain.

18. **What's the Error?** The lengths of the sides of a triangle are 3 inches, 3 inches, and 2 inches. Justin said it is an equilateral triangle. Describe his error.

Maintain Skills

Write <, >, or = for each ●.

19. 51 ● 24
20. 34 ● 74
21. 94 ● 49
22. 16 ● 17

Find each sum or difference.

23. $\begin{array}{r} 167 \\ +648 \\ \hline \end{array}$

24. $\begin{array}{r} 532 \\ -199 \\ \hline \end{array}$

CRCT Test Prep

25. M3N2.b. Use front-end estimation to estimate the difference. (p. 70)

$$\begin{array}{r} 898 \\ -213 \\ \hline \end{array}$$

A. 500
B. 600
C. 700
D. 800

Problem Solving LINKUP . . . to Social Studies

The 5 circles on the Olympic flag represent the 5 regions of the world that join together for the Olympic Games. A circle is a plane figure made of points that are the same distance from a center point.

Follow the directions to draw a circle.

MATERIALS: paper clip, 2 pencils, ruler

1. Draw a point. Draw a circle by placing the pencils in the ends of the paper clip. The pencil on the point should not move.

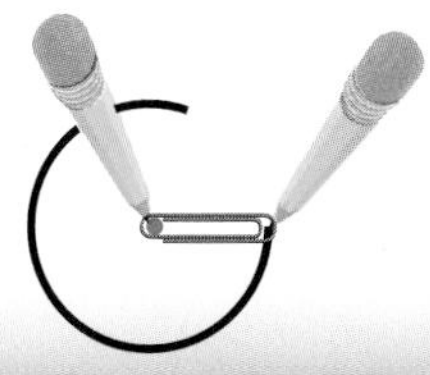

2. Place three points on top of the circle that you drew. Measure the distance from the center point to each of the points on the circle. Are they the same distance from the center?

LESSON 4

Problem Solving Skill
Identify Relationships

M3G1.a. Draw and classify previously learned fundamental geometric figures as well as scalene, isosceles, and equilateral triangles. *also* **M3G1.b., M3P1.a., M3P1.b., M3P1.c., M3P3.a., M3P3.b., M3P3.c., M3P3.d.**

UNDERSTAND › PLAN › SOLVE › CHECK

DIFFERENT VIEWS Mrs. Pine is teaching her students about solid figures. The students looked at the different views of solid figures. Which solid figures could this be?

top view

All of the faces of a cube are squares. So, this could be a cube.

Some rectangular prisms have two faces that are squares. So, this could be a rectangular prism.

Which solid figures could this be?

bottom view

The bottom of a cone is a circle. So, this could be a cone.

The bottom of a cylinder is a circle. So, this could be a cylinder.

The view of a sphere from *any* direction looks like a circle. So, this could be a sphere.

Quick Review

Name each solid figure.

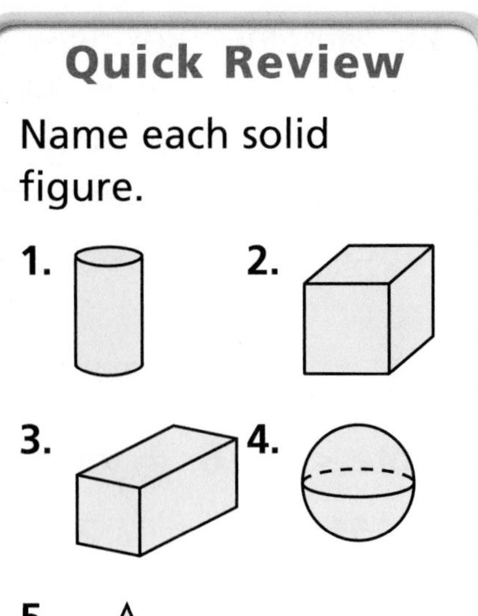

Talk About It

- The figure at the right is the top view of a cone. Explain what you see when you look at the top of a cone.

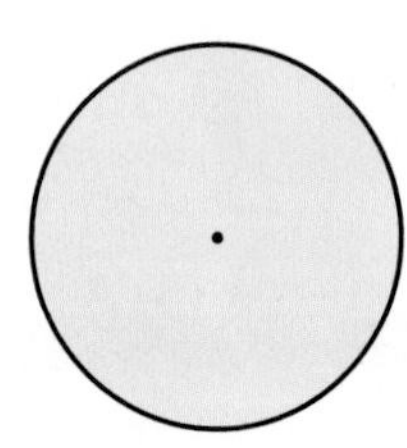

Problem Solving Practice

1. **What if** Mrs. Pine's class looked at the side view of a rectangular prism? What plane figure could be used to describe the shape that the students would see?

2. Look at the cylinder. Even though the side of the cylinder is a curved surface, a plane figure can be used to describe the side view. Name this plane figure.

For 3–4, use the figures below.

Figure Q

Figure R

Figure S

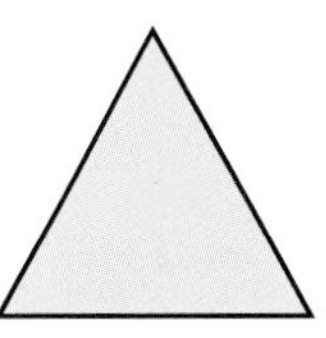
Figure T

3. Which figure is the top view of a cylinder?

   A Figure Q **C** Figure S
   B Figure R **D** Figure T

4. Which figure is the side view of a cube?

   F Figure Q **H** Figure S
   G Figure R **J** Figure T

Mixed Applications

USE DATA For 5–8, use the bar graph.

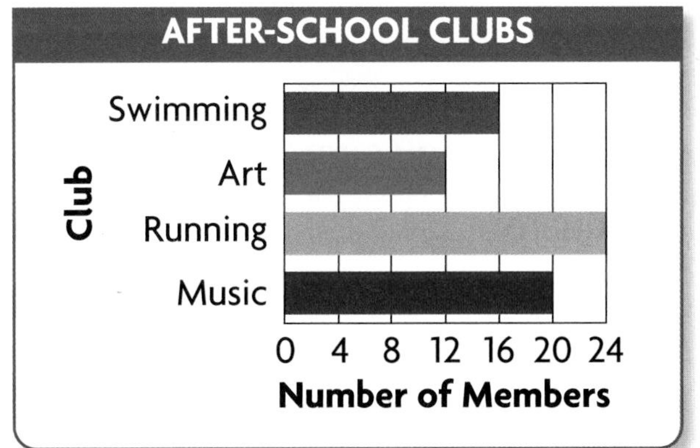

5. How many more members are in the Music Club than in the Swimming Club?

6. How many members are in the four clubs altogether?

7. List the clubs in order from the greatest number of members to the least number of members.

8. **Write a problem** using the data in the bar graph. Explain how to find the answer.

9. **What's the Question?** The answer is 6 faces, 12 edges, and 8 vertices.

Extra Practice

Set A (pp. 332–335)

Name the solid figure that each object looks like.

1. 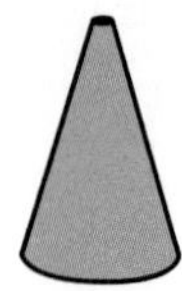

2. 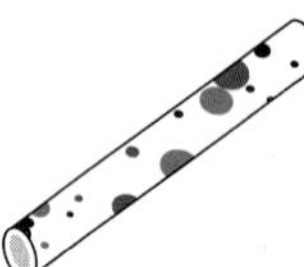

3. 

4. 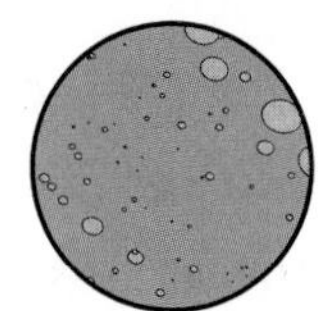

5. 

6. 

7. 

8. 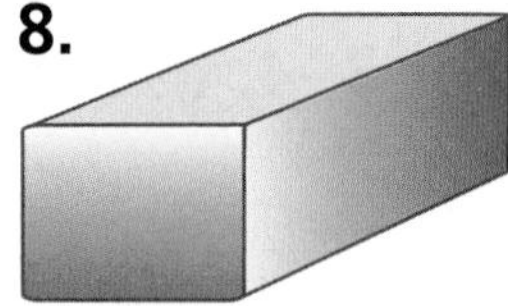

Set B (pp. 336–337)

Name the solid figures used to make each object.

1. 

2. 

3. 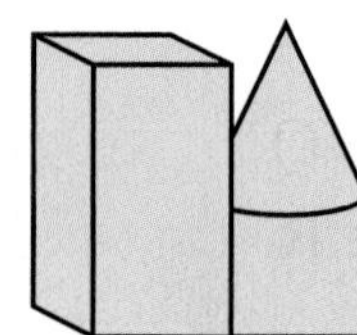

Set C (pp. 338–341)

For 1–6, draw each figure on dot paper. Then, write the number of line segments needed to draw each figure.

1. square
2. hexagon
3. quadrilateral
4. octagon
5. right triangle
6. trapezoid

For 7–9, copy each figure on dot paper. Draw the missing line segments so that the figure matches its label.

7. 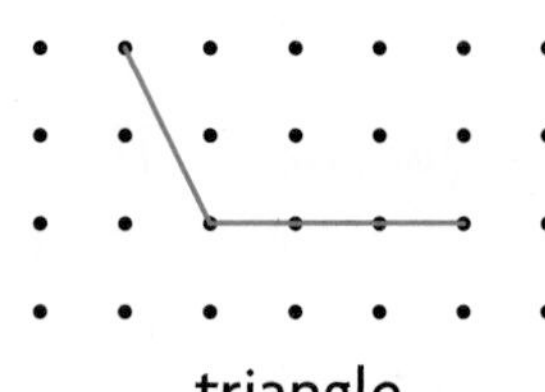

triangle

8. 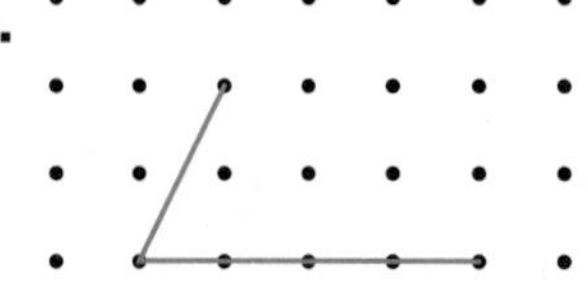

trapezoid

9. 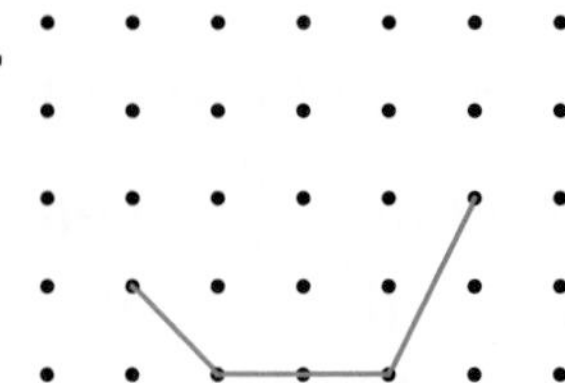

pentagon

Review/Test

CHECK VOCABULARY AND CONCEPTS

For 1–2, choose the best term from the box.

Vocabulary
face
edge
vertex

1. A flat surface of a solid figure is a __?__. (p. 332)
2. The line segment formed where two faces meet is called an __?__. (p. 332)
3. A solid figure has 6 square faces. What is it? (pp. 332–335)
4. A solid figure has 6 rectangular faces. What is it? (pp. 332–335)

CHECK SKILLS

For 5–6, name the solid figures used to make each object. (pp. 336–337)

5. 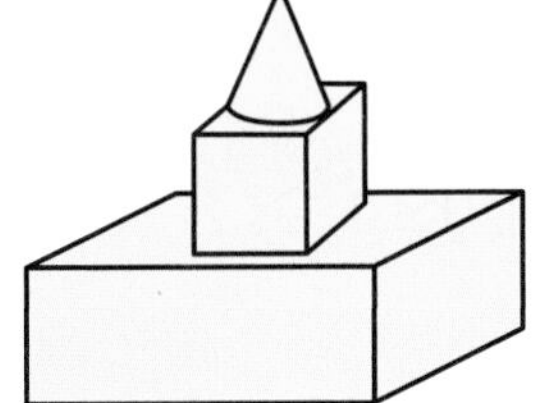

6. 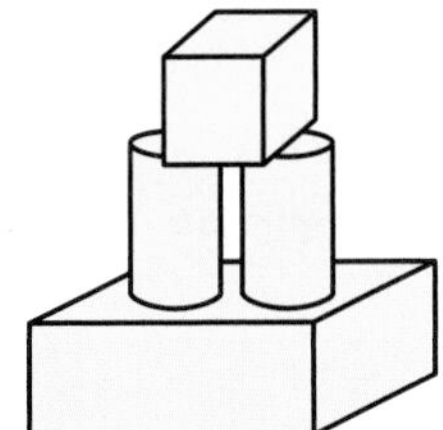

For 7–10, draw each figure on dot paper. Then, write the number of line segments needed to draw each figure. (pp. 338–341)

7. hexagon
8. square
9. trapezoid
10. triangle

For 11–13, copy each figure on dot paper. Draw the missing line segments so that the figure matches its label. (pp. 338–341)

11. rectangle

12. pentagon

13. 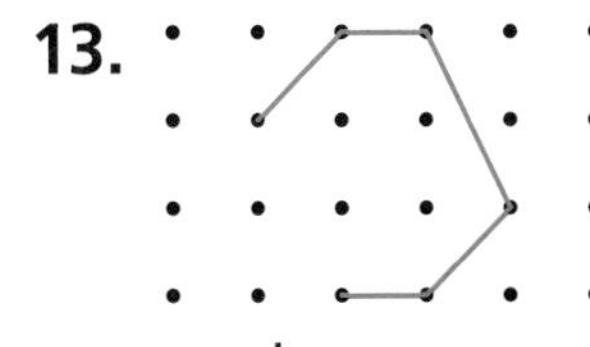
hexagon

CHECK PROBLEM SOLVING

For 14–15, use the figures at the right. (pp. 342–343)

14. Which figure is the bottom view of a cone?
15. Which figure is the side view of a cube?

Figure A

Figure B

Figure C

Chapter CRCT Test Prep

GEOMETRY

1. M3G1.a. Which figure is shown below?

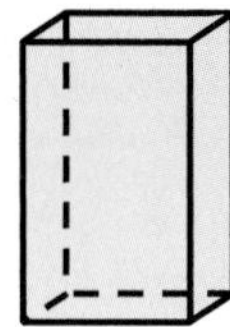

A. cube

B. cone

C. cylinder

D. rectangular prism

2. M3G1.b. How many edges does a cube have?

A. 12

B. 10

C. 8

D. 6

3. M3G1.b. Todd tapes six paper squares together to make a solid figure. Which solid figure did he make?

A. sphere

B. cone

C. cylinder

D. cube

GEOMETRY

4. M3G1.b. Which solid figure is NOT part of the object below?

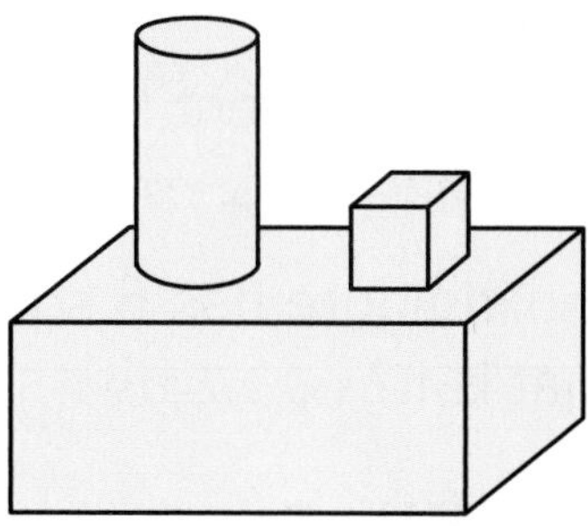

A. cylinder

B. cone

C. cube

D. rectangular prism

5. M3G1.b. One face of Nina's figure is shown below.

Which could be the name of Nina's figure?

A. sphere

B. cylinder

C. cube

D. cone

Cumulative CRCT Test Prep

NUMBERS AND OPERATIONS

6. M3N2.c. Maura bought a pen for \$1.89 and a card for \$1.99. She paid with a \$5 bill. How much change did she receive?

A. \$3.88

B. \$2.12

C. \$1.22

D. \$1.12

7. M3N3.g. A group of students will travel to the aquarium in 3 vans. Each van can hold 9 students. How many students can be taken to the aquarium?

A. 12

B. 18

C. 27

D. 36

8. M3N4.a. Which division sentence belongs to the same fact family as these multiplication sentences?

$$5 \times 4 = 20 \quad 4 \times 5 = 20$$

A. $20 \div 1 = 20$

B. $20 \div 2 = 10$

C. $20 \div 5 = 4$

D. $20 \div 10 = 2$

DATA ANALYSIS

Use the graph below to answer question 9.

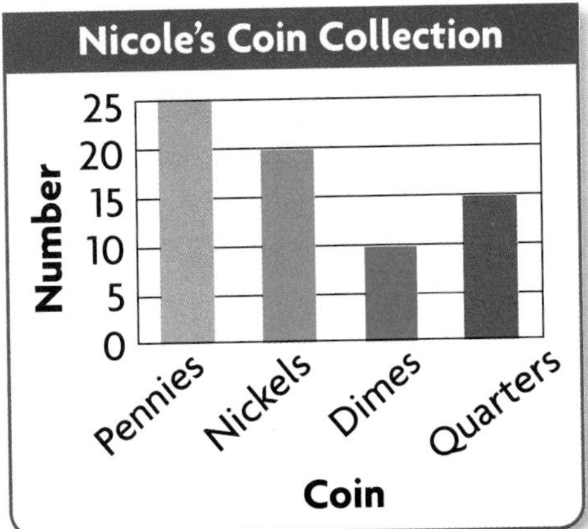

9. M3D1.b. The bar graph shows the number of different coins that Nicole has in her collection. How many nickels does Nicole have?

A. 4

B. 5

C. 20

D. 25

CHAPTER 18 Perimeter and Area

FAST FACT • SOCIAL STUDIES People have grown flowers for thousands of years. In the 1600s, tulips in Holland were so valuable that the bulbs were used as money!

INVESTIGATION Look below at the diagram of a garden. How can you find how many feet of fencing you would need to go around this garden? How can you find about how much land would be needed for this garden?

CHECK WHAT YOU KNOW

Use this page to help you review and remember important skills needed for Chapter 18.

COLUMN ADDITION

Find each sum.

1. $\begin{array}{r} 3 \\ 7 \\ +5 \\ \hline \end{array}$
2. $\begin{array}{r} 2 \\ 4 \\ +8 \\ \hline \end{array}$
3. $\begin{array}{r} 1 \\ 3 \\ +9 \\ \hline \end{array}$
4. $\begin{array}{r} 6 \\ 2 \\ +9 \\ \hline \end{array}$
5. $\begin{array}{r} 6 \\ 7 \\ +3 \\ \hline \end{array}$
6. $\begin{array}{r} 4 \\ 9 \\ +3 \\ \hline \end{array}$
7. $\begin{array}{r} 5 \\ 5 \\ +7 \\ \hline \end{array}$
8. $\begin{array}{r} 9 \\ 8 \\ +1 \\ \hline \end{array}$
9. $4 + 3 + 3 + 5$
10. $8 + 3 + 2 + 9$
11. $5 + 6 + 2 + 5$
12. $9 + 2 + 9$

MULTIPLICATION FACTS

Find each product.

13. $7 \times 4 = \blacksquare$
14. $3 \times 6 = \blacksquare$
15. $2 \times 5 = \blacksquare$
16. $4 \times 9 = \blacksquare$
17. $7 \times 2 = \blacksquare$
18. $6 \times 6 = \blacksquare$
19. $9 \times 8 = \blacksquare$
20. $10 \times 3 = \blacksquare$
21. $4 \times 5 = \blacksquare$

VOCABULARY POWER

REVIEW

square [skwâr] *noun*

A square is a quadrilateral that has 4 right angles and 4 equal sides. On grid paper, draw 2 squares that are different sizes. Include labels showing the lengths of the sides.

PREVIEW

perimeter

square unit

area

www.harcourtschool.com/mathglossary

LESSON 1

Perimeter

M3M3.b. Understand the concept of perimeter as being the boundary of a simple geometric figure. *also* **M3M3.a., M3M3.c., M3P2.a., M3P2.b., M3P2.c., M3P2.d., M3P5.**

Learn

AROUND AND AROUND The distance around a figure is called its **perimeter**.

You can estimate the perimeter of your math book using linear measurement.

Quick Review

1. $2 + 3 + 3 = ■$
2. $5 + 6 + 7 = ■$
3. $7 + 3 + 6 = ■$
4. $4 + 2 + 9 = ■$
5. $10 + 4 + 4 + 2 = ■$

VOCABULARY

perimeter

Activity

MATERIALS: toothpicks, paper clips

STEP 1

Copy the table. Estimate the perimeter of your math book in paper clips and in toothpicks. Record your estimates.

PERIMETER OF MY MATH BOOK		
	Estimate	**Measurement**
Number of paper clips		
Number of toothpicks		

STEP 2

Use paper clips. Record how many paper clips it takes to go around all the edges of your math book.

STEP 3

Use toothpicks. Record how many toothpicks it takes to go around all the edges of your math book.

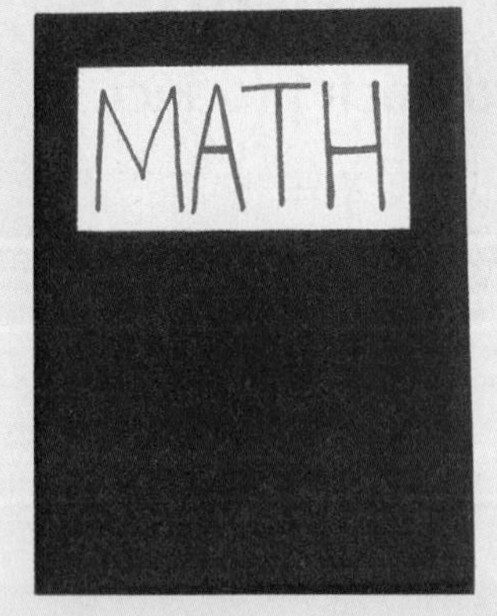

- How does your estimate compare with your actual measurement?
- Did it take more paper clips or more toothpicks to measure the perimeter of your math book? Explain.
- **REASONING** Would it be better to measure the perimeter of your math book with paper clips or with your shoe? Explain.

Other Ways to Find Perimeter

You can count the units to find the perimeter.

Examples Count the units to find the perimeter.

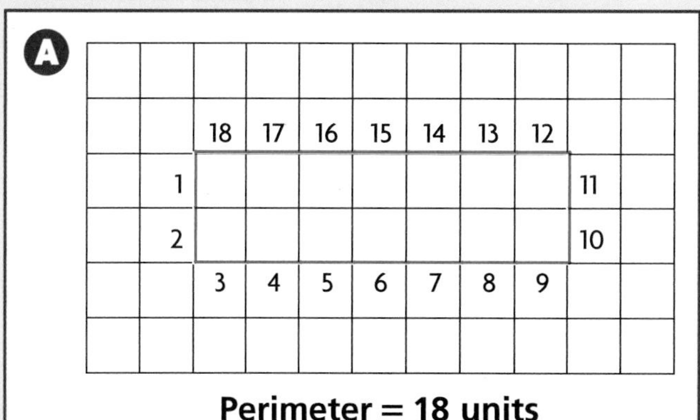

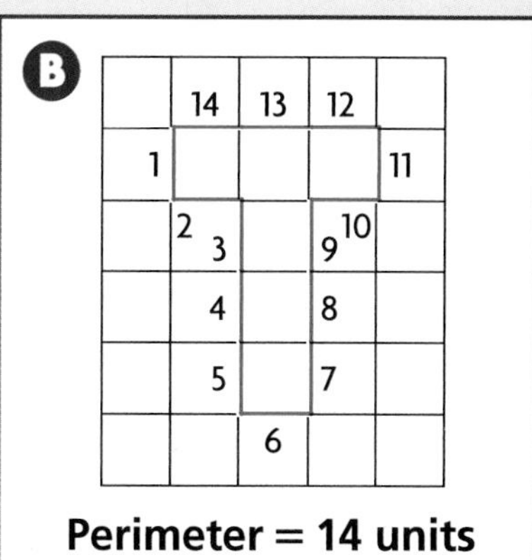

You can add the lengths of the sides to find the perimeter.

More Examples Find the perimeter.

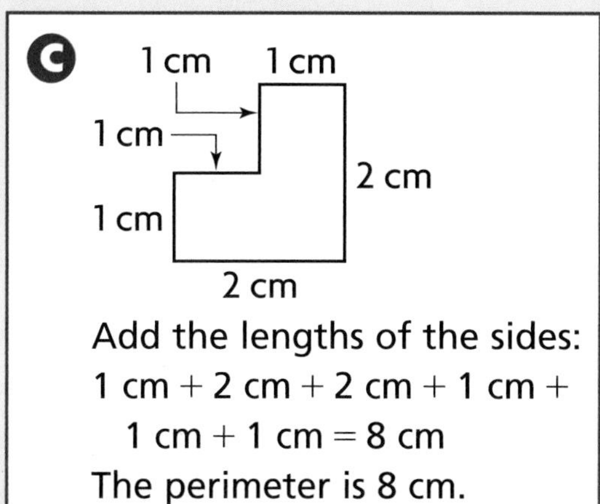

Add the lengths of the sides:
1 cm + 2 cm + 2 cm + 1 cm +
1 cm + 1 cm = 8 cm
The perimeter is 8 cm.

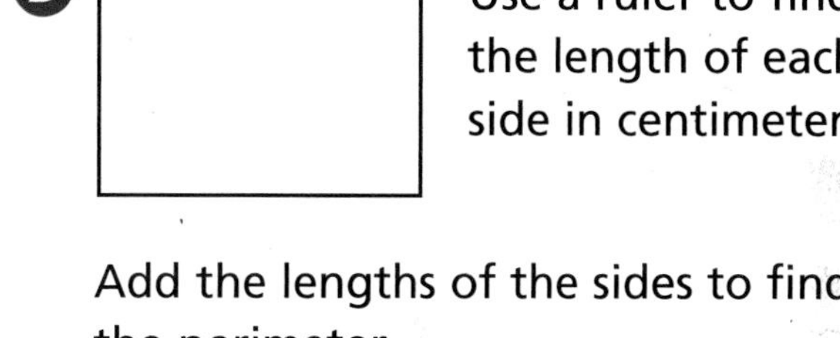

Use a ruler to find the length of each side in centimeters.

Add the lengths of the sides to find the perimeter.
3 cm + 2 cm + 3 cm + 2 cm = 10 cm
The perimeter is 10 cm.

- **REASONING** Explain how to find the perimeter of a square if the length of one side is 5 inches.

Check

1. **Explain** how you could measure only 2 sides to find the perimeter in Example D.

Find the perimeter.

2. 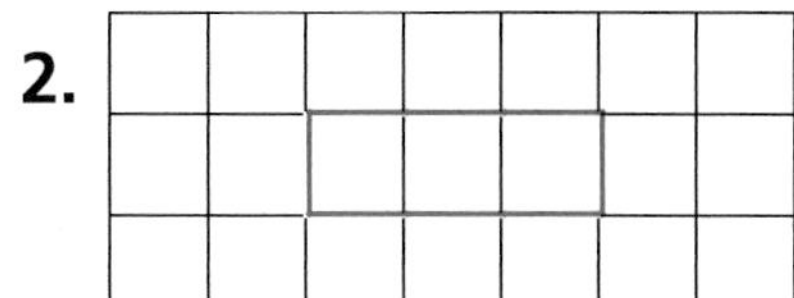

3. 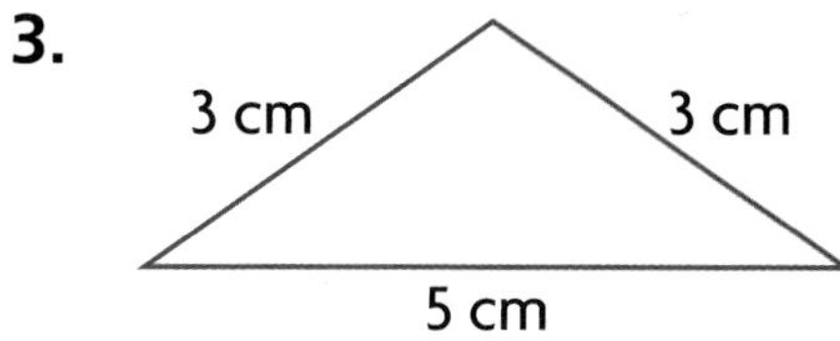

LESSON CONTINUES

Practice and Problem Solving

Extra Practice, page 364, Set A

Find the perimeter.

4. 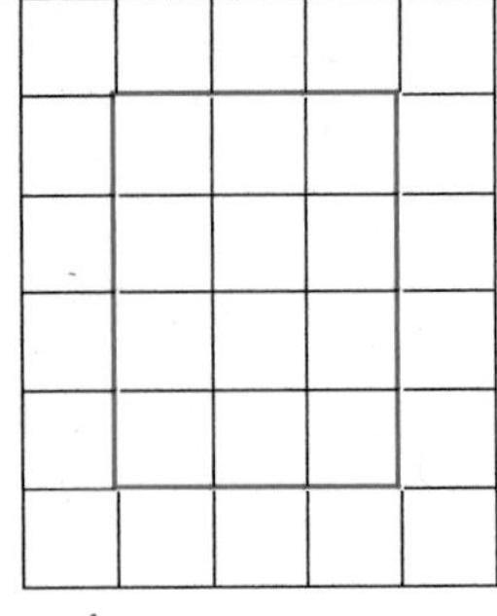

5. 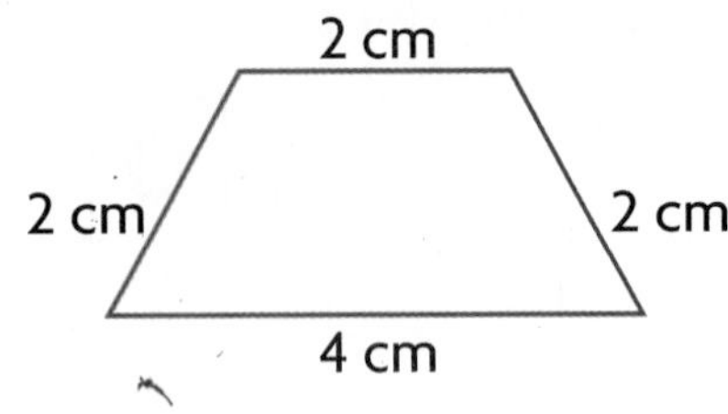

6. 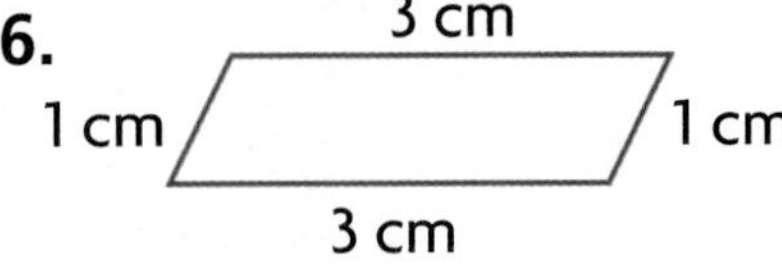

7. 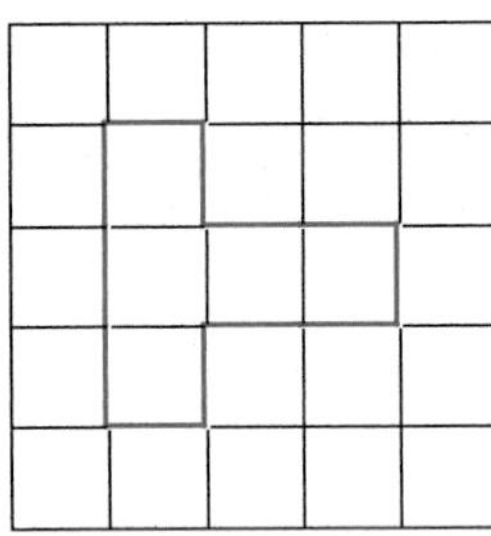

8. 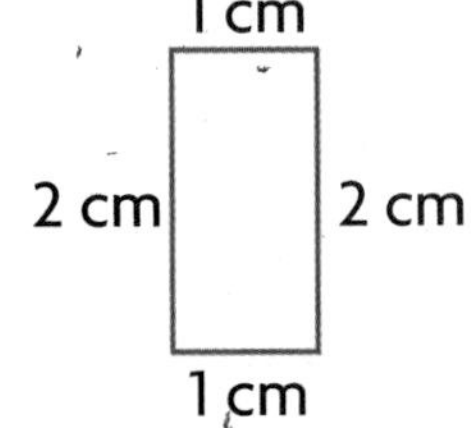

9. 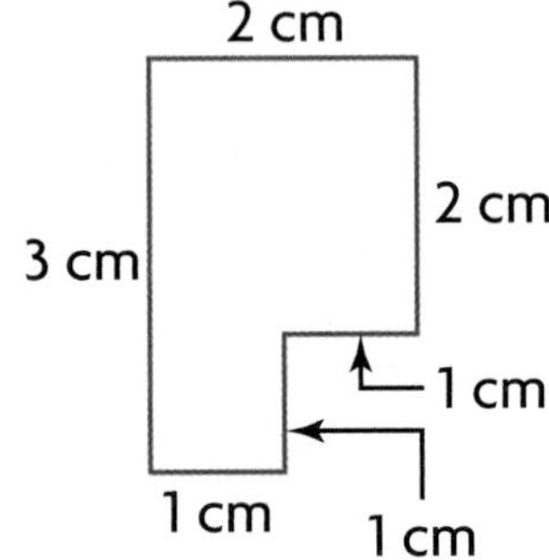

Estimate the perimeter in millimeters. Then use your centimeter ruler to find the perimeter.

10.

11. 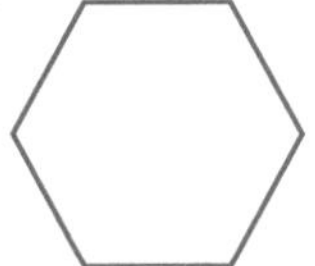

12. **USE DATA** The drawing at the right shows the size of Mrs. Gibson's vegetable garden. She wants to put a fence around her garden. Use the scale to find how many yards of fencing she will need.

Mrs. Gibson's Garden

Scale: ⊢⊣ = 1 yard

13. **ALGEBRA** This triangle has a perimeter of 8 cm. How long is Side C?

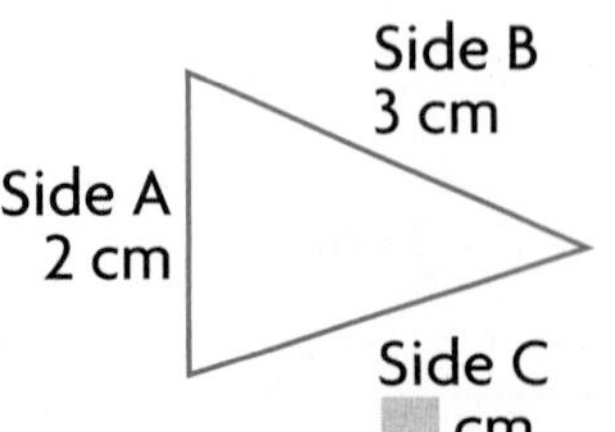

14. **Write About It** Choose an object. Explain how to estimate and measure its perimeter. Then use a ruler to measure its perimeter in inches.

15. Use grid paper. Draw a rectangle with a perimeter of 12 units.

16. Jana's beach towel is 5 feet long and 3 feet wide. What is its perimeter?

Maintain Skills

Find each sum or difference.

17. $\begin{array}{r} 34 \\ +19 \\ \hline \end{array}$

18. $\begin{array}{r} 641 \\ +222 \\ \hline \end{array}$

19. $\begin{array}{r} 325 \\ +149 \\ \hline \end{array}$

20. $\begin{array}{r} 86 \\ -49 \\ \hline \end{array}$

21. $\begin{array}{r} 826 \\ -312 \\ \hline \end{array}$

22. $\begin{array}{r} 733 \\ -306 \\ \hline \end{array}$

23. Write the amount.

CRCT Test Prep

Use the graph below to answer question 24.

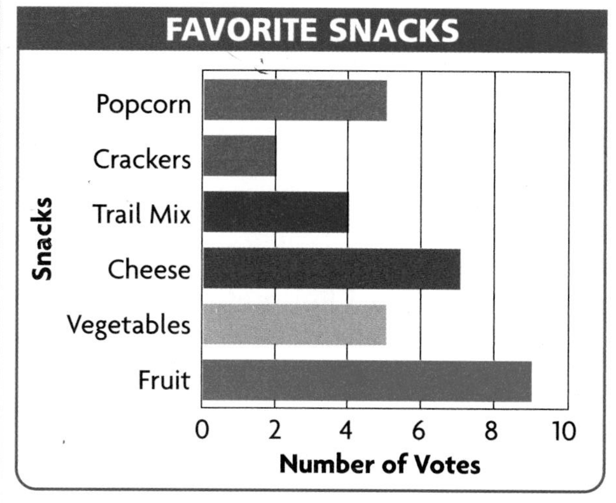

24. M3D1.b. How many students did NOT vote for popcorn? (p. 268)

A. 21 B. 24 C. 27 D. 31

Problem Solving LiNKUP . . . to Social Studies

In 1806, Thomas Jefferson built a house in the Blue Ridge Mountains of Virginia. In the center of the house, Jefferson built a special room that is a perfect cube. This room is 20 feet long, 20 feet wide, and 20 feet tall. Jefferson's granddaughter would draw in this room because a large window called a skylight was in the ceiling.

1. The floor of the center room is a square with each side measuring 20 feet. What is the perimeter of this floor?

2. Around the house, Jefferson built a circular road that measured 540 yards. Write an expression to find how many feet this is. Find the value of the expression.

LESSON 2

Use a Formula

M3A1.b. Describe and explain a quantitative relationship represented by a formula (such as the perimeter of a geometric figure). *also* M3P2.a., M3P3.d.

Quick Review

1. $4 \times 3 = \blacksquare$
2. $4 \times 5 = \blacksquare$
3. $(2 \times 5) + (2 \times 3) = \blacksquare$
4. $(2 \times 2) + (2 \times 4) = \blacksquare$
5. $(2 \times 6) + (2 \times 2) = \blacksquare$

Learn

MEASURING MATH You can use a formula, or rule, to find the perimeter of a square and of a rectangle.

Polygon	Perimeter	Formula
rectangle 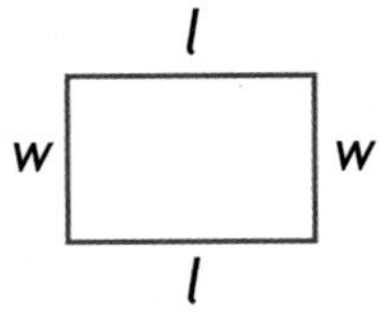 (sides labeled l, w, l, w)	Perimeter = length + width + length + width	$P = l + w + l + w$
square 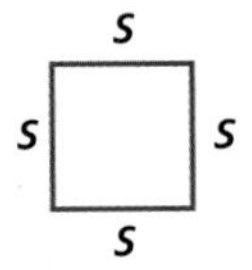 (sides labeled s, s, s, s)	Perimeter = side + side + side + side	$P = s + s + s + s$

Janine wants to put a ribbon border around two pictures in her scrapbook. One picture is a square that is 3 inches on each side. The other picture is a rectangle that is 6 inches long and 4 inches wide. How much ribbon does she need for each picture?

Square Picture

(3 in., 3 in., 3 in., 3 in.)

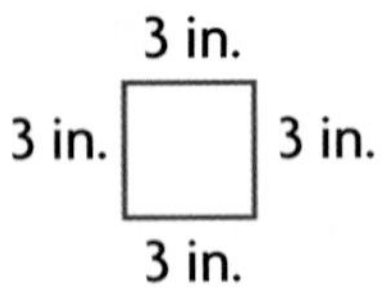

Use the formula.

$P = s + s + s + s$

$P = 3 + 3 + 3 + 3$

$P = 12$

So, Janine needs 12 inches of ribbon for the square picture.

Rectangular Picture

(6 in., 4 in., 4 in., 6 in.)

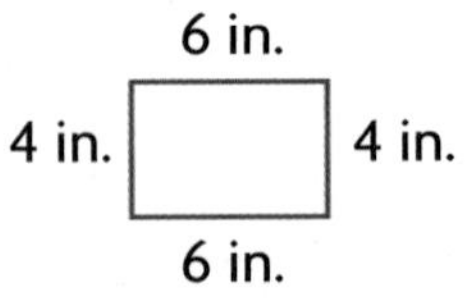

Use the formula.

$P = l + w + l + w$

$P = 6 + 4 + 6 + 4$

$P = 20$

So, Janine needs 20 inches of ribbon for the rectangular picture.

Check

1. **Explain** how you would find the perimeter of a square if the length of one side is 6 centimeters.

Use a formula to find the perimeter.

2. 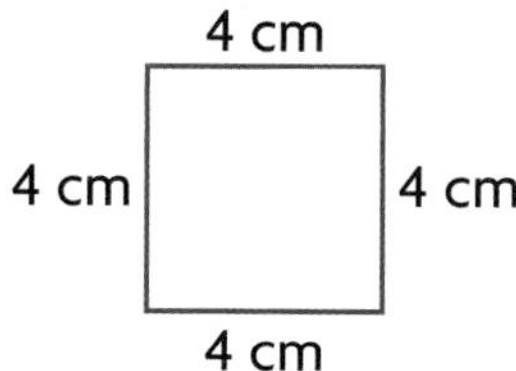

3. 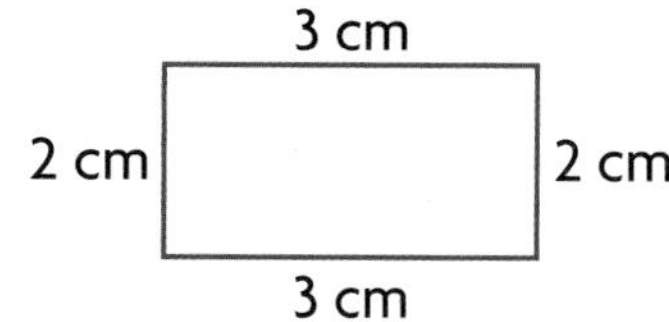

Practice and Problem Solving

Extra Practice, page 364, Set B

Use a formula to find the perimeter.

4. 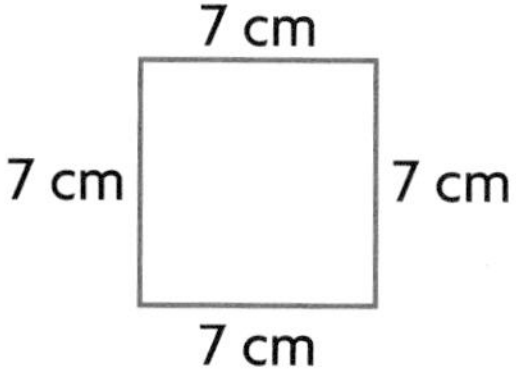

5. 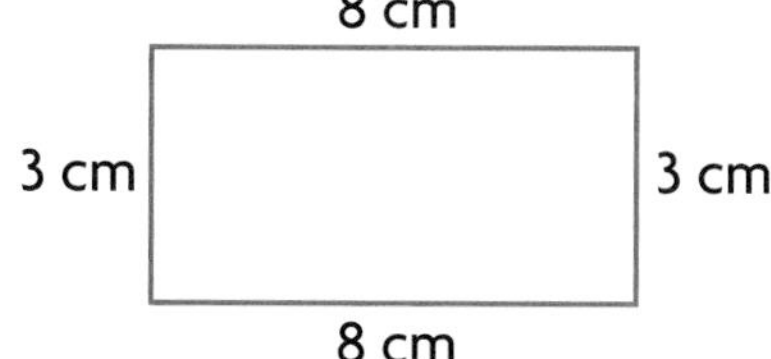

6. 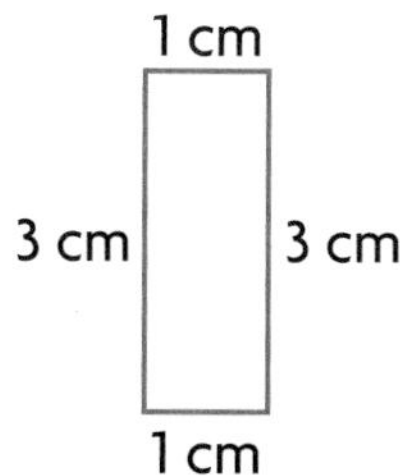

7. 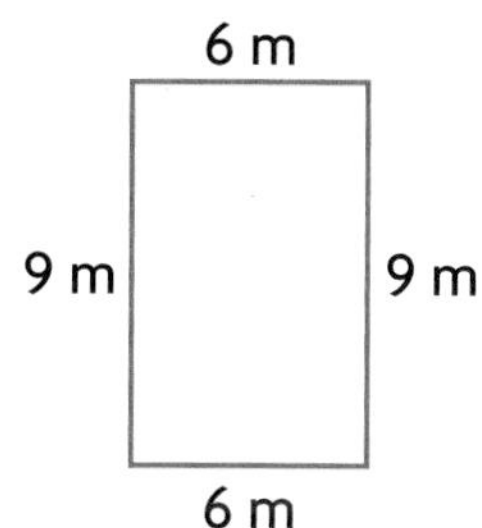

8. 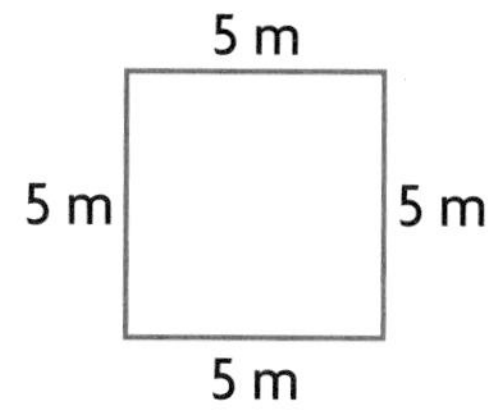

9. 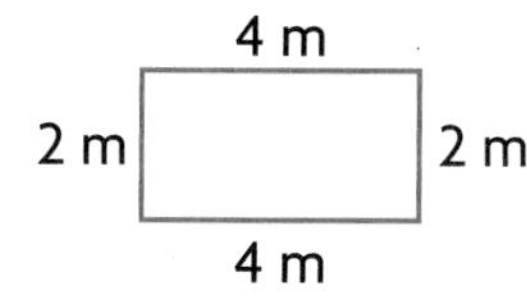

10. **Reasoning** The shape of Jake's bedroom floor is a square. The perimeter of the floor is 36 feet. What is the length of one side of Jake's bedroom floor?

11. Kim measured a rug on her floor. The width was 5 feet and the length was 8 feet. What is the perimeter of Kim's rug?

12. **Multistep** Amy sent her grandmother a birthday card. The card has a perimeter of 24 inches. The longer sides are each 7 inches long. What is the length of each of the shorter sides?

Maintain Skills

Compare. Write <, >, or = for each ●.

13. 45 ● 54 **14.** 93 ● 98

15. 36 ● 63 **16.** 87 ● 81

CRCT Test Prep

17. M3M3.c What is the perimeter of a square if each side is 8 inches? (p. 350)

A. 8 inches C. 24 inches
B. 16 inches D. 32 inches

LESSON 3

Area

M3M4.b. Model (by tiling) the area of a simple geometric figure using square units (square inch, square foot, etc.). *also* M3M4.a., M3M4.c., M3P2.a., M3P2.b., M3P2.c., M3P2.d., M3P3.a., M3P3.b., M3P3.c., M3P3.d., M3P5.

Quick Review

1. $5 \times 8 = ■$
2. $7 \times 6 = ■$
3. $3 \times 3 = ■$
4. $2 \times 8 = ■$
5. $6 \times 4 = ■$

VOCABULARY
square unit
area

MATERIALS
square tiles
grid paper

Explore

A **square unit** is a square with a side length of 1 unit. You use square units to measure area. **Area** is the number of square units needed to cover a flat surface.

1 square unit:

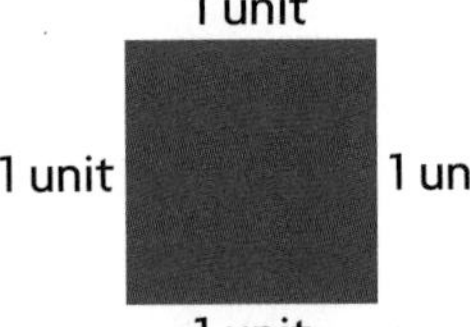

Activity

Use 1-inch square tiles to find the area of your math book cover.

STEP 1

Estimate how many squares will cover your math book. Then place square tiles in rows on the front of your math book. Cover the whole surface.

STEP 2

Use grid paper. Draw a picture to show how you covered the math book.

STEP 3

Count and record the number of square tiles you used. This number is the book cover's area in square inches.

- Look at the picture you made. How could you use multiplication to find the area?

How many rows of tiles do I need to cover an index card?

MATH IDEA You can find the area of a surface by counting the number of square units needed to cover the surface.

Try It

Use square tiles to find the area of each.

a. an index card **b.** a sheet of paper

Connect

To find the area of a rectangle, add the number of tiles in each row.

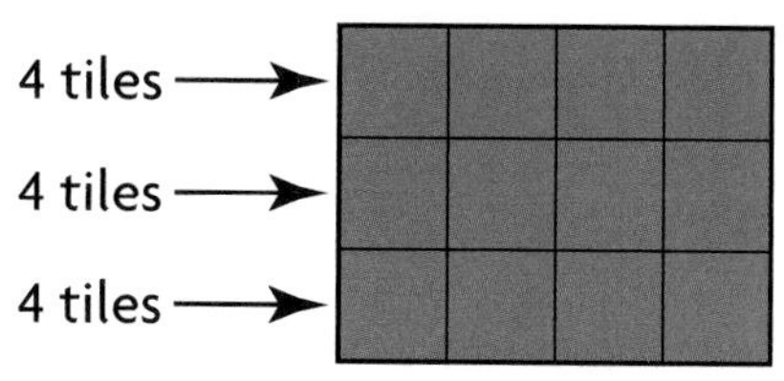

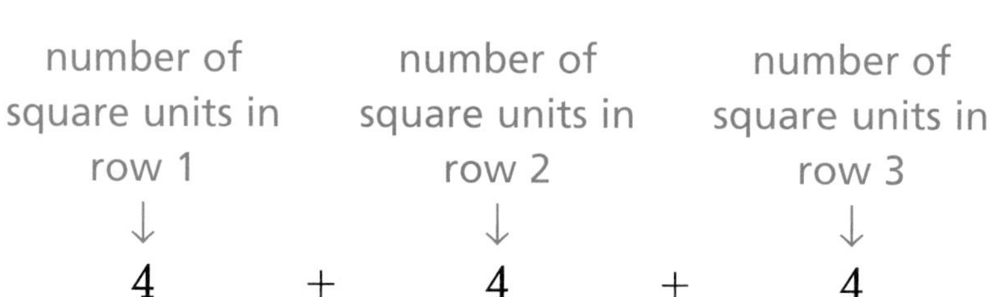

Practice and Problem Solving

Find the area of each figure. Write the area in square units.

1. 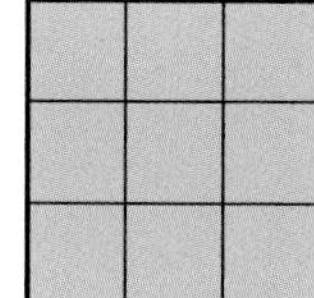

2. 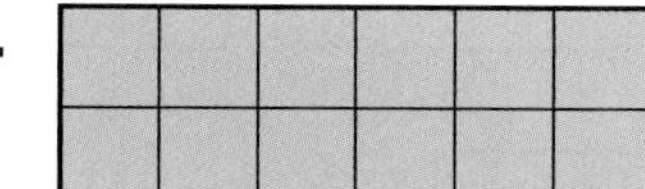

3. 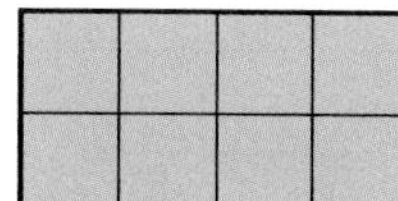

4. 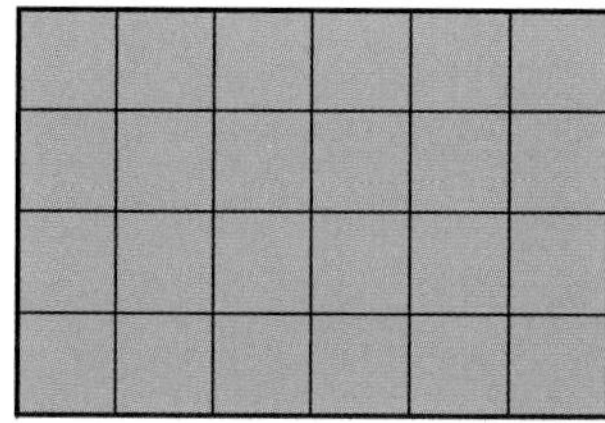

5. 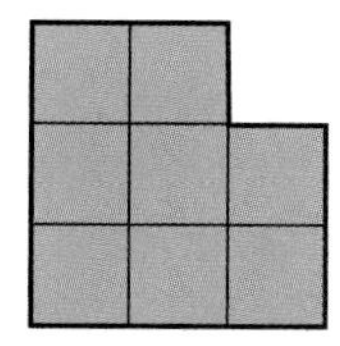

6. 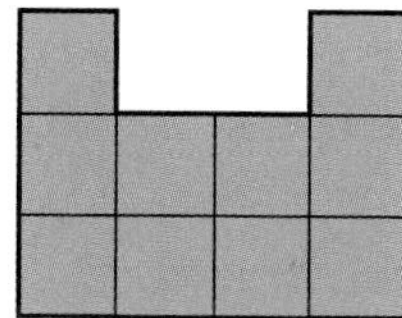

7. **REASONING** For which of the figures in Exercises 1–6 could you use multiplication to find the area? Explain.

8. **What's the Question?** Rachel's notebook is 6 square tiles wide and 4 square tiles long. The answer is 24 square tiles.

9. Copy the figure at the right on grid paper. Show the perimeter in red, and show the area in blue. Record the perimeter and area of the figure.

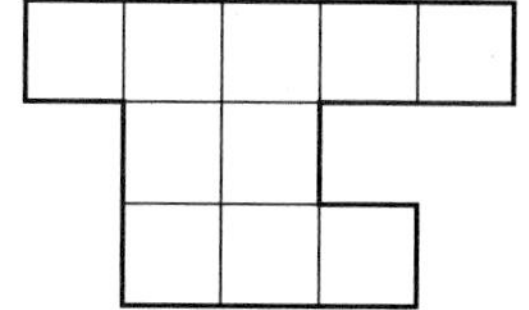

Maintain Skills

10. Write the amount.

CRCT Test Prep

11. M3N4.f. Erma had 45 beads. She put 9 beads on each key chain. How many key chains did she make? (p. 242)

A. 10 B. 9 C. 5 D. 3

LESSON 

Find Area

M3M4.c. Determine the area of squares and rectangles by counting, adding, and multiplying with models. *also* **M3M4.a., M3M4.b., M3P2.a., M3P2.b., M3P2.c., M3P2.d.**

Quick Review

1. $9 \times 8 = \blacksquare$
2. $7 \times 5 = \blacksquare$
3. $4 \times 4 = \blacksquare$
4. $6 \times 5 = \blacksquare$
5. $6 \times 7 = \blacksquare$

Learn

FIND IT! You can find the area of figures using square feet. A square foot is a square with a side length of one foot.

Example 1

Kassie is making a quilt that is made of square patches that each have a side length of 1 foot. What is the area of this quilt in square feet?

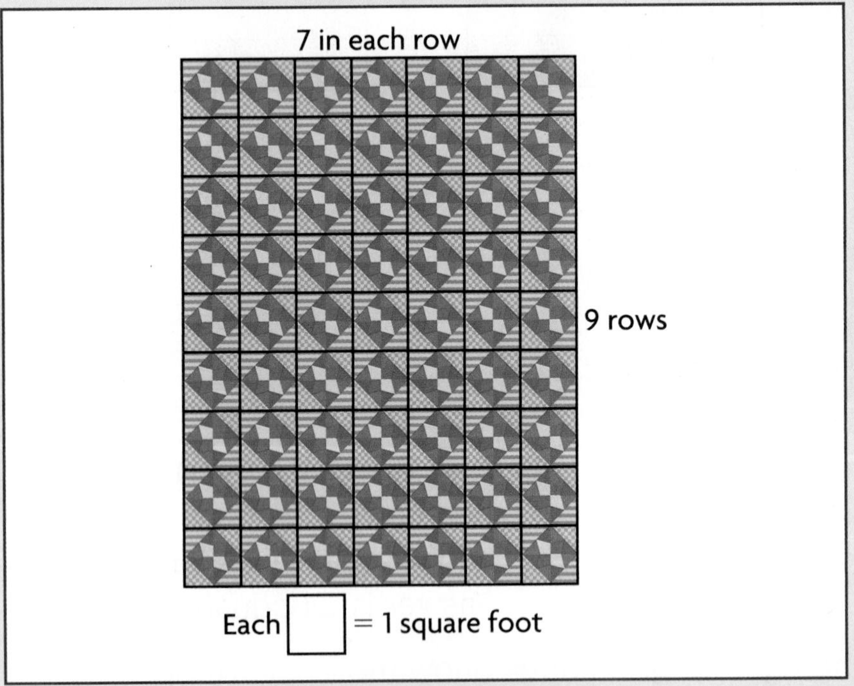

To find the area of a rectangle, multiply the number of rows times the number in each row.

number of rows		number in each row		area
↓		↓		↓
9	×	7	=	63 square feet

So, the area of this quilt is 63 square feet.

- How could you use addition to find the area of this quilt?

Using a Formula

You can also use a formula to find the area of a rectangle.

Area = length × width, or $A = l \times w$

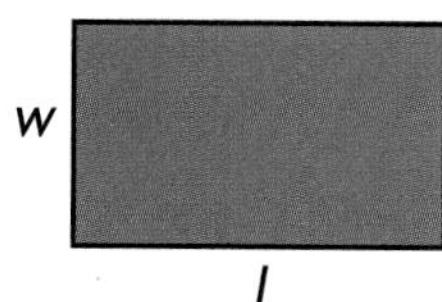

Example 2

Tom has a postcard that is 5 inches wide and 7 inches long. What is the area of Tom's postcard?

Use the formula to find the area.

$A = l \times w$
$A = 7 \times 5$
$A = 35$

So, the area of the postcard is 35 square inches.

- **REASONING** How could you draw an array to show the number of square inches in the postcard?

Check

1. **Explain** two ways to find the area of your math book cover in square inches.

Find the area of each figure. Write the area in square inches.

2. 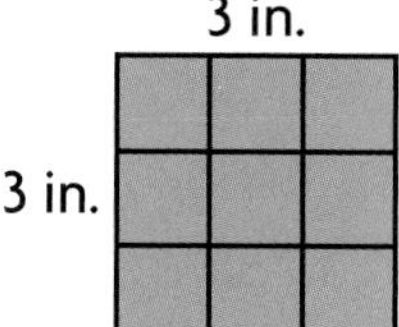

3. 

LESSON CONTINUES

Practice and Problem Solving

Extra Practice, page 364, Set C

Find the area of each figure. Write the area in square inches.

4.

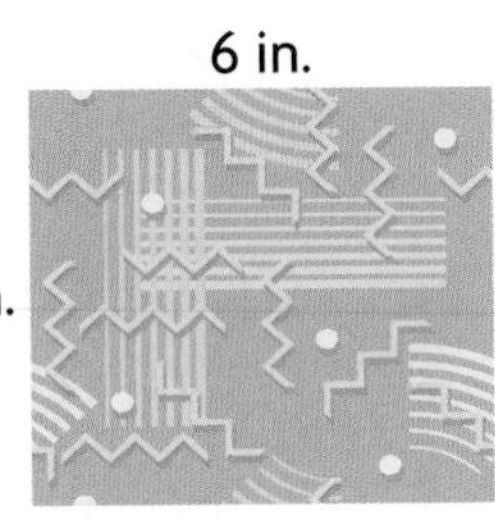

5.

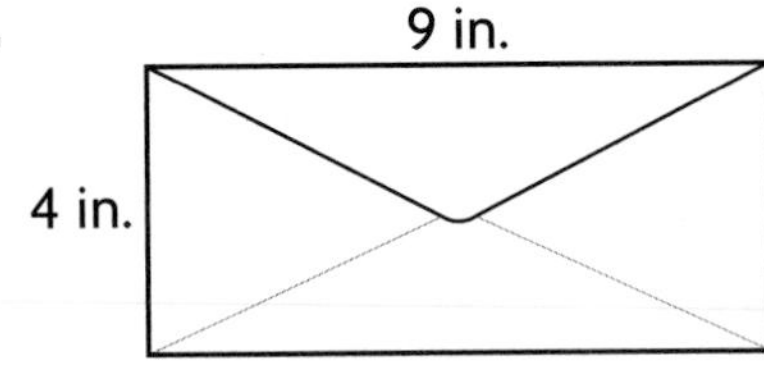

6.

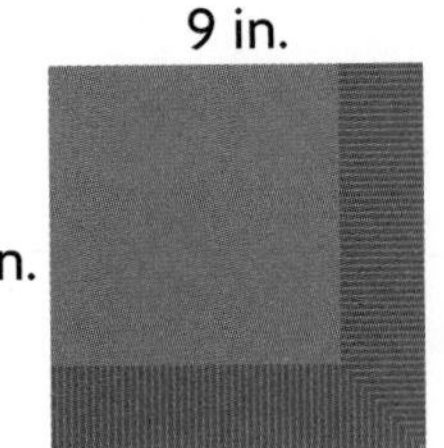

7.

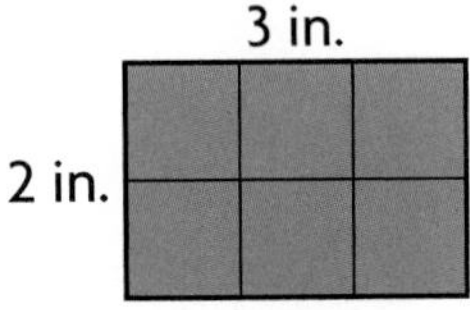

Find the area of each figure. Write the area in square feet.

8.

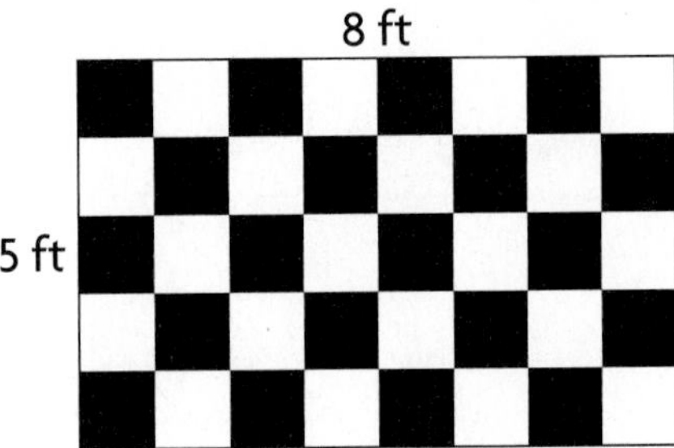

9.

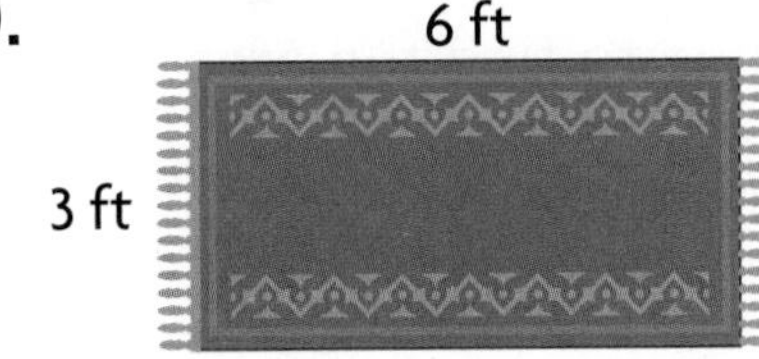

10.

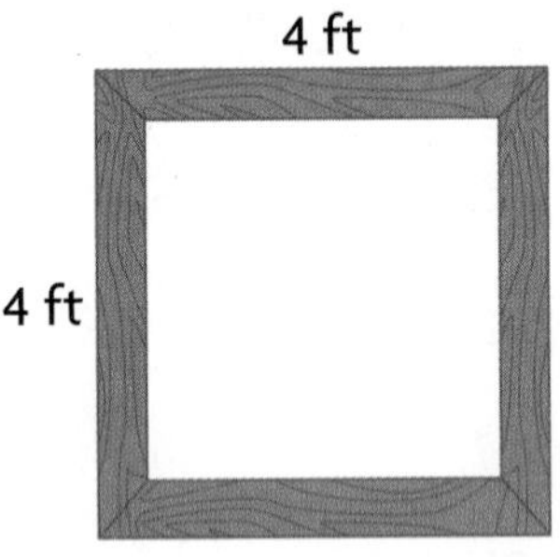

11.

12. **REASONING** A pink strip of paper has a perimeter of 6 inches. A green strip of paper has an area of 4 square inches. Both strips of paper have a width of 1 inch. Which strip of paper is longer? Explain.

13. Patti measured her book cover. Its width is 6 inches and its length is 9 inches. What is the area of her book cover?

14. ALGEBRA The area of the rectangular class mural is 36 feet. Its length is 9 feet. What is its width?

15. Robyn drew the rectangle at the right. What is the area of Robyn's rectangle?

7 in.

2 in.

Maintain Skills

Write the amount.

16.

17.

CRCT Test Prep

18. M3M4.c What is the area of a photograph that is 3 inches wide by 5 inches long? (p. 358)

A. 8 square inches
B. 15 square inches
C. 16 square inches
D. 29 square inches

19. M3N1.b What is the value of the 7 in 16,732? (p. 14)

A. 70
B. 700
C. 7,000
D. 70,000

Problem Solving Thinker's Corner

VEGETABLE GARDEN Carmen has a rectangular garden. She divided her garden into 4 different sections to plant different vegetables. Each section is shown below. What is the total area of Carmen's garden?

4 ft, 6 ft

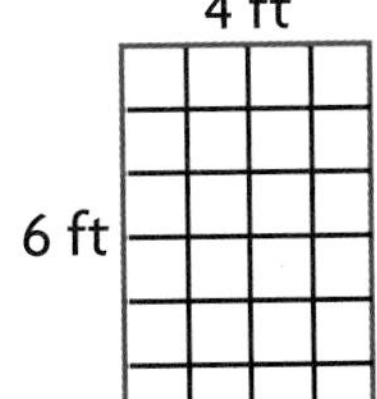

4 ft, 3 ft

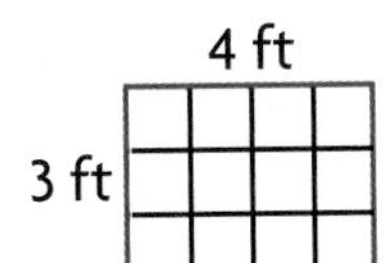

6 ft, 3 ft

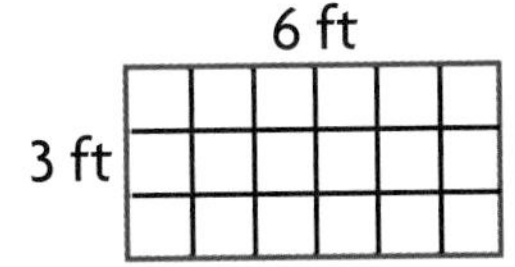

3 ft, 3 ft

Copy each section onto grid paper and cut out each rectangle. Rearrange the sections so they make one large rectangle. Find the area of the large rectangle to find the total area of her garden.

Explain another way you could solve this problem.

LESSON 5

Problem Solving Skill
Make Generalizations

M3M3.b. Understand the concept of perimeter as being the boundary of a simple geometric figure. *also* M3M3.a., M3M3.c., M3M4.a., M3M4.b., M3M4.c., M3P1.a., M3P1.b., M3P1.c., M3P1.d., M3P2.a., M3P2.b., M3P2.c., M3P2.d., M3P3.a., M3P3.b., M3P3.c., M3P3.d., M3P4.c.

UNDERSTAND → PLAN → SOLVE → CHECK

Quick Review

1. $4 + 2 + 4 + 2 = \blacksquare$
2. $8 + 3 + 8 + 3 = \blacksquare$
3. $3 \times 4 = \blacksquare$
4. $7 \times 3 = \blacksquare$
5. $8 \times 4 = \blacksquare$

DON'T FENCE ME IN Maura plans to plant a flower garden and put a fence around it. She has 12 feet of fencing to make a garden. If she wants to have the greatest area possible, should her fence be a rectangle with equal sides (a square) or unequal sides?

Maura draws a picture to show all the rectangular gardens she can make.

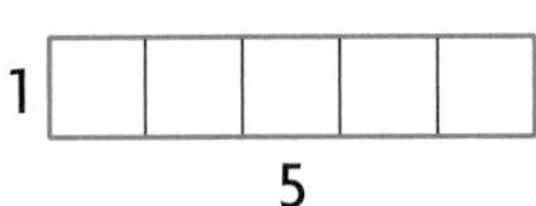

Perimeter:
$1 + 5 + 1 + 5 = 12$ feet

Area:
$1 \times 5 = 5$ square feet

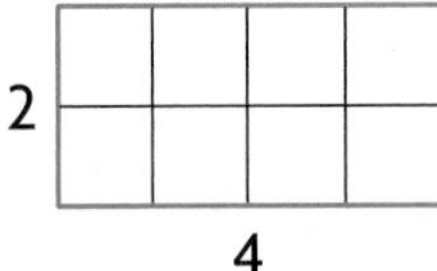

Perimeter:
$2 + 4 + 2 + 4 = 12$ feet

Area:
$2 \times 4 = 8$ square feet

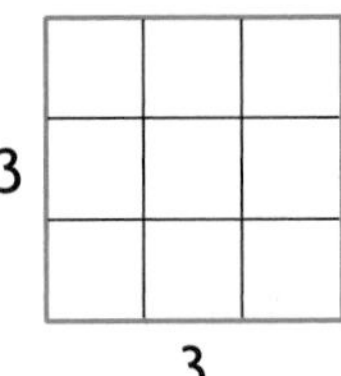

Perimeter:
$3 + 3 + 3 + 3 = 12$ feet

Area:
$3 \times 3 = 9$ square feet

Order the areas: $5 < 8 < 9$

9 square feet is the greatest area.

So, Maura's fence should be a square.

Talk About It

- **Describe** how the area changes when rectangles with the same perimeter change from long and thin to square.
- **What if** Maura had 20 feet of fencing? To have the greatest area, should her fence be a square or a rectangle?

Problem Solving Practice

1. What if Maura had 8 feet of fencing to make a rectangular garden with the greatest possible area? How long should it be? How wide should it be?

2. **MULTISTEP** Kyle used 16 feet of fencing to make a square play yard for his rabbit. What was the length of each side? What was the area of the play yard?

Jane drew some figures on grid paper.

3. Which figure has a perimeter of 16 units?

A

B

C

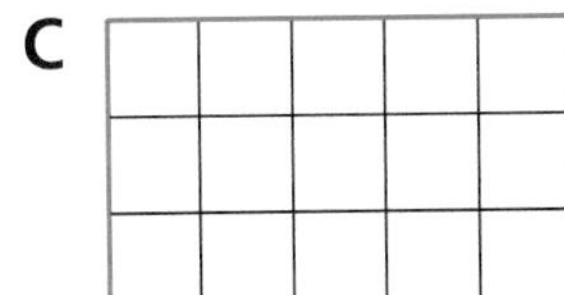

D

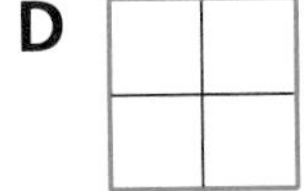

4. Which figure has an area of 15 square units?

F

G

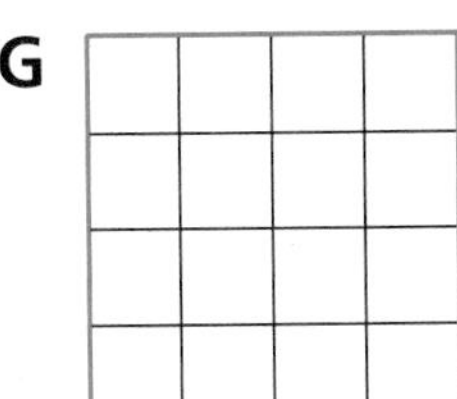

H

J

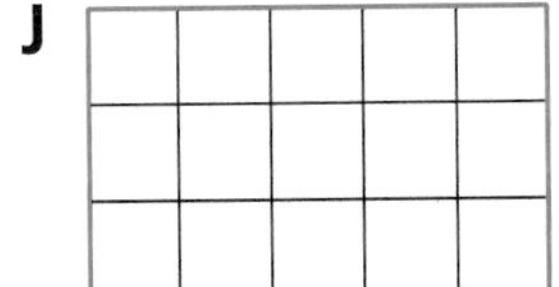

Mixed Applications

5. **MULTISTEP** Abe bought 3 muffins for $1 each and 2 cartons of milk for $0.50 each. How much did he spend in all?

6. Ted eats 1 sandwich and drinks 2 glasses of milk each day. How many glasses of milk does he drink in one week?

7. **REASONING** I am a 2-digit number less than 20. I can be divided evenly into groups of 4. I cannot be divided evenly into groups of 3. What number am I?

8. **Write a problem** about the perimeter and area of a rectangle. Use square tiles to make the rectangle. Then draw a picture of your rectangle.

Extra Practice

Set A (pp. 350–353)

Find the perimeter.

1. 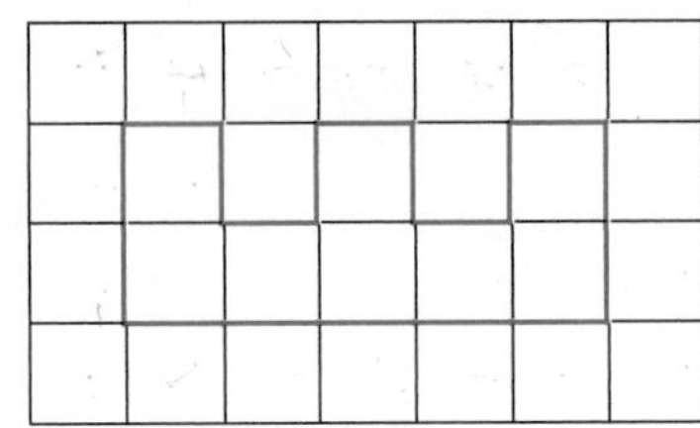

2. 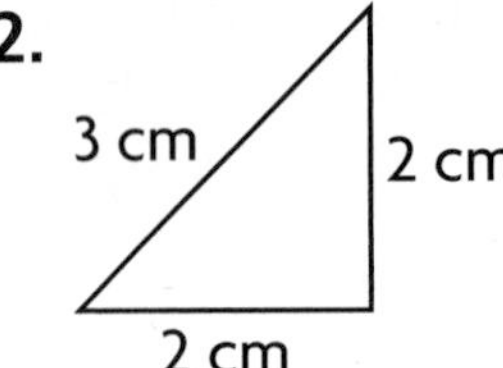

3. 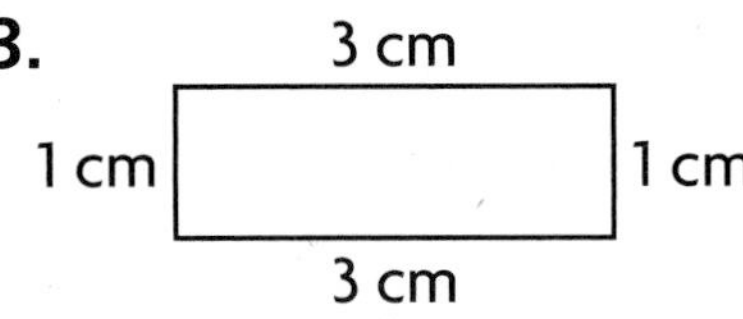

Estimate the perimeter in millimeters. Then use your centimeter ruler to find the perimeter.

4. 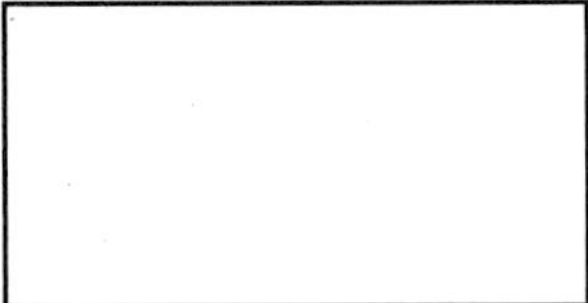

5. 

6. 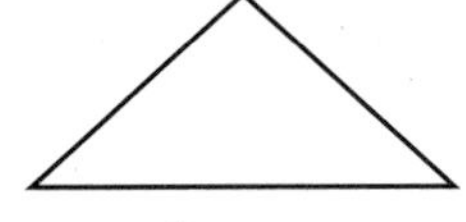

Set B (pp. 354–355)

Use a formula to find the perimeter.

1. 3 cm, 4 cm, 4 cm, 3 cm

2. 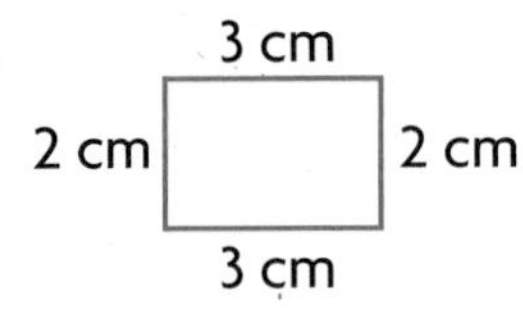

3. 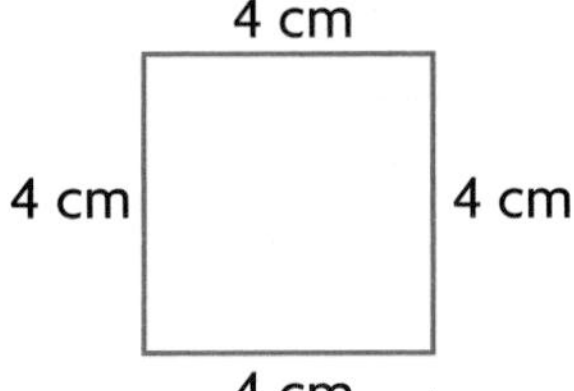

Set C (pp. 358–361)

Find the area of each figure. Write the area in square inches.

1. 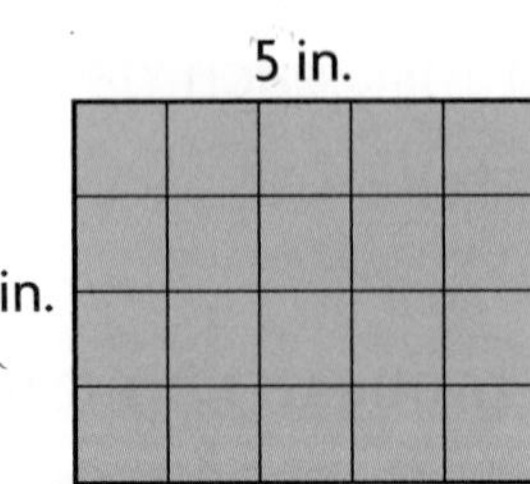

2. 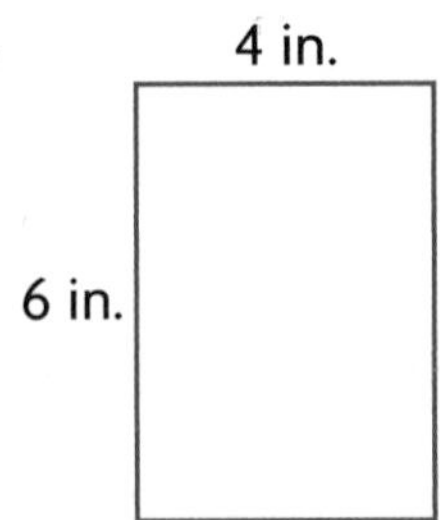

3. 6 in., 2 in.

4. 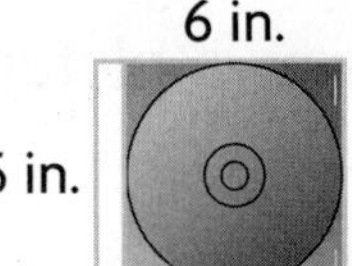

5. 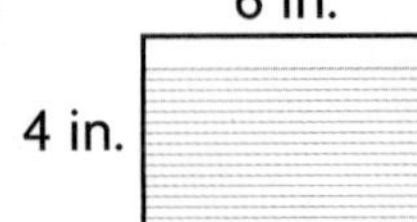

6. 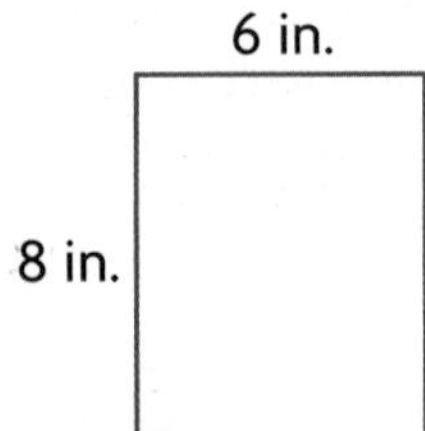

Review/Test

CHECK VOCABULARY

Vocabulary
area
perimeter
square units

Choose the best term from the box.

1. The distance around a figure is called its __?__. (p. 350)
2. The number of square units needed to cover a flat surface is the __?__. (p. 356)

CHECK SKILLS

Find the perimeter. (pp. 350–353, 354–355)

3. 1 cm, 1 cm, 1 cm

4. 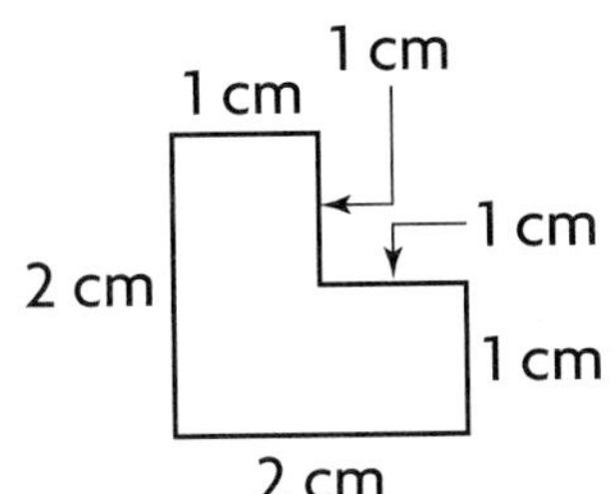

5. 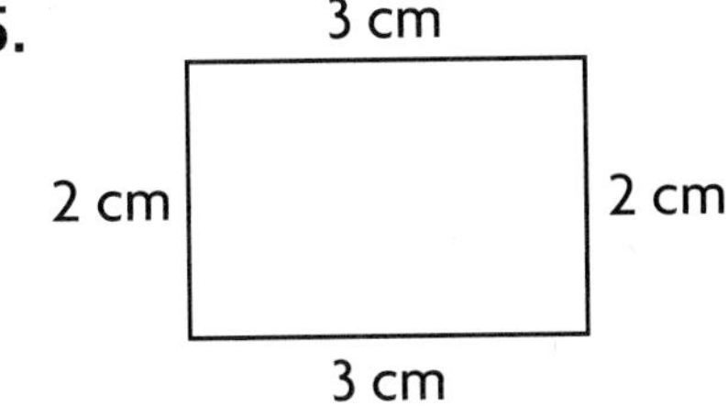

Find the area. Write the area in square inches or square feet. (pp. 358–361)

6. 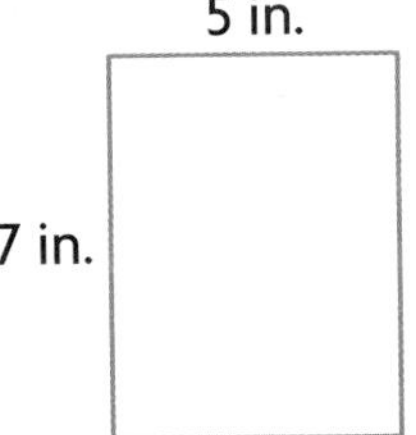

7. 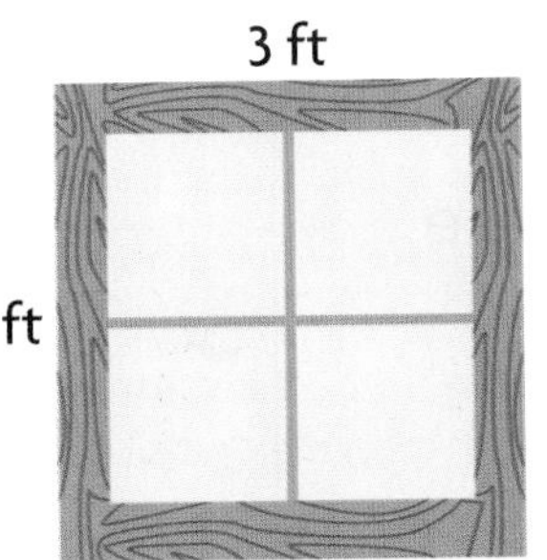

8. 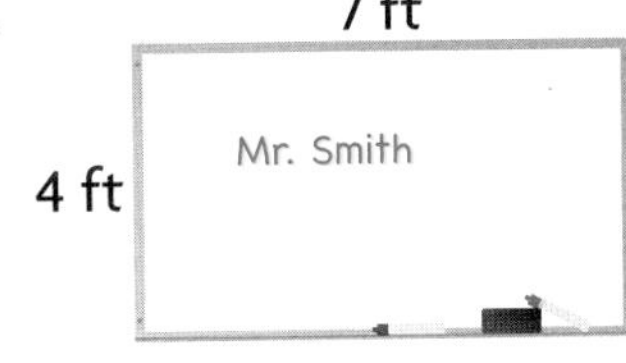

CHECK PROBLEM SOLVING

Solve. (pp. 362–363)

9. Pedro has 20 inches of string. He wants to make a rectangular shape with the greatest possible area. How wide should it be? How long should it be?

10. Nora has 16 inches of ribbon. She wants to make a rectangular shape with the greatest possible area. How long should it be? How wide should it be?

Chapter CRCT Test Prep

MEASUREMENT

1. M3M3.c. Maura drew this figure. The lengths of the sides are measured in centimeters (cm).

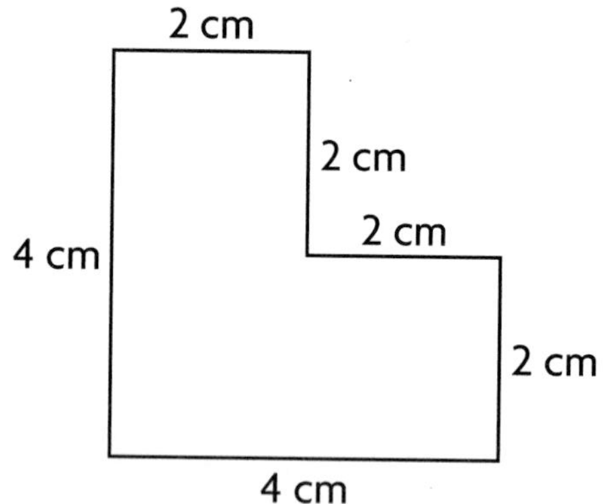

What is the perimeter of Maura's figure?

A. 12 centimeters

B. 16 centimeters

C. 18 centimeters

D. 20 centimeters

2. M3M4.b. What is the area of the figure shown below?

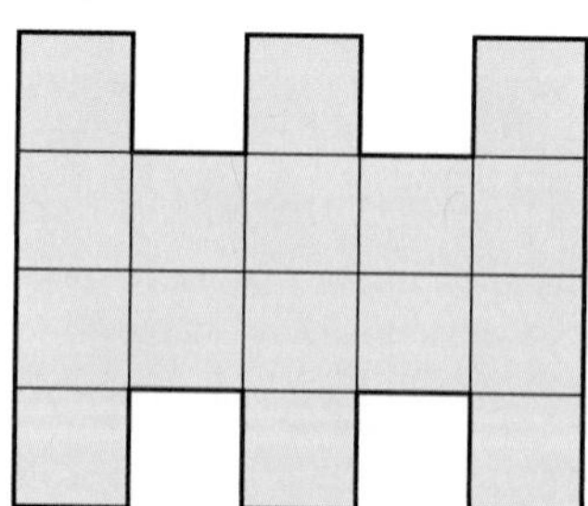

A. 10 square units

B. 12 square units

C. 14 square units

D. 16 square units

MEASUREMENT

3. M3M3.b. Dee has a square garden that measures 8 feet on each side. How many feet of fencing does she need to buy to go around the square garden?

A. 8 feet

B. 16 feet

C. 32 feet

D. 64 feet

4. M3M4.b. Forrest measured a window in the classroom. It was 2 feet wide and 3 feet tall.

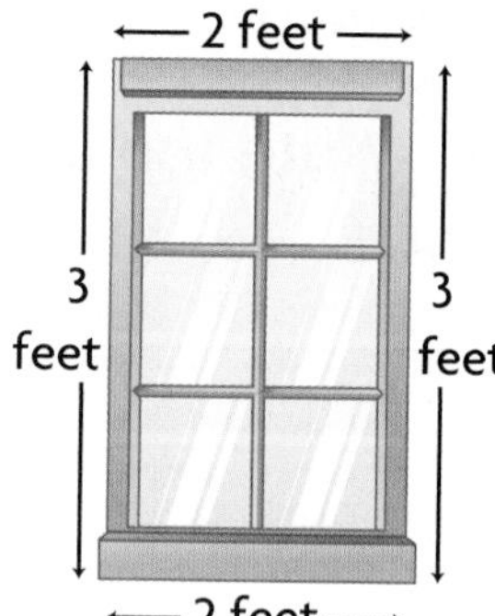

What is the area of the window?

A. 1 square foot

B. 5 square feet

C. 6 square feet

D. 10 square feet

Cumulative CRCT Test Prep

NUMBERS AND OPERATIONS

5. M3N3.g. Lynn sold 8 bracelets at a craft fair. She charged $3 for each bracelet. Which number sentence should you use to find how much money she made at the fair?

A. $8 + 3 = 11$

B. $8 - 3 = 5$

C. $8 \times 3 = 24$

D. $18 \div 3 = 6$

6. M3N3.e. Terry bought 4 packs of markers. Each pack had 8 markers. Jim bought twice as many packs as Terry. Which expression shows how many markers Jim bought?

A. $(4 + 8) + 2$

B. $(8 - 2) + 4$

C. $(4 \times 8) \times 2$

D. $(4 \times 4) \times 8$

7. M3N3.g. Tanya has 8 bags of marbles. Each bag of marbles has 9 marbles. Rob has 55 marbles. How many more marbles does Tanya have than Rob?

A. 17

B. 25

C. 37

D. 72

GEOMETRY

8. M3G1.a. Jessica is making a design with this triangle.

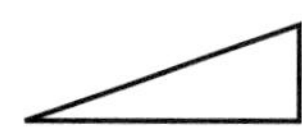

What kind of triangle is she using?

A. obtuse

B. acute

C. right

D. equilateral

9. M3G1.a. A garden is in the shape of a trapezoid. Which figure below shows the shape of the garden?

A. 

B.

C.

D.

Algebra: Patterns

FAST FACT • ART Patterns can be seen in many Native American works of art such as baskets, jewelry, blankets, and pottery. The Pima baskets shown here are woven to be watertight.

INVESTIGATION Look closely at the Navajo serape (shawl) pictured below. Describe the different patterns that you see.

Pima baskets were used for storing food, holding water, and sometimes used as drums.

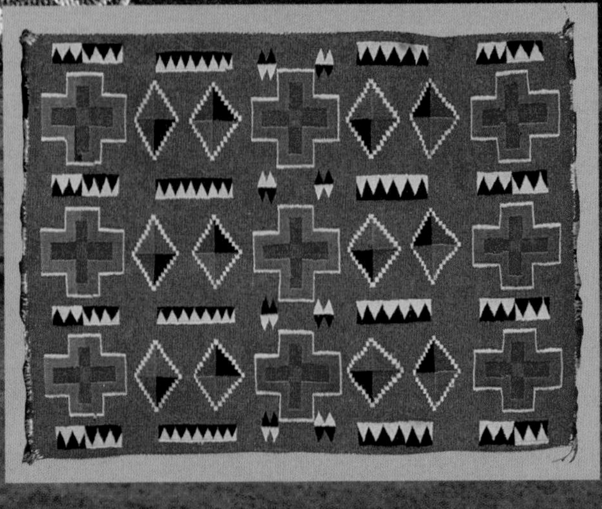

Use this page to help you review and remember important skills needed for Chapter 19.

ORDINAL NUMBERS

For 1–4, use the list of names.

1. Kelly is first on the list. Who is seventh?

2. In which position is Julie on the list?

3. Who is fifth on the list?

4. In which position is Tom on the list?

Kelly
Tom
Sally
Susan
Timothy
Julie
Juan
Matt

USE A RULE

Copy and complete the table.

5.

Dimes	1	2	3	4	5
Nickels	2	4	6	■	■

Rule: Multiply the number of dimes by 2.

6.

Bags	1	2	3	4	5
Marbles	10	20	■	40	■

Rule: Multiply the number of bags by 10.

7.

Baskets	1	2	3	4	5
Oranges	8	16	■	32	■

Rule: Multiply the number of baskets by 8.

8.

Cars	1	2	3	4	5
Tires	4	■	12	16	■

Rule: Multiply the number of cars by 4.

VOCABULARY POWER

REVIEW

pattern [pat′ərn] *noun*

A pattern is an ordered set of numbers or objects that are predictable. Find one example of a pattern and describe the order seen in that pattern.

PREVIEW

pattern unit

GO ON-LINE www.harcourtschool.com/mathglossary

LESSON 1

Geometric Patterns

M3A1.a. Describe and extend numeric and geometric patterns. *also* **M3P2.a., M3P2.b., M3P2.c., M3P2.d.**

Quick Review

Name each polygon.

1. ▭ 2. ⬡

3. ◸ 4. □ 5. ⬠

VOCABULARY

pattern unit

Learn

LOOK CLOSELY Some patterns are made with figures that repeat. The part of a pattern that repeats is called the **pattern unit**.

Ben used pattern blocks to make this pattern. What is the pattern unit?

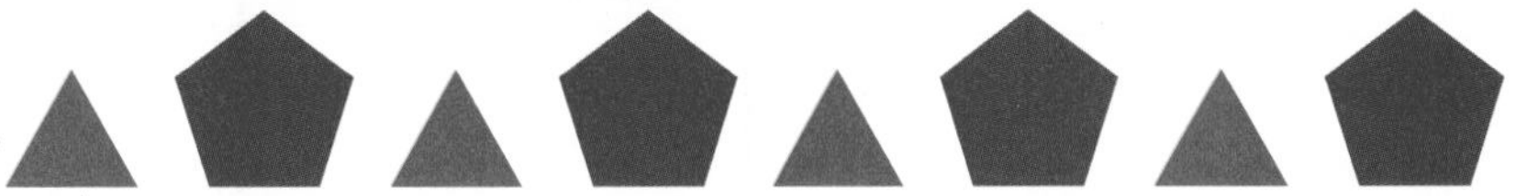

The pattern unit is *green triangle, blue pentagon*.

Carla used tiles and counters to make a pattern. Look for the pattern unit. What will the next two shapes in her pattern be?

The pattern unit is *red circle, green square, yellow circle*. The next two shapes will be a red circle and a green square.

Look at Dee's pattern below. Look for the pattern unit. What shape is missing?

The pattern unit is *blue square, red square, green triangle*. The missing shape is a red square.

- **REASONING** Look closely at the picture of the kingsnake. Do you see a pattern unit? Describe the pattern that you see.

Translating Patterns

The same pattern can be shown using different objects or symbols.

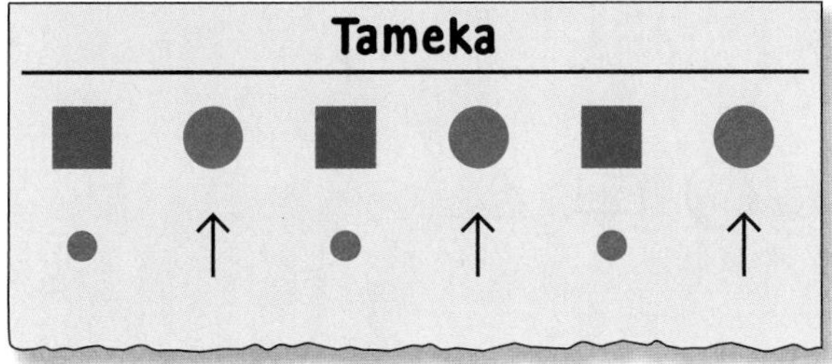

Tameka's pattern is shown using squares and circles and again using dots and arrows.

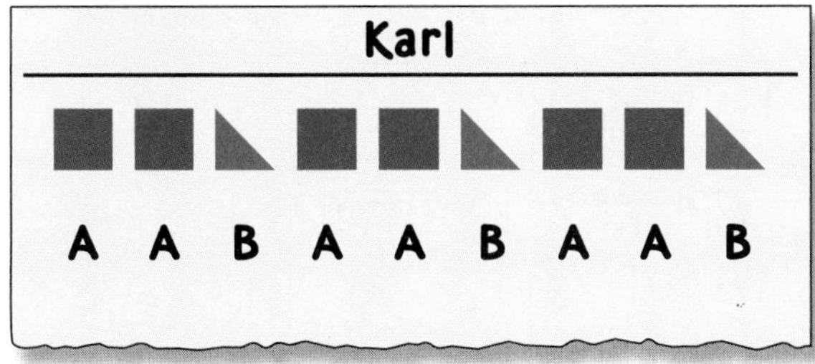

Karl's pattern is shown using squares and triangles and again using the letters A and B.

- **REASONING** How are Tameka's two patterns the same? How are Karl's two patterns the same?

Check

1. **Explain** how you could use rectangles and circles to show the following pattern.

   A B B A B B A B B

Name the pattern unit for each.

2. ○ △ ○ △ ○ △ ○ △
3. ▽ ▯ ⬠ ▽ ▯ ⬠ ▽ ▯ ⬠ ▽ ▯ ⬠

Draw the next two shapes in each pattern.

4. ◺ ◺ □ ◺ ◺ □ ◺ ◺ □ ◺ ◺ □ ? ?
5. □ ○ ▯ □ ○ ▯ □ ○ ▯ □ ○ ▯ ? ?

LESSON CONTINUES

Practice and Problem Solving

Extra Practice, page 380, Set A

Name the pattern unit for each.

6. 

7. 

Draw the next two shapes in each pattern.

8. ? ?

9. ? ?

Copy each pattern on dot paper. Find the pattern unit. Then draw the next two figures in each pattern.

10. 

11. 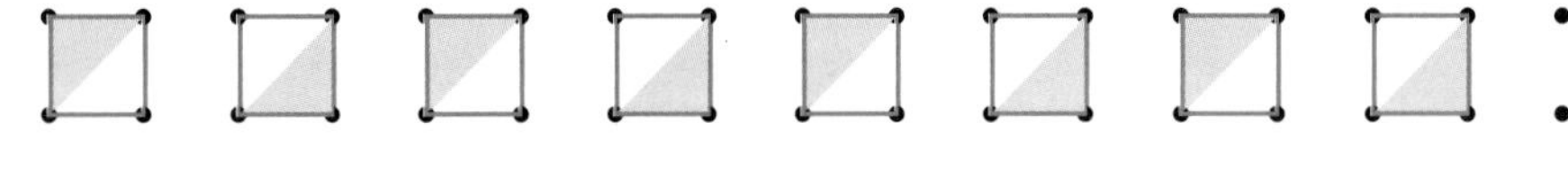

12. Jack drew the pattern below. Show his pattern another way using the letters A and B.

13. **Vocabulary Power** When something *repeats*, it happens again. Explain how this applies to the patterns in this lesson.

14. **REASONING** Mr. Griffin is teaching a sound pattern to his class. The pattern unit is *clap, clap, snap*. What will the eleventh sound be? Explain.

15. **Write a problem** in which a pattern has a missing part. Explain how you know what is missing in the pattern.

16. **MULTISTEP** Four students are working on art projects. There are 3 bags of markers with 8 markers in each bag. Can they share all of the markers equally? Explain.

17. **MULTISTEP** Kelly had a $5 bill, two $1 bills, and three quarters. She bought a snack for $1.35 and a book for $4.55. How much money did Kelly have left?

Maintain Skills

Write the time.

18. 

19. 

Write <, >, or = for each ●.

20. 34 ● 56

21. 87 ● 49

22. 24 ● 72

CRCT Test Prep

23. M3M1. Karson's play began at 6:30 P.M. It lasted 45 minutes. At what time did the play end? (p. 112)

A. 5:45 P.M.
B. 7:00 P.M.
C. 7:15 P.M.
D. 7:30 P.M.

24. M3N4.f. The library ordered six copies of a book for $54. How much did each book cost? (p. 238)

A. $6
B. $7
C. $8
D. $9

Problem Solving Thinker's Corner

VISUAL THINKING

MATERIALS: connecting cubes, grid paper, crayons

Patterns can be made by turning figures. The pattern below is of a figure moving clockwise.

 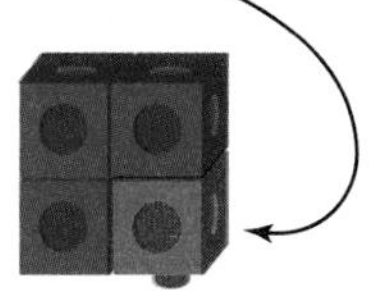   

1. Make a figure using three colors of connecting cubes. On grid paper, draw a pattern in which the figure moves clockwise.

2. Use the figure you made in Exercise 1. On grid paper, draw a pattern in which the figure moves counterclockwise.

LESSON 2

Visual Patterns

M3A1.a. Describe and extend numeric and geometric patterns. *also* M3P3., M3P3.a., M3P3.b., M3P3.c., M3P3.d.

Learn

DESCRIBE IT! A rule can be used to describe a pattern. Look at this pattern made with cubes. How are the figures related?

The number of cubes increases by 1 from one figure to the next. *Add 1 cube to the stack* is a rule that describes the pattern.

- What will the next two figures be?

Look at the pattern on grid paper. What rule describes this pattern?

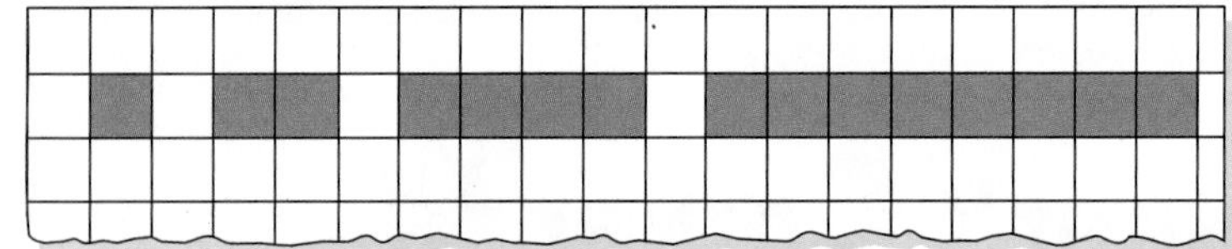

Look at the figures:

1st figure—1 square
2nd figure—2 squares
3rd figure—4 squares
4th figure—8 squares

Each figure has twice as many squares as the figure before it. So, a rule for this pattern is *multiply the number of squares in a row by 2.*

Quick Review

Skip-count to complete.

1. 2, 4, 6, 8, ■
2. 1, 3, 5, 7, 9, ■
3. 4, 8, 12, 16, ■
4. 3, 6, 9, 12, ■
5. 5, 10, 15, 20, ■

Check

1. **Explain** how to find a rule for the dot pattern.

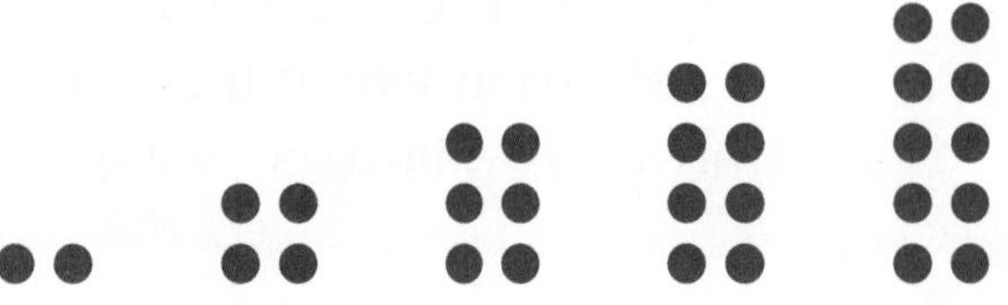

Write a rule for each pattern.

2.    

3. 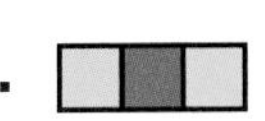 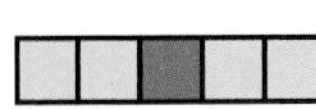 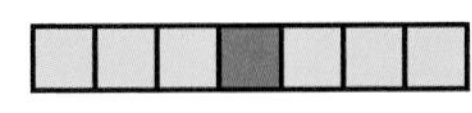

Practice and Problem Solving

Extra Practice, page 380, Set B

Write a rule for each pattern.

4.   

5.  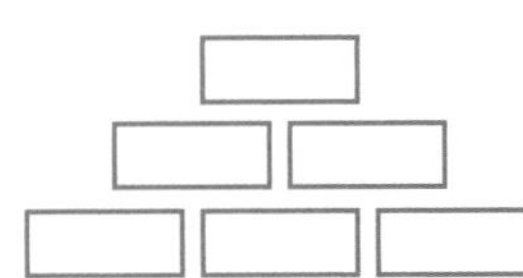 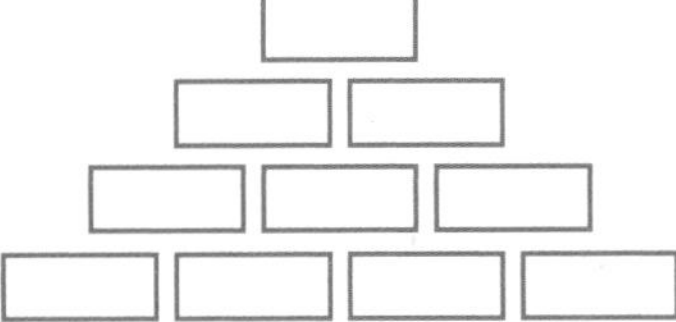

For 6–7, use the tile pattern below.

  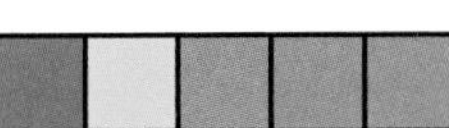 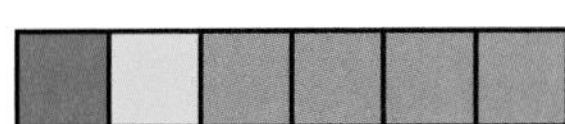

6. What is a rule for the pattern?

7. Describe the next figure in the pattern.

8. **What's the Question?** Ellen has 250 centimeters of red yarn, 510 centimeters of purple yarn, and 120 centimeters of white yarn. The answer is 390 centimeters.

9. **Write About It** Patterns are found in many places. Describe one pattern that you see at school, and one pattern that you see at home.

Maintain Skills

Find each sum.

10. $256 + 188$

11. $349 + 207$

12. $472 + 135$

13. $508 + 364$

CRCT Test Prep

14. M3M1. Jake worked on the computer from 11:30 A.M. to 12:15 P.M. How long did he work on the computer? (p. 112)

A. 50 minutes
B. 45 minutes
C. 40 minutes
D. 35 minutes

LESSON 

3 Number Patterns

M3A1.a. Describe and extend numeric and geometric patterns. *also* M3P3.a., M3P3.b., M3P3.c., M3P3.d., M3P4., M3P4.c.

Learn

NAME THE CHANGE Miss Hart's students made number patterns. How did the numbers change in Derek's pattern? What rule did he use?

Derek
7, 11, 15, 19, 23, 27

7 11 15 19 23 27

+4 +4 +4 +4 +4

The numbers increased by 4. So, Derek used the rule *add 4*.

- Predict the next three numbers in Derek's pattern.

The rule for Nina's pattern is *subtract 3*. What number is missing?

Nina
52, 49, 46, 43, 40, ■, 34

Use the rule to find the missing number.

Since $40 - 3 = 37$, the missing number is 37.

Quick Review

Skip-count by fives to complete.

1. 3, 8, 13, ■, ■
2. 15, 20, 25, ■, ■
3. 12, 17, 22, ■, ■
4. 21, 26, 31, ■, ■
5. 44, 49, 54, ■, ■

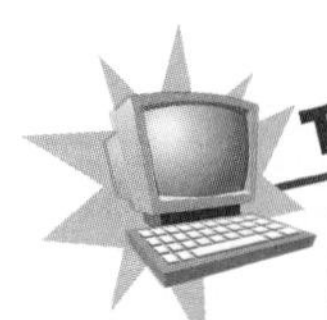

Technology Link

More Practice: Harcourt Mega Math The Number Games, *Tiny's Think Tank*, Level K

Check

1. **Explain** the number pattern on the doors below.

Write a rule for each pattern.

2. 16, 21, 26, 31, 36, 41
3. 52, 50, 48, 46, 44, 42
4. 123, 113, 103, 93, 83, 73
5. 18, 26, 34, 42, 50, 58

Practice and Problem Solving

Extra Practice, page 380, Set C

Write a rule for each pattern.

6. 255, 270, 285, 300, 315, 330
7. 33, 36, 39, 42, 45, 48
8. 54, 63, 72, 81, 90, 99
9. 74, 71, 68, 65, 62, 59

Write a rule for each pattern. Then find the missing numbers.

10. 24, 28, 32, 36, 40, ■, 48, 52, ■, ■
11. 105, 102, 99, 96, ■, ■, 87, 84, 81, ■
12. 937, 917, 897, 877, ■, ■, 817, ■
13. 336, 348, 360, 372, 384, ■, 408, ■, ■

14. There are 2 stacks of boxes with 5 boxes in each stack. If there are 10 books in each box, how many books are there in all?

15. **Write a problem** about a number pattern. Exchange problems with a classmate and solve.

16. **What's the Error?** Tom wrote this pattern:

    8, 25, 42, 59, 75

    He said the rule was *add 17*. Describe his error.

17. **FAST FACT** • SOCIAL STUDIES Games like checkers are played around the world. The pattern on a United States checkerboard has 8 rows of 8 equal-sized squares. How many of these squares are there in all?

Maintain Skills

Write the amount.

18. 

19.   

CRCT Test Prep

20. M3N2.c. Alesha has a journal with 200 pages in it. Forty-three pages are blank. How many pages have been written on? (p. 74)

A. 167
B. 157
C. 143
D. 67

LESSON 4

Problem Solving Strategy
Look for a Pattern

M3A1.a. Describe and extend numeric and geometric patterns.
also **M3P1.a., M3P1.b., M3P1.c., M3P1.d., M3P3.a., M3P3.b., M3P3.c., M3P3.d., M3P4.a., M3P4.b.**

Quick Review

1. 245 + ■ = 253
2. 1,862 + ■ = 1,897
3. 409 + ■ = 422
4. 3,247 + ■ = 3,254
5. 716 + ■ = 727

PROBLEM Mr. Jenson needs to deliver a computer to 2364 Sunshine Circle. He cannot see all of the house numbers. To which house should Mr. Jenson deliver the computer? Use the map to help.

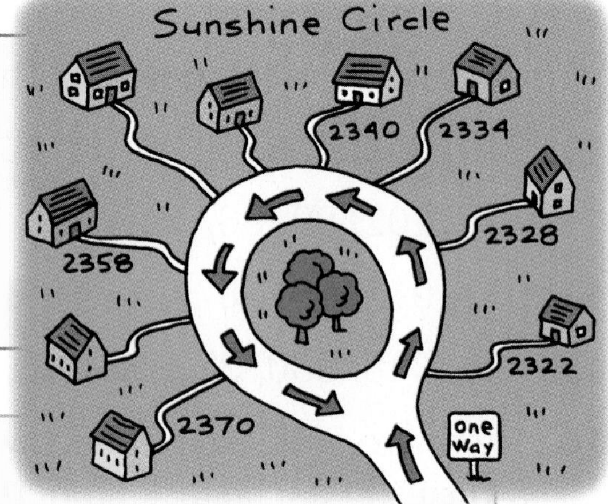

UNDERSTAND

- What are you asked to find?
- What information will you use?
- Is there any information you will not use?

PLAN

- What strategy can you use to solve the problem?

You can *look for a pattern*.

SOLVE

- How can you use the pattern to solve the problem?

Find the rule for the order of the house numbers. Then use the rule to find the missing house numbers.

2322 2328 2334 2340 ■ ■ 2358 ■ 2370

+6 +6 +6

The house numbers increase by 6. The missing house numbers are 2346, 2352, and 2364. The eighth house is numbered 2364. So, Mr. Jenson should deliver the computer to the eighth house on Sunshine Circle.

CHECK

- Look back. How can you check your answer?

Problem Solving Practice

Use *look for a pattern* to solve.

1. **What if** the numbers below were the house numbers that Mr. Jenson saw on Sunshine Circle? Which house would be numbered 2364? What rule describes the pattern?

   2344, 2348, 2352, 2356, ■, ■, 2368, ■, 2376

2. Miss Kane gave her students this pattern. What numbers are missing?

   582, 587, 592, 597, ■, 607, ■

Strategies

Act It Out or Use Objects
Make a Picture or Diagram
Guess and Check
Use or Look for a Pattern
Use Logical Reasoning

Problem Solving

Lisa wrote the following pattern.

142, 139, 136, 133, ■, 127, ■

3. Which is a rule for Lisa's pattern?

   A Add 4.
   B Subtract 3.
   C Add 2.
   D Subtract 4.

4. What numbers are missing in Lisa's pattern?

   F 136, 132
   G 132, 125
   H 130, 124
   J 131, 124

Mixed Strategy Practice

USE DATA For 5–8, use the price list.

5. **MULTISTEP** Mrs. Davis bought two puzzles. She gave the clerk a $20 bill. Her change was $6.25. What puzzles did she buy?

6. **MULTISTEP** José bought 2 large puzzles and 1 medium puzzle. Luke bought 2 medium puzzles and 1 extra large puzzle. Who spent more? Explain.

7. Karen has $9.00 to spend. She wants to buy two puzzles. Which two puzzles could she buy?

THE PUZZLE SHOP

Puzzle Size	Price
Small	$3.00
Medium	$5.25
Large	$6.75
Extra Large	$8.50

8. **MULTISTEP** Vern has a $5 bill and 3 dimes. How much more money does he need to buy a large puzzle?

Extra Practice

Set A (pp. 370–373)

Name the pattern unit for each.

1.

2.

Draw the next two shapes in each pattern.

3. ? ?

4. ? ?

Set B (pp. 374–375)

Write a rule for each pattern.

1.

2.

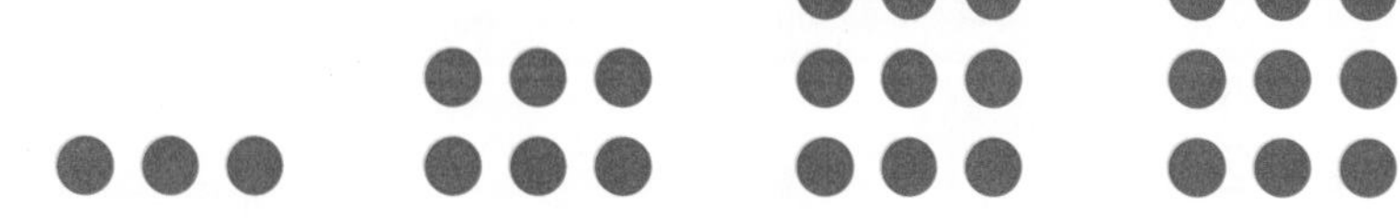

Set C (pp. 376–377)

Write a rule for each pattern.

1. 12, 15, 18, 21, 24, 27
2. 49, 47, 45, 43, 41, 39
3. 235, 241, 247, 253, 259, 265
4. 98, 108, 118, 128, 138, 148

Write a rule for each pattern. Then find the missing numbers.

5. 305, 302, 299, 296, ■, 290, ■, ■
6. 719, 723, 727, 731, ■, ■, 743, ■
7. 89, 98, 107, 116, ■, 134, ■, ■

Review/Test

CHECK VOCABULARY

Choose the best term from the box.

Vocabulary
pattern unit
dividend

1. The part of a pattern that repeats is called the ? . (p. 370)

CHECK SKILLS

Draw the next two shapes in each pattern. (pp. 370–373)

2. □ ◺ □ ◺ □ ◺ □ ◺ ? ?

3. □ □ ○ □ □ ○ □ □ ○ □ □ ○ ? ?

Write a rule for each pattern. (pp. 374–375)

4. ● ●● ●●● ●●●●
   ● ●● ●●● ●●●●

5. ★ ★★★ ★★★★★ ★★★★★★★

Write a rule for each pattern. (pp. 376–377)

6. 49, 51, 53, 55, 57, 59
7. 99, 90, 81, 72, 63, 54
8. 88, 98, 108, 118, 128, 138
9. 340, 325, 310, 295, 280, 265

CHECK PROBLEM SOLVING

Solve. (pp. 378–379)

10. The number is missing from the fifth mailbox. Find a rule for the pattern. What is the missing number?

Chapter CRCT Test Prep

ALGEBRA

1. M3A1.a. Which are the next two shapes in this pattern?

□□△□□△□□△□ ? ?

A. □△

B. △△

C. □□

D. △□

2. M3A1.a. Jan is making a bracelet. She strings the beads according to this pattern.

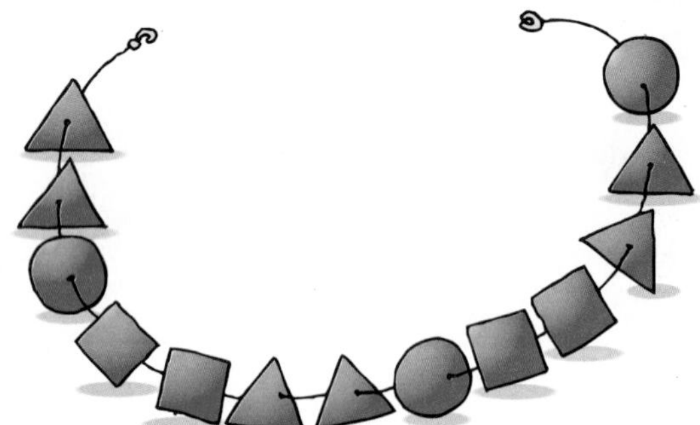

What are the next three beads that she will use?

A. triangle, triangle, circle

B. circle, square, square

C. square, square, triangle

D. square, circle, triangle

ALGEBRA

3. M3A1.a. Which shape is missing from this pattern?

○▭△ ○▭△ ○▭△ ○ ? △

A. ▭

B. □

C. ○

D. △

4. M3A1.a. What are the next two digits in this pattern?

111, 112, 113, 114, 1□□

A. 51

B. 15

C. 56

D. 61

5. M3A1.a. Which number will be next in this pattern?

5, 10, 15, 20, 25, □

A. 20

B. 26

C. 28

D. 30

Cumulative CRCT Test Prep

NUMBERS AND OPERATIONS

6. M3N3.b. Which of the following has the same value as 9×6?

A. $(5 + 6) \times (4 + 6)$

B. $(5 \times 6) + (4 \times 6)$

C. $(5 \times 6) \times (4 \times 6)$

D. $(9 \times 9) + (6 \times 6)$

Use the table below to answer question 7.

×	3	4	5	6	7
9	27	36	□	54	63

7. M3N3.b. Which is the missing product in the table?

A. 39

B. 45

C. 48

D. 49

8. M3N2.c. Tyler read 528 pages over the summer. Liz read 708 pages. How many more pages did Liz read during the summer than Tyler?

A. 140

B. 160

C. 180

D. 200

MEASUREMENT

9. M3M1. Jake has a trumpet lesson at 1:15 P.M. The lesson lasts 1 hour. At what time will Jake be finished with his lesson?

A. 12:15 P.M.

B. 1:30 P.M.

C. 1:45 P.M.

D. 2:15 P.M.

10. M3M2.c. Which units of measure would be the most appropriate to determine the length of a dollar bill?

A. inches

B. feet

C. yards

D. miles

11. M3M3.b. Mrs. Lang wants to put a fence around her square flower garden. Each side of the garden is 4 feet long. How many feet of fencing does she need?

A. 4 feet

B. 8 feet

C. 12 feet

D. 16 feet

GPS/CRCT Vocabulary

ELA3R2 The student acquires and uses grade-level words to communicate effectively. *also* **ELA3R3.b., ELA3R3.h., ELA3R3.r., M3P4.b.**

VOCABULARY

line	**point**
ray	**angle**
circle	**radius**
diameter	**center**
perimeter	**area**
equilateral triangle	
isosceles triangle	
scalene triangle	

VOCABULARY CROSSWORD

MATERIALS *For each student* Unit 6 *Vocabulary Crossword* puzzle

Use the clues to fill in the squares of the crossword puzzle.

- ACROSS
  1. a line segment from a point on a circle to its center
  3. a straight path extending in both directions with no endpoints
  5. a figure formed by two rays or line segments that share an endpoint
  6. an exact position or location
- DOWN
  2. the number of square units needed to cover a flat surface
  4. a point in the middle of a circle that is the same distance from anywhere on the circle

MATH WORD WORK

MATERIALS *For each student* Unit 6 *Math Word Work* puzzle

- Find and circle the terms listed below.

line	**angle**
point	**perimeter**
ray	**area**

L I N E O D S U J P
S I A T T I R W E E
M V E K J V A A Q R
E I I P O I N T U I
R D D G P S G I O M
L E R A Y O L C E E
E N A R Y R E P D T
X D M E L H S D J E
D E Q A A T I O E R
V A R I F O C E T D

WORDS IN ACTION

MATERIALS *For each pair* 4 index cards, markers

- Work with a partner to make a set of vocabulary cards for the terms shown at the right. Write each term on an index card. Place the cards face down on the table.
- Take turns turning over a vocabulary card and drawing a picture of the term on the card.
- Continue until you and your partner have made drawings of all the terms.

circle

radius

center

diameter

GRID GAME

MATERIALS *For each group* definition cards, grid paper, counters

- Look at the terms in the list at the right. Write these terms randomly on your grid, one term in each box. Fill in all the boxes. You will use each word twice.
- Choose one player to be the "caller". The caller mixes up the definition cards, chooses one, and reads it aloud. Each player puts a counter on the word that matches the definition read. Each player can place one counter on his or her grid for each turn.
- The definition card goes back in the pile. Play until someone gets 4 counters in a row, either up and down, across, or diagonally.

Word List
line
point
ray
angle
perimeter
area
diameter
radius

Georgia Tasks

M3G1.a. Draw and classify previously learned fundamental geometric figures as well as scalene, isosceles, and equilateral triangles. *also* **M3A1.a., M3P4.c., M3P5.a., M3P5.b., M3P5.c.**

SS3H1.a. Identify the influence of Greek architecture, law, and the Olympic games on the present.

Task A

GREEK SHAPES

The Old Governor's Mansion in Milledgeville, Georgia, was built in 1838 as a home for the governor. Columns like the ones used here are similar to the columns ancient Greeks used in their buildings.

a. What geometric shapes can you find in the Old Governor's Mansion? Describe each shape by the number of edges and vertices it has.

b. Draw a picture of the front of your school. Describe the shapes you use.

Task B

ADD IT UP!

Martina used base-ten blocks to make a pattern puzzle for her classmates to solve. She placed a piece of paper over the fourth group of blocks.

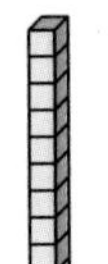 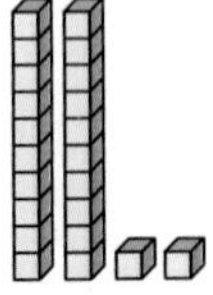 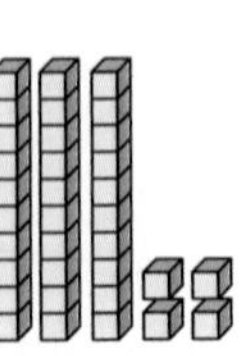 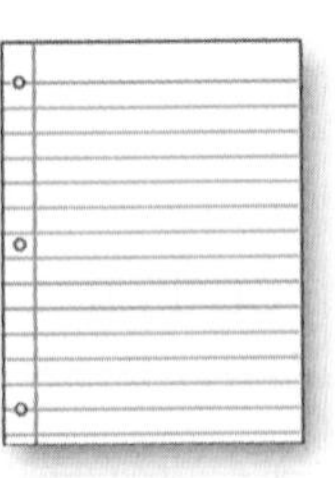 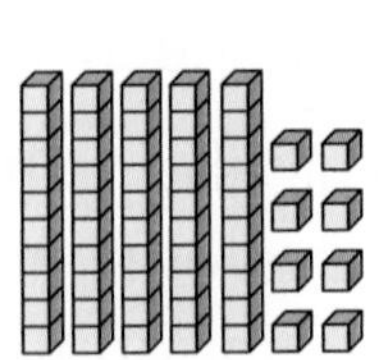

a. Draw a picture of the missing group of blocks. What is a rule for Martina's block pattern?

b. Write a number pattern that shows Martina's pattern. What is a rule for this number pattern?

Maintain/Preview

Maintain

Write as many names for each polygon as you can.

1. 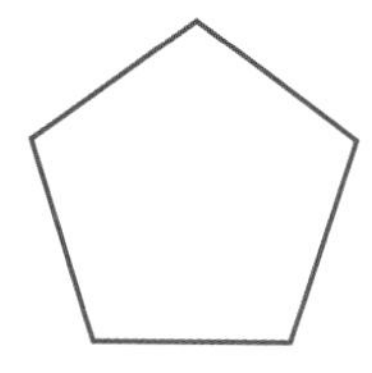

2. 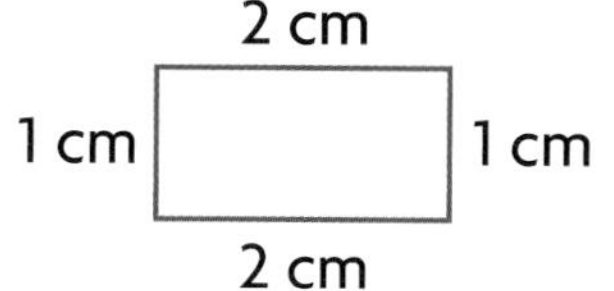

3. 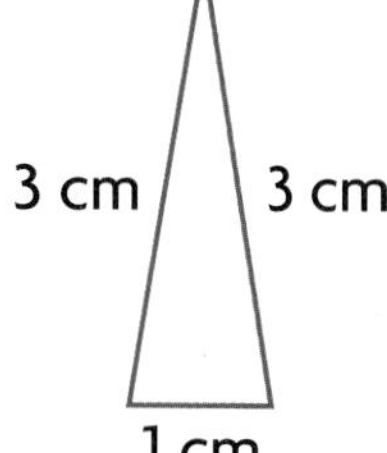

4. 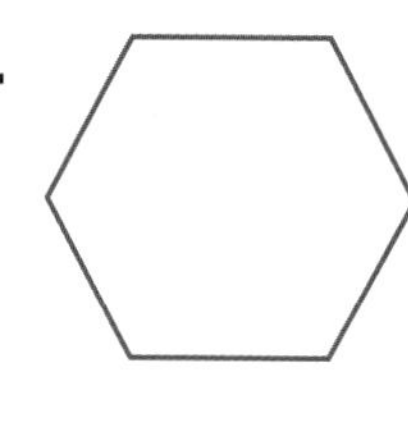

Name each solid figure.

5. 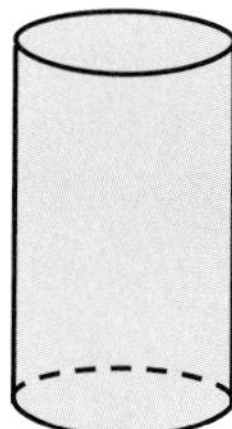

6. 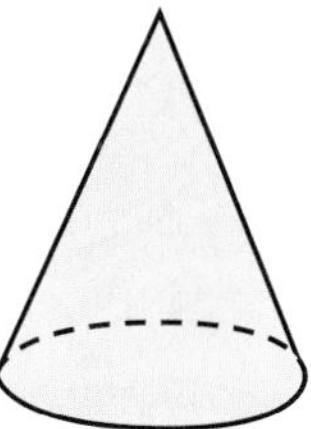

7. 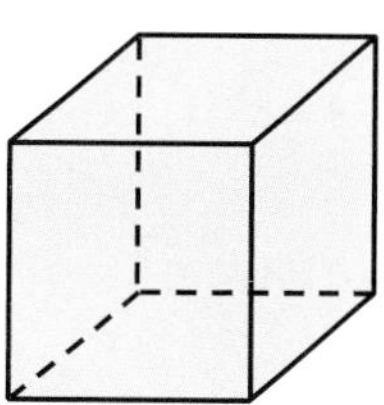

8. 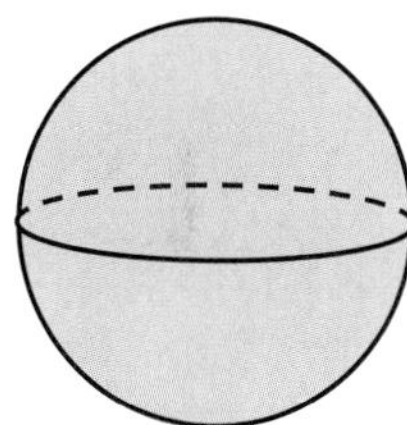

Find the perimeter and area of each figure.

9. 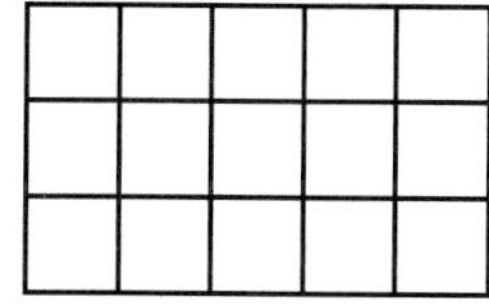

10. 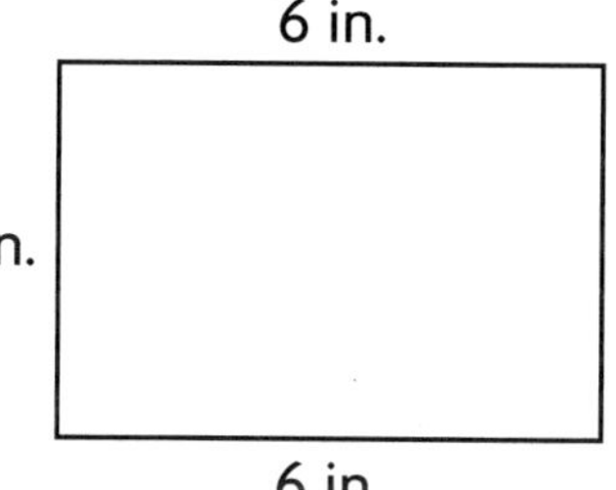

11. 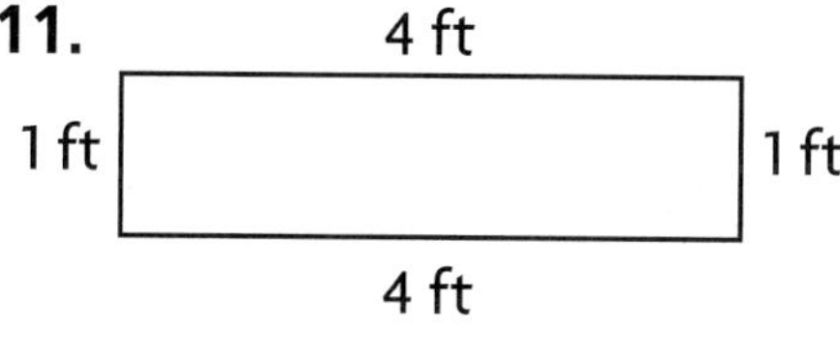

12. **REASONING** Anna drew a circle with a diameter that is 8 centimeters long. What is the length of the radius? Explain how you know.

13. Geoff wrote the number pattern below. What two numbers should Geoff write next?

    85, 74, 63, 52

Preview

Write a fraction for the shaded part.

1. 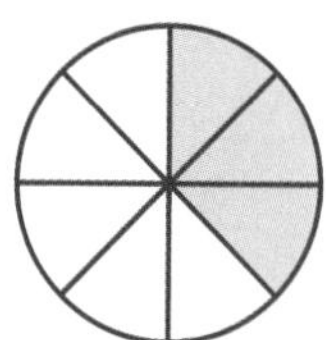

2. 

3. 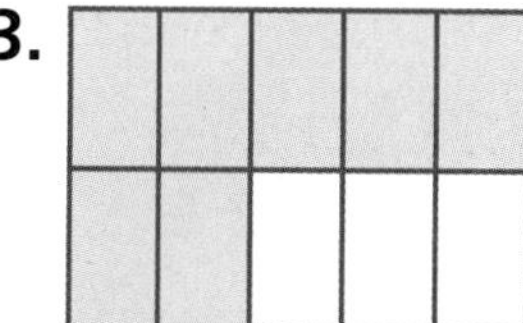

CHAPTER 20 Fractions

FAST FACT • SCIENCE There are thousands of different kinds of insects in the world. Some are very large. Others are so small that we can't even see them.

INVESTIGATION The table shows some insects and their sizes. Which insect is the smallest? Which is the largest? How could you use counters to find the number of ants that would have to line up to equal the length of the grasshopper?

Using Data

SIZES OF INSECTS

Insect	Length
Ant	$\frac{1}{4}$ inch
Mosquito	$\frac{1}{8}$ inch
Grasshopper	2 inches
Goliath beetle	4 inches

African Goliath beetle

Use this page to help you review and remember important skills needed for Chapter 20.

MODEL PARTS OF A WHOLE

Write how many equal parts make up the whole figure. Then write how many parts are shaded.

1. 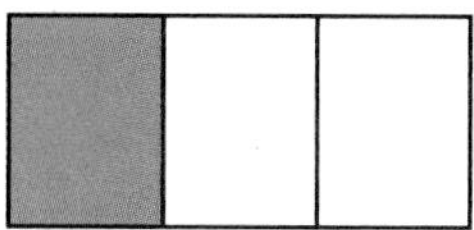

2. 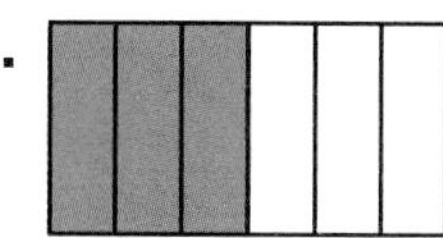

3. 

4. 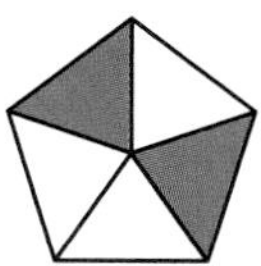

5. 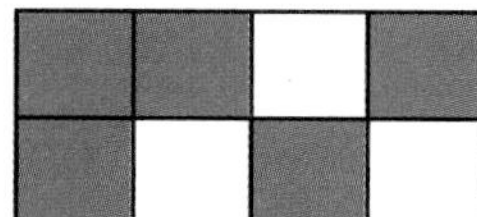

6. 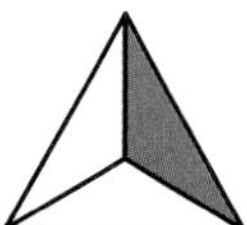

MODEL PARTS OF A GROUP

Write the number in each group. Then write the number in each group that is green.

7. 

8. 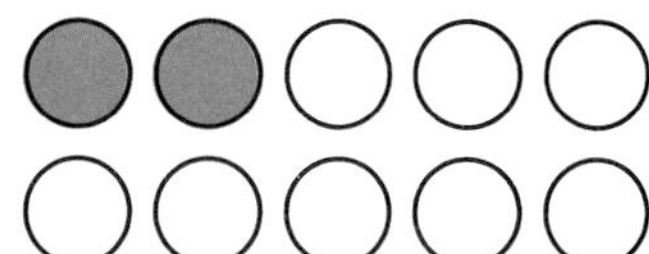

9. 

10. 

11. 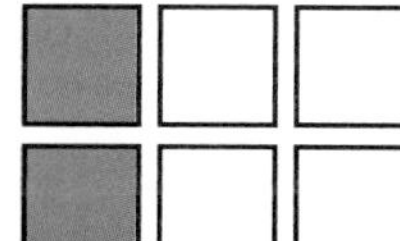

12. 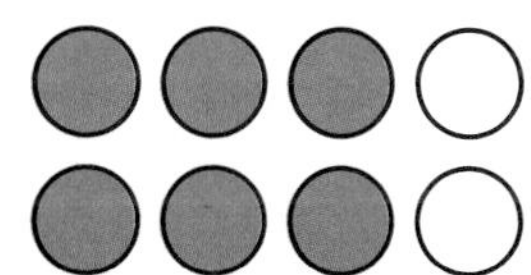

VOCABULARY POWER

REVIEW

fourth [fôrth] *noun*

When there are four equal-sized pieces in one whole, each piece is called one *fourth*. List some things that could be divided into fourths.

PREVIEW

fraction

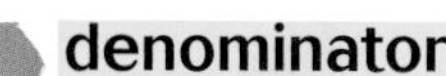

denominator

numerator

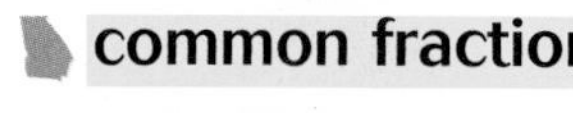

common fraction

like fractions

www.harcourtschool.com/mathglossary

LESSON 1

Parts of a Whole

M3N5.d. Know and use decimals and common fractions to represent the size of parts created by equal divisions of a whole. *also* **M3N5.b.**

Quick Review

Find a rule and the next number in the pattern.

1. 2, 4, 6, 8, ■
2. 12, 11, 10, 9, ■
3. 3, 6, 9, 12, ■
4. 11, 9, 7, 5, ■
5. 4, 8, 12, 16, ■

VOCABULARY

fraction **denominator**
numerator **common fraction**

Learn

ALL TOGETHER A number that names part of a whole is called a **fraction**.

What fraction of this pizza has sausage?

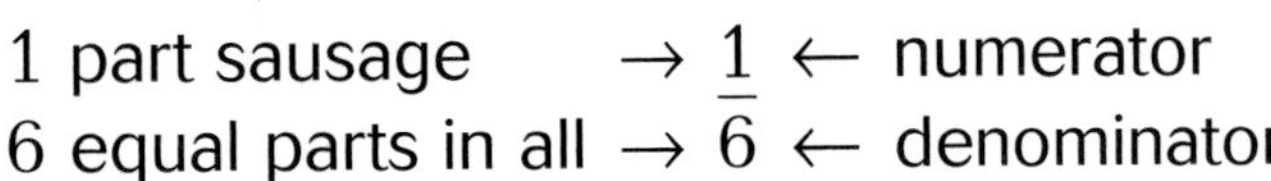

1 part sausage → 1 ← numerator
6 equal parts in all → 6 ← denominator

Read: one sixth **Write:** $\frac{1}{6}$

one part out of six equal parts
1 divided by 6

So, $\frac{1}{6}$ of the pizza has sausage.

The **numerator** tells how many parts are being counted.

The **denominator** tells how many equal parts are in the whole.

A **common fraction** is a fraction that has a whole number for the numerator and the denominator.

- What fraction of the pizza does *not* have sausage? Explain how you know.

These fraction bars show how a whole can be divided into sixths, or six equal parts.

Examples

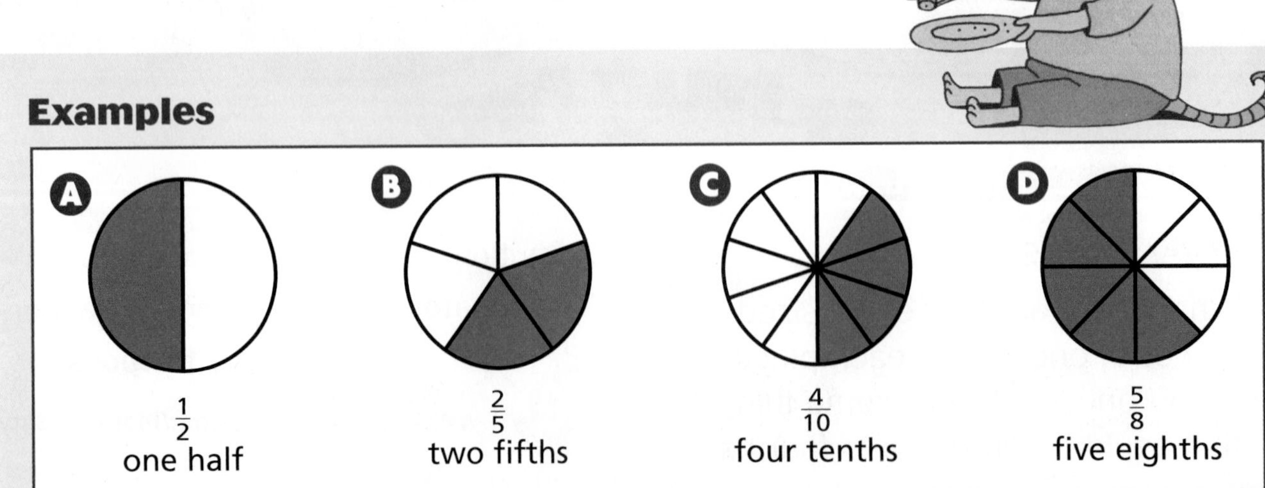

A: $\frac{1}{2}$ one half

B: $\frac{2}{5}$ two fifths

C: $\frac{4}{10}$ four tenths

D: $\frac{5}{8}$ five eighths

Counting Equal Parts

You can count equal parts, such as sixths, to make one whole.

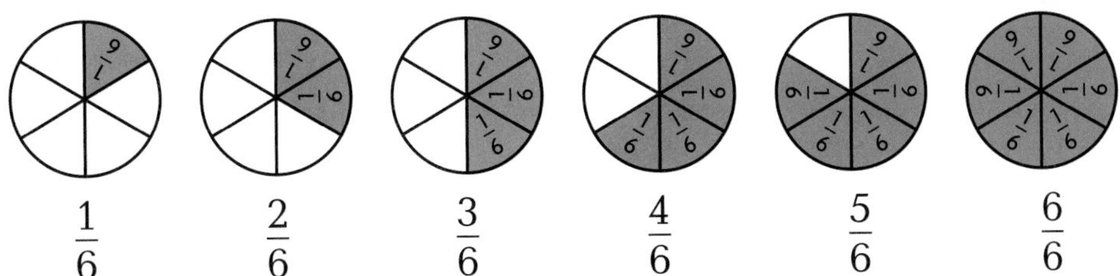

$\frac{6}{6}$ = one whole, or 1

MATH IDEA A number line can show parts of one whole.

The part on a number line from 0 to 1 shows one whole. The line can be divided into any number of equal parts.

This number line is divided into sixths.

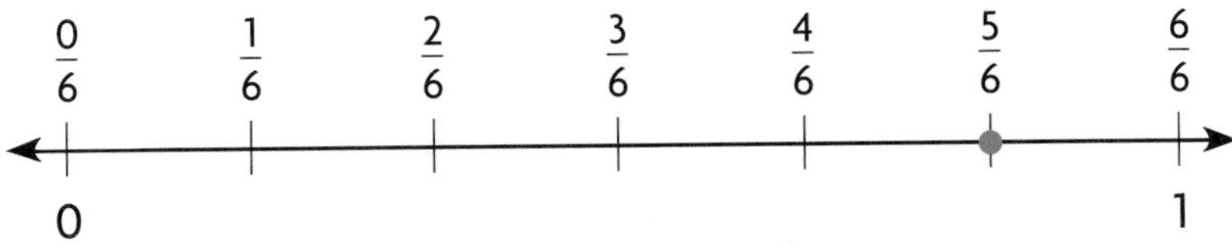

The point shows the location of $\frac{5}{6}$.

Examples

A This number line is divided into thirds.

$\frac{0}{3}$ $\frac{1}{3}$ $\frac{2}{3}$ $\frac{3}{3}$

0 1

The point shows the location of $\frac{1}{3}$.

B This number line is divided into fourths.

$\frac{0}{4}$ $\frac{1}{4}$ $\frac{2}{4}$ $\frac{3}{4}$ $\frac{4}{4}$

0 1

The point shows the location of $\frac{3}{4}$.

Check

1. Write how to count by eighths to make one whole.

Write a fraction in numbers and in words that names the shaded part.

2.

3. 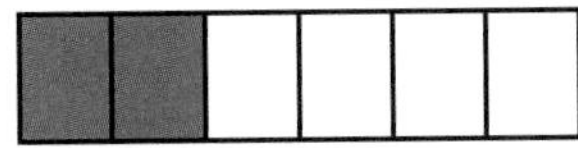

4. 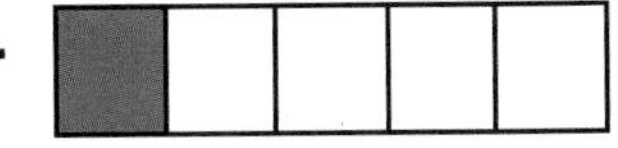

LESSON CONTINUES

Practice and Problem Solving

Extra Practice, page 408, Set A

Write a fraction in numbers and in words that names the shaded part.

5. 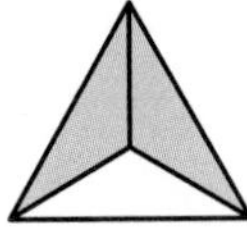

6. 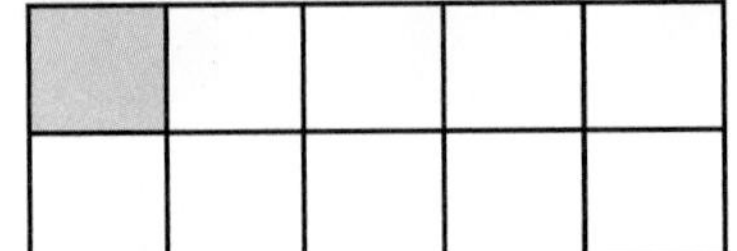

7. 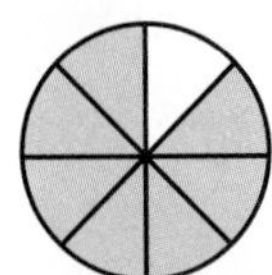

8. 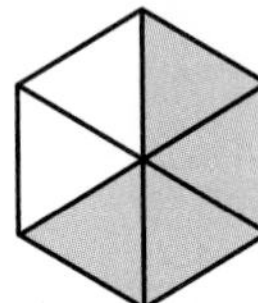

9. 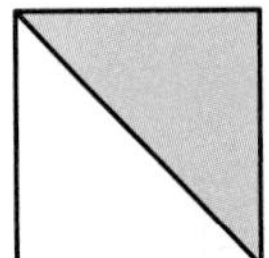

10. 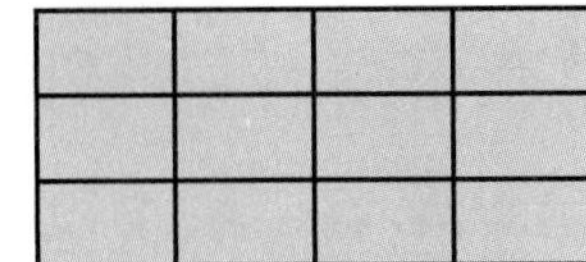

Make a model of each, using fraction circle pieces. Then write the fraction, using numbers.

11. one fourth
12. two out of two
13. six eighths
14. one divided by three
15. three fifths
16. five out of ten

Write a fraction to describe the part of each figure that is shaded.

17. 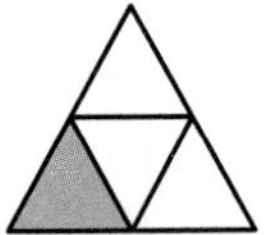 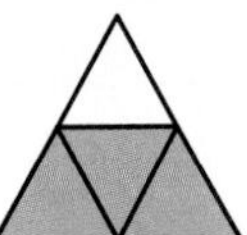 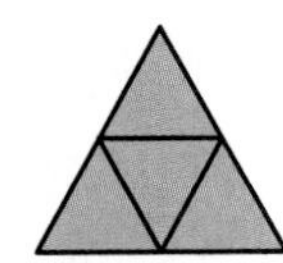

18. 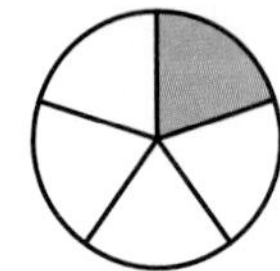 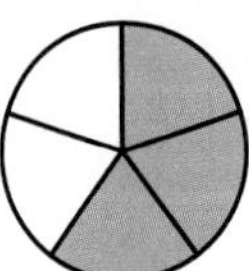 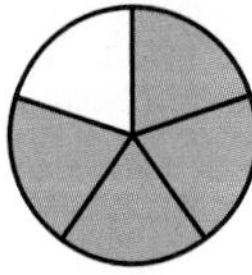 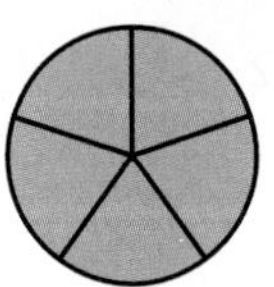

ALGEBRA **Write a fraction that names the point for each letter on the number line.**

19. 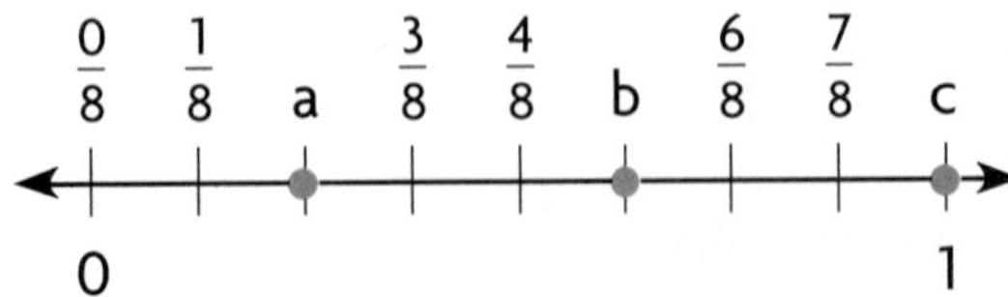

20. 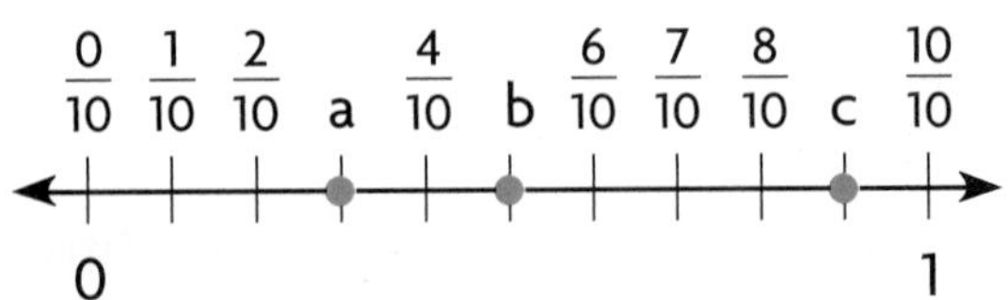

21. **REASONING** There are two pizzas the same size. One is cut into 6 equal pieces. The other is cut into 8 equal pieces. Which pizza has smaller pieces? Explain.

22. **What's the Error?** Lydia said that the fraction $\frac{6}{4}$ names the shaded part of the circle. Explain her error.

23. Suppose you and 4 friends shared equal pieces of a pie. Use fraction circle pieces to model the amount of pie for two people.

24. **REASONING** Mrs. Thomas wants to give $\frac{1}{6}$ of a pie to each visitor. How many whole pies will she need for 6 visitors? 12 visitors?

Maintain Skills

Write the time.

25.

26.

27.

28.

CRCT Test Prep

29. M3G1.b. Which polygon has 4 sides and 4 angles? (p. 310)

A. triangle
B. quadrilateral
C. pentagon
D. hexagon

30. M3N2.c. Larry bought a book for $6.75. He paid with a $10 bill. How much change did he get? (p. 98)

A. $2.25
B. $3.25
C. $4.25
D. $5.25

Problem Solving LINKUP . . . to Social Studies

These alphabet flags are used on ships to send messages in code. For example, if a ship flies the flag for the letter P, that ship is about to sail out of the harbor. Ships carry books that explain the codes in different languages.

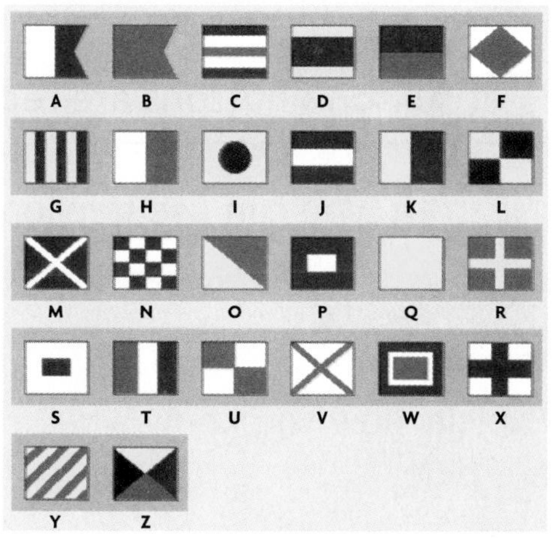

USE DATA For 1–4, use the flags.

1. Look at the flag for the letter G. What fraction names the part of the flag that is yellow?

2. Look at all of the flags. Which of them are divided into four equal parts, or fourths?

3. Look at the flag for the letter N. Into how many equal parts is the flag divided?

4. Write a fraction that names one part of each of these flags: L, O, and T.

LESSON 2

Parts of a Group

M3N5.d. Know and use decimals and common fractions to represent the size of parts created by equal divisions of a whole. *also* **M3P3.a., M3P3.b., M3P3.c., M3P3.d.**

Quick Review

Write the next fraction in the counting pattern.

1. $\frac{0}{3}, \frac{1}{3}, \frac{2}{3}, ■$
2. $\frac{1}{5}, \frac{2}{5}, \frac{3}{5}, ■$
3. $\frac{2}{6}, \frac{3}{6}, \frac{4}{6}, ■$
4. $\frac{3}{8}, \frac{4}{8}, \frac{5}{8}, ■$
5. $\frac{3}{10}, \frac{4}{10}, \frac{5}{10}, ■$

Learn

BUYING BUTTONS Allison and Marsha each bought some buttons at the craft store.

What fraction of Allison's buttons are red?

What fraction of Marsha's buttons are red?

Allison's buttons

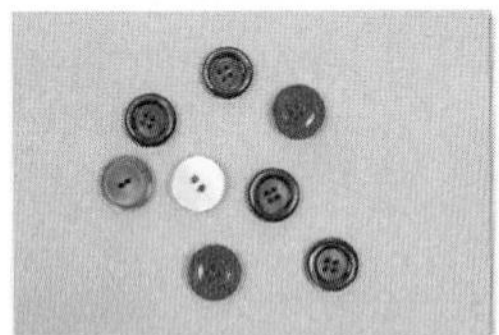

number of red buttons → 2 ← numerator
total buttons → 8 ← denominator

Read: two eighths, or two out of eight

Write: $\frac{2}{8}$

So, $\frac{2}{8}$ of Allison's buttons are red.

Marsha's buttons

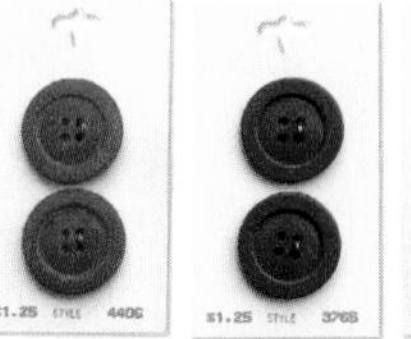

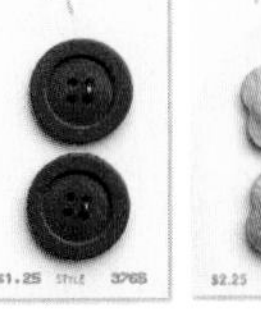

sets of red buttons → 1 ← numerator
total number of sets → 3 ← denominator

Read: one third, or one out of three

Write: $\frac{1}{3}$

So, $\frac{1}{3}$ of Marsha's buttons are red.

MATH IDEA You can use fractions to show parts of a group.

Check

1. **Explain** how you know what fraction of Allison's buttons are blue.

Write a fraction that names the part of each group that is yellow.

2. 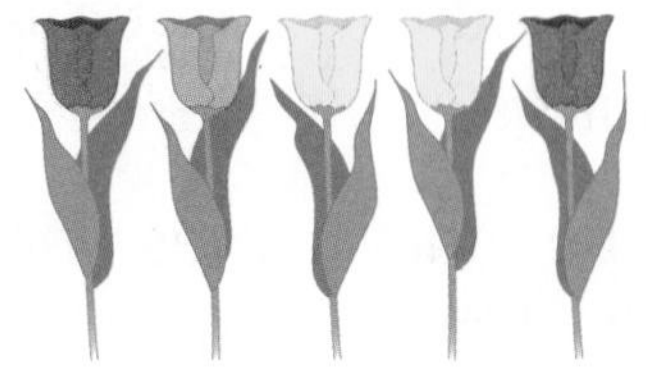

3. 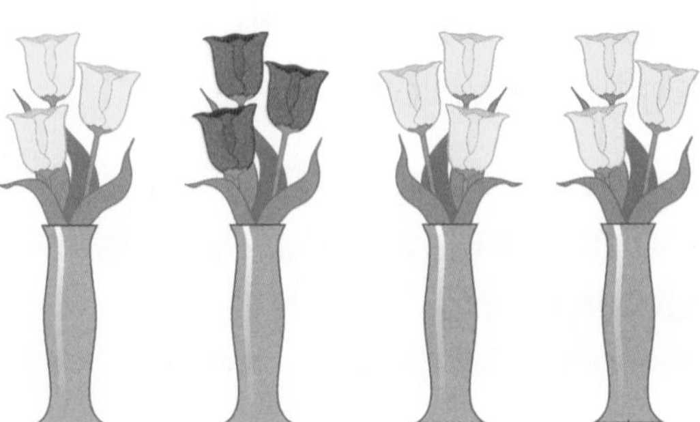

Practice and Problem Solving

Extra Practice, page 408, Set B

For 4–7, write a fraction that names the part of each group that is striped.

4. 

5. 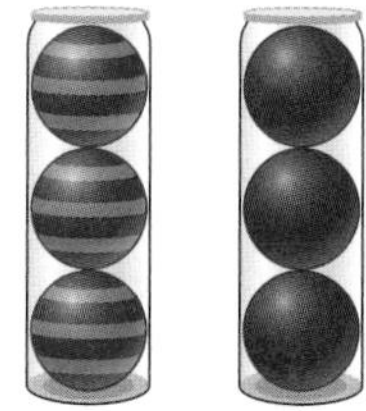

6. 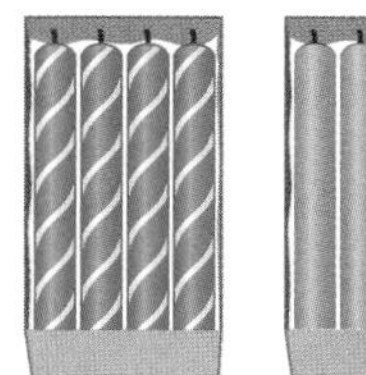 

7. 

8. Draw 8 squares. Circle $\frac{2}{8}$ of them.

9. Draw 6 triangles. Circle $\frac{5}{6}$ of them.

10. Draw 10 rectangles. Circle $\frac{3}{10}$ of them.

Use a pattern to complete the table.

11.	Model	○○○○○	●○○○○	■	●●●○○	●●●●○	●●●●●
12.	Total number of parts	5	■	5	5	5	5
13.	Number of green parts	0	1	2	■	4	5
14.	Fraction of green parts	$\frac{0}{5}$	$\frac{1}{5}$	$\frac{2}{5}$	$\frac{3}{5}$	$\frac{4}{5}$	■

15. Debra has 12 ribbons. Of those ribbons, $\frac{1}{12}$ are red and $\frac{2}{12}$ are blue. The rest are yellow. How many yellow ribbons does she have?

16. **What's the Question?** Jonas has 4 blue tiles, 3 green tiles, and 1 yellow tile. The answer is $\frac{7}{8}$.

17. **Write a problem** in which a fraction is used to name part of a group. Tell what the numerator and denominator mean.

Maintain Skills

Find each sum or difference.

18. $\begin{array}{r} 25 \\ +77 \\ \hline \end{array}$ **19.** $\begin{array}{r} 59 \\ +43 \\ \hline \end{array}$ **20.** $\begin{array}{r} 82 \\ -29 \\ \hline \end{array}$

CRCT Test Prep

21. M3A1.c What number goes in the □? (p. 154)

$$7 \times \square = 21$$

A. 2 B. 3 C. 4 D. 14

LESSON 3

Add Fractions

M3N5.e. Understand the concept of addition and subtraction of decimals and common fractions with like denominators. *also* **M3N5.f., M3P2., M3P3.a., M3P3.b., M3P3.c., M3P3.d., M3P5.a., M3P5.b., M3P5.c.**

Quick Review

Name the fraction for the shaded part.

1\. 2. 3.

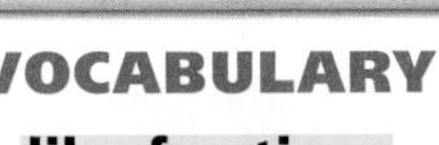

4\. 5.

VOCABULARY

like fractions

MATERIALS

fraction bars

Explore

Fractions that have the same denominator are called **like fractions**.

A fruit punch recipe says to add $\frac{2}{4}$ cup orange juice and $\frac{1}{4}$ cup pineapple juice. How much juice is needed altogether?

Remember

$\frac{1 \rightarrow \text{numerator}}{2 \rightarrow \text{denominator}}$

Activity

Use fraction bars to find $\frac{2}{4} + \frac{1}{4}$.

STEP 1

Line up two $\frac{1}{4}$ fraction bars under the bar for 1.

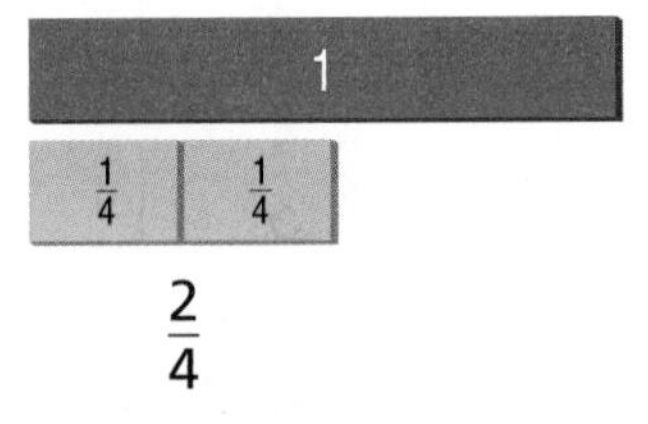

$\frac{2}{4}$

STEP 2

Add one more $\frac{1}{4}$ fraction bar.

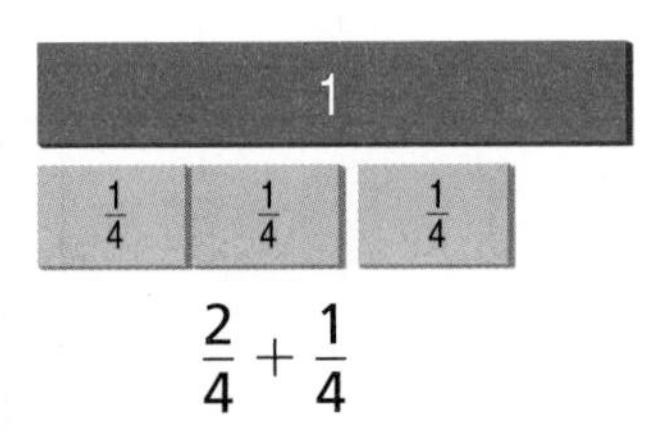

$\frac{2}{4} + \frac{1}{4}$

STEP 3

Count the number of $\frac{1}{4}$ fraction bars.

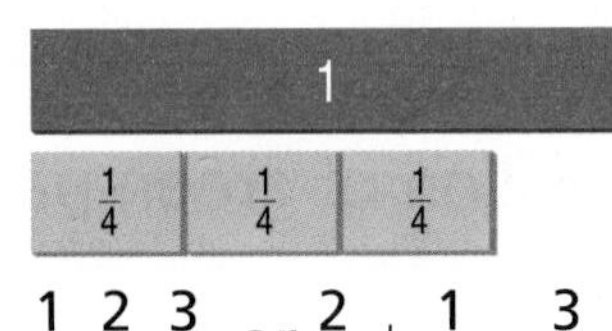

$\frac{1}{4}, \frac{2}{4}, \frac{3}{4}$, or $\frac{2}{4} + \frac{1}{4} = \frac{3}{4}$

So, the recipe calls for $\frac{3}{4}$ cup juice altogether.

- Why doesn't the denominator change when you find the sum?
- Explain how you could use fraction bars to find $\frac{1}{3} + \frac{1}{3}$.

Try It

Use fraction bars to find the sum.

a. $\frac{3}{6} + \frac{1}{6}$ **b.** $\frac{3}{5} + \frac{2}{5}$

Connect

Add like fractions by adding the numerators.

Example

Tom peeled an orange. It had 8 wedges. He ate 1 wedge, or $\frac{1}{8}$ of it. Then he ate 4 more wedges, or $\frac{4}{8}$ of it. What fraction did he eat in all?

Model

Add the number of $\frac{1}{8}$ wedges that Tom ate.

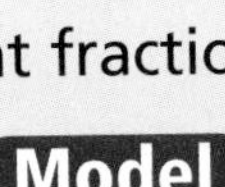

$\frac{1}{8} + \frac{4}{8}$

Record

1 wedge	+	4 wedges	=	5 wedges
↓		↓		↓
$\frac{1}{8}$	+	$\frac{4}{8}$	=	$\frac{5}{8}$

So, Tom ate $\frac{5}{8}$ of the orange.

MATH IDEA When you add *like* fractions, you add the numerators, and the denominators stay the same.

Practice and Problem Solving

Find the sum.

1. $\frac{1}{5} + \frac{2}{5} = ■$

2.  

$\frac{3}{8} + \frac{3}{8} = ■$

3. 

$\frac{1}{3} + \frac{1}{3} = ■$

Use fraction bars to find the sum.

4. $\frac{2}{5} + \frac{2}{5} = ■$
5. $\frac{1}{6} + \frac{4}{6} = ■$
6. $\frac{4}{10} + \frac{3}{10} = ■$
7. $\frac{3}{8} + \frac{2}{8} = ■$

8. Kris has 6 plums and 2 apples. She buys 2 more apples. What fraction of the fruit are apples?

9. A recipe calls for $\frac{1}{4}$ cup sugar. Celia wants to double the recipe. How much sugar will she need?

Maintain Skills

10. Write the product.

$3 \times 8 = ■$

CRCT Test Prep

11. M3G1.c. Which figure has four right angles? (p. 310)

A. triangle
B. rectangle
C. circle
D. ray

LESSON 4

Add Fractions

M3N5.e. Understand the concept of addition and subtraction of decimals and common fractions with like denominators. *also* M3N5.f., M3P2., M3P2.a., M3P2.b., M3P2.c., M3P2.d., M3P3.a., M3P3.b., M3P3.c., M3P3.d., M3P5.a., M3P5.b., M3P5.c.

Quick Review

Find each sum.

1. $3 + 8$ **2.** $2 + 3$

3. $4 + 2$ **4.** $5 + 5$

5. $1 + 3$

Learn

PIECES PLUS Abby and Chris bought a sub sandwich for lunch. The whole sandwich has 8 pieces. Abby ate 2 pieces. Chris ate 2 pieces. How much of the sandwich did they eat?

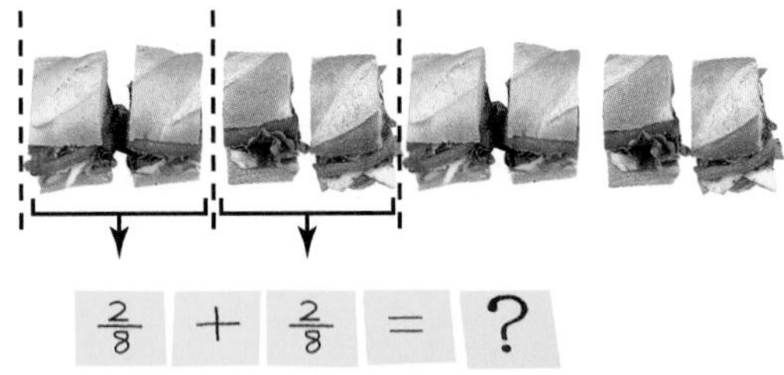

$\frac{2}{8} + \frac{2}{8} = ?$

Find $\frac{2}{8} + \frac{2}{8}$.

HANDS ON

Activity

Materials: fraction bars

STEP 1

Line up two $\frac{1}{8}$ fraction bars under the bar for 1.

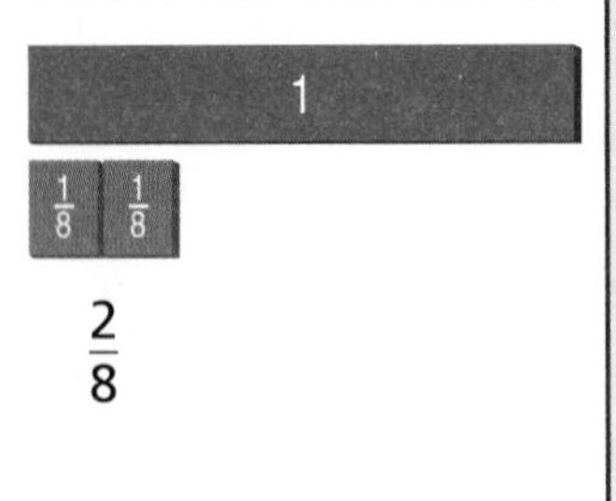

$\frac{2}{8}$

STEP 2

Add two more $\frac{1}{8}$ fraction bars.

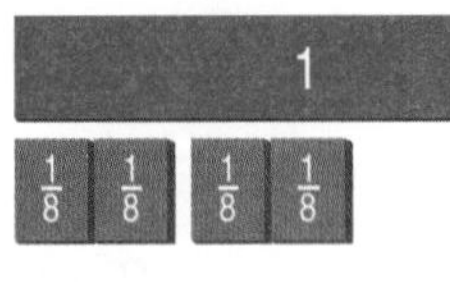

$\frac{2}{8} + \frac{2}{8} = \frac{4}{8}$

So, Abby and Chris ate $\frac{4}{8}$ of the sub sandwich.

Technology Link

More Practice: Harcourt Mega Math Fraction Action, *Fraction Flare Up*, Level H

- Can you name $\frac{4}{8}$ another way? Explain.

MATH IDEA You can use fraction bars to add fractions.

Check

1. Explain how to find $\frac{3}{12} + \frac{1}{12}$.

Find the sum.

2. $\frac{1}{4} + \frac{1}{4} = ■$

3. 

$\frac{2}{6} + \frac{2}{6} = ■$

4. 

$\frac{2}{10} + \frac{2}{10} = ■$

Practice and Problem Solving

Extra Practice, page 408, Set C

Find the sum. Use fraction bars if you wish.

5. $\frac{3}{6} + \frac{1}{6} = ■$

6. 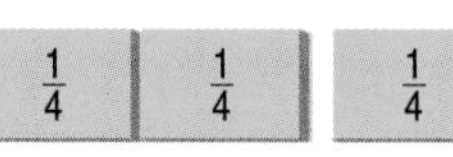

$\frac{2}{4} + \frac{1}{4} = ■$

7. 

$\frac{4}{8} + \frac{3}{8} = ■$

8. $\frac{1}{5} + \frac{1}{5} = ■$
9. $\frac{4}{6} + \frac{1}{6} = ■$
10. $\frac{5}{10} + \frac{4}{10} = ■$
11. $\frac{2}{6} + \frac{2}{6} = ■$
12. $\frac{4}{10} + \frac{4}{10} = ■$
13. $\frac{1}{3} + \frac{1}{3} = ■$
14. $\frac{3}{12} + \frac{6}{12} = ■$
15. $\frac{3}{5} + \frac{1}{5} = ■$

16. **REASONING** Lamar's mother cut a cake into 12 equal pieces. Lamar's family ate 4 pieces. What fraction tells how much of the cake was *not* eaten?

17. **What's the Question?** Sam folded his paper into 8 equal sections. He drew pictures on 3 of the sections. The answer is $\frac{5}{8}$.

Maintain Skills

Write the name of each shape.

18. 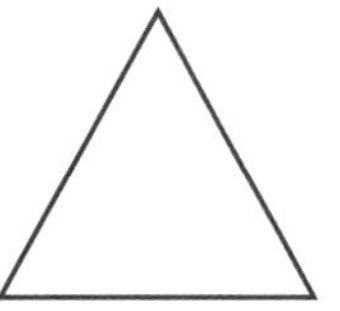

19. 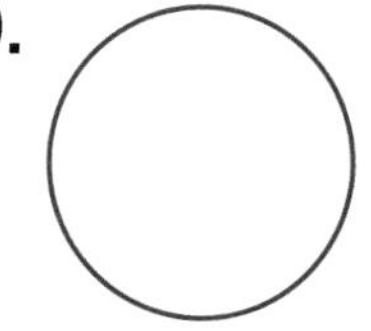

20. 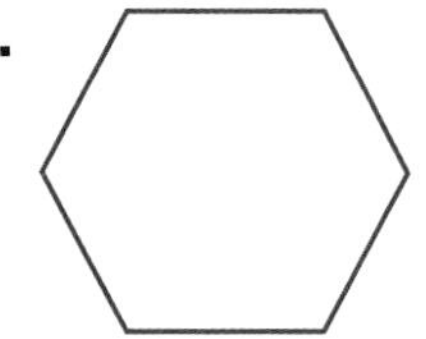

21. 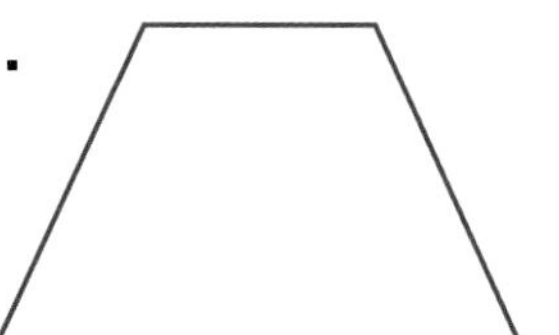

CRCT Test Prep

22. M3N2.c. Gary has $2.78 in his pocket and $3.14 in his bank. He wants to buy a book for $6.50. How much more does he need? (p. 98)

A. $1.58
B. $1.08
C. $0.58
D. $0.08

LESSON 5

Subtract Fractions

M3N5.e. Understand the concept of addition and subtraction of decimals and common fractions with like denominators. *also* M3N5.f., M3P2., M3P2.a., M3P2.b., M3P2.c., M3P2.d., M3P3.a., M3P3.b., M3P3.c., M3P3.d., M3P5.a., M3P5.b., M3P5.c.

Quick Review

Find the difference.

1. 12 – 8
2. 15 – 6
3. 18 – 5
4. 21 – 8
5. 25 – 11

MATERIALS

fraction bars

Explore

Rebecca's dad has $\frac{7}{8}$ of his pan of corn bread to share with the family. If Rebecca eats $\frac{2}{8}$ of the corn bread, how much of the corn bread is left?

Activity

Use fraction bars to find $\frac{7}{8} - \frac{2}{8}$.

STEP 1

Line up seven $\frac{1}{8}$ fraction bars under the bar for 1.

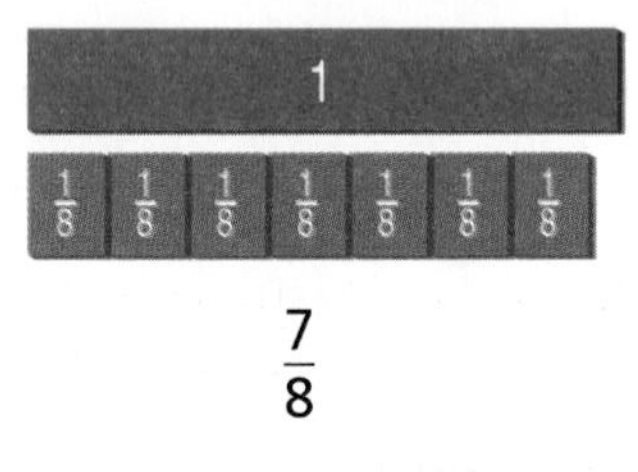

$\frac{7}{8}$

STEP 2

Take away two $\frac{1}{8}$ fraction bars.

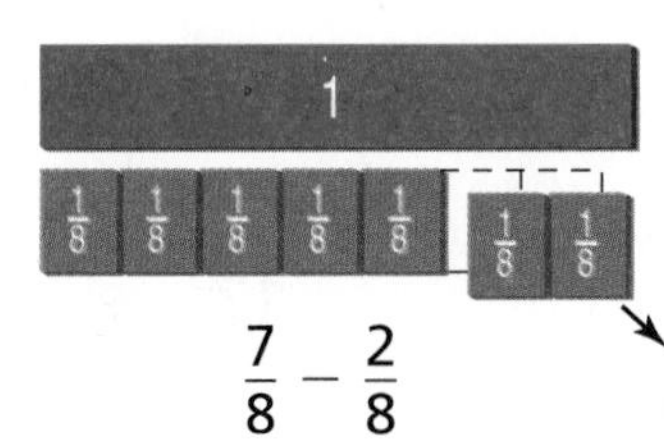

$\frac{7}{8} - \frac{2}{8}$

STEP 3

Count the number of $\frac{1}{8}$ fraction bars left.

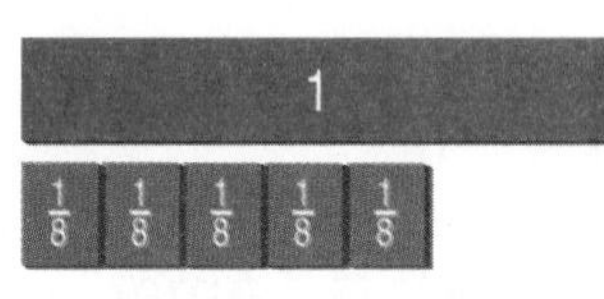

$\frac{7}{8} - \frac{2}{8} = \frac{5}{8}$

So, $\frac{5}{8}$ of the corn bread is left.

- Why doesn't the denominator change when you find $\frac{7}{8} - \frac{2}{8}$?

Try It

Use fraction bars to find the difference.

a. $\frac{3}{6} - \frac{1}{6} = \blacksquare$

b. $\frac{5}{8} - \frac{2}{8} = \blacksquare$

If I take away one of the $\frac{1}{6}$ bars, how many sixths will be left?

Connect

Subtract like fractions by subtracting the numerators.

Example $\frac{7}{10} - \frac{4}{10} = ■$

Model

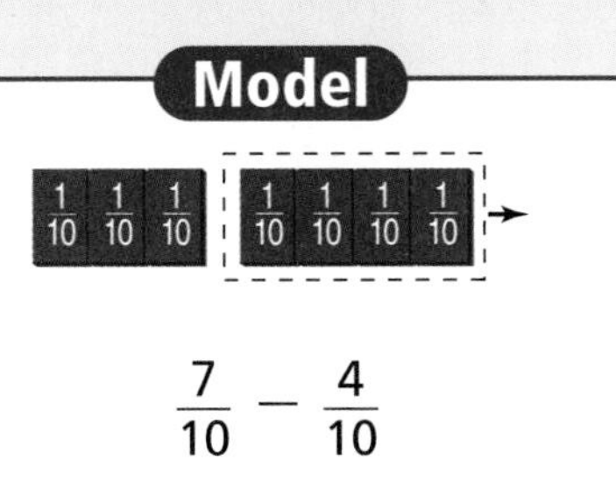

$\frac{7}{10} - \frac{4}{10}$

Record

bars you start with		bars you take away		bars that are left
↓		↓		↓
$\frac{7}{10}$	$-$	$\frac{4}{10}$	$=$	$\frac{3}{10}$

MATH IDEA When you subtract *like* fractions, you subtract the numerators, and the denominators stay the same.

Practice and Problem Solving

Find the difference.

1. $\frac{7}{8} - \frac{4}{8} = ■$
2. $\frac{8}{10} - \frac{3}{10} = ■$
3. $\frac{6}{12} - \frac{2}{12} = ■$

Use fraction bars to find the difference.

4. $\frac{4}{5} - \frac{1}{5} = ■$
5. $\frac{6}{8} - \frac{3}{8} = ■$
6. $\frac{9}{10} - \frac{7}{10} = ■$
7. $\frac{2}{3} - \frac{1}{3} = ■$
8. $\frac{4}{6} - \frac{2}{6} = ■$
9. $\frac{11}{12} - \frac{6}{12} = ■$
10. $\frac{7}{8} - \frac{4}{8} = ■$
11. $\frac{8}{10} - \frac{7}{10} = ■$

12. **MULTISTEP** Wilson earned \$30 mowing lawns and \$25 raking leaves. How much more does Wilson need to have a total of \$100?

Maintain Skills

Find each sum or difference.

13. $286 + 195$
14. $519 + 73$
15. $124 + 436$
16. $724 - 182$
17. $400 - 63$
18. $186 - 29$

CRCT Test Prep

19. M3M1. Malcolm practiced guitar from 11:45 A.M. to 1:00 P.M. How long did he practice? (p. 112)

A. 15 minutes
B. 1 hour 5 minutes
C. 1 hour 15 minutes
D. 2 hours 15 minutes

LESSON 6

Subtract Fractions

M3N5.e. Understand the concept of addition and subtraction of decimals and common fractions with like denominators.
also M3N5.f., M3P2., M3P4.a., M3P4.b., M3P5.a., M3P5.b., M3P5.c.

Find the sum.

1. $\frac{3}{12} + \frac{1}{12} = ■$
2. $\frac{1}{4} + \frac{2}{4} = ■$
3. $\frac{5}{8} + \frac{1}{8} = ■$
4. $\frac{3}{10} + \frac{6}{10} = ■$
5. $\frac{2}{6} + \frac{3}{6} = ■$

Learn

MANY MORE Kara and Eli shared 10 graham crackers. Kara ate 5 of them. Eli ate 3 of them. What fraction tells how many more of the crackers Kara ate than Eli?

Find $\frac{5}{10} - \frac{3}{10}$.

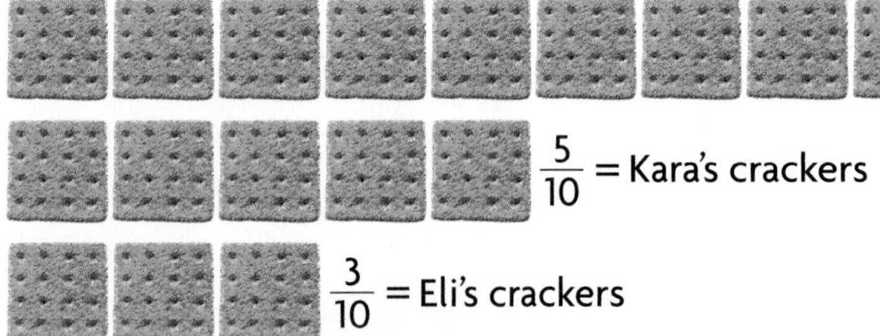

HANDS ON

Activity

Materials: fraction bars

STEP 1

Line up the fraction bars for $\frac{5}{10}$ and $\frac{3}{10}$ under the bar for 1.

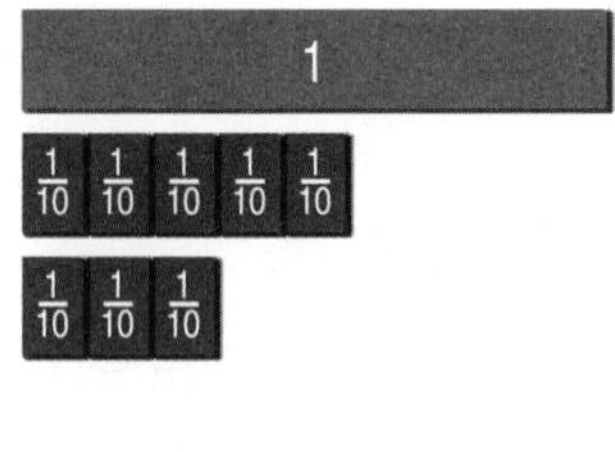

STEP 2

Compare the bars to find the difference.

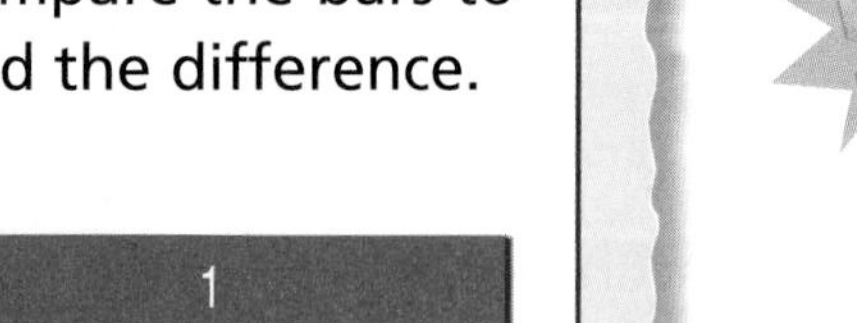

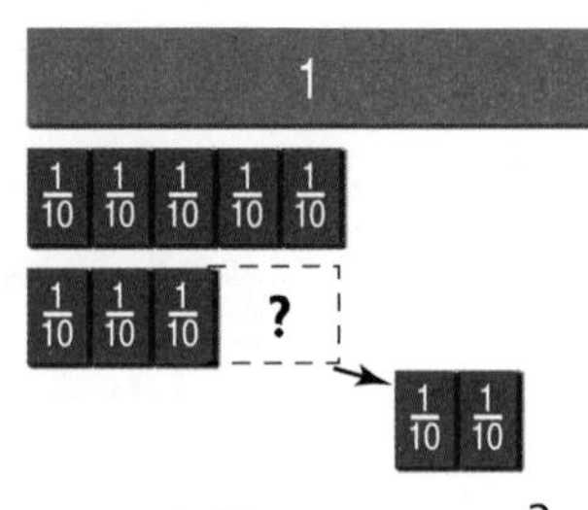

The difference is $\frac{2}{10}$.

Technology Link

More Practice: Harcourt Mega Math Fraction Action, *Fraction Flare Up*, Level H

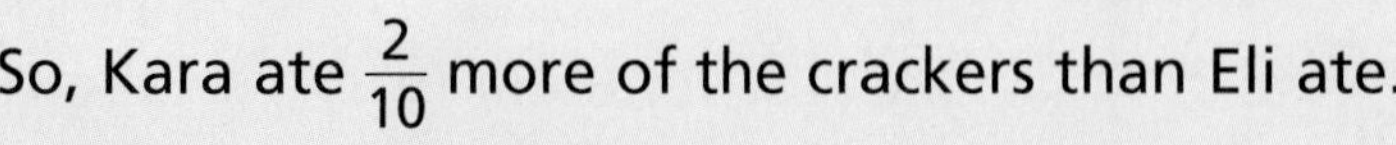

So, Kara ate $\frac{2}{10}$ more of the crackers than Eli ate.

- How many crackers did Kara and Eli eat altogether? How many are left?

Subtracting Fractions

What if Kara and Eli made 8 peanut butter crackers and ate 4 of the crackers? What fraction of the crackers are left?

Use fraction bars to find $\frac{8}{8} - \frac{4}{8}$.

$\frac{8}{8}$ = the total number of crackers

$\frac{4}{8}$ = the 4 crackers they ate

$\frac{4}{8}$ = the crackers that are left

$$\frac{8}{8} - \frac{4}{8} = \frac{4}{8}$$

So, $\frac{4}{8}$ of the crackers are left.

MATH IDEA You can compare fraction bars to subtract fractions.

Check

1. **Explain** how you can use fraction bars to find $\frac{3}{4} - \frac{1}{4}$.

Compare. Find the difference.

2. 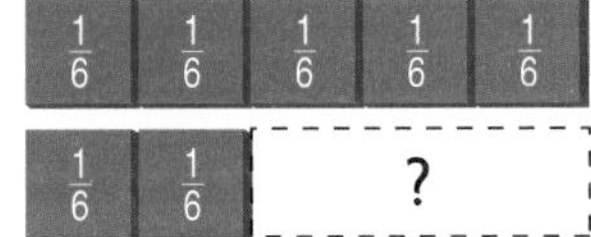

$\frac{5}{6} - \frac{2}{6} = ■$

3. 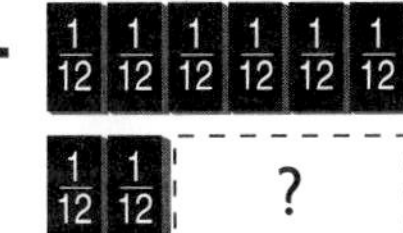

$\frac{6}{12} - \frac{2}{12} = ■$

4. 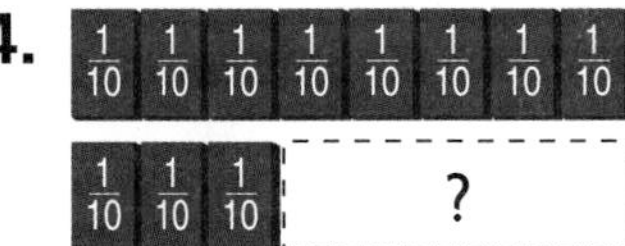

$\frac{8}{10} - \frac{3}{10} = ■$

5.

$\frac{1}{4}$	$\frac{1}{4}$	$\frac{1}{4}$
$\frac{1}{4}$	$\frac{1}{4}$	?

$\frac{3}{4} - \frac{2}{4} = ■$

6. 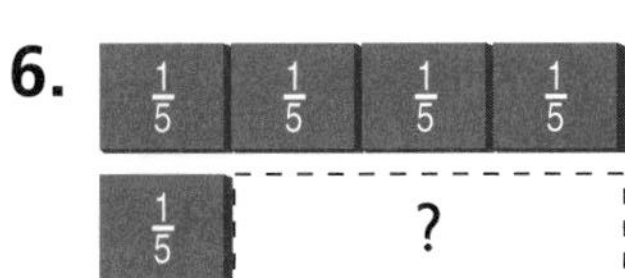

$\frac{4}{5} - \frac{1}{5} = ■$

7. 

$\frac{5}{8} - \frac{4}{8} = ■$

Find the difference. Use fraction bars if you wish.

8. $\frac{7}{8} - \frac{4}{8} = ■$

9. $\frac{9}{12} - \frac{3}{12} = ■$

10. $\frac{9}{10} - \frac{4}{10} = ■$

LESSON CONTINUES

Practice and Problem Solving

Extra Practice, page 408, Set D

Compare. Find the difference.

11. 

$\frac{4}{6} - \frac{1}{6} = \blacksquare$

12. 

$\frac{6}{12} - \frac{3}{12} = \blacksquare$

13. 

$\frac{3}{8} - \frac{2}{8} = \blacksquare$

14. 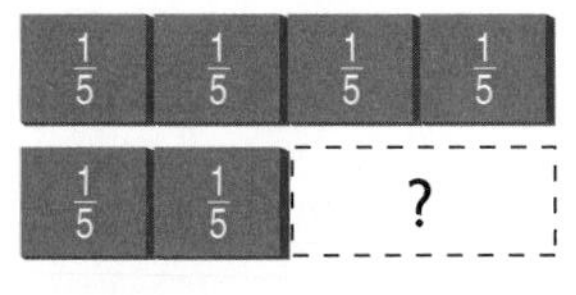

$\frac{4}{5} - \frac{2}{5} = \blacksquare$

15. 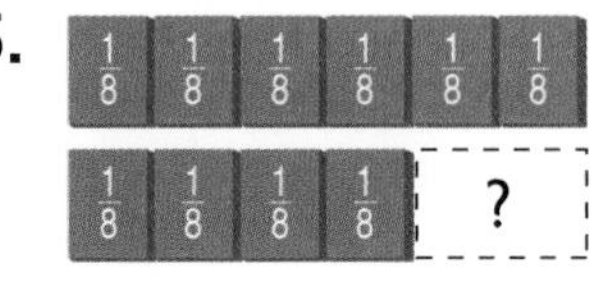

$\frac{6}{8} - \frac{4}{8} = \blacksquare$

16. 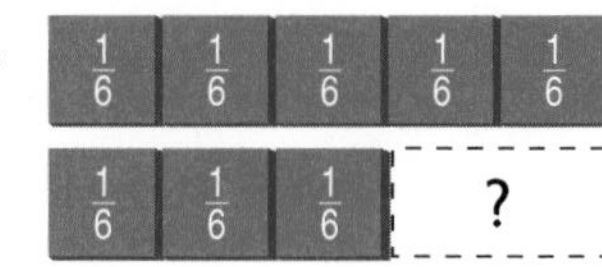

$\frac{5}{6} - \frac{3}{6} = \blacksquare$

Find the difference. Use fraction bars if you wish.

17. $\frac{2}{3} - \frac{1}{3} = \blacksquare$

18. $\frac{4}{5} - \frac{1}{5} = \blacksquare$

19. $\frac{4}{6} - \frac{2}{6} = \blacksquare$

20. $\frac{5}{6} - \frac{1}{6} = \blacksquare$

21. $\frac{7}{10} - \frac{2}{10} = \blacksquare$

22. $\frac{7}{8} - \frac{5}{8} = \blacksquare$

23. $\frac{10}{12} - \frac{7}{12} = \blacksquare$

24. $\frac{6}{8} - \frac{1}{8} = \blacksquare$

25. $\frac{11}{12} - \frac{9}{12} = \blacksquare$

26. $\frac{8}{10} - \frac{5}{10} = \blacksquare$

27. $\frac{5}{6} - \frac{3}{6} = \blacksquare$

28. $\frac{6}{8} - \frac{2}{8} = \blacksquare$

29. REASONING There are 8 letters in the word *Virginia*. The letter *i* is $\frac{3}{8}$ of the word, and the letter *a* is $\frac{1}{8}$ of the word. What fraction of the word are the vowels?

30. MULTISTEP Dana cut an apple pie into 8 equal pieces. She shared the pie with 4 of her friends. Dana and each of her friends ate 1 piece of pie. What fraction of the pie is left?

31. Vocabulary Power The *denominator* in a fraction tells how many equal parts in all. Draw a picture to show the fraction two-fifths. Write the fraction and label the denominator.

32. What's the Error? Haley wrote $\frac{5}{12} - \frac{3}{12} = 2$. What was her error?

33. **Write About It** Explain how you can find the difference of two fractions that have the same denominator.

34. **REASONING** An apple was cut into equal-size slices. Kinji ate 3 of them. If 6 slices of apple are left, what fraction of the apple did Kinji eat?

Maintain Skills

Write the amount.

35. 

36.  

37.  

CRCT Test Prep

38. M3A1.c. What number goes in the $\square$ to make the sentence true? (p. 154)

$$\square \times 9 = 27$$

A. 2 B. 3 C. 4 D. 5

39. M3N2.c. Roller-coaster tickets cost $1.50 each. Samantha bought 2 tickets. How much change should she receive from $5.00? (p. 98)

A. $2.00 C. $3.50
B. $3.00 D. $4.00

Problem Solving LINKUP... to Geography

You can use what you know about adding and subtracting fractions to find distances on a map. The scale tells you how distances are measured. On this map each unit represents $\frac{1}{10}$ of a mile.

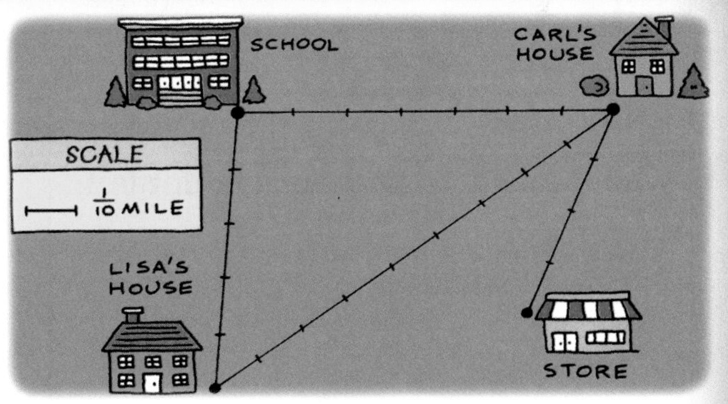

What if you are visiting your friend Carl at his house after school? Use the map to answer the questions.

1. How much farther is the school than the store from Carl's house?

2. How far is Lisa's house from the school?

3. Which is farther from Carl's house, Lisa's house or the school? How much farther?

4. **REASONING** Carl says the store is $\frac{1}{2}$ mile from his house. Is he right? Explain your reasoning.

LESSON 7

Problem Solving Skill
Reasonable Answers

M3N5.g. Solve problems involving fractions. *also* M3P1.a., M3P1.b., M3P1.c., M3P1.d., M3P2.a., M3P2.b., M3P2.c., M3P2.d., M3P3., M3P3.a., M3P3.b., M3P3.c., M3P3.d.

UNDERSTAND | PLAN | SOLVE | CHECK

Quick Review

Find the difference.

1. $\frac{8}{12} - \frac{3}{12}$
2. $\frac{9}{10} - \frac{2}{10}$
3. $\frac{5}{6} - \frac{4}{6}$
4. $\frac{7}{8} - \frac{4}{8}$
5. $\frac{2}{3} - \frac{1}{3}$

SOUNDS GOOD Whenever you solve a problem, always check to see that your answer is reasonable and makes sense.

Tanya's mother made a very large chocolate chip cookie. Tanya and Allie each ate $\frac{3}{8}$ of the cookie. What fraction of the cookie was left?

1 whole cookie = $\frac{8}{8}$

Example

STEP 1

Find out what the problem asks.

What fraction of the cookie was left after Tanya and Allie each ate $\frac{3}{8}$ of it?

STEP 2

Add to find how much of the cookie was eaten.

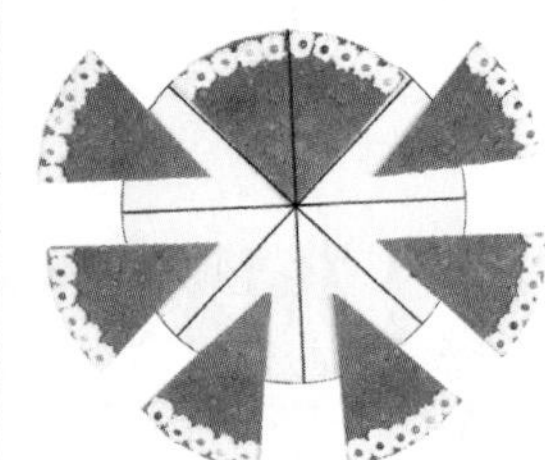

$\frac{3}{8} + \frac{3}{8} = \frac{6}{8}$

STEP 3

Subtract the amount eaten from the whole cookie to find the amount left.

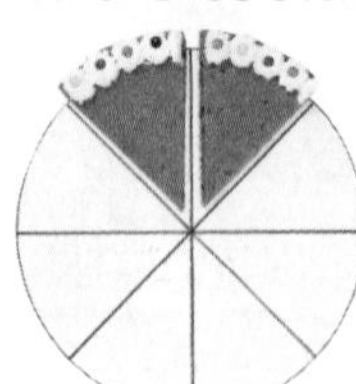

$\frac{8}{8} - \frac{6}{8} = \frac{2}{8}$

So, $\frac{2}{8}$, or $\frac{1}{4}$, of the cookie was left.

STEP 4

Check to see that your answer is reasonable and makes sense.

Think: If I put back $\frac{3}{8}$ for Tanya and $\frac{3}{8}$ for Allie then I get the whole cookie.

Talk About It

- Why is $\frac{8}{8}$ used for the whole cookie?
- Would it be reasonable to decide that $\frac{1}{2}$ of the cookie was left? Explain.

Problem Solving Practice

Solve. Tell how you know your answer is reasonable.

1. Gil hiked $\frac{2}{5}$ of the mountain trail and rested. Then he hiked another $\frac{1}{5}$ of the trail. How much of the trail does he have left to hike?

2. Clyde opened a new box of cereal. He ate $\frac{1}{3}$ of the cereal in the box. How much cereal was left?

Amy planted $\frac{1}{4}$ of her garden on Monday and $\frac{1}{4}$ of her garden on Tuesday. She planted the rest on Wednesday. How much of the garden did she plant on Wednesday?

3. How can you solve the problem?

   A Compare $\frac{1}{4}$ and $\frac{1}{4}$.

   B Find $\frac{1}{4} + \frac{1}{4}$.

   C Find $\frac{1}{4} + \frac{1}{4}$, and then subtract from $\frac{4}{4}$.

   D Find $\frac{1}{4} - \frac{1}{4}$.

4. What is the answer to the question?

   F $\frac{1}{4}$ **G** $\frac{2}{4}$ **H** $\frac{3}{4}$ **J** $\frac{4}{4}$

Mixed Applications

5. **REASONING** Selma cut a pan of brownies into 3 equal pieces. Then she cut each of those pieces in half. She ate 2 of the pieces. What fraction of the brownies were left? Explain.

6. ALGEBRA The total number of Satoko's apples and pears was 12. She traded each pear for 2 apples. Then she had 15 apples in all. How many of each fruit did Satoko have to begin with?

7. **Write About It** Describe the pattern below. What will the fourteenth shape in the pattern be?

Extra Practice

Set A (pp. 390–393)

Write a fraction in numbers and in words that names the shaded part.

1. 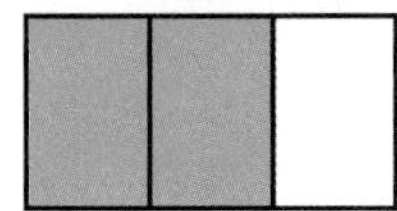

2. 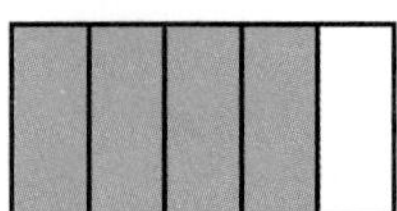

3. 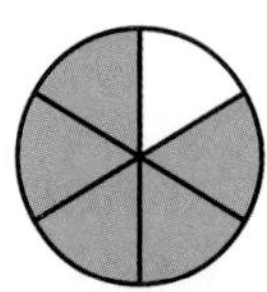

Make a model of each, using fraction circle pieces. Then write the fraction, using numbers.

4. one eighth
5. four out of six
6. two divided by five

Set B (pp. 394–395)

1. Draw 4 nickels. Circle $\frac{3}{4}$ of them.
2. Draw 5 rectangles. Circle $\frac{1}{5}$ of them.
3. Draw 8 triangles. Circle $\frac{5}{8}$ of them.

Set C (pp. 398–399)

Find the sum. Use fraction bars if you wish.

1. $\frac{2}{4} + \frac{1}{4} = \blacksquare$
2. $\frac{2}{5} + \frac{1}{5} = \blacksquare$
3. $\frac{4}{8} + \frac{1}{8} = \blacksquare$
4. $\frac{4}{10} + \frac{2}{10} = \blacksquare$
5. $\frac{1}{3} + \frac{1}{3} = \blacksquare$
6. $\frac{6}{12} + \frac{1}{12} = \blacksquare$
7. Miles gave $\frac{1}{5}$ of the cake to Molly and $\frac{2}{5}$ to Sarah. What fraction of the cake did Miles give away?
8. Gwen says that $\frac{1}{4} + \frac{1}{4} = \frac{2}{8}$. Is she correct? Explain.

Set D (pp. 402–405)

Compare. Find the difference.

1. 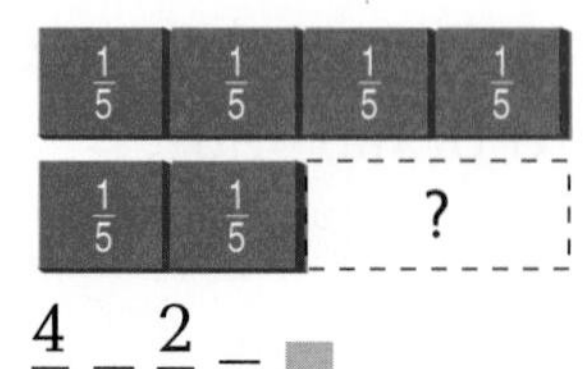

$\frac{4}{5} - \frac{2}{5} = \blacksquare$

2. 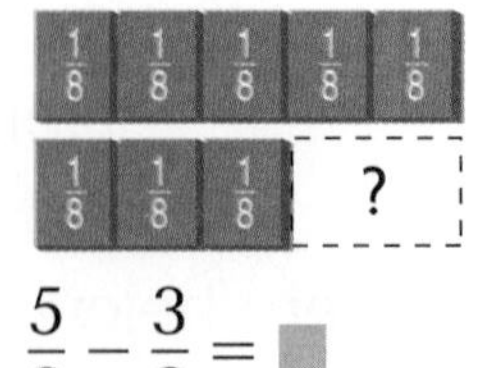

$\frac{5}{8} - \frac{3}{8} = \blacksquare$

3. 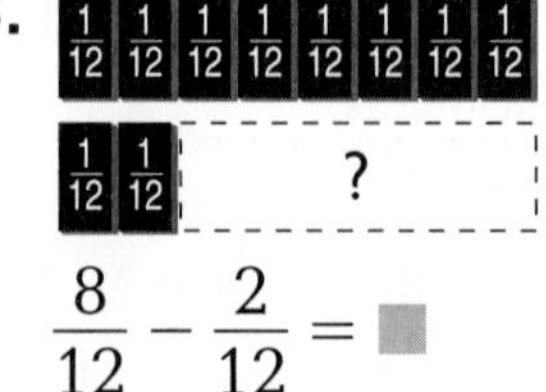

$\frac{8}{12} - \frac{2}{12} = \blacksquare$

Find the difference. Use fraction bars if you wish.

4. $\frac{2}{3} - \frac{1}{3} = \blacksquare$
5. $\frac{5}{6} - \frac{2}{6} = \blacksquare$
6. $\frac{3}{4} - \frac{2}{4} = \blacksquare$
7. $\frac{5}{10} - \frac{3}{10} = \blacksquare$

Review/Test

CHECK VOCABULARY

Choose the best term from the box.

Vocabulary
- fraction
- numerator
- denominator

1. In the fraction $\frac{3}{8}$, the 3 is called the __?__. (p. 390)
2. A number that names part of a whole or part of a group is a __?__. (p. 390)

CHECK SKILLS

Write a fraction in numbers and in words that names the shaded part. (pp. 390–393, 394–395)

3. 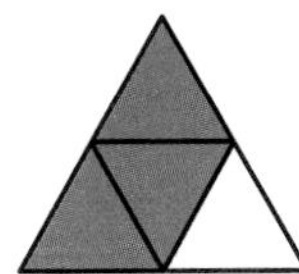
4. 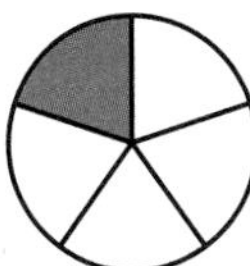
5. 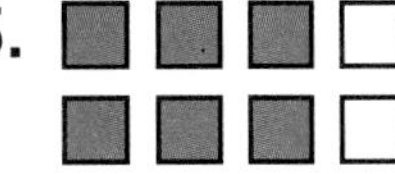
6. 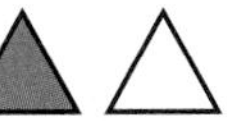

Find the sum or difference. Use fraction bars if you wish.
(pp. 398–399, 402–405)

7. $\frac{2}{4} + \frac{1}{4} = \blacksquare$
8. $\frac{3}{5} + \frac{1}{5} = \blacksquare$
9. $\frac{2}{8} + \frac{4}{8} = \blacksquare$
10. $\frac{2}{6} + \frac{1}{6} = \blacksquare$
11. $\frac{3}{8} + \frac{2}{8} = \blacksquare$
12. $\frac{2}{10} + \frac{7}{10} = \blacksquare$
13. $\frac{4}{6} - \frac{2}{6} = \blacksquare$
14. $\frac{7}{10} - \frac{3}{10} = \blacksquare$
15. $\frac{6}{8} - \frac{4}{8} = \blacksquare$
16. $\frac{10}{12} - \frac{7}{12} = \blacksquare$
17. $\frac{2}{4} - \frac{1}{4} = \blacksquare$
18. $\frac{8}{10} - \frac{5}{10} = \blacksquare$

CHECK PROBLEM SOLVING

Solve. Tell how you know your answer is reasonable.
(pp. 406–407)

19. Joe gave $\frac{1}{8}$ of his football cards to Pete and $\frac{3}{8}$ of his cards to Ron. What fraction of his cards did he keep for himself?

20. On Monday Raquel read $\frac{1}{10}$ of her library book. On Tuesday she read $\frac{1}{10}$ of her book. What fraction of her book does she have left to read?

Chapter CRCT Test Prep

NUMBERS AND OPERATIONS

1. M3N5.b. Which fraction names the part of the figure below that is shaded?

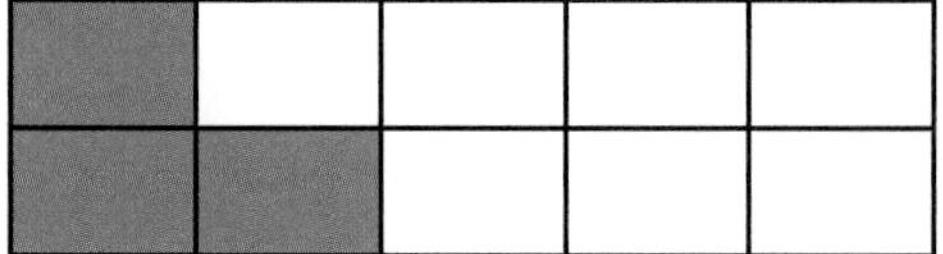

A. $\frac{3}{5}$

B. $\frac{3}{8}$

C. $\frac{3}{10}$

D. $\frac{3}{12}$

2. M3N5.d. Nick made this spinner.

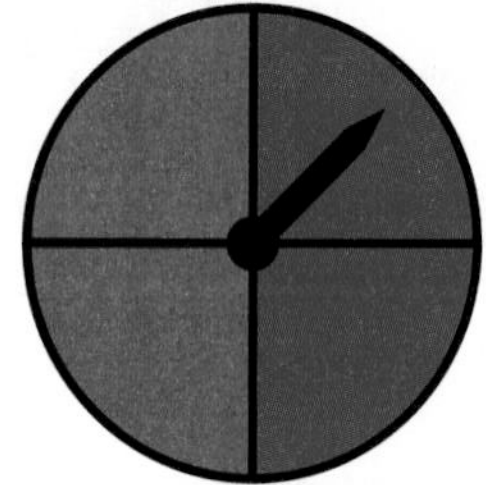

Which fraction names the part of the spinner that is blue?

A. $\frac{1}{4}$

B. $\frac{2}{4}$

C. $\frac{3}{4}$

D. $\frac{4}{4}$

NUMBERS AND OPERATIONS

3. M3N5.g. Aaron and Lana ordered a pizza. Aaron ate $\frac{2}{8}$ of the pizza. Lana ate $\frac{3}{8}$ of the pizza. How much of the pizza did Aaron and Lana eat?

A. $\frac{2}{8}$

B. $\frac{3}{8}$

C. $\frac{5}{8}$

D. $\frac{7}{8}$

4. M3N5.g. Ben has these coins.

Which fraction names the part of Ben's coins that are dimes?

A. $\frac{3}{12}$

B. $\frac{4}{12}$

C. $\frac{5}{12}$

D. $\frac{6}{12}$

Cumulative CRCT Test Prep

GEOMETRY

5. M3G1.a. Which solid figure does a globe look like?

A. cube

B. cone

C. cylinder

D. sphere

6. M3G1.b. Mrs. Conner put this poster on a wall of her classroom.

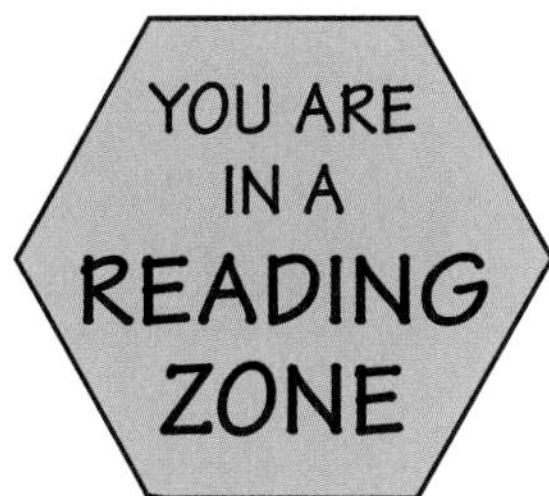

Which polygon describes the shape of this poster?

A. triangle

B. pentagon

C. hexagon

D. octagon

7. M3G1.a. Which solid figure does a soup can look like?

A. cube

B. cylinder

C. sphere

D. rectangular prism

ALGEBRA

8. M3A1.a. Robin wrote this number pattern.

24, 21, 18, 15, 12

Which is a rule that she could have used to make the pattern?

A. Add 4.

B. Subtract 3.

C. Multiply by 2.

D. Divide by 5.

9. M3A1.a. What are the next two shapes in the pattern?

A. ★■

B. ■★

C. ■■

D. ★★

10. M3A1.c. Blanca spent $24 on plants. Each plant cost $3. Which number sentence could be used to find the number of plants that she bought?

A. □ − 3 = 24

B. 24 − 3 = □

C. 24 ÷ 3 = □

D. □ + 3 = 24

CHAPTER 21 Decimals

FAST FACT • SCIENCE The world's smallest mammal is the bumblebee bat. It weighs less than a penny! Bumblebee bats are very rare. They are found in only 3 caves in the country of Thailand. Georgia is home to 16 different types of bats.

INVESTIGATION The table shows the weights, in ounces, of different bats. How can you find the number of silver-haired bats it would take to equal the weight of one hoary bat? Hint: 0.1 ounce means the same as $\frac{1}{10}$ ounce.

Using Data

WEIGHTS OF BATS

Bat	Weight
Silver-haired Bat	0.3 ounces
Seminole Bat	0.4 ounces
Hoary Bat	0.9 ounces
Evening Bat	0.2 ounces

Bumblebee Bat

CHECK WHAT YOU KNOW

Use this page to help you review and remember important skills needed for Chapter 21.

NAME THE FRACTION

Write a fraction for the shaded part.

1. 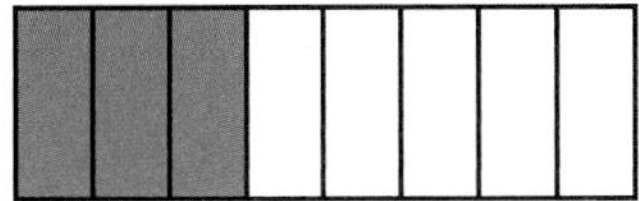

2. 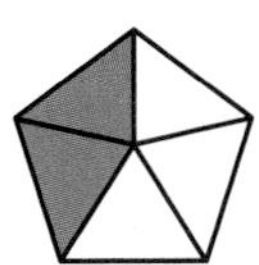

3. 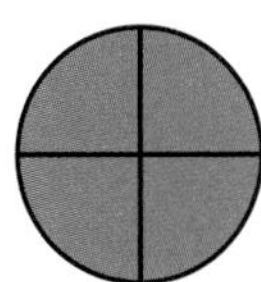

Write a fraction that names the part of each group that is shaded.

4. 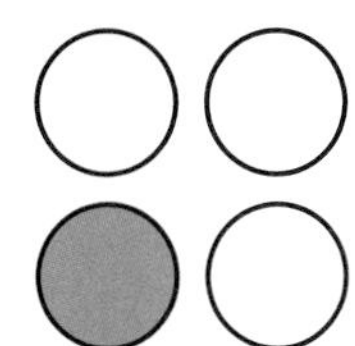

5. 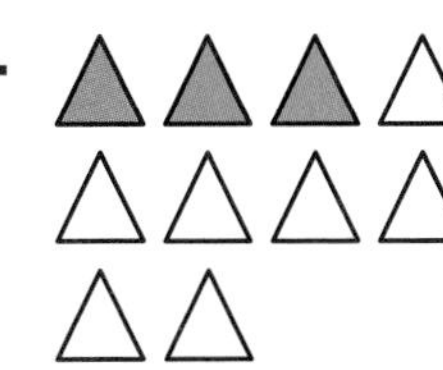

6. 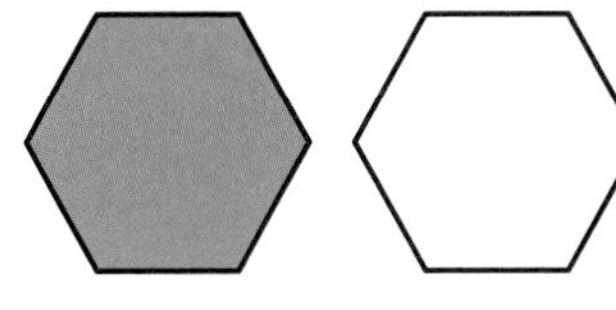

READ THE FRACTION

Write each fraction in words.

7. $\frac{1}{2}$ 8. $\frac{8}{10}$ 9. $\frac{1}{6}$ 10. $\frac{3}{8}$ 11. $\frac{1}{4}$

12. $\frac{5}{6}$ 13. $\frac{5}{10}$ 14. $\frac{4}{8}$ 15. $\frac{3}{4}$ 16. $\frac{9}{10}$

VOCABULARY POWER

REVIEW

digit [di′jət] *noun*

The word *digit* can mean "a finger or a toe." What is the meaning of *digit* in your math book? Write a sentence to describe the math meaning of *digit*.

PREVIEW

decimal

tenth

www.harcourtschool.com/mathglossary

LESSON 1

Fractions and Decimals

M3N5.a. Understand a decimal (i.e., 0.1) and a common fraction (i.e., 1/10) represent parts of a whole. *also* **M3N5.c., M3N5.d., M3P3., M3P4., M3P4.a., M3P4.b.**

Quick Review

Write each fraction in words.

1. $\frac{1}{3}$ **2.** $\frac{2}{5}$ **3.** $\frac{2}{10}$

4. $\frac{3}{8}$ **5.** $\frac{1}{2}$

VOCABULARY

decimal
tenth

Learn

FAIR SHARE A **decimal** is a fraction with a denominator of 10 or 100 written in place-value notation and with a decimal point. A decimal uses place value to show values less than one, such as tenths.

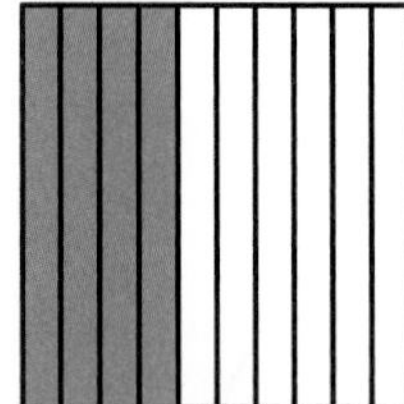

This square has 10 equal parts. Each equal part is one **tenth**.

Fraction	**Decimal**
Write: $\frac{4}{10}$	**Write:** 0.4 (decimal point)
Read: four tenths	**Read:** four tenths

The fraction $\frac{4}{10}$ and the decimal 0.4 name the same amount.

MATH IDEA You can use a fraction or a decimal to show values in tenths.

Examples

A

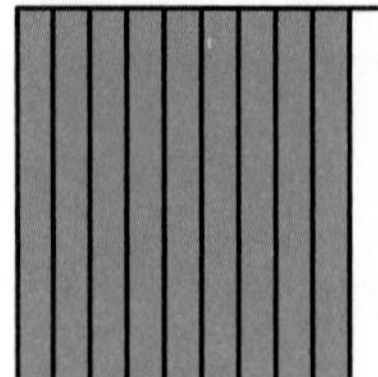

Fraction: $\frac{9}{10}$
Decimal: 0.9
Read: nine tenths

B

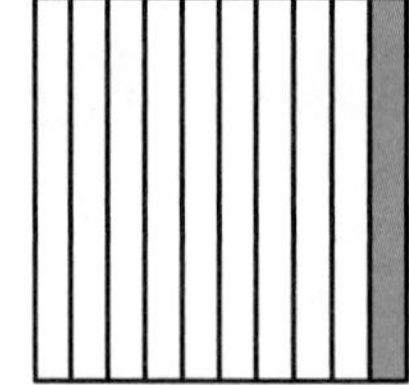

Fraction: $\frac{1}{10}$
Decimal: 0.1
Read: one tenth

C

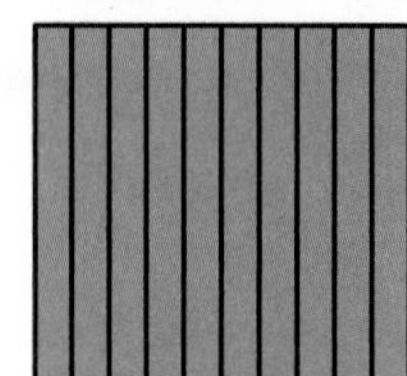

Fraction: $\frac{10}{10}$
Decimal: 1.0, or 1
Read: ten tenths, or one

- How many parts on the square would you shade to show 0.3?

Check

1. **Write** a fraction that shows the amount of crispy treats that are left. Then write the same amount as a decimal.

Write the fraction and decimal for the shaded part.

2. 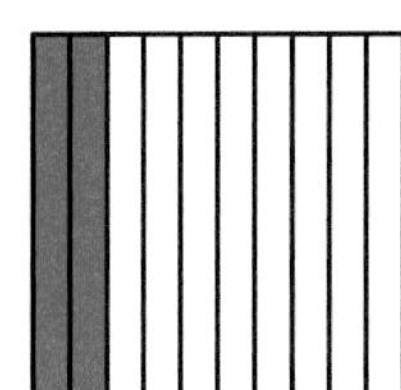

3. 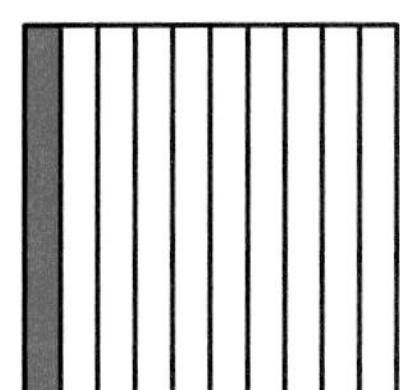

4. 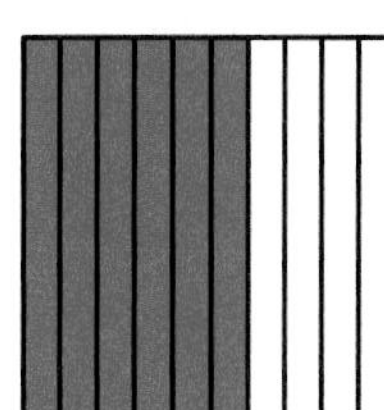

Practice and Problem Solving

Extra Practice, page 424, Set A

Write the fraction and decimal for the shaded part.

5. 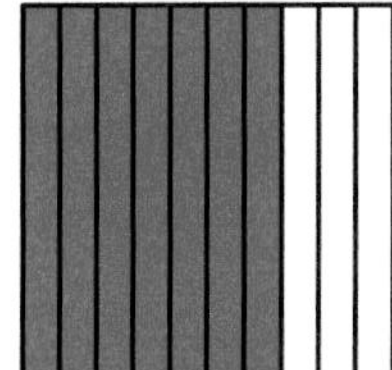

6. 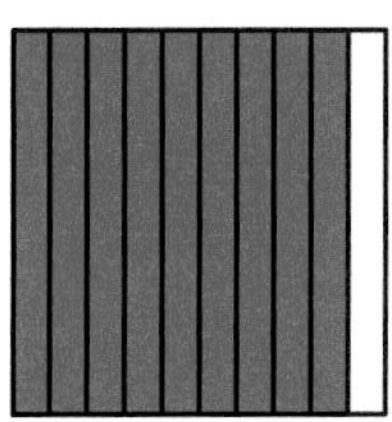

7. 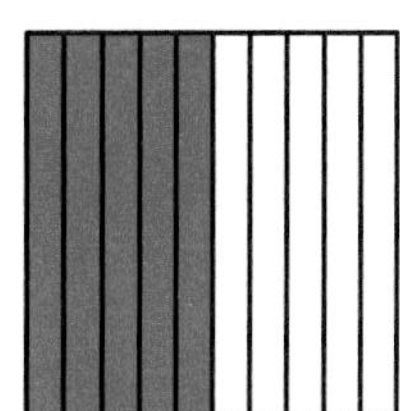

8. 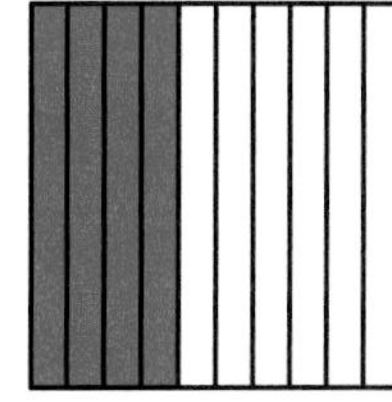

9. ***FAST FACT*** • SCIENCE In 2002, a new kind of centipede was identified. It was found in Central Park in New York. It has 82 legs and is four tenths of an inch long. Write this length as a decimal.

10. **REASONING** Look at the decimal model in Exercise 8 above. How could subtraction be used to find the decimal amount that is NOT shaded?

11. **Write About It** Look at the fraction bars at the right. Explain why 0.5 is the same as $\frac{1}{2}$.

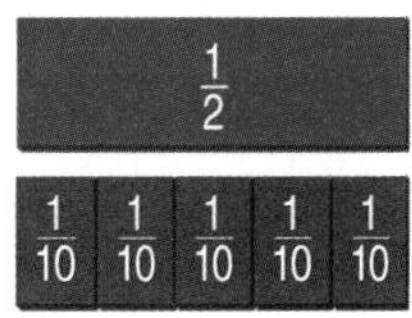

Maintain Skills

Find each sum or difference.

12. $\begin{array}{r} 167 \\ +492 \\ \hline \end{array}$

13. $\begin{array}{r} 649 \\ -263 \\ \hline \end{array}$

14. $\begin{array}{r} 822 \\ -387 \\ \hline \end{array}$

CRCT Test Prep

15. M3N3.g Frieda puts 5 beads on each of 9 necklaces. How many beads does she use? (p. 128)

A. 45 B. 54 C. 72 D. 81

Tenths

M3N5.c. Understand a one place decimal represents tenths, i.e., 0.3 = 3/10. *also* **M3N5.a., M3N5.d., M3P2., M3P2.a., M3P2.b., M3P2.c., M3P2.d., M3P3.a., M3P3.b., M3P3.c., M3P3.d., M3P5.b., M3P5.c.**

Quick Review

Write each fraction in words.

1. $\frac{2}{10}$
2. $\frac{5}{10}$
3. $\frac{1}{10}$
4. $\frac{4}{10}$
5. $\frac{7}{10}$

MATERIALS
decimal models
markers

Explore

You can use a decimal model to show part of a whole. This model shows six tenths.

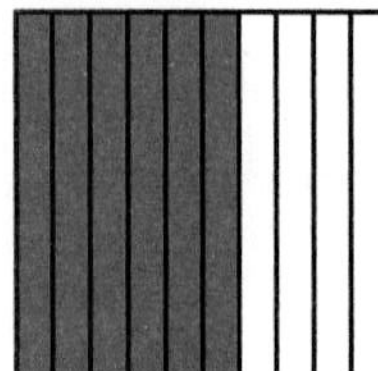

Write: 0.6, or $\frac{6}{10}$

Activity

Use a decimal model to show 0.2, or $\frac{2}{10}$.

STEP 1

Shade the decimal model to show two tenths.

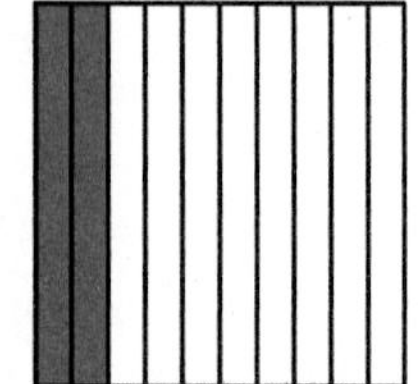

STEP 2

Below your decimal model, write the fraction and decimal amount you have shown.

- Use a new decimal model. Shade and label the decimal model to show 0.8, or $\frac{8}{10}$.

Technology Link
More Practice:
Harcourt Mega Math
Fraction Action,
Fraction Flare Up,
Level L

Try It

Shade and label decimal models to show each amount.

a. 0.9, or $\frac{9}{10}$ **b.** 0.5, or $\frac{5}{10}$

c. 0.7, or $\frac{7}{10}$ **d.** 0.1, or $\frac{1}{10}$

Connect

You can show tenths in different ways.

Use a model.

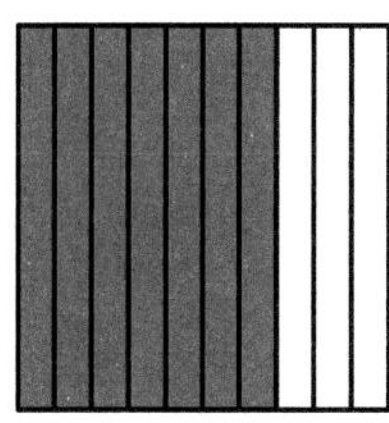

Use a fraction.

$\frac{7}{10}$

Use a place-value chart.

ONES	.	TENTHS
0	.	7

Write: 0.7

Read: seven tenths

Practice and Problem Solving

Use decimal models to show each amount. Then write each fraction as a decimal.

1. $\frac{3}{10}$ **2.** $\frac{8}{10}$ **3.** $\frac{4}{10}$ **4.** $\frac{6}{10}$

Write each decimal as a fraction.

5.

ONES	.	TENTHS
0	.	2

6.

ONES	.	TENTHS
0	.	9

7. 0.5 **8.** 0.4 **9.** 0.3 **10.** 0.1

11. **What's the Question?** Greg has a total of 10 blueberry and pumpkin muffins. Two tenths of the muffins are blueberry. The answer is 8.

12. **MULTISTEP** Hannah had 64 party favors. She put an equal number in each of 8 bags. How many party favors were in 2 bags?

Maintain Skills

13. Write the amount.

CRCT Test Prep

14. M3N2.c. Sara had $4.08. She bought a sticker for $0.29. How much money did she have left? (p. 98)

A. $3.89 C. $3.79
B. $3.81 D. $3.70

LESSON 3

Add Decimals

M3N5.f. Model addition and subtraction of decimals and common fractions. *also* M3N5.e., M3N5.g., M3P2., M3P2.a., M3P2.b., M3P2.c., M3P2.d., M3P3., M3P3.a., M3P3.b., M3P3.c., M3P3.d., M3P4.b., M3P5.b., M3P5.c.

Learn

SNIPPING AWAY Lauren and Amy used ribbon to decorate birthday cards. Lauren used 0.3 foot of ribbon. Amy used 0.2 foot of ribbon. How much ribbon did they use in all?

Quick Review

Write each fraction as a decimal.

1. $\frac{2}{10}$
2. $\frac{9}{10}$
3. $\frac{4}{10}$
4. $\frac{5}{10}$
5. $\frac{3}{10}$

Activity

Materials: decimal models, markers

Use decimal models to find 0.3 + 0.2.

STEP 1

Shade the decimal model to show three tenths, or 0.3.

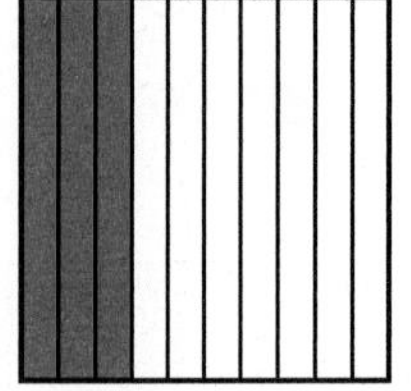

STEP 2

Shade two tenths, or 0.2. Add the shaded parts.

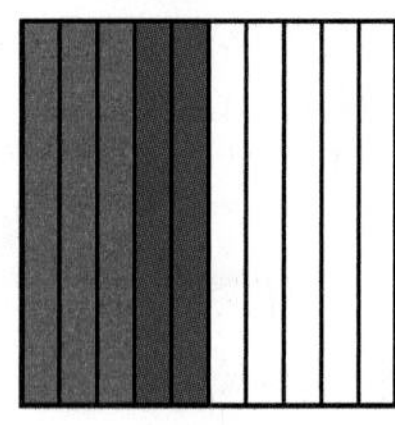

0.3 + 0.2 = 0.5

So, they used 0.5 foot of ribbon.

MATH IDEA You can add decimals the same way you add whole numbers if you line up the decimal points first.

Example

Find 0.1 + 0.5.

STEP 1

Line up each place value and the decimal points.

decimal point
↓

$$\begin{array}{r} 0.1 \\ +0.5 \\ \hline \end{array}$$

STEP 2

Add decimals like whole numbers.

$$\begin{array}{r} 0.1 \\ +0.5 \\ \hline 0\ 6 \end{array}$$

STEP 3

Write the decimal point in the sum.

$$\begin{array}{r} 0.1 \\ +0.5 \\ \hline 0.6 \end{array}$$

Check

1. **Explain** how you could use a decimal model to find $0.3 + 0.4$.

Find each sum.

2. $\begin{array}{r} 0.1 \\ +0.4 \\ \hline \end{array}$

3. $\begin{array}{r} 0.5 \\ +0.2 \\ \hline \end{array}$

4. $\begin{array}{r} 0.8 \\ +0.1 \\ \hline \end{array}$

5. $\begin{array}{r} 0.3 \\ +0.3 \\ \hline \end{array}$

Practice and Problem Solving

Extra Practice, page 424, Set B

Find each sum.

6. $\begin{array}{r} 0.4 \\ +0.2 \\ \hline \end{array}$

7. $\begin{array}{r} 0.1 \\ +0.7 \\ \hline \end{array}$

8. $\begin{array}{r} 0.3 \\ +0.6 \\ \hline \end{array}$

9. $\begin{array}{r} 0.2 \\ +0.3 \\ \hline \end{array}$

10. $0.6 + 0.2 = \blacksquare$

11. $0.3 + 0.4 = \blacksquare$

12. $0.2 + 0.1 = \blacksquare$

ALGEBRA **Write the missing number.**

13. $0.2 + \blacksquare = 0.7$

14. $\blacksquare + 0.4 = 0.9$

15. $0.3 + \blacksquare = 0.9$

16. Jami used 0.3 yard of fabric to make a purse. Ellen used 0.5 yard of fabric to make a bigger purse. How much fabric did they use in all?

17. **MULTISTEP** Joe and Kim shared a pizza. Joe ate $\frac{4}{10}$ of the pizza, and Kim ate $\frac{2}{10}$. What fraction of the pizza is left? Write the answer as a fraction and a decimal.

18. **Write About It** The sum $0.4 + 0.6$ is 1. What are some other pairs of decimals that add up to 1? How are the decimal models for all these sums different? How are they the same?

Maintain Skills

19. Write the amount.

CRCT Test Prep

20. M3M3.c What is the perimeter of the triangle below? (p. 350)

A. 12 inches
B. 15 inches
C. 17 inches
D. 20 inches

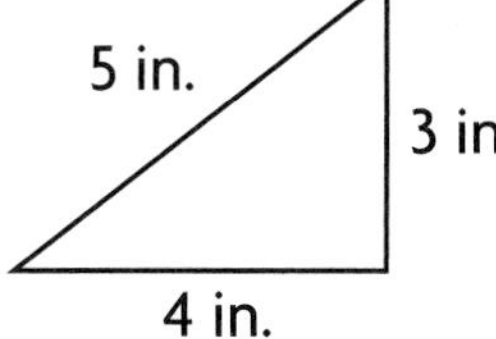

LESSON 4

Subtract Decimals

M3N5.f. Model addition and subtraction of decimals and common fractions. *also* M3N5.e., M3N5.g., M3P2., M3P2.a., M3P2.b., M3P2.c., M3P2.d., M3P3.a., M3P3.b., M3P3.c., M3P3.d., M3P4.b., M3P5.b., M3P5.c.

Quick Review

1. 0.2 + 0.3 = ■
2. 0.8 + 0.1 = ■
3. 0.2 + 0.2 = ■
4. 0.4 + 0.5 = ■
5. 0.1 + 0.7 = ■

Learn

MOVING RIGHT ALONG Gary walked from his house to the playground. Dan walked from his house to the playground. How much farther did Dan walk than Gary?

HANDS ON

Activity

Materials: decimal models, markers, scissors

Use decimal models to find 0.6 − 0.3.

STEP 1

Shade six tenths, or 0.6.

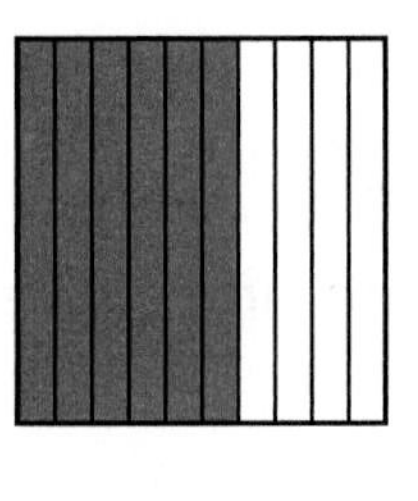

STEP 2

Take away three tenths. There are three tenths left.

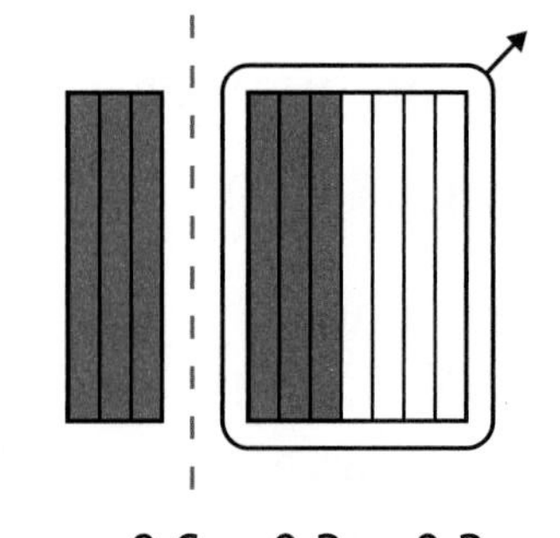

0.6 − 0.3 = 0.3

So, Dan walked 0.3 kilometer farther than Gary.

MATH IDEA You can subtract decimals the same way you subtract whole numbers if you line up the decimal points first.

Example

Find 0.9 − 0.2.

STEP 1

Line up each place value and the decimal points.

decimal point ↓

$$\begin{array}{r} 0.9 \\ -0.2 \\ \hline \end{array}$$

STEP 2

Subtract decimals like whole numbers.

$$\begin{array}{r} 0.9 \\ -0.2 \\ \hline 0\ 7 \end{array}$$

STEP 3

Write the decimal point in the difference.

$$\begin{array}{r} 0.9 \\ -0.2 \\ \hline 0.7 \end{array}$$

Check

1. **Explain** how you can use a decimal model to find $0.6 - 0.2$.

Find each difference.

2. $\begin{array}{r} 0.9 \\ -0.6 \\ \hline \end{array}$

3. $\begin{array}{r} 0.5 \\ -0.3 \\ \hline \end{array}$

4. $\begin{array}{r} 0.7 \\ -0.4 \\ \hline \end{array}$

5. $\begin{array}{r} 0.8 \\ -0.2 \\ \hline \end{array}$

Practice and Problem Solving

Extra Practice, page 424, Set C

Find each difference.

6. $\begin{array}{r} 0.3 \\ -0.2 \\ \hline \end{array}$

7. $\begin{array}{r} 0.6 \\ -0.1 \\ \hline \end{array}$

8. $\begin{array}{r} 0.8 \\ -0.4 \\ \hline \end{array}$

9. $\begin{array}{r} 0.4 \\ -0.3 \\ \hline \end{array}$

10. $0.6 - 0.4 = ■$

11. $0.9 - 0.5 = ■$

12. $0.7 - 0.3 = ■$

ALGEBRA **Write the missing number.**

13. $0.8 - ■ = 0.3$

14. $0.7 - ■ = 0.2$

15. $0.4 - ■ = 0.1$

16. Rhea lives 0.9 kilometer from school. She has walked 0.3 kilometer so far this morning. How much farther must she walk to get to school?

17. **Write a Problem** that can be solved by using the decimal model shown.

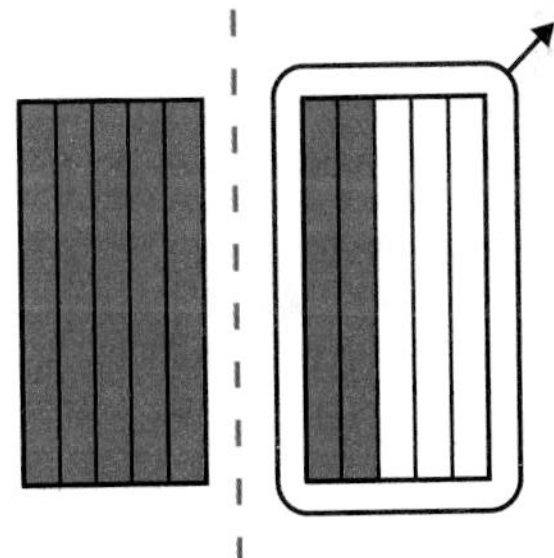

18. **MULTISTEP** Ed bought 4 packs of plain marbles and 5 packs of swirled marbles. Each pack had 10 marbles. How many marbles did he buy in all?

Maintain Skills

Find each sum or difference.

19. $\begin{array}{r} 29 \\ +79 \\ \hline \end{array}$

20. $\begin{array}{r} 82 \\ +37 \\ \hline \end{array}$

21. $\begin{array}{r} 63 \\ +78 \\ \hline \end{array}$

22. $\begin{array}{r} 94 \\ -62 \\ \hline \end{array}$

23. $\begin{array}{r} 43 \\ -18 \\ \hline \end{array}$

24. $\begin{array}{r} 53 \\ -24 \\ \hline \end{array}$

CRCT Test Prep

25. M3N3.g. Pilar put 6 olives on each pizza. If she made 8 pizzas, how many olives did she use? (p. 162)

A. 14
B. 24
C. 40
D. 48

LESSON 5

Problem Solving Skill
Too Much/Too Little Information

M3P1.a. Build new mathematical knowledge through problem solving.
also **M3P1.b., M3P1.c., M3P1.d., M3P3.a., M3P3.b., M3P3.c., M3P3.d., M3P4.a.**

Quick Review

Find the sum or difference.

1. $0.4 + 0.2 = \blacksquare$
2. $0.9 - 0.2 = \blacksquare$
3. $0.4 + 0.4 = \blacksquare$
4. $0.7 - 0.1 = \blacksquare$
5. $0.5 + 0.3 = \blacksquare$

UNDERSTAND | PLAN | SOLVE | CHECK

FIND THE INFORMATION Mr. Dixon went to the store. He bought 0.4 pound of grapes and 0.5 pound of cherries. He also bought 2 pounds of sugar. How many pounds of fruit did Mr. Dixon buy?

STEP 1

Find what the problem asks.
- How many pounds of fruit did Mr. Dixon buy?

STEP 2

Find the information that you need to solve the problem.
- Look for the weights of the fruit:
  0.4 pound of grapes
  0.5 pound of cherries

STEP 3

Look for extra information.
- Look for any items that are not fruit:
  2 pounds of sugar

STEP 4

Solve the problem.
- Add the weights of the fruit to find the total weight.
  0.4 pound + 0.5 pound = 0.9 pound

So, Mr. Dixon bought 0.9 pound of fruit.

Talk About It

- Read the problem below. Is there too much, too little, or the right amount of information? Explain.

Jim and his friends shared a pizza. They each ate 2 slices. There were 2 slices left over. How many slices were in the whole pizza?

Problem Solving Practice

For 1–4, write *a*, *b*, or *c* to tell whether the problem has

a. too much information. **b.** too little information. **c.** the right amount of information.

Solve those with too much or the right amount of information. Tell what is missing for those with too little information.

1. Mrs. Brody made a birthday cake and cut it into equal-size pieces. She gave 8 pieces to Robert and his friends. How many pieces were left?

2. Mrs. Brody bought 10 party hats and 20 noisemakers. She gave 8 hats to Robert and his friends. What fraction of the hats were NOT used?

3. Mr. Grant bought two shirts and a tie. Each shirt cost $19. He gave the clerk $60. What was his change?

4. At practice, Jill swam 0.8 mile, Trish swam 0.6 mile, and Heather swam 0.9 mile. How much further did Jill swim than Trish?

Mixed Applications

5. Ms. Cortez built a fence around her garden. The length of the garden is 4 feet and the width is 3 feet. What is the perimeter of her fence?

6. Mia baked 30 cookies. She gave 6 cookies to each of 4 teachers. Then she gave half of the rest of the cookies to her sister. How many cookies did Mia keep?

USE DATA **For 7–9, use the graph.**

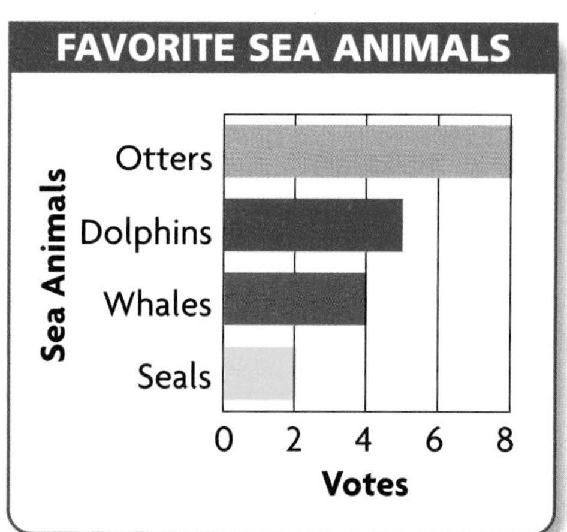

7. How many more students voted for otters and seals than voted for whales and dolphins?

8. How many students did NOT vote for dolphins?

9. **Write a problem** using the data in the bar graph. Then explain how to solve the problem.

Extra Practice

Set A (pp. 414–415)

Write the fraction and decimal for the shaded part.

1. 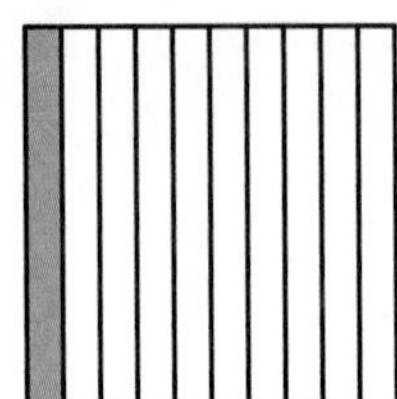
2. 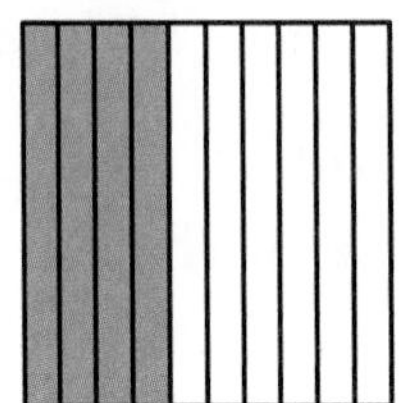
3. 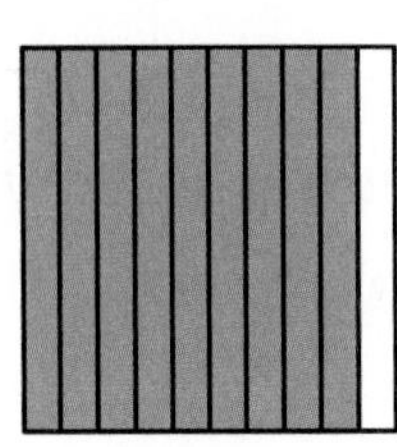
4. 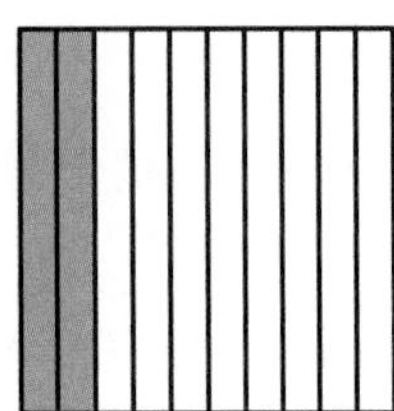

5. What decimal names the amount in Exercise 1 that is NOT shaded?
6. How many more parts would you shade in Exercise 2 to show 0.6?
7. What decimal names the amount in Exercise 4 that is NOT shaded?
8. How many more parts would you shade in Exercise 4 to show 0.8?

Set B (pp. 418–419)

Find each sum.

1. $\begin{array}{r} 0.7 \\ +0.2 \\ \hline \end{array}$
2. $\begin{array}{r} 0.2 \\ +0.5 \\ \hline \end{array}$
3. $\begin{array}{r} 0.4 \\ +0.5 \\ \hline \end{array}$
4. $\begin{array}{r} 0.2 \\ +0.6 \\ \hline \end{array}$
5. $\begin{array}{r} 0.2 \\ +0.2 \\ \hline \end{array}$
6. $\begin{array}{r} 0.3 \\ +0.6 \\ \hline \end{array}$
7. $\begin{array}{r} 0.3 \\ +0.2 \\ \hline \end{array}$
8. $\begin{array}{r} 0.1 \\ +0.1 \\ \hline \end{array}$

Set C (pp. 420–421)

Find each difference.

1. $\begin{array}{r} 0.8 \\ -0.1 \\ \hline \end{array}$
2. $\begin{array}{r} 0.7 \\ -0.2 \\ \hline \end{array}$
3. $\begin{array}{r} 0.5 \\ -0.3 \\ \hline \end{array}$
4. $\begin{array}{r} 0.4 \\ -0.2 \\ \hline \end{array}$

5. On Tuesday, 0.1 foot of snow fell. On Wednesday, 0.4 foot of snow fell. How many more feet of snow fell on Wednesday than Tuesday?
6. Amy bought 0.9 pound of cherries. She used 0.6 pound to make cherry pies. How many pounds of cherries did she have left?

Review/Test

✓ CHECK VOCABULARY AND CONCEPTS

Vocabulary
decimal
tenth

Choose the best term from the box.

1. A number with one or more digits to the right of the decimal point is a __?__. (p. 414)

Write each decimal as a fraction. (pp. 416–417)

2. 0.3
3. 0.8
4. 0.5
5. 0.9

✓ CHECK SKILLS

Write the fraction and decimal for the shaded part. (pp. 414–415)

6. 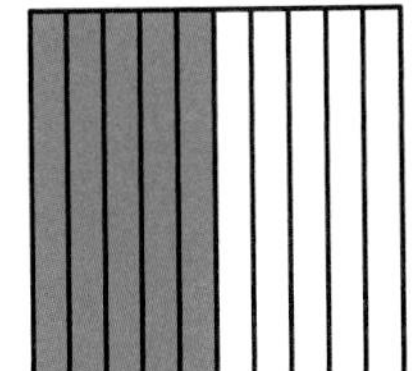
7. 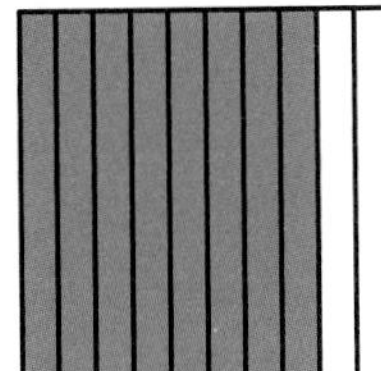
8. 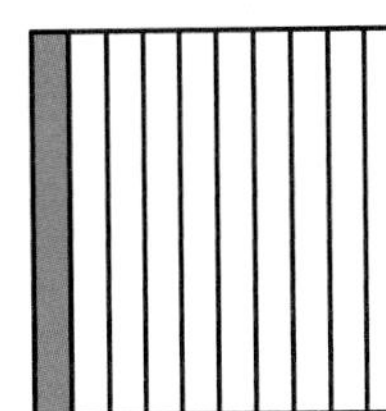
9. 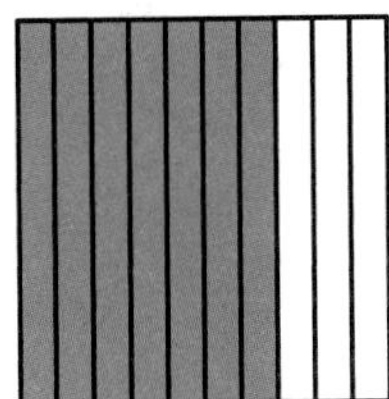

Find each sum or difference. (pp. 418–419, 420–421)

10. $0.4 + 0.3$
11. $0.9 - 0.4$
12. $0.3 + 0.1$
13. $0.8 - 0.2$

✓ CHECK PROBLEM SOLVING

Write *a*, *b*, or *c* to tell whether the problem has

a. too much information.
b. too little information.
c. the right amount of information.

Solve those with too much or the right amount of information. Tell what is missing for those with too little information. (pp. 422–423)

14. Mark paid $6.25 for a book, $4.50 for a sandwich, and $1.00 for crackers. How much did he spend on food in all?

15. Tia made a salad with 0.9 pound of lettuce, 0.3 pound of cucumber, and some carrots. How many pounds of vegetables did she use in all?

Chapter CRCT Test Prep

NUMBERS AND OPERATIONS

1. M3N5.c. How is the fraction $\frac{8}{10}$ written as a decimal?

A. 0.5

B. 0.6

C. 0.7

D. 0.8

2. M3N5.a. What decimal does the model show?

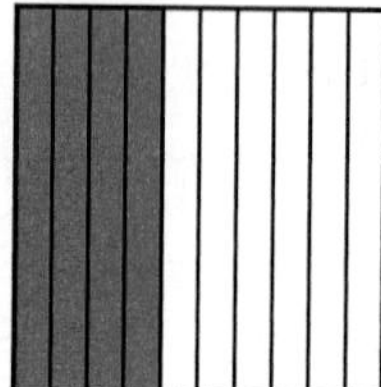

A. 0.3

B. 0.4

C. 0.5

D. 0.6

3. M3N5.e. Kayla walked 0.1 mile in the morning and 0.5 mile in the afternoon. How many miles did she walk in all?

A. 0.4 mile

B. 0.5 mile

C. 0.6 mile

D. 0.7 mile

NUMBERS AND OPERATIONS

4. M3N5.c. How is the fraction $\frac{5}{10}$ written as a decimal?

A. 0.1

B. 0.2

C. 0.5

D. 0.6

5. M3N5.f. What addition does the model show?

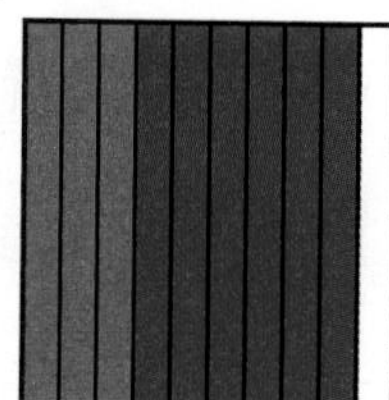

A. $0.2 + 0.5 = 0.7$

B. $0.3 + 0.5 = 0.8$

C. $0.4 + 0.4 = 0.8$

D. $0.3 + 0.6 = 0.9$

6. M3N5.e. Rod bought 0.2 pound of Swiss cheese and 0.4 pound of American cheese. How much cheese did Rod buy?

A. 0.6 pound

B. 0.5 pound

C. 0.4 pound

D. 0.3 pound

Cumulative CRCT Test Prep

MEASUREMENT

7. M3M4.b. Each small square of the figure below is one square centimeter.

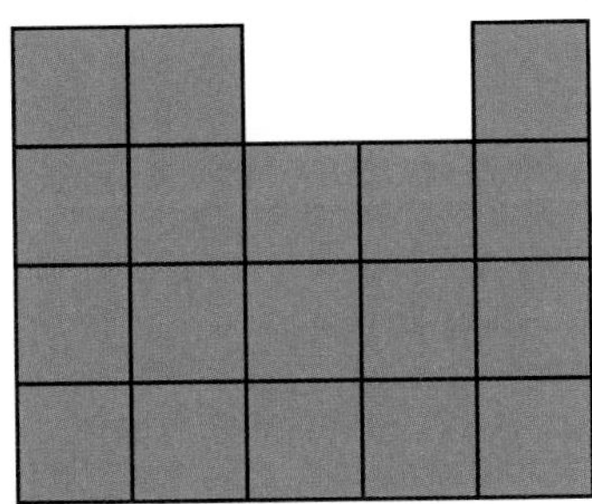

What is the area of the figure?

A. 15 square centimeters

B. 16 square centimeters

C. 18 square centimeters

D. 20 square centimeters

8. M3M4.c. Ryan has a rectangular garden that is 6 feet wide and 8 feet long. What is the area of Ryan's garden?

A. 14 square feet

B. 28 square feet

C. 46 square feet

D. 48 square feet

DATA ANALYSIS

Use the graph below to answer question 9.

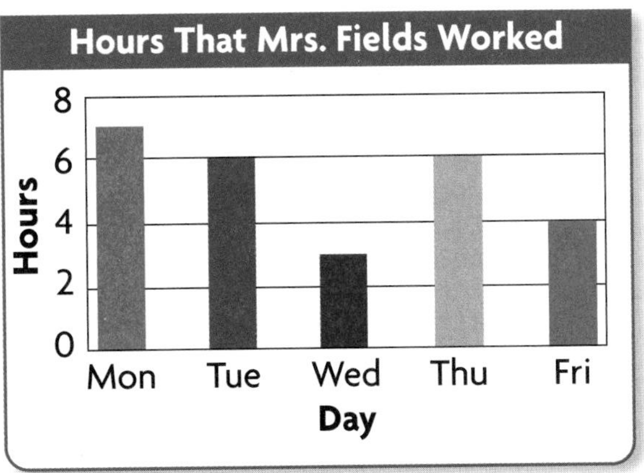

9. M3D1.b. The bar graph shows the number of hours Mrs. Fields worked during one week. How many hours did Mrs. Fields work in all?

A. 18 hours

B. 23 hours

C. 26 hours

D. 29 hours

GPS/CRCT Vocabulary

ELA3R2 The student acquires and uses grade-level words to communicate effectively. *also* **ELA3R3.b., ELA3R3.h., ELA3R3.r.**

VOCABULARY
- fraction
- numerator
- denominator
- common fraction
- like fractions
- tenth
- decimal

VOCABULARY MATCH

MATERIALS *For each pair* vocabulary cards, definition cards

- Shuffle the word cards and the definition cards together.
- Deal 4 cards to each player. Place the rest of the cards face down in a pile on the table.
- The players should match terms with their definitions to make pairs from their cards and set them aside.
- Take turns drawing a card from the pile. If it matches a card in your hand, keep it and set the pair aside. If not, return it to the bottom of the pile.

MATH WORD WORK (MEMORY)

MATERIALS *For each group* vocabulary cards

- Mix up the cards and place them face down. Arrange them in 4 rows and 4 columns.
- Take turns turning over a pair of cards. If the cards are a match, the player must give the definition of the term on the cards. If the definition is correct, the player takes the cards. The player with the greatest number of pairs wins!

WHAT'S IN THE BOX?

MATERIALS *For each pair* Unit 7 *What's in the Box?* puzzle

- With a partner, use the clues and terms in the Vocabulary box on page 428 to help fill in the blanks on your sheet.
- The letters in the boxes will spell the city in Georgia that is known as "The Watermelon Capital of the World."

1. A fraction that has a whole number as the numerator and the denominator is called a __?__ **fraction**.
2. The __?__ of a fraction tells how many equal parts are in the whole.
3. A __?__ names a part of a group or a whole.
4. The fraction $\frac{7}{10}$ written as a __?__ is 0.7.
5. One of 10 equal parts is called a __?__.
6. $\frac{1}{8}$ and $\frac{5}{8}$ are __?__ **fractions**.
7. The __?__ of the fraction $\frac{3}{4}$ is 3.

1. ☐ _ _ _ _ _
2. _ _ _ ☐ _ _ _ _ _ _ _
3. _ ☐ _ _ _ _ _ _
4. ☐ _ _ _ _ _ _
5. _ ☐ _ _ _
6. ☐ _ _ _
7. _ _ _ ☐ _ _ _ _ _

CLUES

- Each partner should come up with an example or a clue for each vocabulary terms shown at the right. For example, a clue for *denominator* could be "the total number of equal parts." A clue for *tenth* could be "a dime is one __?__ of a dollar."
- Take turns giving your partner clues. The partner that correctly names the most vocabulary terms wins!

Word List
fraction
numerator
denominator
like fractions
decimal
tenth

Georgia Tasks

M3N5.g. Solve problems involving fractions. *also* **M3P5.a.**

SS3G1.b. Identify major mountains of the United States of America: Appalachian, Rocky. *also* **ELA3R3.h.**

Task A

MMMM ... BROWNIES!

Jeff made a pan of brownies to share with Carla and Keith. The brownies were cut into equal pieces. The three friends each ate a different number of pieces.

a. Make a drawing of the pan of brownies. Label each piece with J, C, or K. Make sure that there is a different number of pieces for each letter. What fraction of the brownies did each child eat?

b. Write an addition or subtraction word problem about the brownies. Use fractions in your word problems. Trade with a partner and solve.

Task B

TAKE A HIKE!

The Appalachian Mountains are the oldest mountains in North America. They run from Maine down to Georgia. There are many hiking trails that go through the mountains. Linda and her friends are hiking on some of these trails.

Hiking Trails	
Trail	**Length**
Black Trail	0.3 mile
Blue Trail	0.2 mile
Red Trail	0.5 mile
Yellow Trail	0.4 mile

a. Linda hiked the Black Trail and the Red Trail. Gary hiked the Yellow Trail and the Blue Trail. Who hiked the farthest? Explain how you found your answer.

b. Susan wants to hike on 2 trails that are a total of more than 0.5 mile. Which trails could she hike?

Maintain/Preview

Maintain

Find each sum or difference. Use fraction bars if you wish.

1. $\frac{3}{5} + \frac{1}{5} = \blacksquare$ **2.** $\frac{2}{4} + \frac{1}{4} = \blacksquare$ **3.** $\frac{8}{10} - \frac{2}{10} = \blacksquare$ **4.** $\frac{5}{6} - \frac{3}{6} = \blacksquare$

Write each decimal as a fraction.

5. 0.4 **6.** 0.9 **7.** 0.5 **8.** 0.3

Find each sum or difference.

9. $\begin{array}{r} 0.4 \\ +0.3 \\ \hline \end{array}$ **10.** $\begin{array}{r} 0.6 \\ +0.2 \\ \hline \end{array}$ **11.** $\begin{array}{r} 0.9 \\ -0.3 \\ \hline \end{array}$ **12.** $\begin{array}{r} 0.8 \\ -0.6 \\ \hline \end{array}$

13. Carmen lives 0.9 kilometer from the library. So far, she has walked 0.6 kilometer. How much farther must she walk to get to the library?

14. Nathan has a box of 8 doughnuts. One doughnut is frosted, 2 are powdered, and 5 are jelly. What fraction of the doughnuts are jelly?

Preview

Find each product.

1. $\begin{array}{r} 10 \\ \times 4 \\ \hline \end{array}$ **2.** $\begin{array}{r} 8 \\ \times 7 \\ \hline \end{array}$ **3.** $\begin{array}{r} 4 \\ \times 9 \\ \hline \end{array}$ **4.** $\begin{array}{r} 6 \\ \times 8 \\ \hline \end{array}$

5. $\begin{array}{r} 9 \\ \times 8 \\ \hline \end{array}$ **6.** $\begin{array}{r} 2 \\ \times 6 \\ \hline \end{array}$ **7.** $\begin{array}{r} 7 \\ \times 4 \\ \hline \end{array}$ **8.** $\begin{array}{r} 3 \\ \times 5 \\ \hline \end{array}$

9. $2 \times 2 = \blacksquare$ **10.** $6 \times 3 = \blacksquare$ **11.** $7 \times 7 = \blacksquare$ **12.** $10 \times 5 = \blacksquare$

Find each quotient.

13. $6\overline{)36}$ **14.** $4\overline{)28}$ **15.** $6\overline{)42}$ **16.** $9\overline{)81}$

17. $8\overline{)64}$ **18.** $4\overline{)20}$ **19.** $7\overline{)70}$ **20.** $5\overline{)45}$

CHAPTER 22

Multiply by 1-Digit Numbers

FAST FACT • SOCIAL STUDIES **4-H is a club for young people. It stands for *head, heart, hands,* and *health*.**

INVESTIGATION **Some 4-H members raise animals, such as goats, cows, or sheep. Suppose 4-H members are showing goats at a fair. Look at the diagram. If there is 1 goat in each stall and there are 4 barns like this one, how many goats can be kept at the fair?**

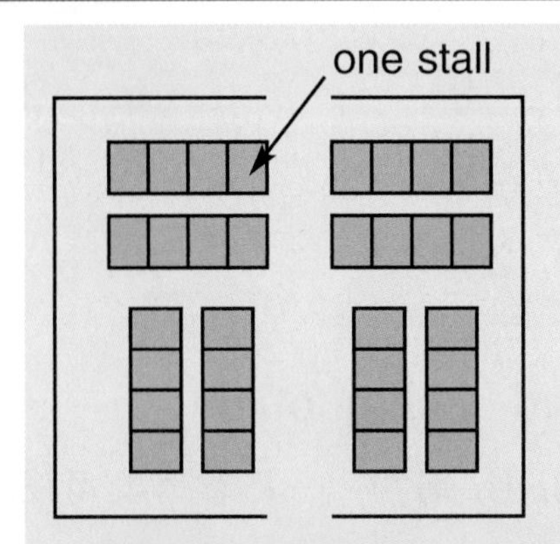

CHECK WHAT YOU KNOW

Use this page to help you review and remember important skills needed for Chapter 22.

ADDITION

Find the sum.

1. $\begin{array}{r} 47 \\ +64 \\ \hline \end{array}$
2. $\begin{array}{r} 29 \\ +81 \\ \hline \end{array}$
3. $\begin{array}{r} 52 \\ +119 \\ \hline \end{array}$
4. $\begin{array}{r} 28 \\ +253 \\ \hline \end{array}$
5. $\begin{array}{r} 88 \\ +93 \\ \hline \end{array}$
6. $\begin{array}{r} 346 \\ +389 \\ \hline \end{array}$
7. $\begin{array}{r} 284 \\ +172 \\ \hline \end{array}$
8. $\begin{array}{r} 314 \\ +726 \\ \hline \end{array}$
9. $\begin{array}{r} 672 \\ +361 \\ \hline \end{array}$
10. $\begin{array}{r} 521 \\ +229 \\ \hline \end{array}$

MULTIPLICATION FACTS

Find the product.

11. $6 \times 7 = \blacksquare$
12. $5 \times 5 = \blacksquare$
13. $\blacksquare = 9 \times 4$
14. $9 \times 1 = \blacksquare$
15. $7 \times 10 = \blacksquare$
16. $\blacksquare = 8 \times 6$
17. $5 \times 9 = \blacksquare$
18. $\blacksquare = 2 \times 3$
19. $\blacksquare = 4 \times 5$
20. $4 \times 8 = \blacksquare$
21. $\blacksquare = 0 \times 6$
22. $8 \times 7 = \blacksquare$
23. $\begin{array}{r} 5 \\ \times 7 \\ \hline \end{array}$
24. $\begin{array}{r} 8 \\ \times 4 \\ \hline \end{array}$
25. $\begin{array}{r} 4 \\ \times 9 \\ \hline \end{array}$
26. $\begin{array}{r} 10 \\ \times\ 3 \\ \hline \end{array}$
27. $\begin{array}{r} 8 \\ \times 8 \\ \hline \end{array}$

VOCABULARY POWER

REVIEW

multiple [mul′tə•pəl]

Part of the word *multiple* is *multi,* which means "many times over." Look in a dictionary and find another word that begins with *multi*. What does the word mean?

PREVIEW

partial products

www.harcourtschool.com/mathglossary

LESSON 1

Algebra: Multiply Multiples of 10 and 100

M3N3.d. Understand the effect on the product when multiplying by multiples of 10. *also* M3P2., M3P2.a., M3P2.b., M3P2.c., M3P2.d., M3P3.a., M3P3.b., M3P3.c., M3P3.d., M3P4.a., M3P4.b., M3P5., M3P5.b., M3P5.c.

Quick Review

1. $2 \times 4 = ■$
2. $5 \times 7 = ■$
3. $■ = 2 \times 10$
4. $10 \times 7 = ■$
5. $■ = 6 \times 10$

MATERIALS
base-ten blocks

Explore

You can use models or drawings to find multiples. A multiple is the product of a given whole number and another whole number.

$3 \times 2 = \mathbf{6} \leftarrow$ 6 is a multiple of 3 and 2.

Activity 1

Model or draw the first three multiples of 10 and 100.

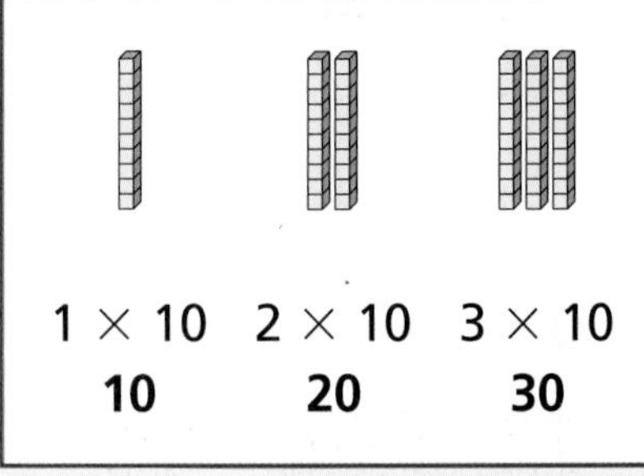

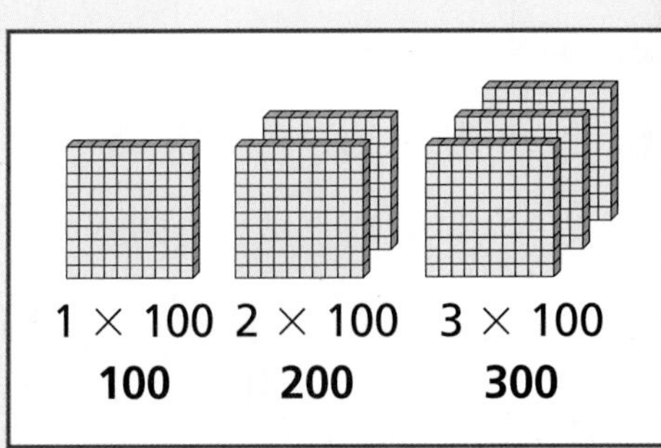

- What are the first nine multiples of 10? the first nine multiples of 100?

Activity 2 You can multiply by multiples of 10 and 100.
Find 4×30.

STEP 1

Model 4 groups of 30.

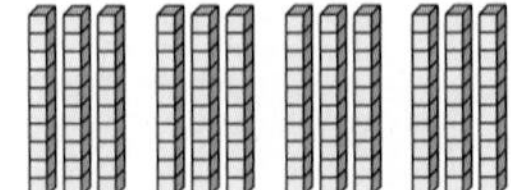

STEP 2

Combine the tens. Regroup 12 tens as 1 hundred 2 tens.

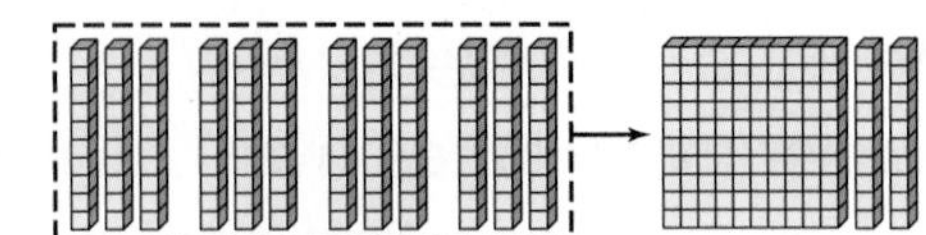

So, $4 \times 30 = 120$.

Try It Use base-ten blocks to find each product.

a. $5 \times 20 = ■$ b. $4 \times 200 = ■$ c. $6 \times 30 = ■$

Connect

You can use multiplication facts and patterns to help you multiply multiples of 10 and 100.

Examples Use a basic fact. Then use a pattern.

$3 \times 2 = 6$ $3 \times 20 = 60$ $3 \times 200 = 600$	The product has the same number of zeros as the factor.
$2 \times 5 = 10$ $2 \times 50 = 100$ $2 \times 500 = 1{,}000$	When a basic fact has a zero in the product, all products in the pattern have an additional zero.

Practice and Problem Solving

Copy and complete. Use patterns and mental math to help.

1. $6 \times 1 = ■$ $6 \times 10 = ■$ $6 \times 100 = ■$
2. $4 \times 5 = ■$ $4 \times 50 = ■$ $4 \times 500 = ■$

Use mental math and basic facts to find the product.

3. $2 \times 70 = ■$
4. $■ = 6 \times 400$
5. $4 \times 800 = ■$
6. $■ = 5 \times 300$
7. $5 \times 60 = ■$
8. $■ = 3 \times 90$
9. **USE DATA** Emilio wants to save money for a new bicycle. How many dollars does he need to save? Use the table.

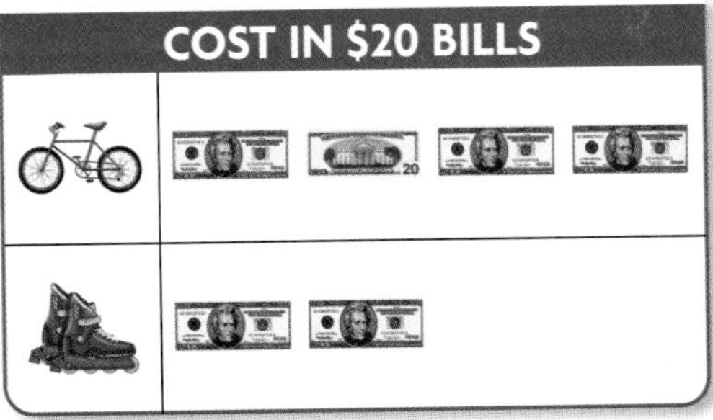

10. **REASONING** Tom adds a number to itself and then subtracts 13. The answer is 37. What is Tom's number?
11. **What's the Question?** A case of popcorn contains 80 boxes. The answer is 480 boxes.

Maintain Skills

Write <, >, or = for each ●.

12. 81 ● 64
13. 73 ● 92
14. 57 ● 98
15. 35 ● 25
16. 16 ● 61
17. 44 ● 43

CRCT Test Prep

18. M3N2.c. The parking lot can hold 132 cars. There are 84 cars in the lot. How many more cars can park in the lot? (p. 74)

A. 36 B. 46 C. 48 D. 58

LESSON 2

Estimate Products

M3N3.f. Use mental math and estimation strategies to multiply. *also* M3P2.a., M3P2.b., M3P2.c., M3P2.d., M3P3.a., M3P3.b., M3P3.c., M3P3.d.

Learn

BUNCHES OF BISCUITS There are 28 dogs at the pet fair. If each dog gets 4 biscuits, about how many biscuits will be needed?

$4 \times 28 = \blacksquare$ or $\begin{array}{r} 28 \\ \times\ 4 \\ \hline \end{array}$

MATH IDEA When you don't need an exact answer, you can estimate.

Quick Review

1. $4 \times 20 = \blacksquare$
2. $7 \times 40 = \blacksquare$
3. $2 \times 90 = \blacksquare$
4. $4 \times 60 = \blacksquare$
5. $8 \times 30 = \blacksquare$

Example

STEP 1

Estimate the first factor.

$\begin{array}{r} 28 \\ \times\ 4 \\ \hline \end{array} \rightarrow \begin{array}{r} 30 \\ \times\ 4 \\ \hline \end{array}$

STEP 2

Find the estimated product.

$\begin{array}{r} 30 \\ \times\ 4 \\ \hline 120 \end{array}$

So, about 120 biscuits are needed.

- Is the actual answer less than or greater than 120? How do you know?

More Examples

A Estimate. 7×52

$\begin{array}{r} 52 \\ \times\ 7 \\ \hline \end{array} \rightarrow \begin{array}{r} 50 \\ \times\ 7 \\ \hline 350 \end{array}$

B Estimate. 4×213

$\begin{array}{r} 213 \\ \times\ 4 \\ \hline \end{array} \rightarrow \begin{array}{r} 200 \\ \times\ 4 \\ \hline 800 \end{array}$

Check

1. Explain how to estimate 7×65.

Estimate the product.

2. $\begin{array}{r} 47 \\ \times\ 3 \\ \hline \end{array}$

3. $\begin{array}{r} 58 \\ \times\ 4 \\ \hline \end{array}$

4. $\begin{array}{r} 64 \\ \times\ 2 \\ \hline \end{array}$

5. $\begin{array}{r} 396 \\ \times\ \ 5 \\ \hline \end{array}$

Practice and Problem Solving

Extra Practice, page 450, Set A

Estimate the product.

6. $\begin{array}{r} 38 \\ \times\ 5 \\ \hline \end{array}$

7. $\begin{array}{r} 73 \\ \times\ 8 \\ \hline \end{array}$

8. $\begin{array}{r} 44 \\ \times\ 3 \\ \hline \end{array}$

9. $\begin{array}{r} 89 \\ \times\ 4 \\ \hline \end{array}$

10. $\begin{array}{r} 169 \\ \times\ \ 6 \\ \hline \end{array}$

11. $\begin{array}{r} 228 \\ \times\ \ 7 \\ \hline \end{array}$

12. $\begin{array}{r} 514 \\ \times\ \ 4 \\ \hline \end{array}$

13. $\begin{array}{r} 682 \\ \times\ \ 8 \\ \hline \end{array}$

14. $\begin{array}{r} 37 \\ \times\ 2 \\ \hline \end{array}$

15. $\begin{array}{r} 83 \\ \times\ 4 \\ \hline \end{array}$

16. $\begin{array}{r} 286 \\ \times\ \ 7 \\ \hline \end{array}$

17. $\begin{array}{r} 267 \\ \times\ \ 5 \\ \hline \end{array}$

18. $3 \times 29 = \blacksquare$

19. $\blacksquare = 3 \times 78$

20. $5 \times 173 = \blacksquare$

21. $\blacksquare = 7 \times 731$

22. $\blacksquare = 9 \times 395$

23. $6 \times 419 = \blacksquare$

24. $4 \times 59 = \blacksquare$

25. $\blacksquare = 8 \times 612$

26. **REASONING** Gretchen says that $7 \times 43 = 3{,}001$. Estimate to decide if you agree or disagree. Explain.

27. **Write a Problem** for which you can estimate the answer by finding 400×7.

28. Mr. Cory has 29 students and Miss Jan has 27 students. Each student needs 4 jars for an experiment. About how many jars are needed for all students?

29. **What's the Error?** Tui said that the product 7×488 is less than 2,800. Describe her error and give a more reasonable estimate.

Maintain Skills

Find each sum or difference.

30. $\begin{array}{r} 942 \\ -258 \\ \hline \end{array}$

31. $\begin{array}{r} 604 \\ -465 \\ \hline \end{array}$

32. $\begin{array}{r} 731 \\ -283 \\ \hline \end{array}$

33. $\begin{array}{r} 234 \\ +625 \\ \hline \end{array}$

34. $\begin{array}{r} 324 \\ +576 \\ \hline \end{array}$

35. $\begin{array}{r} 658 \\ +394 \\ \hline \end{array}$

CRCT Test Prep

36. M3N3.g. Leroy has a scrapbook with 8 pages. Each page has 7 stickers. How many stickers does he have in all? (p. 164)

A. 52
B. 54
C. 56
D. 64

LESSON 3

Arrays

M3N3.c. Use arrays...to develop understanding of the distributive property.... *also* M3P2., M3P4.a., M3P4.b., M3P5.a., M3P5.b., M3P5.c.

Quick Review

1. $6 \times 5 =$ ■
2. ■ $= 4 \times 3$
3. $10 \times 6 =$ ■
4. ■ $= 6 \times 8$
5. $4 \times 10 =$ ■

MATERIALS
base-ten blocks

Explore

You can use an array to multiply a 2-digit number by a 1-digit number.

Activity Find 4×16.

STEP 1

Use 1 ten 6 ones to show 16. Make 4 rows of 16 to show 4×16.

STEP 2

Combine the ones and the tens to find the product.

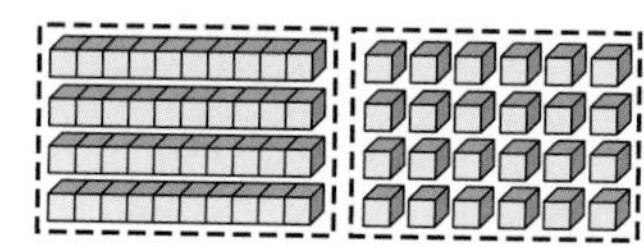

$4 \times 10 = 40$ $4 \times 6 = 24$

$40 + 24 = 64$

So, $4 \times 16 = 64$.

- How did you combine the ones and tens to find the product?

Try It

Use base-ten blocks to find the product.

a. $3 \times 12 =$ ■

b. $4 \times 13 =$ ■

c. $2 \times 36 =$ ■

d. $5 \times 23 =$ ■

e. $6 \times 14 =$ ■

f. $3 \times 27 =$ ■

g. $2 \times 21 =$ ■

h. $4 \times 19 =$ ■

Connect

You can use the Distributive Property to combine tens and ones.

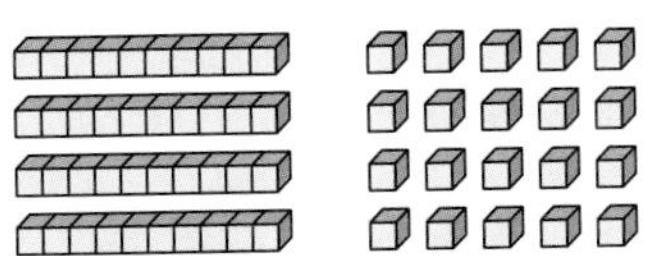

$4 \times 15 = (4 \times 10) + (4 \times 5)$
$40 + 20 = 60$

So, $4 \times 15 = 60$.

Practice and Problem Solving

Find the product. Use base-ten blocks.

1. $3 \times 18 = ■$ **2.** $5 \times 31 = ■$ **3.** $6 \times 40 = ■$ **4.** $8 \times 19 = ■$

5. $9 \times 14 = ■$ **6.** $2 \times 43 = ■$ **7.** $3 \times 17 = ■$ **8.** $5 \times 38 = ■$

9. 21×4 **10.** 18×2 **11.** 28×4 **12.** 25×3

13. Kimberly has 5 bags. Each bag has 27 marbles in it. Write a multiplication sentence that Kimberly can use to find the number of marbles she has in all.

14. Jason bought 3 boxes of crayons. Each box contains 64 crayons. How many crayons did Jason buy?

15. **Vocabulary Power** One meaning of product is "a result of something." A cake is the result of ingredients baked in an oven. What is the product in multiplication the result of?

16. **MULTISTEP** Marla bought 2 pounds of apples for \$1.29 per pound. She paid with a \$5 bill. How much change did she receive?

Maintain Skills

Write the time.

17.

18.

CRCT Test Prep

19. M3N1.a. What is the value of the digit 8 in 28,051? (p. 14)

A. 80
B. 800
C. 8,000
D. 80,000

LESSON 4

Partial Products

M3N3.c. Use arrays and area models to develop understanding of the distributive property and to determine partial products for multiplication of 2- or 3-digit numbers by a 1-digit number. *also* **M3P3.a., M3P3.b., M3P3.c., M3P3.d., M3P4.a., M3P4.b.**

Learn

CHORUS LINE UP Students in the school chorus stand in 3 rows of 14. How many students are in the chorus?

You can multiply by using the Distributive Property to find **partial products**.

Quick Review

Find each sum.

1. $40 + 16 = ■$
2. $80 + 45 = ■$
3. $240 + 32 = ■$
4. $350 + 49 = ■$
5. $150 + 80 = ■$

VOCABULARY

partial products

Example Find 3×14.

STEP 1

Draw an array on grid paper to model the problem.

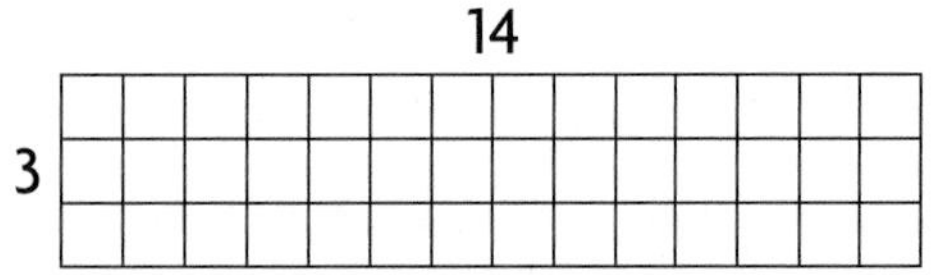

STEP 2

Use the Distributive Property to break apart the array. Multiply to find the partial products.

$$3 \times 14 = (3 \times 10) + (3 \times 4)$$

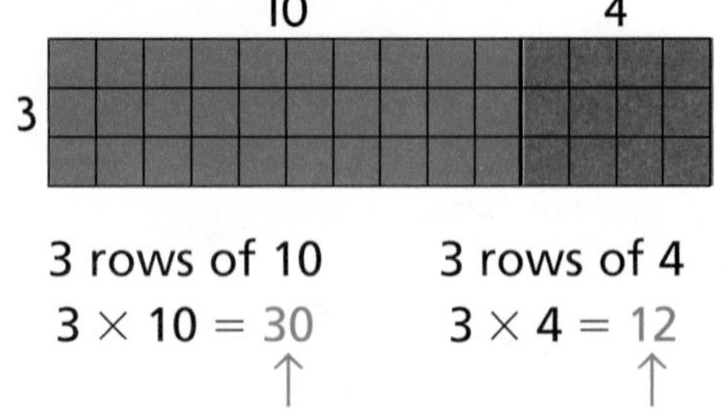

3 rows of 10
$3 \times 10 = 30$
↑
partial product

3 rows of 4
$3 \times 4 = 12$
↑
partial product

STEP 3

Find the sum of the partial products.

$$30 + 12 = 42$$

So, there are 42 students in the chorus.

- How does using the Distributive Property help you solve the problem?

Check

1. **Model** 3×18 on grid paper. Write the partial products.

Use the Distributive Property to find each product. You may wish to use grid paper.

2. $2 \times 38 = \blacksquare$
3. $5 \times 21 = \blacksquare$
4. $4 \times 14 = \blacksquare$
5. $3 \times 26 = \blacksquare$

Practice and Problem Solving

Extra Practice, page 450, Set B

Use the Distributive Property to find each product. You may wish to use grid paper.

6. $3 \times 23 = \blacksquare$
7. $3 \times 15 = \blacksquare$
8. $2 \times 35 = \blacksquare$
9. $4 \times 28 = \blacksquare$
10. $3 \times 16 = \blacksquare$
11. $5 \times 22 = \blacksquare$
12. $6 \times 31 = \blacksquare$
13. $6 \times 92 = \blacksquare$
14. $\begin{array}{r} 42 \\ \times\ 4 \\ \hline \end{array}$
15. $\begin{array}{r} 71 \\ \times\ 6 \\ \hline \end{array}$
16. $\begin{array}{r} 28 \\ \times\ 7 \\ \hline \end{array}$
17. $\begin{array}{r} 18 \\ \times\ 9 \\ \hline \end{array}$

18. A recipe for a cake calls for 2 cups of flour. How many cups of flour would a baker need to make 35 cakes?
19. **MULTISTEP** Alice bought 3 DVDs for $15 each and 2 CDs for $10 each. How much did Alice spend?
20. Brett has 18 packs of baseball cards. Each pack has 8 cards. How many baseball cards does he have in all?
21. **Write About It** Explain how to use the Distributive Property to find the product 31×6.

Maintain Skills

Find each sum or difference

22. $\begin{array}{r} 275 \\ +376 \\ \hline \end{array}$
23. $\begin{array}{r} 382 \\ -158 \\ \hline \end{array}$
24. $\begin{array}{r} 822 \\ -568 \\ \hline \end{array}$
25. $\begin{array}{r} 936 \\ +826 \\ \hline \end{array}$
26. $\begin{array}{r} 492 \\ +378 \\ \hline \end{array}$
27. $\begin{array}{r} 907 \\ -713 \\ \hline \end{array}$

CRCT Test Prep

28. M3M3.b. What is the perimeter of a square that has one side that is 3 centimeters long? (p. 354)

A. 3 centimeters
B. 6 centimeters
C. 9 centimeters
D. 12 centimeters

LESSON 5

Record Multiplication

M3N3.c. Use arrays and area models to develop understanding of the distributive property and to determine partial products for multiplication of 2- or 3-digit numbers by a 1-digit number. *also* **M3P2.a., M3P2.b., M3P2.c., M3P2.d.**

Quick Review

1. $6 \times 5 = ■$
2. $■ = 4 \times 3$
3. $10 \times 6 = ■$
4. $■ = 6 \times 8$
5. $4 \times 10 = ■$

Learn

ARE WE THERE YET? Ann's class is going on a field trip. There are 5 buses with 23 people on each bus. How many people in all are going on the trip?

Example

Find 5×23.

STEP 1

Model 5 groups of 23. Multiply the ones.

	T	O
	2	3
×		5
	1	5

(5 × 3 ones)

STEP 2

Multiply the tens.

	H	T	O
		2	3
×			5
		1	5
	1	0	0

(5 × 2 tens)

STEP 3

Add to find the product.

	H	T	O
		2	3
×			5
		1	5
+	1	0	0
	1	1	5

So, there are 115 people are going on the field trip.

- How does knowing 5×2 help you find 5×20?

More Examples

A

```
   32
 ×  4
    8 (4 × 2 ones)
 +120 (4 × 3 tens)
  128
```

B

```
   73
 ×  5
   15 (5 × 3 ones)
 +350 (5 × 7 tens)
  365
```

Check

1. **Model** 3×28 with base-ten blocks. Use paper and pencil to record what you did.

Find the product.

2. 26×2

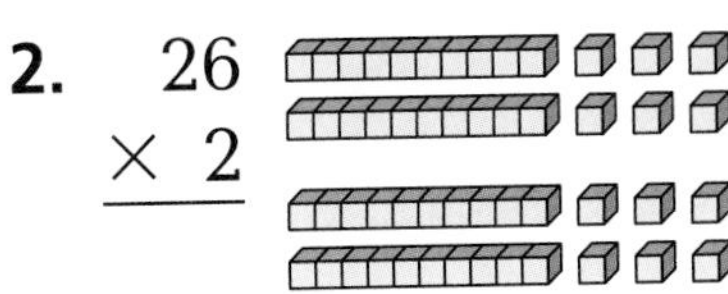

3. 24×3

4. 38×2

Practice and Problem Solving

Extra Practice, page 450, Set C

Find the product.

5. 13×5

6. 22×4

7. 47×2

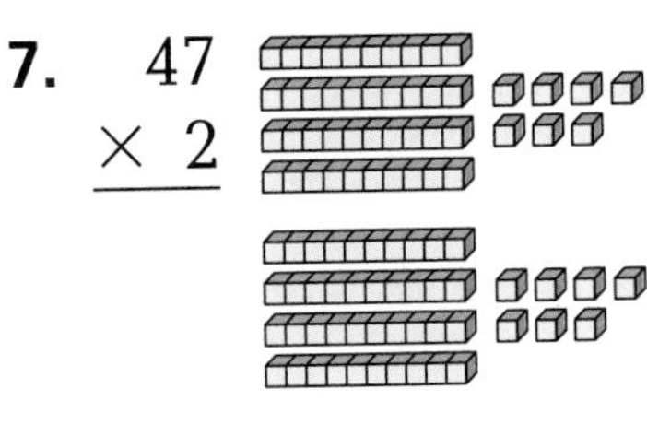

8. 23×6

9. 34×3

10. 57×2

11. 19×4

12. 38×5

13. 15×9

14. 28×4

15. 21×3

16. 42×2

17. 53×4

18. **MULTISTEP** Tanya bought 2 pairs of jeans for \$18 each, a shirt for \$12, and a sweatshirt for \$8. How much did Tanya spend?

19. **REASONING** The sum of two numbers is 20. The product of the two numbers is 75. What are the numbers?

20. **Write a problem** There are 24 hours in a day. There are 7 days in a week. Write a multiplication problem using this information. Solve your problem.

21. **What's the Error?** Lori says that the product 3×16 is the same as the sum $3 + 18$. Describe Lori's error and then find the product.

Maintain Skills

22. Write the amount.

CRCT Test Prep

23. M3M2.c. Which unit would you use to measure the length of your finger? (p. 282)

A. foot
B. yard
C. inch
D. mile

LESSON 6

Problem Solving Skill
Choose the Operation

M3P1.c. Apply and adapt a variety of appropriate strategies to solve problems. *also* M3N3.g., M3P1.a., M3P1.b., M3P1.d.

UNDERSTAND · PLAN · SOLVE · CHECK

Quick Review

1. $\begin{array}{r} 15 \\ \times\ 6 \\ \hline \end{array}$
2. $\begin{array}{r} 72 \\ \times\ 8 \\ \hline \end{array}$
3. $\begin{array}{r} 232 \\ +125 \\ \hline \end{array}$
4. $\begin{array}{r} 495 \\ -208 \\ \hline \end{array}$
5. $18 \div 9 = \blacksquare$

GRAND CHAMP Steve will work 28 hours each week to get his cattle ready for the State Fair. The fair is in 4 weeks. How many hours will Steve work to get his cattle ready?

This chart can help you decide which operation to use.

Add	• Join groups of different amounts.
Subtract	• Take away. • Compare amounts.
Multiply	• Join equal groups.
Divide	• Separate into equal groups. • Find the number in each group.

Since you are joining equal groups, you multiply.

number of weeks worked ↓	×	number of hours worked per week	=	total number of hours
4	×	28	=	■

or $\begin{array}{r} 28 \\ \times\ 4 \\ \hline 112 \end{array}$

So, Steve will work 112 hours to get his cattle ready.

MATH IDEA Before you solve a problem, decide what operation to use.

Talk About It

- What other operation could you use to solve the problem? Explain.
- **What if** Steve will work 8 more hours during the week before the fair? How many hours will he work to get ready?

Problem Solving Practice

Write whether you would *add, subtract, multiply,* or *divide*. Then solve.

1. Tamara spends 30 minutes each day grooming her horse. How many minutes does she spend grooming her horse in 5 days?

2. Drew paid \$12.99 for a state fair T-shirt and \$10.95 for a cap. How much more did the T-shirt cost than the cap?

Mieko bought 3 flowers for 75¢ each. How much did she spend for the flowers?

3. Which number sentence can you use to solve the problem?
   - **A** $75¢ + 3¢ = ■$
   - **B** $75¢ - 3¢ = ■$
   - **C** $3 \times 75¢ = ■$
   - **D** $75¢ \div 3 = ■$

4. How much did Mieko spend for the flowers?
   - **F** 25¢
   - **G** 75¢
   - **H** \$1.50
   - **J** \$2.25

Mixed Applications

USE DATA For 5–9, use the table.

ANIMAL CONTEST ENTRIES	
Animals	**Number of Entries**
Horses	60
Hogs	55
Sheep	50
Rabbits	30

5. Six rabbits were entered in a special contest. The others were put into 3 equal groups for the Largest Rabbit Contest. How many rabbits were in each of the 3 groups?

6. The horses are shown in groups of 6. How many groups of horses will there be?

7. Make a bar graph using the data in the table. Be sure to write a title and labels.

8. Llamas were added to the contest. They were put into 2 equal groups. Do you have enough information to find the number of llamas in each group? Explain.

9. **? What's the Question?** The answer is 10 more horses. What is the question? What operation would you use to solve the problem?

LESSON 7

Multiply 3-Digit Numbers

M3N3.c. Use arrays and area models to develop an understanding of the distributive property and to determine partial products for multiplication of 2- or 3-digit numbers by a 1-digit number.

Quick Review

Find each product.

1. 28×5
2. 51×7
3. 81×4
4. 67×6
5. 17×5

Learn

FULL HOUSE Brook Elementary School is presenting a play. There will be 2 shows, and 165 people can attend each show. How many people can attend all of the shows?

$2 \times 165 = \blacksquare$

Estimate. $2 \times 200 = 400$

Example

STEP 1

Multiply the ones.

	H	T	O
	1	6	5
×			2
		1	0

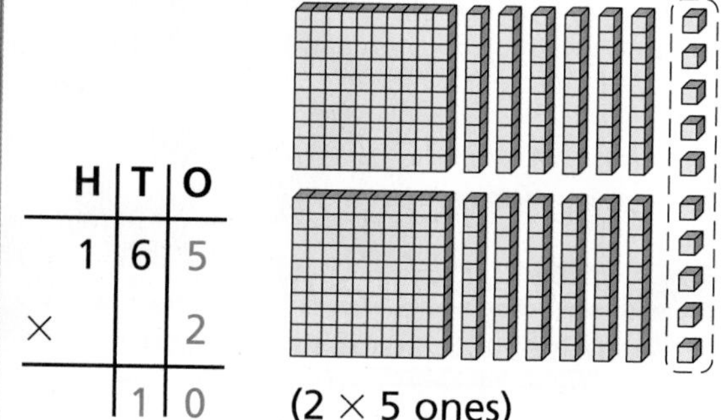

(2 × 5 ones)

STEP 2

Multiply the tens.

	H	T	O
	1	6	5
×			2
		1	0
	1	2	0

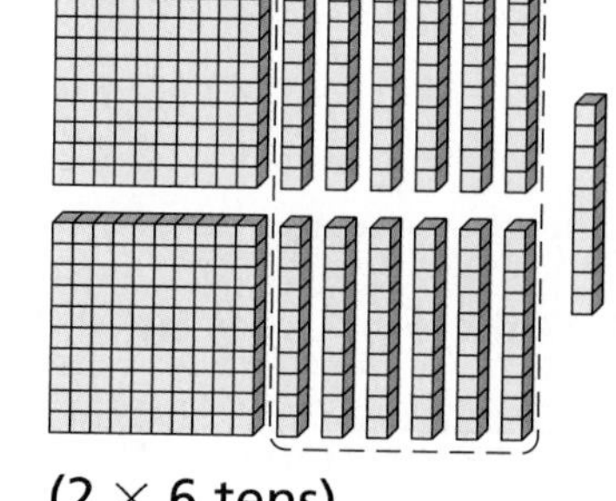

(2 × 6 tens)

STEP 3

Multiply the hundreds.

	H	T	O
	1	6	5
×			2
		1	0
	1	2	0
	2	0	0

(2 × 1 hundred)

STEP 4

Add to find the product.

	H	T	O
	1	6	5
×			2
		1	0
	1	2	0
+	2	0	0
	3	3	0

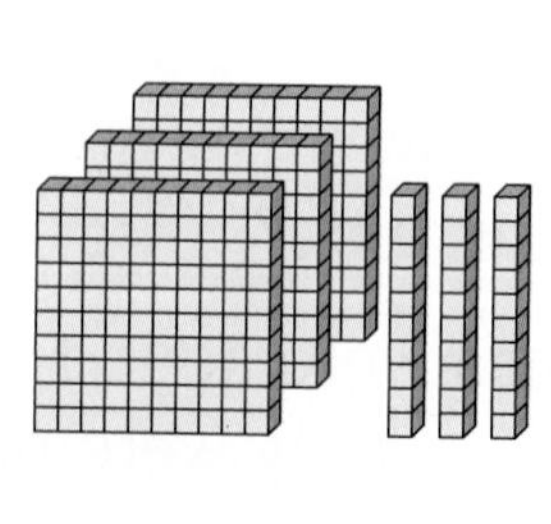

So, 330 people can attend the play. Since 330 is close to the estimate 400, the product is reasonable.

Check

1. Write a 3-digit number you could multiply by 3 and get a 6 in the tens place.

Find the product.

2. $4 \times 135 = \blacksquare$ 3. $6 \times 413 = \blacksquare$ 4. $8 \times 215 = \blacksquare$ 5. $3 \times 142 = \blacksquare$

Practice and Problem Solving

Extra Practice, page 450, Set D

Find the product.

6. $4 \times 114 = \blacksquare$ 7. $7 \times 327 = \blacksquare$ 8. $6 \times 218 = \blacksquare$ 9. $2 \times 847 = \blacksquare$

10. $\begin{array}{r} 194 \\ \times \quad 5 \\ \hline \end{array}$ 11. $\begin{array}{r} 216 \\ \times \quad 3 \\ \hline \end{array}$ 12. $\begin{array}{r} 823 \\ \times \quad 2 \\ \hline \end{array}$ 13. $\begin{array}{r} 275 \\ \times \quad 4 \\ \hline \end{array}$

14. $\begin{array}{r} 313 \\ \times \quad 8 \\ \hline \end{array}$ 15. $\begin{array}{r} 481 \\ \times \quad 3 \\ \hline \end{array}$ 16. $\begin{array}{r} 527 \\ \times \quad 7 \\ \hline \end{array}$ 17. $\begin{array}{r} 316 \\ \times \quad 6 \\ \hline \end{array}$

USE DATA For 18–21, use the table.

18. Anna and her family took a train to Washington, D.C. How many seats were on the train in all?

19. How many deluxe seats are there on 4 trains?

20. **What's the Question?** The answer is 192 seats.

21. **MULTISTEP** Claudia orders 2 pillows for each seat in the sleeper car and in the deluxe car. How many pillows does she order?

TRAIN

Type of Car	Total Seats
Coach	360
Sleeper	168
Deluxe	90

Maintain Skills

Write the name of each shape.

22. 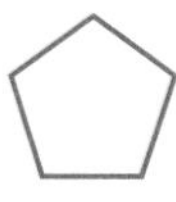

23. 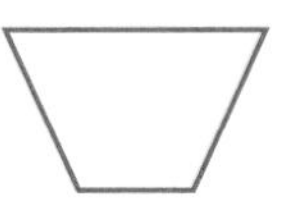

24.

25. 

CRCT Test Prep

26. M3N3.g. Jami bought 4 necklaces for \$18 each. How much money did she spend? (p. 442)

A. \$22 C. \$54
B. \$36 D. \$72

LESSON 8

Mental Math: Multiplication

 M3N3.f. Use mental math and estimation strategies to multiply.

Quick Review

1. 40×3
2. 70×6
3. 90×2
4. 50×7
5. 80×4

Learn

PRINTER PURCHASE Mr. Velasquez is buying 7 new printers for the school's computer lab. Each printer costs \$98. How can you use mental math to find how much the printers will cost?

$7 \times \$98 = \blacksquare$

Estimate: $7 \times \$100 = \$700$

One Way Write 98 as a sum and multiply.

$$\begin{aligned} 7 \times 98 &= 7 \times (90 + 8) \\ &= (7 \times 90) + (7 \times 8) \\ &= 630 + 56 \\ &= 686 \end{aligned}$$

Another Way Write 98 as a difference and multiply.

$$\begin{aligned} 7 \times 98 &= 7 \times (100 - 2) \\ &= (7 \times 100) - (7 \times 2) \\ &= 700 - 14 \\ &= 686 \end{aligned}$$

So, the printers will cost \$686. Since 686 is close to the estimate 700, the answer is reasonable.

 **MATH IDEA** You can use the Distributive Property to find products using mental math.

Examples

A

$$\begin{aligned} 3 \times 34 &= 3 \times (30 + 4) \\ &= (3 \times 30) + (3 \times 4) \\ &= 90 + 12 \\ &= 102 \end{aligned}$$

B

$$\begin{aligned} 4 \times 49 &= 4 \times (50 - 1) \\ &= (4 \times 50) - (4 \times 1) \\ &= 200 - 4 \\ &= 196 \end{aligned}$$

- Describe how knowing $10 \times 42 = 420$ can help you find 9×42.

Check

1. **Explain** how to find the product 4×97 using mental math.

Write each 2-digit factor as a sum or difference.

2. $7 \times 39 = 7 \times (■ - ■)$

3. $6 \times 52 = 6 \times (■ + ■)$

Use mental math to find the product.

4. $7 \times 14 = ■$
5. $4 \times 32 = ■$
6. $5 \times 28 = ■$
7. $2 \times 58 = ■$

Practice and Problem Solving

Extra Practice, page 450, Set E

Write each 2-digit factor as a sum or difference.

8. $4 \times 78 = 4 \times (■ - ■)$

9. $3 \times 64 = 3 \times (■ + ■)$

Use mental math to find the product.

10. $5 \times 49 = ■$
11. $6 \times 91 = ■$
12. $9 \times 13 = ■$
13. $8 \times 34 = ■$
14. $7 \times 98 = ■$
15. $4 \times 52 = ■$
16. $4 \times 85 = ■$
17. $6 \times 28 = ■$
18. $\begin{array}{r} 28 \\ \times\ 7 \\ \hline \end{array}$
19. $\begin{array}{r} 26 \\ \times\ 8 \\ \hline \end{array}$
20. $\begin{array}{r} 47 \\ \times\ 2 \\ \hline \end{array}$
21. $\begin{array}{r} 45 \\ \times\ 4 \\ \hline \end{array}$

22. Kareem bought 4 ink cartridges for his printer. Each cartridge cost \$28. How much did the cartridges cost altogether?

23. **REASONING** Since $100 \times 4 = 400$ and $99 \times 4 = 396$, what is 98×4? How do you know?

24. **MULTISTEP** Michele made 3 necklaces using 15 beads on each. She also made 6 bracelets using 10 beads on each. How many beads did she use in all?

25. **What's the Error?** Renee wants to find 32×6 by finding $(30 - 2) \times 6$. Explain her error. What is the correct product?

Maintain Skills

Find each sum or difference.

26. $\begin{array}{r} 37 \\ +67 \\ \hline \end{array}$
27. $\begin{array}{r} 52 \\ +49 \\ \hline \end{array}$
28. $\begin{array}{r} 66 \\ +28 \\ \hline \end{array}$
29. $\begin{array}{r} 91 \\ -62 \\ \hline \end{array}$
30. $\begin{array}{r} 64 \\ -36 \\ \hline \end{array}$
31. $\begin{array}{r} 73 \\ -55 \\ \hline \end{array}$

CRCT Test Prep

32. M3N3.g. At a garage sale, Paul bought 3 toy cars for 49¢ each. He paid with a \$5 bill. How much change did Paul receive? (p. 442)

A. \$1.47
B. \$2.47
C. \$3.53
D. \$4.53

Extra Practice

Set A (pp. 436–437)

Estimate the product.

1. 38×4 **2.** 32×8 **3.** 104×6 **4.** 281×6 **5.** 528×7

6. $3 \times 77 = \blacksquare$ **7.** $2 \times 497 = \blacksquare$ **8.** $4 \times 19 = \blacksquare$ **9.** $7 \times 315 = \blacksquare$

Set B (pp. 440–441)

Use the Distributive Property to find each product. You may wish to use grid paper.

1. 27×5 **2.** 82×3 **3.** 34×2 **4.** 51×7 **5.** 76×3

6. $5 \times 34 = \blacksquare$ **7.** $8 \times 21 = \blacksquare$ **8.** $6 \times 38 = \blacksquare$ **9.** $4 \times 63 = \blacksquare$

Set C (pp. 442–443)

Find the product.

1. 34×8 **2.** 73×2 **3.** 23×7 **4.** 45×5 **5.** 99×3

6. $6 \times 14 = \blacksquare$ **7.** $5 \times 29 = \blacksquare$ **8.** $7 \times 37 = \blacksquare$ **9.** $3 \times 22 = \blacksquare$

Set D (pp. 446–447)

Find the product.

1. 213×3 **2.** 128×4 **3.** 412×8 **4.** 155×8 **5.** 654×3

6. $2 \times 449 = \blacksquare$ **7.** $3 \times 164 = \blacksquare$ **8.** $6 \times 547 = \blacksquare$ **9.** $5 \times 155 = \blacksquare$

Set E (pp. 448–449)

Use mental math to find the product.

1. $3 \times 97 = \blacksquare$ **2.** $7 \times 26 = \blacksquare$ **3.** $5 \times 48 = \blacksquare$ **4.** $9 \times 28 = \blacksquare$

CHAPTER 22

Review/Test

✓ CHECK CONCEPTS

Use the array to help find the product. (pp. 438–439, 440–441)

1. $3 \times 24 = ■$

2. 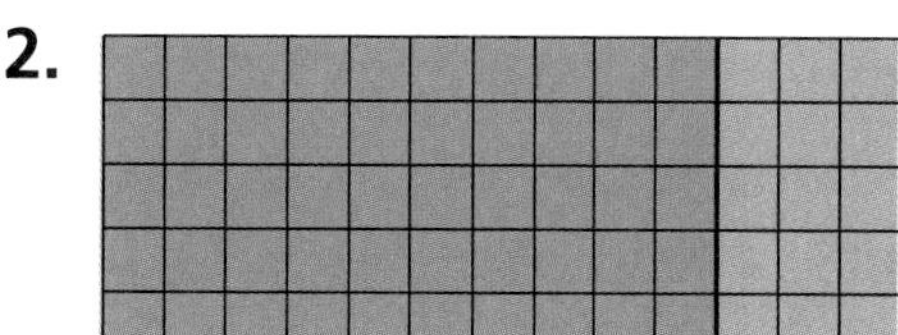

$5 \times 13 = ■$

Use mental math and basic facts to find the product. (pp. 434–435)

3. $3 \times 50 = ■$
4. $6 \times 20 = ■$
5. $7 \times 300 = ■$

✓ CHECK SKILLS

Estimate the product. (pp. 436–437)

6. $\begin{array}{r} 32 \\ \times\ 6 \\ \hline \end{array}$
7. $\begin{array}{r} 87 \\ \times\ 4 \\ \hline \end{array}$
8. $\begin{array}{r} 381 \\ \times\ \ 5 \\ \hline \end{array}$
9. $\begin{array}{r} 506 \\ \times\ \ 8 \\ \hline \end{array}$
10. $\begin{array}{r} 78 \\ \times\ 2 \\ \hline \end{array}$

Find the product. (pp. 442–443, 446–447, 448–449)

11. $4 \times 18 = ■$
12. $3 \times 34 = ■$
13. $7 \times 40 = ■$
14. $6 \times 312 = ■$
15. $5 \times 27 = ■$
16. $4 \times 145 = ■$
17. $5 \times 67 = ■$
18. $9 \times 53 = ■$
19. $\begin{array}{r} 14 \\ \times\ 2 \\ \hline \end{array}$
20. $\begin{array}{r} 275 \\ \times\ \ 3 \\ \hline \end{array}$
21. $\begin{array}{r} 136 \\ \times\ \ 6 \\ \hline \end{array}$
22. $\begin{array}{r} 20 \\ \times\ 4 \\ \hline \end{array}$
23. $\begin{array}{r} 56 \\ \times\ 8 \\ \hline \end{array}$

✓ CHECK PROBLEM SOLVING

Write whether you would *add, subtract, multiply,* or *divide.* Then solve. (pp. 444–445)

24. Caitlin practices the flute for 45 minutes each day. How many minutes does she practice in 4 days?

25. Lee has 64 photos in an album. There are 8 pages with the same number of photos on each page. How many photos are on each page?

Chapter CRCT Test Prep

NUMBERS AND OPERATIONS

1. M3N3.d. Each of the 3 third-grade classes at Blue Hill School collected 1,000 aluminum cans. How many cans did the classes collect?

A. 30

B. 100

C. 300

D. 3,000

2. M3N3.f. Rita bought 4 boxes of straws for a school fair. Each box holds 196 straws. About how many straws did Rita buy?

A. 800

B. 600

C. 400

D. 200

3. M3N3.f. Which shows how you could find the product 3×23 mentally?

A. $(3 \times 2) + (3 \times 3)$

B. $(3 \times 20) + (3 \times 3)$

C. $(2 \times 20) + (1 \times 3)$

D. $(1 \times 2) + (3 \times 3)$

NUMBERS AND OPERATIONS

4. M3N3.c. Use the array to find the product.

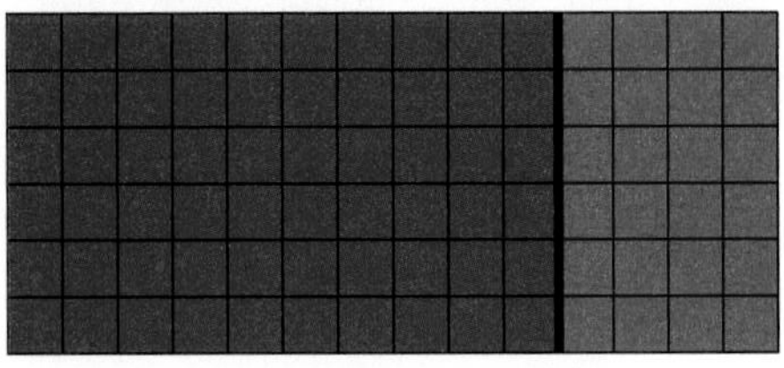

$6 \times 14 = \square$

A. 60

B. 74

C. 84

D. 90

5. M3N3.g. Jay took 5 packs of napkins to a picnic. There were 250 napkins in each pack. How many napkins did Jay bring in all?

A. 1,000

B. 1,250

C. 1,500

D. 1,750

6. M3N3.g. Christy has 8 packs of stickers. Each pack contains 36 stickers. How many stickers does Christy have?

A. 244

B. 262

C. 278

D. 288

Cumulative CRCT Test Prep

NUMBERS AND OPERATIONS

7. M3N1.a. Shelli picked 4 number cards and made this number. What is the value of the digit 6?

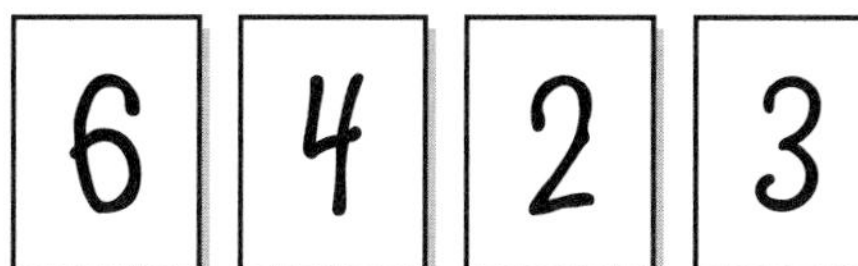

A. 6

B. 60

C. 600

D. 6,000

8. M3N4.a. Which division sentence belongs to the same fact family as these multiplication facts?

$$3 \times 9 = 27 \qquad 9 \times 3 = 27$$

A. $9 \div 3 = 9$

B. $9 \div 9 = 1$

C. $27 \div 9 = 3$

D. $27 \div 1 = 27$

9. M3N2.c. Ken's book has 367 pages. Al's book has 411 pages. How many more pages does Al's book have?

A. 44

B. 56

C. 144

D. 156

ALGEBRA

10. M3A1.a. Which figure comes next in this pattern?

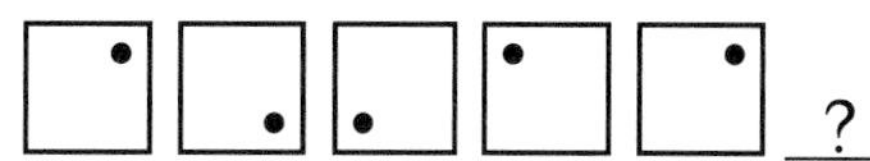

A.

B.

C.

D.

11. M3A1.c. Which number belongs in the □ to make the number sentence true?

$$6 \times \square = 42$$

A. 8

B. 7

C. 6

D. 5

12. M3A1.a. The first four houses on Joan's block are numbered 13, 15, 17, and 19. What are the numbers on the next two houses?

A. 20 and 22

B. 20 and 23

C. 21 and 22

D. 21 and 23

Divide by 1-Digit Numbers

FAST FACT • SOCIAL STUDIES Soccer is the world's most popular sport. A game like soccer was played in China about 2,500 years ago.

INVESTIGATION The table shows a shopping list of soccer supplies a coach wants to buy. Make a shopping list like this one showing items you want to buy. Find how much one of each item on your list costs.

Using Data

SOCCER SUPPLIES SHOPPING LIST

Item	Quantity	Cost
Corner flags	8	$64
Goal nets	4	$120
Soccer balls	3	$48
Air pumps	3	$60
Shin guards	4 pairs	$48

CHECK WHAT YOU KNOW

Use this page to help you review and remember important skills needed for Chapter 23.

SUBTRACTION

Find the difference.

1. $\begin{array}{r} 9 \\ -7 \\ \hline \end{array}$ **2.** $\begin{array}{r} 41 \\ -\ 4 \\ \hline \end{array}$ **3.** $\begin{array}{r} 34 \\ -\ 8 \\ \hline \end{array}$ **4.** $\begin{array}{r} 52 \\ -\ 6 \\ \hline \end{array}$ **5.** $\begin{array}{r} 75 \\ -\ 8 \\ \hline \end{array}$

6. $\begin{array}{r} 92 \\ -63 \\ \hline \end{array}$ **7.** $\begin{array}{r} 64 \\ -29 \\ \hline \end{array}$ **8.** $\begin{array}{r} 73 \\ -55 \\ \hline \end{array}$ **9.** $\begin{array}{r} 43 \\ -26 \\ \hline \end{array}$ **10.** $\begin{array}{r} 95 \\ -52 \\ \hline \end{array}$

MULTIPLICATION AND DIVISION FACTS

Find the product.

11. $6 \times 6 = \blacksquare$ **12.** $\blacksquare = 3 \times 9$ **13.** $6 \times 8 = \blacksquare$ **14.** $7 \times 3 = \blacksquare$

15. $6 \times 7 = \blacksquare$ **16.** $5 \times 5 = \blacksquare$ **17.** $\blacksquare = 2 \times 9$ **18.** $8 \times 8 = \blacksquare$

19. $\blacksquare = 9 \times 7$ **20.** $6 \times 4 = \blacksquare$ **21.** $5 \times 6 = \blacksquare$ **22.** $\blacksquare = 9 \times 9$

Find the quotient.

23. $8\overline{)56}$ **24.** $9\overline{)45}$ **25.** $4\overline{)32}$ **26.** $7\overline{)49}$

27. $6\overline{)54}$ **28.** $5\overline{)40}$ **29.** $6\overline{)42}$ **30.** $8\overline{)48}$

VOCABULARY POWER

REVIEW

divisor [di • vī′ zər] *noun*

In a division problem, the *divisor* is the number being used to divide another number, called the dividend. What is the answer in a division problem called?

PREVIEW

remainder

www.harcourtschool.com/mathglossary

LESSON 1

Divide with Remainders

M3N4.e. Divide a 2 and 3-digit number by a 1-digit divisor. *also* M3P2.a., M3P2.b., M3P2.c., M3P2.d., M3P5., M3P5.a., M3P5.b., M3P5.c.

Quick Review

1. $3\overline{)9}$
2. $6\overline{)12}$
3. $4\overline{)24}$
4. $5\overline{)35}$
5. $7\overline{)28}$

VOCABULARY
remainder

MATERIALS
counters

Explore

Noah collected all 19 dinosaur toys from Crispy Crunch cereal. He wants to keep an equal number of toys in each of 3 shoe boxes. Can Noah divide them equally among the 3 boxes? Why or why not?

Activity

Use counters to find 19 ÷ 3.

STEP 1

Use 19 counters. Draw 3 circles.

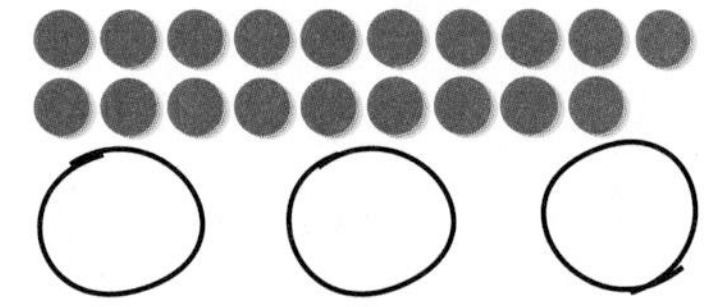

STEP 2

Divide the 19 counters into 3 equal groups by putting them in the circles.

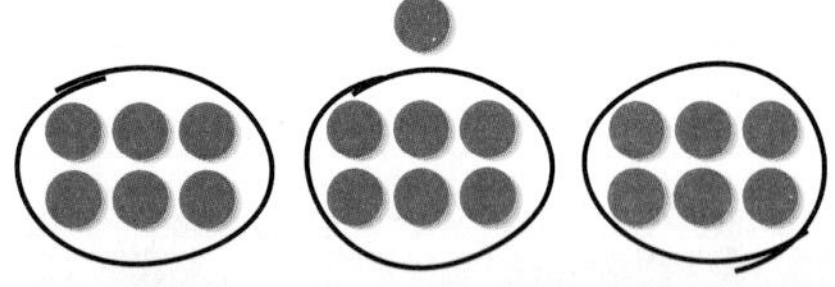

No, Noah cannot divide the toys equally because there will be 6 toys in each shoe box, with 1 toy left over.

Remember

30	÷	6	=	5
↑		↑		↑
dividend		*divisor*		*quotient*

Try It

Use counters to make equal groups. Draw a picture of the model you made.

a. 11 ÷ 2 **b.** 15 ÷ 4 **c.** 26 ÷ 3

Connect

In division, the amount left over when a number cannot be divided evenly is called the **remainder**.

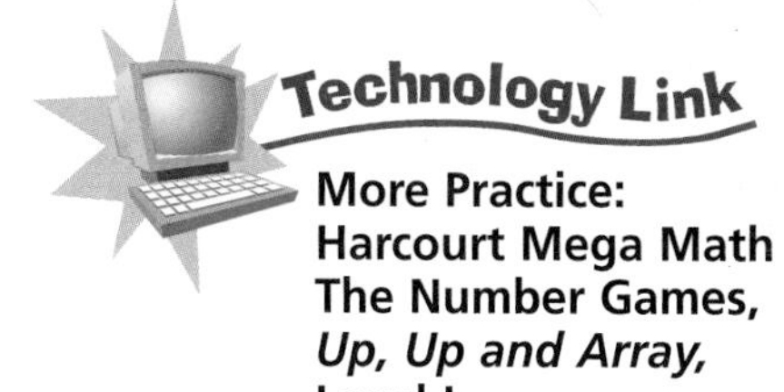

More Practice: Harcourt Mega Math The Number Games, *Up, Up and Array,* Level L

Activity

Find 20 ÷ 6.

STEP 1

Use 20 counters. Draw 6 circles.

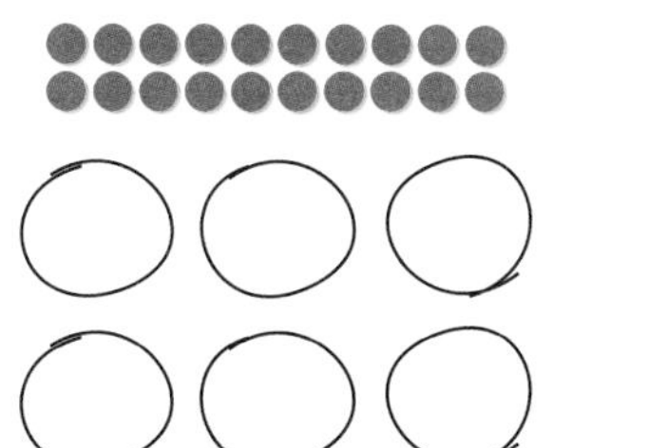

STEP 2

Divide the 20 counters into 6 equal groups.

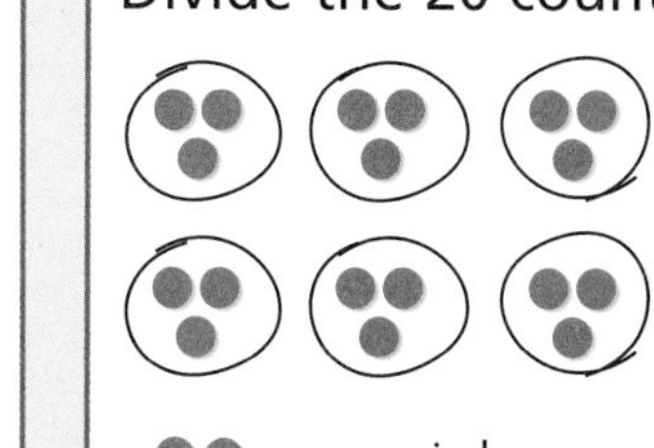

The quotient is 3.
The remainder is 2.

Practice and Problem Solving

Use counters to find the quotient and remainder.

1. $9 \div 2 = \blacksquare$
2. $17 \div 4 = \blacksquare$
3. $10 \div 3 = \blacksquare$
4. $20 \div 3 = \blacksquare$
5. $4\overline{)18}$
6. $5\overline{)19}$
7. $5\overline{)27}$
8. $6\overline{)21}$

Find the quotient and remainder. Use counters or draw a picture to help.

9. $16 \div 3 = \blacksquare$
10. $21 \div 5 = \blacksquare$
11. $2\overline{)15}$
12. $4\overline{)22}$
13. Carmen baked 38 cookies to sell at the bake sale. She put 4 cookies in each bag. How many cookies will Carmen have left over?
14. **What's the Question?** Darnell has 14 Beastie Buddies in his collection. He puts 4 of them in each of 3 drawers. The answer is 2 Beastie Buddies.

Maintain Skills

Find each sum or difference.

15. $\begin{array}{r} 129 \\ +565 \end{array}$

16. $\begin{array}{r} 346 \\ +299 \end{array}$

17. $\begin{array}{r} 737 \\ -158 \end{array}$

18. $\begin{array}{r} 620 \\ -311 \end{array}$

CRCT Test Prep

19. M3N3.g. Hector ran 3 miles each day for 5 days. How many miles did he run in all? (p. 128)

A. 8 miles
B. 10 miles
C. 15 miles
D. 20 miles

LESSON 2

Model Division

M3N4.e. Divide a 2 and 3-digit number by a 1-digit divisor.
also M3P2., M3P5.b., M3P5.c.

Quick Review

1. 18 ÷ 3 = ■
2. 30 ÷ 6 = ■
3. 32 ÷ 4 = ■
4. 49 ÷ 7 = ■
5. 63 ÷ 9 = ■

Learn

DOG DAYS A third-grade class collected 48 dog toys to donate to 3 animal shelters. Each shelter will get the same number of toys. How many toys will each shelter receive?

Activity

Materials: base-ten blocks

48 ÷ 3 = ■ $\quad 3\overline{)48}$

STEP 1

Model 48 with base-ten blocks. Put an equal number of tens in each of 3 groups.

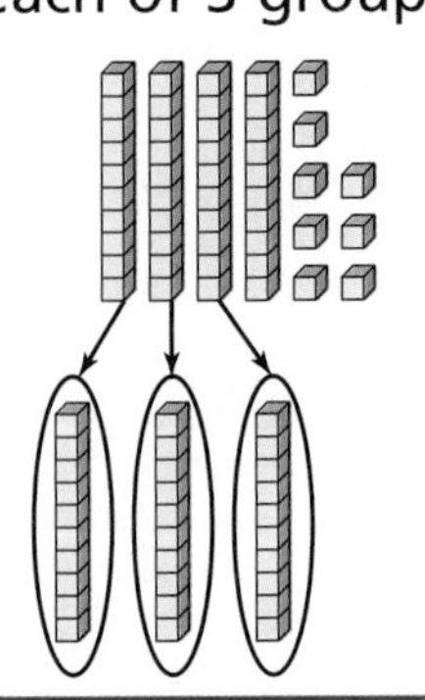

STEP 2

There is one ten left over. Regroup it as 10 ones.

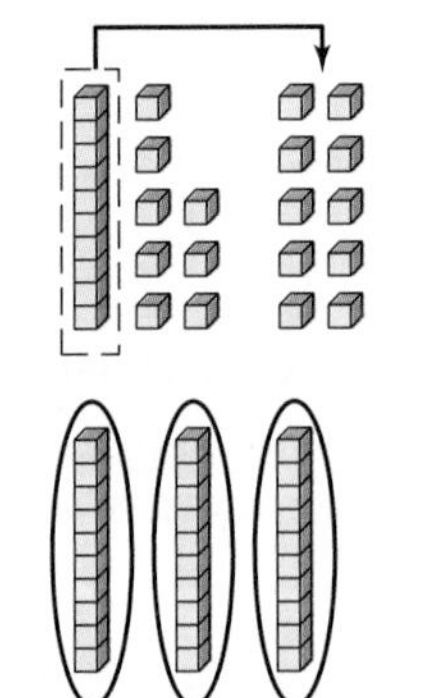

STEP 3

Put an equal number of ones into each of the 3 groups.

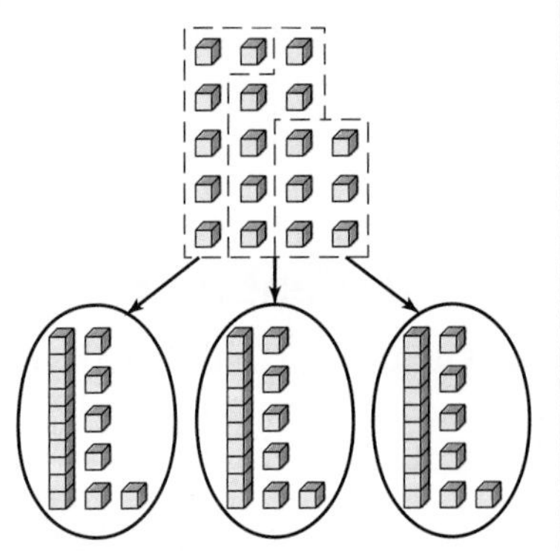

So, each shelter will receive 16 toys.

- How can you use multiplication to check your answer?

Examples

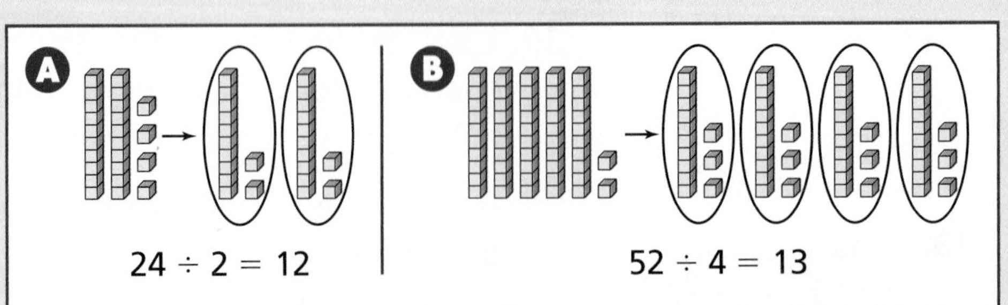

A 24 ÷ 2 = 12

B 52 ÷ 4 = 13

Recording Division

Katie had 72 dog treats. She put 4 in each bag to give to the shelters. How many bags did she use?

Example

Find $72 \div 4$. **Read:** 72 divided by 4 **Write:** $4\overline{)72}$

STEP 1

Divide the 7 tens first. $4\overline{)7}$

Think: $4 \times 1 = 4$

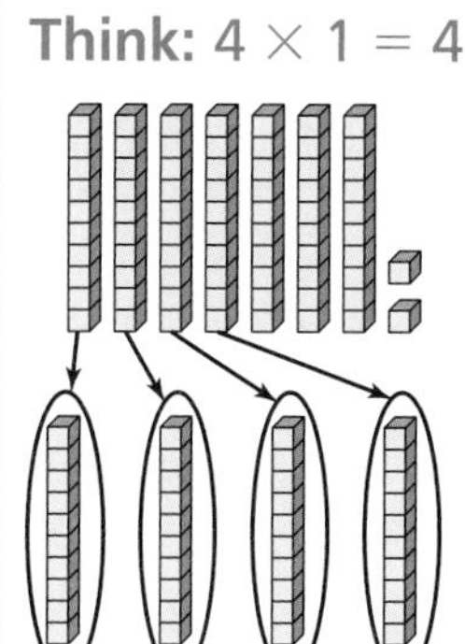

$$\begin{array}{r} 1 \\ 4\overline{)72} \\ -4 \\ \hline 3 \end{array}$$

1 ten in each group.

Divide. $4\overline{)7}$

Multiply. 4×1

Subtract. $7 - 4$

Compare. $3 < 4$

The difference, 3, must be less than the divisor, 4.

STEP 2

Bring down the 2 ones.

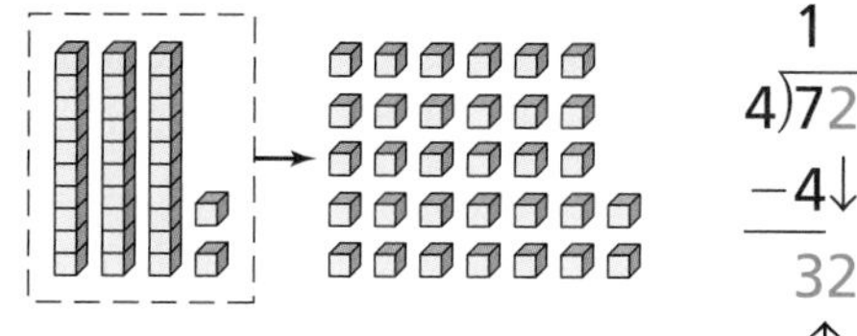

$$\begin{array}{r} 1 \\ 4\overline{)72} \\ -4\downarrow \\ \hline 32 \end{array}$$

Regroup 3 tens 2 ones as 32 ones.

STEP 3

Divide the 32 ones. $4\overline{)32}$

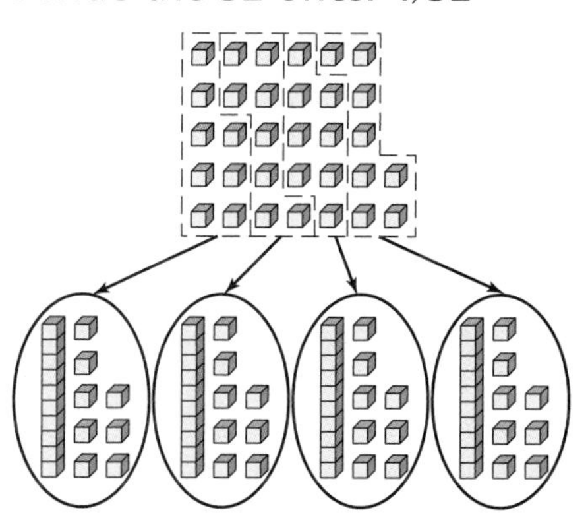

$$\begin{array}{r} 18 \\ 4\overline{)72} \\ -4 \\ \hline 32 \\ -32 \\ \hline 0 \end{array}$$

8 ones in each group.

Divide. $4\overline{)32}$

Multiply. 4×8

Subtract. $32 - 32 = 0$

Compare. $0 < 4$

STEP 4

Multiply to check your answer.

$$\begin{array}{r} 18 \\ \times\ 4 \\ \hline 72 \end{array}$$

18 ← quotient

× 4 ← divisor

72 ← This should equal the dividend.

So, Katie used 18 bags.

More Examples

A
$$\begin{array}{r} 14 \\ 4\overline{)56} \\ -4 \\ \hline 16 \\ -16 \\ \hline 0 \end{array}$$

B
$$\begin{array}{r} 15 \\ 5\overline{)75} \\ -5 \\ \hline 25 \\ -25 \\ \hline 0 \end{array}$$

C
$$\begin{array}{r} 28 \\ 3\overline{)84} \\ -6 \\ \hline 24 \\ -24 \\ \hline 0 \end{array}$$

LESSON CONTINUES

Check

1. **Explain** why you should compare the difference with the divisor before dividing the ones.

Use the model. Write the quotient.

2. $36 \div 2$

3. $42 \div 3$

Divide. You may use base-ten blocks to help.

4. $51 \div 3 = \blacksquare$
5. $60 \div 4 = \blacksquare$
6. $75 \div 3 = \blacksquare$
7. $98 \div 7 = \blacksquare$

Practice and Problem Solving

Extra Practice, page 476, Set A

Use the model. Write the quotient.

8. 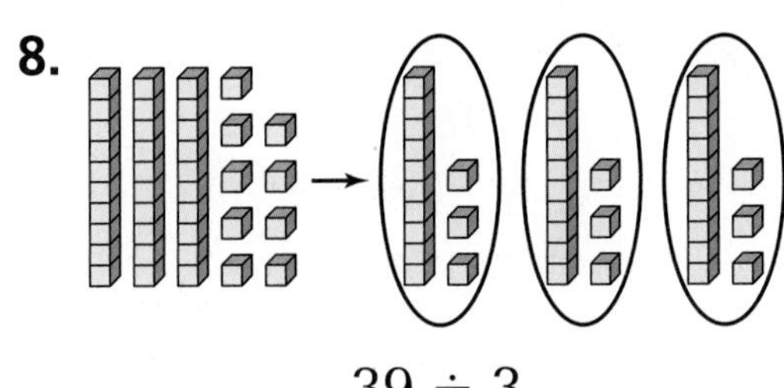

$39 \div 3$

9. $28 \div 2$

Divide. You may use base-ten blocks to help.

10. $36 \div 3 = \blacksquare$
11. $88 \div 4 = \blacksquare$
12. $26 \div 2 = \blacksquare$
13. $57 \div 3 = \blacksquare$
14. $4\overline{)64}$
15. $5\overline{)80}$
16. $3\overline{)78}$
17. $8\overline{)96}$

Divide and check.

18. $5\overline{)75}$
19. $4\overline{)68}$
20. $7\overline{)91}$
21. $3\overline{)63}$
22. $4\overline{)56}$
23. $6\overline{)90}$
24. $3\overline{)87}$
25. $7\overline{)84}$
26. ALGEBRA Find the missing digit.

$$\begin{array}{r} 32 \\ 3\overline{)9\blacksquare} \end{array}$$

27. Mrs. Ramsey bakes pies at a bakery. She has 95 cups of apples. If 5 cups of apples are needed for one pie, how many pies can she make?

28. Austin has 4 days to read 96 pages. He wants to read the same number of pages each day. How many pages should Austin read each day?

29. **MULTISTEP** Amy has 27 blue marbles and 33 red marbles. She puts the same number of marbles into each of 3 bags. How many marbles are in each bag?

Maintain Skills

Find each sum or difference.

30. $47 + 92$ **31.** $39 + 84$ **32.** $54 + 55$

33. $62 - 26$ **34.** $95 - 38$ **35.** $33 - 16$

CRCT Test Prep

36. M3N1.b. What is the value of the 8 in 68,725? (p. 14)

A. 80
B. 800
C. 8,000
D. 80,000

Problem Solving Thinker's Corner

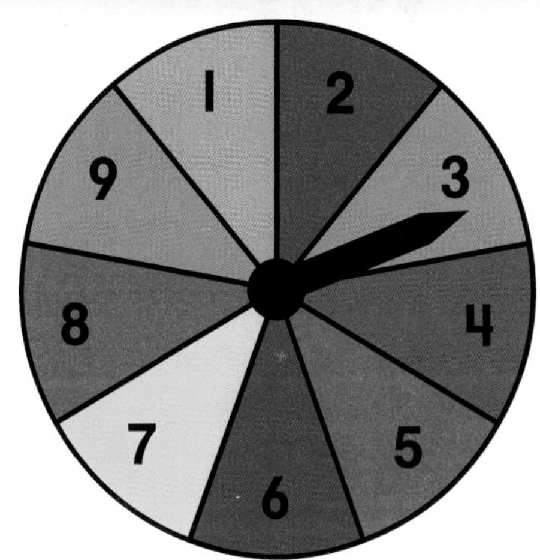

Try to make a greater quotient than your partner's.

MATERIALS spinner with nine sections, labeled 1–9.

- Player 1 spins the spinner 3 times and chooses one of the digits to be the divisor. The remaining two digits are used to write a 2-digit number. This number will be the dividend.
- Player 2 repeats the first step.
- Both players divide. The player with the greater quotient wins. Play this game several times. See if you can find a winning strategy.
- Repeat this game. Try to make the lesser quotient.

1. When making the greater quotient, where is the best place to use a 1?
2. When making the lesser quotient, where is the best place to use a 1?

LESSON 3

Model Division with Remainders

M3N4.e. Divide a 2 and 3-digit number by a 1-digit divisor.
also M3P2., M3P2.a., M3P2.b., M3P2.c., M3P2.d., M3P5.b., M3P5.c.

Quick Review

1. 16 ÷ 4 = ■
2. 14 ÷ 7 = ■
3. 15 ÷ 3 = ■
4. 32 ÷ 4 = ■
5. 18 ÷ 6 = ■

Learn

COOL COLLECTIONS Suppose you have a collection of 63 hockey cards. You display an equal number of cards on each of 5 shelves. How many cards are on each shelf? How many cards are left over?

Activity

Materials: base-ten blocks

63 ÷ 5 = ■ $5\overline{)63}$

STEP 1

Model 63 with base-ten blocks. Put an equal number of tens in each of 5 groups.

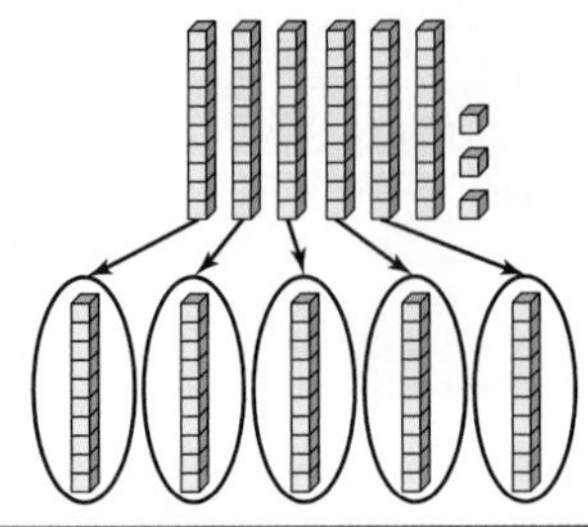

STEP 2

One ten is left. Regroup it as 10 ones. Put an equal number of ones in each of 5 groups.

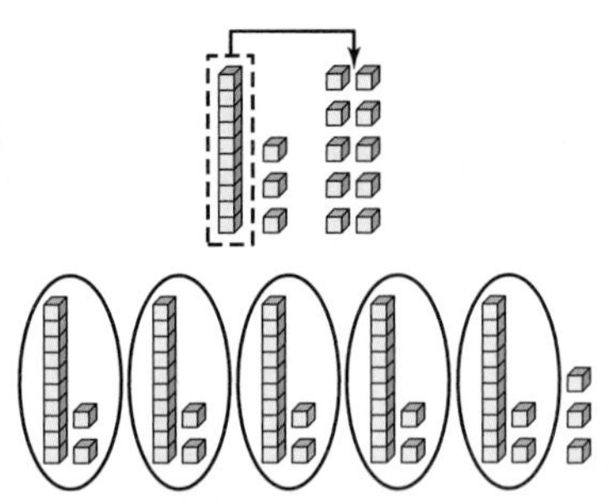

STEP 3

Use the letter *r* to show the remainder.

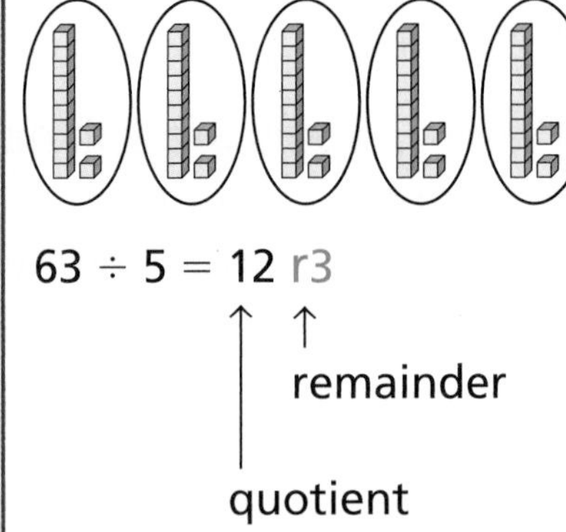

63 ÷ 5 = 12 r3

12 — quotient; r3 — remainder

So, there are 12 cards on each shelf. There are 3 cards left over.

- In Step 2, why was the 1 ten regrouped into 10 ones?

Examples

A

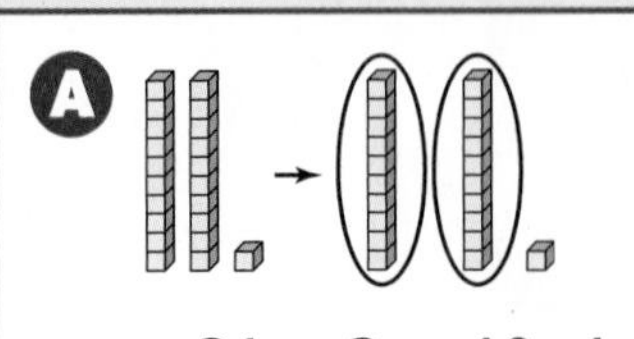

21 ÷ 2 = 10 r1

B

44 ÷ 3 = 14 r2

Recording Division

You use the same steps to record division with remainders as you do when there are no remainders.

Example 1

Find 58 ÷ 3 = ■. **Read:** 58 divided by 3 **Write:** $3\overline{)58}$

STEP 1

Divide the 5 tens first. $3\overline{)5}$

Think: 3 × 1 = 3

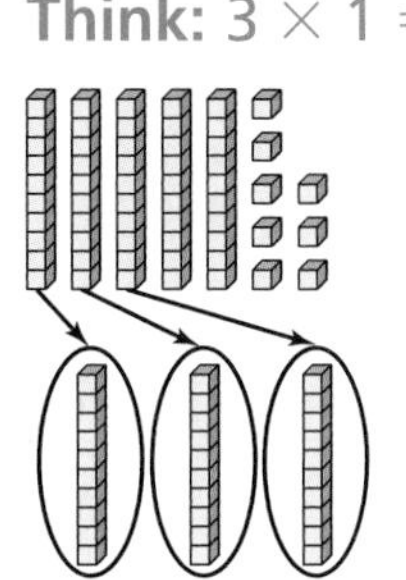

$$\begin{array}{r} 1 \\ 3\overline{)58} \\ -3 \\ \hline 2 \end{array}$$

1 ten in each group.

Divide. $3\overline{)5}$
Multiply. 3 × 1
Subtract. 5 − 3
Compare. 2 < 3

The difference, 2, must be less than the divisor, 3.

STEP 2

Bring down the 8 ones.

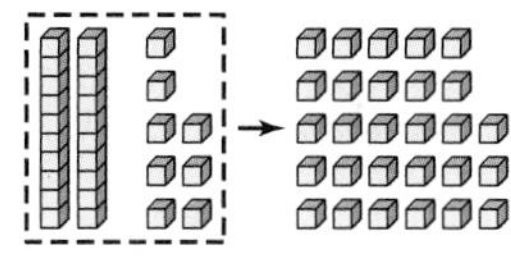

$$\begin{array}{r} 1 \\ 3\overline{)58} \\ -3\downarrow \\ \hline 28 \end{array}$$

Regroup 2 tens 8 ones as 28 ones.

STEP 3

Divide the 28 ones. $3\overline{)28}$ **Think:** 3 × 9 = 27

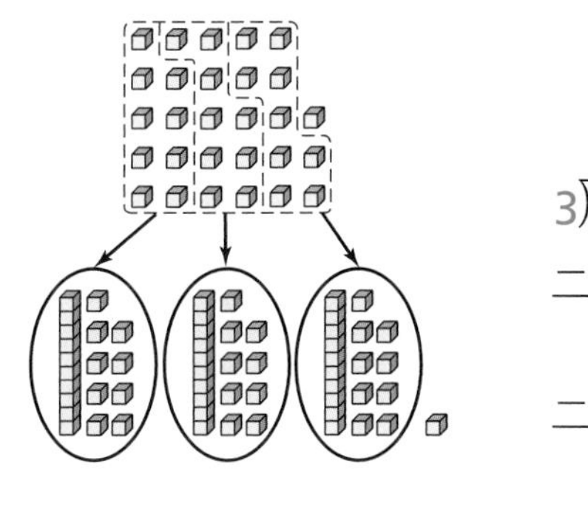

$$\begin{array}{r} 19\text{ r}1 \\ 3\overline{)58} \\ -3 \\ \hline 28 \\ -27 \\ \hline 1 \end{array}$$

9 ones in each group.

Divide. $3\overline{)28}$
Multiply. 3 × 9
Subtract. 28 – 27
Compare. 1 < 3

STEP 4

Multiply to check your answer.

$$\begin{array}{r} 19 \\ \times\ 3 \\ \hline 57 \end{array}$$

19 ← quotient
3 ← divisor

$$\begin{array}{r} 57 \\ +\ 1 \\ \hline 58 \end{array}$$

1 ← Add the remainder.
58 ← This should equal the dividend.

Example 2

Find 35 ÷ 4 = ■. **Read:** 35 divided by 4 **Write:** $4\overline{)35}$

STEP 1

Since there are not enough tens to divide, start with ones.

$4\overline{)35}$ 4 > 3, so place the first digit in the ones place.

STEP 2

Divide the 35 ones.

$$\begin{array}{r} 8\text{ r}3 \\ 4\overline{)35} \\ -32 \\ \hline 3 \end{array}$$

Divide. $4\overline{)35}$
Multiply. 4 × 8
Subtract. 35 – 32
Compare. 3 < 4

STEP 3

Multiply to check.

$$\begin{array}{r} 8 \\ \times 4 \\ \hline 32 \end{array}$$

8 ← quotient
4 ← divisor

$$\begin{array}{r} 32 \\ +\ 3 \\ \hline 35 \end{array}$$

3 ← Add the remainder.

Check

1. **Explain** why $63 \div 5$ has a remainder.

Use the model. Write the quotient and remainder.

2. $43 \div 2$

3. $38 \div 3$

Divide. You may use base-ten blocks to help.

4. $31 \div 2 = \blacksquare$
5. $86 \div 3 = \blacksquare$
6. $29 \div 4 = \blacksquare$
7. $32 \div 4 = \blacksquare$

Practice and Problem Solving

Extra Practice, page 476, Set B

Use the model. Write the quotient and remainder.

8. $62 \div 4$

9. $71 \div 5$

Divide. You may use base-ten blocks to help.

10. $23 \div 2 = \blacksquare$
11. $25 \div 2 = \blacksquare$
12. $39 \div 3 = \blacksquare$
13. $43 \div 4 = \blacksquare$
14. $4\overline{)77}$
15. $6\overline{)52}$
16. $5\overline{)73}$
17. $3\overline{)66}$

Divide and check.

18. $5\overline{)48}$
19. $2\overline{)71}$
20. $7\overline{)92}$
21. $9\overline{)89}$
22. $2\overline{)87}$
23. $7\overline{)34}$
24. $8\overline{)99}$
25. $6\overline{)39}$

26. **What's the Error?** Lou began to solve this problem. What is his error? Solve the problem.

$$\begin{array}{r} 1 \\ 2\overline{)53} \\ 2 \\ \hline 3 \end{array}$$

27. **ALGEBRA** Find the missing digit.

$$\begin{array}{r} 15 \text{ r}2 \\ 3\overline{)4\blacksquare} \end{array}$$

28. **REASONING** Alyssa divided 79 jelly beans equally into 6 jars. She kept 1 jar and the leftover jelly beans. How many jelly beans did she keep?

29. **FAST FACT** • SOCIAL STUDIES Strawberries have been grown in the United States since 1834. Today every state in the United States grows strawberries. In how many states are strawberries not grown?

30. It takes Grant 12 minutes to get to his friend's house. It takes him 4 times as long to get to his uncle's house. How long does it take Grant to get to his uncle's?

Maintain Skills

Write the amount.

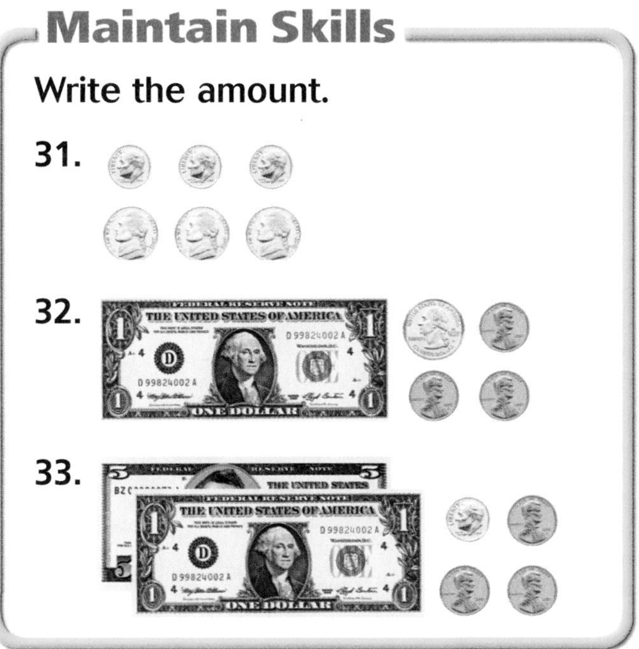

31.

32.

33.

CRCT Test Prep

34. M3N5.g Elise cut a pie into 8 equal pieces. She gave 2 pieces to her teacher. Elise ate 1 piece. What fraction of the pie was left? (p. 402)

A. $\frac{5}{8}$

B. $\frac{3}{8}$

C. $\frac{2}{8}$

D. $\frac{1}{8}$

Problem Solving LINKUP . . . to Reading

STRATEGY • USE GRAPHIC AIDS
The steps for making crayons have not changed much since 1903. Wax in different colors is heated to 240°F. Workers pour the hot wax across crayon molds. In $7\frac{1}{2}$ minutes, the wax cools into 72 rows of 8 crayons.

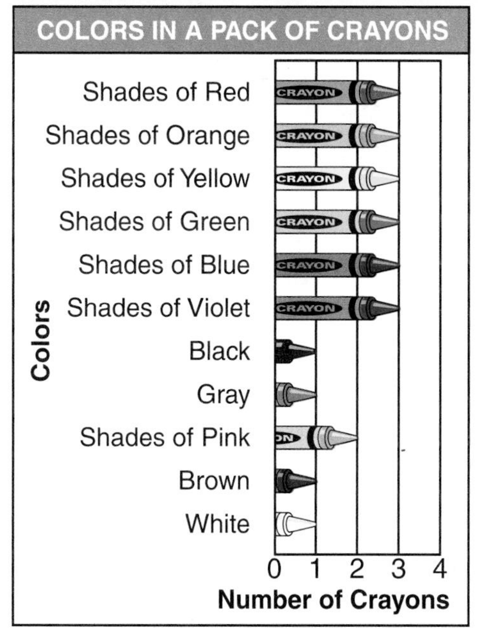

USE DATA For 1–2, use the bar graph.

1. How many crayons are in the pack shown in the bar graph?
2. **Write a problem** about the bar graph. Use division. Trade with a partner and solve.
3. How many crayons are made in each mold of 72 rows of 8 crayons?
4. The pack of 64 crayons has 4 equal rows. How many crayons are in each row?

LESSON 4

Mental Math: Divide

M3N4.e. Divide a 2 and 3-digit number by a 1-digit divisor.

Quick Review

1. 5×10
2. 10×7
3. 3×10
4. 9×10
5. 10×6

Learn

PARTY TRAYS Brandon made 56 sandwiches for a party. He has 4 trays and wants to put the same number of sandwiches on each tray. How many sandwiches should he put on each tray?

You can use mental math to help you divide.

Example 1

Find $56 \div 4$.

You can break apart the dividend and use basic facts.

Think: $56 = 40 + 16$ Use a multiple of 10.

You can divide 40 and 16 by 4.

$40 \div 4 = 10$ $16 \div 4 = 4$

Add to find the quotient.

$10 + 4 = 14$

$56 \div 4 = 14$

So, Brandon should put 14 sandwiches on each tray.

Example 2

Find $95 \div 8$.

Think: $95 = 80 + 15 = 80 + 8 + 7$

You can divide 80 and 8 by 8. Since 7 is less than 8, 7 is the remainder.

$80 \div 8 = 10$ $8 \div 8 = 1$

Add to find the quotient.

$10 + 1 = 11$

So, $95 \div 8 = 11$ r7.

Check

1. **Explain** how to use mental math to find $35 \div 2$.

Use mental math to divide.

2. $5\overline{)67}$
3. $3\overline{)55}$
4. $6\overline{)76}$
5. $3\overline{)43}$

Practice and Problem Solving

Extra Practice, page 476, Set C

Use mental math to divide.

6. $4\overline{)51}$ **7.** $2\overline{)37}$ **8.** $7\overline{)91}$ **9.** $5\overline{)64}$

10. $3\overline{)45}$ **11.** $6\overline{)98}$ **12.** $7\overline{)80}$ **13.** $3\overline{)74}$

14. $41 \div 3 = \blacksquare$ **15.** $33 \div 2 = \blacksquare$ **16.** $64 \div 5 = \blacksquare$ **17.** $52 \div 2 = \blacksquare$

18. $67 \div 4 = \blacksquare$ **19.** $79 \div 5 = \blacksquare$ **20.** $82 \div 6 = \blacksquare$ **21.** $73 \div 3 = \blacksquare$

Divide and check.

22. $7\overline{)89}$ **23.** $5\overline{)72}$ **24.** $5\overline{)81}$ **25.** $8\overline{)97}$

26. $4\overline{)62}$ **27.** $5\overline{)95}$ **28.** $2\overline{)39}$ **29.** $3\overline{)49}$

30. Kayla made 94 jars of peach jam. She stored them in boxes. Each box holds 8 jars. How many boxes does she fill with jam jars? How many jars are leftover?

31. ALGEBRA Write the missing digit.

$$\begin{array}{r} 20 + \blacksquare \text{ r1} \\ 4\overline{)80 + 17} \end{array}$$

32. The school band has 78 band members. For a parade, they marched in rows, and each row had 6 students. How many rows were there?

33. **MULTISTEP** Rudy bought a comic book for \$3.50 and a snack for \$1.49. He paid with a \$5 bill. How much change did he receive?

34. **REASONING** Masao thought of this number pattern. What is his rule? What is the next number?

2, 6, 18, 54, $\blacksquare$

35. **MULTISTEP** Jackie has 35 crackers. She divides them equally among 5 plates. How many crackers are on 2 plates?

Maintain Skills

36. Write the amount.

CRCT Test Prep

37. M3M3.c. Tara's quilt is 3 feet long and 4 feet wide. What is the perimeter of her quilt? (p. 350)

A. 16 feet C. 12 feet
B. 14 feet D. 10 feet

LESSON 5

Problem Solving Skill
Interpret the Remainder

M3N4.d. Explain the meaning of a remainder in division in different circumstances. *also* M3N4.e., M3P1.a., M3P1.b., M3P1.c., M3P1.d.

UNDERSTAND | PLAN | SOLVE | CHECK

Quick Review

1. $3\overline{)55}$
2. $4\overline{)18}$
3. $2\overline{)61}$
4. $5\overline{)60}$
5. $7\overline{)32}$

PICNIC PLANS Clare needs to take 50 cans of juice to the picnic. The juice is sold in packages of 6 cans. How many packages must she buy?

Since you need to know how many groups of 6 are in 50, you divide.

Find $50 \div 6$.

$$\begin{array}{r} 8 \text{ r}2 \\ 6\overline{)50} \\ -48 \\ \hline 2 \end{array}$$

The 8 packages of juice will have only 48 cans.

If Clare buys 8 packages of juice, she will still need 2 more cans of juice. So, Clare must buy 9 packages of juice.

Rico is making crispy treats for the picnic. He needs 2 cups of cereal for each pan of treats. If he has 13 cups of cereal, how many pans of treats can he make?

Find $13 \div 2$.

$$\begin{array}{r} 6 \text{ r}1 \\ 2\overline{)13} \\ -12 \\ \hline 1 \end{array}$$

Making 6 pans of treats uses 12 cups of cereal.

If Rico makes 6 pans of treats, he will have only 1 cup of cereal left. This is not enough for another pan of treats. So, he can make 6 pans of treats.

MATH IDEA When you divide, sometimes you have to decide how to use the remainder to solve the problem.

Problem Solving Practice

1. **What if** Clare had to take 56 cans of juice to the picnic? If there are 6 cans in each package, how many packages would she need to buy?

2. Simon has 63 bird stamps in a collection. He can fit 8 stamps on a page. How many pages does he need?

3. Beth is making bows to decorate a float in a parade. It takes 5 feet of ribbon to make a bow. She has 89 feet of ribbon. How many bows can Beth make?

4. Dimitri worked on a math puzzle for 32 minutes. If each part of the puzzle took 5 minutes to solve, how many parts did he solve?

A class of 28 students is going on a field trip. Each van can hold 8 students. How many vans does the class need?

5. Which number sentence can help solve the problem?

   A $28 - 28 = 0$
   B $28 \times 8 = 224$
   C $28 \div 8 = 3$ r4
   D $8 \div 8 = 1$

6. How many vans does the class need?

   F 3 vans
   G 4 vans
   H 8 vans
   J 28 vans

Mixed Applications

USE DATA For 7–9, use the price list.

7. **MULTISTEP** Tomas bought 1 pound of peanuts and 1 pound of cashews. He paid with $5. How much change did he get?

8. **MULTISTEP** Sheila has $5.36. Does she have enough to buy 1 pound of raisins, 1 pound of peanuts, and 1 pound of cashews? Explain.

9. **MULTISTEP** Cole bought 2 pounds of raisins. The checker charged him $1.19. Is this price reasonable? Explain.

PRICE LIST	
Raisins	$0.85 per lb
Peanuts	$1.99 per lb
Cashews	$2.50 per lb

LESSON 6

Divide 3-Digit Numbers

M3N4.e. Divide a 2 and 3-digit number by a 1-digit divisor. *also* M3P2.a., M3P2.b., M3P2.c., M3P2.d.

Quick Review

1. 56 ÷ 7
2. 45 ÷ 5
3. 24 ÷ 6
4. 72 ÷ 9
5. How many twos are in 15? What is left over?

Learn

FAIR TRADE Roger and his sister have 358 trading cards. They want to divide them evenly. How many cards does each one get?

Example

Divide. 358 ÷ 2 = ■ or $2\overline{)358}$

STEP 1

Decide where to place the first digit in the quotient.

```
   ■
2)358   3 > 2, so divide the hundreds.
```

STEP 2

Divide 3 hundreds by 2.

```
   1
2)358
 -2      Multiply.
  1      Subtract.
         Compare.
         1 < 2
```

STEP 3

Bring down the 5 tens. Divide 15 tens.

```
   17
2)358
 -2↓
  15
 -14     Multiply.
   1     Subtract.
         Compare.
         1 < 2
```

STEP 4

Bring down the 8 ones. Divide 18 ones.

```
   179
2)358
 -2
  15
 -14↓    Multiply.
   18    Subtract.
  -18    Compare.
    0    0 < 2
```

So, each one gets 179 trading cards.

• In Step 1, where would you place the first digit if the divisor was 4 instead of 2? Explain.

More Examples

A

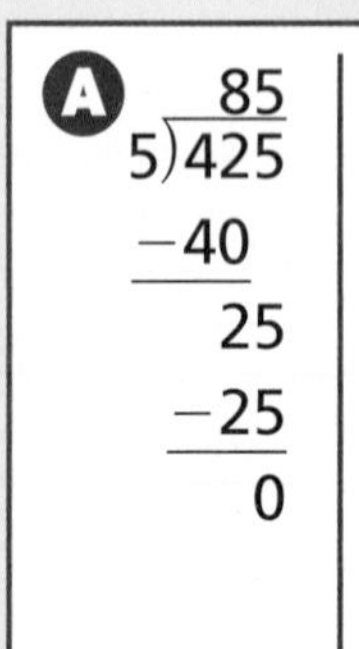

```
   85
5)425
 -40
  25
 -25
   0
```

B

```
  116 r1
6)697
 -6
  09
 - 6
  37
 -36
   1
```

C You can also use a calculator to divide greater numbers.

161 ÷ 7 = ■

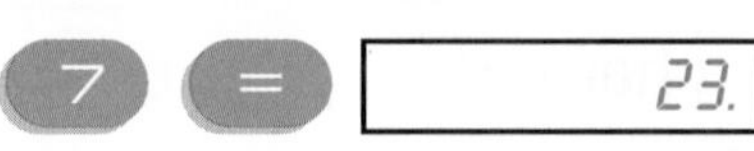

Check

1. **Explain** how you can decide where to place the first digit in this problem. $3\overline{)216}$

Divide.

2. $5\overline{)365}$
3. $3\overline{)354}$
4. $4\overline{)156}$
5. $6\overline{)138}$

Practice and Problem Solving

Extra Practice, page 476, Set D

Divide.

6. $5\overline{)155}$
7. $2\overline{)384}$
8. $3\overline{)844}$
9. $4\overline{)472}$
10. $8\overline{)680}$
11. $4\overline{)136}$
12. $7\overline{)294}$
13. $5\overline{)757}$
14. $3\overline{)726}$
15. $4\overline{)475}$
16. $9\overline{)819}$
17. $6\overline{)294}$
18. $7\overline{)158}$
19. $2\overline{)784}$
20. $5\overline{)905}$
21. $9\overline{)558}$

22. **Write a problem** in which the dividend has 3 digits and the first digit of the quotient is in the tens place.

23. **Vocabulary Power** The word *remainder* means "something left over." Use $26 \div 4$ and explain what a remainder is in division.

24. **MULTISTEP** Bonnie has $2.35. John has $1.20 less than Bonnie. How much money do they have altogether?

25. **REASONING** Julie bought cards for $3.00. She paid for them with the same number of dimes as nickels. She received no change. How many of each coin did she use?

Maintain Skills

Write the time.

26. 

27. 

CRCT Test Prep

28. M3N3.g Max's team had practice 3 days a week for 9 weeks. Max missed 2 practices. How many practices did he go to? (p. 190)

A. 3
B. 24
C. 25
D. 27

LESSON 7

Choose a Method

M3N4.e. Divide a 2 and 3-digit number by a 1-digit divisor. *also* M3P4.b.

Quick Review

1. $5\overline{)122}$
2. $6\overline{)316}$
3. $2\overline{)822}$
4. $3\overline{)417}$
5. $4\overline{)921}$

Learn

You can find a quotient by drawing a picture, making a model, or using mental math.

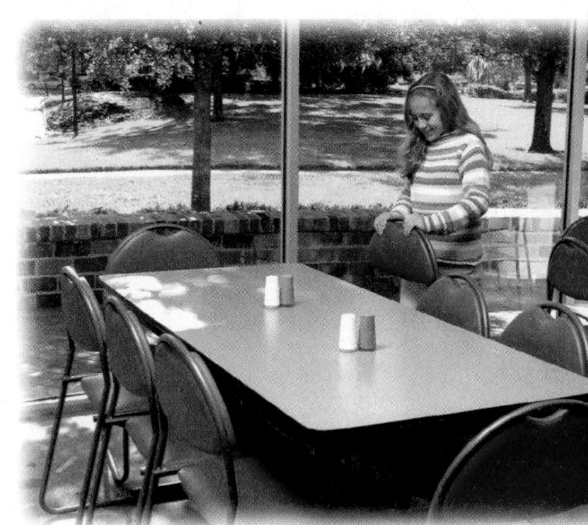

MEET AND GREET Emily is in charge of setting up tables for a Science Club meeting. There will be 35 people at the meeting, and each table holds 8 people. How many tables are needed?

$$35 \div 8 = \blacksquare$$

Draw a Picture The numbers are small. So, drawing a picture is a good choice.

Draw 35 squares to show 35 people. Circle groups of 8 to show how many people can sit at each table.

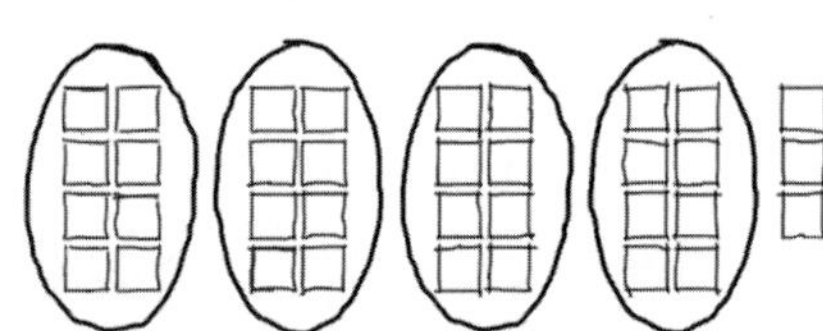

Look at your picture. Four tables will be filled. There are 3 people left over, so they need one more table. So, Emily should set up 5 tables.

Use Mental Math

$57 \div 4 = \blacksquare$

The dividend can be broken apart into numbers that are easy to divide, so using mental math is a good choice.

Think: $57 = 40 + 17 = 40 + 16 + 1$
You can divide 40 and 16 by 4. Since 1 is less than 4, 1 is the remainder.
$40 \div 4 = 10$ $16 \div 4 = 4$
Add to find the quotient.
$10 + 4 = 14$

So, $57 \div 4 = 14$ r1.

Make a Model

$76 \div 2 = \blacksquare$

The numbers are large. Making a model is a good choice.

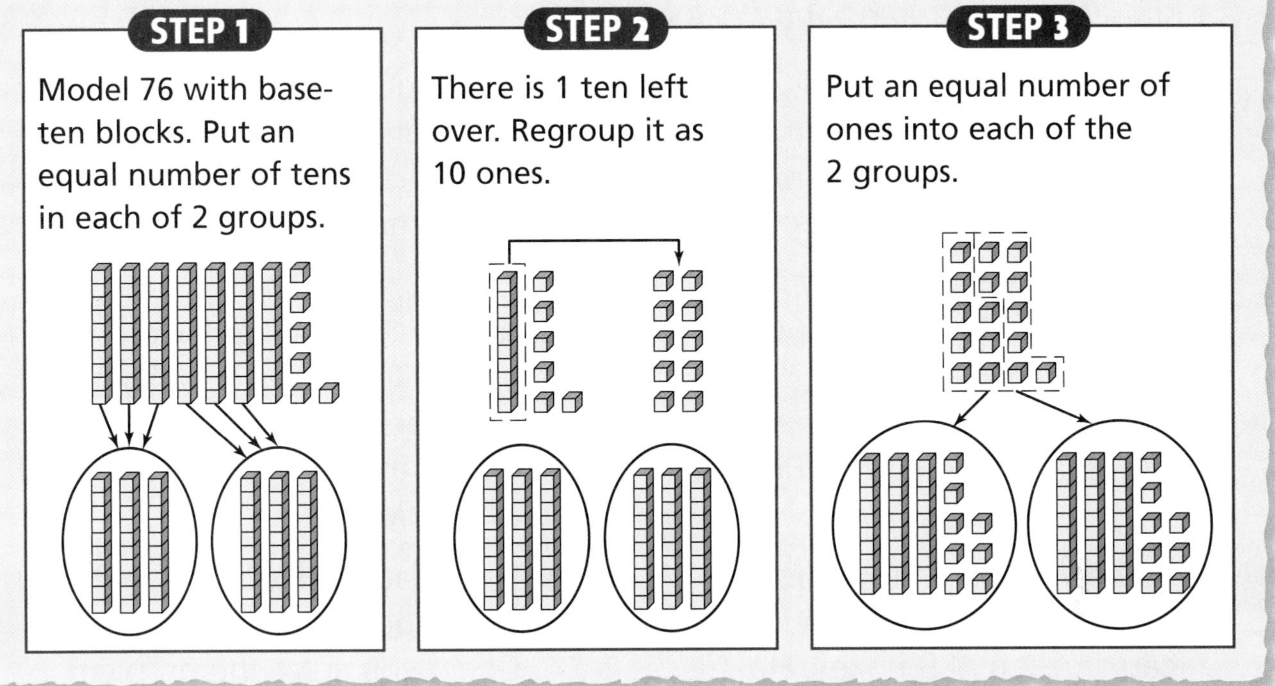

So, $76 \div 2 = 38$.

- Write a division problem you could solve by drawing a picture. Then draw a picture to solve.

Check

1. **Explain** what method you would use to divide 76 by 4.

Tell whether each problem can be solved by using mental math, pictures, or models. Then solve each problem using the method you chose.

2. Students raised $87 to buy 3 new trees for their school. How much can they spend for each tree?

3. Karen had 58 photos. She put 4 pictures on each page to go into her photo album. How many pages did she use?

4. Look back at Problems 2 and 3. Did you choose the best method? Could you solve the problem another way? Explain.

LESSON CONTINUES

Practice and Problem Solving

Extra Practice, page 476, Set E

Tell whether each problem can be solved by using mental math, pictures, or models. Then solve each problem using the method you chose.

5. Sarah is putting 82 oranges into boxes. Each box can hold 6 oranges. How many boxes does Sarah need to pack all the oranges?

6. Mrs. Hubbard wants to divide her class into 3 equal groups. There are 36 students in her class. How many students will be in each group?

7. Tiffany has 78 ounces of fruit punch to give to her friends. Each glass can hold 8 ounces of juice. How many glasses can Tiffany fill?

8. Jacob is arranging flowers. He has 57 flowers and wants to put 5 flowers in each vase. How many vases will he need to hold all the flowers?

9. Catherine has 72 toy cars. She wants to put the same number of cars in each of 3 boxes. How many cars will Catherine put in each box? Will she have any cars left over?

10. Look back at Problems 5–9. Did you choose the best method? Could you solve the problem another way? Explain.

USE DATA For 11–13, use the table.

SHELLS WE COLLECTED	
Jarrod	62
Gina	45
Tim	60

11. Jarrod wants to make flower pictures out of the shells he collected. Each large flower will take 8 shells to make. How many flowers can he make? How many shells will he have left over?

12. Gina made small flower pictures using 4 shells for each flower. How many flowers did she make? How many shells were left over?

13. **MULTISTEP** Tim made 4 small flowers using 4 shells each and 5 large flowers using 8 shells each. How many shells did he have left over?

14. **REASONING** Gustavo had 15 cookies. He gave 3 cookies to each of his friends. He kept 3 cookies for himself. With how many friends did he share his cookies?

15. **REASONING** Heather went to the mall and bought 3 tapes. Each tape cost $9. Then she bought lunch for $6. She has $4 left. How much money did Heather start with?

Maintain Skills

Find each sum or difference.

16. $\begin{array}{r} 241 \\ +382 \\ \hline \end{array}$ **17.** $\begin{array}{r} 698 \\ +473 \\ \hline \end{array}$ **18.** $\begin{array}{r} 634 \\ +118 \\ \hline \end{array}$

19. $\begin{array}{r} 809 \\ -224 \\ \hline \end{array}$ **20.** $\begin{array}{r} 347 \\ -198 \\ \hline \end{array}$ **21.** $\begin{array}{r} 766 \\ -438 \\ \hline \end{array}$

22. Write the amount.

CRCT Test Prep

23. M3N2.c. Katya bought a card for $1.85 and ribbon for $0.98. She paid with a $10 bill. How much change should she get? (p. 98)

A. $5.71
B. $6.77
C. $7.07
D. $7.17

Problem Solving Thinker's Corner

SOLVE THE RIDDLE!

Find each product or quotient.

75×3 **K**	$4\overline{)116}$ **B**			
$2\overline{)382}$ **O**	19×7 **F**	$6\overline{)306}$ **Q**	43×2 **C**	37×6 **A**
24×5 **U**	$8\overline{)328}$ **E**	22×9 **S**	$9\overline{)108}$ **R**	$4\overline{)224}$ **X**

To answer the riddle, match the letters from the products and quotients above to the numbers below.

What do you call a crate of ducks?

___   ___ ___ ___   ___ ___   ___ ___ ___ ___ ___ ___ ___ ___!

222   29 191 56   191 133   51 120 222 86 225 41 12 198

Extra Practice

Set A (pp. 458–461)

Use the model. Write the quotient.

1. $45 \div 3 = \blacksquare$

2. $38 \div 2 = \blacksquare$

Set B (pp. 462–465)

Use the model. Write the quotient and remainder.

1. $33 \div 2 = \blacksquare$

2. $55 \div 3 = \blacksquare$

Divide. You may use base-ten blocks to help.

3. $3\overline{)57}$
4. $8\overline{)92}$
5. $4\overline{)71}$
6. $7\overline{)68}$
7. $6\overline{)32}$

Set C (pp. 466–467)

Use mental math to divide.

1. $3\overline{)49}$
2. $5\overline{)70}$
3. $2\overline{)39}$
4. $6\overline{)84}$
5. $5\overline{)93}$

Set D (pp. 470–471)

Divide.

1. $2\overline{)684}$
2. $3\overline{)108}$
3. $5\overline{)250}$
4. $9\overline{)279}$

Set E (pp. 472–475)

Tell whether each problem can be solved by using mental math, pictures, or models. Then solve each problem using the method you chose.

1. Ms. Payne divides 65 crayons equally among 9 students. How many crayons does each student get? How many are left over?

2. Marian has 83 sunflower seeds. How many seeds can she put in each of 3 bags? How many seeds will be left over?

Review/Test

CHECK VOCABULARY AND CONCEPTS

Choose the best term from the box.

Vocabulary
divisor
remainder

1. In division, the amount left over is called the ___?___. (p. 457)

Find the quotient and remainder. Use counters or draw a picture to help. (pp. 456–457)

2. $11 \div 2 = \blacksquare$ **3.** $26 \div 4 = \blacksquare$ **4.** $38 \div 5 = \blacksquare$ **5.** $14 \div 5 = \blacksquare$

CHECK SKILLS

Divide and check. (pp. 458–461, 462–465, 466–467)

6. $26 \div 2 = \blacksquare$ **7.** $41 \div 3 = \blacksquare$ **8.** $59 \div 4 = \blacksquare$

9. $6\overline{)84}$ **10.** $3\overline{)77}$ **11.** $7\overline{)67}$ **12.** $8\overline{)39}$

Divide. (pp. 470–471)

13. $4\overline{)253}$ **14.** $9\overline{)747}$ **15.** $3\overline{)744}$ **16.** $6\overline{)678}$

Tell whether each problem can be solved by using mental math, pictures, or models. Then solve each problem using the method you chose. (pp. 472–475)

17. Marty has 81 coins. He puts an equal number of coins into 3 jars. How many coins does he put in each jar?

18. Alana divided 46 stickers into 4 piles. How many stickers did she put in each pile? How many stickers are left over?

CHECK PROBLEM SOLVING

19. A class of 33 students is going to the science museum. If each van holds 9 students, how many vans does the class need? (pp. 468–469)

20. Caroline needs 4-inch pieces of yarn for an art project. She has 58 inches of yarn. How many 4-inch pieces can she make? (pp. 468–469)

Chapter CRCT Test Prep

NUMBERS AND OPERATIONS

1. M3N4.b. Karen made this model. What division sentence does it show?

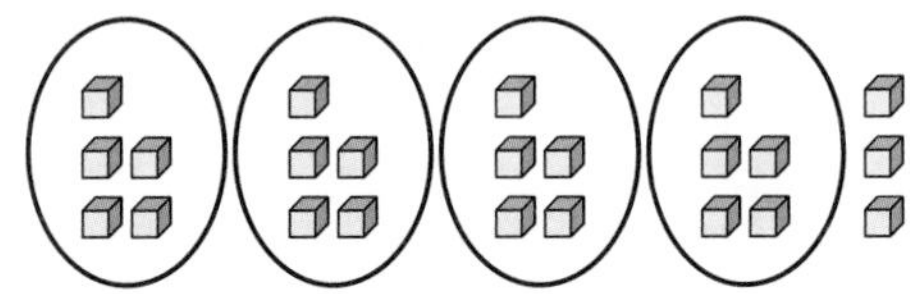

A. $18 \div 4 = 4$ r2

B. $20 \div 3 = 6$ r2

C. $20 \div 4 = 5$

D. $23 \div 4 = 5$ r3

2. M3N4.f. Tim has 91 coins. He puts an equal number of coins into 7 albums. How many coins does Tim put in each album?

A. 38

B. 21

C. 13

D. 7

3. M3N4.e. Find the quotient.

$2\overline{)380}$

A. 175

B. 180

C. 185

D. 190

NUMBERS AND OPERATIONS

4. M3N4.d. Michael wants to take 30 hot dogs to a picnic. The hot dogs are sold in packages of 8. How many packages should Michael buy?

A. 5

B. 4

C. 3

D. 2

5. M3N4.e. Find the quotient and remainder.

$3\overline{)248}$

A. 72 r2

B. 76 r1

C. 82 r2

D. 86 r1

6. M3N4.f. Carl has 68 toy cars. He put the same number of cars into each of 4 boxes. How many boxes did he use?

A. 17

B. 18

C. 19

D. 20

Cumulative CRCT Test Prep

ALGEBRA

Use the table below to answer question 7.

Hours Worked	1	2	3	4
Money Earned	\$8	\$16	\$24	\$32

7. M3A1.a. Which rule decribes the pattern in this table?

A. Subtract \$7.

B. Multiply by \$8.

C. Add \$7.

D. Divide by \$4.

8. M3A1.a. Laura drew this pattern.

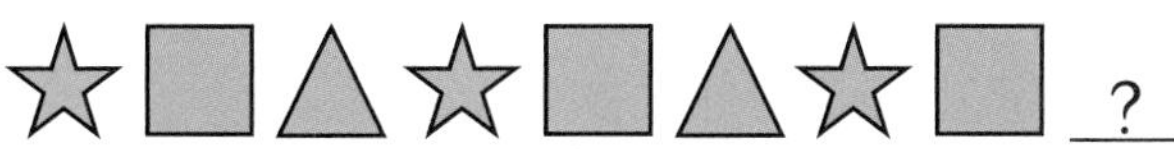

What is the next shape in her pattern?

A. ☆

B. ■

C. △

D. ▬

DATA ANALYSIS

Use the table below to answer question 9.

Number of Books Read	
Number of Books	Number of Students
6	𝍸 |
7	𝍸 ||||
8	𝍸 ||
9	|||

9. M3D1.a. The table shows the number of books read by the students in Ms. Sullivan's class. How many more students read 6 or 7 books than read 8 or 9 books?

A. 1

B. 5

C. 6

D. 7

GPS/CRCT Vocabulary

ELA3R2 The student acquires and uses grade-level words to communicate effectively. *also* **ELA3R3.b., ELA3R3.h., ELA3R3.r.**

VOCABULARY

- multiply (×)
- multiple
- partial products
- quotient
- divisor
- product
- factors
- divide (÷)
- dividend
- remainder

VOCABULARY CONCENTRATION

MATERIALS *For each group* vocabulary cards, definition cards

- Mix up the vocabulary and definition cards, and place them face down in 4 rows and 3 columns.
- Take turns turning over two cards at a time. The player that matches a term with the correct definition removes the cards. If a term does not match the definition, turn both cards face down, and continue playing.
- Play the game until all the terms and definitions have been matched.
- The player with the most pairs of matched cards wins the game.

	remainder	
the amount left over when a number cannot be divided evenly		

MATH WORD WORK

MATERIALS *For each student* Unit 8 *Math Word Work* puzzle

- Find and circle the words listed below.

multiply	**product**
multiple	**divide**
quotient	**remainder**

A	M	U	L	T	I	P	L	Y	B
M	U	O	M	L	X	Q	M	R	A
P	L	E	O	A	V	P	Q	L	T
L	T	I	R	P	M	L	U	S	R
D	I	V	I	D	E	Q	O	C	A
Q	P	R	L	B	I	E	T	L	Y
A	L	C	P	A	V	M	I	E	R
R	E	M	A	I	N	D	E	R	I
M	O	N	E	C	T	S	N	Y	E
L	P	R	O	D	U	C	T	A	S

GRID GAME

MATERIALS *For each group* definition cards, counters, grid paper

- Look at the terms in the Vocabulary box on page 480. Write the terms randomly on your grid, one term to a box. Fill in all the boxes. You will use 6 terms more than once.
- Choose one player to be the "caller". The caller mixes up the definition cards, chooses one, and reads it aloud. Each player puts a counter on the term that matches the definition read. Each player can place one counter on his or her grid for each turn.
- The definition card goes back in the pile. Play until someone gets 4 counters in a row, either up and down, across, or diagonally.

WHAT'S IN THE BOX?

MATERIALS *For each pair* Unit 8 *What's in the Box?* puzzle

- With a partner, use the clues and the words in the Vocabulary box on page 480 to help you fill in the blanks.
- The letters in the boxes will spell the last name of the only U.S. president who was born in Georgia.

1. In the number sentence $3 \times 4 = 12$, 12 is the __?__.
2. You can multiply by using the Distributive Property to find __?__ **products**.
3. The numbers multiplied together to find a product are called __?__.
4. In the number sentence $45 \div 9 = 5$, the __?__ is 5.
5. To __?__ means to separate into equal groups.
6. The number that divides the dividend is called the __?__.

1. _ _ _ _ _ _ □ _
2. _ □ _ _ _ _ _ _
3. _ _ _ _ _ _ □ _
4. _ _ _ □ _ _ _ _
5. _ _ _ _ _ _ _ □
6. _ _ _ _ _ _ _ _ □

Georgia Tasks

M3N3.c. Use arrays and area models to develop understanding of the distributive property and to determine partial products for multiplication of 2- or 3-digit numbers by a 1-digit number. *also* **M3N3.g., M3N4.c., M3N4.e., M3N4.f., M3P4.c.**

SS3G1.a. Identify major rivers of the United States of America: Mississippi, Ohio, Rio Grande, Colorado, Hudson. *also* **ELA3R3.h.**

Task A

TABLETOP TILES

Evan has 90 square tiles to make a rectangular design for a tabletop. So far, his design has 4 rows with 18 tiles in each row.

a. How many tiles has Evan used so far? Draw an array and write a multiplication sentence to show that your answer is correct. How many more rows of 18 tiles can Evan make?

b. Draw a model and write a multiplication sentence to show a different rectangular design Evan could make using 90 tiles.

Task B

RIVER RUN

The Mississippi is one of the longest rivers in the United States. It is about 2,300 miles long. If you paddled 9 miles each day down the Mississippi, it would take you over 250 days to reach the other end! The table shows some of the lengths of longest rivers in Georgia.

a. If Clark paddled 9 miles each day, how many days would it take him to go from one end of the Chattahoochee River to the other? Explain how you found your answer.

b. If Susan paddled 5 miles each day, how many more days would it take her to paddle the Savannah River than it would take her to paddle the Suwannee River? Explain how you found your answer.

Georgia River Lengths

River	Length
Suwannee	207 miles
Chattahoochee	430 miles
Savannah	314 miles

Maintain/Preview

Maintain

Use mental math to multiply and divide.

1. $4 \times 60 = \blacksquare$
2. $3 \times 500 = \blacksquare$
3. $\blacksquare = 7 \times 20$
4. $5 \times 400 = \blacksquare$
5. $6\overline{)73}$
6. $2\overline{)35}$
7. $5\overline{)72}$
8. $7\overline{)88}$

Find each product.

9. $\begin{array}{r} 62 \\ \times\ 5 \\ \hline \end{array}$
10. $\begin{array}{r} 143 \\ \times\ 7 \\ \hline \end{array}$
11. $\begin{array}{r} 28 \\ \times\ 4 \\ \hline \end{array}$
12. $\begin{array}{r} 294 \\ \times\ 3 \\ \hline \end{array}$
13. $\begin{array}{r} 632 \\ \times\ 8 \\ \hline \end{array}$

Divide.

14. $7\overline{)54}$
15. $3\overline{)296}$
16. $4\overline{)35}$
17. $6\overline{)271}$

18. Jeff used 32 ounces of milk to make 4 milkshakes. Each milkshake has the same amount of milk. How many ounces of milk are in each milkshake?

19. There is a group of 45 people going to the Atlanta Zoo. Each van can hold 8 people. How many vans do they need to take them to the zoo?

20. Theresa bought 5 sweaters. Each sweater cost $29. How much did Theresa spend in all?

21. Sophia swims 1 lap in 2 minutes. How long will it take her to swim 13 laps?

Preview

Write the value of the blue digit.

1. 54,602
2. 29,374
3. 13,916
4. 48,538
5. 69,713

Estimate each sum or difference.

6. $\begin{array}{r} 2{,}493 \\ +4{,}758 \\ \hline \end{array}$
7. $\begin{array}{r} 8{,}162 \\ +9{,}275 \\ \hline \end{array}$
8. $\begin{array}{r} 7{,}349 \\ -1{,}066 \\ \hline \end{array}$
9. $\begin{array}{r} 1{,}527 \\ +7{,}399 \\ \hline \end{array}$
10. $\begin{array}{r} 8{,}246 \\ -4{,}312 \\ \hline \end{array}$
11. $\begin{array}{r} 9{,}267 \\ -4{,}570 \\ \hline \end{array}$
12. $\begin{array}{r} 3{,}021 \\ +3{,}492 \\ \hline \end{array}$
13. $\begin{array}{r} 2{,}752 \\ +5{,}119 \\ \hline \end{array}$
14. $\begin{array}{r} 8{,}434 \\ -1{,}672 \\ \hline \end{array}$
15. $\begin{array}{r} 4{,}924 \\ -2{,}882 \\ \hline \end{array}$

GEORGIA CRCT HANDBOOK

The tips and the problems on the following pages will help you succeed on the Georgia CRCT.

Before working on the CRCT Practice problems and before taking the CRCT, sharpen your test-taking skills by reviewing these pages. Here you can find tips such as how to get ready for the test, how to understand the directions, and how to keep track of time.

The problems in this section cover the mathematics content standards from the Georgia Performance Standards.

Other Resources

Tips for Taking the Georgia CRCT

Being a good test-taker is like being a good problem solver. When you answer test questions, you are solving problems. Remember to **UNDERSTAND, PLAN, SOLVE,** and **CHECK.**

UNDERSTAND

Read the problem.

- Look for math terms and recall their meanings.
- Reread the problem and think about the question.
- Use the details in the problem and the question.

1. The sum of the digits of a number is 14. The ones digit is 4 less than the tens digit. What is the number?

A. 59 C. 86

B. 77 D. 95

TIP! Understand the problem.

Remember the meanings of *sum* and *digits*. Reread the problem to compare the details to the answer choices. Since all choices have a sum of 14, look for a ones digit that is 4 less than the tens digit. The answer is D.

- Each word is important. Missing a word or reading it incorrectly could cause you to get the wrong answer.
- Pay attention to words that are in **bold** type, all CAPITAL letters, or *italics*.
- Some other words to look for are estimate, about, only, best, or least to greatest.

2. Mr. Karza drew a diagram of 8 squares. He made 3 squares red, 2 squares blue, 2 squares yellow, and 1 square green. What fraction of the squares was NOT green?

A. $\frac{7}{8}$ C. $\frac{1}{2}$

B. $\frac{5}{8}$ D. $\frac{1}{8}$

TIP! Look for important words.

The word NOT is important. Without the word NOT, the answer would be $\frac{1}{8}$. Find the number of squares that were NOT green. The answer is A.

PLAN

Think about how you can solve the problem.

- See if you can solve the problem with the information given.
- Pictures, charts, tables, and graphs may have the information you need.
- You may need to think about information you already know.
- The answer choices may have information you need.

3. Soccer practice started at 12:00. The clock shows the time practice ended. How long did soccer practice last?

A. 10 minutes C. 35 minutes

B. 20 minutes D. 45 minutes

TIP! Get the information you need.
Use the clock to find how long soccer practice lasted. You can find out how much time passed by counting by fives. The answer is D.

- You may need to write a number sentence and solve it.
- Some problems have two steps or more.
- In some problems you need to look at relationships instead of computing an answer.
- If the path to the solution isn't clear, choose a problem solving strategy and use it to solve the problem.

4. June always has 30 days. Mary takes swimming lessons every three days in June, starting on June 3. How many times will she have lessons?

A. 5 C. 12

B. 10 D. 30

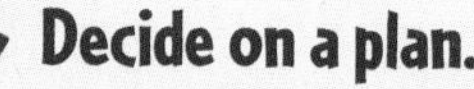

TIP! Decide on a plan.
Lessons every three days sounds like a pattern. Use the strategy *look for a pattern*. Count by 3 beginning with June 3 until you reach 30. You need to count 10 numbers, so the answer is B.

SOLVE

Follow your plan, working logically and carefully.

- Estimate your answer. Look for unreasonable answer choices.
- Use logical reasoning to find the most likely choices.
- Solve all steps needed to answer the problem.
- If your answer does not match any answer choice, check your numbers and your computation.

5. The cafeteria served 76 lunches each day for a week. How many lunches were served in 5 days?

A. 76 C. 380

B. 353 D. 1,380

TIP! Eliminate choices.

Estimate the product (5 × 80). The only reasonable answers are B. and C. Since 5 times the ones digit 6 is 30, the answer must end in zero. If you are still not certain, multiply and check your answer against B. and C. The answer is C.

- If your answer still does not match, look for another form of the number, such as a decimal instead of a fraction.
- If answer choices are given as pictures, look at each one by itself while you cover the other three.
- Read answer choices that are statements and relate them to the problem one by one.
- If your strategy isn't working, try a different one.

6. Mr. Rodriguez is putting a fence around a garden. The garden is 9 feet wide and 12 feet long. How many feet of fencing does he need?

A. 21 feet C. 84 feet

B. 42 feet D. 108 feet

TIP! Choose the answer.

The fence goes around all four sides, two that are 9 feet and two that are 12 feet. Add the lengths of the four sides (9 + 9 + 12 + 12). Find the answer choice that shows this sum. The answer is B.

CHECK

Take time to catch your mistakes.

- Be sure you answered the question asked.
- Check for important words you might have missed.
- Did you use all the information you needed?
- Check your computation by using a different method.
- Draw a picture when you are unsure of your answer.

7. Katy is buying 3 books. Their prices are $4.95, $3.25, and $7.49. What is the total cost of the books?

A. $14.59 C. $15.59
B. $14.69 D. $15.69

TIP! Check your work.
To check column addition, write the numbers in a different order. Then you will be adding different basic facts. For example, add $7.49 + $3.25 + $4.95. The answer is D.

Don't Forget!

Before the test

- Listen to the teacher's directions and read the instructions.
- Write down the ending time if the test is timed.
- Know where and how to mark your answers.
- Know whether you should write on the test page or use scratch paper.
- Ask any questions you may have before the test begins.

During the test

- Work quickly but carefully. If you are unsure how to answer a question, leave it blank and return to it later.
- If you cannot finish on time, read the questions that are left. Answer the easiest ones first. Then answer the others.
- Fill in each answer space carefully. Erase completely if you change an answer. Erase any stray marks.
- Check that the answer number matches the question number, especially if you skip a question.

CRCT Practice

NUMBERS AND OPERATIONS

1. M3N1.a. Which of these numbers has a 5 in the thousands place?

   A. 18,275

   B. 25,187

   C. 51,728

   D. 72,581

2. M3N2.b. Which way lets you use mental math to find the sum?

$$\begin{array}{r} 295 \\ +426 \\ \hline \end{array}$$

   A. 300 + 400

   B. 300 + 421

   C. 200 + 400

   D. 300 + 431

3. M3N2.c. Tomas and his friends spent $28.00 at the movie theater. They paid $14.80 for the tickets. They spent the rest of the money on snacks. How much money did they spend on snacks?

   A. $34.80

   B. $14.20

   C. $13.20

   D. $4.80

4. M3N5.c. How do you write the fraction $\frac{3}{10}$ as a decimal?

   A. 0.2

   B. 0.3

   C. 0.4

   D. 0.5

Use the word problem in the box below to answer question 5.

> There are 20 party guests. Four people can sit at each table. How many tables are needed to seat all the guests?

5. M3N4.c. Which expression can be used to solve the problem?

   A. $20 \div 4$

   B. 4×4

   C. $20 + 4$

   D. 20×4

Study and Review	
Item	Lesson Pages
1	14–15
2	52–53
3	98–99
4	416–417
5	224–225

6. M3N3.c. Which multiplication sentence is shown by the array?

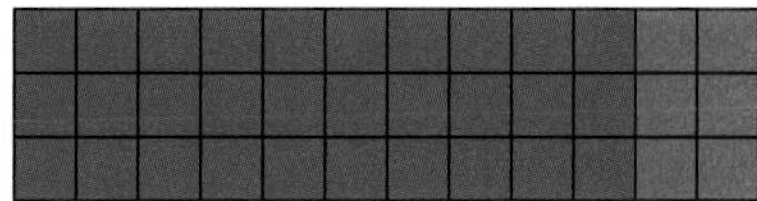

A. $3 \times 2 = 6$

B. $3 \times 10 = 30$

C. $2 \times 16 = 32$

D. $3 \times 12 = 36$

7. M3N2.a. What number should Jolene write in the □ to make the sentence true?

$$184 + \square = 184$$

A. 0

B. 1

C. 4

D. 8

8. M3N5.e. Find the sum.

$$\frac{4}{8} + \frac{1}{8} = \square$$

A. $\frac{5}{8}$

B. $\frac{6}{8}$

C. $\frac{5}{16}$

D. $\frac{6}{16}$

9. M3N2.c. A book store sold 4,506 books in March and 3,298 books in April. How many more books were sold in March than in April?

A. 1,528

B. 1,208

C. 905

D. 321

Use the picture below to answer question 10.

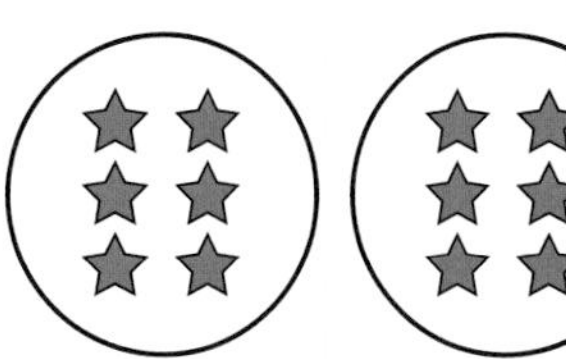

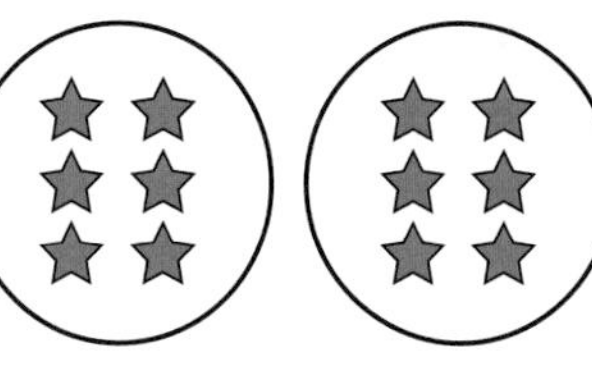

10. M3N4.b. Which division sentence does the picture show?

A. $6 \div 3 = 2$

B. $9 \div 3 = 3$

C. $12 \div 6 = 2$

D. $18 \div 3 = 6$

Study and Review	
Item	Lesson Pages
6	438–439
7	46–47
8	398–399
9	74–75
10	202–203

CRCT Practice

NUMBERS AND OPERATIONS

11. M3N2.b. Use front-end estimation to estimate the difference.

$$\begin{array}{r} 8{,}199 \\ -2{,}276 \\ \hline \end{array}$$

A. 6,000
B. 5,900
C. 5,800
D. 5,700

12. M3N3.f. Which of these gives the best estimate of the product 31×5?

A. 30×10
B. 40×10
C. 30×5
D. 40×5

13. M3N3.e. Which number sentence is NOT true?

A. $1 \times 9 = 9$
B. $(2 \times 4) \times 7 = 2 \times (4 \times 7)$
C. $5 \times 6 = 6 \times 5$
D. $3 \times 0 = 3$

14. M3N1.b. What is the value of the digit 6 in 4,762?

A. 6,000
B. 600
C. 60
D. 6

Use the picture below to answer question 15.

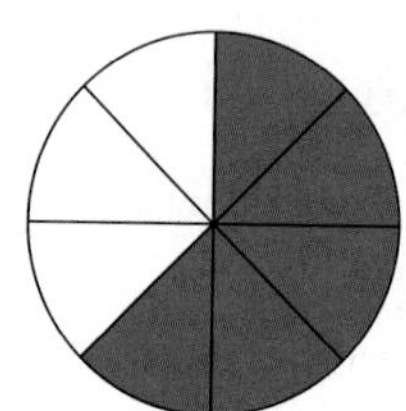

15. M3N5.b. What fraction of the circle is shaded?

A. $\frac{1}{5}$
B. $\frac{1}{3}$
C. $\frac{3}{8}$
D. $\frac{5}{8}$

Study and Review	
Item	Lesson Pages
11	70–71
12	436–437
13	188–189
14	6–9
15	390–393

16. M3N3.b. A multiplication sign correctly completes which number sentence?

A. 3 ○ 4 = 7

B. 8 ○ 2 = 4

C. 7 ○ 6 = 42

D. 10 ○ 5 = 5

17. M3N3.a. What multiplication sentence matches the addition sentence?

$$6 + 6 + 6 + 6 + 6 = 30$$

A. $6 \times 6 = 36$

B. $5 \times 5 = 25$

C. $6 \times 4 = 24$

D. $5 \times 6 = 30$

18. M3N5.a. What decimal does the shaded part of the picture show?

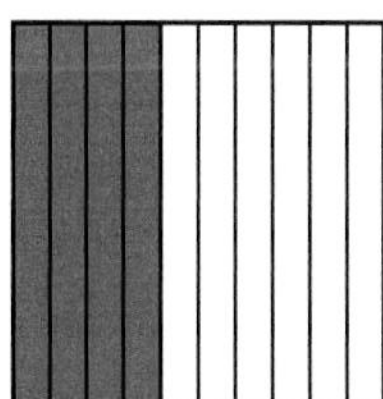

A. 0.4

B. 0.5

C. 0.6

D. 0.7

19. M3N2.a. Which number should Elly write in the box?

$$26 + (51 + 37) = 114$$
$$(26 + \square) + 37 = 114$$

A. 26

B. 37

C. 51

D. 114

Use the word problem in the box below to answer question 20.

Mr. Ruiz bought 10 pairs of socks. Each pair of socks cost $2. How much did Mr. Ruiz spend in all?

20. M3N3.g. Which number sentence can be used to solve the word problem?

A. $10 + 2 = 12$

B. $10 - 2 = 8$

C. $10 \times 2 = 20$

D. $10 \div 2 = 5$

Study and Review	
Item	Lesson Pages
16	170–171
17	126–127
18	414–415
19	46–47
20	230–231

NUMBERS AND OPERATIONS

21. M3N3.f. Which shows how you can use mental math to find the product?

$$99 \times 4 = \square$$

A. $(100 - 1) \times 4$

B. $(100 + 1) \times 4$

C. $100 - (1 \times 4)$

D. $100 + (1 \times 4)$

22. M3N5.f. What is the sum $0.6 + 0.2$?

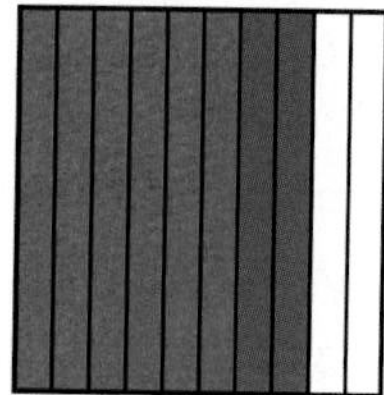

A. 0.6

B. 0.7

C. 0.8

D. 0.9

23. M3N4.e. Find the quotient and remainder.

$$4\overline{)721}$$

A. 105 r1

B. 162 r2

C. 180 r1

D. 185 r2

24. M3N4.a. Which division sentence belongs to the same fact family as these multiplication facts?

$$8 \times 4 = 32 \quad 4 \times 8 = 32$$

A. $8 \div 2 = 4$

B. $8 \div 4 = 2$

C. $32 \div 1 = 32$

D. $32 \div 4 = 8$

Use the table below to answer question 25.

Park Attendance	
Day	**Number of People**
Saturday	2,549
Sunday	3,607

25. M3N2.c. How many people in all went to the park on Saturday and Sunday?

A. 1,058

B. 1,142

C. 5,156

D. 6,156

Study and Review	
Item	**Lesson Pages**
21	448–449
22	418–419
23	470–471
24	210–213
25	54–55

26. M3N3.d. Jason brought 4 boxes of napkins to a picnic. Each box had 300 napkins. How many napkins did Jason bring?

A. 12
B. 120
C. 1,200
D. 12,000

27. M3N4.a. Which division sentence represents these subtractions?

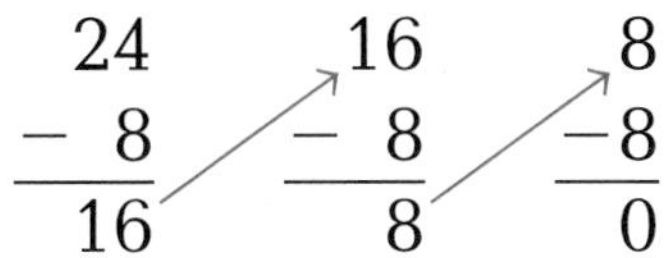

A. $24 \div 6 = 4$
B. $16 \div 2 = 8$
C. $24 \div 8 = 3$
D. $8 \div 8 = 1$

28. M3N4.f. Eva had 18 balloons. She gave the same number of balloons to each of 6 friends. How many balloons did each friend get?

A. 12
B. 9
C. 4
D. 3

Use the model below to answer question 29.

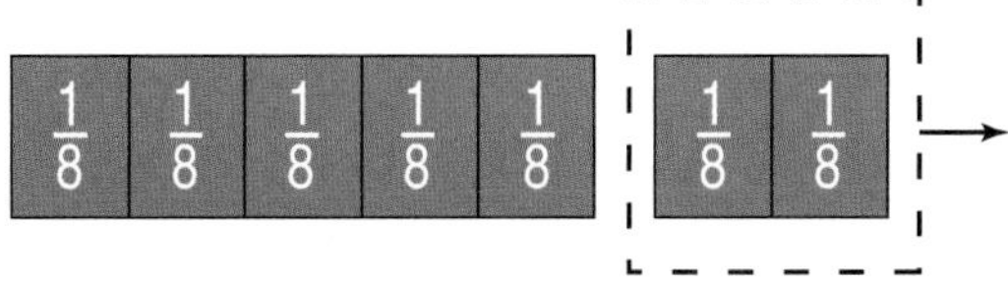

29. M3N5.f. Which subtraction sentence is shown by the model?

A. $\frac{8}{8} - \frac{2}{8} = \frac{6}{8}$
B. $\frac{7}{8} - \frac{2}{8} = \frac{5}{8}$
C. $\frac{6}{8} - \frac{2}{8} = \frac{4}{8}$
D. $\frac{5}{8} - \frac{2}{8} = \frac{3}{8}$

30. M3N1.b. In 2004, the population of Macon, Georgia was 94,990. What is the value of the digit 4 in 94,990?

A. 40
B. 400
C. 4,000
D. 40,000

Study and Review	
Item	Lesson Pages
26	434–435
27	204–205
28	238–241
29	400–401
30	14–15

NUMBERS AND OPERATIONS

31. M3N4.b. How many groups of 5 are in 45?

A. 9

B. 8

C. 7

D. 6

32. M3N5.d. Ms. Jackson cut a pie into 10 equal slices. She ate 1 slice of the pie. Which of these fractions represent the amount of the pie that Ms. Jackson ate?

A. $\frac{1}{9}$

B. $\frac{1}{2}$

C. $\frac{1}{3}$

D. $\frac{1}{10}$

33. M3N5.g. Carmen walked $\frac{2}{8}$ mile before school and $\frac{5}{8}$ mile after school. How much farther did Carmen walk after school than before school?

A. $\frac{2}{8}$

B. $\frac{3}{8}$

C. $\frac{5}{8}$

D. $\frac{7}{8}$

34. M3N4.e. Find the quotient.

$$3\overline{)84}$$

A. 31

B. 30

C. 29

D. 28

35. M3N5.b. Which does NOT show $\frac{4}{10}$ shaded?

A.

B.

C.

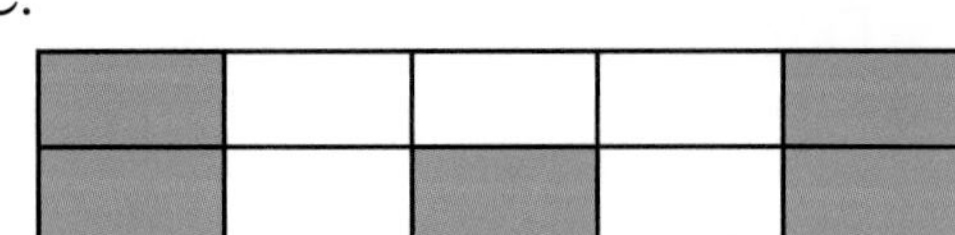

D.

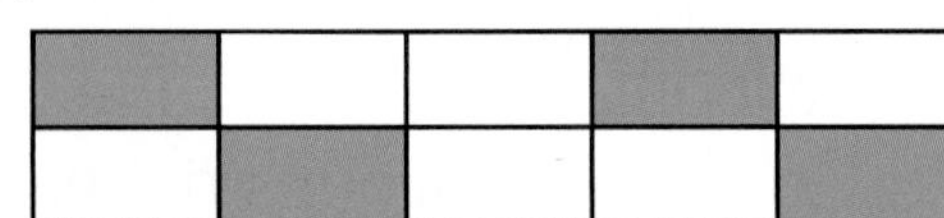

Study and Review	
Item	**Lesson Pages**
31	222–223
32	390–393
33	402–405
34	458–461
35	390–393

36. M3N2.b. Which shows how to use front-end estimation to find the sum?

$$\begin{array}{r} 2{,}052 \\ +5{,}418 \\ \hline \end{array}$$

A. 2,000 + 5,000

B. 2,000 + 6,000

C. 3,000 + 5,000

D. 3,000 + 6,000

37. M3N3.c. Kevin made the array below to help him find the product 5 × 17.

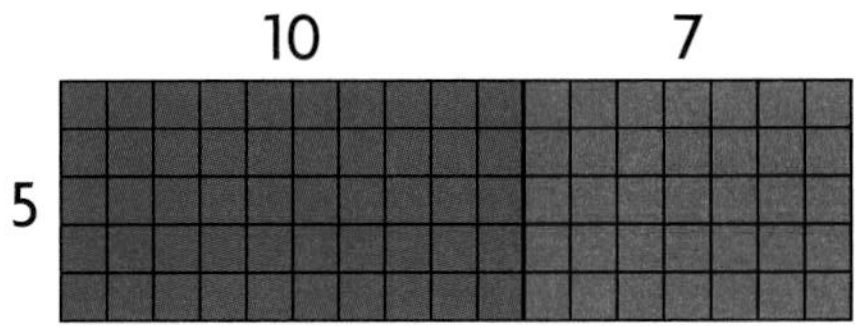

Which shows how Kevin can use the distributive property to find the product?

A. (5 × 10) + (10 × 7)

B. (5 × 10) + (5 × 7)

C. (7 × 10) + (7 × 5)

D. (10 × 5) + (10 × 7)

38. M3N1.a. Which of these numbers has a 2 in the hundreds place?

A. 82,046

B. 64,820

C. 48,206

D. 20,468

39. M3N3.b. Find the product.

$$9 \times 4 = \square$$

A. 32

B. 36

C. 45

D. 49

Use the graph below to answer question 40.

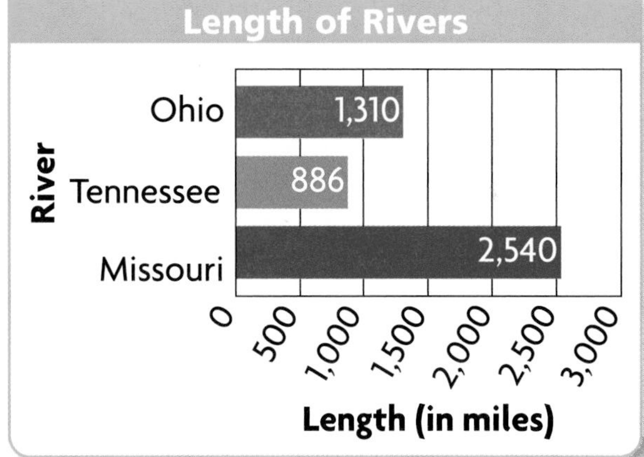

40. M3N2.c. How much longer is the Missouri River than the Ohio River?

A. 424 miles

B. 886 miles

C. 1,230 miles

D. 1,654 miles

Study and Review	
Item	Lesson Pages
36	50–51
37	440–441
38	14–15
39	146–147
40	74–75

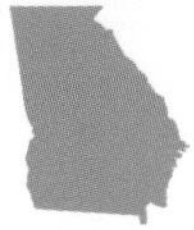

NUMBERS AND OPERATIONS

41. M3N5.g. Robin and Katie have a box of muffins. Robin ate $\frac{4}{8}$ of the muffins and Katie ate $\frac{3}{8}$ of the muffins. What fraction tells how many more of the muffins Robin ate than Katie?

A. $\frac{1}{8}$

B. $\frac{2}{8}$

C. $\frac{3}{8}$

D. $\frac{4}{8}$

42. M3N4.f. Emily has 30 books. She wants to put the same number of books onto each of 5 shelves. How many books should she put on each shelf?

A. 7

B. 6

C. 4

D. 5

43. M3N1.b. What is the value of the digit 3 in 34,265?

A. 30,000

B. 3,000

C. 300

D. 30

Use the word problem in the box below to answer question 44.

Ms. Daley packed 64 plants in boxes. Each box has 8 plants. How many boxes did she use?

44. M3N4.c. Which number sentence can be used to solve the word problem?

A. $8 + 8 = 16$

B. $64 + 8 = 72$

C. $64 \times 8 = 512$

D. $64 \div 8 = 8$

45. M3N2.c. Eddie's book has 313 pages. So far, he has read 192 pages. How many pages does Eddie have left to read?

A. 121

B. 181

C. 221

D. 281

Study and Review	
Item	**Lesson Pages**
41	402–405
42	222–223
43	14–15
44	230–231
45	74–75

46. M3N4.f. There are 24 students in Lucy's class. The students split into 4 equal reading groups. How many students are in each reading group?

A. 3

B. 4

C. 5

D. 6

47. M3N2.a. What number should Janine write in the box?

$$4 + 5 = 5 + \square$$

A. 1

B. 4

C. 5

D. 9

48. M3N5.d. What fraction of the picture is shaded?

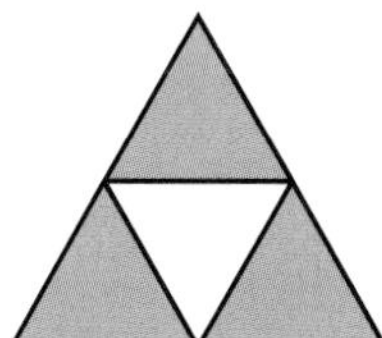

A. $\frac{1}{4}$

B. $\frac{2}{4}$

C. $\frac{3}{4}$

D. $\frac{4}{4}$

49. M3N3.d. Find the product.

$$400 \times 9 = \square$$

A. 36

B. 360

C. 3,600

D. 36,000

50. M3N4.d. Amy has 95 inches of yarn to make bracelets. It takes 6 inches of yarn to make each bracelet. She divides 95 ÷ 6 to find the number of bracelets she can make. What does the remainder tell you?

A. the number of bracelets she can make

B. the number of inches of yarn she will have left over

C. the number of inches of yarn she will use

D. the number of inches of yarn it takes to make each bracelet

Study and Review	
Item	**Lesson Pages**
46	224–225
47	46–47
48	390–393
49	434–435
50	468–469

MEASUREMENT

1. M3M1. Scott started reading a book at 6:15 P.M. He stopped reading at 7:30 P.M. For how long did Scott read?

   A. 1 hour

   B. 1 hour 15 minutes

   C. 1 hour 30 minutes

   D. 1 hour 45 minutes

2. M3M2.d. Which of these units of measure is the smallest?

   A. meter

   B. kilometer

   C. millimeter

   D. centimeter

3. M3M1. Tasha left her house at 4:20 P.M. The car ride to her grandmother's house lasted 1 hour. At what time did Tasha get to her grandmother's house?

   A. 3:20 P.M.

   B. 5:20 P.M.

   C. 6:20 P.M.

   D. 6:30 P.M.

Use the drawing below to answer question 4.

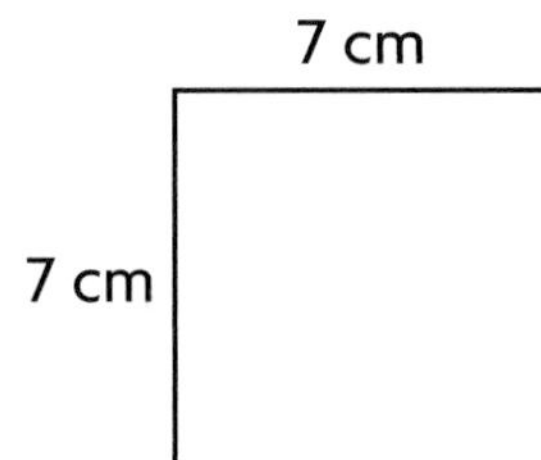

4. M3M3.b. Which number sentence can be used to find the perimeter of the square shown above?

   A. $1 \times 7 = 7$

   B. $7 + 7 = 14$

   C. $7 + 7 + 7 = 21$

   D. $7 + 7 + 7 + 7 = 28$

5. M3M2.c. Which is the best estimate for the length of a teacher's desk?

   A. 4 inches

   B. 4 feet

   C. 4 yards

   D. 4 miles

Study and Review	
Item	Lesson Pages
1	112–113
2	290–291
3	112–113
4	354–355
5	282–283

6. M3M2.b. What is the length of this nail to the nearest half inch?

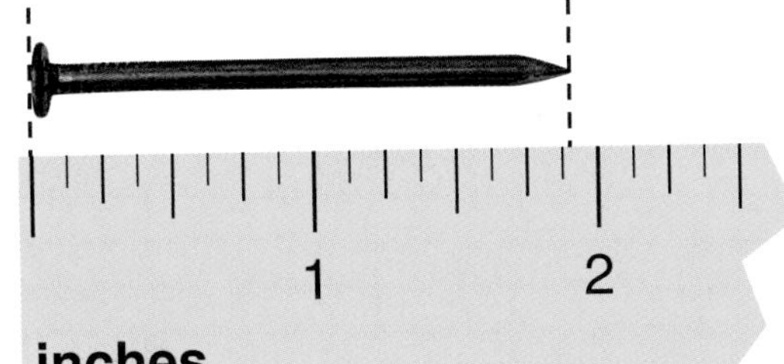

A. $\frac{1}{2}$ inch

B. 1 inch

C. $1\frac{1}{2}$ inches

D. 2 inches

Use the picture below to answer question 7.

30 ft

10 ft 10 ft

30 ft

7. M3M3.c. The flower garden at the state park is 30 feet long by 10 feet wide, as shown above. Cory started at one corner of the garden and walked all the way around. How far did Cory walk?

A. 40 feet

B. 50 feet

C. 60 feet

D. 80 feet

Use the clocks below to answer question 8.

start

end

8. M3M1. The clocks show the start and end times of Brandon's math class. How long is his math class?

A. 15 minutes

B. 30 minutes

C. 45 minutes

D. 60 minutes

9. M3M2.d. How many centimeters are in 2 meters?

A. 20

B. 200

C. 2,000

D. 20,000

Study and Review	
Item	Lesson Pages
6	280–281
7	350–353
8	112–113
9	290–291

MEASUREMENT

10. M3M4.c The rug in Joe's room is shown below.

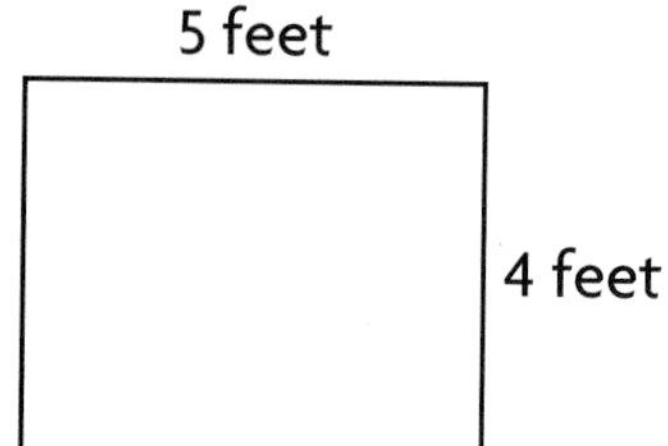

Which of these could Joe use to find the area of his rug?

A. $5 + 4$

B. 5×4

C. $5 \times 2 \times 4$

D. $5 + 5 + 4 + 4$

Use the picture below to answer question 11.

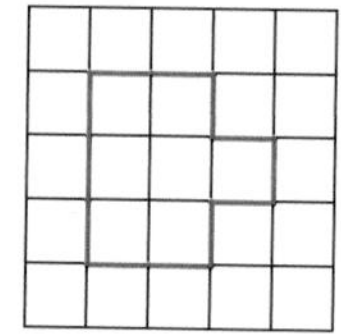

11. M3M3.a What is the perimeter of the figure above?

A. 7 units

B. 7 square units

C. 12 units

D. 12 square units

Use the picture below to answer question 12.

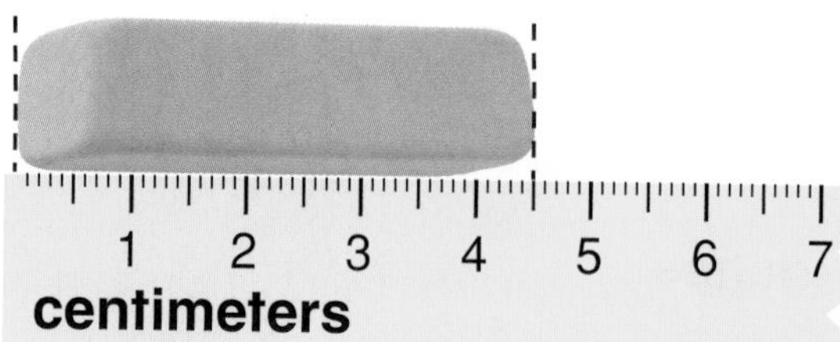

12. M3M2.b What is the length of the eraser shown above to the nearest millimeter?

A. 4 millimeters

B. 5 millimeters

C. 40 millimeters

D. 45 millimeters

13. M3M2.d How many feet are in 3 yards?

A. 9

B. 8

C. 6

D. 3

Study and Review	
Item	Lesson Pages
10	358–361
11	350–353
12	286–289
13	284–285

14. M3M1. Sara started working on her science project at 6:30 P.M. She worked on it for a half hour. What time did she stop?

A. 7:00 A.M.

B. 7:00 P.M.

C. 8:00 A.M.

D. 8:00 P.M.

15. M3M3.c. What is the perimeter of this piece of ribbon?

A. 12 centimeters

B. 24 centimeters

C. 27 centimeters

D. 81 centimeters

16. M3M2.d. Which of these units of measure is the largest?

A. foot

B. inch

C. mile

D. yard

Use the schedule below to answer question 17.

Camp Activity Schedule	
Activity	**Time**
Hiking	10:00 A.M.–11:15 A.M.
Canoeing	12:45 P.M.– 1:45 P.M.
Swimming	3:15 P.M.– 3:45 P.M.
Sing-Along	7:15 P.M.– 8:00 P.M.

17. M3M1. Which activity is 30 minutes long?

A. hiking

B. canoeing

C. swimming

D. sing-along

18. M3M2.c. Which is the best estimate for the length of an ant?

A. 8 millimeters

B. 8 centimeters

C. 8 meters

D. 8 kilometers

Study and Review	
Item	**Lesson Pages**
14	112–113
15	350–353
16	282–283
17	114–115
18	286–289

MEASUREMENT

Use the picture below to answer question 19.

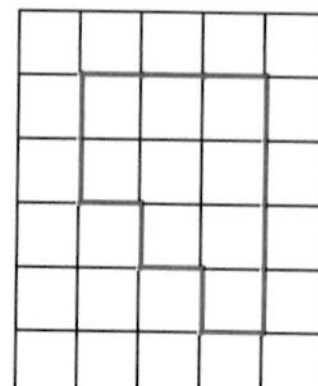

19. M3M4.a. What is the area of the figure above?

A. 9 units

B. 9 square units

C. 14 units

D. 14 square units

20. M3M2.a. Which unit of measure would be most appropriate to measure the distance you travel on a highway?

A. inch

B. foot

C. yard

D. mile

21. M3M2.d. How many meters are in 1 kilometer?

A. 10

B. 100

C. 1,000

D. 10,000

Use the picture below to answer question 22.

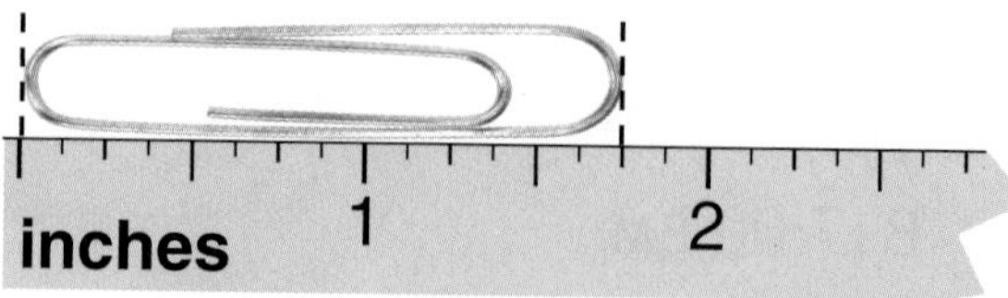

22. M3M2.b. What is the length of the paper clip to the nearest quarter inch?

A. $1\frac{1}{4}$ inches

B. $1\frac{1}{2}$ inches

C. $1\frac{3}{4}$ inches

D. 2 inches

23. M3M2.a. Which unit would you use to measure the distance between two towns?

A. meter

B. kilometer

C. millimeter

D. centimeter

Study and Review	
Item	Lesson Pages
19	356–357
20	282–283
21	290–291
22	280–281
23	286–289

24. M3M4.b. Sue wants to paint the top of her picnic table. The table is 7 feet long and 4 feet wide.

Each □ = 1 square foot

What is the area of the table Sue will be painting?

A. 22 feet

B. 22 square feet

C. 28 feet

D. 28 square feet

Use the schedule below to answer question 25.

Saturday Schedule	
Activity	**Time**
Breakfast	8:00 A.M.– 8:30 A.M.
Chores	8:45 A.M.–10:00 A.M.
Lunch	11:45 A.M.–12:30 P.M.
Movie	1:15 P.M.– 3:15 P.M.

25. M3M1. Which activity lasts 45 minutes?

A. breakfast

B. chores

C. lunch

D. movie

26. M3M2.c. Which of these is the best estimate for the length of a car?

A. 4 inches

B. 4 feet

C. 4 yards

D. 4 miles

Use the clock below to answer question 27.

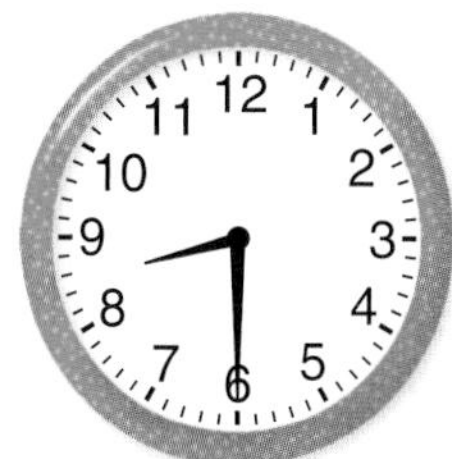

27. M3M1. The clock shows the time the band started playing. They played for 1 hour 15 minutes. What time did the band stop playing?

A. half past nine

B. quarter to ten

C. quarter past ten

D. quarter past nine

Study and Review	
Item	**Lesson Pages**
24	358–361
25	114–115
26	282–283
27	112–113

MEASUREMENT

28. M3M2.c Carly wants to measure the length of her baby gerbil. What units of measure would be the most appropriate for her to use?

A. yards

B. feet

C. inches

D. miles

29. M3M2.c Which is the best estimate for the length of a ladybug?

A. 5 meters

B. 5 kilometers

C. 5 millimeters

D. 5 centimeters

30. M3M3.b Bethany made a quilt that is 6 feet long and 4 feet wide. She wants to put a ribbon border around the outside of the quilt. How many feet of ribbon does she need?

A. 10 feet

B. 14 feet

C. 20 feet

D. 24 feet

Use the figure below to answer question 31.

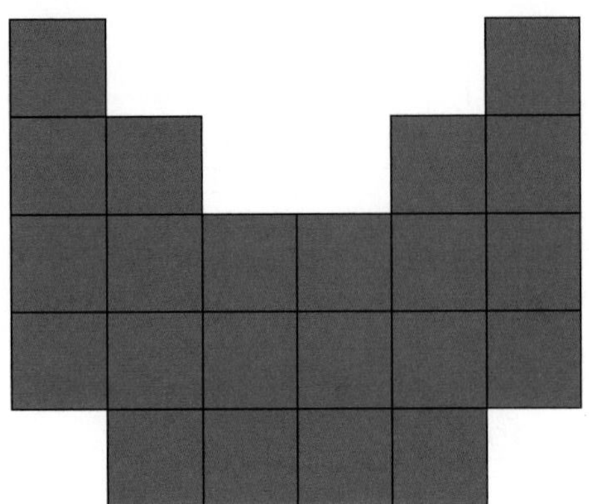

= 1 square centimeter

31. M3M4.b Each small square of the figure above is one square centimeter. What is the area of this figure?

A. 22 square centimeters

B. 24 square centimeters

C. 26 square centimeters

D. 30 square centimeters

Study and Review	
Item	Lesson Pages
28	282–283
29	286–289
30	354–355
31	356–357

GEOMETRY

1. M3G1.a. Which of these is an equilateral triangle?

A. 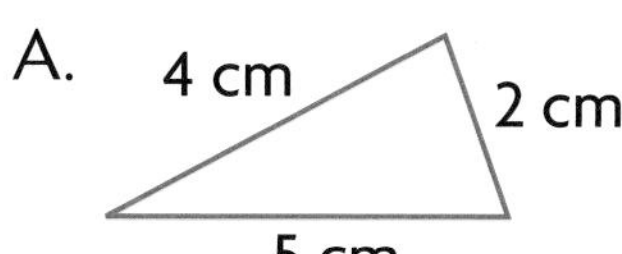

B. 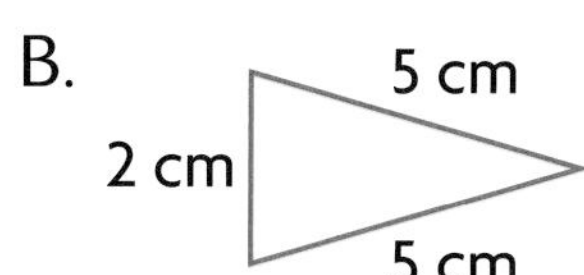

C. 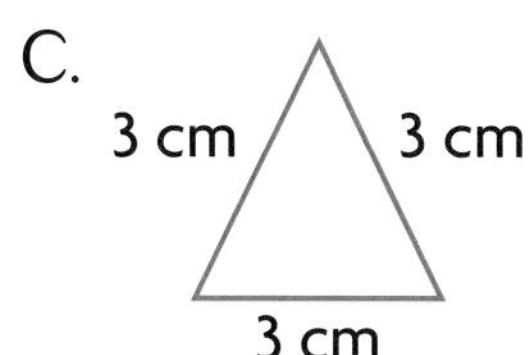

D. 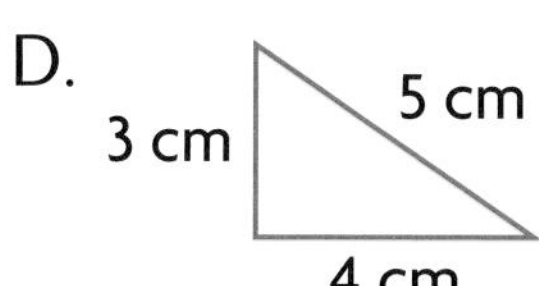

Use the figure below to answer question 2.

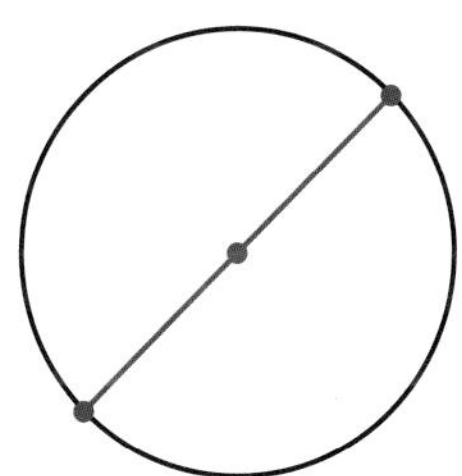

2. M3G1.d. What is the name for the part of the figure that is blue?

A. diameter

B. radius

C. circle

D. center

3. M3G1.b. How many sides does a quadrilateral have?

A. 3

B. 4

C. 5

D. 6

4. M3G1.a. Nina made this castle out of blocks.

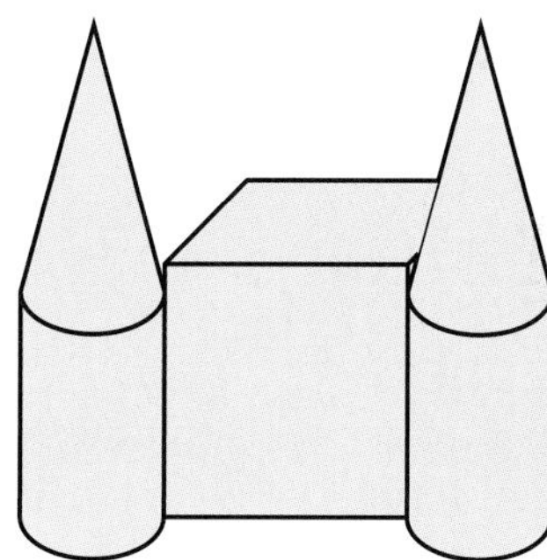

Which of these solid figures is NOT a part of Nina's castle?

A. cone

B. cube

C. sphere

D. cylinder

Study and Review	
Item	**Lesson Pages**
1	314–317
2	322–323
3	310–313
4	336–337

CRCT Practice

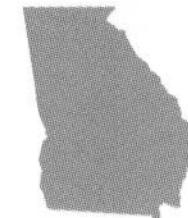

GEOMETRY

5. M3G1.b. Kelly traced over the faces of a solid figure.

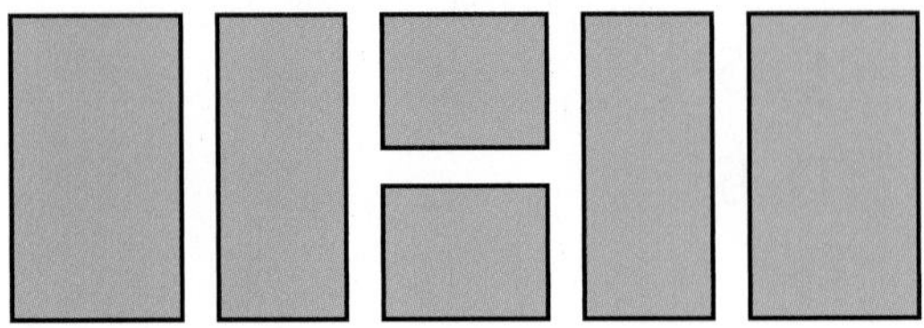

What solid figure did Kelly trace?

A. rectangular prism

B. sphere

C. cube

D. cone

6. M3G1.c. Which of these is a right triangle?

A. 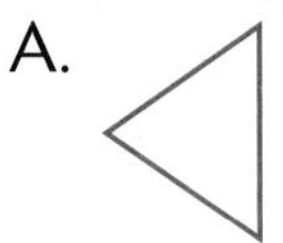

B. 

C. 

D. 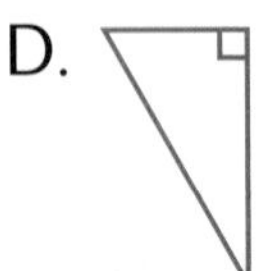

Use the picture below to answer question 7.

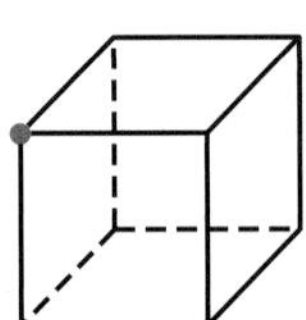

7. M3G1.b. Which part of the cube is shown in red?

A. edge

B. face

C. line

D. vertex

8. M3G1.a. What is the name of a polygon that has 6 sides?

A. quadrilateral

B. hexagon

C. pentagon

D. octagon

Study and Review	
Item	**Lesson Pages**
5	332–335
6	314–317
7	332–335
8	310–313

9. M3G1.b. Which does NOT describe a square?

A. 2 pairs of sides that are the same distance apart

B. 4 right angles

C. 4 equal sides

D. 2 obtuse angles

10. M3G1.b. How many angles does an octagon have?

A. 8

B. 6

C. 5

D. 4

Use the figure below to answer question 11.

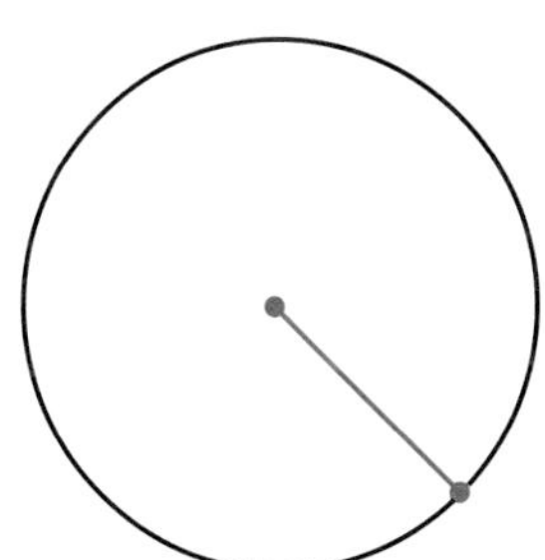

11. M3G1.d. What is the name for the part of the figure that is red?

A. center

B. radius

C. diameter

D. circle

12. M3G1.c. Maya's sandbox has 5 sides. It has 2 right angles and 3 obtuse angles. Which of these could be the shape of Maya's sandbox?

A.

B.

C.

D.

13. M3G1.a. Which of these figures is NOT a polygon?

A. trapezoid

B. hexagon

C. circle

D. triangle

Study and Review	
Item	Lesson Pages
9	318–321
10	310–313
11	322–323
12	310–313
13	310–313

CRCT Practice

GEOMETRY

14. M3G1.a. Mara drew the triangle shown below.

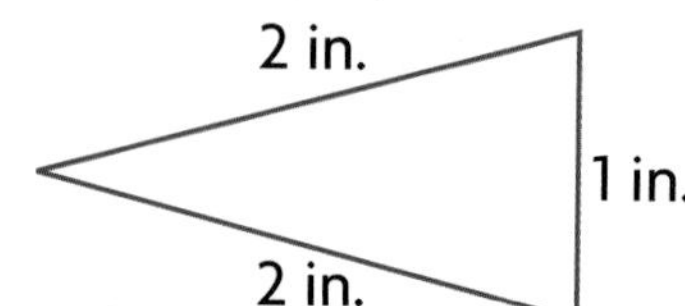

What kind of triangle did Mara draw?

A. obtuse

B. equilateral

C. isosceles

D. scalene

Use the picture below to answer question 15.

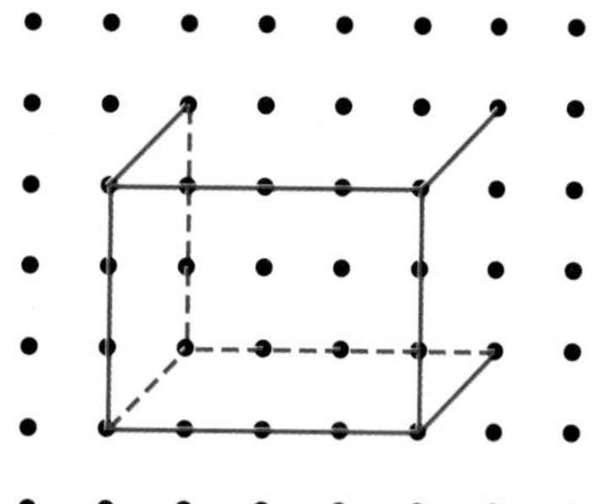

15. M3G1.a. How many more line segments are need to finish drawing this rectangular prism?

A. 1

B. 2

C. 3

D. 4

Use the diagram below to answer question 16.

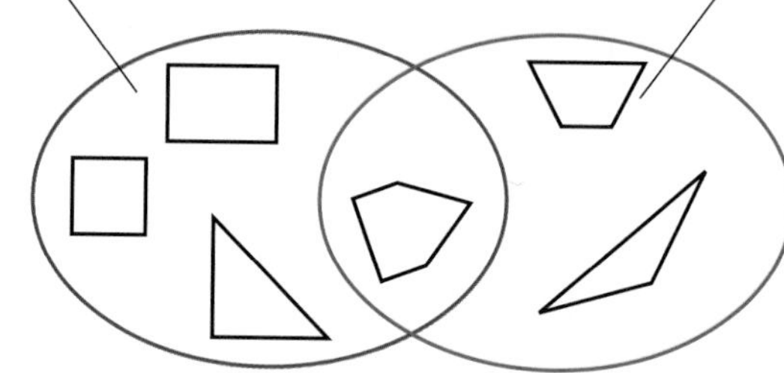

16. M3G1.c. Which of these figures would be inside the area of the Venn diagram where both sets overlap?

A.

B.

C.

D.

Study and Review	
Item	Lesson Pages
14	314–317
15	338–341
16	324–325

GEOMETRY

Use the figure below to answer question 17.

17. M3G1.b. Which of these correctly describes the figure above?

    A. It has one vertex.

    B. It has six faces.

    C. It has eight edges.

    D. It is a cylinder.

Use the figure below to answer question 18.

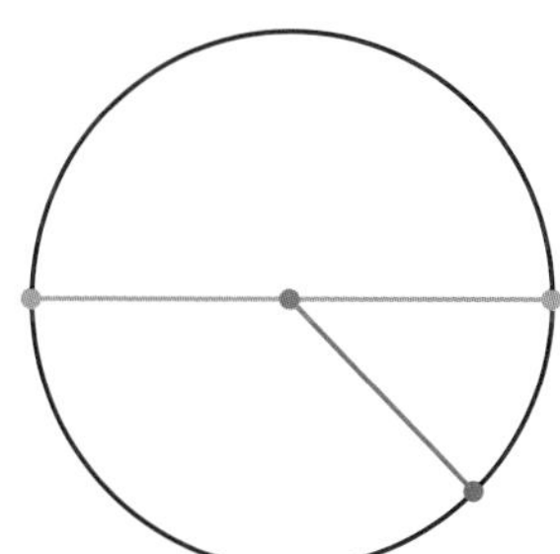

18. M3G1.d. What is the name for the part of the figure that is blue?

    A. circle

    B. radius

    C. diameter

    D. center

19. M3G1.a. Which solid figure does a roll of paper towels look like?

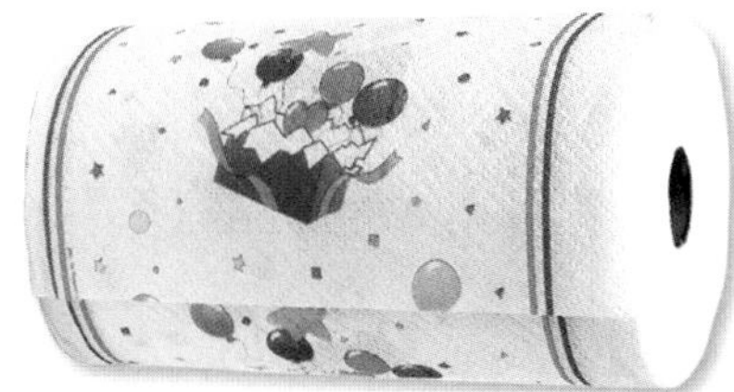

    A. cube

    B. sphere

    C. cylinder

    D. rectangular prism

20. M3G1.a. Mrs. Hobb's garden is shown below.

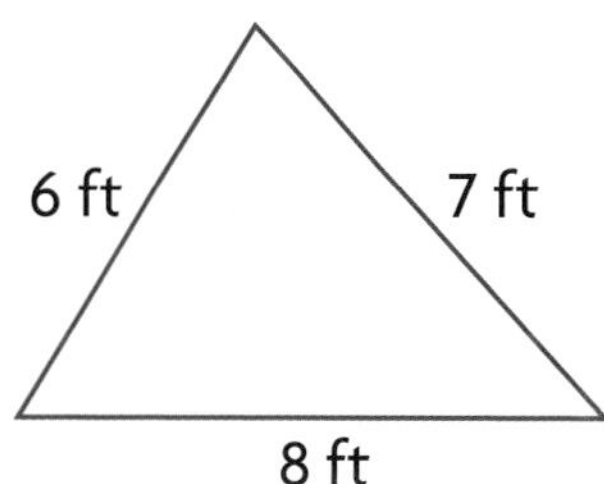

    What kind of triangle is Mrs. Hobb's garden?

    A. isosceles

    B. equilateral

    C. right

    D. scalene

Study and Review	
Item	Lesson Pages
17	332–335
18	322–323
19	332–335
20	314–317

CRCT Practice

ALGEBRA

1. M3A1.c. Which number belongs in the □ to make the number sentence true?

$$16 + \square = 43$$

A. 17

B. 27

C. 49

D. 59

Use the pattern below to answer question 2.

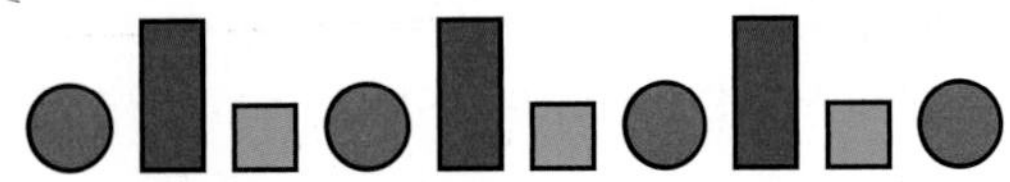

2. M3A1.a. Which are the next two figures in the pattern?

A. 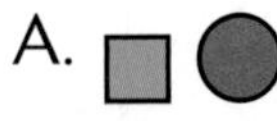

B. 

C. 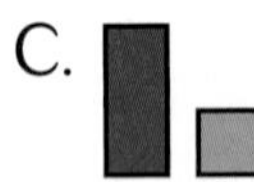

D.

Use the drawing below to answer question 3.

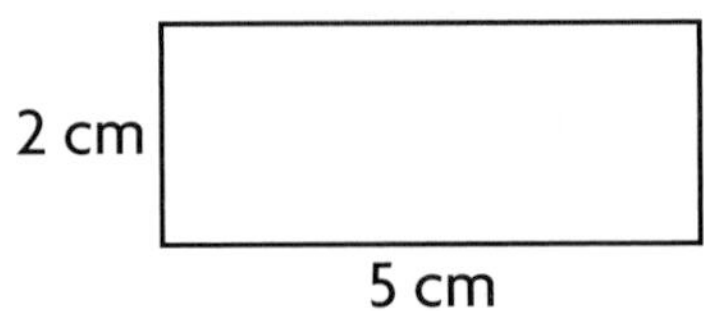

3. M3A1.b. Which number sentence can you use to find the perimeter of the rectangle?

A. $(2 \times 2) + (2 \times 2) = 8$

B. $2 \times 5 = 10$

C. $(2 \times 2) + (2 \times 5) = 14$

D. $(2 \times 5) + (2 \times 5) = 20$

4. M3A1.c. Which number belongs in the □ to make the number sentence true?

$$3 + 3 + 3 + 3 = \square \times 3$$

A. 1

B. 3

C. 4

D. 12

Study and Review	
Item	Lesson Pages
1	48–49
2	370–373
3	354–355
4	126–127

ALGEBRA

5. M3A1.a. Nikki wrote this number pattern. Which number is missing?

114, 124, 134, □, 154

A. 135

B. 144

C. 164

D. 254

6. M3A1.b. Cathy made a quilt square that is 6 inches long on each side. Which of these could Cathy use to find the area of her quilt square in square inches?

A. $6 + 6 + 6 + 6$

B. $6 + 6$

C. $(6 \times 6) + (6 \times 6)$

D. 6×6

7. M3A1.c. Which number belongs in the □ to make the number sentence true?

16 = (□ × 2) × 8

A. 4

B. 3

C. 2

D. 1

8. M3A1.a. John wrote this pattern. What rule did John use to make the pattern?

1, 2, 4, 8, 16

A. Subtract 2.

B. Add 4.

C. Multiply by 2.

D. Multiply by 4.

Use the word problem in the box below to answer question 9.

The Smith family went on a 2-week vacation. They drove 873 miles during the first week. They drove 1,801 miles in all. How many miles did they drive during the second week?

9. M3A1.c. Which number sentence can be used to solve the word problem?

A. 1,801 + □ = 873

B. 873 + □ = 1,801

C. 873 × □ = 1,801

D. 1,801 ÷ □ = 873

Study and Review	
Item	**Lesson Pages**
5	12–13
6	354–355
7	188–189
8	376–377
9	230–231

ALGEBRA

10. M3A1.a. What are the next three numbers in the pattern?

500, 503, 506, 509

A. 510, 511, 512

B. 512, 515, 518

C. 515, 520, 525

D. 516, 520, 524

Use the table below to answer question 11.

Flower	1	2	3	4	5
Petals	5	10	15	20	25

11. M3A1.a. Susie made the table above to show the number of petals on different numbers of flowers. What is the rule for the table?

A. Subtract 4 from the number of flowers.

B. Add 4 to the number of flowers.

C. Multiply the number of flowers by 2.

D. Multiply the number of flowers by 5.

12. M3A1.c. Which number belongs in the □ to make the number sentence true?

$$(2 + 4) + 6 = 2\ (\square + 6)$$

A. 0

B. 2

C. 4

D. 6

13. M3A1.b. If a square has a perimeter of 28 cm, which number sentence can be used to find the length of one side of the square?

A. $4 \times \square = 28$

B. $4 \div \square = 28$

C. $4 - \square = 28$

D. $4 + \square = 28$

Study and Review	
Item	**Lesson Pages**
10	12–13
11	184–185
12	46–47
13	354–355

ALGEBRA

14. M3A1.c. Which number belongs in the □ to make the number sentence true?

$$\square \times 40 = 80$$

A. 2

B. 4

C. 10

D. 20

15. M3A1.a. Terence is skip-counting by hundreds. He starts with 2,150. The next number he counts is 2,250. What are the third and fourth numbers in Terence's pattern?

A. 3,350 and 3,450

B. 3,150 and 3,250

C. 2,260 and 2,270

D. 2,350 and 2,450

16. M3A1.c. Kira has 72 beads to make bracelets. She wants to put 8 beads on each bracelet. Which number sentence can Kira use to find the number of bracelets she can make?

A. $\square + 8 = 72$

B. $8 \times \square = 72$

C. $72 - \square = 8$

D. $\square \div 72 = 8$

Use the pattern below to answer question 17.

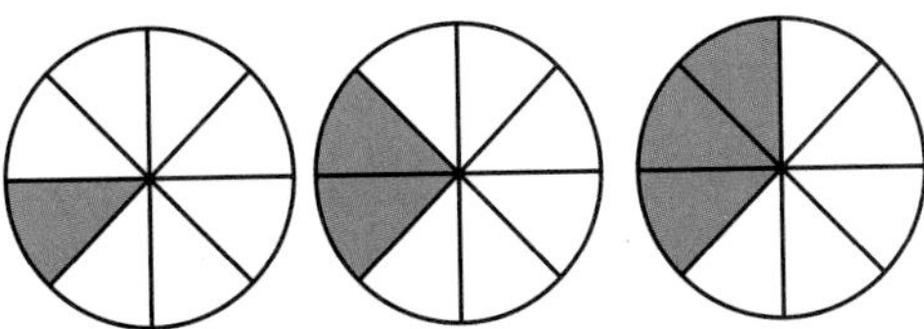

17. M3A1.a. Which figure will be next in the pattern above?

A.
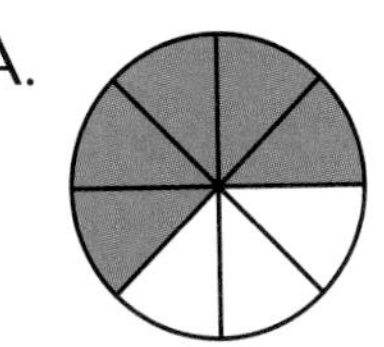

B.
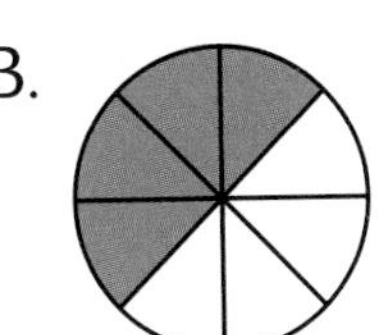

C.
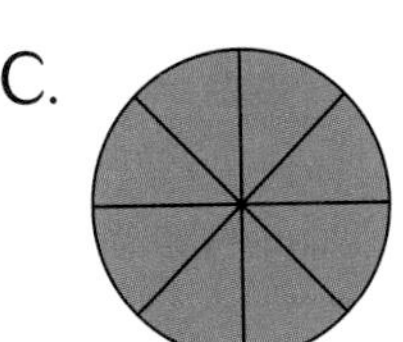

D.
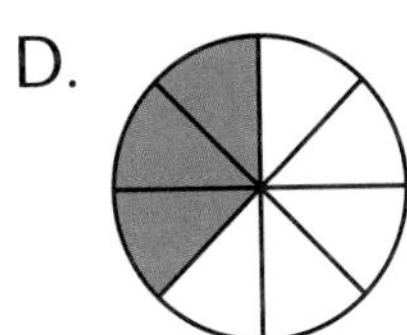

Study and Review	
Item	Lesson Pages
14	434–435
15	376–377
16	228–229
17	370–373

CRCT Practice

DATA ANALYSIS

Use the table below to answer question 1.

Favorite Animal	
Animal	**Tally**
Dog	𝍸
Cat	𝍸 𝍸 |
Horse	||
Rabbit	𝍸 ||

1. M3D1.a. How many more votes did cats get than rabbits?

   A. 4

   B. 6

   C. 7

   D. 11

Use the table below to answer question 2.

Favorite Season	
Season	**Number of Votes**
Spring	32
Summer	36
Fall	28
Winter	14

2. M3D1.a. How many people voted in all?

   A. 80

   B. 90

   C. 100

   D. 110

Use the graph below to answer question 3.

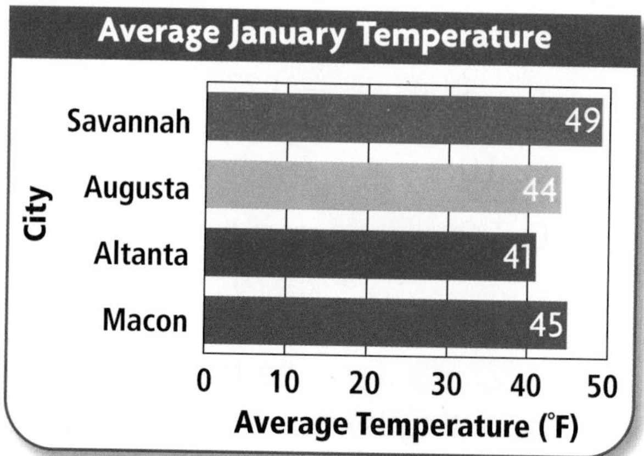

3. M3D1.b. The graph shows the average January temperature for different cities in Georgia. What city's average January temperature is higher than Atlanta's but not as high as Macon's?

   A. Savannah

   B. Augusta

   C. Atlanta

   D. Macon

Study and Review	
Item	**Lesson Pages**
1	264–265
2	264–265
3	268–269

DATA ANALYSIS

Use the table below to answer question 4.

Favorite Music	
Type of Music	**Number**
Rock	29
Classical	27
Jazz	10
Pop	16

4. M3D1.a. How many people were surveyed?

A. 82

B. 56

C. 29

D. 10

Use the graph below to answer question 5.

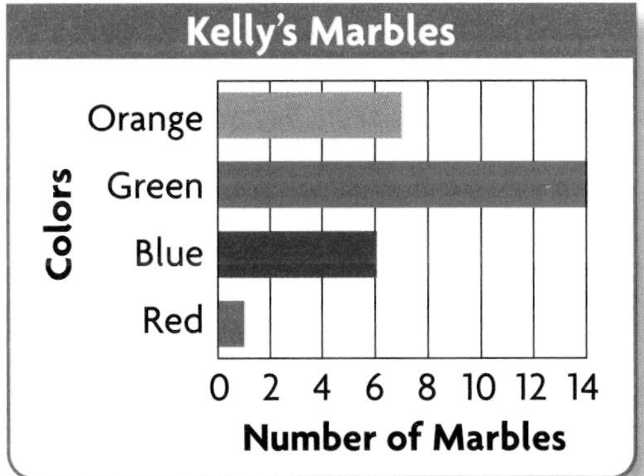

5. M3D1.b. How many green and blue marbles does Kelly have?

A. 6

B. 8

C. 14

D. 20

Use the graph below to answer question 6.

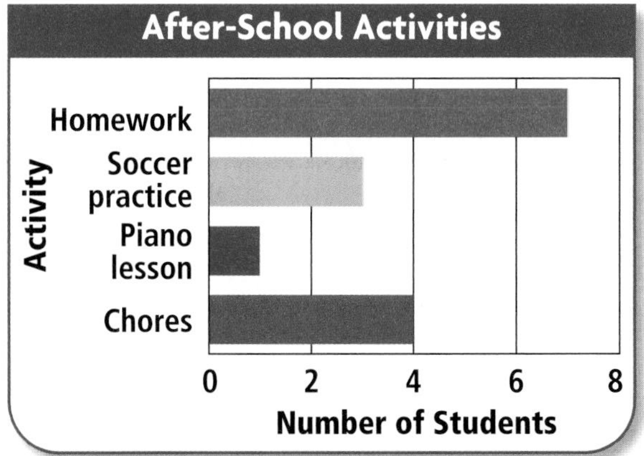

6. M3D1.b. April made this graph to show what her classmates do when they get home from school. What scale did she use for her graph?

A. scale of 1

B. scale of 2

C. scale of 5

D. scale of 10

Study and Review	
Item	**Lesson Pages**
4	264–265
5	268–269
6	268–269

DATA ANALYSIS

Use the table below to answer question 7.

Field Trip Votes	
Place	**Number**
Piedmont Park	47
Zoo Atlanta	82
State Capitol	64
Georgia Dome	51

7. M3D1.a. How many more students want to go to Zoo Atlanta than Piedmont Park?

A. 64

B. 35

C. 31

D. 18

Use the table below to answer question 8.

Main Street School	
Grade	**Number of Students**
Third	419
Fourth	487
Fifth	425

8. M3D1.a. How many students are in the third and fourth grades?

A. 844

B. 896

C. 906

D. 912

Use the graph below to answer question 9.

9. M3D1.b. The graph shows the number of movie tickets sold during five days. On which two days were the most tickets sold?

A. Wednesday and Thursday

B. Friday and Saturday

C. Thursday and Sunday

D. Saturday and Sunday

Study and Review	
Item	**Lesson Pages**
7	264–265
8	54–55
9	268–269

DATA ANALYSIS

Use the table below to answer question 10.

Favorite Subject	
Subject	**Number**
Science	4
Art	3
Reading	2
Math	3

10. M3D1.a. Which bar graph shows the information in the table?

A. Favorite Subject

Number: 0, 2, 4, 6

Science, Art, Reading, Math

Subject

B. 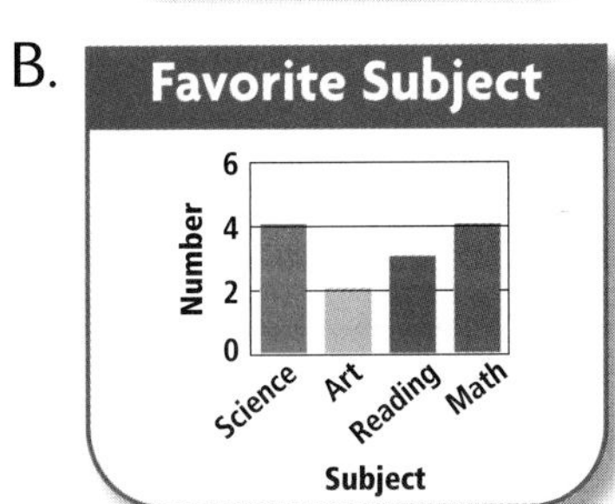

C. Favorite Subject

Number: 0, 2, 4, 6

Science, Art, Reading, Math

Subject

D. 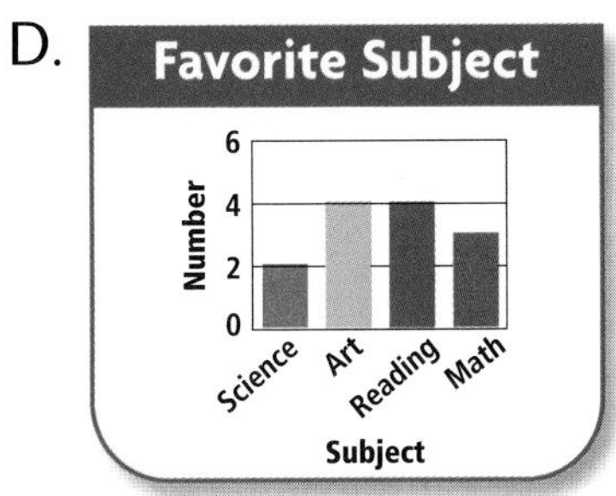

Use the graph below to answer question 11.

11. M3D1.b. Miss Kaley's students are writing poems for a class book. How many poems have these four students written in all?

A. 12

B. 20

C. 21

D. 23

Study and Review	
Item	**Lesson Pages**
10	270–271
11	268–269

TABLE OF MEASURES

METRIC	CUSTOMARY
Length	
1 centimeter (cm) = 10 millimeters (mm)	1 foot (ft) = 12 inches (in.)
1 decimeter (dm) = 10 centimeters	1 yard (yd) = 3 feet, or 36 inches
1 meter (m) = 100 centimeters	1 mile (mi) = 1,760 yards, or 5,280 feet
1 meter (m) = 10 decimeters	
1 kilometer (km) = 1,000 meters	
Mass/Weight	
1 kilogram (kg) = 1,000 grams (g)	1 pound (lb) = 16 ounces (oz)
Capacity	
1 liter (L) = 1,000 milliliters (mL)	1 pint (pt) = 2 cups (c)
	1 quart (qt) = 2 pints
	1 gallon (gal) = 4 quarts

TIME

1 minute (min) = 60 seconds (sec)	1 year (yr) = 12 months (mo), or about 52 weeks
1 hour (hr) = 60 minutes	1 year = 365 days
1 day = 24 hours	1 leap year = 366 days
1 week (wk) = 7 days	

MONEY

1 penny = 1 cent (¢)
1 nickel = 5 cents
1 dime = 10 cents
1 quarter = 25 cents
1 half dollar = 50 cents
1 dollar ($) = 100 cents

SYMBOLS

$<$ is less than
$>$ is greater than
$=$ is equal to
$\neq$ is not equal to
°F degrees Fahrenheit
°C degrees Celsius
(2,3) ordered pair

Pronunciation Key

a	add, map	f	fit, half	n	nice, tin	p	pit, stop	yo͞o	fuse, few
ā	ace, rate	g	go, log	ng	ring, song	r	run, poor	v	vain, eve
â(r)	care, air	h	hope, hate	o	odd, hot	s	see, pass	w	win, away
ä	palm, father	i	it, give	ō	open, so	sh	sure, rush	y	yet, yearn
b	bat, rub	ī	ice, write	ô	order, jaw	t	talk, sit	z	zest, muse
ch	check, catch	j	joy, ledge	oi	oil, boy	th	thin, both	zh	vision, pleasure
d	dog, rod	k	cool, take	ou	pout, now	t͟h	this, bathe		
e	end, pet	l	look, rule	o͝o	took, full	u	up, done		
ē	equal, tree	m	move, seem	o͞o	pool, food	û(r)	burn, term		

ə the schwa, an unstressed vowel representing the sound spelled *a* in above, *e* in sicken, *i* in possible, *o* in melon, *u* in circus

Other symbols:
• separates words into syllables
ʹ indicates stress on a syllable

A

acute angle [ə•kyo͞otʹ angʹgəl] An angle that has a measure less than a right angle (p. 305)
Example:

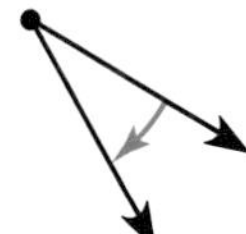

Word History

When the letter "g" is replaced with the letter "k" in the word *angle*, the word becomes *ankle*. Both words come from the same Latin root, *angulus*, which means "a sharp bend."

acute triangle [ə•kyo͞otʹ trīʹang•gəl] A triangle that has three acute angles (p. 315)

addend [aʹdend] Any of the numbers that are added
Example: 2 + 3 = 5
(2 and 3 are each labeled: addend)

addition [ə•dishʹən] The process of finding the total number of items when two or more groups of items are joined; the opposite operation of subtraction

A.M. [ā em] The hours between midnight and noon (p. 110)

angle [angʹgəl] A figure formed by two rays or line segments that share an endpoint (p. 304)
Example:

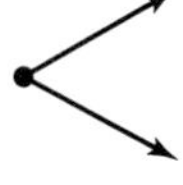

area [ârʹē•ə] The number of square units needed to cover a flat surface (p. 356)
Example:

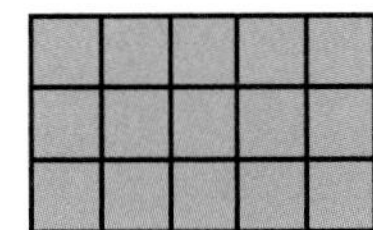

area = 15 square units

array [ə•rāʹ] An arrangement of objects in rows and columns (p. 130)
Example:

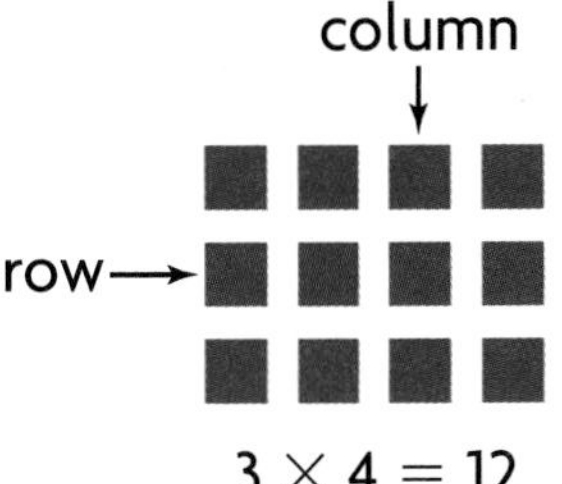

Associative Property of Addition [a•sō′shē•ā•tiv prä′pər•tē əv ə•dish′ən] The property that states that you can group addends in different ways and still get the same sum (p. 46)
Example:
4 + (2 + 5) = 11 and
(4 + 2) + 5 = 11

Associative Property of Multiplication [a•sō′shē•ā•tiv prä′pər•tē əv mul•tə•plə•kā′shən] The property that states that when the grouping of factors is changed, the product remains the same (p. 186)
Example:
(3 × 2) × 4 = 24
3 × (2 × 4) = 24

bar graph [bär graf] A graph that uses bars to show data (p. 30)
Example:

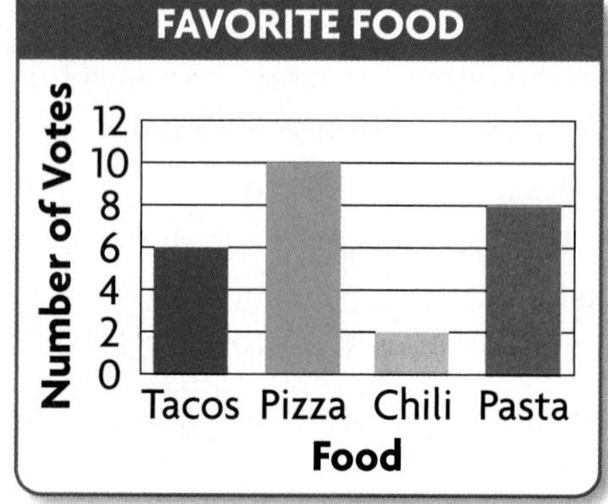

benchmark numbers [bench′märk num′bərz] Numbers that help you estimate the number of objects without counting them, such as 25, 50, 100, 1,000 (p. 22)

calendar [ka′lən•dər] A chart that shows the days, weeks, and months of a year

center [sen′tər] A point in the middle of a circle that is the same distance from anywhere on the circle (p. 322)
Example:

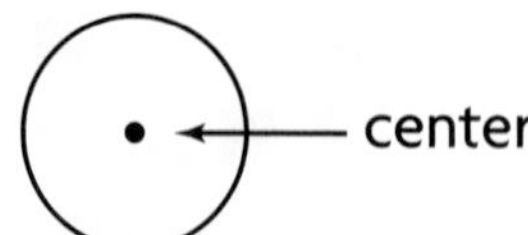

centimeter (cm) [sen′tə•mē•tər] A metric unit that is used to measure length or distance (p. 286)
Example:

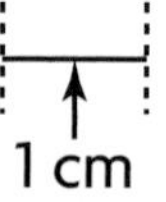

circle [sər′kəl] A plane figure made up of points that are the same distance from the center (p. 322)

clockwise [klok′wīz′] In the same direction in which the hands of a clock move (p. 109)

closed figure [klōzd fi′•gyər] A shape that begins and ends at the same point
Examples:

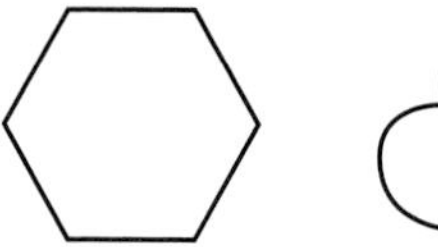

common fraction [kä′mən frak′shən] A fraction having a whole number as the numerator and a whole number as the denominator. (p. 390)

Commutative Property of Addition [kə•myōō•tə•tiv prä′pər•tē əv ə•dish′ən] The property that states that you can add two numbers in any order and get the same sum (p. 46)
Example: 6 + 7 = 13
7 + 6 = 13

Commutative Property of Multiplication [kə•myōō•tə•tiv prä′pər•tē əv mul•tə•plə•kā′shən] The property that states that you can multiply two factors in any order and get the same product (p. 131)
Examples: 2 × 4 = 8
4 × 2 = 8

compare [kəm•pâr′] To describe whether numbers are equal to, less than, or greater than each other

compensation [käm•pən•sā′shən] A mental math strategy in which you change one addend to a multiple of ten and then adjust the other addend to keep the balance (p. 52)
Example: 24 + 98 = (24 − 2) + (98 + 2)
= 22 + 100
= 122

cone [kōn] A solid, pointed figure that has a flat, round base
Example:

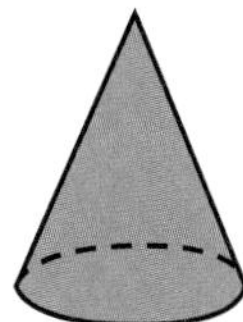

counterclockwise [koun′tər•klok′wīz′] In the opposite direction in which the hands of a clock move (p. 109)

counting back [koun′ting bak] A way to find the difference when you subtract 1, 2, or 3
Example: 8 − 3 = ■ Count: 8 . . . 7, 6, 5

counting on [koun′ting on] A way to find the sum when one of the addends is 1, 2, or 3
Example: 5 + 2 = ■ Count: 5 . . . 6, 7

counting up [koun′ting up] A way to find the difference by beginning with the smaller number
Example: 7 − 4 = ■
Count: 4 . . . 5, 6, 7 ← 3 is the difference.

cube [kyōōb] A solid figure with six congruent square faces
Example:

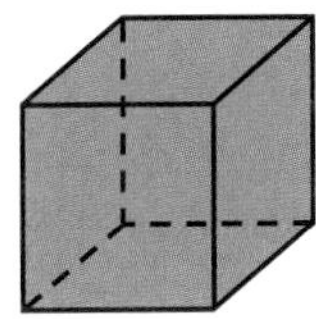

cylinder [sil′in•dər] A solid or hollow object that is shaped like a can
Example:

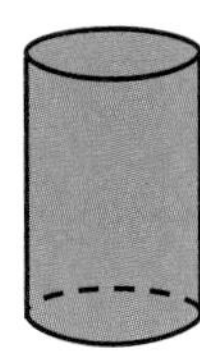

D

data [dā′tə] Information collected about people or things (p. 262)

decimal [de′sə•məl] A number with one or more digits to the right of the decimal point (p. 414)

decimal point [de′sə•məl point] A symbol used to separate dollars from cents in money and to separate the ones place from the tenths place in decimals (p. 88)
Example: 4.5
↑decimal point

denominator [di•nä′mə•nā•tər] The part of a fraction below the line, which tells how many equal parts there are in the whole or in the group (p. 390)
Example: $\frac{3}{4}$ ←denominator

diameter [di•a′mə•tər] A line segment that passes through the center of a circle and has its endpoints on the circle. (p. 322)
Example:

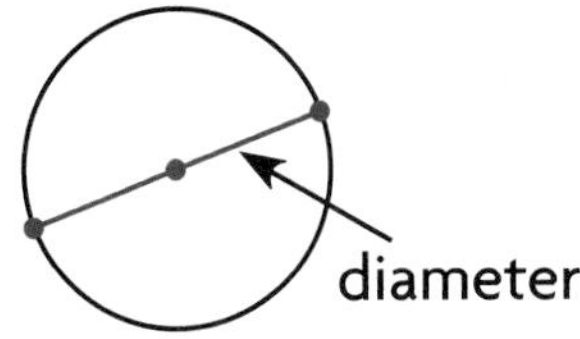

difference [dif′rən(t)s] The answer in a subtraction problem
Example: 6 − 4 = 2
↑difference

digits [di′jəts] The symbols 0, 1, 2, 3, 4, 5, 6, 7, 8, and 9

Word History

The word *distributive* comes from the Latin word *distribuere* which means "to divide up." When you use the Distributive Property, you *divide up* one factor and multiply each part by the other factor.

Distributive Property [di•strib′yə•tiv prä′pər•tē] The property that states that multiplying a sum by a number is the same as multiplying each addend by the number and then adding the products (p. 188)
Examples:
3 × (4 + 2) = (3 × 4) + (3 × 2)
3 × 6 = 12 + 6
18 = 18

divide (÷) [di•vīd′] To separate into equal groups; the opposite operation of multiplication (p. 202)

dividend [di′və•dend] The number that is to be divided in a division problem (p. 206)
Example: 35 ÷ 5 = 7
↑ dividend

divisor [di•vī′zər] The number that divides the dividend (p. 206)
Example: 35 ÷ 5 = 7
↑ divisor

E

edge [ej] A line segment formed where two faces meet (p. 332)
Example:

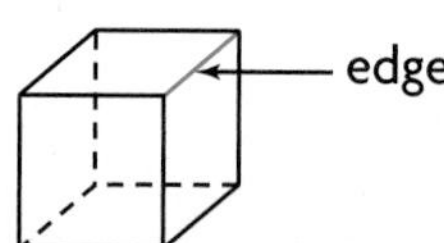

elapsed time [i•lapst′ tīm] The amount of time that passes from the start of an activity to the end of that activity (p. 112)

equilateral triangle [ē•kwə•lat′ər•əl trī′ang•gəl] A triangle that has three equal sides (p. 315)
Examples:

equivalent [ē•kwiv′ə•lənt] Two or more sets that name the same amount (p. 89)

estimate [es′tə•māt] *verb*: To find about how many or how much (p. 50)

estimate [es′tə•mit] *noun*: A number close to an exact amount (p. 50)

even [ē′vən] A whole number that has a 0, 2, 4, 6, or 8 in the ones place

expanded form [ik•spand′id fôrm] A way to write numbers by showing the value of each digit (p. 4)
Example: 7,201 = 7,000 + 200 + 1

expression [ik•spre′shən] The part of a number sentence that combines numbers and operation signs, but doesn't have an equal sign (p. 62)
Example: 5 × 6

F

face [fās] A flat surface of a solid figure (p. 332)
Example:

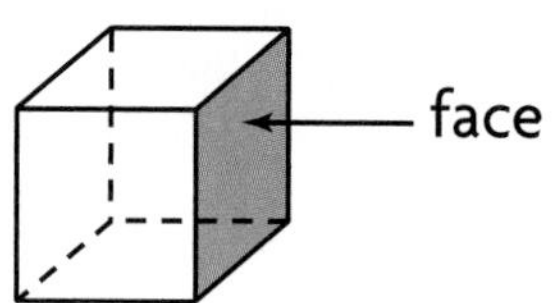

fact family [fakt fam′ə•lē] A set of related addition and subtraction, or multiplication and division, number sentences (p. 210)
Example:

4 × 7 = 28	28 ÷ 7 = 4
7 × 4 = 28	28 ÷ 4 = 7

factor [fak′tər] A number that is multiplied by another number to find a product (p. 128)
Example: 3 × 8 = 24
↑ factor ↑ factor

foot (ft) [fo͝ot] A customary unit used to measure length or distance;
1 foot = 12 inches (p. 282)

fraction [frak′shən] A number that names part of a whole or part of a group (p. 390)
Example:

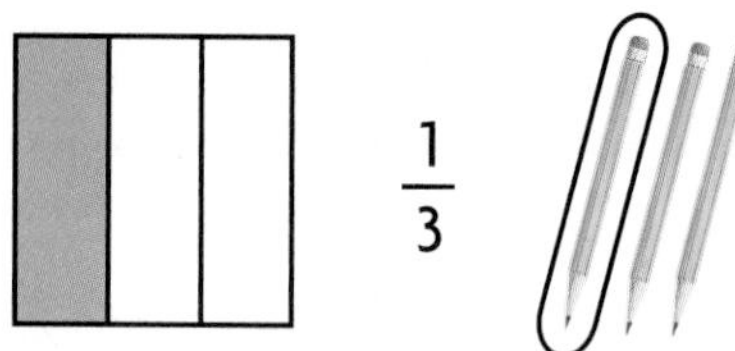

Word History

A *fraction* is a part of a whole, or a whole that is broken into pieces. *Fraction* comes from the Latin word *frangere,* which means "to break".

frequency table [frē′kwen•sē tā′bəl] A table that uses numbers to record data (p. 262)
Example:

FAVORITE COLOR	
Color	**Number**
blue	10
red	7
green	8
yellow	4

front-end estimation [frunt-end es•tə•mā′shən] A method of estimating a sum or difference by using the front digit of the number and adding zeros for the other digits (p. 50)
Example:

$$\begin{array}{r} 4{,}496 \\ +3{,}745 \\ \hline \end{array} \rightarrow \begin{array}{r} 4{,}000 \\ +3{,}000 \\ \hline 7{,}000 \end{array}$$

half hour [haf our] 30 minutes
Example: Between 4:00 and 4:30 is one half hour.

hexagon [hek′sə•gän] A polygon with six sides (p. 310)
Examples:

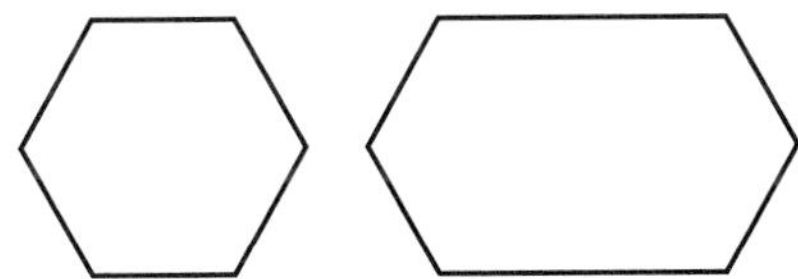

horizontal bar graph [hôr•ə•zän′təl bär graf] A bar graph in which the bars go from left to right (p. 268)

hour (hr) [our] A unit used to measure time; in one hour, the hour hand on a clock moves from one number to the next;
1 hour = 60 minutes

hour hand [our hand] The short hand on an analog clock

Identity Property of Addition [ī•den′tə•tē prä′pər•tē əv ə•dish′ən] The property that states that when you add zero to a number, the result is that number (p. 46)
Example: $24 + 0 = 24$

Identity Property of Multiplication [ī•den′tə•tē prä′pər•tē əv mul•tə•plə•kā′shən] The property that states that the product of any number and 1 is that number (p. 188)
Example: $5 \times 1 = 5$
$1 \times 8 = 8$

inch (in.) [inch] A customary unit used for measuring length or distance
Example:

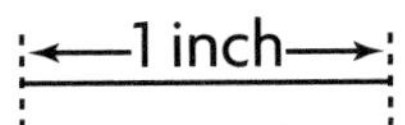

intersecting lines [in•tər•sek′ting līnz] Lines that cross (p. 308)
Example:

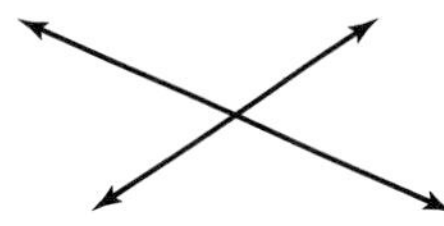

inverse operations [in′vərs ä•pə•rā′shənz] Opposite operations, or operations that undo each other, such as addition and subtraction or multiplication and division (pp. 48, 206)

is equal to (=) [iz ē′kwəl to͞o] Having the same value (p. 24)
Example: $4 + 4 = 3 + 5$

is greater than (>) [iz grā′tər than] A symbol used to compare two numbers, with the greater number given first (p. 24)
Example: $6 > 4$

is less than (<) [iz les than] A symbol used to compare two numbers, with the lesser number given first (p. 24)
Example: $3 < 7$

is not equal to (≠) [iz not ē′kwəl to͞o] A number or set of numbers that is not equal to another number or set of numbers (p. 62)
Examples:

$$4 \neq 5$$
$$3 + 3 \neq 3 + 8$$
$$217 \neq 271$$

isosceles triangle [ī•sos′ə•lēz trī′ang•gəl] A triangle that has two equal sides (p. 315)
Example:

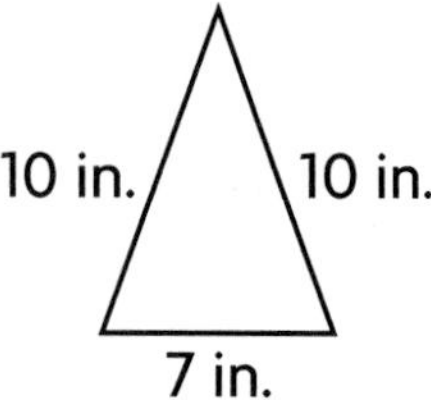

kilometer (km) [kə•lä′mə•tər] A metric unit for measuring length or distance;
1 kilometer = 1,000 meters (p. 286)

like fractions [līk frak′shənz] Fractions that have the same denominator (p. 396)
Example: $\frac{3}{8}$ and $\frac{7}{8}$

line [līn] An undefined term; description: a straight path extending in both directions with no endpoints (p. 304)
Example:

Word History

The word *line* comes from *linen,* a thread spun from the fibers of the flax plant. In early times thread was held tight to mark a straight line between two points.

line segment [līn seg′mənt] A part of a line that includes two points, called endpoints, and all of the points between them (p. 304)
Example:

meter (m) [mē′tər] A metric unit for measuring length or distance;
1 meter = 100 centimeters (p. 286)

midnight [mid′nīt] 12:00 at night (p. 110)

mile (mi) [mīl] A customary unit for measuring length or distance;
1 mile = 5,280 feet (p. 282)

millimeter (mm) [mi′lə•mē•tər] A metric unit for measuring length or distance;
1 centimeter = 10 millimeters (p. 286)

minute (min) [min′it] A unit used to measure short amounts of time; in one minute, the minute hand moves from one mark to the next

minute hand [mi′nət hand] The long hand on an analog clock

multiple [mul′tə•pəl] A number that is the product of a given number and a whole number (p. 146)
Example:

$$\begin{array}{r}10\\ \times 1\\ \hline 10\end{array}\quad\begin{array}{r}10\\ \times 2\\ \hline 20\end{array}\quad\begin{array}{r}10\\ \times 3\\ \hline 30\end{array}\quad\begin{array}{r}10\\ \times 4\\ \hline 40\end{array}\leftarrow \text{multiples of 10}$$

multiply (×) [mul′tə•plī] When you combine equal groups, you can multiply to find how many in all; the opposite operation of division. (p. 126)

multistep problem [mul′tē•step prä′bləm] A problem with more than one step (p. 190)

noon [no͞on] 12:00 in the day (p. 110)

number sentence [num′bər sen′təns] A sentence that includes numbers, operation symbols, and a greater than or less than symbol or an equal sign
Example:
5 + 3 = 8 is a number sentence.

numerator [no͞o′mə•rā•tər] The part of a fraction above the line, which tells how many parts are being counted (p. 390)
Example: $\frac{3}{4}$ ←numerator

obtuse angle [əb•t(y)o͞os′ ang′gəl] An angle that has a measure greater than a right angle (p. 305)

Example:

obtuse triangle [əb•t(y)o͞os′ trī′ang•gəl] A triangle that has 1 obtuse angle (p. 315)

octagon [äk′tə•gän] A polygon with eight sides (p. 310)

Example:

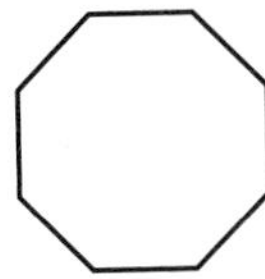

odd [od] A whole number that has a 1, 3, 5, 7, or 9 in the ones place

open figure [ō•pən fi′•gyər] A figure that does not begin and end at the same point

Examples:

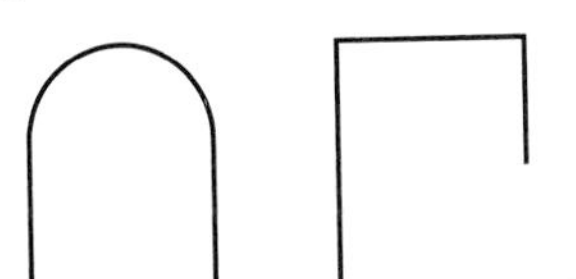

partial products [pär′shəl prä′dəkts] The products that result from multiplying the ones and tens separately; the *product* is found by adding the partial products (p. 440)

Example:

```
  24
×  3
  12  } partial products
 +60
  72
```

pattern [pat′ərn] An ordered set of numbers or objects; the order helps you predict what will come next. (p. 12)

Examples:

2, 4, 6, 8, 10

pattern unit [pat′ərn yo͞o′nət] The part of a pattern that repeats (p. 370)

Example:

pentagon [pen′tə•gän] A polygon with five sides (p. 310)

Example:

perimeter [pə•ri′mə•tər] The distance around a figure (p. 350)

Example:

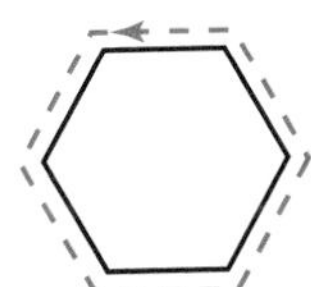

pictograph [pik′tə•graf] A graph that uses pictures to show and compare information

Example:

HOW WE GET TO SCHOOL

Walk	❋ ❋ ❋
Ride a Bike	❋ ❋ ❋ ❋
Ride a Bus	❋ ❋ ❋ ❋ ❋ ❋
Ride in a Car	❋ ❋

Key: Each ❋ = 10 students.

place value [plās val′yo͞o] The value of each digit in a number, based on the location of the digit

place value of $\frac{1}{10}$ (tenth) See *place value* and *tenth.*

plane figure [plāne fi′•gyər] A closed figure in a plane that is formed by lines that are curved, straight, or both
Example:

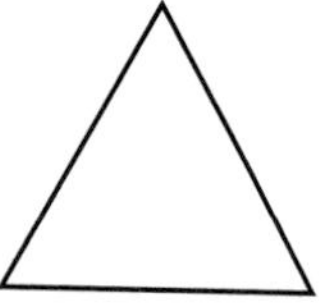

P.M. [pē em] The hours between noon and midnight (p. 110)

point [point] An undefined term; description: an exact position or location (p. 304)

polygon [pol′ē•gän] A closed plane figure with straight sides that are line segments (p. 310)
Examples:

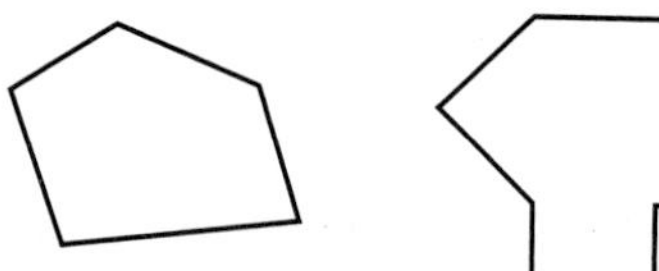

Word History

Did you ever notice that a *polygon* looks like a bunch of knees that are bent? This is how the term got its name. *Poly-* is from the Greek root, *poli,* that means "many". The ending *-gon* is from the Latin, *gonus,* which means "to bend the knee".

product [prä′dəkt] The answer in a multiplication problem (p. 128)
Example: $3 \times 8 = 24$
↳ product

quadrilateral [kwa•drə•lat′ər•əl] A polygon with four sides (p. 310)
Example:

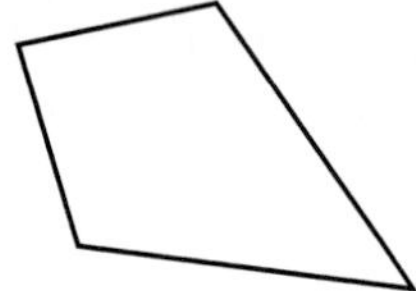

quarter hour [kwôr•tər our] 15 minutes
Example: Between 4:00 and 4:15 is one quarter hour.

quotient [kwō′shənt] The number, not including the remainder, that results from division (p. 206)
Example: $8 \div 4 = 2$
↳ quotient

radius [rā′dē•əs] A line segment with one endpoint at the center of a circle and the other endpoint on the circle (p. 322)
Example:

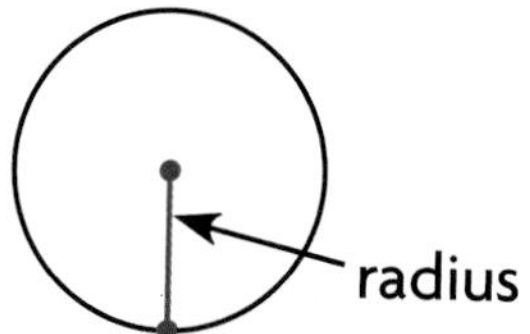

ray [rā] A part of a line, with one endpoint, that is straight and continues in one direction (p. 304)
Example:

rectangle [rek′tang•gəl] A quadrilateral with 2 pairs of parallel sides, 2 pairs of equal sides, and 4 right angles
Example:

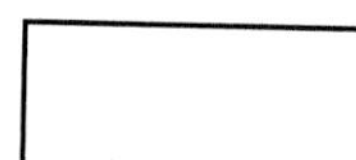

rectangular prism [rek•tan′gyə•lər pri′zəm] A solid figure with six faces that are all rectangles
Example:

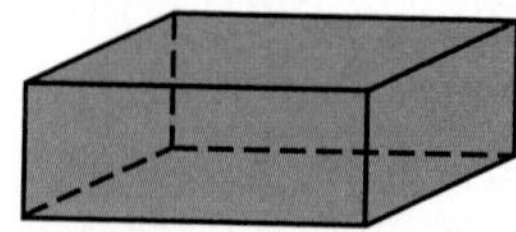

regroup [rē•grōōp′] To exchange amounts of equal value to rename a number
Example: $5 + 8 = 13$ ones or 1 ten 3 ones

remainder [ri•mān′dər] The amount left over when a number cannot be divided evenly (p. 456)

results [ri•zults′] The answers from a survey (p. 264)

right angle [rīt ang′gəl] A special angle that forms a square corner (p. 304)
Example:

right triangle [rīt trī′ang•gəl] A triangle with one right angle (p. 315)
Example:

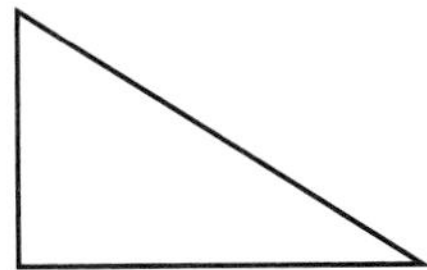

scale [skāl] The numbers on a bar graph that help you read the number each bar shows (p. 268)

scalene triangle [skā′lēn trī′ang•gəl] A triangle in which no sides are equal (p. 315)
Example:

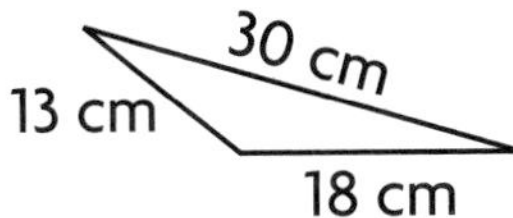

schedule [ske′•jool] A table that lists activities or events and the times they happen (p. 114)

second [sek′ənd] A unit of time that is equal to $\frac{1}{60}$ of a minute

second [sek′ənd] An ordinal number, coming next after first

sphere [sfir] A solid figure that has the shape of a round ball
Example:

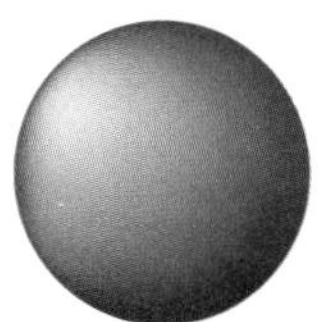

square [skwâr] A quadrilateral with 2 pairs of parallel sides, 4 equal sides, and 4 right angles
Example:

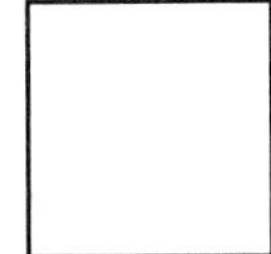

square unit [skwâr yoo′nət] A square with a side length of one unit; used to measure area (p. 356)

standard form [stan′dərd fôrm] A way to write numbers by using the digits 0–9, with each digit having a place value (p. 4)
Example: 345 ← standard form

subtraction [səb•trak′shən] The process of finding how many are left when a number of items are taken away from a group of items; the process of finding the difference when two groups are compared; the opposite operation of addition

sum [sum] The answer to an addition problem

survey [sər′vā] A method of gathering information (p. 264)

tally table [ta′lē tā′bəl] A table that uses tally marks to record data (p. 262)
Example:

FAVORITE SPORT	
Sport	**Number**
Soccer	~~IIII~~ III
Baseball	III
Football	~~IIII~~
Basketball	~~IIII~~ I

tenth [tenth] One of ten equal parts (p. 414)
Example:

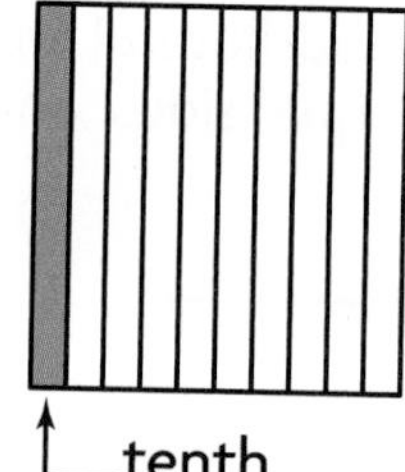

tenths [tenths] The place to the right of the ones place
Example:

ONES	.	TENTHS
0	•	7

trapezoid [trap′ə•zoid] A quadrilateral with one pair of parallel sides (p. 318)
Example:

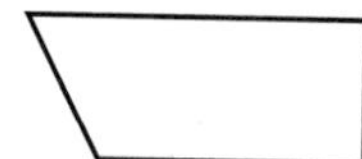

triangle [trī′ang′gəl] A polygon with three sides (p. 314)
Examples:

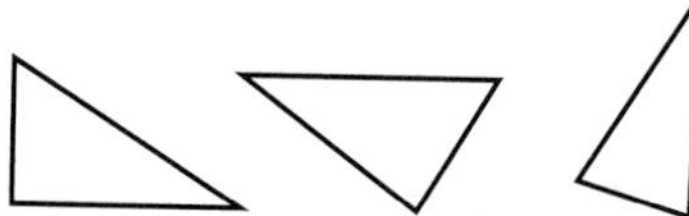

Venn diagram [ven dī′ə•gram] A diagram that shows relationships among sets of things (p. 324)
Example:

2-Digit Numbers **Even Numbers**

35, 17, 29 | 12, 10 | 8, 6, 4

vertex [vûr′teks] The point at which two or more line segments meet in a plane figure or where three or more edges meet in a solid figure (p. 332)
Examples:

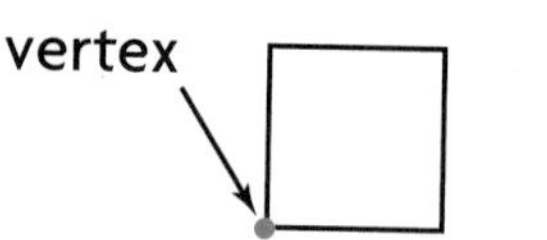

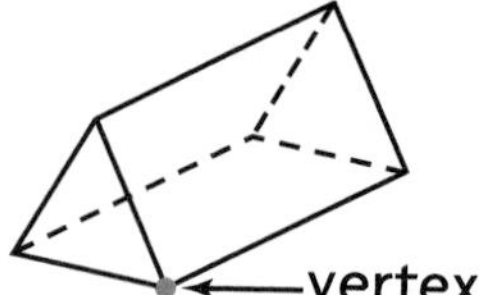

vertical bar graph [vûr′ti•kəl bär graf] A bar graph in which the bars go up from bottom to top (p. 268)

whole number [hōl nəm′bər] One of the numbers 0, 1, 2, 3, 4, ... The set of whole numbers goes on without end (p. 4)

word form [wûrd form] A way to write numbers by using words (p. 4)
Example: The word form of 212 is two hundred twelve.

yard (yd) [yärd] A customary unit for measuring length or distance; 1 yard = 3 feet (p. 282)

Zero Property of Multiplication [zir′ō prä′pər•tē əv mul•tə•plə•kā′shən] The property that states that the product of zero and any number is zero (p. 188)
Example: $0 \times 6 = 0$

D

E

F

G

H

K

L

M

N

Q

R

S

Photography Credits

Page placement key: (t) top, (c) center, (b) bottom, (l) left, (r) right, (bg) background, (i) inset.

xx (tr) ©Spencer Grant/PhotoEdit; xxi (tl) Photo by Harry Goeller for Live Oak Public Libraries; xxi (cr) ©Michael Barley/CORBIS; xxi (bl) The University of Georgia, Faculty of Engineering; 20 (bg) ©James Randlev/CORBIS; 42 (tr) ©Royalty-Free/Corbis; 52 (cr) age fotostock/SuperStock; 72 (tr) Tom Rickles/Index Stock Imagery, Inc.; 104 (bg) Greater Rome Convention and Visitors Bureau; 142 (bg) Gustavo Vanderput-Abranches; 166 (cr) Henry Westheim Photography/Alamy; 258 (tr) Michael Newman/PhotoEdit Inc.; 266 (cr) Christopher Arnesen/Stone/Getty Images; 267 (br) Stockdisc/Getty Images; 330 (bg) ©SuperStock, Inc./SuperStock; 334 (tl) Rachel Epstein/PhotoEdit Inc.; 359 (tc) ©David Muench/CORBIS; 361 (bl) Copyright ©Michael Newman/PhotoEdit Inc.—All rights reserved; 386 (tr) Tim Vacula/GC&SU; 412 (c) Merlin Tuttle/Photo Researchers, Inc.; 418 (bl) ©Michael Newman/PhotoEdit; 442 (br) "O'Brien Productions/CORBIS Photographer Kevin Cozad"; 448 (tr) ©Myrleen Ferguson Cate/PhotoEdit, Inc.